L3308

75060 9.765

Analysis and Design of Electronic Circuits

McGraw-Hill Electrical and Electronic Engineering Series

Fredrick Emmons Terman, Consulting Editor
W. W. Harman and J. G. Truxal, Associate Consulting Editors

Ahrendt and Savant · Servomechanism Practice
Angelo · Electronic Circuits
Aseltine · Transform Method in Linear System Analysis
Atwater · Introduction to Microwave Theory
Bailey and Gault · Alternating-current Machinery
Beranek · Acoustics
Brenner and Javid · Analysis of Electric Circuits
Brown · Analysis of Linear Time-invariant Systems
Bruns and Saunders · Analysis of Feedback Control Systems
Cage · Theory and Application of Industrial Electronics
Cauer · Synthesis of Linear Communication Networks
Chen · The Analysis of Linear Systems
Chen · Linear Network Design and Synthesis
Chirlian · Analysis and Design of Electronic Circuits
Chirlian and Zemanian · Electronics
Clement and Johnson · Electrical Engineering Science
Cote and Oakes · Linear Vacuum-tube and Transistor Circuits
Cuccia · Harmonics, Sidebands, and Transients in Communication Engineering
Cunningham · Introduction to Nonlinear Analysis
Eastman · Fundamentals of Vacuum Tubes
Evans · Control-system Dynamics
Feinstein · Foundations of Information Theory
Fitzgerald and Higginbotham · Basic Electrical Engineering
Fitzgerald and Kingsley · Electric Machinery
Frank · Electrical Measurement Analysis
Friedland, Wing, and Ash · Principles of Linear Networks
Geppert · Basic Electron Tubes
Ghose · Microwave Circuit Theory and Analysis
Greiner · Semiconductor Devices and Applications
Hammond · Electrical Engineering
Hancock · An Introduction to the Principles of Communication Theory
Happell and Hesselberth · Engineering Electronics
Harman · Fundamentals of Electronic Motion
Harman · Principles of the Statistical Theory of Communication
Harman and Lytle · Electrical and Mechanical Networks
Harrington · Introduction to Electromagnetic Engineering
Harrington · Tlme-harmonic Electromagnetic Fields
Hayashi · Nonlineal Oscillations in Physical Systems
Hayt · Engineering Electromagnetics
Hayt and Kemmerly · Engineering Circuit Analysis
Hill · Electronics in Engineering
Javid and Brenner · Analysis, Transmission, and Filtering of Signals
Javid and Brown · Field Analysis and Electromagnetics
Johnson · Transmission Lines and Networks
Koenig and Blackwell · Electromechanical System Theory
Kraus · Antennas
Kraus · Electromagnetics

Paul M. Chirlian

Associate Professor of Electrical Engineering

Stevens Institute of Technology

McGraw-Hill Book Company

New York   St. Louis   San Francisco   Toronto   London

Analysis

and

Design of

Electronic

Circuits

Analysis and Design of Electronic Circuits

To my wife

BARBARA

Preface

This book is an undergraduate college textbook on electronic circuits for use in junior or senior level courses. Its object is to provide the student with a thorough understanding of the circuits of electronic devices. This includes not only a knowledge of these circuits and the techniques used for analyzing them, but also an understanding of the basic principles involved in their design. This textbook is by no means a design handbook since it fundamentally develops and analyzes the circuits of electronic devices. However, there are numerous design examples and discussions. It is hoped that the student will obtain a general design philosophy from these sections. The book can also be of considerable help to the practicing electronics engineer. Although there is not a design example for every circuit, such things as amplifier design (including the effects of bypass capacitors), feedback system stabilization, and oscillator design are discussed in considerable detail. Numerous other thorough design discussions are also given.

A unified treatment of semiconductor and vacuum-tube circuits is given whenever possible. This makes for an efficient presentation and emphasizes the similarities of many vacuum-tube and semiconductor circuits. At times, vacuum-tube circuits are discussed first because they are conceptually simpler. However, the reader should not consider them to be more important than the semiconductor circuits. In fact, in many circumstances, the vacuum-tube circuits can be omitted from classroom discussion and merely be assigned for reading. When fundamental differences exist between semiconductor and vacuum-tube circuits, they are stressed. Particular emphasis is placed upon the approximations which can be made in electronic circuits. If semiconductor and vacuum-tube circuits require different approximations, these are presented.

A knowledge of the physical behavior and characteristics of electronic

*devices is necessary if their circuits are to be discussed.   Chapter 1 presents
this material in sufficient detail so that the discussions of the remainder of the
book can be followed.   If this course follows a course in electronic physics,
then Chap. 1 can be omitted.   As a matter of fact, this book can be used as a
companion to "Electronics" by P. M. Chirlian and A. H. Zemanian,
(McGraw-Hill Book Company, New York, 1961), which discusses the fundamentals of electronic devices in considerable detail.*

*Chapters 2, 3, and 4 develop the basic techniques for the analysis of elec-
tronic circuits.   Chapter 2 presents graphical analysis techniques.   The
analysis of nonlinear distortion is also discussed here.   Linear equivalent
circuits are discussed in Chap. 3.   Various forms of low- and high-frequency
equivalent circuits are developed, and their advantages and disadvantages are
discussed.   Linear-circuit theory is related to the equivalent circuits of electronic devices.   In the case of the transistor, the h-parameter equivalent circuit is stressed since it is felt that it has the most important practical applications.   The hybrid-π high-frequency equivalent circuit is also presented.
Basic amplifier circuits are also given in this chapter.   Chapter 4 consists of
a study of piecewise linear equivalent circuits.   Such circuits for the commonly used electronic devices are developed.*

*Chapter 5 is an introduction to electronic amplifiers.   Basic terminology
and amplifier structures are given.   Decibel notation, logarithmic plots, and
concepts of efficiency are also introduced.*

*Chapter 6 discusses linear class A amplifiers.   This is a lengthy chapter
since there has been an attempt made at completeness here.   The analysis and
design of many amplifier configurations are discussed.   In addition, poles
and zeros are introduced and their relation to the transient response is given.
The ideas of transformed gain and time functions are also presented.*

Chapters 7 and 8 discuss the analysis and design of power amplifiers.

*Chapter 9 introduces signal-flow graphs.   These are used in Chap. 10,
which is a discussion of feedback.   Every attempt is made in this chapter to
present a rigorous, accurate discussion of feedback amplifiers.   The complete
mathmatic theory of feedback cannot be presented on an undergraduate level.
However, sufficient material is included to enable the student to have a basic
understanding of what he is doing.   For instance, stability is discussed in
terms of poles and zeros.   The Nyquist criterion is presented as a procedure
for determining the differences between the number of right half-plane zeros and
poles.   In addition, the design of feedback systems is presented in some detail
here.*

*Chapter 11 uses and simplifies the principles of Chap. 10 in a discussion
of sinusoidal oscillators.*

*Pulse and switching circuits are discussed in Chap. 12.   Discussion of
these circuits has been limited to avoid undue length.   Fundamentals of
vacuum-tube and semiconductor switching circuits, including transient*

response, are discussed. Several basic switching, counting, logic, and wave-shaping circuits are then presented.

Amplitude, frequency, and phase modulation are discussed in Chap. 13. The mathematics of these modulation systems is rigorously given. Modulation and demodulation systems are discussed here in considerable detail.

Chapter 14 consists of a discussion of power supplies. This chapter not only contains the analysis and design of rectifiers and filters, but also such things as regulated-power supplies and controlled rectifiers.

If the instructor so desires, he need not exactly follow the order of these chapters. For instance, Chap. 4 can be omitted until pulse circuits (Chap. 12) are discussed. Chapters 7 and 8 can follow the discussion of feedback in Chap. 10. Much of the discussion of power supplies can precede the chapters on amplifiers.

Instead of including the characteristics of electronic devices in an appendix, they are distributed throughout the text where they are most useful. However, the student should encounter no difficulty in finding the characteristics necessary for the solution of problems. Usually, the characteristics are close to the problems themselves. In any event, the necessary characteristics are referred to (by figure number) in a specific problem or set of problems. Many varied problems have been included at the end of each chapter.

The author would like to acknowledge the fact that he has drawn on his book "Electronics" for much of the material in Chaps. 1, 2, and 4. Part of Chap. 3 is also taken from this book. The author expresses his thanks to Prof. A. H. Zemanian, the coauthor of "Electronics," who coauthored the first draft of Chap. 1 and Sect. 2-2 of this book. Particular thanks are due Dr. John Truxal for his several reviews and help with the manuscript on Chap. 3 especially.

Loving thanks are due my wife, Barbara, who not only provided me with continuous encouragement and saw to it that my time was free from interruption, but also typed the rough draft and the final draft of the manuscript, and corrected the punctuation and grammar of the copy.

Paul M. Chirlian

Contents

2 *Graphical Analysis of Electronic Circuits* 47

3 *Linear Equivalent Circuits of Electronic Devices* 84

7   *Untuned Large-signal Amplifiers*   *320*

8   *Tuned Large-signal Amplifiers*   *362*

Analysis and Design of Electronic Circuits

A Summary
of Electronic
Devices

1

This chapter is an introduction to a text on the circuits of electronic devices. It presents their characteristics and ratings. The physical phenomena occurring in these devices will be discussed briefly here so that the physical discussions in the book can be followed. The electronic engineer should certainly know the physics of electronic devices. For further information, the reader should consult a textbook that considers the subject more completely. One such is "Electronics" by P. M. Chirlian and A. H. Zemanian. It uses the notation and point of view adopted here.

1-1   The vacuum-tube diode

The simplest vacuum tube is the *vacuum-tube diode*. It is composed of a *cathode* which is heated so that it emits electrons and a metallic *anode*, or *plate*, that gathers the electrons. These elements are enclosed in an evacuated chamber. The cathode may be heated directly by a current through

1

Fig. 1-1   Circuit symbols for the vacuum-tube diode (a) with directly heated cathode; (b) with indirectly heated cathode.

it or indirectly by a heating element which is electrically insulated from it. The circuit symbols for the two types of vacuum-tube diodes are shown in Fig. 1-1. Often, to avoid cluttering the diagram, the heater circuit is omitted when an indirectly heated cathode is used.

The current through a vacuum-tube diode depends upon both the temperature of the emitting cathode and the potential between the plate and the cathode. This current, called the *plate current*, is designated by i_b. The potential difference between the plate and the cathode, called the *plate voltage*, is designated by e_b. Usually, in vacuum tubes, the cathode is taken as the reference electrode and therefore double-subscript notation is not used for these voltages. The standard polarities for i_b and e_b are indicated in Fig. 1-2.

A typical plot of diode characteristics is shown in Fig. 1-3. If the plate-to-cathode voltage E_b is high enough to attract all the emitted electrons to the plate, the temperature of the emitter essentially determines the current. Under these conditions, the diode is said to be *temperature-limited*, since its operation is essentially independent of the plate voltage. For instance, in Fig. 1-3 (if the temperature is equal to or less than T_3) the operation will be temperature-limited if the plate voltage is greater than E_{b2}. On the other hand, if the potential applied to the diode is not sufficient to attract all the emitted electrons, a *space-charge cloud* will form around the cathode. Many of the electrons emitted will be repelled back into the cathode by the field set up by the space-charge cloud. Under these conditions, if the temperature of the cathode is increased, the number of electrons in the space-charge cloud

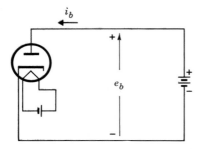

Fig. 1-2   A simple vacuum-tube-diode circuit.

will also increase. This, in turn, will repel still more electrons back to the cathode. An equilibrium is set up such that the total number of electrons reaching the plate remains essentially constant and dependent almost entirely on the plate voltage. In this case, we have *space-charge-limited* operation. Such operation takes place in Fig. 1-3 if the temperature is equal to or greater than T_1 and the plate voltage is less than E_{b1}. If $E_{b1} < e_b < E_{b2}$, there is a transition between these two types of operation. Finally, for negative values of e_b, i_b is essentially zero, since the plate does not emit electrons, and the vacuum tube is said to be *cut off*.

In general, it is desirable to have the plate current dependent only upon the applied potential and not upon the temperature of the cathode. Temperature dependence of the current leads to erratic operation, since it is difficult to maintain a desired cathode temperature. On the other hand, a given potential of the plate with respect to the cathode can be established quite readily. Hence, vacuum tubes are usually operated in the space-charge-limited region. A theoretical relation that describes the current-voltage characteristics in this region is called the Child-Langmuir law[1] and is given by

$$i_b = K e_b^{3/2} \tag{1-1}$$

where K is a constant that depends upon the geometry of the vacuum-tube diode. For actual vacuum-tube diodes, i_b does not vary precisely with the three-halves power of e_b and a more accurate relation is

$$i_b = K e_b^n \tag{1-2}$$

where the constants K and n may be determined empirically.

Fig. 1-3   *Plate current versus plate voltage for a vacuum-tube diode. The cathode temperature is taken as a parameter.*

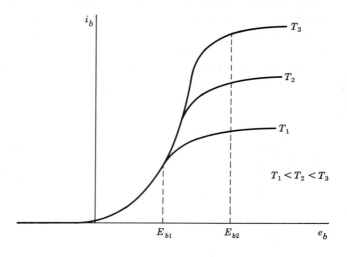

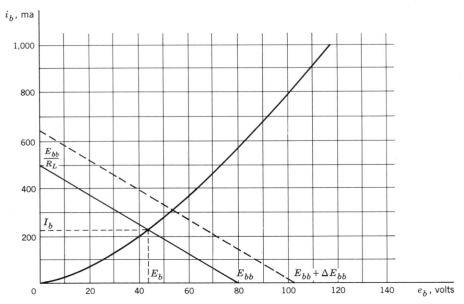

Fig. 1-4   The plate characteristic of the 5U4-GB vacuum-tube diode.   (Courtesy General Electric Company.)

Since the actual variation of plate current with plate voltage is not a simple function, diode characteristics are usually presented graphically.   A plot of plate current versus plate voltage is called the *plate characteristic* (often, *static plate characteristic*).   A typical one is shown in Fig. 1-4.   Thus, if the plate voltage E_b is known, the plate current I_b can be found directly from the curve.   (Note that we shall, in general, use lowercase letters to indicate time-varying quantities and uppercase letters for time-invariant quantities.)   In the simple diode circuit shown in Fig. 1-5, even though the battery voltage E_{bb}, the series resistor R_L, and the vacuum-tube-diode plate characteristic are given, the plate voltage and the plate current (E_b and I_b) are not known.   Two relations between them must be obtained.   The first

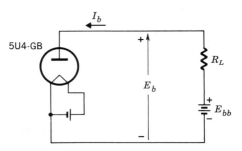

Fig. 1-5   A simple vacuum-tube-diode circuit.

of these is given by the plate characteristic of Fig. 1-4, and the second is provided by the application of Kirchhoff's voltage law to the circuit of Fig. 1-5. This yields

$$E_b = E_{bb} - I_b R_L \tag{1-3}$$

An alternative way of writing this equation is

$$I_b = -\frac{E_b}{R_L} + \frac{E_{bb}}{R_L} \tag{1-4}$$

Equation (1-4) plots as a straight line on Fig. 1-4 and is shown there. The resulting intersection of the two graphs is the solution for E_b and I_b. This straight line is called the *load line*, since R_L usually represents the load resistance of the circuit. The slope of the load line is $-1/R_L$, its abscissa intercept is E_{bb}, and its ordinate intercept is E_{bb}/R_L. This information may be used in plotting it. In many applications, the supply voltage E_{bb} is not fixed but varies, whereas the load resistance R_L remains constant. In this case, the slope of the load line remains constant, while the abscissa intercept varies. If the supply voltage is increased by the amount ΔE_{bb}, then the load line shifts parallel to itself as is shown in Fig. 1-4. Conversely, if the load resistance R_L varies but the battery voltage E_{bb} remains fixed, the load line changes its slope but not its abscissa intercept.

Under static (i.e., time-invariant) conditions, the actual plate voltage and its corresponding plate current determine a point on the graph. This point is called the *static operating point* or *quiescent operating point*.

In many instances, involving a varying plate voltage, the operating point varies instantaneously about some quiescent operating point. For example, in the circuit of Fig. 1-5, let us consider that the supply voltage increases by a small amount ΔE_{bb}. The changes in the plate current and plate voltage depend upon the slope of the plate characteristic of the diode. For this reason, a parameter called the *dynamic plate resistance*, r_p, is defined. It is the reciprocal of the slope of the static plate characteristic at the operating point. Thus,

$$r_p = \frac{de_b}{di_b} \tag{1-5}$$

The reciprocal of r_p is called the *dynamic plate conductance* and is denoted by the symbol g_p. These parameters are functions of the operating point. The plate resistance increases as the plate voltage decreases.

When the applied voltage varies, it is often desirable to have a plot of the plate current versus the supply voltage for a given value of load resistance. Such a plot may be obtained from the static characteristic by drawing many parallel load lines corresponding to different values of E_{bb} to determine corresponding values of I_b. This plot of I_b versus E_{bb} is called the *dynamic characteristic*. A typical set of these curves, for various load resistances, is shown in Fig. 1-6. It should be noted that the curve for $R_L = 0$ is the static

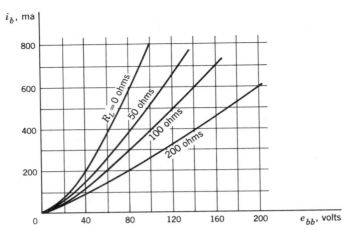

Fig. 1-6   The dynamic characteristics of the 5U4-GB vacuum-tube diode.

plate characteristic.   The dynamic characteristic is more linear than the static plate characteristic, since the dynamic characteristic is obtained for a device that consists of the nonlinear vacuum tube in series with a linear resistance.

1-2   Vacuum-tube-diode ratings

In order to ensure a reasonable vacuum-tube life, manufacturers specify maximum operating conditions.   The factors that affect the ratings of a vacuum-tube diode will be discussed in turn.

Plate dissipation

The kinetic energy of the electrons is converted into heat as they strike the plate of the vacuum-tube diode.   The kinetic energy that an electron gains in falling through the difference of potential between the cathode and the plate is E_b ev.   The abbreviation ev stands for the *electron volt*—the amount of kinetic energy gained by an electron in falling through a potential difference of one volt.   Electron volts can be converted to joules by multiplying by ε, the magnitude of the electronic charge ($\varepsilon = 1.602 \times 10^{-19}$ coul). Therefore, if the plate voltage is held constant at E_b, and if N electrons arrive at the plate in one second, the total power delivered to the plate in the form of heat is $N\varepsilon E_b$ watts.   Since $N\varepsilon$ is the amount of charge transferred per second, it is also the plate current.   Thus, the total power dissipated at the plate under static conditions is

$$P_p = N\varepsilon E_b = I_b E_b \qquad \text{watts} \tag{1-6}$$

If the plate voltage varies with time, then the instantaneous values of plate voltage and plate current must be used to obtain the instantaneous value of plate dissipation. Using lowercase letters to denote instantaneous values, we have

$$p_p = i_b e_b \tag{1-7}$$

Increased plate dissipation increases the anode operating temperature. Excessive heating can liberate residual gases from the anode at a rapid rate. This can substantially reduce the tube life by contaminating the vacuum. Of course, excessive operating temperatures will tend to melt the anode. The heat radiated from the anode may be sufficient to damage the envelope, or to cause it to *outgas*. For these reasons, manufacturers specify a maximum plate dissipation.

Special means are sometimes employed to cool high-power transmitting tubes. In some cases, the anode is made a part of the envelope and cooling fins are attached to it. The cooling due to convection may be improved by forcing air through the fins. A more efficient water-cooling system may be employed, wherein water is circulated over surfaces of the vacuum tube.

Filament heating

Excessive heating of the filament will cause its rapid evaporation and its eventual rupture. Manufacturers specify voltage and current ratings for these filaments to ensure a reasonable tube life and a reasonable amount of electron emission from the cathode. Of course, the heat radiated from the filament will also heat the envelope and the anode and, thus, tend to increase the effects of plate dissipation. However, the ratings of the plate dissipation take this into account.

Breakdown voltages

The voltages applied to the elements of a diode must be limited, since excessive voltages will cause breakdown of the insulating materials. This breakdown may take place either in the insulating materials, or through the air surrounding the diode, or within the diode.

In tubes with indirectly heated cathodes, the insulation between the heating element and the cathode may also break down if the voltage between them is too high; thus, its value is also specified.

Cathode emissivity

The cathode size, material, and operating temperature determine the maximum amount of current that can be drawn from the vacuum tube and, thus, a maximum current rating is also given.

1-3   Semiconductors

Many electronic devices make use of semiconductor materials. We shall briefly discuss their physics in this section. The atoms of the principal materials of semiconductor devices form a uniform geometric pattern or crystalline structure called the *lattice structure*, shown symbolically in Fig. 1-7. Materials of valence 4, such as carbon, silicon, and germanium, may form such patterns. In this case, each atom forms one *covalent*, or electron-pair, bond with each of the four adjacent atoms. This is a stable crystalline structure and it is electrically neutral. With this ideal structure, a small applied voltage will produce no current, because each valence electron is bound to a pair of atoms, and so there are no free electrons available. Conduction can take place in these materials because imperfections in their crystalline structure occur. The magnitude of the current is considerably less than that in a conductor, all other conditions being the same. Hence, they are called *semiconductors*.

In all materials, conduction can take place when some electrons have sufficient energy to permit them to move throughout the material without being bound to any atom. Thus, the difference between conductors, semiconductors, and insulators can be discussed by means of energy considerations. In a single isolated atom, the electrons cannot possess any arbitrary energy but can have only certain discrete energy values. Thus, a single isolated atom is said to possess a set of *discrete energy levels*. When several atoms are brought together, the energy levels split. That is, other allowable energy levels are formed. When many atoms are brought together, their

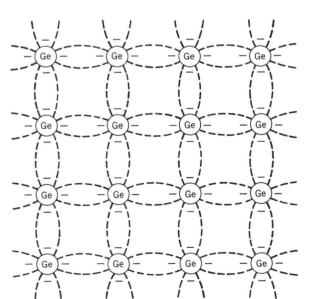

Fig. 1-7   A symbolic representation of the germanium crystal structure.

energy levels split further.   Thus, in any material where the number of atoms is extremely large, the difference between allowable energy levels becomes so small that for all practical purposes the allowable energy levels may be considered to be a continuous band of energies.   However, these energy bands are finite and there exist continuous regions of prohibited energy.   Thus, we speak of *allowable energy bands* and *prohibited energy bands*. Figure 1-8*a* and *b* illustrates such energy bands.   A principle of quantum mechanics is that no more than one electron can possess a particular energy. Since any allowable energy band consists of a finite number of very closely spaced energy levels, there is a maximum number of electrons that can have energies in this band.   When exactly this number of electrons have energies lying in this band, the band is said to be *filled*.   The sizes of the prohibited bands and whether or not the occupied bands are completely filled determine whether a material is a conductor, semiconductor, or an insulator.

Figure 1-8*a* illustrates the energy bands in an *insulator*.   These materials

Fig. 1-8   (*a*) *Energy levels in an insulator or in a semiconductor;* (*b*) *energy levels in a conductor.*

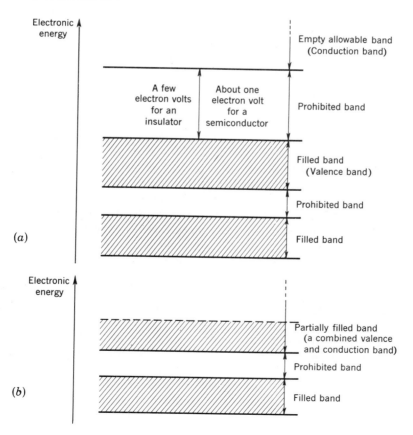

are characterized by the fact that those bands which have electrons in them are completely filled at a temperature of absolute zero, and there is a gap of at least several electron volts between the highest filled energy band, called the *valence band*, and the next higher allowable energy band, called a *conduction band*. The electrons in a completely filled energy band cannot contribute to electrical conduction, because an electron which is accelerated by an electric field must gain energy, and it can do this only if it is able to shift to a higher allowable energy level. There are no empty levels in a completely filled band. If, however, the electric field is sufficiently large to raise the energy of some electrons into the next higher, empty allowable band, then conduction can take place. It may seem that this separation of a few electron volts between the allowable energy bands is not unduly large. However, this potential difference must occur over lengths of the orders of an atomic distance. Thus, a field intensity of the order of hundreds of millions of volts per centimeter is required to break down the insulator. Electrons may be transferred from a filled band to an empty band by other means, such as the application of light or heat energy. However, in the case of insulators, the energy available from light or heat in ordinary cases is too small to accomplish this to any great extent.

On the other hand, in a *conductor* the highest allowable energy band containing electrons is only partially filled at a temperature of absolute zero, as shown in Fig. 1-8*b*. These allowable bands consist of discrete energy levels which are extremely close together. Thus, some electrons in the partially filled band require only extremely small energy increments to be raised to a higher energy level. Hence, small applied electric fields will produce conduction. Increasing the temperature of a conductor increases the thermal agitation of the electrons and atoms. This, in turn, increases the probability of a collision between these particles, hampering their motion and increasing the electrical resistance of the material.

If all the bands having electrons are completely filled at a temperature of absolute zero and the energy gap between the highest filled band (the valence band) and the next higher conduction band is small (in the order of 1 ev), then this material is called a *semiconductor*. In such materials, some conduction can ordinarily take place, because the excitations due to the usually present heat and light are sufficient to raise the energies of some of the electrons from the highest filled band to the next higher allowable band. These electrons may then contribute to conduction. The energy diagram from such a material is shown in Fig. 1-8*a*. Increasing the operating temperature substantially increases the number of electrons available for conduction. This more then outweighs the hampering effect on conduction due to the increased thermal agitation of the atoms and electrons. Thus, the electrical resistance of semiconductors decreases with an increase in temperature.

In the perfect lattice structure of a semiconductor at a temperature of absolute zero, all electrons are bound and, therefore, there are no free-charge carriers. In order for there to be electrical conduction in this pure semiconductor, electrons must be liberated from their bound positions. That is, imperfections must be introduced into the lattice structure. When an electron is liberated from its covalent bond and begins to wander with a random motion throughout the material, the atom from which it came will have a net positive charge. As long as this free electron remains some distance away from any atom lacking an electron, it will not be attracted by the net positive charge of any such atom, since the surrounding neutral atoms will shield it from the resulting electric field. Thus, these free electrons behave as the free electrons in a conductor, and they carry current by responding to any externally applied electric field.

In addition to the conduction due to these free electrons, another type of conduction may take place in a pure semiconductor. The absence of an electron in a covalent bond, caused by the liberation of an electron, is called a *hole*. It is possible for an adjacent electron, which does not have sufficient energy to become a free electron, to move into this hole. The net effect is that the hole moves in the opposite direction. This process will continue in a random manner; so the hole also wanders throughout the material. Although the dynamics of the motion of a hole is considerably different from that of a free electron (that is, the continued movement of a single hole corresponds to a series of movements of many electrons), an analysis of its behavior by quantum mechanics indicates that a hole may be considered to be a free, positively charged particle in the material. The magnitude of its charge equals that of the electron and its apparent mass is somewhat less than that of the electron. When the semiconductor is pure (i.e., when it contains no foreign substances) and when the lattice structure remains unaffected, the number of free electrons will equal the number of holes, since each hole is produced by the liberation of a free electron. Such pure materials are called *intrinsic semiconductors* and their electrical properties are modified by the adjective *intrinsic*.

Impurities in a semiconductor

If charge carriers are to be present in a semiconductor, imperfections must be produced in the lattice structure. Thermal agitation may cause these imperfections, but a better way is to introduce very small amounts of chemical impurities that are distributed throughout the crystalline structure. Usually these impurities are elements that have a valence of 3 or 5.

Donors

Consider a crystalline lattice structure made up of a semiconductor material such as germanium or silicon, into which a small quantity of another element has been introduced. If the impurity has a valence of 5, it is called a *donor*. Commonly used donors are arsenic, antimony, and phosphorus. In general, the donors form an extremely small proportion of the total crystal. A donor atom takes its place in the lattice structure in the same fashion as an ordinary atom of the semiconductor material; however, only four of the donor's five valence electrons may form covalent bonds with the adjacent four atoms of the semiconductor material. The remaining valence electron is held more loosely than those electrons that enter into covalent bonds. At normal operating temperatures, this electron possesses sufficient energy to escape from its atom and to become a conduction electron. The donor atom is thus ionized and acquires a positive charge. This excess positive charge resides in the nucleus and is, therefore, not available for conduction. A donor atom is so called because it may supply a free electron. The number of conduction electrons provided by the donors usually far exceeds the number of free-electron–hole pairs generated intrinsically by thermal agitation. Such semiconductors are called *n-type*, since there is a greater number of free electrons than holes. For this reason, in *n*-type material the free electrons are called the *majority carriers* and the holes are called the *minority carriers*.

Acceptors

Another general class of impurities are those elements that have a valence of 3, such as boron, aluminum, and gallium. When an atom of one of these elements replaces an atom of the intrinsic semiconductor, a hole will be produced in one of the covalent bonds, since each impurity element has only three valence electrons. Thus, these impurities usually produce a preponderance of holes. This is called *p-type* material because most of the charge carriers are positively charged. In this case, the holes are called the majority carriers and the free electrons are called the minority carriers. The impurity atoms are called *acceptors* because they may accept an electron. Once this occurs, each acceptor atom becomes ionized and it represents a fixed negative charge in the structure.

1-4   The semiconductor diode

The junction of *p*-type and *n*-type semiconductors results in a device that has electrical properties which are similar to those of the vacuum-tube diode. This semiconductor is called a *p-n junction diode* or a *semiconductor diode*. Consider the *p-n* junction of Fig. 1-9*a*. The densities of the donor and acceptor atoms are shown in Fig. 1-9*b* and *c*, respectively. Now consider that the *n*-type and *p*-type materials are brought into physical contact to form a junction. (Junctions are not actually formed in this way.) Thermal agitation causes the free electrons and holes to diffuse throughout the material. Since the *n*-type and *p*-type materials were electrically neutral before the junction was formed, the diffusion of a free electron from the *n*-type region into the *p*-type material will add an excess negative charge to the *p*-type material and will leave behind an excess positive charge, due to an ionized donor atom. Conversely, the holes leaving the *p*-type material will tend to make it negative and cause the n-type material to acquire a positive charge. Of course, some of the free electrons formed intrinsically in the p-type material and some of the holes formed intrinsically in the n-type material will also diffuse across the junction. However, since the number of free electrons and holes generated by the impurities is so much greater than the number produced intrinsically, the initial current will be predominantly comprised of free electrons flowing into the p-type material and holes flowing into the n-type material. Thus, the n-type material becomes positively charged and the p-type material becomes negatively charged. This, in turn, sets up a potential difference across the junction, which tends to retard any further diffusion of free electrons into the p-type material and holes into the n-type material. An equilibrium condition is

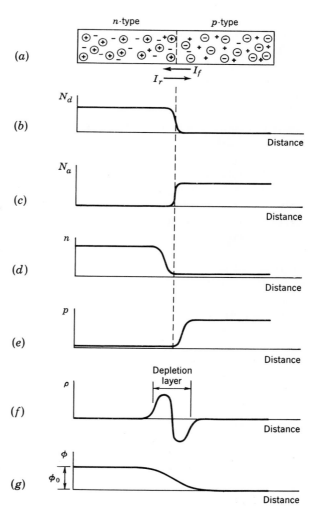

Fig. 1-9 Various distributions in a p-n junction. (a) The p-n junction; (b) donor density; (c) acceptor density; (d) free-electron density; (e) hole density; (f) total charge density; (g) potential distribution.

achieved where the potential barrier across the junction reduces the free-electron flow from the n-type material into the p-type material, until it equals the intrinsic free-electron flow from the p-type material into the n-type material. A similar equality will hold for the hole currents in both directions across the junction.

The electrostatic field caused by the charge imbalance between the n-type and the p-type materials will drive the free electrons in the n-type region and the holes in the p-type region away from the junction. This will leave a small zone in the vicinity of the junction in which the charge concentration is due mainly to the fixed donor and acceptor atoms. Such regions are called *depletion layers,* because they are almost divested of mobile charge carriers. The resulting concentrations of donors, acceptors, free electrons, and holes are shown in Fig. 1-9b to e. The total charge-density variation is shown in Fig. 1-9f. The electric field within the depletion layer is due to the ionized donors and acceptors residing there. The resulting potential distribution ϕ for the p-n junction is shown in Fig. 1-9g.

Two currents may be said to cross the p-n junction. One of these is the *forward current I_f,* composed of the free electrons leaving the n-type region and the holes leaving the p-type region. The other is the *reverse current I_r,* composed of the free electrons leaving the p-type region and the holes leaving the n-type region. It should be noted that the reverse current is aided by the potential difference across the junction. That is, it is due to the minority carriers in either region reaching the depletion layer. These carriers are caused to drift across the junction by the potential difference. On the other hand, the forward current consists of majority carriers leaving these respective regions. Although there are a much greater number of these carriers, only a few of them have sufficient kinetic energy to overcome the potential barrier and cross the junction.

Consider that a battery is connected to the p-n junction as shown in Fig. 1-10a. The potential barrier ϕ_0 will be reduced by e_b and the forward current will increase. Because of the large majority-carrier density a small increase in e_b will greatly increase I_f. The reverse current will remain essentially constant, since the potential barrier does not retard it. The total current i_b increases rapidly with increases in e_b. If the battery is

Fig. 1-10   (a) *A forward-biased p-n junction;* (b) *a reversed-biased p-n junction.*

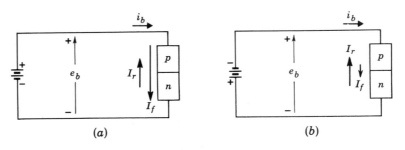

(a)   (b)

Fig. 1-11 The symbol for the p-n junction diode.

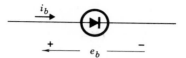

reversed, so that e_b is negative, then ϕ_0 will be increased. This will reduce I_f, but I_r will remain unchanged. Thus, i_b will be negative. Since I_r is quite small, the maximum magnitude that i_b can have, for negative e_b, is limited. Thus, for positive values of e_b there is substantial current; this is the *forward direction* of conduction and the diode is said to be *forward-biased.* For the negative e_b the current has an extremely small magnitude; this is the *reverse direction* of conduction and now the diode is said to be *reverse-biased.* In the forward direction the current increases quite rapidly with applied voltage, whereas in the reverse direction the magnitude of the current approaches the small constant value I_r. For this reason, I_r is called the *reverse saturation current.* Although I_r is independent of the applied voltage, it varies widely with temperature.

One factor concerning the current is quite important and we shall discuss it further. That is, the electrons and holes whose motion constitute the forward current do not move under the application of an electric field but wander randomly through the material. Those charge carriers that have enough energy to surmount the potential barrier at the junction, and which *are at* the junction, and which *happen* to have a sufficiently large component of velocity directed across the potential barrier, constitute the forward current. Such random motion is termed *diffusion.* The reverse current is somewhat different. In this case, the charge carriers move by diffusion to the potential barrier. However, its polarity is such that these charge carriers are swept across the junction by the electric field there. Motion of charge carriers due to an electric field is termed *drift.*

The symbol for the semiconductor diode is shown in Fig. 1-11. The arrow points in the forward direction for conventional current (i.e., it is forward-biased if the arrow points toward the negative side of the diode). In theory, the current i_b is given by the relation

$$i_b = I_s(\epsilon^{\varepsilon e_b/kT} - 1) \tag{1-8}$$

where ε = magnitude of the charge of electron, 1.602×10^{-19} coul
     k = Boltzmann constant, 1.380×10^{-23} joule/°K
     T = temperature, °K
     I_s = reverse saturation current = I_r

Characteristics of actual semiconductor diodes differ somewhat from the ideal ones. A typical characteristic is shown in Fig. 1-12. The actual characteristic follows Eq. (1-8) fairly closely except for the *reverse breakdown,* which is illustrated by the almost vertical portion of the characteristic on the left-hand side of the diagram.

Consider the circuit of Fig. 1-13. The graphical procedure of Sec. 1-1 can be used to determine the current through, and the voltage across, a

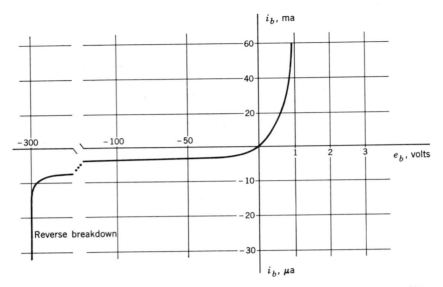

Fig. 1-12   *A typical current-voltage characteristic for a p-n junction diode.   (Note the scale changes on the axes.)*

semiconductor diode.   Note that the semiconductor diode allows current in the reverse direction in contrast to the vacuum-tube diode.   A load line can be drawn on the reverse portion of the characteristics to calculate it.

Dynamic resistance of the semiconductor diode is defined in just the same way as it is for the vacuum-tube diode.   That is, the dynamic resistance r_p is the reciprocal of the slope of the static characteristic at the operating point.

$$r_p = \frac{de_b}{di_b} \tag{1-9}$$

1-5   Ratings of semiconductor diodes

The useful lifetime of a semiconductor diode is, generally, much longer than that of a vacuum-tube diode, since the vacuum-tube diode has a heater

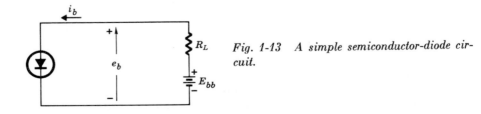

Fig. 1-13   *A simple semiconductor-diode circuit.*

which evaporates and a cathode whose emissivity decreases with use. However, if the ratings of a semiconductor diode are exceeded, its useful lifetime may be drastically shortened.   This is essentially due to excessive heating of the diode.   To limit this, the maximum allowable power dissipation is specified.   Since this power is a product of the voltage and current applied to the diode, it is these quantities that are generally limited.   In particular, maximum allowable voltage and current ratings in both the forward and reverse directions are given.   Since the ambient temperature affects the characteristics of the diode and its operating temperature, a range of allowable ambient temperatures may also be specified.

Finally, the reverse-breakdown voltage may be given, since the diode will not operate properly as a rectifier if this reverse voltage is exceeded.   It should be noted, however, that in many cases this voltage may be exceeded without necessarily damaging the diode.

1-6   The tunnel diode

Another type of semiconductor diode is the *tunnel diode*, which is sometimes called the *Esaki diode*.   Its principle of operation is considerably different from that of the semiconductor junction diode.   The tunnel diode is a *p-n* junction diode whose impurity concentrations in both the *p*-type and *n*-type regions are much larger than those of the conventional *p-n* junction diode and whose depletion region is considerably narrower.

A typical current-voltage characteristic for the tunnel diode is shown in Fig. 1-14.   This characteristic is radically different from the previously discussed diode characteristics in that the current does not increase monotonically with increasing forward bias.   The dynamic resistance (see Sec. 1-1) is of importance when the response to small signals is of interest. Between points *a* and *b* of Fig. 1-14, the dynamic resistance is negative, and it is this property of the tunnel diode that makes it important as an electronic device.   As an example of the use of negative resistance, see Sec. 11-1.

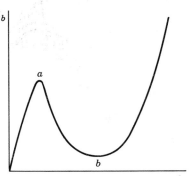

Fig. 1-14   The current-voltage characteristic of a tunnel diode.

1-7 The vacuum-tube triode

Vacuum-tube triodes consist of three elements, the cathode, the *grid*, and the plate, placed within an evacuated envelope. The cathode may be heated directly or indirectly, although the indirectly heated type is far more common. The grid, which surrounds the cathode, usually consists of a wire wound in the form of a helix. At times, other constructions are used for grids, such as a wire mesh. Characteristically the area presented to the electron stream by the wires of these grids is much less than the area of the space between the wires. The plate encloses both of these elements, and the grid is usually closer to the cathode than it is to the plate. These elements are most often in the form of concentric right cylinders whose cross sections are generally circular, elliptical, or polygonal. The entire configuration is placed within an evacuated chamber whose envelope is made of metal, glass, or ceramic material. A typical triode structure is shown in Fig. 1-15.

The grid of the vacuum-tube triode is usually operated at a negative potential with respect to the cathode. As a consequence, electrons are repelled from it, and current to it is negligible. Since the grid is physically closer to the cathode than the plate is, the grid-to-cathode potential e_c has a greater effect upon the current leaving the cathode than does the plate-to-cathode potential e_b. The voltages e_b and e_c are always measured with respect to the cathode and, hence, double subscripts need not be used. If the grid current is zero, then the current leaving the cathode is the same as the plate current i_b. A theoretical equation that relates these quantities is similar to the Child-Langmuir law; in addition, it takes into account the fact that the grid potential is more effective than the plate potential in controlling the plate current. This relationship is given by

$$i_b = \begin{cases} k(e_b + \mu e_c)^n & \text{for } e_b + \mu e_c \geqslant 0 \\ 0 & \text{for } e_b + \mu e_c < 0 \end{cases} \tag{1-10}$$

The exponent n is approximately $\frac{3}{2}$ in the usual cases. The constant μ is

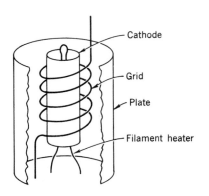

Fig. 1-15 Typical structure of a vacuum-tube triode.

in general much greater than unity and is given approximately by

$$\mu \approx \frac{C_{gk}}{C_{pk}} \tag{1-11}$$

where C_{gk} = capacitance between grid and cathode

$\qquad C_{pk}$ = capacitance between plate and cathode

Since the grid current is negligible, no power is dissipated in the grid. Hence, a voltage generator connected to the grid can control the plate current without supplying any measurable power.

1-8   Static characteristics of the vacuum-tube triode

In the operation of a vacuum-tube triode, the variables of interest are the plate current i_b, the plate voltage e_b, the grid current i_c, and the grid voltage e_c where, as usual, all voltages are referred to the cathode. In most operations, the grid is maintained at a negative potential, so the grid current is negligible. Thus, a relation among the remaining three variables is all that is needed to characterize the tube. Such a relation is given by Eq. (1-10). However, this is an idealization and is not sufficiently accurate for most practical applications. For greater accuracy, the relation among these three variables is presented in an empirically determined graphical form, as in the case of the vacuum-tube diode. A three-dimensional plot may be used to relate the three parameters, e_b, e_c, and i_b. Such a three-dimensional plot is impractical, and, therefore, information is usually presented by a family of curves on a two-dimensional plot. For instance, a curve of plate current i_b versus plate voltage e_b may be plotted for a constant value of grid voltage e_c. Then, other curves for different constant values of e_c are plotted on the same

Fig. 1-16   Typical plate characteristics for a vacuum-tube triode. The grid current i_c is plotted as the dashed curves.

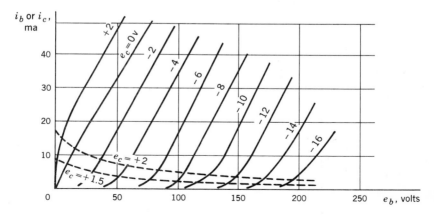

set of axes. This family of curves characterizes the operation of the vacuum-tube triode and is called the *plate characteristics* (or sometimes the *static plate characteristics*). A typical set of plate characteristics is shown in Fig. 1-16 by the solid curves. It should be noted that for a given plate voltage the plate current decreases as the grid voltage is made more negative.

In a similar way, the vacuum-tube triode may be characterized by plotting any two of the variables, while the third is held constant. By using different constant values for the third parameter, another family of curves may be obtained. Thus, the vacuum-tube triode may be completely characterized by any one of the three families of curves obtained by using either the grid voltage, the plate voltage, or the plate current as the constant parameter. When the plate voltage is used as the constant parameter, the family of curves is called the *transfer characteristics;* a typical set is shown in Fig. 1-17 by the solid curves. When the plate current is used as the parameter, the family of curves is called the *constant-current characteristics;* these are illustrated by the solid curves of Fig. 1-18. It should be noted that a knowledge of any one of these sets of curves is sufficient to determine the other two. However, it may be much more convenient and/or accurate to use one of these families for any given example.

Although we have assumed in this discussion that the grid current is negligible, this is not the case when the grid voltage becomes positive. In this case, grid-current curves may be plotted on the aforementioned characteristics. Typical sets of curves for grid current are shown dashed in Figs. 1-16 to 1-18.

At any instant during its operation, a vacuum-tube triode will have a certain plate current, plate voltage, and grid voltage. This determines a point on each of the static characteristics which is called the *instantaneous operating point.* Quite often, the electrode potentials and currents consist of a small alternating component added to a direct component. The posi-

Fig. 1-17   Typical transfer characteristics for a vacuum-tube triode. The grid current is plotted as the dashed curves.

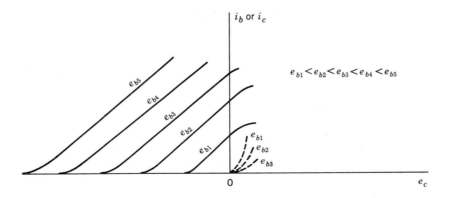

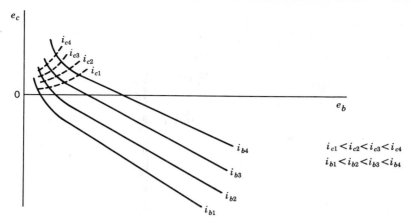

*Fig. 1-18   Typical constant-current characteristics for a vacuum-tube triode.
The grid current is plotted as the dashed curves.*

tion assumed by the instantaneous operating point when the alternating
components are zero is called the *quiescent operating point.*

1-9   Dynamic parameters of the vacuum-tube triode

The operation of the vacuum-tube triode is often such that the element
potentials vary only slightly around a quiescent operating point. In order
to calculate these variations the vacuum-tube triode is often approximately
characterized by a linear device whose characteristics are straight lines.
The parameters used to define the triode are determined by the slopes of
each of the characteristics at the quiescent operating point.

Amplification factor μ

The amplification factor is the negative of the rate of change of the plate
voltage with respect to the grid voltage (at some operating point) such that
the plate current remains constant.   That is,

$$\mu = -\left.\frac{de_b}{de_c}\right|_{i_b,\,\text{const}} = -\frac{\partial e_b}{\partial e_c} \tag{1-12}$$

Thus, the amplification factor is the negative reciprocal of the slope of the
constant-current characteristic at the operating point. This definition is
compatible with that given in Eq. (1-10). This can be seen by partially
differentiating Eq. (1-10). The amplification factor is a dimensionless ratio;
typical values for conventional vacuum-tube triodes usually lie between 2
and 100.

Dynamic plate resistance r_p

This parameter is defined at a given operating point by

$$r_p = \frac{de_b}{di_b}\bigg|_{e_c,\,\text{const}} = \frac{\partial e_b}{\partial i_b} \tag{1-13}$$

Its units are ohms and typical values lie between 50 and 100,000 ohms. The plate resistance is the reciprocal of the slope of the plate characteristic at the operating point. The similarity of this definition to that of the dynamic plate resistance of the vacuum-tube diode should be noted.

Transconductance or mutual conductance g_m

The slope of the transfer characteristic at the operating point determines the *grid-plate transconductance*, which is usually called the *transconductance* or *mutual conductance*. It is defined by

$$g_m = \frac{di_b}{de_c}\bigg|_{e_b,\,\text{const}} = \frac{\partial i_b}{\partial e_c} \tag{1-14}$$

The units of transconductance are mhos. It is usually given in micromhos (μmhos). Typical values lie between 500 and 30,000 μmhos.

A relationship exists among these three parameters for any given vacuum-tube triode. Consider an operation of a vacuum-tube triode in which the variations around the operating point are differentially small. When the plate and grid potentials change by differential amounts, the incremental change in the plate current is given by

$$di_b = \frac{\partial i_b}{\partial e_b}\,de_b + \frac{\partial i_b}{\partial e_c}\,de_c \tag{1-15}$$

Substituting the appropriate dynamic parameters for the partial derivatives, we obtain

$$di_b = \frac{1}{r_p}\,de_b + g_m\,de_c \tag{1-16}$$

This equation indicates that, for infinitesimal variations, the dynamic parameters may be used instead of the static characteristics to determine the operation of the tube.

If the incremental changes in the plate and the grid voltages are of opposite sign and of such magnitude that the plate current remains constant, di_b may be set equal to zero in Eq. (1-16). This yields

$$-\frac{de_b}{de_c}\bigg|_{i_b,\,\text{const}} = g_m r_p$$

Then using Eq. (1-12) the relationship among the dynamic parameters is found to be

$$\mu = g_m r_p \tag{1-17}$$

1-10   Variations of the dynamic parameters of the vacuum-tube triode with changes in the operating point

Any vacuum-tube triode will have static characteristics that resemble the nonlinear curves of Figs. 1-16, 1-17, and 1-18. Since the dynamic parameters represent the slopes of these characteristics at the operating point, a shift in the operating point will result in a variation of these quantities. Approximate expressions for the plate resistance and transconductance in terms of the currents and voltages of the tube can be obtained if we assume that the theoretical expression for the plate current in a vacuum-tube triode given by Eq. (1-10) is valid. In this discussion, we shall assume that the exponent n is equal to $\frac{3}{2}$ and the potentials are such that $e_b + \mu e_c$ is nonnegative. Thus,

$$i_b = k(e_b + \mu e_c)^{\frac{3}{2}} \tag{1-18}$$

Theoretically μ is a constant that is given approximately by Eq. (1-11). To obtain r_p, partially differentiate Eq. (1-18) with respect to e_b and then substitute for $e_b + \mu_c e$ using Eq. (1-18). Thus,

$$r_p = (\tfrac{2}{3})k^{-\frac{2}{3}}i_b^{-\frac{1}{3}} \tag{1-19}$$

Similarly, g_m may be obtained from Eq. (1-17). Thus,

$$g_m = (\tfrac{3}{2})\mu k^{\frac{2}{3}}i_b^{\frac{1}{3}} \tag{1-20}$$

In summary, μ is theoretically independent of plate current, while r_p and g_m vary as $i_b^{-\frac{1}{3}}$ and $i_b^{\frac{1}{3}}$, respectively. In actual vacuum-tube triodes this statement is only approximately correct.

1-11   Graphical analysis of a simple vacuum-tube-triode amplifier

A very simple circuit, which is the basis for many common vacuum-tube-triode circuits, is shown in Fig. 1-19. The notation used in this circuit follows the terminology commonly in use. That is, lowercase letters represent the instantaneous values of time-varying quantities, whereas

Fig. 1-19   A simple vacuum-tube-triode amplifier. Note that E_{cc} is defined as a negative number.

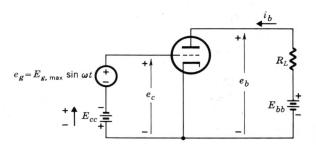

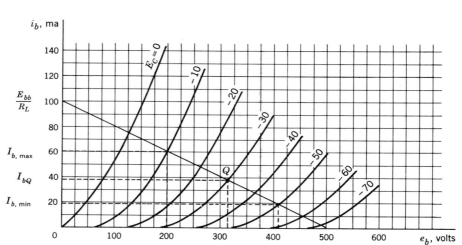

Fig. 1-20 *The plate characteristics of the type 7027-A vacuum-tube triode (connected).*
(Courtesy Radio Corporation of America.)

uppercase letters indicate quantities that do not vary with time. As before,
all vacuum-tube voltages are measured with respect to the cathode, and so
the plate-to-cathode voltage is simply called the plate voltage and the
grid-to-cathode voltage is simply called the grid voltage. The direct-
voltage sources, indicated by E_{bb} and E_{cc}, are used to develop the appropriate
direct potentials on the plate and grid, respectively, where E_{cc} is negative.
The purpose of this circuit is to increase the magnitude of the alternating
voltage $e_g = E_{g,\max} \sin \omega t$. This amplified voltage is developed across the
resistance R_L, which is called the *load resistance*. If R_L were not present,
the plate voltage would remain fixed at the value E_{bb}.

To analyze this circuit, we shall use the plate characteristics for the
vacuum-tube triode shown in Fig. 1-20. For any given grid voltage the
triode is characterized by the single curve corresponding to that grid voltage.
The analysis then proceeds in exactly the same manner as the analysis of the
vacuum-tube diode that was presented in Sec. 1-1. That is, a load line may
be drawn. The intersection of this load line with the appropriate grid-
voltage curve yields the plate voltage and the plate current. As before, the
load line is the straight line that passes through the points $i_b = 0, e_b = E_{bb}$ and
$i_b = E_{bb}/R_L, e_b = 0$. For example, in Fig. 1-19, assume that $E_{bb} = 500$ volts,
$E_{cc} = -30$ volts, $e_g = 20 \sin \omega t$ volts, and $R_L = 5,000$ ohms. Thus, the
total instantaneous grid voltage is $e_c = -30 + 20 \sin \omega t$. The load line for
this circuit intersects the abscissa at 500 volts and intersects the ordinate at
100 ma. At the instant when e_g is zero volts, the grid voltage is equal to
$E_{cc} = -30$ volts. Hence, at this instant, $e_b = 315$ volts and $i_b = 38$ ma.
This is also the condition that would exist if there were no applied alternating

voltages. Thus, this point is the quiescent operating point and is indicated in Fig. 1-20 by point Q, whose coordinates are E_{bQ} and I_{bQ}. The grid voltage will vary sinusoidally between the values -10 and -50 volts. The plate voltage will swing between the values $E_{b,\min} = 200$ volts and $E_{b,\max} = 410$ volts, while the plate current varies between $I_{b,\max} = 60$ ma and $I_{b,\min} = 19$ ma. These variations are indicated in Fig. 1-20 and, in addition, are sketched to corresponding time axes in Fig. 1-21.

It should be pointed out that, even though the grid voltage has a sinusoidal variation, the plate current and plate voltage are only approximately sinusoidal, because of the nonlinearity of the characteristics. Furthermore, the plate voltage e_b reaches its minimum value when the grid voltage e_c reaches its maximum (least negative) value. Thus, there is a 180° phase shift between the alternating components of the grid and plate voltages. This happens because an increase in grid voltage (in the positive direction) increases the plate current, which results in an increased voltage drop across R_L. This, in turn reduces the plate voltage. The most important characteristic of this circuit is its amplifying ability. Indeed, the peak-to-peak variation in plate voltage, $E_{b,\max} - E_{b,\min}$, is 210 volts, while the peak-to-peak grid voltage, $E_{c,\max} - E_{c,\min}$, is only 40 volts. The *voltage amplification*

Fig. 1-21   Instantaneous values of grid voltage, plate current, and plate voltage for the circuit of Fig. 1-19. Note the 180° phase shift between the grid voltage and the plate voltage.

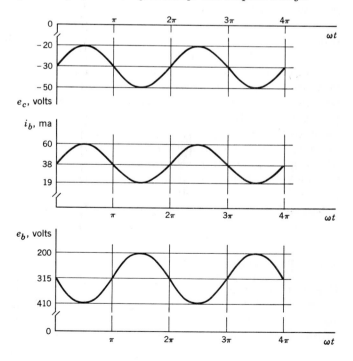

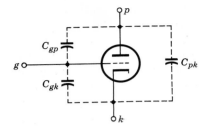

Fig. 1-22   *The interelectrode capacitances of a vacuum-tube triode.*

or *voltage gain* of this circuit is $-210/40 = -5.25$.   The minus sign is used to indicate the 180° phase shift.

1-12   Shortcomings of the vacuum-tube triode

In the preceding section we have ignored the capacitances that always exist between the electrodes of any triode.   These *interelectrode capacitances* are inherent in the structure of the triode; they are called *stray capacitances* or *parasitic capacitances*, since they are not deliberately placed there.   In a vacuum-tube triode, three such capacitances exist: the *grid-to-plate capacitance* C_{gp}, the *grid-to-cathode capacitance* C_{gk}, and the *plate-to-cathode capacitance* C_{pk}.   These are shown in Fig. 1-22.

In an ideal vacuum-tube triode, voltages and currents in the plate circuit will not affect the grid circuit.   Moreover, voltages and currents in the grid circuit will affect the plate circuit only through the amplification property of the tube.   This unilateral coupling, which isolates the grid circuit from signals in the plate circuit, is not perfect in an actual triode when alternating signals are present, because of the stray capacitance C_{gp}.   This stray capacitance may markedly impair the operation of the circuit.   We shall discuss these effects in Secs. 3-12, 6-26, 8-7, and in Chap. 10.   These effects can cause a substantial reduction in the gain of the circuit or may cause it to oscillate (i.e., produce an output voltage that is independent of the input voltage).   To reduce these effects, other types of vacuum tubes have been developed.   These other tubes are, in general, more costly and require more complicated circuits.   In many cases, the vacuum-tube triode performs quite satisfactorily.   Hence, these tubes merely supplement the vacuum-tube triode and do not render it obsolete.

1-13   The vacuum-tube tetrode

Grid-to-plate capacitance is the cause of several of the vacuum-tube triode's disadvantages.   Although the magnitude of this capacitance is usually about 10 or 20 $\mu\mu$f, it may be decreased by a factor of a thousand or more by adding a second grid that electrostatically shields the first grid from the plate. This second grid is connected to the cathode and placed between the first grid and the plate. Thus, it will decrease the effect of the varying plate voltage on the electric field in the vicinity of the first grid. Vacuum tubes having such an additional grid are called *vacuum-tube tetrodes*. Since the alternating input signal is usually connected to the first grid, which thereafter controls the alternating component of the plate current, this grid is known as the *control grid*. The second grid is called the *screen grid*, since it shields or "screens" the plate from the control grid. The screen grid is similar to the control grid in that the area between the grid wires is much greater than the area presented by the grid wires to the electronic current.

If the screen grid is connected directly to the cathode, the electric field from the plate will be shielded not only from the control grid but also from the cathode. Thus, negligible current will reach the plate and the tube will not operate. This difficulty can be overcome by maintaining the screen grid at a fixed positive direct potential and connecting it to the cathode through a circuit that has a low impedance for the frequencies of interest and a high resistance to direct current. Such a circuit is indicated in Fig. 1-23, where C_s acts essentially as a short circuit between the screen grid and the cathode for alternating signals.

A plot of plate current i_b, screen-grid current i_{c2}, and total current from the cathode i_t for a fixed value of screen-grid voltage is shown in Fig. 1-24. The dip in the plate current characteristics between points a and b is due to secondary emission. That is, electrons reaching the plate may impart enough energy to some of the internal electrons so as to emit them. For a low value of plate voltage, this secondary emission is quite small since the primary electrons have low energies. At higher values of plate voltage, the secondary emission can become appreciable. Moreover, if the plate voltage is less than the screen grid voltage, then most of the secondary electrons will be attracted to the screen grid, thereby reducing the plate current. Since each electron impinging upon the plate may produce more than one secondary electron, the plate current can decrease appreciably. As the plate voltage is increased still higher, more of the secondary electrons will be attracted

Fig. 1-23 *A simple vacuum-tube-tetrode circuit. Note that E_{cc} is defined as a negative number.*

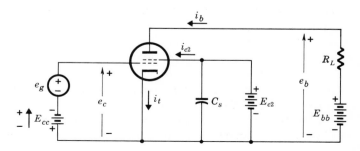

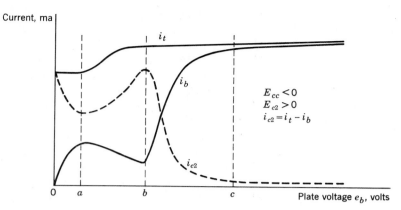

Fig. 1-24   Plate current i_b, screen-grid current i_{c2}, and cathode current i_t versus plate voltage e_b for fixed control-grid and screen-grid voltages in a vacuum-tube tetrode.

back to the plate.   In addition, secondary electrons emitted from the screen grid will also be attracted to the plate.   Hence, at sufficiently high plate voltages, the plate current will be almost equal to the current leaving the cathode.

The total current i_t (i.e., the current leaving the cathode) is almost independent of the plate voltage, since the screen grid shields the cathode as well as the control grid from the plate.   The screen-grid current i_{c2} is given by $i_t - i_b$.

Static characteristics and dynamic parameters of the vacuum-tube tetrode

The variables of interest in a vacuum-tube tetrode are the voltages and currents of the control grid, the screen grid, and the plate.   This requires a six-dimensional plot, which is, of course, impossible to draw.   However, the control grid is usually maintained at a negative potential, so its current is negligible.   Moreover, the screen-grid current and voltage characteristics are often not required, since the screen grid is maintained at a fixed positive potential.   This leaves the three variables that were used for the static characteristics of the vacuum-tube triode and, in fact, the same sets of static characteristics can be drawn for the vacuum-tube tetrode.   Figure 1-25 illustrates the plate characteristics for a typical vacuum-tube tetrode with a constant screen-grid voltage and the control-grid voltage as a parameter.   For a different value of screen-grid voltage, a different set of plate characteristics would be required.   The transfer characteristics and the constant-current characteristics can be obtained from the plate characteristics.

The dynamic parameters μ, r_p, and g_m for a vacuum-tube tetrode are defined in the same way as they were for a vacuum-tube triode, with the additional provision that the screen-grid voltage is maintained constant. It should be noted that because of the nonlinearity of the static characteristics, the dynamic parameters can vary greatly as the operating point is shifted. In fact, the dynamic plate resistance r_p, which is the reciprocal of the slope of the plate characteristics, even becomes negative over certain regions. This nonlinearity of the static characteristics is a distinct disadvantage. For instance, the operation of the amplifier indicated in Fig. 1-23 will be along the load line shown in Fig. 1-25. (The procedure for drawing this load line is the same as that for a vacuum-tube triode.) If the output waveform is to be a reasonably good representation of the input waveform, the region of operation must be restricted to the right of the line $\overline{AB}$ in Fig. 1-25. This considerably limits the useful operating region of the tube. This serious drawback led to the development of the vacuum-tube pentode and the beam power tube and resulted in the subsequent decline in the use of the vacuum-tube tetrode.

1-14 The vacuum-tube pentode

If the current due to secondary emission between the plate and the screen grid in a vacuum-tube tetrode could be eliminated, the characteristics would

Fig. 1-25   Typical plate characteristics for a vacuum-tube tetrode.

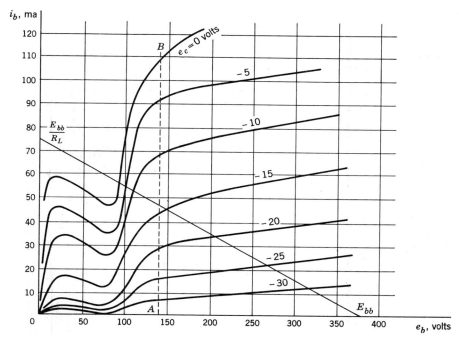

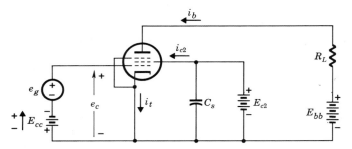

Fig. 1-26   *A simple vacuum-tube-pentode circuit.   Note that E_{cc} is defined as a negative number.*

be considerably more linear.   A third grid, placed between the screen grid and the plate and maintained at a potential that is considerably less than the potentials of either, would accomplish this, since the force on the electrons between the new grid and the plate would be strongly toward the plate.   A vacuum tube having such a third grid is known as a *vacuum-tube pentode* and this third grid is called a *suppressor grid*.   In order to maintain the suppressor grid at a low potential, it is often connected to the cathode, as is indicated in the simple vacuum-tube-pentode amplifier circuit of Fig. 1-26.

1-15   Static characteristics of the vacuum-tube pentode

Vacuum-tube pentodes are usually operated with a fixed voltage on the screen and suppressor grids.   The suppressor-grid voltage is usually zero, since it is commonly connected to the cathode.   The screen-grid potential is maintained at a fixed positive potential, as it is in a vacuum-tube tetrode. The variation in the curve of plate current versus the plate voltage because of secondary-emission current will now be absent and the resulting plate characteristics will appear as in Fig. 1-27.   The curve of screen-grid current versus plate voltage for constant control-grid voltage and screen-grid voltage, which is shown by the dashed curve of Fig. 1-27, also indicates the absence of secondary-emission currents.

1-16   Dynamic parameters of the vacuum-tube pentode

When the screen and suppressor grids are maintained at constant potentials, as is usually the case, the plate current is a function of only the control-grid and plate voltages.   Differentially small changes in these voltages will produce a change in the plate current according to the following equation:

$$di_b = \frac{\partial i_b}{\partial e_c} de_c + \frac{\partial i_b}{\partial e_b} de_b \tag{1-21}$$

Equation (1-21) is the same relationship that applies to vacuum-tube triodes. Therefore, the same parameters that were used to characterize the vacuum-tube triode may also be used for the vacuum-tube pentode. These are the *control-grid–to–plate amplification factor*

$$\mu = -\left.\frac{de_b}{de_c}\right|_{i_b,e_{c2},e_{c3},\,\text{const}} = -\frac{\partial e_b}{\partial e_c} \tag{1-22}$$

the *control-grid–to–plate transconductance*

$$g_m = \left.\frac{di_b}{de_c}\right|_{e_b,e_{c2},e_{c3},\,\text{const}} = \frac{\partial i_b}{\partial e_c} \tag{1-23}$$

and the *dynamic plate resistance*

$$r_p = \left.\frac{de_b}{di_b}\right|_{e_c,e_{c2},e_{c3},\,\text{const}} = \frac{\partial e_b}{\partial i_b} \tag{1-24}$$

where e_{c2} and e_{c3} are the screen-grid and the suppressor-grid voltages, respectively. The relation $\mu = g_m r_p$ may be derived in exactly the same way as it was for the vacuum-tube triode.

Since the control-grid voltage affects the current from the cathode in the same way for both the vacuum-tube triode and the vacuum-tube pentode, the transconductances of similarly constructed vacuum-tube triodes and

Fig. 1-27   The plate characteristics of the 6AU6 vacuum-tube pentode.   The screen-grid current i_{c2} is indicated by the dashed curve.   (Courtesy Westinghouse Electric Corporation.)

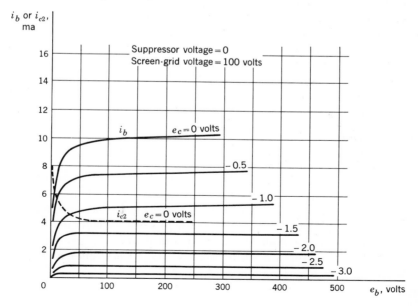

Table 1-1

	Triodes	*Pentodes*
μ	2–100	100–20,000
g_m, μmhos	500–30,000	500–30,000
r_p, ohms	50–100,000	50,000–2,000,000

vacuum-tube pentodes are about the same.   However, the plate voltage has much less effect upon the plate current in a vacuum-tube pentode than it does in a vacuum-tube triode.   Thus, plate resistance is generally much larger in vacuum-tube pentodes than it is in vacuum-tube triodes.   Since $\mu = g_m r_p$, it follows that vacuum-tube pentodes have larger amplification factors than vacuum-tube triodes.   Common values of these parameters for triodes and pentodes are compared in Table 1-1.

If differentially small changes are made in the potentials of all three grids and the plate, the incremental change in the plate current may be written as

$$di_b = \frac{\partial i_b}{\partial e_c}\, de_c + \frac{\partial i_b}{\partial e_{c2}}\, de_{c2} + \frac{\partial i_b}{\partial e_{c3}}\, de_{c3} + \frac{\partial i_b}{\partial e_b}\, de_b \tag{1-25}$$

Hence, additional tube parameters may be defined.   For instance, the *screen-grid–to–plate transconductance g_{ps}* is

$$g_{ps} = \frac{\partial i_b}{\partial e_{c2}}$$

the *screen-grid–to–plate amplification factor μ_{ps}* is

$$\mu_{ps} = -\frac{\partial e_b}{\partial e_{c2}}$$

and the *dynamic screen-grid resistance r_s* is

$$r_s = \frac{\partial e_{c2}}{\partial i_{c2}}$$

Similarly, a transconductance and an amplification factor may be defined between any two pairs of electrodes other than the reference electrode (usually the cathode).   A dynamic resistance also may be defined for any of these electrodes.   Since the screen and suppressor grids have constant potentials in most applications, these other parameters are not commonly used.   Thus, the control-grid–to–plate transconductance and the control-grid–to–plate amplification factor are called simply *transconductance* and *amplification factor*.

1-17　The beam power tube

The static plate characteristics of vacuum-tube pentodes are fairly linear, except for comparatively low plate voltages, where they exhibit a fairly broad "knee" or gradual bending of the curve. The allowable instantaneous plate voltage must be restricted to higher values if linear operation is desired. (However, this restriction is nowhere as severe as it is in the vacuum-tube tetrode.) For large power output in an amplifier, large swings in voltage and current are required, and this usually carries the instantaneous operating point into the region where the knees of the plate characteristics occur. On the other hand, a certain type of vacuum tube called the *beam power tube* has plate characteristics that are similar to those of the vacuum-tube pentode but have sharper knees and, therefore, larger regions of linearity. These tubes were developed for power applications. The beam power tube has a pair of beam-forming plates instead of a suppressor grid. Often these are omitted from the schematic diagram.

1-18　Ratings of vacuum tubes

The ratings of the conventional multielectrode vacuum tubes studied thus far, including the vacuum-tube triode, are determined by the same considerations as those of the vacuum-tube diode, which were discussed in Sec. 1-2, except that now the maximum allowable values of voltage and power dissipation for each of the grids must also be considered.

　　The instantaneous plate dissipation is $e_b i_b$. The maximum allowable plate dissipation limits the average value of $e_b i_b$ and thereby limits the choice of the operating point. Similarly, in tetrodes, pentodes, and beam power tubes, the average screen-grid dissipation, which is the average value of the product of the screen-grid voltage and screen-grid current, is limited by the heat-dissipating ability of the screen grid. The other grids have similar power ratings. However, these are not generally exceeded, since the suppressor grid is usually at the cathode potential and the control grid is at a negative potential. Thus, these ratings are not usually specified. Sometimes, the control-grid voltage does become positive and, for tubes designed for such operation, the control-grid dissipation is specified.

　　To prevent insulation breakdown and arcing, maximum ratings should be given for the voltages between each pair of electrodes.

1-19　The junction transistor

The transistor is a solid-state device which performs many of the functions of vacuum tubes. In comparable applications the transistor is smaller, lighter,

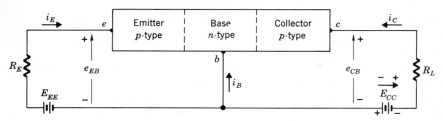

Fig. 1-28   A representation of a p-n-p junction transistor.

more rugged, and freer from microphonic noise.   In addition, the transistor requires no filament-heating power, with the associated warmup time.   The life of the vacuum tube is limited by the life of its cathode, but the transistor has no such limitation.   Lower power-supply voltages may be used with the transistor, and its efficiency is higher.   On the other hand, the vacuum tube can, in general, operate satisfactorily at higher frequencies with higher power levels.   Under some circumstances, it has lower noise, with the exception of microphonics, and is capable of operating at much higher power levels. Finally, the vacuum tube is relatively insensitive to temperature change, whereas the operation of the transistor varies markedly with temperature. Thus, the transistor and the vacuum tube complement each other.

There are many varieties of transistors.   One type that has found wide application is the *junction transistor*.   A knowledge of its operation is basic for understanding the behavior of all types of transistors.

The junction transistor consists of a region of *n*-type material between two regions of *p*-type material, as shown in Fig. 1-28.   The *n*-type and *p*-type regions may be interchanged.   These constructions are called the *p-n-p* junction transistor and the *n-p-n* junction transistor, respectively.   Both types are commonly used, and the theory of operation for each is essentially the same.   That is, the theory of the *n-p-n* junction transistor may be obtained from that of the *p-n-p* junction transistor by reversing all polarities and by interchanging the roles played by the free electrons and holes.   Usually, one junction is forward-biased while the other is reverse-biased.   The middle region is called the *base*, the end region that is adjacent to the forward-biased junction is called the *emitter*, and the other end region is called the *collector*.   The base region is very thin; in fact, its width is much smaller than the average *diffusion length* of the minority carriers in the base.   Note that this diffusion length is the average distance that a minority carrier travels before combining with a majority carrier.

When the connections to a *p-n-p* junction transistor are open-circuited, the *p*-type emitter and collector regions attain a negative potential with respect to the *n*-type base.   This occurs because of the distribution of the free electrons and holes throughout the transistor, as was explained in the discussion of the junction diode (Sec. 1-4).   The resulting potential distribution is shown in Fig. 1-29a, where it may be noted that the potential differences across the junctions are different, since the emitter is, in general, more highly doped than the collector. The potential drop ϕ_{01} from the base to the emitter is a positive quantity as is the potential drop ϕ_{02} from the base to the collector.

If a comparatively large reverse-biasing voltage e_{CB} is connected between the base and collector leads, the potential difference across the collector-base junction increases to $\phi_{02} - e_{CB}$, where e_{CB} is negative. This large reverse potential makes the forward current (electrons flowing from base to collector and holes flowing from collector to base) negligibly small. The collector current will practically achieve its saturation value. In the transistor, this saturation current I_{CO} is called the *collector-cutoff current* and is the current across the collector-base junction when the collector is strongly reverse-biased and the emitter is open-circuited. For a *p-n-p* transistor, the current I_{CO} is negative. If in addition to e_{CB} a small forward-biasing voltage e_{EB} is connected between the emitter and base leads, as shown in Fig. 1-28, the potential distribution becomes that shown in Fig. 1-29b. Since the emitter junction is now forward-biased, its forward current is very much larger than its reverse current. This forward current is composed of two components. One is the electron current which is from the base to the emitter. The other component, the hole current from emitter to base, accounts for the major portion of the current in the transistor which is conventionally biased. Since the width of the base is very much less than the diffusion length of the holes in the *n*-type region and since the other dimensions of the base are very much larger than this diffusion length, most of the hole current from the emitter will *diffuse across the base* without recombining and will be swept into the collector by the strong potential across the collector junction. This is a crucial property of the junction transistor, and deserves repetition. Consider a hole which has entered the base region from the emitter. Three

Fig. 1-29 (a) The potential distribution in an unbiased transistor; (b) the potential distribution in a conventionally biased transistor. Note that e_{CB} is negative.

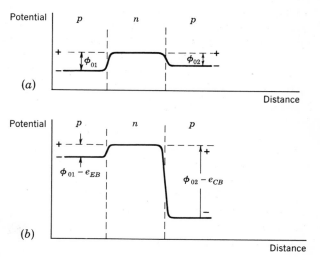

possibilities exist for the behavior of this hole. First, it may wander back to the emitter region. Holes that behave in this fashion do not produce any net current from the emitter. Secondly, it may diffuse to the collector junction, where it will be swept into the collector region. Thirdly, the hole may recombine in the base region. This is unlikely, since the base width is much less than the diffusion length. The second case, that of hole current from the emitter to the collector, is by far the predominant current through the transistor.

A consideration of this current leads to an explanation of the amplifying ability of the junction transistor. Consider the elementary amplifier circuit shown in Fig. 1-28. The collector current i_C has essentially the same magnitude as the emitter current i_E, while the resistance of the forward-biased emitter junction is very much less than the resistance of the reverse-biased collector junction. Thus, a comparatively large resistance R_L may be inserted into the collector circuit without appreciably altering the collector current i_C. Suppose now that E_{EE} is increased by an amount ΔE_{EE}. The emitter current will be increased by an amount Δi_E, resulting in an approximately equal change in the magnitude of collector current ($-\Delta i_C \approx \Delta i_E$). This will produce a change in the voltage drop across R_L that is considerably greater than ΔE_{EE}, because the resistance R_L is considerably larger than that of the emitter junction. Similarly, there is also a power gain from the emitter circuit to the collector circuit.

The changes in the emitter and collector currents are not exactly the same and their ratio for incremental changes at a fixed collector potential defines the *common-base short-circuit forward-current transfer ratio (or amplification factor)* α. This is

$$\alpha = -\left.\frac{di_C}{di_E}\right|_{e_{CB},\,\text{const}} = -\frac{\partial i_C}{\partial i_E} \tag{1-26}$$

The magnitude of α is usually slightly less than unity.

The circuit symbols for the *p-n-p* transistor and the *n-p-n* transistor are shown in Fig. 1-30a and b. The conventional polarities are also shown there. For normal operation of a *p-n-p* transistor i_E is positive, i_C and i_B are negative, e_{CB} is negative, and e_{EB} is positive.

Fig. 1-30 (a) The circuit symbol for the p-n-p transistor; (b) the circuit symbol for the n-p-n transistor.

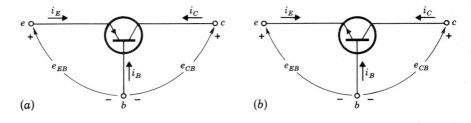

(a)　　　　　　　　　　　　　　　　　　(b)

1-20　Current relations for a transistor

In this section we shall discuss some equations that relate the currents into a transistor to the applied potentials. Ebers and Moll[2] have developed such equations, which are fairly accurate for most operating conditions of transistors. These are, for the *p-n-p* transistor

$$i_E = c_{11}(\epsilon^{\varepsilon e_{EB}/kT} - 1) + c_{12}(\epsilon^{\varepsilon e_{CB}/kT} - 1) \tag{1-27}$$

$$i_C = c_{21}(\epsilon^{\varepsilon e_{EB}/kT} - 1) + c_{22}(\epsilon^{\varepsilon e_{CB}/kT} - 1) \tag{1-28}$$

The quantity k is the Boltzmann constant, ε is the magnitude of the charge of an electron, and T is the temperature in degrees Kelvin. The parameters c_{11}, c_{12}, c_{21}, and c_{22} are assumed to be constants. The current entering the base lead is

$$i_B = -i_E - i_C \tag{1-29}$$

The coefficients in Eqs. (1-27) and (1-28) may be expressed in terms of some previously defined parameters for the transistor. In particular, eliminating e_{EB} from these equations, the expression for i_C is found to be

$$i_C = \frac{c_{11}c_{22} - c_{21}c_{12}}{c_{11}} \left(\epsilon^{\varepsilon e_{CB}/kT} - 1\right) + \frac{c_{21}}{c_{11}} i_E \tag{1-30}$$

If the emitter lead is open-circuited, i_E becomes zero. By definition, the collector-cutoff current I_{CO} is the value of i_C with i_E equal to zero and e_{CB} equal to a large negative quantity. Under these conditions, the exponential term in Eq. (1-30) is negligible as compared to unity and, therefore,

$$I_{CO} = \frac{c_{21}c_{12} - c_{11}c_{22}}{c_{11}} \tag{1-31}$$

For a *p-n-p* transistor, I_{CO} is a negative number. Moreover, if we partially differentiate Eq. (1-30) with respect to i_E and multiply by -1, we obtain the current-amplification factor α.

$$\alpha = -\frac{\partial i_C}{\partial i_E} = -\frac{c_{21}}{c_{11}} \tag{1-32}$$

Thus

$$i_C = I_{CO}(1 - \epsilon^{\varepsilon e_{CB}/kT}) - \alpha I_E \tag{1-33}$$

Similarly, i_E may be expressed in terms of I_{EO} (where we define the *emitter-cutoff current* I_{EO} as the emitter current with the emitter junction strongly reverse-biased and the collector lead open-circuited) and the *common-base reverse-current amplification factor* α_r which is

$$\alpha_r = -\frac{di_E}{di_C}\bigg|_{e_{EB},\text{ const}} = -\frac{\partial i_E}{\partial i_C} \tag{1-34}$$

It has been tacitly assumed that the parameters c_{11}, c_{12}, c_{21}, c_{22}, α, and α_r are independent of the operating point. Actually, they are not, so Eqs. (1-27) and (1-28) are only approximate.

1-21   Static characteristics of transistors

A common means of specifying the behavior of the transistor is by presenting graphical characteristics that relate its external voltages and currents. For the transistor, two families of curves are required, since there are four variables (two voltages and two currents) that are needed to specify its operating condition. Since the transistor has three leads, there is an additional voltage and an additional current, but these may be obtained by algebraic combinations of the other two voltages or currents. The quantities that are chosen as the independent variables are picked, for convenience and accuracy, according to the circuit configuration.

One circuit used with transistors is the *common-base circuit*. In it, the base lead is common to the input and the output circuits and is taken as the voltage-reference node (see Fig. 1-31). The corresponding family of characteristic curves that is most often used is called the *common-base output characteristics*. They are given in Fig. 1-32a. Here, the two independent variables are e_{CB} and i_E; the dependent variable is i_C. Note that both axes are negative.

These characteristics are usually divided into three regions. When the common-base circuit is used for amplifying, its operation is restricted to the *active region*, the first quadrant of the figure. In this region, the emitter is forward-biased, while the collector is reverse-biased. The collector current is essentially independent of the collector voltage and is nearly equal to the emitter current. The difference between these two currents is the base current, which is quite small. From Eq. (1-26) we see that α may be determined from these characteristics by taking the negative of the ratio of the change in i_C to a small incremental change in i_E for a fixed value of e_{CB}. Often, the quantity of interest is $1 - \alpha$ and not α. Since α is quite close to unity, the precision of this graphical technique is usually not adequate for determining $1 - \alpha$.

The fourth quadrant of these characteristics is known as the *cutoff*

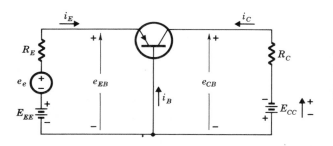

Fig. 1-31 A common-base-transistor amplifier. Note that E_{CC} is defined as negative.

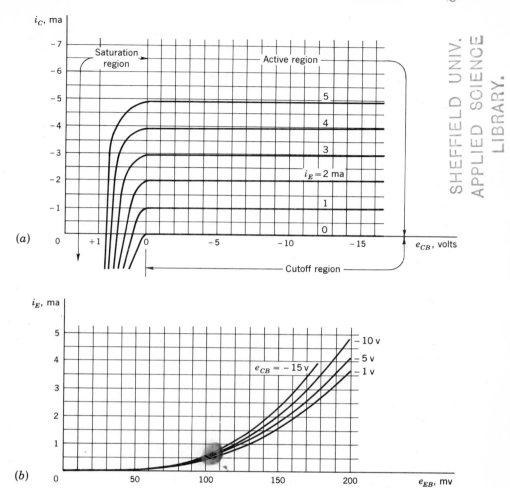

Fig. 1-32 *Common-base characteristics of a typical p-n-p junction transistor. (a) Output characteristics; (b) input characteristics. (By permission from D. DeWitt and A. L. Rossoff, "Transistor Electronics," McGraw-Hill Book Company, 1957.)*

region. Here, both the emitter and collector junctions are reverse-biased, so the currents in the transistor are negligible.

The second and third quadrants constitute the *saturation region.*   In this region, the collector junction is forward-biased.

A detailed discussion of graphical procedures for the analysis of transistor circuits will be given in Chap. 2.

The common-base output characteristics give no information about the emitter-to-base voltage e_{EB}.   Thus, to characterize the transistor completely, an additional set of characteristics is needed.   Such a set is the *common-base*

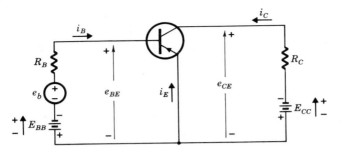

Fig. 1-33   A common-emitter-transistor amplifier.   Note that the E_{CC} and E_{BB} are defined as negative.

input characteristics (see Fig. 1-32*b*).   In this case, the two independent variables are e_{EB} and e_{CB}.   The emitter current is the dependent variable.

Since the emitter and collector currents of a transistor are nearly the same, the base current is quite small.   Thus, if the base is used as the input lead, as shown in Fig. 1-33, the input current will be considerably less than the output (collector) current.   For this configuration, there is a high current gain from the input to the output (i.e., the ratio of the output alternating current to the input alternating current), and the operation is somewhat analogous to that of the conventional vacuum-tube-triode amplifier.   The *common-emitter circuit* is the most often used type of transistor amplifier. Figure 1-34 shows the *common-emitter characteristics* for a typical *p-n-p* transistor.   To produce approximately zero ($i_C = I_{CO}$) collector current with a negative collector-to-emitter voltage, the base current must be reversed and made essentially equal in magnitude to $|I_{CO}|$.   That is, the base current, which cuts off the transistor, is equal to the negative of the collector-cutoff current.   (Note that this value of i_B is *positive* for a *p-n-p* transistor.)   The *active region* of Fig. 1-34*a* lies between the curve of $i_B = -I_{CO}$ and the almost vertical line where all the characteristics approach each other.   The *cutoff region* lies below (or essentially on) the $i_B = -I_{CO}$ curve.   Finally, the *saturation region* occurs in the vicinity of the ordinate where the constant base-current curves approach each other.

The curves of Figs. 1-32 and 1-34 present the same information.   However, there are times when we are *required* to use one or the other.   For instance, the common-emitter output characteristics often provide more precision than the common-base output characteristics.   The determination of the base current from the common-base output characteristics requires the subtraction of two practically equal numbers.   On the other hand, the base current can be read directly from the common-emitter output characteristics.   Since $i_E = -i_C - i_B$, the forward-current amplification factor α may be obtained quite accurately from these characteristics by using the relation

$$\alpha \approx -\left.\frac{\Delta i_C}{\Delta i_E}\right|_{e_{CB},\ \text{const}}$$

Note that the lines of constant abscissa in Fig. 1-34a represent constant values of e_{CE}. However, in conventional operation, the magnitude of e_{CE} is much greater than the magnitude of e_{BE}; so for most of the active region, $e_{CE} \approx e_{CB}$. Thus,

$$\alpha \approx \frac{\Delta i_C}{\Delta(i_C + i_B)}\bigg|_{e_{CE},\ \text{const}} \tag{1-35}$$

The quantity α relates the corresponding changes in the output and input currents for the common-base configuration. In a similar way, we may define a current-amplification factor β for the common-emitter configura-

Fig. 1-34   Common-emitter characteristics of a typical p-n-p junction transistor. (a) Output characteristics; (b) input characteristics. (By permission from D. DeWitt and A. L. Rossoff, "Transistor Electronics," McGraw-Hill Book Company, 1957.)

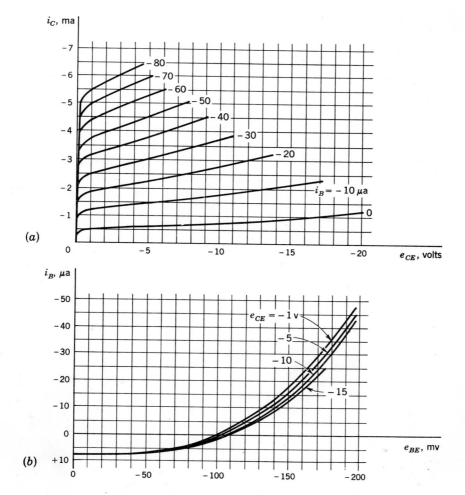

tion. This quantity, called the *common-emitter short-circuit forward-current transfer ratio*, is defined by

$$\beta = \frac{di_C}{di_B}\bigg|_{e_{CE},\ \text{const}} = \frac{\partial i_C}{\partial i_B} \tag{1-36}$$

This parameter is readily obtained from the common-emitter characteristics by taking the ratio of the change in collector current to the change in base current along a line of constant e_{CE}.

For infinitesimally small increments, Eq. (1-35) may be used to relate α to β as follows:

$$\frac{1}{\alpha} \approx \frac{\Delta(i_C + i_B)}{\Delta i_C} = 1 + \frac{1}{\beta}$$

$$\beta \approx \frac{\alpha}{1 - \alpha} \tag{1-37}$$

Equations (1-35) and (1-37) can be used to determine α accurately if the common-emitter output characteristics are supplied. There are times when the common-base or common-emitter input characteristics are not required. Often, manufacturers do not specify them.

1-22   Transistor ratings

The ratings of the transistor are similar to those of the junction diode. The power dissipation in the junctions is important since excessive heating can damage the transistor or alter its characteristics. The amount of heating depends not only upon the power dissipated but also upon the means provided for removing heat from the transistor. This latter topic is discussed in detail in Sec. 7-8; here we shall concentrate on the power dissipation. It will be assumed that almost all the voltage drops in the transistor occur across the junctions and not in the bulk of the semiconductor material. Hence, under quiescent conditions, we can write the collector-base junction power dissipation as

$$P_{oC} = E_{CBQ}I_{CQ}$$

Similarly, the emitter-base junction power dissipation is given by

$$P_{oE} = E_{EBQ}I_{EQ}$$

Usually, $|i_E| \approx |i_C|$ but $|e_{CB}| \gg |e_{EB}|$ so that P_{oC} is much greater than P_{oE}. Often, the emitter junction rating is not specified.

A reverse-biased transistor junction can break down in the same way that a reverse-biased *p-n* junction diode can (see Sec. 1-4). Since the collector junction is normally reverse-biased, the maximum value of E_{CB} or E_{CE} is often specified. Note that $E_{CB} \approx E_{CE}$, since E_{BE} is usually quite small. If the emitter-base junction is reverse-biased, then breakdown can occur here also. In such circumstances a maximum voltage rating would be specified.

The power dissipation can be related to the current through the junction. However, no actual equation can be written for the power, since the junction voltage is a function of other things than the current through it. Maximum current ratings are usually specified. If these are exceeded, ratings will be exceeded for all usual operating conditions.

1-23   High-frequency transistors

When a signal of fairly low frequency is impressed on the input of a transistor amplifier, it is amplified. However, if the frequency of the signal is increased, the amplification falls off. Several factors are responsible for this. The operation of the junction transistor depends fundamentally upon the diffusion of the minority carriers through the base. This process is comparatively slow and it leads to the distortion of high-frequency signals. Consider the input signal shown in Fig. 1-35a, which is a low-frequency pulse train. Random diffusion will smooth the signal and round off the edges of each pulse. However, if the period T of the pulse train is sufficiently long, the output signal will still have essentially the same shape as

Fig. 1-35   The distortion of high-frequency signals by a transistor. (a) Transmission of a low-frequency pulse train through a transistor; (b) transmission of a high-frequency pulse train through a transistor.

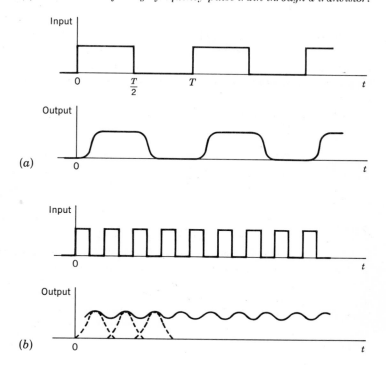

the input signal.   On the other hand, if the period of the pulse train is too short, as in Fig. 1-35*b*, the distortion will cause excessive overlapping between pulses, which attenuates the signal.

Capacitances at the emitter and collector junctions also decrease amplification as frequency increases, since these capacitances tend to load down the input and output circuits.   The manner in which this loading occurs depends upon the configuration of the transistor amplifier circuit.   Generally, it is the collector capacitance which produces the predominant capacitive deterioration.

The high-frequency response of transistors can be improved by several means.   Two important methods involve reducing the time of transit of the minority carriers across the base region by introducing fields there or by reducing the base width.   The collector junction capacitance can also be reduced.

REFERENCES

[1] D. C. Child, Discharge from Hot CaO, *Phys. Rev.*, vol. 32, pp. 492–511, May, 1911.   I. Langmuir: The Effect of Space Charge and Residual Gases on Thermionic Currents in High Vacuum, *Phys. Rev.*, ser. 2, vol. 2, pp. 450–486, December, 1913.   I. Langmuir and K. B. Blodgett: Currents Limited by Space Charge between Coaxial Cylinders, *Phys. Rev.*, ser. 2, vol. 22, pp. 347–356, October, 1923.   I. Langmuir and K. B. Blodgett: Currents Limited by Space Charge between Concentric Spheres, *Phys. Rev.*, ser. 2, vol. 24, pp. 49–59, July, 1924.

[2] J. J. Ebers and J. L. Moll, Large-signal Behavior of Junction Transistors, *Proc. IRE*, vol. 42, pp. 1761–1772, December, 1954.

BIBLIOGRAPHY

Chirlian, P. M., and A. H. Zemanian: "Electronics," chaps. 1–9, McGraw-Hill Book Company, New York, 1961.

Greiner, R. A.: "Semiconductor Devices and Applications," chaps. 1–10, McGraw-Hill Book Company, New York, 1961.

Millman, J.: "Vacuum-tube and Semiconductor Electronics," chaps. 1–7, 9, and 11, McGraw-Hill Book Company, New York, 1958.

PROBLEMS

1-1. A diode is characterized by Eq. (1-2).   Obtain expressions for the maximum allowable plate voltage and plate current in terms of the maximum allowable plate dissipation.

1-2. The characteristics of the vacuum-tube diode of Fig. 1-5 are given in Fig. 1-4.   If $E_{bb} = 90$ volts and $R_L = 120$ ohms, what are the values of the plate voltage, the plate current, and the plate dissipation?

1-3. Repeat Prob. 1-2, but now use a value of $E_{bb} = 50$ volts.

1-4. Repeat Prob. 1-2, but now use a value of $R_L = 10$ ohms.

1-5. Repeat Prob. 1-2, but now use a value of $E_{bb} = -90$ volts.

1-6. Plot a curve of dynamic plate resistance r_p versus plate voltage e_b for the 5U4-GB vacuum-tube diode whose characteristics are given in Fig. 1-4.

1-7. Repeat Prob. 1-6, but now plot a curve of r_p versus plate current i_b.

1-8. Obtain the dynamic characteristic of the 5U4-GB vacuum-tube diode whose characteristics are given in Fig. 1-4. Use a value of $R_L = 300$ ohms.

1-9. The characteristics of the semiconductor diode of Fig. 1-13 are given in Fig. 1-12. If $E_{bb} = 3$ volts and $R_L = 75$ ohms, what are E_b and I_b?

1-10. Repeat Prob. 1-9, but now assume that $E_{bb} = -50$ volts. Why does the load line of this problem *appear* not parallel with that of Prob. 1-9?

1-11. Plot a curve of the dynamic resistance r_p versus e_b for the semiconductor diode of Fig. 1-12. Use both positive and negative values of e_b.

1-12. Plot a curve of junction dissipation versus e_b for the semiconductor diode whose characteristics are given in Fig. 1-12. Assume that all the power is dissipated at the junction.

1-13. A vacuum-tube triode is characterized by Eq. (1-10). If $e_b = 250$ volts, it is found that $i_b = 0$ when e_c becomes more negative than 25 volts. When $e_b = 250$ volts and $e_c = -10$ volts, $i_b = 30$ ma and when $e_b = 250$ volts and $e_c = -5$ volts, $i_b = 50$ ma. Compute the values of k, μ, and n for this triode.

1-14. The vacuum-tube triode of Prob. 1-13 has a grid-to-cathode capacitance of $10 \, \mu\mu\text{f}$. What is the approximate value of its plate-to-cathode capacitance?

1-15. Construct the transfer characteristics and the constant-current characteristics of the type 7027-A vacuum-tube triode. The plate characteristics of this vacuum tube are given in Fig. 1-20.

1-16. For the type 7027-A vacuum-tube triode, determine the value of μ, g_m, and r_p at an operating point of $E_b = 350$ volts, $E_c = -30$ volts. The plate characteristics of this vacuum tube are given in Fig. 1-20.

1-17. Repeat Prob. 1-16 for an operating point of $E_b = 450$ volts, $E_c = -60$ volts.

1-18. The vacuum-tube-triode amplifier of Fig. 1-19 is such that $E_{cc} = -20$ volts, $E_{bb} = 400$ volts, and $R_L = 5,000$ ohms. Determine E_{bQ}, I_{bQ}, and E_{cQ}, the coordinates of the quiescent operating point. If $e_g = 20 \sin \omega t$ volts, determine the maximum and minimum values of e_b and i_b. Draw curves of the instantaneous values of e_b and i_b. What is the voltage amplification of this circuit? Assume that the plate characteristics of the vacuum tube are those given in Fig. 1-20.

1-19. If $e_g = 0$ in the amplifier of Prob. 1-18, what will the plate dissipation be?

1-20. Plot a curve of r_p, μ, and g_m versus plate voltage e_b for the vacuum-tube tetrode whose characteristics are given in Fig. 1-25. Use a constant value of e_c equal to -10 volts.

1-21. The vacuum-tube-tetrode amplifier of Fig. 1-23 has the following element values: $E_{bb} = 300$ volts, $E_{cc} = -15$ volts, $R_L = 4,285$ ohms, and $e_g = 15 \sin \omega t$ volts. Draw curves of the instantaneous values of e_b, i_b, and e_c. Do the curves of e_b and i_b vary sinusoidally? Assume that the plate characteristics of the vacuum-tube tetrode are those given in Fig. 1-25.

1-22. Plot curves of μ, g_m, and r_p versus plate voltage e_b for the 6AU6 vacuum-tube pentode. Use a constant control-grid voltage of -1.0 volt and a screen-grid voltage of 100 volts. The characteristics of this vacuum tube are given in Fig. 1-27.

1-23. Repeat Prob. 1-22, but now use a constant plate voltage of 250 volts and plot the parameters versus e_c. Discuss the accuracy of these calculations.

1-24. Draw the transfer characteristics and the constant-current characteristics for the 6AU6 vacuum-tube pentode whose characteristics are given in Fig. 1-27.

1-25. The vacuum-tube amplifier of Fig. 1-26 is such that $E_{bb} = 400$ volts, $E_{cc} = -1.0$ volt, $E_{c2} = 100$ volts, $e_g = 1 \sin \omega t$ volt, and $R_L = 40,000$ ohms. Compute E_{bQ} and I_{bQ}, the quiescent plate voltage and plate current, respectively. What are the maximum and minimum values of i_b and e_b? Plot the instantaneous values of e_b, i_b, and e_c. What is the voltage amplification of this circuit? The plate characteristics of the vacuum tube are given in Fig. 1-27.

1-26. Repeat Prob. 1-25, but now use a value of $R_L = 66,700$ ohms. Compare the results of this problem with those of Prob. 1-25. Is there distortion produced?

1-27. If $e_g = 0$ for the amplifier of Prob. 1-25, what will be the value of the plate dissipation?

1-28. A *p-n-p* transistor is characterized by Eqs. (1-27) and (1-28). If $i_E = 0$ and e_{CB} is a large negative value, then $i_C = -100 \, \mu a$. The short-circuit forward-current transfer ratio for this transistor is 0.98. Write an expression for i_C in terms of i_E, e_{CB}, the temperature, and any necessary constants. If e_{CB} is a large negative number, what does this expression become?

1-29. Determine the values of c_{11}, c_{12}, c_{21}, and c_{22} of Eqs. (1-27) and (1-28) in terms of α, α_r, I_{CO} and I_{EO}. (These quantities are defined in Secs. 1-19 and 1-20.) Compute the value of α at the operating point $e_{CB} = -5$ volts and $i_E = 3$ ma for the transistor whose characteristics are given in Fig. 1-32. Is this a very accurate calculation?

1-31. The parameters of the transistor amplifier of Fig. 1-31 are such that $i_E = 3 + 2 \sin \omega t$ ma, $E_{CC} = -10$ volts, and $R_C = 1,500$ ohms. Compute the coordinates of the quiescent operating point and the maximum and minimum values of i_C and e_{CB}. Plot the instantaneous waveforms of e_{CB}, i_C, and i_E. What is the current gain of this amplifier? The characteristics of the transistor are given in Fig. 1-32. If $i_E = 3$ ma, what will the collector junction dissipation be?

1-32. Compute the value of α at an operating point of $e_{CB} = -5$ volts and $i_B = -40 \, \mu a$ for the transistor whose characteristics are given in Fig. 1-34. Compare the accuracy of this calculation with that of Prob. 1-30.

1-33. The parameters of the transistor amplifier of Fig. 1-33 are such that $i_B = -40 + 20 \sin \omega t \, \mu a$. The values of the circuit elements are $E_{CC} = -15$ volts and $R_C = 3,000$ ohms. Compute the coordinates of the quiescent operating point and the maximum and minimum values of i_C and e_{CB}. Sketch the instantaneous waveforms of e_{CB}, i_C and i_B. What is the current gain of this amplifier? The characteristics of the transistor are given in Fig. 1-34. If $i_B = -40 \, \mu a$, what will the value of the collector junction dissipation be?

1-34. Repeat Prob. 1-33, but now use a base current of $i_B = -40 + 40 \sin \omega t \, \mu a$.

Graphical Analysis of Electronic Circuits

2

The purpose of this chapter is to develop methods of graphically analyzing electronic circuits. The characteristics of electronic devices are nonlinear. Hence, graphical techniques are generally used when the signal level in the device is so large that its nonlinearity cannot be ignored. We shall discuss basic graphical methods here and will reserve for Chap. 3 the widely used linear techniques of analysis, which are valid only when the signal is sufficiently small.

2-1 Rules for notation

At this point, it is appropriate to establish some standard rules of notation for the voltages and currents.

1. Capital letters indicate time-invariant voltages and currents, such as direct quantities and the maximum and effective values of alternating quantities. Lowercase letters indicate time-varying quantities.

2. The current-reference direction is indicated by an arrow, whereas the voltage-reference polarity is indicated by plus and minus signs or by an arrow that points from the negative to the positive terminal. The first subscript on the current symbol indicates the lead in which the current is. Moreover, the voltage-reference polarity is indicated by the usual double-subscript notation. That is, the first subscript indicates the positive terminal and the second subscript the negative terminal. Often, all voltages are given with respect to one reference node, and, in this case, the second subscript is usually omitted. For instance, in a vacuum tube, the alternating grid-to-cathode voltage drop can be written as e_{gk}, but when the cathode is taken as the reference node, as is usual, this quantity is given by e_g.

3. Additional subscripts may be added to the afore-mentioned ones to identify a type of quantity. The most common of these are the subscript max, which represents a maximum value for an alternating quantity, and the subscript Q, which represents conditions at a quiescent operating point.

4. A voltage or current symbol having two subscripts that are the same represents a direct-voltage or a direct-current supply. For instance, E_{bb} is the symbol used for the plate supply voltage in a vacuum-tube circuit.

2-2 Biasing techniques for vacuum tubes

An elementary vacuum-tube-pentode amplifier using a type 5879 tube is shown in Fig. 2-1a. Its plate characteristics are shown in Fig. 2-1b. A load line corresponding to a load resistance $R_L = 80,000$ ohms and a plate supply voltage $E_{bb} = 400$ volts is indicated. The method for obtaining this load line and the quiescent operating point Q has been discussed in Sec. 1-11.

Three separate voltage supplies are used for biasing in the circuit of Fig. 2-1a. This is impractical. In most systems, these bias voltages are obtained from a single, direct-voltage power supply. A circuit which accomplishes this is shown in Fig. 2-2. The total direct tube current I_T, which is the sum of the direct plate current I_b and the direct screen current I_{c2}, through R_k produces the direct-voltage drop $I_T R_k$. Using Kirchhoff's voltage law around the grid-cathode circuit, it is seen that $-I_T R_k$ is the grid bias E_{cQ}. The purpose of the capacitor C_k is to prevent any signal voltage from appearing across R_k. For instance, if C_k were absent and e_g represented a sinusoidal input voltage, then the total current i_T through the vacuum tube would have a sinusoidal component that would be in phase with e_g. Thus, the voltage drop across R_k would buck the voltage e_g, thereby reducing the actual grid-cathode alternating voltage and, hence, the gain of the amplifier. To eliminate this effect, a sufficiently

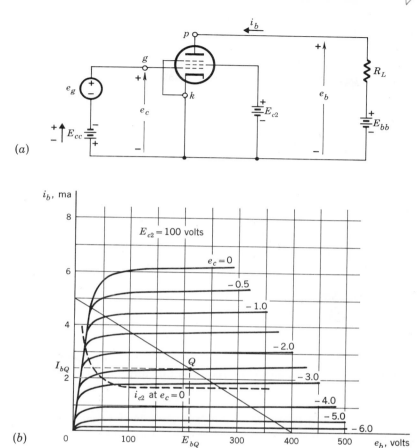

Fig. 2-1 (a) *An elementary vacuum-tube-pentode amplifier using a type 5879 vacuum tube.   All biasing voltages are obtained from separate voltage sources. Note that* E_{cc} *is defined as negative; (b) the plate characteristics of the type 5879 vacuum-tube pentode.   The load line is drawn for* $E_{bb} = 400$ *volts,* $R_L = 80,000$ *ohms,   and* $E_{cQ} = E_{cc} = -2.5$ *volts.   (Courtesy   Radio   Corporation   of America.)*

large capacitor C_k, usually called a *bypass capacitor*, is put in parallel with R_k so that the impedance to the alternating current and, hence, the alternating-voltage drop are both negligible.   This capacitor acts as an open circuit at zero frequency and does not affect the direct bias.   Techniques for computing the effect of C_k will be discussed in Chaps. 3 and 6.   Bias obtained in this way is called *cathode bias* or *self-bias*, in contrast to battery bias.

Another advantage of self-bias over battery bias is that it provides a degree of stabilization of the operating point, which compensates for varia-

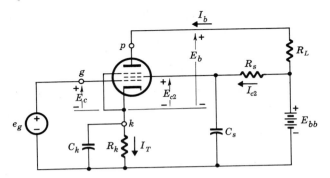

Fig. 2-2   *Biasing connections for a vacuum-tube-pentode amplifier using a single direct-voltage power supply.*

tions due to aging or replacement of the vacuum tube.   For instance, if a change in the characteristics increases the plate current, then the voltage drop across R_k will increase.   This will increase the negative bias on the grid, which will tend to decrease the plate current.   Consequently, the plate current will increase less than it would have if battery bias had been used.

The battery voltage E_{bb} is, in general, larger than the required screen-grid-bias voltage.   Thus, a resistance R_s is inserted between it and the screen grid to drop the voltage to the required amount.   Hence,

$$E_{c2} = E_{bb} - I_{c2}R_s - I_T R_k \tag{2-1}$$

If C_s were not present, R_s would act as a load resistance for the screen circuit.   This would produce an alternating component of the screen potential that would be 180° out of phase with the input alternating voltage e_g.   The effect of the alternating screen voltage on the plate current will oppose the effect of e_g and thus reduce the voltage gain.   To prevent this, the capacitor C_s is used to bypass the alternating current in the screen-grid circuit so that no alternating voltage appears across R_s.

To illustrate the procedure for calculating the quiescent operating point, we shall use the vacuum-tube-triode circuit of Fig. 2-3a.   The total resistance in series with the E_{bb} is $R_L + R_k$.   Thus, the equation for the load line is

$$E_b = E_{bb} - I_b(R_L + R_k) \tag{2-2}$$

This load line is indicated in Fig. 2-3b.   Since the grid bias E_{cQ} is not known at this point, the quiescent operating point is still unknown.   However, it must lie on the load line; hence, the following cut-and-try procedure can be used to determine it.   Choose a point on the load line.   The product of the ordinate I_b and the resistance R_k is then compared with the value of the grid bias read from the plate characteristics at the chosen operating point.   If these two values are equal, the correct choice has been made. If they are not equal, repeat the process until a fairly good choice is obtained.

An equivalent procedure, which is not a cut-and-try one, is first to choose a plate current I_b and then compute the value of $E_{cQ} = -I_b R_k$. The coordinates I_b and E_{cQ} will establish a point on the plane of Fig. 2-3b. By repeating this procedure, a curve is generated. The intersection of this curve with the load line yields the operating point E_{cQ}. An example of such a *grid-bias curve* is shown in Fig. 2-3b. Note that the i_b and e_b axes are not used to plot this curve; instead, the i_b axis and the e_c curves are employed.

In the case of a vacuum-tube pentode, the method of finding the operating point is more involved, since the screen-grid current affects the position of the d-c load line and the control-grid bias. The equation for the d-c load line is similar to that for the vacuum-tube triode, except that now the drop in the cathode-bias resistor, due to the screen-grid current I_{c2}, must also be taken into account. Applying Kirchhoff's voltage law around

Fig. 2-3   (a) *A vacuum-tube-triode amplifier using a 6C4 vacuum tube;* (b) *the plate characteristics of a type 6C4 vacuum-tube triode. The load line and grid-bias curve are drawn for $E_{bb} = 400$ volts, $R_L = 12,333$ ohms, and $R_k = 1000$ ohms. (Courtesy Radio Corporation of America.)*

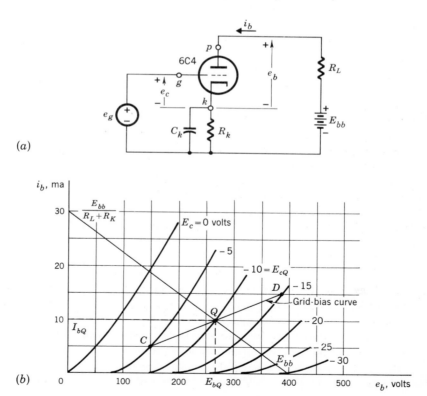

the output circuit of Fig. 2-2, we obtain

$$E_b = (E_{bb} - I_{c2}R_k) - I_b(R_L + R_k) \tag{2-3}$$

Comparing this expression with Eq. (2-2) we see that E_{bb} is replaced by $E_{bb} - I_{c2}R_k$. That is, the ordinate intercept of the load line is now $(E_{bb} - I_{c2}R_k)/(R_L + R_k)$, and the abscissa intercept is now $E_{bb} - I_{c2}R_k$. The fact that the load line shifts with variations in the unknown I_{c2} complicates the problem of finding the operating point. Fortunately, however, in almost all cases, the value of $I_{c2}R_k$ is very much less than E_{bb}, so that $I_{c2}R_k$ may be ignored. Hence, Eq. (2-2) may be used as the expression for the load line. Thus, the load line may be drawn as before.

The control-grid bias is given by

$$E_c = -(I_{c2} + I_b)R_k \tag{2-4}$$

In this case, I_{c2} often cannot be ignored, since $I_{c2}R_k$ is often a substantial fraction of E_c. To draw the grid-bias line, assume a value for E_c. The value of the screen-grid current I_{c2} can be obtained from the screen-current characteristics, such as the dashed curve of Fig. 2-1b. (Values of I_{c2} corresponding to values of E_c other than for $E_c = 0$ may be estimated by assuming I_{c2} varies with E_c in the same way as I_b varies with E_c.) The value I_{c2} is also a function of the unknown plate voltage E_b. However, over most of the operating region, the curves are essentially independent of E_b. Generally, the value for I_{c2} lies in this region. Since the values of E_c and I_{c2} have now been assumed, the value of I_b can be obtained from Eq. (2-4). The point determined by I_b and E_c specifies one point on the grid-bias curve. Repeating this procedure, the entire grid-bias curve can be drawn; again, its intersection with the load line determines the operating point. If the abscissa of this operating point E_{bQ} falls within the region of constant screen-grid current, then this procedure will be valid. If this is not the case, we may resort to a cut-and-try procedure. For this method, a point is chosen on the load line. The corresponding E_b and E_c determine I_{c2}. Then, $-(I_b + I_{c2})R_k$ is compared with the chosen value of E_c. This procedure is repeated until the calculated and assumed values of E_c agree.

If the assumption that $E_{bb} \gg I_{c2}R_k$—which was made to allow the use of Eq. (2-2) as the expression of the load line—is not valid, the following cut-and-try procedure may be used. Choose an operating point. This assumes values for the variables E_b, E_c, I_b, and I_{c2}. If Eqs. (2-3) and (2-4) are simultaneously satisfied by these assumed values, then the correct operating point has been chosen. If not, other choices for the operating point must be tried until these equations are satisfied. This procedure is, in general, tedious.

In many cases the voltage applied to the input of an amplifier contains a large direct component in addition to the alternating signal. This will occur, for instance, if the input signal is the output of a previous amplifier stage. To prevent this large direct voltage from appearing at the grid, while permitting the alternating signal to pass, the input circuit shown in

Fig. 2-4   A vacuum-tube circuit illustrating a grid-leak resistance.

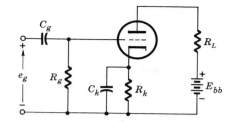

Fig. 2-4 is used.   The direct voltage is blocked by the voltage divider consisting of the capacitor C_g and the resistor R_g.   The capacitor C_g should be made sufficiently large so that its reactance at the signal frequency is small compared with the resistance R_g.   This will prevent appreciable attenuation of the alternating signal.

The resistance R_g cannot be made arbitrarily large, for several reasons. There will always be some electrons that succeed in overcoming the negative potential of the grid.   If R_g were absent, these electrons would accumulate on the grid, producing a large negative grid potential.   This will radically shift the operating point.   Thus, the size of R_g must be limited so that the voltage drop produced across it by this electron flow is comparatively small.   Since R_g allows the electrons to leave the grid, it is called a *grid-leak resistance*.   There are other sources for grid current. For instance, some of the positive ions from residual gas in the vacuum tube strike the grid.   The resulting current produces a voltage drop in R_g, which tends to bias the grid positively.   A similar effect is produced if there is any electronic emission from the grid.   This may occur if cathode material accumulates on the grid over a period of time.   If R_g is too large, the voltage drop produced by such grid-emission current may cause the grid bias to become positive and increase the grid current.   The resulting heating of the grid will increase the grid emission still more.   Thus, this phenomenon is cumulative, and the vacuum tube may actually be destroyed. If sufficiently small values of R_g are used, the grid voltage will not become positive.   Typical maximum allowable values for R_g lie in the range of $\frac{1}{2}$ to 2 megohms.

2-3   Biasing techniques for transistors

An elementary transistor circuit which provides the necessary forward bias for the emitter-base junction and the reverse bias for the collector-base junction is shown in Fig. 2-5a.   This circuit has the disadvantage that two biasing supplies are used.   If E_{BB} is set equal to E_{CC}, then their two negative terminals can be connected without changing the circuit conditions; thus, one power supply can be eliminated.   Such a circuit is shown in Fig. 2-5b.   Note that the second voltage subscript for e_B and e_C has not been used in Fig. 2-5b.   This is often done once the reference electrode has been established. To determine the location of the quiescent operating point, we shall use the input and output characteristics of Fig. 2-6a and b. Consider that, in Fig. 2-5a, $E_{CC} = -15$ volts, $E_{BB} = -443 \times 10^{-3}$ volt, $R_C = 3{,}000$ ohms, and $R_B = 8{,}850$ ohms. Then, the load line shown in Fig. 2-6a can be drawn. The quiescent operating point cannot be obtained, since i_B is not known. The values of R_B and E_{BB} can be used to draw a load line on the input characteristic. This load line is the solid straight line of Fig. 2-6b. Its intercepts are $e_{BE} = E_{BB}$ and $i_B = E_{BB}/R_B$ and its slope is $-1/R_B$. Note that the abscissa intercept does not fall on the curve of Fig. 2-6b. If the value of e_{CE} were known, the base current could be obtained from the intersection of the load line and the appropriate characteristic of Fig. 2-6b. Since e_{CE} is not known, a cut-and-try procedure is used. That is, assume a value of e_{CE}. Then use Fig. 2-6b to determine i_B. The quiescent operating point can then be found on Fig. 2-6a. The value of e_{CE} can be read from this curve and checked with the assumed one. If they agree, the quiescent operating point is correct. Otherwise, a new value of e_{CE} should be chosen and the procedure repeated. In general, the curves of i_B versus e_{BE} do not vary greatly with e_{CE}. Thus, the correct value of i_B can usually be obtained on the first trial.

The value of E_{BB} in the last example was quite small. Usually the circuit of Fig. 2-5b is used. In this case, $E_{BB} = E_{CC}$. Let us now recalculate the problem using the same values of $E_{CC} = -15$ volts, and $R_C = 3{,}000$ ohms, but we shall now use $E_{BB} = -15$ volts and $R_B = 494{,}000$ ohms. The load line on the input characteristic is drawn as the dashed straight line.

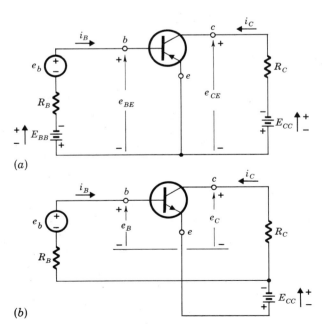

Fig. 2-5 (a) An elementary transistor amplifier using two direct-voltage bias sources; (b) a modification of this amplifier using only one direct-voltage bias source. Note that E_{BB} and E_{CC} are defined as negative.

(a)

(b)

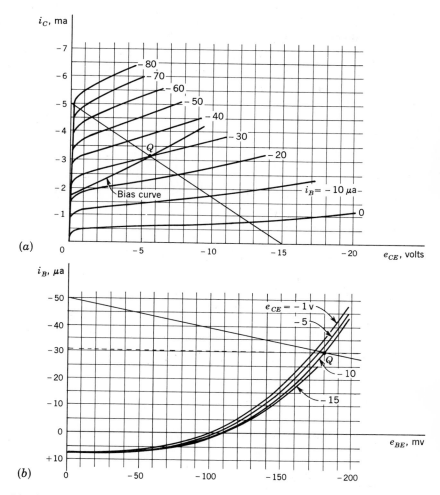

Fig. 2-6   *Common-emitter characteristics of a typical p-n-p junction transistor.
(a) Output characteristics (the bias curve is a plot of Eq. (2-16) with $E_{CC} = -15$
volts, $R_C = 2,000$ ohms, $R_E = 1,000$ ohms, $R_{B1} = 328,600$ ohms, and $R_{B2} =
511,100$ ohms); (b) input characteristics. (By permission from D. DeWitt and
A. L. Rossoff, "Transistor Electronics," McGraw-Hill Book Company, 1957.)*

It is almost horizontal. Hence, i_B is essentially independent of the curve
of i_B versus e_{BE} and it can be determined directly. Thus, $i_B = -30$ μa
as before. The quiescent operating point is shown in Fig. 2-6a and b.

Let us now ascertain when the input characteristics can be ignored in
the calculations of i_B. From Fig. 2-5a we have

$$I_{BQ} = \frac{E_{BB} - E_{BEQ}}{R_B} \tag{2-5}$$

If

$$|E_{BB}| \gg |E_{BEQ}| \tag{2-6}$$

then

$$I_{BQ} \approx \frac{E_{BB}}{R_B} \tag{2-7}$$

In general, the approximation of relation (2-6) is valid and the input characteristics are not needed.

Another very commonly used transistor circuit is shown in Fig. 2-7 (see Sec. 2-5). To simplify the analysis we shall replace the circuit consisting of E_{CC}, R_{B1}, and R_{B2} by its Thévenin's equivalent. Thus, we obtain the circuit of Fig. 2-8, where

$$R_B = \frac{R_{B1}R_{B2}}{R_{B1} + R_{B2}} \tag{2-8}$$

and

$$E = \frac{E_{CC}R_{B2}}{R_{B1} + R_{B2}} \tag{2-9}$$

Then, writing mesh equations, we have

$$\begin{aligned} E - e_{BE} &= i_B(R_B + R_E) + i_C R_E \\ E_{CC} - e_{CE} &= i_B R_E + i_C(R_C + R_E) \end{aligned} \tag{2-10}$$

Solving for i_C, we obtain

$$i_C = \frac{(E_{CC} - e_{CE})(R_B + R_E) - (E - e_{BE})R_E}{R_B R_C + R_B R_E + R_E R_C} \tag{2-11}$$

If

$$|(E_{CC} - e_{CE})(R_B + R_E) - R_E E| \gg |e_{BE} R_E| \tag{2-12}$$

then

$$i_C = \frac{E_{CC}(R_B + R_E) - E R_E}{R_B R_C + R_B R_E + R_E R_C} - \frac{e_{CE}(R_B + R_E)}{R_B R_C + R_B R_E + R_C R_E} \tag{2-13}$$

Thus, this equation is of the form $i_C = E_1 - e_{CE}/R$ and can be plotted as a load line on the output characteristic of Fig. 2-6a. If $R_B \gg R_E$ and thus $R_B(R_C + R_E) \gg R_E R_C$, then Eq. (2-13) reduces to

$$i_C = \frac{E_{CC}}{R_C + R_E} - \frac{e_{CE}}{R_C + R_E}$$

This is equivalent to neglecting the drop in R_E due to the base current. If the value of i_B could be established, the quiescent operating point would be obtained. Solving Eqs. (2-10) for i_B, we have

$$i_B = \frac{(E - e_{BE})(R_C + R_E) - (E_{CC} - e_{CE})R_E}{R_B R_C + R_B R_E + R_E R_C} \tag{2-14}$$

If $|E(R_C + R_E) - (E_{CC} - e_{CE})R_E| \gg |e_{BE}(R_C + R_E)|$ (2-15)

then

$$i_B = \frac{E(R_C + R_E) - (E_{CC} - e_{CE})R_E}{R_B R_C + R_B R_E + R_E R_C} \tag{2-16}$$

This relation can be plotted on the plane of Fig. 2-6a. The e_{CE} axis and the i_B curves are used here. Thus, the curve is similar to the grid-bias curve for a vacuum tube. Its intersection with the load line determines the quiescent operating point.

In almost all cases, relations (2-12) and (2-15) will be satisfied. If they are not, then input characteristics such as those of Fig. 2-6b will also be required. In this case, a cut-and-try procedure is used. That is, choose a value of e_{BE}. Then Eqs. (2-11) and (2-14) can be used—as Eqs. (2-13) and (2-16) were used—to determine the operating point. The value of e_{BE} at this operating point is then compared with the assumed value. If they are equal, the correct operating point has been obtained. If not, a new value of e_{BE} should be assumed and the procedure repeated. This procedure is quite tedious. Fortunately, it rarely has to be used.

As an example, let us consider that $E_{CC} = -15$ volts, $R_C = 2,000$ ohms, $R_E = 1,000$ ohms, $R_{B1} = 328,600$ ohms, and $R_{B2} = 511,100$ ohms. Thus, $E = -9.13$ volts and $R_B = 200,000$ ohms. The transistor whose output characteristics are given in Fig. 2-6 will be used. Since $R_B \gg R_E$, we can write

$$i_C = -5 \times 10^{-3} - \frac{e_{CE}}{3,000}$$

Thus, the load line drawn in Fig. 2-6a applies here. Let us assume that relation (2-15) is satisfied. Then, the bias curve can be obtained by substituting in Eq. (2-16). This yields

$$e_{CE} = 602,000i_B + 12.39$$

This bias curve is plotted in Fig. 2-6a. The point Q is the quiescent operating point.

Let us verify that relation (2-15) is satisfied. By substituting and rearranging, we obtain $33.4 \gg 1$. Thus, our results will be accurate within about 3 percent. This is probably well within the accuracy of the graph and is usually quite satisfactory. If greater accuracy is desired, the cut-and-try procedure should be used.

It should be noted that an alternating component of voltage appearing across R_E will reduce the alternating component of the base current and thus reduce the gain of the circuit (see Sec. 6-6). The bypass capacitor C_E is included to eliminate this effect.

2-4   Operating-point instability

Transistors possess a thermal instability which is of such magnitude that additional circuits must be used to compensate for it. This thermal instability occurs mainly because the collector saturation current I_{co} varies markedly with temperature. Other parameters, such as the forward-current amplification factor α, are also dependent upon temperature, but these variations are usually of secondary importance. This thermal instability causes a variation in the transistor's characteristics, which manifests itself as a shift in the operating point. This is undesirable, since the operating point may drift into an excessively nonlinear region. In addition, this temperature dependence may cause a phenomenon known as *thermal runaway*. For instance, an increase in the temperature will cause I_{co} to increase, which increases the collector current I_c. This, in turn, may increase the transistor's temperature, which further increases I_{co}. This cumulative process may, at times, result in such large currents that the transistor may be destroyed. Also, transistors of the same type have somewhat different characteristics, such as I_{co}, and, hence, transistor amplifiers using the same circuit may have different operating points.

A measure of the effect of these variations in I_{co} is called the *stability factor S*. It is defined by

$$S = \frac{dI_c}{dI_{co}} \tag{2-17}$$

Thus, a small value of S implies a high degree of stability. The quantity S depends not only upon the transistor but also upon the associated circuitry. We shall attempt to choose some circuits that minimize S.

Since for normal operation the collector junction is strongly reverse-biased, the collector current is the sum of the collector saturation current I_{co} and the current $-\alpha I_E$ [see Eq. (1-33)].

$$I_C = -\alpha I_E + I_{co} \tag{2-18}$$

Because the emitter current is the negative of the sum of the base and collector currents, this equation becomes

$$I_C = \frac{\alpha}{1-\alpha} I_B + \frac{1}{1-\alpha} I_{co} \tag{2-19}$$

For the circuit of Fig. 2-5b, I_B is essentially constant, since it is mainly determined by the external circuitry and not by the transistor characteristics. Thus, the stability factor is

$$S = \frac{1}{1-\alpha} = \beta + 1 \tag{2-20}$$

where β is given by Eq. (1-37). Since α is usually only slightly less than

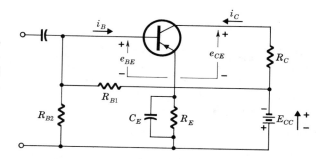

Fig. 2-7 An emitter-stabi-lized common-emitter tran-sistor amplifier. Note that E_{CC} is defined as negative.

unity, $1/(1 - \alpha)$ will be quite large (i.e., if $\alpha = 0.98$, $S = 50$). (If the transistor circuit were such that I_E were constant, then $S = 1$, which is quite small.)

2-5 Operating-point stabilization using an emitter resistance

A circuit that tends to stabilize the location of the quiescent operating point is shown in Fig. 2-7. An equivalent circuit that can be more easily discussed is shown in Fig. 2-8 (see Sec. 2-3 for definitions). If the magnitude of I_C should increase, for any reason, then the magnitude of the voltage across R_E, E_{RE} will also increase. (Capital letters are used here since it is assumed that these quantities represent quiescent operating conditions.) If we neglect E_{BE}, the base current is given by $(E - E_{RE})/R_B$. Thus, any increase in the magnitude of I_C will cause the magnitude of I_B to decrease, which will tend to reduce I_C. Thus, stabilization has been introduced into this circuit.

For this circuit, the stability factor S can be obtained as follows. Summing the voltage drops around the loop that contains E, R_B, and R_E and again neglecting the voltage across the emitter-base junction, we obtain

$$E = I_B R_B + (I_B + I_C)R_E \qquad\qquad (2\text{-}21)$$

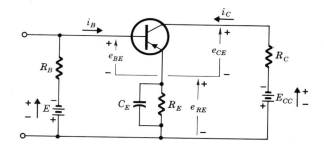

Fig. 2-8 A circuit that is equivalent to Fig. 2-7. Note that E_{CC} and E are defined as negative.

Then, using Eq. (2-19) to eliminate I_B, we obtain

$$I_C = \frac{\alpha E + (R_B + R_E)I_{co}}{(1 - \alpha)R_B + R_E} \tag{2-22}$$

Thus, from Eq. (2-17), the stability factor is

$$S = \frac{1}{1 - \alpha R_B/(R_B + R_E)} = \frac{\beta + 1}{1 + \beta R_E/(R_B + R_E)} \tag{2-23}$$

This stability factor is less than $1/(1 - \alpha)$. For instance, if $\alpha = 0.98$, $R_B = 10{,}000$ ohms, and $R_E = 1{,}000$ ohms, then $S = 9.16$. This is a considerable reduction from the unstabilized case. The factor S may be decreased by decreasing R_B or by increasing R_E. Since R_E is effectively in series with E_{CC}, an increase in R_E would require an increase in E_{CC} to maintain the necessary bias. Consequently, practical considerations limit the size of R_E. On the other hand, R_B cannot be made too small, because this will reduce the gain of the preceding stage. This phenomenon will be discussed in Chaps. 3 and 6.

2-6 Operating-point stabilization using a collector-to-base resistance

The circuit shown in Fig. 2-9 also stabilizes the operating point of a transistor amplifier. It is similar to the unstabilized circuit of Fig. 2-5b, except that the resistor R_1 is connected to the collector instead of to the negative terminal of E_{CC}. If the magnitude of the direct collector current increases, then the magnitude of the voltage drop across R_C will increase. This will decrease $|E_{CE}|$, resulting in a decrease in $|I_B|$, since I_B is essentially equal to E_{CE}/R_1. This will tend to counteract the original increase in $|I_C|$. Consequently, a degree of stabilization has been introduced. The capacitor C_1 acts as a short circuit at the signal frequencies. Hence, it prevents any alternating signals at the collector from affecting those at the base (through R_1).

To calculate the stability factor, we may proceed as in Sec. 2-5. Since $I_B \approx E_{CE}/R_1$, an application of Kirchhoff's voltage law yields

$$I_B = \frac{E_{CC} - R_C I_C}{R_1 + R_C} \tag{2-24}$$

Substituting this into Eq. (2-19), solving for I_C, and differentiating, we obtain

$$S = \frac{1}{1 - \alpha R_1/(R_1 + R_C)} = \frac{\beta + 1}{1 + \beta R_C/(R_1 + R_C)} \tag{2-25}$$

Increasing R_C and/or decreasing R_1 will improve the stability. In many applications, the resistor R_C is quite small. In such cases, S will be large,

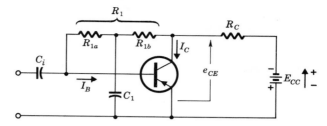

Fig. 2-9 *A collector-stabilized common-emitter transistor amplifier. Note that E_{CC} is defined as negative.*

and another stabilization system, such as that discussed in Sec. 2-5, should be used. On the other hand, the circuit of Fig. 2-9 has no resistance in series with the emitter lead and, consequently, E_{CC} does not have to be increased to compensate for an additional voltage drop. For alternating signals R_{1a} will shunt the input circuit and R_{1b} will shunt the output circuit. This can result in a significant loss in gain.

The equation for the load line of the circuit of Fig. 2-9 is

$$E_{CE} = E_{CC} - (I_B + I_C)R_C \tag{2-26}$$

Since $|I_B|$ is very much smaller than $|I_C|$, this equation for the load line is given quite accurately by

$$E_{CE} = E_{CC} - I_C R_C \tag{2-27}$$

Thus, the load line may be determined in the usual way. In this case, the bias curve is given by the expression $I_B = E_{CE}/R_1$ and its intersection with the load line determines the operating point.

Fig. 2-10 *(a) A generalized device; (b) a generalized input representation; (c) a voltage-generator input representation; (d) a current-generator input representation.*

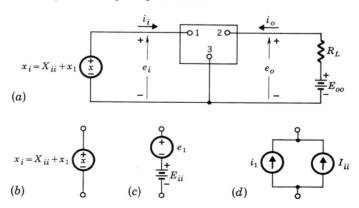

2-7   The generalized device and generalized output characteristics

Most vacuum tubes and transistors are essentially three-terminal devices. For instance, two of the three grids in a vacuum-tube pentode are usually maintained at a constant potential and, hence, do not contribute to its dynamic operation.   Often, there will be no need to distinguish whether the device in question is a vacuum tube or a transistor.   In such cases, the device will be represented by the symbol shown in Fig. 2-10a and the analysis will apply to either the vacuum tube or the transistor.   In the rest of this chapter, we shall refer to this generalized element as the *generalized device*. The input to it will be represented by the letter x_i, which may be either a voltage or a current.   Examples of actual input representations are shown in Figs. 2-10c and d.   At times, the generalized device can represent an entire amplifier circuit.

Usually, the currents and voltages in an electronic circuit consist of both a direct and an alternating part.   The symbols that we shall use to designate the various components of these signals for a generalized device

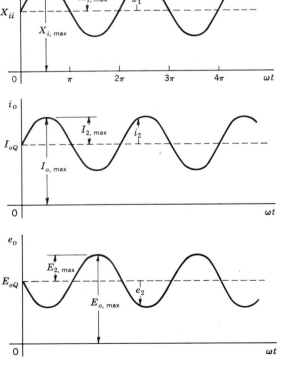

Fig. 2-11   An illustration of the input and output quantities of the generalized device.

Table 2-1   *Definitions of symbols*

	Generalized device	Common-cathode vacuum-tube amplifier	Common-emitter transistor amplifier
Input quantities:			
Total instantaneous value	x_i	e_c	i_B
Quiescent component	X_{iQ}	E_{cQ}	I_{BQ}
Average component	X_{iA}	E_{cA}	I_{BA}
Direct input bias supply	X_{ii}	E_{cc}	I_{BB}
Instantaneous alternating component	x_1	e_g	i_b
Rms value of alternating component	X_1	E_g	I_b
Peak value of alternating component	$X_{1,max}$	$E_{g,max}$	$I_{b,max}$
Output voltage:			
Total instantaneous voltage	e_o	e_b	e_C
Quiescent component	E_{oQ}	E_{bQ}	E_{CQ}
Average component	E_{oA}	E_{bA}	E_{CA}
Direct bias supply	E_{oo}	E_{bb}	E_{CC}
Instantaneous alternating component	e_2	e_p	e_c
Rms value of alternating component	E_2	E_p	E_c
Peak value of alternating component	$E_{2,max}$	$E_{p,max}$	$E_{c,max}$
Output current:			
Total instantaneous current	i_o	i_b	i_C
Quiescent component	I_{oQ}	I_{bQ}	I_{CQ}
Average component	I_{oA}	I_{bA}	I_{CA}
Instantaneous alternating component	i_2	i_p	i_c
Rms value of alternating component	I_2	I_p	I_c
Peak value of alternating component	$I_{2,max}$	$I_{p,max}$	$I_{c,max}$

In addition, the subscript s may be used in some circuits to designate an input quantity.

are defined in the first column of Table 2-1. Some of these are illustrated in Fig. 2-11, where, for convenience, a sinusoidal variation is assumed. The notation follows the general rules stated in Sec. 2-1. Since all voltages are measured with respect to the common terminal 3, the double-subscript notation for indicating voltage polarity will not be used here. The subscripts i and 1 are used to designate input quantities, whereas the subscripts o and 2 are used for output quantities. The subscripts i and o designate the *total* signal, whereas the subscripts 1 and 2 designate only the *alternating* portion of the signal.

As an example, consider the output voltage. The symbol e_o represents its instantaneous value, E_{oA} is its average value, and $E_{o,max}$ its peak value. The voltage of the bias supply in the output is E_{oo}. The instantaneous, rms, and peak values of the alternating component of the output voltage are designated by e_2, E_2, and $E_{2,max}$, respectively.

Table 2-1 also indicates the symbols used for a grounded-cathode vacuum-tube amplifier and a grounded-emitter transistor amplifier.

The most commonly used characteristics for both vacuum tubes and

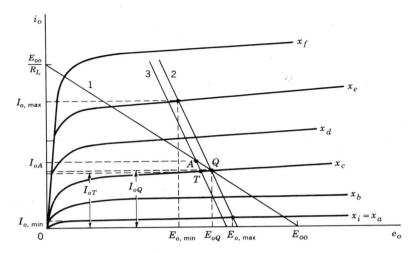

Fig. 2-12   *The generalized-device output characteristics with (1) the d-c load line, (2) the a-c load line, and (3) the a-c load line shifted by distortion. The increments in the input parameters for each curve are equal and are given by* Δx, *that is,* $x_b - x_a = x_c - x_b = x_d - x_c = \cdots = \Delta x$, *where* Δx *may be either positive or negative.*

transistors are the output characteristics (i.e., the output current versus the output voltage). For common-cathode vacuum tubes, the grid voltage is used as the input parameter, whereas for common-emitter transistors the base current is used. Generalized output characteristics may represent either device. The input quantity remains undesignated. Such characteristics are shown in Fig. 2-12. In fact, this type of generalized characteristic may be used no matter which terminal of the device is common to the input and output circuits. In each case, the parameter x_i represents the appropriate input quantity. For instance, x_i represents the input-base current for a grounded-emitter transistor. The characteristics shown in Fig. 2-12 have the general shape of those for either the vacuum-tube pentode or for the transistor. Of course, they can also be used for the vacuum-tube triode.

It should be emphasized here that, when the instantaneous value of

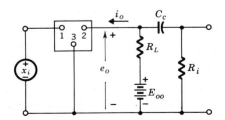

Fig. 2-13   *The RC-coupled amplifier.*

the input parameter x_i is known, the analysis for the output quantities is exactly the same whether the device is a vacuum tube or a transistor.

2-8 A-C load lines

Previously, whenever a load line was drawn, it was assumed that a single resistance was used as the load. This is usually not the case. In general, a more complex coupling circuit is employed. One such is the RC-coupling network shown in Fig. 2-13. The resistance R_i is the input resistance of the next stage. The coupling capacitor C_c is so large that it is usually a good approximation to assume that it is a short circuit at the signal frequencies. Thus, under quiescent operating conditions, the load resistance is R_L, whereas for alternating signals it is the parallel combination of R_L and R_i. The load line that we have previously discussed has a slope of $-1/R_L$ and is the locus of all quiescent operating points for this load resistance. However, when an alternating signal x_1 is impressed, the effective load resistance is now R_{ac}.

$$R_{ac} = \frac{R_L R_i}{R_L + R_i} \tag{2-28}$$

The locus of the instantaneous values of the output voltage e_o and of the output current i_o will lie along a straight line whose slope is $-1/R_{ac}$. The coordinates of the point where the a-c load line intersects the d-c load line are the average values of the output voltage and current. (The average values of a voltage or current are their direct values.) If x_1 is a sinusoid and if distortion is negligible, then the variations in the output are also purely sinusoidal. In this case, since the average value of a sinusoid is zero, the average values of the output voltage and current are the coordinates of the quiescent operating point Q. Thus, if the direct input bias X_{ii} is x_c and the alternating input signal x_1 is $2\Delta x \sin \omega t$, then the quiescent operating point Q is at the intersection of the d-c load line and the characteristic curve for which $x_i = x_c$. The a-c load line is determined by drawing a line having a slope $-1/R_{ac}$ through the point Q. The alternating variation in voltage is between $E_{o,\max}$ and $E_{o,\min}$, as shown in Fig. 2-12. The variation in current is similarly indicated.

When the nonlinearity of the output characteristics is taken into account, there will be a distortion in the output waveform. An example of a distorted output for a sinusoidal input is shown in Fig. 2-14. In this case, the lower portion of the output wave tends to be flattened. Since the direct current is the average value of the waveform, the direct output current shifts from its quiescent value I_{oQ} to the average value I_{oA}, as indicated in Fig. 2-14. The amount of this d-c shift depends upon the magnitude of the input signal. The direct current I_{oA} must lie on the d-c load line. Hence, its value determines the point of intersection A between the d-c and the a-c load lines, as shown in Fig. 2-12. Thus, the effect of distortion

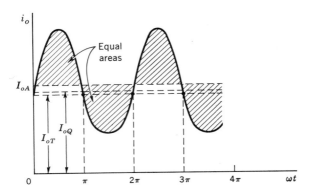

Fig. 2-14   A distorted output of a sinusoidal input.

is to shift the a-c load line, without changing its slope.   Values of the output waveform may be obtained from the shifted a-c load line, as before. It should be noted that, when the input sinusoid is instantaneously zero (i.e., $\omega t = 0, \pi, 2\pi, \ldots$), the output current does not assume the quiescent value I_{oQ} or the average value I_{oA}, but rather is I_{oT}.   This is the value at the intersection T of the shifted a-c load line with the characteristic curve corresponding to the direct bias (i.e., $X_{ii} = x_c$ in Fig. 2-12).   Methods of calculating the amount of this d-c shift will be given in Sec. 2-10.   Often it is so small that it can be neglected.

Another commonly used coupling network is the transformer coupling shown in Fig. 2-15.   The input resistance of this transformer for direct current is merely the resistance of the primary winding R_p.   At signal frequencies, the input resistance is the sum of R_p and the reflected load resistance $R_L(n_1/n_2)^2$.   The resistance of the secondary winding is included in the value of R_L.   Thus, this a-c resistance is greater than the d-c resistance; hence, the slope of the a-c load line has a smaller magnitude than that of the d-c load line.   This is the reverse of the situation for the RC-coupled amplifier.   The procedure for drawing the load lines is the same as before. Once again, because of nonlinearities in the output characteristics, the a-c load line will shift as the input-signal level is varied.   (Additional material about transformers is given in Secs. 6-17 and 6-18.)

When the load impedance is a pure resistance, the sinusoidal components of the instantaneous output voltage e_2 and output current i_2 are exactly

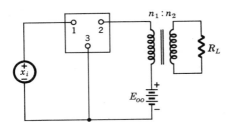

Fig. 2-15   The transformer-coupled amplifier.

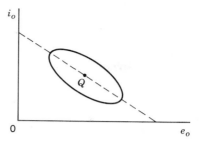

Fig. 2-16   The elliptical locus of instantaneous operating points produced by a load containing a reactive component.

180° out of phase and may be written as

$$e_2 = -E_{2,\max} \sin \omega t$$
$$i_2 = I_{2,\max} \sin \omega t \tag{2-29}$$

where $E_{2,\max}$ and $I_{2,\max}$ are the peak values of these sinusoids. This is the situation we have just discussed; as we have seen, the locus of instantaneous operating points lies along a straight line. This is also borne out by the fact that Eqs. (2-29) are the parametric equations of a straight line. If, however, the load has a reactive component, then a phase shift θ occurs between $-e_2$ and i_2.

$$e_2 = -E_{2,\max} \sin \omega t$$
$$i_2 = I_{2,\max} \sin (\omega t + \theta) \tag{2-30}$$

These are the parametric equations of an ellipse, so the resulting locus of instantaneous operating points is the ellipse shown in Fig. 2-16. When the load is purely reactive (and the scales are correct), the locus is a circle. If the nonlinearities of the output characteristics are taken into account, the ellipse becomes distorted. In this case, the procedure for determining the exact operating locus is, in general, too complicated to be useful.

2-9   Graphical calculation of output quantities

We shall now consider a graphical means of calculating the output voltage, current, and power for an amplifier. In addition, we shall consider what limitations are imposed upon the operation by the ratings of the generalized device. The procedures given here apply to any output circuit whose operation is along a straight a-c load line. For the sake of definiteness, we shall refer to the circuit of Fig. 2-13 for the RC-coupled amplifier. It is assumed in this section that the effects of distortion can be neglected and that the device is never cut off (i.e., the operation remains within the first quadrant of the output characteristics). The effects of distortion will be analyzed in the next section.

Let the device be characterized by the curves of Fig. 2-17 and let the input bias supply X_{ii} equal x_c. The output circuit determines the d-c

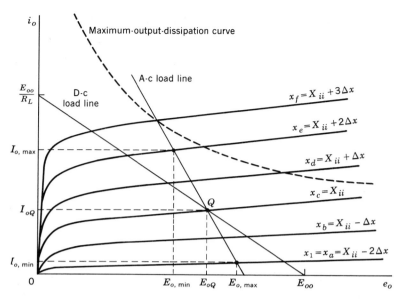

Fig. 2-17   The output characteristics of a generalized device.

and a-c load lines shown. Since distortion is neglected, these curves intersect at the quiescent operating point Q. The alternating component of the input signal is assumed to be

$$x_1 = 2\Delta x \sin \omega t$$

Thus, the alternating components of output voltage and current are

$$e_2 = -\frac{E_{o,\max} - E_{o,\min}}{2} \sin \omega t = \frac{-E_{2,\max}}{2} \sin \omega t \tag{2-31}$$

$$i_2 = \frac{I_{o,\max} - I_{o,\min}}{2} \sin \omega t = \frac{I_{2,\max}}{2} \sin \omega t \tag{2-32}$$

where $E_{2,\max}$ and $I_{2,\max}$ are the peak values of the sinusoidal components. The rms values of these quantities are

$$E_2 = \frac{E_{o,\max} - E_{o,\min}}{2\sqrt{2}} \tag{2-33}$$

$$I_2 = \frac{I_{o,\max} - I_{o,\min}}{2\sqrt{2}} \tag{3-34}$$

Thus, the average alternating (signal) power delivered to the load is

$$P_2 = \frac{(E_{o,\max} - E_{o,\min})(I_{o,\max} - I_{o,\min})}{8} \tag{2-35}$$

In a transformer-coupled amplifier this represents the power delivered to both the load and the transformer.

To compute the power P_{oo} supplied by the source whose voltage is E_{oo}, we note that the current through it is the direct current I_{oQ} plus a fraction of the alternating current through the device. Let us designate this alternating component $I_{ac,max} \sin \omega t$. Hence, the instantaneous power supplied by the voltage source is

$$p_{oo} = E_{oo}(I_{oQ} + I_{ac,max} \sin \omega t)$$

Thus, the average power supplied by the voltage source is

$$P_{oo} = \frac{1}{2\pi} \int_0^{2\pi} E_{oo}(I_{oQ} + I_{ac,max} \sin \omega t) \, d(\omega t)$$

Hence

$$P_{oo} = E_{oo}I_{oQ} \tag{2-36}$$

If distortion is present then I_{oQ} should be replaced by I_{oA}. The amount of power dissipated in the output portion of the generalized device is called the *device-output dissipation*. It corresponds to the *plate dissipation* in a vacuum tube and the *collector dissipation* in a transistor. Maximum dissipation specified by manufacturers should not be exceeded. Under quiescent conditions, the device-output dissipation P_{oD} is given by

$$P_{oD} = E_{oQ}I_{oQ} = P_{oo} - I_{oQ}{}^2 R_L \tag{2-37}$$

The right-hand side of this equation may be obtained by the application of the conservation-of-energy principle to the output circuit. When an alternating signal is impressed, the average value of the device-output dissipation P_{oD} differs from the value given by Eq. (2-37). It is the difference between the power $P_{oo} = E_{oo}I_{oQ}$ and the sum of the alternating output power P_2 and the direct power dissipated in R_L.

$$P_{oD} = P_{oo} - P_2 - I_{oQ}{}^2 R_L \tag{2-38}$$

Hence, when an alternating signal is applied, the average device-output dissipation is reduced by P_2. In order not to exceed the maximum rating of P_{oD} during periods when the alternating signal is not present, the greater value given by Eq. (2-37) is used for design purposes. Thus, a relation that limits the choice of the quiescent operating point is

$$E_{oQ}I_{oQ} \leqslant P_{oD,max} \tag{2-39}$$

where $P_{oD,max}$ is the maximum allowable device-output dissipation. The equation $E_{oQ}I_{oQ} = P_{oD,max}$ defines a hyperbola on the output characteristics. An example of such a hyperbola is shown in Fig. 2-17. Any quiescent operating point should lie below this hyperbola.

Maximum instantaneous voltage and current ratings, which are usually specified, should not be exceeded.

Another useful quantity is the *output-circuit efficiency* η_2, which is the ratio of the alternating power output to the direct power supplied by the voltage source.

$$\eta_2 = \frac{(E_{o,\max} - E_{o,\min})(I_{o,\max} - I_{o,\min})}{8E_{oo}I_{oQ}} \qquad (2\text{-}40)$$

2-10   Nonlinear distortion

Distortion of the output signal due to the nonlinearities of the generalized device characteristics is called *nonlinear distortion* or *amplitude distortion*. Other types of distortion are caused by the frequency dependence of the characteristics of the device and the external circuitry. These effects will be discussed in Chaps. 5 and 6.

If the input signal is a sinusoid, the output signal will be a periodic function having the same fundamental frequency; hence, it can be represented by a Fourier series. It will be assumed that the load is purely resistive at the frequencies of interest, so the operation is along a straight a-c load line. Thus, the output waveform will have even symmetry around its peak value. Choosing the origin of the time axis to coincide with this peak value, we can represent the output current by the following Fourier cosine series:

$$i_o = I_{oA} + \sqrt{2}(I_{o1} \cos \omega t + I_{o2} \cos 2\omega t + I_{o3} \cos 3\omega t + \cdots) \qquad (2\text{-}41)$$

where I_{oA} = the average value of i_o when signal is impressed and I_{ok} = the rms value of the kth harmonic. For the moment, we shall assume that the position of the a-c load line is known (i.e., that the shift in the a-c load line has been predetermined). In some cases (often, for the vacuum-tube triode), the harmonics higher than the second are negligible and the output current can be represented with sufficient accuracy by

$$i_o = I_{oA} + \sqrt{2}\,(I_{o1} \cos \omega t + I_{o2} \cos 2\omega t) \qquad (2\text{-}42)$$

Expressions for the three unknown coefficients I_{oA}, I_{o1}, and I_{o2} can be obtained by evaluating Eq. (2-42) at three different points on the a-c load line. Let the magnitude of the input signal be $2\Delta x$ and the input bias be X_{ii}. Choosing the time origin as mentioned above, the input signal is

$$x_i = X_{ii} + 2\Delta x \cos \omega t \qquad (2\text{-}43)$$

Then, choosing the values for ωt as 0, $\pi/2$, and π, the corresponding values of the alternating component x_1 are $2\Delta x$, $0\Delta x$, and $-2\Delta x$. These, in turn, yield three values of output current $I_{o,\max}$, I_{oT}, and $I_{o,\min}$, which are illustrated in Fig. 2-18. Hence, the following three simultaneous equations may be written:

For $\omega t = 0$

$$I_{o,\max} = I_{oA} + \sqrt{2}\,I_{o1} + \sqrt{2}\,I_{o2} \qquad\qquad (2\text{-}44)$$

For $\omega t = \pi/2$

$$I_{oT} = I_{oA} - \sqrt{2}\,I_{o2} \qquad\qquad (2\text{-}45)$$

For $\omega t = \pi$

$$I_{o,\min} = I_{oA} - \sqrt{2}\,I_{o1} + \sqrt{2}\,I_{o2} \qquad\qquad (2\text{-}46)$$

Solving these equations, we obtain

$$I_{oA} = \frac{I_{o,\max} + I_{o,\min}}{4} + \frac{I_{oT}}{2} \qquad\qquad (2\text{-}47)$$

$$\sqrt{2}\,I_{o1} = \frac{I_{o,\max} - I_{o,\min}}{2} \qquad\qquad (2\text{-}48)$$

$$\sqrt{2}\,I_{o2} = \frac{I_{o,\max} + I_{o,\min}}{4} - \frac{I_{oT}}{2} \qquad\qquad (2\text{-}49)$$

It was assumed above that the position of the a-c load line was known. This requires a knowledge of I_{oA} which, in turn, depends upon the position of the a-c load line. To determine the above quantities, a cut-and-try procedure must be used. That is, as a first trial, we assume that the a-c

Fig. 2-18   *The output characteristics for a generalized device showing the points used in the calculation of second-, third-, and fourth-harmonic distortion.*

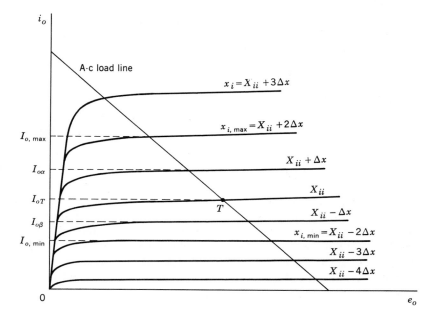

load line passes through the point Q. If the calculated value of I_{oA} differs substantially from I_{oQ}, a new a-c load line is drawn through that point on the d-c load line whose ordinate is the calculated value of I_{oA}. The procedure for obtaining I_{oA} (hence, the position of the load line) is repeated until the calculated and assumed values of I_{oA} are sufficiently close. In many cases, the shift in the position of the a-c load line is so small that it is sufficiently accurate to assume that $I_{oA} = I_{oQ}$. If there is a cathode-bias resistor, or an emitter-stabilizing resistor, then a shift in I_{oA} will change the input bias. This should be taken into account when the instantaneous operating points are determined.

For the cases where the higher harmonics are not negligible (e.g., when using vacuum-tube pentodes and transistors), the same basic procedure may be used to determine the magnitudes of these harmonics. For example, let us assume that the harmonics higher than the fourth are negligible. Thus, we may write

$$i_o = I_{oA} + \sqrt{2}\,(I_{o1} \cos \omega t + I_{o2} \cos 2\omega t + I_{o3} \cos 3\omega t + I_{o4} \cos 4\omega t) \tag{2-50}$$

Since there are now five unknown harmonic magnitudes, we need five independent simultaneous equations. We shall choose for ωt the values 0, $\pi/3$, $\pi/2$, $2\pi/3$, and π. Since x_i is given by Eq. (2-43), the corresponding values for x_i are $X_{ii} + 2\Delta x$, $X_{ii} + \Delta x$, X_{ii}, $X_{ii} - \Delta x$, and $X_{ii} - 2\Delta x$; the corresponding values for i_o are $I_{o,\max}$, $I_{o\alpha}$, I_{oT}, $I_{o\beta}$, and $I_{o,\min}$ (see Fig. 2-18). Inserting these values for ωt and i_o into Eq. (2-50) and inverting the resulting five simultaneous equations, we obtain the expressions for the harmonic magnitudes.

$$I_{oA} = \frac{I_{o,\max} + I_{o,\min}}{6} + \frac{I_{o\alpha} + I_{o\beta}}{3} \tag{2-51}$$

$$\sqrt{2}\,I_{o1} = \frac{I_{o,\max} - I_{o,\min}}{3} + \frac{I_{o\alpha} - I_{o\beta}}{3} \tag{2-52}$$

$$\sqrt{2}\,I_{o2} = \frac{I_{o,\max} + I_{o,\min}}{4} - \frac{I_{oT}}{2} \tag{2-53}$$

$$\sqrt{2}\,I_{o3} = \frac{I_{o,\max} - I_{o,\min}}{6} - \frac{I_{o\alpha} - I_{o\beta}}{3} \tag{2-54}$$

$$\sqrt{2}\,I_{o4} = \frac{I_{o,\max} + I_{o,\min}}{12} - \frac{I_{o\alpha} + I_{o\beta}}{3} + \frac{I_{oT}}{2} \tag{2-55}$$

Note that the expressions for I_{oA} given by Eqs. (2-47) and (2-51) differ, as do the corresponding expressions for I_{o1}. This is simply because the assumptions made in deriving these two sets of equations are different. In general, both sets of equations yield only approximate values for the harmonics, since the higher harmonics are not identically zero.

The magnitudes of the various harmonics are not a good measure of distortion unless expressed as a percentage of the fundamental, I_{o1}. The *percent harmonic distortion* for the second, third, and fourth harmonics is defined as

$$D_2 = \left| \frac{I_{o2}}{I_{o1}} \right| \times 100\% \qquad D_3 = \left| \frac{I_{o3}}{I_{o1}} \right| \times 100\% \qquad D_4 = \left| \frac{I_{o4}}{I_{o1}} \right| \times 100\%$$

$$(2\text{-}56)$$

Another quantity of interest is the *percent total harmonic distortion D*, which is defined as the ratio of the rms value of the sum of the harmonics to the fundamental component in percent. Hence, D is given by

$$D = \frac{\sqrt{I_{o2}^2 + I_{o3}^2 + I_{o4}^2 + \cdots}}{I_{o1}} \times 100\% \qquad (2\text{-}57)$$

$$D = \sqrt{D_2^2 + D_3^2 + D_4^2 + \cdots} \qquad (2\text{-}58)$$

The total alternating power output $P_{2,tot}$ is the sum of the powers of the fundamental and higher harmonics. Hence,

$$P_{2,tot} = I_{o1}^2 R_{ac} + I_{o2}^2 R_{ac} + I_{o3}^2 R_{ac} + \cdots \qquad (2\text{-}59)$$

where R_{ac} is the negative of the reciprocal of the slope of the a-c load line. The power of the harmonic distortion is the sum $I_{o2}^2 R_{ac} + I_{o3}^2 R_{ac} + \cdots$.

Another means of analyzing nonlinear distortion is to write the output current as a Taylor's series expansion of the input quantity x_1. This is a power-series expansion involving the instantaneous alternating component of the input signal $x_1 = x_i - X_{ii}$.

$$i_o = I_{oT} + a_1 x_1 + a_2 x_1^2 + a_3 x_1^3 + \cdots \qquad (2\text{-}60)$$

When the signal x_1 is instantaneously zero, the output current i_o assumes the value I_{oT}. However, the average value of i_o (i.e., I_{oA}) is I_{oT} plus tne direct components of the remaining terms in Eq. (2-60). Note that I_{oT} is a function of the signal (see Fig. 2-12).

This power-series analysis of nonlinear distortion is somewhat more general than the previous harmonic analysis, since the distortion components may be readily calculated when the input signal has more than one frequency present. We shall assume that i_o can be adequately represented by a finite number of terms in Eq. (2-60). The coefficients a_i may be calculated by substituting values for i_o and x_1 obtained from the a-c load line.

For example, terminating Eq. (2-60) after the third term, we obtain

$$i_o = I_{oT} + a_1 x_1 + a_2 x_1^2 \qquad (2\text{-}61)$$

There are two unknowns, a_1 and a_2. Hence, substituting any two points from the a-c load line into Eq. (2-61) yields values for a_1 and a_2. These values will vary depending upon which two points are chosen. We shall choose the maximum and minimum values, $x_{1,max}$ and $x_{1,min}$, of the signal x_1. Hence, the simultaneous equations which determine a_1 and a_2 are

$$I_{o,max} = I_{oT} + a_1 x_{1,max} + a_2 x_{1,max}^2$$

$$I_{o,min} = I_{oT} + a_1 x_{1,min} + a_2 x_{1,min}^2 \qquad (2\text{-}62)$$

where

$$x_{1,\max} = x_{i,\max} - X_{ii} \quad \text{and} \quad x_{1,\min} = x_{i,\min} - X_{ii}$$

Some of these values are illustrated in Fig. 2-18. If, for greater accuracy, a larger number of terms of Eq. (2-60) are used, the unknown coefficients may be determined in a similar fashion.

Let us use Eq. (2-61) to determine the output when the input is

$$x_i = X_{ii} + X_{1,\max} \cos \omega t \tag{2-63}$$

This yields

$$i_o = I_{oT} + a_1 X_{1,\max} \cos \omega t + \frac{a_2 X_{1,\max}^2}{2} (1 + \cos 2\omega t)$$

$$i_o = \left(I_{oT} + \frac{a_2 X_{1,\max}^2}{2} \right) + a_1 X_{1,\max} \cos \omega t + \frac{a_2 X_{1,\max}^2}{2} \cos 2\omega t \tag{2-64}$$

Equation (2-64) demonstrates the shift in the average current and also the generation of a second-harmonic component. If higher power terms are included in the finite series for i_o, higher order harmonics will also appear.

Let us now consider the output current i_o when the input signal x_i has two sinusoidal components of different frequencies.

$$x_i = X_{ii} + X_{1a} \cos \omega_a t + X_{1b} \cos \omega_b t$$

Substituting this into Eq. (2-61) and rearranging the result by using some trigonometric identities, we obtain

$$i_o = I_{oT} + \frac{a_2}{2} (X_{1a}^2 + X_{1b}^2) + a_1(X_{1a} \cos \omega_a t + X_{1b} \cos \omega_b t)$$

$$+ \frac{a_2}{2} (X_{1a}^2 \cos 2\omega_a t + X_{1b}^2 \cos 2\omega_b t)$$

$$+ a_2 X_{1a} X_{1b} [\cos (\omega_a - \omega_b)t + \cos (\omega_a + \omega_b)t] \tag{2-65}$$

In addition to the second-harmonic components of ω_a and ω_b, other frequencies which are the sum and difference frequencies of ω_a and ω_b are generated by the nonlinear distortion. This second type of frequency generation is called *intermodulation distortion*, in contrast to harmonic distortion. If more terms are used for the finite series for i_o, additional intermodulation or "*beat*" frequencies will appear.

In this analysis, it has been assumed that the position of the shifted a-c load line is known. If this is not the case, a cut-and-try procedure similar to the one discussed in harmonic-distortion analysis should be used to determine it.

2-11   Effect of the input circuit on nonlinear distortion

The calculations of Sec. 2-10 were made under the assumption that the input signal x_i varied as a cosinusoid. However, the input circuit may

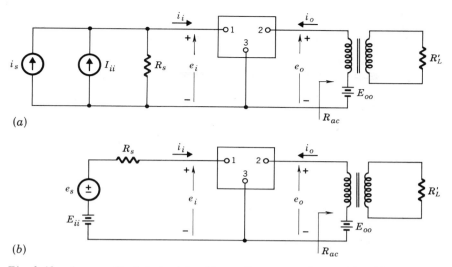

Fig. 2-19 A generalized device (a) with a voltage source input; (b) with a current source input.

distort the effective input waveform. This occurs in a transistor, because input impedance varies with signal level. If the grid voltage of a vacuum tube becomes positive, then there will be grid current for a portion of a cycle and distortion of the grid voltage will result. The effects of the input circuit must be considered when computing the distortion of the amplifier. Figure 2-19 indicates a generalized device with either a voltage source or a current source input. Even if i_s or e_s is sinusoidal, e_i and i_i may not be. The direct generators, I_{ii}, E_{ii}, and E_{oo} are used for biasing purposes. The methods of Secs. 2-2 and 2-3 can be used to determine the quiescent operating point.

The static characteristics of the generalized device are shown in Fig. 2-20. For this discussion, the output characteristics are drawn with i_i as the controlling parameter, and the input characteristic is drawn so that e_o is the controlling parameter. A trial a-c load line is drawn, assuming no distortion. A curve of i_i versus e_o is found using Fig. 2-20a and the trial load line. It is then plotted as the dotted curve of Fig. 2-20b. This is called the *dynamic input characteristic*. The load line is then drawn on the input characteristics. Its slope is $-1/R_s$ and its ordinate intercept is $i_s + I_{ii}$ if a current source is used. The abscissa intercept is $e_s + E_{ii}$ for a voltage source. The instantaneous values of e_i and i_i can be obtained from the intersection of the load line and the dynamic characteristic. As i_s or e_s varies in time, the load line shifts parallel to itself. Thus, a plot of e_i and/or i_i versus time can be obtained. Once the instantaneous values of i_i are known, the instantaneous values of e_o and i_o can be obtained from Fig. 2-20a. For instance, if $R_s = 1$ ohm, $i_s = 3 \cos \omega t$, and $I_{ii} = 4$, and the five-point schedule of

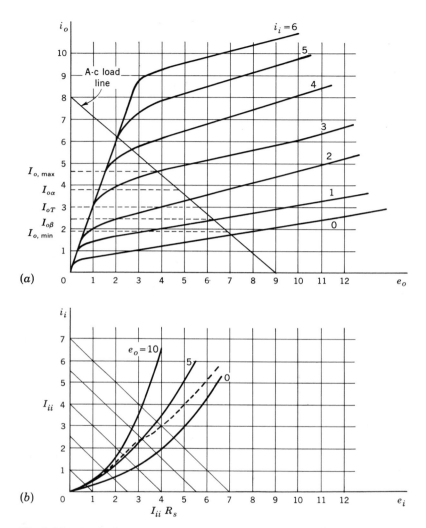

Fig. 2-20   Static characteristics of a generalized device.   (a) Output charac-teristics with an a-c load line; (b) input characteristics with load lines and with the dynamic characteristics shown dotted.

Eqs. (2-51) to (2-55) is used, then the five load lines shown in Fig. 2-20b would be drawn.   These correspond to values of $\omega t = 0$, $\pi/3$, $\pi/2$, $2\pi/3$, and π.   The corresponding values of $I_{o,\max}$, $I_{o\alpha}$, I_{oT}, $I_{o\beta}$, and $I_{o,\min}$ are obtained from Fig. 2-20a.   If the calculated value of I_{oA} causes the output a-c load line to shift appreciably, then a new one should be drawn, a new dynamic characteristic should be calculated, and the procedure should be repeated. If the d-c and a-c resistances of the input circuit differ, then an a-c load line must be drawn on the input characteristics.   The location of this load line will depend upon the instantaneous signal level and the distortion, which affects E_{iA} and I_{iA}. It may be necessary to use a cut-and-try procedure similar to the one used in determining the position of the output-circuit load line.

At times, the distortion created by the input circuit is quite severe. However, there are circumstances when the distortion of the input and output circuits tend to cancel one another.

BIBLIOGRAPHY

DeWitt, D., and A. L. Rossoff: "Transistor Electronics," chap. 6, McGraw-Hill Book Company, New York, 1957.

Greiner, R. A.: "Semiconductor Devices and Applications," chap. 11, McGraw-Hill Book Company, New York, 1961.

Millman, J.: "Vacuum-tube and Semiconductor Electronics," pp. 230–237, 402–408, 419–420, McGraw-Hill Book Company, New York, 1958.

PROBLEMS

In all the following problems it can be assumed that the reactance of any capacitances shown in any circuit is zero at the signal frequency.

2-1. The circuit elements of the 6C4 vacuum-tube-triode circuit of Fig. 2-3a are $E_{bb} = 350$ volts, $R_L = 15,000$ ohms, and $R_k = 625$ ohms. Determine E_{bQ}, I_{bQ}, and E_{cQ}, the coordinates of the quiescent operating point. The plate characteristics of the type 6C4 vacuum-tube triode are given in Fig. 2-3b.

2-2. The 6C4 vacuum-tube triode of Fig. 2-3a is to be operated such that $E_{bQ} = 300$ volts, $I_{bQ} = 15$ ma. The value of the load resistance is $R_L = 10,000$ ohms. Determine the values of R_k and E_{bb}. The plate characteristics of the 6C4 vacuum-tube triode are given in Fig. 2-3b.

2-3. Repeat Prob. 2-2, but now assume that the coordinates of the operating point are $E_{bQ} = 250$ volts, $E_{cQ} = -10$ volts.

2-4. The type 6C4 vacuum-tube triode is operated in the circuit of Fig. 2-3a such that $E_{bb} = 405$ volts, $R_L = 20,000$ ohms, and $E_{cQ} = -5$ volts. Compute the value of R_k that produces the required operating point. The plate characteristics of the type 6C4 vacuum-tube triode are given in Fig. 2-3b.

2-5. The type 5879 vacuum-tube pentode is used in the circuit of Fig. 2-2. The circuit values are $E_{bb} = 350$ volts, $E_{c2} = 100$ volts, $R_L = 50,000$ ohms, and $R_k = 500$ ohms. Assume that I_{c2} is constant at 0.5 ma. Compute E_{bQ}, I_{bQ}, and E_{cQ} (i.e., the coordinates of the quiescent operating point) and the value of R_s. The plate characteristics of the 5879 vacuum-tube pentode are given in Fig. 2-1b.

2-6. Repeat Prob. 2-5, but now do not assume that I_{c2} is constant at 0.5 ma. Assume that the variation of the screen-grid current with e_c is the same as the variation of i_b with e_c.

2-7. The type of 5879 vacuum-tube pentode of Fig. 2-2 is to be operated such that $E_{bQ} = 350$ volts, $E_{cQ} = -2$ volts, and $E_{c2Q} = 100$ volts. The value of R_L is 30,000 ohms. Assume that the screen-grid current is 1.0 ma. Determine the values of E_{bb}, R_k, and R_s. The characteristics of the type 5879 vacuum-tube pentode are given in Fig. 2-1*b*.

2-8. Repeat Prob. 2-7, but now do not assume that the screen-grid current is 1.0 ma. Use the assumption of Prob. 2-6 to determine the screen-grid current.

2-9. Discuss the operation of the vacuum-tube circuit of Fig. 2-4 if R_g becomes open-circuited.

2-10. The circuit values of the transistor circuit of Fig. 2-5*a* are $E_{CC} = -20$ volts, $R_C = 4,000$ ohms, $E_{BB} = -200 \times 10^{-3}$ volt and $R_B = 2,000$ ohms. Determine the coordinates of the quiescent operating point, E_{CQ}, I_{CQ}, E_{BQ}, and I_{BQ}. The characteristics of the transistor are given in Fig. 2-6.

2-11. Repeat Prob. 2-10, but now assume that $E_{BB} = -20$ volts and $R_B = 500,000$ ohms. Are the common-emitter input characteristics required to solve this problem?

2-12. The transistor whose characteristics are supplied in Fig. 2-6 is operated in the circuit of Fig. 2-5*b*. The element values are $E_{CC} = -20$ volts, $R_C = 4,000$ ohms, and $R_B = 500,000$ ohms. Compute E_{CQ}, I_{CQ}, E_{BQ}, and I_{BQ}, the coordinates of the quiescent operating point. Are the common-emitter input characteristics required to solve this problem? Compare this problem with Prob. 2-11.

2-13. The transistor circuit of Fig. 2-5*b* is operated such that $E_{CQ} = -10$ volts, $I_{BQ} = -20 \,\mu a$, and $R_C = 1,500$ ohms. Compute the values of E_{CC} and R_B. The characteristics of the transistor are given in Fig. 2-6. Make any appropriate approximations.

2-14. The circuit values of Fig. 2-7 are $E_{CC} = -20$ volts, $R_C = 4,000$ ohms, $R_E = 1,000$ ohms, $R_{B1} = 10^6$ ohms, and $R_{B2} = 10^6$ ohms. Determine the coordinates of the quiescent operating point E_{CQ}, I_{CQ}, and I_{BQ}. The characteristics of the transistor are given in Fig. 2-6. Make any appropriate approximations.

2-15. The transistor of Fig. 2-7 is operated such that $E_{CEQ} = -10$ volts, and $I_{BQ} = -20 \,\mu a$. The value of R_L is 2,000 ohms and $E_{CC} = -20$ volts. Determine the value of R_E. Determine a set of values of R_{B1} and R_{B2} that produce the required base current. The characteristics of the transistor are given in Fig. 2-6. Make any appropriate approximations.

2-16. Repeat the calculations for R_{B1} and R_{B2} of Prob. 2-15, but now choose them so that the value of $R_B = R_{B1}R_{B2}/(R_{B1} + R_{B2})$ is a maximum. Then repeat the calculations so that R_B is a minimum.

In Probs. 2-17 through 2-43, assume that $e_{BE} = 0$ volts.

2-17. The elements of the circuit of Fig. 2-7 are $R_C = 2,000$ ohms, $R_E = 2,000$ ohms, $R_{B1} = 10,000$ ohms, and $R_{B2} = 10,000$ ohms. The transistor has an α of 0.99. Compute the stability factor of this circuit.

2-18. Repeat Prob. 2-17, but now assume that $R_E = 0$. Compare this result with that of Prob. 2-17.

2-19. Repeat Prob. 2-17, but now assume that $R_{B1} = 10^6$ ohms and $R_{B2} = 10^6$ ohms. Compare this result with that of Prob. 2-17.

2-20. The transistor of Fig. 2-7 is operated at the quiescent operating point $E_{CE} = -10$ volts, $I_C = -5$ ma, and $I_B = -100 \,\mu a$. The value of α

is 0.99 and $R_L = 1,000$ ohms. If $R_B = R_{B1}R_{B2}/(R_{B1} + R_{B2}) = 20,000$ ohms and the maximum magnitude of E_{CC} is 25 volts, what is the smallest stability factor that can be obtained with this circuit?

2-21. The transistor circuit of Fig. 2-9 is such that $R_C = 2,000$ ohms, $R_1 = 20,000$ ohms, and $\alpha = 0.99$. Compute the stability factor of the circuit. What will the stability factor become if $R_C = 1,000$ ohms and $R_1 = 10^6$ ohms?

2-22. The transistor circuit of Fig. 2-9 is operated such that $E_{CEQ} = -10$ volts, $I_{CQ} = -1.0$ ma, and $I_{BQ} = -100\,\mu$a. If $E_{CC} = -20$ volts, compute the stability factor of the circuit. Assume that $\alpha = 0.99$.

2-23. Derive an expression for the stability factor of Fig. 2-21.

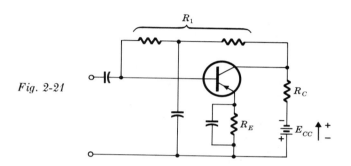

Fig. 2-21

2-24. A 6C4 vacuum-tube triode, whose plate characteristics are given in Fig. 2-3b, is connected into the circuit of Fig. 2-22. If $E_{bb} = 400$ volts, $R_L = 20,000$ ohms, $R_k = 500$ ohms, and $R_g = 20,000$ ohms, draw the d-c and a-c load lines. Assume that the signal e_g is small enough so that distortion can be neglected. If e_g is $5 \sin \omega t$ volts, plot the waveforms of i_b, e_b, and e_c.

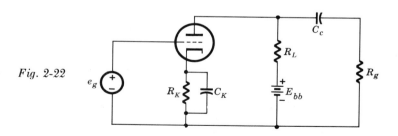

Fig. 2-22

2-25. Repeat Prob. 2-24, but now assume that distortion causes I_{bA} to be 2 ma greater than I_{bQ}. Note that the grid bias will also shift.

2-26. The transistor whose characteristics are given in Fig. 2-6 is operated in the circuit of Fig. 2-23. If $E_{CC} = -20$ volts, $R_C = 4,000$ ohms, $R_i = 3000$ ohms, $R_B = 667,000$ ohms, and $R_E = 0$, draw the a-c and d-c load lines.

If the alternating component of the base current is 20 sin ωt μa, plot i_C, e_{CE}, and i_B.

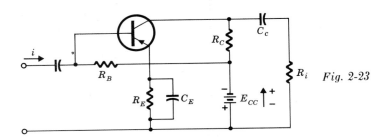

Fig. 2-23

2-27. Repeat Prob. 2-26, but now assume that distortion causes I_{CA} to be 0.5 ma greater in magnitude than I_{CQ}.

2-28. Repeat Prob. 2-26, but now assume that $R_E = 1,000$ ohms and $E_{CC} = -23.3$ volts.

2-29. Repeat Prob. 2-27, but now assume that $R_E = 1,000$ ohms and $E_{CC} = -23$ volts. Note that the distortion also shifts the voltage across R_E.

2-30. The type 7027-A beam power tube is connected into the circuit of Fig. 2-24, where $E_{bb} = 315$ volts and $E_{cQ} = -15$ volts. The primary resistance of the transformer is 100 ohms and the secondary resistance is zero. The values of $R_1 = 4$ ohms and n_1/n_2 is 22.4. Draw the a-c and d-c load lines and determine the value of R_k. Assume that e_g is small enough so that shifts in the operating point can be neglected. If $e_g = 5 \sin \omega t$ volts, plot the instantaneous curves of e_b, i_b, and e_c. The plate characteristics of the type 7027-A vacuum tube are given in Fig. 2-25.

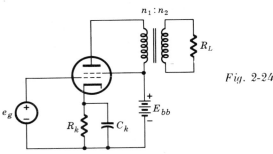

Fig. 2-24

2-31. The transistor whose characteristics are given in Fig. 2-6 is connected into the circuit of Fig. 2-26. Assume that the transformer is ideal. If $E_{cQ} = -8$ volts, $I_{BQ} = -20$ μa, $R_E = 1,000$ ohms, find the value of R_B. If $n_1/n_2 = 26.6$ and $R_L = 4$ ohms, draw the a-c load line.

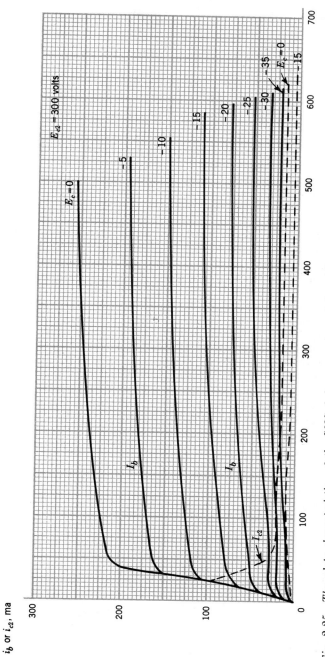

Fig. 2-25 The plate characteristics of the 7027-A beam-power pentode. (Courtesy Radio Corporation of America.)

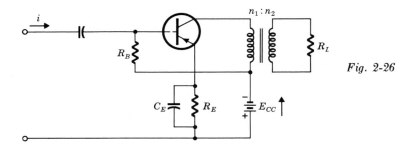

Fig. 2-26

2-32. A type 7027-A vacuum tube is operated as discussed in Prob. 2-30. If $e_g = 15 \sin \omega t$ volts, compute the power delivered to R_L, the plate dissipation, the screen-grid dissipation, the power supplied by the battery, and the plate circuit efficiency.   Neglect any effects of distortion.

2-33. Repeat Prob. 2-32, but now assume that $e_g = 0$.   Compare these results with those of Prob. 2-32.

2-34. The maximum rated plate dissipation of the type 7027-A vacuum tube is 35 watts.   Draw a curve on the plate characteristics of Fig. 2-24 showing an upper limit of the location of the quiescent operating point.

2-35. The transistor whose characteristics are given in Fig. 2-6 is operated as discussed in Prob. 2-31.   If the alternating component of the base current is $20 \sin \omega t$ μa, compute the power delivered to R_L, the collector dissipation, the power supplied by the battery, and the collector circuit efficiency.   Neglect any shift in the operating point due to distortion.

2-36. Repeat Prob. 2-35, but now assume that the alternating component of the base current is zero.   Compare the results with those of Prob. 2-35.

2-37. The 6C4 vacuum-tube triode, whose plate characteristics are given in Fig. 2-3*b*, is connected into the circuit of Fig. 2-27.   If $E_{bb} = 400$ volts, $E_{cc} = -10$ volts, $R_L = 13,333$ ohms, and $e_g = 10 \cos \omega t$ volts, compute the magnitude of the second-harmonic distortion of e_b and i_b.

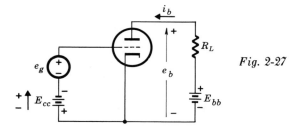

Fig. 2-27

2-38. Repeat Prob. 2-37 using a power-series expansion.   Then, if $e_g = 10 \sin \omega_1 t + 15 \sin \omega_2 t$ volts, use the power series to calculate the output current.   Do the "constants" of the power series vary if the signal level changes?   Explain your answer.

2-39. The transistor whose characteristics are given in Fig. 2-6 is connected into the circuit of Fig. 2-28, where $E_{CC} = -15$ volts, $R_C = 3,000$ ohms, $R_B = 500,000$ ohms, and $i_1 = 30 \cos \omega t \, \mu$a. Calculate the magnitude of the second-, third-, fourth-, and total harmonic distortion of i_C.

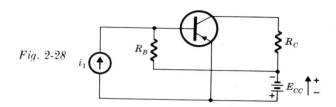

Fig. 2-28

2-40. Repeat Prob. 2-39 using a power-series expansion. Then use three terms of the power series to obtain the output current if $i_1 = 30 \cos \omega_1 t + 15 \cos \omega_2 t \, \mu$a.

2-41. The 7027-A beam power tube is operated in the circuit of Fig. 2-25 where $E_{bb} = 315$ volts and $R_L = 4$ ohms. Under quiescent conditions, $E_{cQ} = -15$ volts. Assume that the transformer is ideal and $n_1/n_2 = 26.8$. Draw the a-c and d-c load lines. If $e_g = 15 \cos \omega t$ volts, draw the shifted a-c load line and calculate the magnitude of the second, third, fourth, and total harmonic distortion of the output voltages. Assume that the characteristics of Fig. 2-24 can be used at all times.

2-42. Repeat Prob. 2-41 using a power-series expansion.

2-43. The transistor whose characteristics are given in Fig. 2-6 is connected into the circuit of Fig. 2-26. Under quiescent conditions $E_{CQ} = -5$ volts and $I_{BQ} = -40 \, \mu$a. The value of R_E is 1,000 ohms and $R_L = 4$ ohms. The transformer is ideal with a turns ratio of $n_1/n_2 = \sqrt{1,000}$. Draw the a-c and d-c load lines. A signal is applied so that the alternating component, of the base current is $40 \cos \omega t \, \mu$a. What are the magnitudes of the second-, third-, fourth-, and total harmonic distortion of the output voltage? Do not neglect the shift in the a-c load line.

2-44. The generalized device of Fig. 2-19a, whose characteristics are given in Fig. 2-20, is operated such that $R_{ac} = 1$ ohm, $E_{oo} = 5$ volts, $R_s = 1.5$ ohms, $I_{ii} = 4$ amp, and $i_s = 3 \cos \omega t$ amp. Assume that the primary resistance of the transformer is zero. Compute the magnitude of the second-, third-, fourth-, and total harmonic distortion. Neglect the shift in the a-c load line due to distortion.

2-45. Repeat Prob. 2-44, but do not neglect the shift in the a-c load line due to distortion.

Linear Equivalent Circuits of Electronic Devices

3

If electronic devices are operated so that the nonlinear distortion is small, then they can often be approximated by linear equations and circuits. In such cases, all of the procedures of linear-circuit analysis can be applied and complex circuits can be analyzed with a minimum of effort. In this chapter, we shall develop linear equivalent circuits that can often be used to replace electronic devices in analysis procedures. It is important to realize that these equivalent circuits can be used to determine the effect of the electronic device on the external circuit. In general, they *do not* actually represent the internal behavior of the device. Basic amplifier circuits will also be presented and analyzed. We shall begin with a discussion of the techniques for representing linear circuits. These procedures will then be applied to electronic devices.

3-1 Equivalent circuits for three-terminal linear networks

For the time being, we shall concern ourselves with networks that have only three terminals, as shown in Fig. 3-1. Thus, there are only two independent voltages and two independent currents. Usually, a knowledge of any two of these quantities is sufficient to determine the other two.

z parameters

Since this is a linear circuit, we can usually write the voltages as linear functions of the currents. (Exceptions occur when open or short circuits are present.) Thus,

$$\mathbf{E}_1 = \mathbf{z}_{11}\mathbf{I}_1 + \mathbf{z}_{12}\mathbf{I}_2 \tag{3-1}$$

$$\mathbf{E}_2 = \mathbf{z}_{21}\mathbf{I}_1 + \mathbf{z}_{22}\mathbf{I}_2 \tag{3-2}$$

The terms $\mathbf{z}_{11}$, $\mathbf{z}_{12}$, $\mathbf{z}_{21}$, and $\mathbf{z}_{22}$ have the dimensions of impedance. Boldface letters are used to indicate complex quantities such as voltage or current phasors or complex impedances and admittances. These elements are called the *z parameters* of the network and are sometimes represented by a *z-parameter matrix*.

$$\begin{bmatrix} \mathbf{z}_{11} & \mathbf{z}_{12} \\ \mathbf{z}_{21} & \mathbf{z}_{22} \end{bmatrix} \tag{3-3}$$

The z parameters can be obtained by a mesh analysis of the circuit within the "black box" of Fig. 3-1. An alternative procedure would be to make two sets of independent measurements of $\mathbf{E}_1$, $\mathbf{E}_2$, $\mathbf{I}_1$, and $\mathbf{I}_2$. These could be substituted into Eqs. (3-1) and (3-2) and the z parameters solved for. Since these parameters are constants, we can use any independent sets of voltages and currents to make the calculations. If we set $\mathbf{I}_2$ and $\mathbf{I}_1$ alternately equal to zero, the calculations become quite simple. For instance,

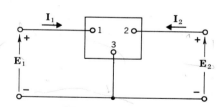

Fig. 3-1 A three-terminal network.

consider the circuit of Fig. 3-2.   A current generator is applied to the input, and the output is open-circuited.   Thus, $\mathbf{I}_2 = 0$ and

$$\mathbf{Z}_{11} = \left.\frac{\mathbf{E}_1}{\mathbf{I}_1}\right|_{\mathbf{I}_2=0} \tag{3-4}$$

$$\mathbf{Z}_{21} = \left.\frac{\mathbf{E}_2}{\mathbf{I}_1}\right|_{\mathbf{I}_2=0} \tag{3-5}$$

Thus, z_{11} is simply the impedance (or driving-point impedance) of the input with the output open-circuited.   For this reason, z_{11} is called the *open-circuit input driving-point impedance*.   Note that side 1 (terminals 1 and 3) is called the input side while side 2 (terminals 2 and 3) is called the output side.   The parameter z_{12} also has the dimensions of an impedance.   However, it is the ratio of the voltage at one part of a network to the current at another part.   (It is assumed that the current is the driving function.)   Hence, z_{12} is called a *transfer impedance*.   In particular, z_{12} is the *open-circuit forward-transfer impedance*.   The word "forward" is used since this is the response at the output terminals when a signal is impressed at the input terminals.

In a similar way, we can open-circuit the input terminals and apply a current generator to the output terminals.   Thus,

$$\mathbf{Z}_{12} = \left.\frac{\mathbf{E}_1}{\mathbf{I}_2}\right|_{\mathbf{I}_1=0} \tag{3-6}$$

and

$$\mathbf{Z}_{22} = \left.\frac{\mathbf{E}_2}{\mathbf{I}_2}\right|_{\mathbf{I}_1=0} \tag{3-7}$$

where z_{12} is the *open-circuit reverse-transfer impedance*, and z_{22} is the *open-circuit output driving-point impedance*.

Equations (3-1) and (3-2) characterize the behavior of the network of Fig. 3-1.   It is often convenient to represent a network by an *equivalent circuit*, that is, one whose equations are given by Eqs. (3-1) and (3-2).   Such a circuit is shown in Fig. 3-3a.   It is equivalent to the black box of Fig. 3-1 as far as its external behavior is concerned.   *In general, it is not representative of its internal behavior*.   The voltage generators of this circuit are dependent generators.   That is, their voltages depend upon currents in the network.   They are treated as ordinary voltage generators.   Their volt-

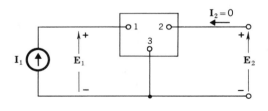

Fig. 3-2   *A network used to measure* z_{11} *and* z_{21}.

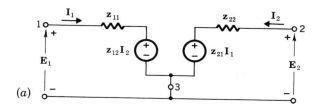

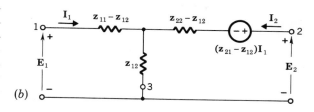

Fig. 3-3 Equivalent circuits for three terminal networks, using the z parameters. (a) The two-voltage-generator form; (b) the single-voltage-generator form; (c) the single-current-generator form.

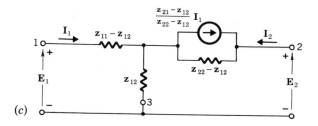

ages are unknown and are grouped with the unknown terms in the mesh equations.

Another circuit that is equivalent to the one in Fig. 3-3a is shown in Fig. 3-3b. A simple mesh analysis demonstrates this equivalency. It is sometimes more convenient to use this circuit, since there is only one voltage generator. In the circuit of Fig. 3-3c the voltage generator and series impedance have been replaced by a current generator and shunt impedance. If the network is reciprocal (that is, $z_{12} = z_{21}$), then the generators are eliminated from Fig. 3-3b and c.

As an example, consider the network of Fig. 3-4. Its z parameters are given by $z_{11} = Z_a + Z_c$, $z_{12} = z_{21} = Z_c$, and $z_{22} = Z_b + Z_c$.

y parameters

The currents of the network of Fig. 3-1 can usually be represented as linear functions of the voltages. Thus,

$$I_1 = y_{11}E_1 + y_{12}E_2 \tag{3-8}$$

$$I_2 = y_{21}E_1 + y_{22}E_2 \tag{3-9}$$

The parameters in these equations are called *y parameters*. They have the dimensions of admittances. It is most convenient to measure these

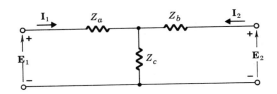

Fig. 3-4   A T section.

parameters under short-circuit conditions.   That is, apply a voltage generator to the input side and short circuit the output side or vice versa. Thus,

$$\mathbf{y}_{11} = \frac{\mathbf{I}_1}{\mathbf{E}_1}\bigg|_{\mathbf{E}_2=0} \qquad \mathbf{y}_{21} = \frac{\mathbf{I}_2}{\mathbf{E}_1}\bigg|_{\mathbf{E}_2=0} \qquad\qquad (3\text{-}10)$$

$$\mathbf{y}_{12} = \frac{\mathbf{I}_1}{\mathbf{E}_2}\bigg|_{\mathbf{E}_1=0} \qquad \mathbf{y}_{22} = \frac{\mathbf{I}_2}{\mathbf{E}_2}\bigg|_{\mathbf{E}_1=0} \qquad\qquad (3\text{-}11)$$

We define these quantities as: $\mathbf{y}_{11}$ is the *short-circuit input driving-point admittance;* $\mathbf{y}_{21}$ is the *short-circuit forward-transfer admittance;* $\mathbf{y}_{12}$ is the *short-*

Fig. 3-5   *Equivalent circuits for three-terminal networks using the y parameters.* (a) *The two-current-generator form;* (b) *the single-current-generator form;* (c) *the single-voltage-generator form.   The y parameters have the dimensions of admittances.*

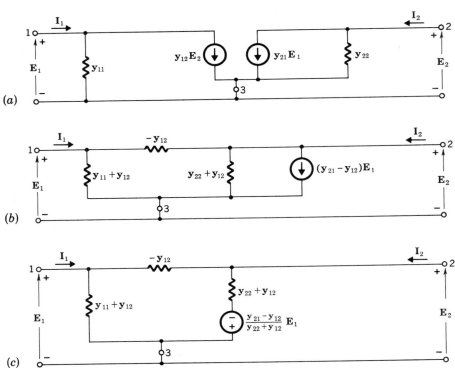

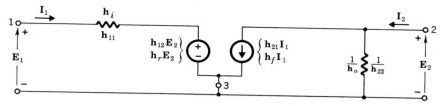

Fig. 3-6 *An equivalent circuit for three-terminal networks using the h parameters. Note that both passive elements are impedances, and that there is a voltage generator on the input side and a current generator on the output side.*

circuit reverse-transfer admittance; and y_{22} is the *short-circuit output driving-point admittance.* Three equivalent circuits for networks characterized by Eqs. (3-8) and (3-9) are given in Fig. 3-5. Dependent generators are used in these networks, and their currents or voltages depend upon a voltage at some point in the network. If the network is reciprocal ($y_{12} = y_{21}$), the generators are eliminated from Fig. 3-5b and c.

h parameters

Another convenient set of parameters is called the *hybrid parameters* or *h parameters.* These relate E_2 and I_1 to E_1 and I_2. Hence,

$$E_1 = h_{11}I_1 + h_{12}E_2 \tag{3-12}$$

$$I_2 = h_{21}I_1 + h_{22}E_2 \tag{3-13}$$

In this case, it is most convenient to determine h_{11} and h_{21} by short-circuiting the output and applying a current generator at the input. Conversely, h_{12} and h_{22} are conveniently determined by open-circuiting the input and applying a voltage generator at the output. Thus,

$$h_{11} = \frac{E_1}{I_1}\bigg|_{E_2=0} \qquad h_{21} = \frac{I_2}{I_1}\bigg|_{E_2=0} \tag{3-14}$$

$$h_{12} = \frac{E_1}{E_2}\bigg|_{I_1=0} \qquad h_{22} = \frac{I_2}{E_2}\bigg|_{I_1=0} \tag{3-15}$$

The dimensions of h_{11} and h_{22} are of an impedance and an admittance, respectively, while h_{21} and h_{12} are dimensionless. They relate currents (voltages) at one part of the network to currents (voltages) at another part. Hence, they are called transfer current (voltage) ratios. Thus: h_{11} is the *short-circuit input driving-point impedance*, h_{21} is the *short-circuit forward-transfer current ratio*, h_{12} is the *open-circuit reverse-transfer voltage ratio*, and h_{22} is the *open-circuit output driving-point admittance*. To avoid the use of double subscripts, the following notation is often used.

$$\begin{bmatrix} h_{11} & h_{12} \\ h_{21} & h_{22} \end{bmatrix} = \begin{bmatrix} h_i & h_r \\ h_f & h_o \end{bmatrix} \tag{3-16}$$

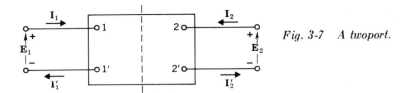

Fig. 3-7   A twoport.

where the subscripts i, f, r, and o stand for input, forward, reverse, and output, respectively. An equivalent circuit using h parameters is shown in Fig. 3-6.

Twoports

The parameters that we have been discussing are often used to characterize a special case of networks with four terminals. Such a network is shown in Fig. 3-7. The dashed line is considered to isolate the input and output sides of the network, so that $I_1 = I_1'$ and $I_2 = I_2'$ and we cannot measure E_{12} or $E_{1'2'}$. In this case, we can consider that E_1, E_2, I_1, and I_2 are the only independent variables and use the previously developed parameters to characterize the network. The term *twoport* is used since the four-terminal network is considered to have only two ports of entry.

There are other parameters which relate different combinations of E_1, E_2, I_1, and I_2. However, the ones that have been considered here are the ones commonly used for electronic devices.

3-2   Relations among network parameters

One set of network parameters can be obtained from another by writing their defining equations in the same form. For instance, if Eqs. (3-1) and (3-2) are solved for I_1 and I_2 in terms of E_1 and E_2, the y parameters can be obtained as functions of the z parameters. Thus,

$$y_{11} = \frac{z_{22}}{\Delta_z} \qquad y_{12} = -\frac{z_{12}}{\Delta_z}$$

$$y_{21} = -\frac{z_{21}}{\Delta_z} \qquad y_{22} = \frac{z_{11}}{\Delta_z} \tag{3-17}$$

where

$$\Delta_z = z_{11}z_{22} - z_{12}z_{21} \tag{3-18}$$

Note that $y_{11} \neq 1/z_{11}$, since one is measured under short-circuit conditions while the other is measured under open-circuit conditions. Equations (3-12) and (3-13) can be manipulated into the form of Eqs. (3-1) and (3-2), so that

$$z_{11} = \frac{h_{11}h_{22} - h_{21}h_{12}}{h_{22}} \qquad z_{12} = \frac{h_{12}}{h_{22}}$$

$$z_{21} = -\frac{h_{21}}{h_{22}} \qquad\qquad z_{22} = \frac{1}{h_{22}} \qquad\qquad (3\text{-}19)$$

In a similar way, all the relationships among the parameters can be obtained.

3-3 Low-frequency equivalent-circuit representations of electronic devices

Electronic devices (e.g., vacuum tubes or transistors) are not linear. However, if the signal voltages and currents are small variations about a quiescent operating point, then the signal quantities can usually be obtained by a linear analysis. *The quiescent operating point cannot be obtained by these procedures.* Consider the electronic device represented by the generalized device of Fig. 3-8. For the time being, we shall ignore reactive elements and work with instantaneous quantities. For most electronic devices, the reactive frequency-dependent elements behave as resistive frequency-independent terms at sufficiently low frequencies. Thus, the equivalent circuits that we shall develop here are *low-frequency equivalent circuits.* As in the case of the linear network, any two variables can, in general, be expressed as functions of the other two. For instance,

$$e_i = f_1(i_i, i_o)$$
$$e_o = f_2(i_i, i_o) \qquad\qquad (3\text{-}20)$$

Now, let us obtain relations for increments in e_i and e_o as functions of the increments in i_i and i_o about an operating point $i_i = I_{iQ}$, $i_o = I_{oQ}$. Since f_1 and f_2 are not linear, we must use a double Taylor's series. Hence,

$$\Delta e_i = \frac{\partial e_i}{\partial i_i} \Delta i_i + \frac{\partial e_i}{\partial i_o} \Delta i_o + \frac{\partial^2 e_i}{\partial i_i\, \partial i_o} \Delta i_i\, \Delta i_o + \frac{1}{2}\frac{\partial^2 e_i}{\partial i_i^2} \Delta i_i^2 + \frac{1}{2}\frac{\partial^2 e_i}{\partial i_o^2} \Delta i_o^2 + \cdots$$

$$(3\text{-}21)$$

$$\Delta e_o = \frac{\partial e_o}{\partial i_i} \Delta i_i + \frac{\partial e_o}{\partial i_o} \Delta i_o + \frac{\partial^2 e_o}{\partial i_i\, \partial i_o} \Delta i_i\, \Delta i_o + \frac{1}{2}\frac{\partial^2 e_o}{\partial i_i^2} \Delta i_i^2 + \frac{1}{2}\frac{\partial^2 e_o}{\partial i_o^2} \Delta i_o^2 + \cdots$$

$$(3\text{-}22)$$

where the derivatives are evaluated as indicated in Eq. (3-28). If the

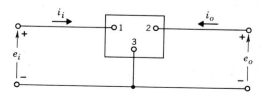

Fig. 3-8 A generalized electronic device.

deviations are small and/or the higher order derivatives are very small, then all the terms in these equations, except the first two, can be ignored. Thus, we obtain

$$\Delta e_i \approx \frac{\partial e_i}{\partial i_i} \Delta i_i + \frac{\partial e_i}{\partial i_o} \Delta i_o \tag{3-23}$$

$$\Delta e_o \approx \frac{\partial e_o}{\partial i_i} \Delta i_i + \frac{\partial e_o}{\partial i_o} \Delta i_o \tag{3-24}$$

The variation Δe_i can be considered to be the signal component of e_i. We shall write it as e_1. Then, proceeding similarly for all four variables

$$\begin{aligned} \Delta e_i &= e_1 & \Delta e_o &= e_2 \\ \Delta i_i &= i_1 & \Delta i_o &= i_2 \end{aligned} \tag{3-25}$$

Thus

$$e_1 = \frac{\partial e_i}{\partial i_i} i_1 + \frac{\partial e_i}{\partial i_o} i_2 \tag{3-26}$$

and

$$e_2 = \frac{\partial e_o}{\partial i_i} i_1 + \frac{\partial e_o}{\partial i_o} i_2 \tag{3-27}$$

If we compare these equations with Eqs. (3-1) and (3-2), we obtain

$$\begin{aligned} z_{11} &= \frac{\partial e_i}{\partial i_i} \bigg|_{i_i = I_{iQ},\ i_o = I_{oQ}} & z_{12} &= \frac{\partial e_i}{\partial i_o} \bigg|_{i_i = I_{iQ},\ i_o = I_{oQ}} \\ z_{21} &= \frac{\partial e_o}{\partial i_i} \bigg|_{i_i = I_{iQ},\ i_o = I_{oQ}} & z_{22} &= \frac{\partial e_o}{\partial i_o} \bigg|_{i_i = I_{iQ},\ i_o = I_{oQ}} \end{aligned} \tag{3-28}$$

where the derivatives are evaluated at the operating point $i_o = I_{oQ}$, $i_i = I_{iQ}$. Thus, we can use the z-parameter equivalent circuits of Fig. 3-3 to obtain the relations for the incremental variation of voltage and current of the electronic device of Fig. 3-8. In this case, the z parameters represent slopes of the static characteristics of the device at the operating point. We shall relate these to open-circuit measurement for the z parameters in the next section, where we shall also consider the effect of reactive components.

The other equivalent circuits can also be used to characterize the electronic devices. For instance, using the procedure of Eqs. (3-20) to (3-27) we can approximately write:

$$i_1 = \frac{\partial i_i}{\partial e_i} e_1 + \frac{\partial i_i}{\partial e_o} e_2 \tag{3-29}$$

$$i_2 = \frac{\partial i_o}{\partial e_i} e_1 + \frac{\partial i_o}{\partial e_o} e_2 \tag{3-30}$$

If these equations are compared with Eqs. (3-8) and (3-9) we have

$$y_{11} = \frac{\partial i_i}{\partial e_i}\bigg|_{e_i = E_{iQ}, \, e_o = E_{oQ}} \qquad y_{12} = \frac{\partial i_i}{\partial e_o}\bigg|_{e_i = E_{iQ}, \, e_o = E_{oQ}}$$

$$y_{21} = \frac{\partial i_o}{\partial e_i}\bigg|_{e_i = E_{iQ}, \, e_o = E_{oQ}} \qquad y_{22} = \frac{\partial i_o}{\partial e_o}\bigg|_{e_i = E_{iQ}, \, e_o = E_{oQ}}$$

(3-31)

where the derivatives are the appropriate slopes of the static characteristics at the operating point. Thus, the y-parameter equivalent circuits of Fig. 3-5 can be used to characterize the electronic device of Fig. 3-8 for incremental changes about the operating point.

Similarly, we can relate the h parameters to the approximate slopes of the static characteristics. For instance, we can approximately write:

$$e_1 = \frac{\partial e_i}{\partial i_i} i_1 + \frac{\partial e_i}{\partial e_o} e_2 \tag{3-32}$$

$$i_2 = \frac{\partial i_o}{\partial i_i} i_1 + \frac{\partial i_o}{\partial e_o} e_2 \tag{3-33}$$

Comparing these equations with Eqs. (3-12) and (3-13), we have

$$h_{11} = \frac{\partial e_i}{\partial i_i}\bigg|_{i_i = I_{iQ}, \, e_o = E_{oQ}} \qquad h_{12} = \frac{\partial e_i}{\partial e_o}\bigg|_{i_i = I_{iQ}, \, e_o = E_{oQ}}$$

$$h_{21} = \frac{\partial i_o}{\partial i_i}\bigg|_{i_i = I_{iQ}, \, e_o = E_{oQ}} \qquad h_{22} = \frac{\partial i_o}{\partial e_o}\bigg|_{i_i = I_{iQ}, \, e_o = E_{oQ}}$$

(3-34)

These derivatives are evaluated at the operating point $e_o = E_{oQ}$, $i_i = I_{iQ}$. Hence, the h-parameter equivalent circuit of Fig. 3-6 can be used to calculate incremental changes in voltage and current for the electronic device of Fig. 3-8.

The parameters developed in this section are all real numbers. In the next section, they will be extended to complex, frequency-dependent terms.

3-4   General equivalent circuits of electronic devices

The equations that were developed in the last section are valid only for instantaneous, frequency-independent terms. However, if the instantaneous voltages and currents are replaced by phasors indicated by boldface symbols and the constant partial derivatives are replaced by frequency-dependent complex quantities, then the equivalent circuit will be valid at all frequencies. In this case, Eqs. (3-1) and (3-2), or (3-8) and (3-9), or (3-12) and (3-13) replace Eqs. (3-26) and (3-27), or (3-29) and (3-30), or (3-32) and (3-33), respectively. The discussion of Sec. 3-1 applies to the equivalent circuits of electronic devices, with one difference. When $\mathbf{I}_1 = 0$ or $\mathbf{I}_2 = 0$ for an electronic device, the signal components of the current are zero. *However,*

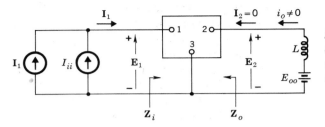

Fig. 3-9 A circuit which can be used for open-circuit measurements with electronic devices.

the total currents are not. That is, if i_i and i_o are constant, so that $i_i = I_{iQ}$ and $i_o = I_{oQ}$, then $\mathbf{I}_1 = 0$ and $\mathbf{I}_2 = 0$. A similar statement can be made when $\mathbf{E}_1 = 0$ or $\mathbf{E}_2 = 0$. Thus, when the equivalent circuits of Sec. 3-1 are applied to electronic devices, the open-circuit and short-circuit measurements are made with respect to signal quantities but _not_ with respect to quiescent voltages and currents. This is to be expected, since the equivalent circuit is used to obtain the incremental variations about the operating point. If we wish to make the open-circuit measurement of Fig. 3-2 on an electronic device without disturbing the quiescent operating point, then the circuit of Fig. 3-9 can be used. The generators E_{oo} and I_{ii} are direct-bias generators. The inductance L should be essentially an open circuit at the frequency of $\mathbf{I}_1$, but it should act as a short circuit for direct current. Thus, the direct bias of the electronic device has not been disturbed, but the output lead has been effectively open-circuited for signal quantities. Note that voltage sources could be used instead of current sources (or vice versa) in the circuit. Similarly, a capacitor can produce a short circuit without disturbing the quiescent operating point. The circuit of Fig. 3-10 will accomplish this. If the capacitance C acts as a short circuit at the frequency of $\mathbf{I}_1$, then the desired measurements can be obtained. The output circuits of Figs. 3-9 and 3-10 can be placed on the input side of the electronic device to obtain open- or short-circuited input measurements (i.e., $\mathbf{I}_1 = 0$ or $\mathbf{E}_1 = 0$, respectively).

Accuracy of open-circuit or short-circuit measurements

If the equivalent circuits of electronic devices are to be valid over a wide range of frequencies, then the open-circuit and/or short-circuit measure-

Fig. 3-10 A circuit which can be used for short-circuit measurements with electronic devices.

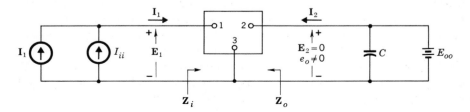

ments must be made over the same frequency range. An inductance or capacitance (or any real circuit) will not be exactly an infinite impedance or a zero impedance at any frequency. Thus, the measurements will be in error. Let us see how large or how small the impedance of L or C must be if the parameter values are to be accurate. Consider the circuit of Fig. 3-10. If the voltage $\mathbf{E}_2$ is to be essentially zero, then the magnitude of the reactance X_C of the capacitor must be very much less than the magnitude of the output impedance $\mathbf{Z}_o$ of the electronic device. Thus, for accuracy,

$$|X_C| \ll |Z_o| \tag{3-35}$$

Similarly, if X_L, the reactance of the inductor L of Fig. 3-9, is to be large enough to cause $\mathbf{I}_2$ to essentially be zero, then

$$|X_L| \gg |Z_o| \tag{3-36}$$

In general, we can state that the "short circuit" measurement can be accurate if the impedance of the electronic device, in shunt with the short circuit, is quite high, while the open-circuit measurement can be accurate if the impedance of the electronic device, in series with the open circuit, is quite low.

Let us now consider which equivalent circuits are appropriate to use with vacuum tubes and transistors.

The vacuum tube

In most vacuum-tube circuits, the grid is terminal 1 of the generalized device, the plate is terminal 2, and the cathode is terminal 3. Thus, $\mathbf{Z}_i$ of Fig. 3-9 or 3-10 will be very high. The output impedance $\mathbf{Z}_o$ is of the magnitude of r_p, which is very high for vacuum-tube pentodes and beam power tubes. It is usually fairly large for triodes also. Thus, it is desirable to make short-circuit measurements at both input and output sides of the network. The y parameters should be used to characterize the vacuum tube [see Eqs. (3-10) and (3-11)]. Actually, if the grid is considered to be an open circuit, the z parameters and the h parameters cannot be used, since the input impedance is infinite.

The transistor

In most transistor configurations, we shall see that the magnitude of the input impedance is fairly low, while the magnitude of the output impedance is high. Thus, we desire an equivalent circuit whose parameters are obtained by open-circuit measurements at the input side and by short-circuit measurements at the output side. Thus, the h-parameter equivalent circuit is very often used for analysis of transistor circuits. The z-parameter equivalent circuit was used in the early days of the transistor. However, it is now very rarely used for actual circuit calculations.

3-5   The low-frequency equivalent circuit for the vacuum-tube triode, tetrode, pentode, and beam power tube—the common-cathode vacuum-tube amplifier

We shall use the methods of Sec. 3-3 to obtain the low-frequency equivalent circuits of the vacuum-tube triode, tetrode, and pentode and of the beam power tube. In doing this we shall neglect the effect of interelectrode capacitances and other high-frequency effects. These shall be considered later in Secs. 3-12 to 3-14. It will be assumed that the control grid of the vacuum tube is biased so that the control-grid current is zero. We shall use the y parameters to obtain the equivalent circuits. Consider the vacuum-tube-triode circuit of Fig. 3-11. The subscripts g and p refer to the signal components of the grid and plate voltages and currents. The subscripts c and b are used for total quantities. Then, proceeding as in Eqs. (3-29) and (3-30), we obtain

$$i_g = 0$$

$$i_p = \frac{\partial i_b}{\partial e_c} e_g + \frac{\partial i_b}{\partial e_b} e_p$$

Since $i_g = 0$, $\partial i_c/\partial e_g = 0$, and $\partial i_c/\partial e_b = 0$. The derivatives are evaluated at the operating point $e_b = E_{bQ}$, $e_c = E_{cQ}$. Then, substituting Eqs. (1-13) and (1-14), we have

$$i_p = g_m e_g + \frac{e_p}{r_p} \tag{3-37}$$

Then, using Eqs. (3-29), (3-30), (3-8), and (3-9) and Fig. 3-5a, we obtain the equivalent circuit for the vacuum-tube triode, given in Fig. 3-12a. If a voltage generator is desirable, then the circuit of Fig. 3-12b can be used. It is obtained from Fig. 3-12a using the relation $\mu = g_m r_p$.

Consider the vacuum-tube-pentode circuit of Fig. 3-13. If the capacitor C_s is a short circuit at the signal frequency, then the screen-grid potential will be independent of the signal voltage. Since the suppressor grid is often connected to the cathode, its potential does not vary. Then, if the control-grid current is zero, the vacuum-tube pentode is characterized by Eq. (3-37).

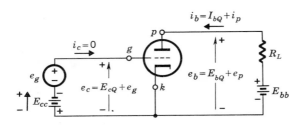

Fig. 3-11 An elementary vacuum-tube-triode amplifier.

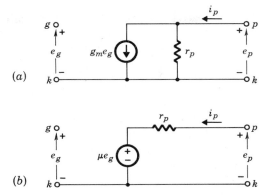

Fig. 3-12 (a) A current-generator equivalent circuit for the vacuum tube; (b) a voltage-generator equivalent circuit for the vacuum tube.

Thus, it can be represented by the equivalent circuits of Fig. 3-12. The general equivalent circuit for the vacuum-tube pentode, where the potential of all the grids is allowed to vary, will be discussed in Sec. 3-19. The equivalent circuits of Fig. 3-12 can also be used for vacuum-tube tetrodes and beam power tubes if the screen-grid potential does not vary with the signal.

When equivalent circuits are drawn, all direct-bias supplies are replaced by their internal impedances at the signal frequencies. Ideally, voltage-source power supplies can be replaced by short circuits, and current sources can be replaced by open circuits. All the other elements remain unchanged. The vacuum tube is removed from the circuit and the equivalent circuit is interconnected in its place. Hence, the amplifiers of Figs. 3-11 and 3-13 are characterized by the equivalent circuit of Fig. 3-14. Phasor notation can be used as well as instantaneous notation. In this way, the effect of reactive circuit elements can be easily analyzed.

Let us calculate the *voltage amplification*, or *voltage gain*, $\mathbf{A}_v$, of these amplifiers. This is the ratio of the output-voltage phasor to the input-voltage phasor when the input is a sinusoid. Thus, $\mathbf{A}_v$ is a complex quantity which has a magnitude and a phase angle. Boldface letters are used for phasors throughout this book. The magnitude of a voltage or current phasor will usually be its rms value unless the subscript max is added. In addition, the notation of Table 2-1 will be used. Then, for the circuit of Fig. 3-14, the

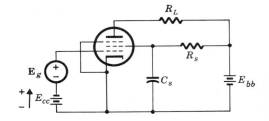

Fig. 3-13 An elementary vacuum-tube-pentode voltage amplifier.

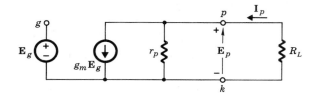

Fig. 3-14 An equivalent circuit for the amplifiers of Figs. 3-11 and 3-13.

input voltage is $\mathbf{E}_g$ and the output voltage is $\mathbf{E}_p$. Hence,

$$\mathbf{A}_v = \frac{\mathbf{E}_p}{\mathbf{E}_g} = -\frac{g_m R_L}{1 + R_L/r_p} \qquad (3\text{-}38)$$

Using the relation $\mu = g_m r_p$ we obtain the equivalent expression

$$\mathbf{A}_v = -\frac{\mu}{1 + r_p/R_L} \qquad (3\text{-}39)$$

The minus signs in Eqs. (3-38) and (3-39) indicate the 180° phase shift between the input and output voltages. The maximum magnitude of $\mathbf{A}_v$ occurs when $R_L \gg r_p$ and is equal to μ. Thus, the amplification factor is the maximum voltage gain that this circuit can have. When vacuum-tube pentodes are used, the value of r_p is often quite large. If $r_p \gg R_L$, then Eq. (3-38) becomes

$$\mathbf{A}_v \approx -g_m R_L \qquad (3\text{-}40)$$

The cathode lead is common to both the input and output circuits in the

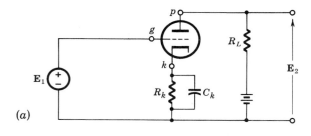

(a)

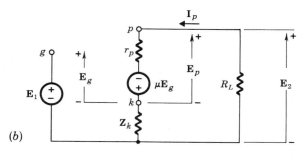

(b)

Fig. 3-15 (a) A common-cathode vacuum-tube amplifier with a cathode-bias impedance; (b) its equivalent circuit

$$\mathbf{Z}_k = \frac{R_k}{1 + j\omega C_k R_k}$$

amplifiers of Figs. 3-11 and 3-13. For this reason, they are called *common-cathode amplifiers*.

Let us now consider the circuit of Fig. 3-15a, which includes a self-bias circuit. The equivalent circuit is shown in Fig. 3-15b. Writing mesh equations, we obtain

$$\mu \mathbf{E}_g = \mathbf{I}_p(r_p + R_L + \mathbf{Z}_k) \tag{3-41}$$

The quantity $\mathbf{E}_g$ is unknown. It should be substituted for before Eq. (3-41) is solved. *If this is not done, the "solution" will contain an unknown.* Then, summing the voltage drops from grid to cathode, we obtain

$$\mathbf{E}_g = \mathbf{E}_1 - \mathbf{I}_p\mathbf{Z}_k$$

The output voltage is

$$\mathbf{E}_2 = -\mathbf{I}_pR_L$$

Thus, substituting for $\mathbf{E}_g$ in Eq. (3-41) and solving for $\mathbf{E}_2/\mathbf{E}_1$, we have

$$\mathbf{A}_v = \frac{\mathbf{E}_2}{\mathbf{E}_1} = \frac{-\mu R_L}{r_p + (1 + \mu)\mathbf{Z}_k + R_L} \tag{3-42}$$

Since $\mathbf{Z}_k$ represents a complex number, the phase angle of $\mathbf{A}_v$ will not be 180°. Thus, there will no longer be an exact phase reversal between the input and output voltages.

The impedance $\mathbf{Z}_k$ appears to be a much larger impedance, $\mathbf{Z}_k(1 + \mu)$, because its presence affects the grid circuit as well as the plate circuit. This phenomenon will be discussed in great detail in Chap. 10. The term $(1 + \mu)\mathbf{Z}_k$ in the denominator of Eq. (3-42) tends to reduce the voltage gain. The value of R_k is fixed by bias requirements. However, the value of C_k is usually made large enough so that $(1 + \mu)\mathbf{Z}_k$ is small at all frequencies of interest. This is discussed in Sec. 6-5.

3-6 The common-plate vacuum-tube amplifier— the cathode follower

Another vacuum-tube-amplifier configuration and its equivalent circuit are illustrated in Fig. 3-16. The plate lead is common to both the input and output circuits; thus, this amplifier is called a *common-plate amplifier*. The circuit of Fig. 3-16b yields the following equations:

$$\mu \mathbf{E}_g = \mathbf{I}_p(r_p + R_L) \tag{3-43}$$

$$\mathbf{E}_g = \mathbf{E}_1 - \mathbf{I}_pR_L \tag{3-44}$$

Then, solving for $\mathbf{I}_p$ and using the relation $\mathbf{E}_2 = \mathbf{I}_pR_L$, we obtain

$$\mathbf{A}_v = \frac{\mu}{1 + \mu} \cdot \frac{1}{1 + r_p/[(1 + \mu)R_L]} \tag{3-45}$$

This is a real positive number, so there is no phase reversal between the input and output voltages. The voltage gain of this circuit approaches its maximum value when R_L becomes so large that $r_p/[(1 + \mu)R_L] \ll 1$. Thus,

$$|A_v| \leqslant A_{v,\text{max}} = \frac{\mu}{1 + \mu} \tag{3-46}$$

This is a number that is less than unity. In many instances $\mu \gg 1$ and the gain is essentially 1. For this reason, the common-plate amplifier is called a *cathode follower*, since the cathode voltage "follows" the input voltage.

Even though there is no actual voltage gain, the cathode follower is commonly used in many electronic devices. We shall see in Sec. 3-13 that, when interelectrode capacitances are considered, the input impedance of the cathode follower is usually very much greater than that of other vacuum-tube amplifiers. In addition, the output impedance of the cathode follower is usually much lower than that of other amplifiers. Common-plate amplifiers are often used as the input stages of high-frequency voltage-measuring devices such as vacuum-tube voltmeters and oscilloscopes where their high input impedance does not "load down" the circuit to be measured. Cathode followers are also frequently used as the output stages of audio preamplifiers. These devices require low output impedances so that they can be connected to low-impedance loads without appreciable loss of signal level. Low-impedance circuits also are used where it is necessary to minimize interference.

When impedance is obtained, all independent generators should be replaced by their internal impedances. However, the dependent generators represent the effect of the electronic device on the circuit. Thus, they are not replaced. The impedance can then be obtained by placing a

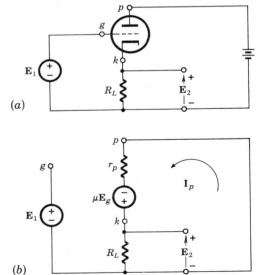

Fig. 3-16 (a) A common-plate vacuum-tube amplifier; (b) its equivalent circuit.

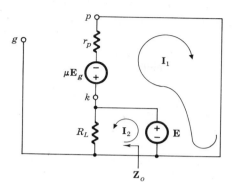

Fig. 3-17 An equivalent circuit used to calculate the output impedance of the cathode follower.

voltage generator across the pair of terminals in question and then determining the current. Impedance is the ratio of the voltage to the current. (Current generators can also be used in these calculations.) Thus, the circuit of Fig. 3-17 can be used to obtain the output impedance of the cathode follower. The output impedance is $\mathbf{Z}_o = \mathbf{E}/(\mathbf{I}_1 + \mathbf{I}_2)$. Hence,

$$\mathbf{Z}_o = \frac{1}{1/r_p + \mu/r_p + 1/R_K} \qquad (3\text{-}47)$$

This is a pure resistance which represents the parallel combination of r_p, $1/g_m$, and R_L. Usually, this is very much less than the parallel combination of r_p and R_L.

If the gain of the cathode follower is to approach unity, then $R_L \gg r_p/(1 + \mu) \approx 1/g_m$. Often, this requires relatively large values of R_L. This resistance not only serves as an output load resistance but also produces the direct-grid bias. If large values of R_L are used, the grid bias often becomes excessive. To prevent this, the circuit of Fig. 3-18, which also illustrates a pentode cathode follower, is often used. The direct current through R_g is zero. Thus, the direct-voltage drop across it is zero. Hence, the direct grid bias is equal to $-I_T R_K$. The value of R_K is chosen to provide

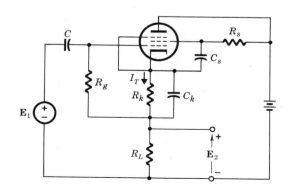

Fig. 3-18 A pentode cathode-follower circuit.

the correct grid bias.   If the capacitors are chosen large enough so that they can be considered short circuits at the signal frequency, and if R_g is chosen large enough so that there is negligible signal current through it, then the equivalent circuit of Fig. 3-16b is valid for this circuit also, provided that R_L is replaced by the parallel combination of R_L and R_s.

3-7   The common-grid vacuum-tube amplifier

Another vacuum-tube-amplifier configuration is shown, with its equivalent circuit, in Fig. 3-19.   Since the grid lead is common to both the input and output circuit, this is called a *common-grid amplifier*.   The voltage gain is R_L is given by

$$\mathbf{A}_v = \frac{(1 + \mu)\,\mathbf{Z}_L}{r_p + (1 + \mu)\mathbf{Z}_K + \mathbf{Z}_L} \tag{3-48}$$

Note that if $\mathbf{Z}_K$ and $\mathbf{Z}_L$ are purely resistive, then the voltage amplification is a real positive number.   That is, there is no 180° phase shift between the input and output waveforms.   The maximum value of $\mathbf{A}_v$ is equal to $1 + \mu$ and is obtained when $|\mathbf{Z}_L| \gg |r_p + (1 + \mu)\mathbf{Z}_K|$.   Thus, the maximum voltage gain of the common-grid amplifier is potentially greater than that of the

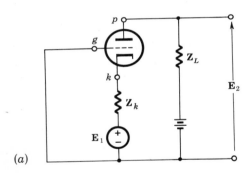

(a)

Fig. 3-19   (a) A common-grid amplifier; (b) its equivalent circuit.

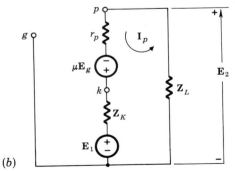

(b)

common-cathode amplifier. However, the common-cathode amplifier finds far more use than the common-grid amplifier. In the common-grid amplifier, the input generator is in series with the cathode lead. This eliminates one of the primary advantages of the vacuum-tube amplifier: its infinite, or extremely high, input impedance. The gain of the common-grid amplifier is usually much less than the maximum value because of the factor $(1 + \mu)\mathbf{Z}_K$. If $\mathbf{Z}_K$ represents the internal impedance of the signal generator, then it cannot be bypassed with a capacitor. Thus, the common-cathode amplifier often provides much more gain than the common-grid amplifier. In a common-grid amplifier, the grid tends to isolate the input (cathode) circuit from the output (plate) circuit, providing the input-output isolation of the vacuum-tube pentode with a vacuum-tube triode. At times, this is quite useful and in such circumstances common-grid circuits are used.

3-8   Physical discussion of transistor equivalent circuits

Before considering the circuit aspects of transistor equivalent circuits we shall develop one using physical arguments. The common-base circuit will be used. In the equivalent circuit of Fig. 3-20a, r'_c represents the dynamic resistance of the reverse-biased collector-base junction with the emitter lead open-circuited. Similarly, r'_e represents the dynamic resistance of the forward-biased emitter-base junction with $e_c = 0$. For incremental changes in

Fig. 3-20   Low-frequency equivalent circuits for the junction transistor developed from physical arguments.   (a) An ideal equivalent circuit that does not include the ohmic resistances; (b) an equivalent circuit with the ohmic resistances, including the base spreading resistance r''_{bb}.

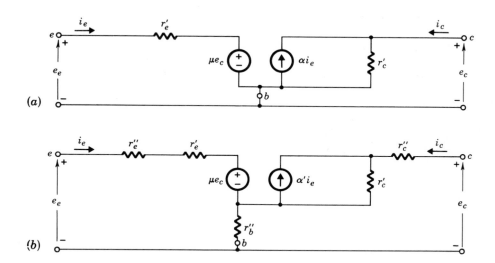

i_e, the change in collector current is α times the emitter current. Thus, the generator αi_e is included. As e_c varies, the collector-base junction depletion-layer width varies. This, in turn, changes the width of the base. This is called the *Early effect*. As the base width changes, the rate of change of minority-carrier density with distance also varies. This changes i_e. Thus, i_e is not independent of e_c. The μe_c generator takes this dependence into account. The equivalent circuit of Fig. 3 20a has the same form as that of the h-parameter equivalent circuit of Fig. 3-6. If Fig. 3-20a were the equivalent circuit of the transistor, then the h parameters would correspond to r'_e, $1/r'_c$, α, and μ. However, we have ignored the ohmic resistance of the semiconductor material in the regions removed from the junction. The largest effect is in the base region, since the base current is transverse in the narrow base region and, thus, the cross-sectional area presented to the current is small. This resistance, called the *base-spreading resistance*, must be added to the equivalent circuit of Fig. 3-20a. It is shown in Fig. 3-20b as r''_b. Resistances also occur in the bulk of the emitter and collector materials. These are shown as r''_e and r''_c in Fig. 3-20b. However, the cross-sectional areas presented to the currents are much larger here and these resistances are often neglected. The value of α has been replaced by α', since by definition $i_c = \alpha i_e$ if $e_c = 0$. In general, $r'_c \gg r''_b + r''_c$, hence $\alpha' \approx \alpha$. The common-base h-parameter equivalent circuit for the transistor will be of the form of Fig. 3-6. However, there will not be a simple relationship between the h parameters and the elements of Fig. 3-20b.

The direct-bias current through the base produces an alternating voltage drop, since the base-spreading resistance varies with base width. This in turn varies with e_c. An additional voltage can be included in the base lead to take this alternating voltage into account. However, it is small and can often be ignored.

3-9   Low-frequency *h*-parameter equivalent circuits for common-base, common-emitter, and common-collector transistors

We shall now obtain h-parameter low-frequency equivalent circuits for the transistor. When the h parameters are used, it is conventional to use the same form of the equivalent circuit for the common-base, common-emitter, and common-collector amplifier configurations, but different numerical values of the h parameters are used in each of the three equivalent circuits. The general form of these three equivalent circuits is shown in Fig. 3-6. It should be stressed that all of these equivalent circuits are general and can be used to represent the transistor, no matter which lead is taken as common, just as the circuits of Fig. 3-12 can always represent the vacuum-tube triode. However, it is often more convenient or more accurate to use one equivalent circuit rather than another. This is why so many forms of equivalent circuits are used. For instance, the generator $\mathbf{h}_{fe}\mathbf{I}_1$ of Fig. 3-6 is of prime importance. Its presence causes the circuit to have a gain.

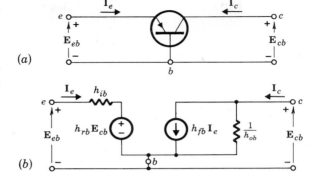

Fig. 3-21 (a) A common-base transistor; (b) its h-parameter equivalent circuit.

Usually, more insight can be gained if I_1 represents the input current. It is usually more accurate to do this, since the generator current can be expressed in terms of the input directly rather than in terms of the difference among variables.

We shall now define the h-parameter equivalent circuits for the common-base, common-emitter, and common-collector transistor amplifiers and relate them to each other. The circuit of Fig. 3-6 can be used as the equivalent circuit for any three-terminal device. Thus, the equivalent circuit for the common-base transistor amplifier of Fig. 3-21a is shown in Fig. 3-21b. The subscript b is added to the voltages and h parameters to avoid confusion, since we shall consider all three configurations in this section. To avoid an excessive number of subscripts, the notation of Eq. (3-16) will be employed. That is, $h_{11} = h_i$, $h_{12} = h_r$, $h_{21} = h_f$, and $h_{22} = h_o$. The equations that characterize Fig. 3-21 are

$$E_{eb} = h_{ib}I_e + h_{rb}E_{cb} \qquad (3\text{-}49)$$

$$I_c = h_{fb}I_e + h_{ob}E_{cb} \qquad (3\text{-}50)$$

Similarly, Fig. 3-22 illustrates the common-emitter transistor and its equiva-

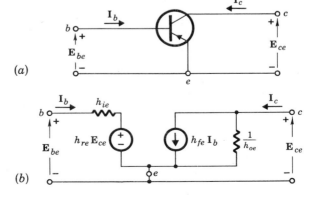

Fig. 3-22 (a) A common-emitter transistor; (b) its h-parameter equivalent circuit.

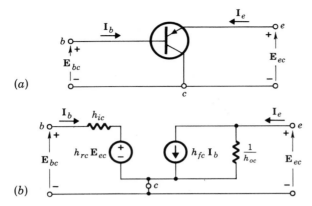

(b)

Fig. 3-23 (a) A common-collector transistor; (b) its h-parameter equivalent circuit.

lent circuit.   The equations that characterize it are

$$\mathbf{E}_{be} = h_{ie}\mathbf{I}_b + h_{re}\mathbf{E}_{ce} \tag{3-51}$$

$$\mathbf{I}_c = h_{fe}\mathbf{I}_b + h_{oe}\mathbf{E}_{ce} \tag{3-52}$$

Finally, Fig. 3-23 shows the common-collector transistor and its equivalent circuit.   The equations that characterize it are

$$\mathbf{E}_{bc} = h_{ic}\mathbf{I}_b + h_{rc}\mathbf{E}_{ec} \tag{3-53}$$

$$\mathbf{I}_e = h_{fc}\mathbf{I}_b + h_{oc}\mathbf{E}_{ec} \tag{3-54}$$

The h parameters for one configuration can be related to those for another configuration simply by making some elementary substitutions and rearranging the equations.   For instance, to relate the common-emitter h parameters to the common-base h parameters, use the following substitutions:

$$\begin{aligned}
\mathbf{E}_{eb} &= -\mathbf{E}_{be} \\
\mathbf{E}_{cb} &= \mathbf{E}_{ce} - \mathbf{E}_{be} \\
\mathbf{I}_e &= -(\mathbf{I}_c + \mathbf{I}_b)
\end{aligned} \tag{3-55}$$

Substitute Eqs. (3-55) into Eqs. (3-49) and (3-50) and rearrange them into the form of Eqs. (3-51) and (3-52).   We then obtain

$$\mathbf{E}_{be} = \frac{h_{ib}}{(1 + h_{fb})(1 - h_{rb}) + h_{ob}h_{ib}}\,\mathbf{I}_b + \frac{h_{ib}h_{ob} - h_{rb}(h_{fb} + 1)}{(1 + h_{fb})(1 - h_{rb}) + h_{ob}h_{ib}}\,\mathbf{E}_{ce} \tag{3-56}$$

$$\mathbf{I}_c = \frac{-h_{ob}h_{ib} - h_{fb}(1 - h_{rb})}{(1 + h_{fb})(1 - h_{rb}) + h_{ob}h_{ib}}\,\mathbf{I}_b + \frac{h_{ob}}{(1 + h_{fb})(1 - h_{rb}) + h_{ob}h_{ib}}\,\mathbf{E}_{ce} \tag{3-57}$$

Comparing these with Eqs. (3-51) and (3-52), we have

$$h_{ie} = \frac{h_{ib}}{(1 + h_{fb})(1 - h_{rb}) + h_{ob}h_{ib}}$$

$$h_{re} = \frac{h_{ib}h_{ob} - h_{rb}(h_{fb} + 1)}{(1 + h_{fb})(1 - h_{rb}) + h_{ob}h_{ib}}$$

$$h_{fe} = \frac{-h_{ib}h_{ob} - h_{fb}(1 - h_{rb})}{(1 + h_{fb})(1 - h_{rb}) + h_{ob}h_{ib}}$$

$$h_{oe} = \frac{h_{ob}}{(1 + h_{fb})(1 - h_{rb}) + h_{ob}h_{ib}}$$

(3-58)

If we proceed in a similar fashion, we can relate any two sets of h parameters. These relationships are given below.[1]

$$h_{ib} = \frac{h_{ie}}{(1 + h_{fe})(1 - h_{re}) + h_{ie}h_{oe}} = \frac{h_{ic}}{h_{ic}h_{oc} - h_{fc}h_{rc}}$$

$$h_{rb} = \frac{h_{ie}h_{oe} - h_{re}(1 + h_{fe})}{(1 + h_{fe})(1 - h_{re}) + h_{ie}h_{oe}} = \frac{h_{fc}(1 - h_{rc}) + h_{ic}h_{oc}}{h_{ic}h_{oc} - h_{fc}h_{rc}}$$

$$h_{fb} = \frac{-h_{fe}(1 - h_{re}) - h_{ie}h_{oe}}{(1 + h_{fe})(1 - h_{re}) + h_{ie}h_{oe}} = \frac{h_{rc}(1 + h_{fc}) - h_{ic}h_{oc}}{h_{ic}h_{oc} - h_{fc}h_{rc}}$$

$$h_{ob} = \frac{h_{oe}}{(1 + h_{fe})(1 - h_{re}) + h_{ie}h_{oe}} = \frac{h_{oc}}{h_{ic}h_{oc} - h_{fc}h_{rc}}$$

(3-59)

and

$$h_{ie} = \frac{h_{ib}}{(1 + h_{fb})(1 - h_{rb}) + h_{ob}h_{ib}} = h_{ic}$$

$$h_{re} = \frac{h_{ib}h_{ob} - h_{rb}(1 + h_{fb})}{(1 + h_{fb})(1 - h_{rb}) + h_{ob}h_{ib}} = 1 - h_{rc}$$

$$h_{fe} = \frac{-h_{fb}(1 - h_{rb}) - h_{ob}h_{ib}}{(1 + h_{fb})(1 - h_{rb}) + h_{ob}h_{ib}} = -(1 + h_{fc})$$

$$h_{oe} = \frac{h_{ob}}{(1 + h_{fb})(1 - h_{rb}) + h_{ob}h_{ib}} = h_{oc}$$

(3-60)

and

$$h_{ic} = \frac{h_{ib}}{(1 + h_{fb})(1 - h_{rb}) + h_{ob}h_{ib}} = h_{ie}$$

$$h_{rc} = \frac{1 + h_{fb}}{(1 + h_{fb})(1 - h_{rb}) + h_{ob}h_{ib}} = 1 - h_{re}$$

$$h_{fc} = \frac{h_{rb} - 1}{(1 + h_{fb})(1 - h_{rb}) + h_{ob}h_{ib}} = -(1 + h_{fe})$$

$$h_{oc} = \frac{h_{ob}}{(1 + h_{fb})(1 - h_{rb}) + h_{ob}h_{ib}} = h_{oe}$$

(3-61)

With the exception of the relationships between the common-emitter and common-collector h parameters, these equations are quite cumbersome.

Table 3-1   *Values of the h parameters for a typical transistor*[2]

Parameter	Common base	Common emitter	Common collector
h_i, ohms	39	2,000	2,000
h_r	3.8×10^{-4}	6×10^{-4}	1
h_f	-0.9804	50	-51
h_o, mhos	0.49×10^{-6}	25×10^{-6}	25×10^{-6}

The h parameters of actual transistors are such that approximations can often be made which simplify these equations greatly. Let us consider some typical values (see Table 3-1) in order to see what approximations can be made.

$$h_{re} \ll 1$$
$$h_{ie}h_{oe} \ll 1$$
$$h_{rb} \ll 1$$
$$h_{ib}h_{ob} \ll 1 \tag{3-62}$$
$$h_{rc} \approx 1$$
$$h_{ic}h_{oc} \ll 1$$

Thus, we can use the following approximate relationships

$$h_{ib} \approx \frac{h_{ie}}{1 + h_{fe}} \qquad \approx -\frac{h_{ic}}{h_{fc}}$$

$$h_{rb} \approx \frac{h_{ie}h_{oe}}{1 + h_{fe}} - h_{re} \approx h_{rc} - 1 - \frac{h_{ic}h_{oc}}{h_{fc}}$$

$$h_{fb} \approx \frac{-h_{fe}}{1 + h_{fe}} \qquad \approx -\frac{1 + h_{fc}}{h_{fc}} \tag{3-63}$$

$$h_{ob} \approx \frac{h_{oe}}{1 + h_{fe}} \qquad \approx -\frac{h_{oc}}{h_{fc}}$$

and

$$h_{ie} \approx \frac{h_{ib}}{1 + h_{fb}}$$

$$h_{re} \approx \frac{h_{ib}h_{ob}}{1 + h_{fb}} - h_{rb}$$

$$h_{fe} \approx \frac{-h_{fb}}{1 + h_{fb}} \tag{3-64}$$

$$h_{oe} \approx \frac{h_{ob}}{1 + h_{fb}}$$

and

$$h_{ic} \approx \frac{h_{ib}}{1 + h_{fb}}$$

$$h_{rc} \approx 1$$

$$h_{fc} \approx \frac{-1}{1 + h_{fb}} \tag{3-65}$$

$$h_{oc} \approx \frac{h_{ob}}{1 + h_{fb}}$$

Although the *h*-parameter equivalent circuits are now most commonly used, at one time the *r*-parameter equivalent circuits were used. The *z*-parameter equivalent circuit of the common-base amplifier was used here. Since all the elements were real the notation *r* parameter was adopted.

3-10   Comparison of the *h* parameters

Let us now compare the *h* parameters for the various configurations and relate them to other parameters of the transistor. The amplifying ability of the transistor, in any configuration, depends directly upon h_f, since it relates the output circuit current and voltage to the input current. From Fig. 3-21, we have

$$h_{fb} = \frac{\mathbf{I}_c}{\mathbf{I}_e}\bigg|_{\mathbf{E}_{cb}=0} \tag{3-66}$$

The currents and voltages represent incremental changes. Then, if this is compared with Eq. (1-26), we have

$$h_{fb} = -\alpha \tag{3-67}$$

Thus, the significance of α is again illustrated. Then, using Eqs. (3-64) and (3-65), we have

$$h_{fe} = \frac{\alpha}{1 - \alpha} \tag{3-68}$$

$$h_{fc} = -\frac{1}{1 - \alpha} \tag{3-69}$$

The value of h_{fe} is the *common-emitter short-circuit forward-current amplification factor*, and is denoted by the symbol β. This is to the common-emitter circuit what α is to the common-base circuit. Thus,

$$\beta = \frac{\alpha}{1 - \alpha} \tag{3-70}$$

In the usual transistor, α is a positive number that is slightly less than unity. Thus, h_{fe} and h_{fc} are usually very much greater than 1. We shall see that the common-emitter and common-collector amplifier configurations are capable of much greater current gains than the common-base configuration. In the transistor, the current gain is usually of prime importance. We are usually concerned with the gain of cascaded amplifiers (where the output of one amplifier is connected to the input of the next). The output generator of the transistor is controlled by the input current (not by the input voltage). Thus, knowledge of current gains can be used directly to obtain the gain of a cascaded amplifier. The input current can be obtained from the input voltage, but this involves tedious calculations involving the input admittance.

Now let us consider the admittance h_o that shunts the output current generator. In general,

$$h_{oe} \approx h_{oc} \approx \frac{h_{ob}}{1 - \alpha} \tag{3-71}$$

Thus, the shunting effect of h_{oe} and h_{oc} are considerably greater than that of h_{ob}. The resistance that is in series with the input generator is h_{ie}. Here we have

$$h_{ie} \approx h_{ic} \approx \frac{h_{ib}}{1 - \alpha} \tag{3-72}$$

Here h_{ie} and h_{ic} are considerably greater than h_{ib}. At first glance, Eqs. (3-71) and (3-72) seem quite similar. However, it should be remembered that h_o represents an admittance whereas h_i represents an impedance.

3-11 An analysis of elementary common-base, common-emitter, and common-collector transistor amplifiers

Since the form of the h-parameter equivalent circuits of the common-base, common-emitter, and common-collector transistor configurations are the same, a single equivalent circuit will suffice for the three elementary amplifiers. That is, the amplifier circuits of Figs. 3-24 to 3-26 can be represented by the equivalent circuit of Fig. 3-27a, provided that the substitutions of Table 3-2 are used.

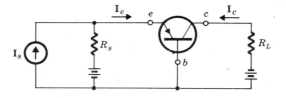

Fig. 3-24   An elementary common-base transistor amplifier.

**Table 3-2   Substitutions to be used with the h parameter
equivalent circuits of Fig. 3-27**

Quantity	Common base	Common emitter	Common collector
h_i	h_{ib}	h_{ie}	h_{ic}
h_r	h_{rb}	h_{re}	h_{rc}
h_f	h_{fb}	h_{fe}	h_{fc}
h_o	h_{ob}	h_{oe}	h_{oc}
E_1	E_{eb}	E_{be}	E_{bc}
E_2	E_{cb}	E_{ce}	E_{ec}
I_1	I_e	I_b	I_b
I_2	I_c	I_c	I_e

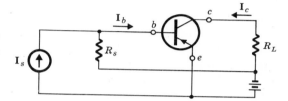

*Fig. 3-25 An elementary com-
mon-emitter transistor amplifier.*

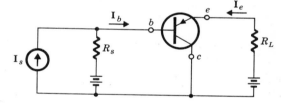

*Fig. 3-26 An elementary com-
mon-collector transistor amplifier.*

*Fig. 3-27   (a) An h-parameter equivalent circuit that can be used to represent the
elementary common-base, common-emitter, and common-collector transistor amplifiers;
(b) the same circuit with a voltage generator input.*

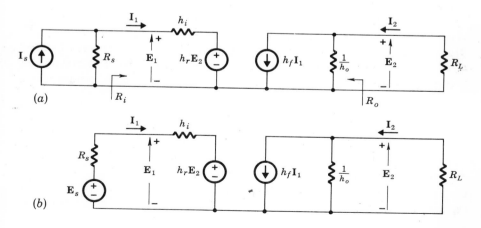

Writing a mesh equation for the input side and a nodal equation for the output side of Fig. 3-27a, we obtain

$$\mathbf{I}_s R_s = (R_s + h_i)\mathbf{I}_1 + h_r \mathbf{E}_2 \tag{3-73}$$

$$0 = h_f \mathbf{I}_1 + \left(h_o + \frac{1}{R_L} \right) \mathbf{E}_2 \tag{3-74}$$

As we discussed in Sec. 3-10, the current gains are of prime importance. There are two different ones that can be considered. The first is the *current amplification (or gain)* $\mathbf{A}_i$, which is defined as

$$\mathbf{A}_i = \frac{\mathbf{I}_2}{\mathbf{I}_1} \tag{3-75}$$

This is the ratio of the transistor output current to its input current and is quite useful in calculating the current gain of cascaded amplifier stages. The other current gain is $\mathbf{K}_i$, the *composite-current amplification (or gain)*, which is defined as

$$\mathbf{K}_i = \frac{\mathbf{I}_2}{\mathbf{I}_s} \tag{3-76}$$

This is the ratio of the circuit's output current to its input current. Thus, $\mathbf{K}_i$ is the current gain for the complete circuit. Then, solving Eqs. (3-73) and (3-74) for $\mathbf{E}_2$, and dividing by $-\mathbf{I}_s R_L$, we obtain

$$\mathbf{K}_i = \frac{h_f R_s}{(h_i + R_s)(1 + h_o R_L) - h_f h_r R_L} \tag{3-77}$$

The current gain $\mathbf{A}_i$ is different from $\mathbf{K}_i$ because of the current through R_s. $\mathbf{A}_i$ can be obtained from $\mathbf{K}_i$ by letting $R_s \to \infty$. Thus,

$$\mathbf{A}_i = \frac{h_f}{1 + h_o R_L} \tag{3-78}$$

The maximum value of $\mathbf{K}_i$ occurs when R_s is infinite and R_L is zero. Letting $R_s \to \infty$ maximizes $\mathbf{I}_1$ independently of R_L, and setting $R_L = 0$ maximizes $\mathbf{I}_2$ independently of R_s. Similarly, the maximum value of $\mathbf{A}_i$ occurs when $R_L = 0$. Thus,

$$K_{i,\max} = A_{i,\max} = h_f \tag{3-79}$$

These equations again illustrate the significance of the function h_f.

Now let us consider the voltage amplifications of the circuit. We shall use the circuit of Fig. 3-27b, where the current generator input has been replaced by a voltage generator input to permit us to define a composite voltage gain. The *composite voltage amplification (or gain)* $\mathbf{K}_v$ is

$$\mathbf{K}_v = \frac{\mathbf{E}_2}{\mathbf{E}_s} \tag{3-80}$$

The *voltage amplification (or gain)* $\mathbf{A}_v$ is defined by

$$\mathbf{A}_v = \frac{\mathbf{E}_2}{\mathbf{E}_1} \tag{3-81}$$

The significance of $\mathbf{K}_v$ and $\mathbf{A}_v$ is analogous to that of $\mathbf{K}_i$ and $\mathbf{A}_i$. Note that the value of $\mathbf{A}_v$ does not depend on whether Fig. 3-27a or b is used. Then, replacing $\mathbf{I}_s R_s$ by $\mathbf{E}_s$ in Eq. (3-73) and solving Eqs. (3-73) and (3-74), we obtain

$$\mathbf{K}_v = \frac{-h_f R_L}{(h_i + R_s)(1 + h_o R_L) - h_f h_r R_L} \tag{3-82}$$

The voltage gain $\mathbf{A}_v$ can be obtained from $\mathbf{K}_v$ by setting $R_s = 0$. Thus,

$$\mathbf{A}_v = \frac{-h_f R_L}{h_i(1 + h_o R_L) - h_f h_r R_L} \tag{3-83}$$

The maximum value of $\mathbf{K}_v$ occurs when $R_s = 0$ and $R_L \to \infty$. Similarly, the maximum value of $\mathbf{A}_v$ occurs when $R_L \to \infty$. Thus,

$$K_{v,\max} = A_{v,\max} = \frac{-h_r}{h_i h_o - h_f h_r} \tag{3-84}$$

The input and output resistances of transistor circuits can be used to calculate the effect of the external circuit on the amplifier and vice versa (see Sec. 5-2). Solving for these, we obtain

$$R_i = \frac{\mathbf{E}_1}{\mathbf{I}_1}\bigg|_{\mathbf{I}_2 = -\mathbf{E}_2/R_L} = h_i - \frac{h_f h_r R_L}{1 + h_o R_L} \tag{3-85}$$

and

$$R_o = \frac{\mathbf{E}_2}{\mathbf{I}_2}\bigg|_{\mathbf{I}_1 = -\mathbf{E}_1/R_s} = \frac{R_s + h_i}{h_o(h_i + R_s) - h_f h_r} \tag{3-86}$$

where R_o is measured with the input generator replaced by its internal impedance.

Since the input resistance of a transistor circuit is not infinite, power will be taken from the input generator. We can define two operating power gains: K_p, the *composite power gain*, and A_p, the *power gain*. Using Fig. 3-27a, we have

$$K_p = \frac{|E_2|\,|I_2|}{|E_1|\,|I_s|} = |A_v|\,|K_i| \tag{3-87}$$

and

$$A_p = \frac{|E_2|\,|I_2|}{|E_1|\,|I_1|} = |A_v|\,|A_i| \tag{3-88}$$

where K_p is the ratio of the power dissipated in R_L to the power supplied by I_s, and A_p is the ratio of the power dissipated in R_L to the power entering the transistor. These are called *"operating"* gains since they represent the ratios of actual powers. Then, substituting in Eqs. (3-87) and (3-88) we obtain

$$K_p = \frac{h_f{}^2 R_s R_L}{[(h_i + R_s)(1 + h_o R_L) - h_f h_r R_L][h_i(1 + h_o R_L) - h_f h_r R_L]} \qquad (3\text{-}89)$$

The value of A_p can be found from K_p by letting $R_s \to \infty$, since this will cause the power dissipated in R_s to become zero. Hence,

$$A_p = \frac{h_f{}^2 R_L}{h_i(1 + h_o R_L)^2 - h_f h_r R_L(1 + h_o R_L)} \qquad (3\text{-}90)$$

To maximize K_p with respect to R_s, let $R_s \to \infty$, since this will simultaneously maximize the output power and eliminate the power dissipated in R_s, independent of R_L. Thus, the maximum value of A_p will also be the maximum value of K_p. To maximize A_p with respect to R_L, differentiate and set the derivative equal to zero. This yields

$$R_{L,\text{opt}} = \sqrt{\frac{h_i}{h_o(h_i h_o - h_r h_f)}} \qquad (3\text{-}91)$$

Note that this is not equal to R_o given by Eq. (3-86). If $R_L = R_o$, the output power will be maximized. However, the power gain is a ratio of output to input power. Hence, maximizing the output does not necessarily maximize the ratio. Substituting Eq. (3-91) into Eq. (3-90), we obtain

$$K_{p,\text{max}} = A_{p,\text{max}} = \frac{h_f{}^2}{(\sqrt{h_i h_o - h_f h_r} + \sqrt{h_i h_o})^2} \qquad (3\text{-}92)$$

Another type of power gain called the *transducer gain* K_T is defined as the ratio of the output power to the power that the input generator could supply to a matched load. This is *not* an operating power gain, since a matched load is not usually presented. The transducer gain is a measure of the advantage gained by using a transistor, since it is the ratio of the output power to the power that *could* be supplied to a matched load without a transistor.

$$K_T = \frac{|I_2|^2 R_L}{|I_s|^2 \dfrac{R_s}{4}} = \frac{4 K_i{}^2 R_L}{R_s} \qquad (3\text{-}93)$$

Hence

$$K_T = \frac{4 R_s R_L h_f{}^2}{[(h_i + R_s)(1 + h_o R_L) - h_f h_r R_L]^2} \qquad (3\text{-}94)$$

Since the denominator of Eq. (3-93) is independent of the actual circuit conditions, K_T will be maximized with respect to R_L when $R_L = R_o$. This maximized value of K_T is called the *available power gain* K_{AP}. Substituting Eq. (3-86) into Eq. (3-94), we obtain

$$K_{AP} = \frac{h_f{}^2 R_s}{(h_i + R_s)[h_o(h_i + R_s) - h_f h_r]} \tag{3-95}$$

Maximizing this expression with respect to R_s, we have

$$R_{s,\text{opt}} = \sqrt{\frac{h_i(h_i h_o - h_f h_r)}{h_o}} \tag{3-96}$$

Substituting, we obtain

$$K_{AP,\text{max}} = \frac{h_f{}^2}{(\sqrt{h_i h_o - h_f h_r} + \sqrt{h_i h_o})^2} \tag{3-97}$$

This is the same as Eq. (3-92). Thus, $K_{P,\text{max}}$, $A_{p,\text{max}}$, and $K_{AP,\text{max}}$ are all equal. This quantity is sometimes used as a figure of merit for the transistor.

Let us now consider the relative merits of the common-base, common-emitter, and the common-collector amplifiers. The current gain is usually of prime importance. Its maximum value is given by h_f. Thus,

$$K_{ib,\text{max}} = \alpha$$

$$K_{ie,\text{max}} = \frac{\alpha}{1 - \alpha} = \beta \tag{3-98}$$

$$K_{ic,\text{max}} = \frac{1}{1 - \alpha}$$

The subscripts b, e, and c stand for common-base, common-emitter, and common-collector, respectively. Since α is a number that is, in general, less than, but almost equal to, unity, we can write

$$K_{ib,\text{max}} \approx 1$$

$$K_{ie,\text{max}} \approx K_{ic,\text{max}} \gg K_{ib,\text{max}}$$

The maximum current gain available from the common-base amplifier is less than unity, while it is considerably greater than unity for the common-emitter and common-collector amplifiers. The largest value is that for the common-collector amplifier. Before drawing any conclusions about the desirability of one configuration over another, we must consider the actual current gain $\mathbf{K}_i$, rather than the theoretical maximum values of Eqs. (3-98). Equation (3-77) can be written as

$$K_i = \frac{h_f R_s}{(1 + h_o R_L)\left(R_s + h_i - \dfrac{h_f h_r R_L}{1 + h_o R_L}\right)}$$

Substituting Eq. (3-85), we obtain

$$\mathbf{K}_i = h_f \left(\frac{R_s}{R_s + R_i} \right) \left(\frac{1}{1 + h_o R_L} \right) \tag{3-99}$$

Let us interpret the various factors of this equation. h_f represents the value of $\mathbf{I}_2/\mathbf{I}_1$ when R_L is set equal to zero. That is, it is the short-circuit current gain of the transistor. It is also the maximum value of $\mathbf{K}_i$. The other two factors reduce the actual current gain below the maximum value. All of the current that is supplied by the input current generator $\mathbf{I}_s$ does not enter the transistor as $\mathbf{I}_1$. Some of it is shunted by R_s. Thus, the gain is reduced by the fraction

$$\frac{\mathbf{I}_1}{\mathbf{I}_s} = \frac{R_s}{R_s + R_i} \tag{3-100}$$

In the same way, a fraction of the current of the output current generator $h_f\mathbf{I}_1$ is shunted by the resistance $1/h_o$. Thus, the gain is also reduced by

$$\frac{\mathbf{I}_2}{h_f\mathbf{I}_1} = \frac{1/h_o}{1/h_o + R_I} = \frac{1}{1 + h_o R_L} \tag{3-101}$$

In general, $R_{ib} < R_{ie} < R_{ic}$. Some typical values are $R_{ib} = 60$ ohms, $R_{ie} = 1,000$ ohms, and $R_{ic} = 30,000$ ohms. Thus, the value of $R_s/(R_s + R_i)$ will be smallest for the common-collector circuit and largest for the common-base circuit. Of course, if R_s is made large enough, the fraction will be quite close to unity for all three circuits. In general, when cascaded amplifiers are considered, $R_s/(R_s + R_i)$ is almost unity for the common-base circuit, somewhat less than unity for the common-emitter circuit, and very much less than unity for the common-collector circuit. Finally, $h_{ob} < h_{oe} \approx h_{oc}$. Some average values are $h_{ob} = 0.49 \times 10^{-6}$ mho and $h_{oe} = h_{oc} = 25 \times 10^{-6}$ mho. Then $1/(1 + h_o R_L)$ will be the largest for the common-base circuit. Often R_L is such that this ratio is fairly close to unity for all three circuits. In cascaded circuits, one usually finds that $|K_{ie}| > |K_{ic}| > |K_{ib}|$ and, thus, the common-emitter circuit is the one that is usually employed.

Although most transistor amplifiers have the common-emitter configuration, it is by no means the only one that is used. Current gain is not the only factor that is considered when a circuit is chosen. For instance, if a device is to be used to sense voltage, it is desirable that its input impedance be high so that it does not load down the circuit to be measured. In such cases, the input stage of the device would be a common-collector amplifier. Conversely, if the device were to measure current a low-impedance input would be desirable and the common-base circuit would be used as the input stage. The output impedance of the common-collector circuit is often quite low; hence, it is often used as an impedance-match between a high-impedance input and a low-impedance output. The converse is true for the common-base circuit. The voltage gain of the common-base circuit is usually quite

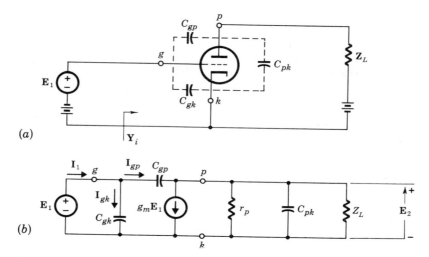

Fig. 3-28   (a) An elementary common-cathode vacuum-tube amplifier which illustrates the interelectrode capacitance; (b) an equivalent circuit for this amplifier.

high.   Thus, in those instances where voltage gain is of prime importance, the common-base circuit is at times used.

3-12   Stray capacitances of vacuum tubes and the Miller effect

Thus far, we have considered only low-frequency effects.   At higher frequencies, the equivalent circuits must be modified.   For vacuum tubes, the phenomena which become important as frequency is increased are stray-capacitive effects, cathode-lead-inductance effects, and transit-time effects. Usually, for frequencies up to 10 Mc/sec, only the stray-capacitive effects need be considered.   The stray capacitances (or parasitic capacitances) between the electrodes of a vacuum-tube triode may be represented by the lumped capacitors shown in Fig. 3-28a.   These capacitances are added to the equivalent circuits of the vacuum-tube triode as if they were external elements, as is indicated in Fig. 3-28b.   The presence of the stray capacitances affects all the properties of the amplifier.   We shall discuss many of these effects in Chap. 6.   As an example, let us consider $\mathbf{Y}_i$, the input admittance of the circuit.   It is given by $\mathbf{Y}_i = \mathbf{I}_1/\mathbf{E}_1$.   The input current $\mathbf{I}_1$ is

$$\mathbf{I}_1 = \mathbf{I}_{gk} + \mathbf{I}_{gp}$$

where

$$\mathbf{I}_{gk} = j\omega C_{gk}\mathbf{E}_1 \qquad\qquad (3\text{-}102)$$

and

$$\mathbf{I}_{gp} = j\omega C_{gp}(\mathbf{E}_1 - \mathbf{E}_2)$$

The quantity $\mathbf{E}_2$ is unknown. However, if we assume that the voltage gain $\mathbf{A}_v = \mathbf{E}_2/\mathbf{E}_1$ is known, we may write the expression for the input admittance $\mathbf{Y}_i$ as follows:

$$\mathbf{Y}_i = j\omega[C_{gk} + (1 - \mathbf{A}_v)C_{gp}] \tag{3-103}$$

The quantity $\mathbf{A}_v$ is, in general, complex. Thus,

$$\mathbf{A}_v = A_R + jA_X$$

We can write the real and imaginary components of $\mathbf{Y}_i$ as

$$Re\ \mathbf{Y}_i = G_i = \omega A_X C_{gp} \tag{3-104}$$
$$Im\ \mathbf{Y}_i = B_i = \omega[C_{gk} + (1 - A_R)C_{gp}]$$

The effective input capacitance C_i is

$$C_i = C_{gk} + (1 - A_R)C_{gp} \tag{3-105}$$

Often the voltage gain $\mathbf{A}_v$ has a negative real component whose magnitude is considerably greater than 1. In this case, the input capacitance C_i is very much greater than the capacitance one might expect from the magnitudes of the stray capacitances. This increase in input capacitance due to the gain of the amplifier is known as the *Miller effect*. Another consequence of these stray capacitances is the presence of a conductive component in the input admittance, as is indicated by Eq. (3-104). This conductance may be either positive or negative, depending upon the sign of A_X, the reactive component of the voltage gain.

In order to use the above expressions, a knowledge of the voltage gain $\mathbf{A}_v$ is required.

$$\mathbf{A}_v = \frac{\mathbf{E}_2}{\mathbf{E}_1} = \frac{-g_m + j\omega C_{gp}}{j\omega(C_{gp} + C_{pk}) + r_p^{-1} + \mathbf{Z}_L^{-1}} \tag{3-106}$$

If the input conductance is negative, then the amplifier may oscillate and no longer function properly (see Sec. 6-26). Even if oscillation does not result, the large input admittance, due to the Miller effect, can cause great reduction in the voltage gain at high frequencies. If the stray capacitances are ignored, then the voltage gain of the amplifier of Fig. 3-28a is $\mathbf{A}_v = -\mu \mathbf{Z}_L/(r_p + \mathbf{Z}_L)$. If $|Z_L|$ decreases, then $|A_v|$ will decrease. If several amplifier stages are cascaded, the effective load impedance consists of $\mathbf{Z}_L$ in parallel with the input admittance of the next amplifier stage. If this input admittance is high, $|A_v|$ will be reduced. This effect, which can severely reduce the high-frequency response of an amplifier, will be discussed in Chap. 6.

If C_{gp} could be made negligibly small, then Y_i would become very much smaller [see Eqs. (3-103) and (3-104)] and its conductive component would become essentially zero. In vacuum-tube pentodes, the stray capacitance

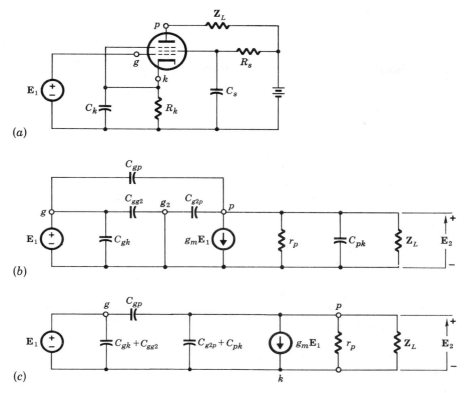

Fig. 3-29   (a) *An elementary vacuum-tube-pentode amplifier; (b) an equivalent circuit showing the stray capacitances (it is assumed that C_k and C_s are short circuits at the signal frequency); (c) the equivalent circuit redrawn.*

C_{gp} between the plate and the control grid is on the order of hundreds to several thousand times smaller than it is in vacuum-tube triodes. Consequently, the Miller effect is, in general, negligible in vacuum-tube pentodes; this is one of their advantages. The presence of the additional grids in a vacuum-tube pentode results in additional stray capacitances. All of the stray capacitances are shown in the equivalent circuit of Fig. 3-29b. Since the suppressor grid is connected to the cathode, capacitances between the suppressor grid and the other electrodes are included in those to the cathode. It is also assumed that the bypass capacitors C_k and C_s are large enough to act as short circuits at the frequencies of interest. Hence, in Fig. 3-29b, the screen-grid node s is connected directly to the cathode node k. This short-circuits the capacitance C_{g2k}, and the other capacitances may be combined as indicated in Fig. 3-29c. If the screen grid is not short-circuited to the cathode, then there will be coupling between the control grid and the plate through C_{gg2} and C_{g2p}. The advantage of the pentode will then be lost. The equivalent circuit of Fig. 3-29c has the same form as that of the vacuum-tube triode shown in Fig. 3-28b.   Consequently, the previous analysis also applies to the vacuum-tube pentode and the expression for the input admittance becomes

$$\mathbf{Y}_i = j\omega[C_{gk} + C_{gg2} + (1 - \mathbf{A}_v)C_{gp}] \tag{3-107}$$

where

$$\mathbf{A}_v = \frac{\mathbf{E}_2}{\mathbf{E}_1} = A_R + jA_X = \frac{-g_m + j\omega C_{gp}}{j\omega(C_{gp} + C_{g2p} + C_{pk}) + r_p^{-1} + \mathbf{Z}_L^{-1}}$$

The input capacitance is

$$C_i = C_{gk} + C_{gg2} + (1 - A_R)C_{gp} \tag{3-108}$$

The input capacitance of a vacuum-tube-pentode amplifier is less than that of the vacuum-tube-triode amplifier, because of the very large reduction in C_{gp} in the pentode.   Note that capacitance to the cathode also represents capacitance to the suppressor grid (g_3).   Thus, Eq. (3-108) can be written as

$$C_i = C_{gk} + C_{gg3} + C_{gg2} + (1 - A_R)C_{gp} \tag{3-109}$$

3-13   High-frequency input admittance of the common-plate amplifier

One of the most important advantages of the common-plate amplifier is that its input admittance is very much lower than that of the other commonly used amplifier configurations, especially when the interelectrode capacitances

Fig. 3-30   (a) A simple cathode-follower amplifier; (b) its equivalent circuit.   Note that the orientation of the vacuum tube has been reversed.

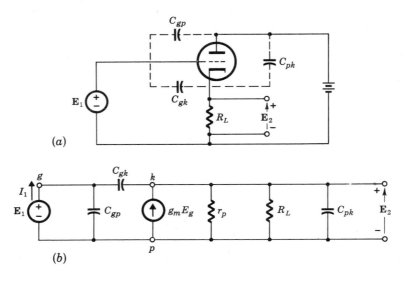

(a)

(b)

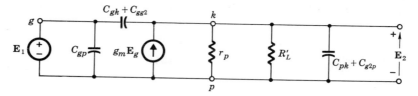

Fig. 3-31   *The equivalent circuit of the pentode cathode-follower amplifier of Fig. 3-18 where it is assumed that the reactances of all bypass capacitors are zero and $R'_L = R_L R_s/(R_L + R_s)$.*

are considered.   We shall demonstrate this with the cathode-follower amplifier and equivalent circuit of Fig. 3-30.   The input admittance is

$$\mathbf{Y}_i = j\omega[C_{gp} + (1 - \mathbf{A}_v)C_{gk}] \tag{3-110}$$

where $\mathbf{A}_v = \mathbf{E}_2/\mathbf{E}_1$.   Equation (3-110) has the same form as Eq. (3-103), except that the roles of C_{gp} and C_{gk} have been interchanged.   However, in the cathode follower, $\mathbf{A}_v$ can often be considered to be approximately unity.   Hence, the factor $(1 - \mathbf{A}_v)$ will be extremely small instead of large.   When triodes are used, the input admittance of Eq. (3-110) can often be approximated by

$$\mathbf{Y}_i \approx j\omega C_{gp} \tag{3-111}$$

In general, $\mathbf{A}_v$ will be a complex number that varies with frequency, so that this approximation is only valid for those frequencies where $\mathbf{A}_v \approx 1$.   However, this approximation usually is quite good over most of the frequencies of interest.

The use of vacuum-tube pentodes in common-plate circuits usually results in a large reduction in the input admittance because of the very low value of C_{gp}.   An equivalent circuit of such an amplifier is shown in Fig. 3-31, where it is assumed that the reactance of all the bypass capacitors is zero at the signal frequency.   (The capacitance between the suppressor grid and the plate and between the suppressor grid and the control grid is included in C_{pk} and C_{gk}, respectively.)   The input admittance of this circuit is given by

$$C_i = j\omega[C_{gp} + (1 - \mathbf{A}_v)(C_{gk} + C_{gg2})] \tag{3-112}$$

Again $1 - \mathbf{A}_v$ is usually extremely small and, in the case of the pentode, C_{gp} will also be quite small.   Hence, the input admittance is very low.   In fact, the input admittance of this circuit may be many times less than that of a comparable common-cathode amplifier.

3-14   Cathode-lead inductance and transit-time effects

The leads to all the electrodes in a vacuum tube have an inductive impedance.   This tends to reduce the gain at high frequencies.   This effect can be accounted for approximately by including series inductances as though they were external elements in the equivalent circuit. The largest effect is produced by the cathode lead, since it causes the output current to affect the grid voltage. At those frequencies where the other lead inductances produce an appreciable effect, the performance has so deteriorated because of the effects of the cathode-lead inductance that these other inductive effects usually need not be considered. The cathode-lead inductance reduces the voltage gain and also, in conjunction with the stray capacitances of the tube, introduces a conductive component into the input admittance, with the disadvantages discussed in Sec. 3-12. The effect of the loss in gain can be approximated by considering that $\mathbf{Z}_K$ represents the inductance in Eq. (3-42). In general, it is the effect of the conductive component that is important, and we shall analyze it here.

For vacuum-tube triodes, cathode-lead inductance effects are usually not considered, since, at those frequencies where they are appreciable, the loading of the input by stray capacitance is so large that it masks the effect of the cathode-lead inductance. At times, in the vacuum-tube pentode, with its negligible Miller effect, cathode-lead inductance effects must be considered. In the succeeding analysis, approximations will be made which are valid for vacuum-tube pentodes, beam power tubes, and vacuum-tube tetrodes.

The input admittance of Fig. 3-32 is $\mathbf{Y}_i = \mathbf{I}_1/\mathbf{E}_1$. If C_{gp} is neglected, then we need only consider the capacitance C_t, which represents the total stray capacitance between the control grid and those electrodes that are effectively connected to the cathode. Thus,

$$\mathbf{I}_1 = j\omega C_t \mathbf{E}_g \tag{3-113}$$

In addition, we shall assume that $\mathbf{I}_k \gg \mathbf{I}_1$ and that the plate resistance r_p is so much greater than the magnitude of the series combination of the load impedance and $j\omega L_k$ that $\mathbf{I}_k$ may be represented by

$$\mathbf{I}_k = g_m \mathbf{E}_g \tag{3-114}$$

Hence

$$\mathbf{E}_1 = \mathbf{E}_g + j\omega L_k \mathbf{I}_k \tag{3-115}$$

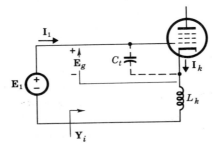

Fig. 3-32 A circuit used in computing the input admittance of a vacuum-tube pentode due to cathode lead inductance.

Substituting Eqs. (3-113) and (3-114) into this expression and rearranging, we obtain

$$\mathbf{Y}_i = \frac{\omega^2 g_m C_t L_k + j\omega C_t}{1 + \omega^2 g_m{}^2 L_k{}^2} \tag{3-116}$$

Usually, at the frequencies of interest, $1 \gg \omega^2 g_m{}^2 L_k{}^2$. Thus

$$\mathbf{Y}_i \approx \omega^2 g_m C_t L_k + j\omega C_t \tag{3-117}$$

The second term is just the susceptance component due to the capacitance C_t. The first term is the conductance component, which is due to the cathode-lead inductance. Note that this component varies directly with L_k, C_t, the transconductance g_m, and with the square of the frequency at sufficiently low frequencies.

Still another phenomenon which hampers the operation of vacuum-tube amplifiers at high frequencies, principally through the conductive component it introduces into the input admittance of the vacuum tube, is the effect due to the time required by the electrons to traverse the distance between the cathode and the plate. This effect becomes important when this transit time is an appreciable fraction of the period of the impressed signal.

A qualitative explanation of this phenomenon is as follows. Assume that the varying component of the grid voltage is sinusoidal. The electronic space current passing between the cathode and plate will then have a sinusoidal alternating component, which, in turn, will induce a sinusoidal current in the control-grid circuit. At low frequencies, this induced current will lead the control-grid voltage by 90°. This current, in addition to the current through the stray capacitances, makes up the total capacitive input current at low frequencies. That is, the stray capacitances of vacuum tubes include not only the effect of the electric fields between the electrodes but also the effects of the space currents.

At higher frequencies, when the transit time of the electrons is an appreciable fraction of the period of the input signal, the phase angle of the induced grid current will lead that of the grid voltage by somewhat less than 90°. This reduction in the leading phase angle is a result of the nonzero transit time of the electrons. Since the phase angle is less than 90°, there is a positive conductive component introduced into the input admittance. A detailed analysis of this phenomenon yields the following relation for the input conductance,[3] which is valid for small values of ωT:

$$G_t = k g_m T^2 \omega^2 \tag{3-118}$$

where k is a constant, depending upon the tube geometry, and T is the transit time of the electrons. This conductance is also proportional to the transconductance g_m and to the square of the frequency. At high frequencies, the equivalent circuit of the vacuum tube should be modified by adding a conductance between the grid and cathode terminals which is the sum of the conductances due to the cathode-lead inductance and the transit-time effects.

Special vacuum-tube triodes designed for use at high frequencies minimize the effects of the stray capacitances, the cathode-lead inductance, and the transit time.

3-15   Variation of alpha with frequency

Transistor performance deteriorates as the frequency is increased. Primarily this is caused by the decrease in the short-circuit forward-current amplification factor α and by the effects of the capacitances that exist within the transistor. We shall consider the variation of α with frequency in this section. An analysis[4] of an ideal planar transistor yields

$$\alpha = \frac{k_1}{\cosh\left[(W/L)(1 + j\omega\tau)^{1/2}\right]} \tag{3-119}$$

where W is the base width; L and τ are the diffusion lengths and the lifetime, respectively, of the minority carriers in the base region; and k_1 is a constant. Note that α is now a phasor. This expression is usually much too cumbersome to use and it is approximated by expanding Eq. (3-119) into a power series.

$$\alpha = k_1\left[1 + \frac{W^2}{2L^2}(1 + j\omega\tau) + \frac{W^4}{24L^4}(1 + j\omega\tau)^2 + \cdots\right]^{-1} \tag{3-120}$$

Eliminating all but the first two terms and manipulating, we obtain

$$\alpha \approx \frac{\alpha_0}{1 + j\omega/\omega_\alpha} = \frac{\alpha_0}{\sqrt{1 + (\omega/\omega_\alpha)^2}} \quad \underline{/ - \tan^{-1}\omega/\omega_\alpha} \tag{3-121}$$

where $\alpha_0 = k_1/(1 + W^2/2L^2)$ and $\omega_\alpha = (2L^2 + W^2)/W^2\tau$. The value of α_0 is the value of α at very low frequencies and is the quantity that was considered in the discussion of Secs. 3-8 to 3-11. As ω increases, the magnitude of α falls off monotonically from α_0 toward zero. ω_α is the angular frequency at which the magnitude of α has decayed to $\alpha_0/\sqrt{2}$. Thus, ω_α is one measure of the ability of a transistor to amplify higher frequencies. The higher ω_α is, the better is the expectation for good high-frequency response.

Transistors are constructed so that $W \ll L$. Hence, ω_α may be approximated by $\omega_\alpha \approx 2L^2/W^2\tau$. Thus, ω_α is almost inversely proportional to the square of the base width. This means that, all other factors considered equal, the thinner the base region is, the better is the high-frequency behavior of the transistor.

To better approximate the theoretical expression for α, additional terms of Eq. (3-120) may be used. Usually, to keep the expression simple, ω_α is the experimentally determined angular frequency, where $|\alpha| = \alpha_0/\sqrt{2}$. Under this condition, Eq. (3-121) usually yields a good approximation of the magnitude of α. However, the error in the phase angle of α is generally somewhat greater. In most instances, this error can be tolerated. In those special cases where more accuracy is required, the right-hand side of Eq.

(3-121) is multiplied by exp $(-jk\omega/\omega_\alpha)$ where k is an experimentally determined correction factor. This expression introduces a linear phase lag into the expression for α. Its value is $-k$ radians at $\omega = \omega_\alpha$. Hence, a more accurate expression for α is

$$\alpha \approx \frac{\alpha_0 \epsilon^{-jk\omega/\omega_\alpha}}{1 + j\omega/\omega_\alpha} \tag{3-122}$$

Ordinarily, a good value for k is 0.2. However, it may vary from this value for certain types of transistors.

The variation of α with frequency yields the variation of $\mathbf{h}_{fb}$ with frequency (see Eq. 3-67). Let us now obtain the variation of $\mathbf{h}_{fe} = \beta$ with frequency. Substituting Eq. (3-121) into Eq. (3-70), we obtain

$$\beta = \frac{\beta_0}{1 + j\omega/\omega_\beta} \tag{3-123}$$

where

$$\beta_0 = \frac{\alpha_0}{1 - \alpha_0} \tag{3-124}$$

and

$$\omega_\beta = \omega_\alpha(1 - \alpha_0) \tag{3-125}$$

Since α_0 is close to unity, β_0 will be considerably greater than α_0. However, ω_β will be considerably smaller than ω_α. We shall see, in Chap. 6, that the common-emitter amplifier has a considerably greater gain over a narrower bandwidth than the comparable common-base amplifier.

3-16 High-frequency equivalent circuits for transistors

The high-frequency equivalent circuit for a transistor can be obtained from the low-frequency equivalent circuit if suitable modifications are made.

Fig. 3-33   A modification of the circuit of Fig. 3-20b which is valid at high frequencies.

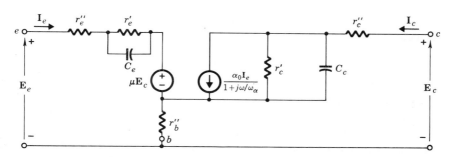

The high-frequency behavior of a transistor is very complex, and any equivalent circuit is a compromise between accuracy and simplicity. At the start, let us consider the equivalent circuit of Fig. 3-20b, which was obtained on a physical basis, and modify it. Such a modification is shown in Fig. 3-33. In general, the quantity α' of Fig. 3-20b is such that $\alpha' \approx \alpha$. Thus, the current generator has been replaced by the value $\alpha_0 I_e/(1 + j\omega/\omega_\alpha)$ which was derived in the last section. In addition, the capacitances that exist across the transistor junctions must also be included. This is done by adding the capacitors C_e and C_c across the appropriate junction resistances. The capacitor C_e is usually larger than C_c. However, r'_c is usually very much greater than r'_e. The value of r'_e is quite small, since the emitter-base junction is forward-biased. For this reason, C_e often can be neglected in high-frequency calculations. Let us obtain the high-frequency h-parameter equivalent circuits. Consider the low-frequency common-base equivalent circuit of Fig. 3-21. The quantity $h_{fb} = -\alpha$. Thus, we shall replace h_{fb} by the complex frequency-dependent quantity

$$\mathbf{h}_{fb} = -\frac{\alpha_0}{1 + j\omega/\omega_\alpha} = \frac{h_{fb}}{1 + j\omega/\omega_\alpha} \tag{3-126}$$

The capacitance C_c of Fig. 3-33 does not appear between the collector and base leads because of r''_{bb} and r''_{cc}. Since they are small, very little error is introduced if we assume that C_c is connected between the collector and base leads. Usually, this capacitance is denoted by C_{ob}. The equivalent circuit is shown in Fig. 3-34. The input circuit has not been modified. That is, the effect of C_e has been ignored. It has also been assumed that h_{rb} does not vary with frequency. Usually, these approximations introduce very little error. Thus, the common-base h parameters that are valid at low and high frequencies are given by

$$\mathbf{h}_{ib} = h_{ib}$$
$$\mathbf{h}_{rb} = h_{rb}$$
$$\mathbf{h}_{fb} = \frac{h_{fb}}{1 + j\omega/\omega_\alpha} \tag{3-127}$$
$$\mathbf{h}_{ob} = h_{ob} + j\omega C_{ob}$$

Fig. 3-34 *A high-frequency h-parameter common-base equivalent circuit for the transistor.*

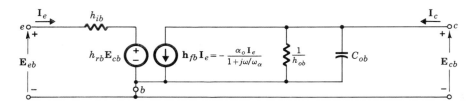

The manipulations of Sec. 3-9 are valid even if the h parameters are complex quantities. Thus, the high-frequency common-emitter h parameters can be obtained by substituting Eqs. (3-127) into Eqs. (3-60). However, the results are considerably simpler and, in almost all cases, quite accurate if the approximate expressions of Eqs. (3-64) are used. Before performing this substitution, let us obtain one more approximation, which is usually quite valid. Consider the quantity $1 + \mathbf{h}_{fb}$.

$$1 + \mathbf{h}_{fb} = 1 - \frac{\alpha_0}{1 + j\omega/\omega_\alpha} = \frac{(1 - \alpha_0)(1 + j\omega/\omega_\beta)}{1 + j\omega/\omega_\alpha} \qquad (3\text{-}128)$$

where ω_β is given in Eq. (3-125). In general, $\omega_\alpha \gg \omega_\beta$. Then, if $\omega/\omega_\alpha \ll 1$, which often characterizes the useful range of frequencies for the common-emitter circuit, we have

$$1 + \mathbf{h}_{fb} \approx (1 - \alpha_0)(1 + j\omega/\omega_\beta) = (1 + h_{fb})(1 + j\omega/\omega_\beta) \qquad (3\text{-}129)$$

Then, substituting Eqs. (3-127) and (3-129) into Eqs. (3-64), we obtain

$$\mathbf{h}_{ie} \approx \frac{h_{ie}}{1 + j\omega/\omega_\beta}$$

$$\mathbf{h}_{re} \approx \frac{h_{ib}h_{ob}}{(1 + h_{fb})(1 + j\omega/\omega_\beta)} - h_{rb} + \frac{jh_{ib}\omega C_{ob}}{(1 + h_{fb})(1 + j\omega/\omega_\beta)}$$

$$\mathbf{h}_{fe} \approx \frac{h_{fe}}{1 + j\omega/\omega_\beta} = \frac{\beta_0}{1 + j\omega/\omega_\beta} \qquad (3\text{-}130)$$

$$\mathbf{h}_{oe} \approx \frac{h_{oe}}{1 + j\omega/\omega_\beta} + j\omega \frac{C_{ob}}{1 + h_{fb}} \frac{1}{1 + j\omega/\omega_\beta}$$

All of these parameters vary with frequency. Often, we can ignore these variations in $\mathbf{h}_{ie}$, $\mathbf{h}_{re}$, and $\mathbf{h}_{oe}$ and approximate them by the following quantities:

$$\mathbf{h}_{ie} \approx h_{ie}$$

$$\mathbf{h}_{re} \approx h_{re}$$

$$\mathbf{h}_{oe} \approx h_{oe} + j\omega \frac{C_{ob}}{1 + h_{fb}} \qquad (3\text{-}131)$$

The parameter $\mathbf{h}_{oe}$ does have a factor of $j\omega$. However, the physical representation of $\mathbf{h}_{oe}$ is as a fixed resistance and a fixed capacitance in parallel. The frequency variation of $\mathbf{h}_{fe}$ must be taken into account. The resulting equivalent circuit is shown in Fig. 3-35. The results obtained with this equivalent circuit are usually accurate enough for many calculations involving common-emitter circuits. The approximations introduced in Eqs. (3-131) become poor at sufficiently high frequencies. If more accuracy is desired, then the parameters of Eqs. (3-130) can be used in the equivalent circuit of Fig. 3-35. Still greater accuracy is obtained if Eqs. (3-60) are used to derive the common-emitter h parameters.

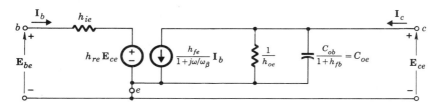

Fig. 3-35   A high-frequency h-parameter common-emitter equivalent circuit for the transistor.

In a manner similar to that used for the common-emitter circuit, we can use Eqs. (3-65) to obtain an approximate high-frequency h-parameter common-collector equivalent circuit.   Thus,

$$\mathbf{h}_{ic} \approx \frac{h_{ic}}{1 + j\omega/\omega_\beta}$$

$$\mathbf{h}_{rc} \approx h_{rc} \approx 1$$

$$\mathbf{h}_{fc} \approx \frac{h_{fc}}{1 + j\omega/\omega_\beta} \tag{3-132}$$

$$\mathbf{h}_{oc} \approx \frac{h_{oc}}{1 + j\omega/\omega_\beta} + \frac{j\omega C_{ob}}{(1 + h_{fb})(1 + j\omega/\omega_\beta)}$$

If we consider only the output capacitance and the variation of $\mathbf{h}_{fc}$ with frequency, then the equivalent circuit given in Fig. 3-36 is a common-collector h-parameter equivalent circuit.

These equivalent circuits are general; any one can be used, no matter which lead of the transistor is taken as common.   Thus, if it is not desired to use any of the approximations of the common-emitter or common-collector equivalent circuits, the common-base circuit can always be used. If still more accuracy is desired, then the equivalent circuit of Fig. 3-33 can be used.

Another equivalent circuit which is commonly used is shown in Fig. 3-37.   Here, the base resistance is divided into two components $r_{bb'}$ and $r_{b'c}$. A current generator whose transconductance g_m is not frequency-dependent may be used.   The frequency dependence of the amplifying properties of

Fig. 3-36   A high-frequency h-parameter common-collector equivalent circuit for the transistor.

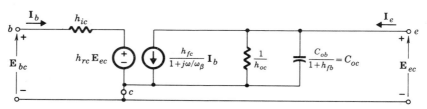

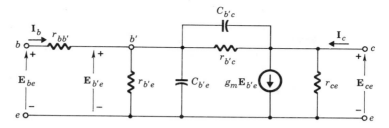

Fig. 3-37 A high-frequency common-emitter hybrid π equivalent circuit for the transistor.

the transistor are obtained by making the current generator proportional to the internal voltage $\mathbf{E}_{b'e}$, rather than to the terminal voltage $\mathbf{E}_{be}$. As frequency is increased, the reactance of the capacitor $C_{b'e}$ falls off, tending to reduce the magnitude of the ratio $\mathbf{E}_{b'e}/\mathbf{E}_{be}$. The magnitude of the current generator also falls off in the same fashion. For grown-junction transistors, the value of $r_{b'c}$ is so large that it may be omitted in Fig. 3-37. This circuit is called a *common-emitter hybrid-π* equivalent circuit. Its parameters tend to be fairly independent of frequency.

In some cases, the stray capacitances between the transistor leads may become important if transistors are operated at sufficiently high frequencies. These capacitances may be taken into account simply by assuming them to be lumped and connected between the appropriate lead terminals.

3-17 An equivalent circuit for the tunnel diode

The tunnel diode acts as a negative resistance in its useful operating range. For small signals at low frequencies, a single negative resistor, which is the dynamic resistance r_p at the operating point, can represent the tunnel diode. This dynamic resistance can be considered to be composed of two resistors $-r_a$ and r_b connected in series. The negative resistor $-r_a$ represents the net effect of the tunneling currents and the ordinary barrier currents at the junction. The resistor r_b represents the ohmic effects at the contacts and within the bulk of the p-type and n-type regions.

At higher frequencies, the junction capacitance must be taken into account. This capacitance appears across $-r_a$. Furthermore, the lead inductance may also be taken into account by a series inductance L. A high-frequency equivalent circuit for the tunnel diode is shown in Fig. 3-38. These parameters for actual tunnel diodes are such that this device is useful up to extremely high frequencies (i.e., of the order of thousands of megacycles per second).

As an example of the use of the equivalent circuit for the tunnel diode, we shall analyze an elementary, low-frequency tunnel-diode amplifier. It

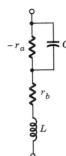

Fig. 3-38   An equivalent circuit for the tunnel diode.   Note that $-r_a$ is negative.

is shown in Fig. 3-39a, where the tunnel diode is placed in parallel with the load resistor R_L. The inductor L_1 and the capacitor C_1 are used merely for biasing purposes. We shall assume that the inductor L_1 acts as an open circuit at all signal frequencies of interest, while acting as a short circuit at zero frequency (i.e., direct current). Thus, the biasing voltage source E_{bb} can establish the operating point for the tunnel diode without

Fig. 3-39   (a) A simple tunnel-diode amplifier; (b) its low-frequency equivalent circuit; (c) a modification of this circuit that uses a current-source input.

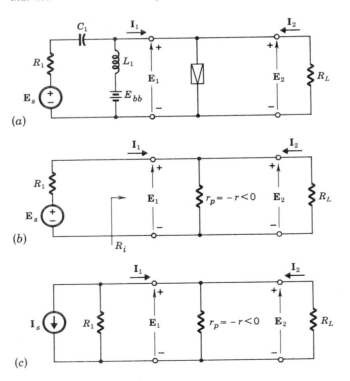

loading down the signal source E_s. We shall also assume that C_1 acts as a short circuit at the signal frequencies of interest. An equivalent circuit for this amplifier is shown in Fig. 3-39b. Assuming that the operation is at sufficiently low frequencies, the effects of the junction capacitor C and the lead inductance L of Fig. 3-38 may be omitted. The resistor $r_p = -r$ represents the series combination of $-r_a$ and r_b, where $r_a > r_b$. In all computations with this circuit, the negative resistance $-r$ is employed exactly as a positive resistance would be.

To obtain the composite voltage gain $K_v = E_2/E_s$, we first note that the input resistance R_i of the amplifier is

$$R_i = -\frac{rR_L}{R_L - r} \tag{3-133}$$

Hence, we have

$$K_v = \frac{R_i}{R_1 + R_i} = \frac{rR_L}{r(R_1 + R_L) - R_1R_L} \tag{3-134}$$

The voltage gain $A_v = E_2/E_1$ can be obtained by setting $R_1 = 0$ in Eq. (3-134).

$$A_v = 1 \tag{3-135}$$

If the input source is replaced by a current generator, as shown in Fig. 3-39c, the composite current gain is

$$K_i = \frac{I_2}{I_s} = \frac{-rR_1}{r(R_1 + R_L) - R_1R_L} \tag{3-136}$$

Furthermore, the current gain is

$$A_i = \frac{I_2}{I_1} = \frac{-r}{r - R_L} \tag{3-137}$$

Note that, by choosing the parameters appropriately (i.e., by setting the denominators equal to zero), some of these gains can be made infinite. Actually, this is the borderline case of unstable operation for the amplifier, and it is avoided.

One problem has been ignored in this analysis. When tunnel diodes are used, the negative resistance in conjunction with the circuit elements can cause the circuit to oscillate and not function properly. Such oscillation is discussed in Sec. 11-1.

3-18 Two examples of the use of equivalent circuits

As an example of the use of equivalent circuits to analyze linear amplifiers, we shall compute the voltage gain of the feedback amplifier of Fig. 3-40a. This is called a feedback amplifier, since a portion of the output signal is impressed upon the input through the resistor R_2. This particular circuit

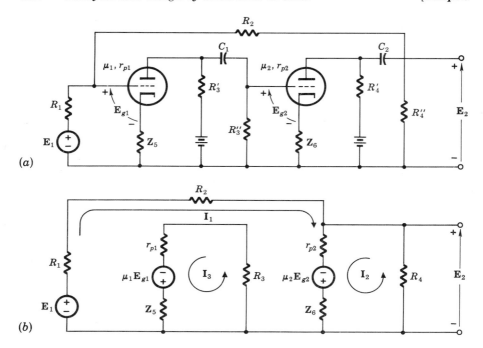

Fig. 3-40   (a) *A two-stage vacuum-tube feedback amplifier;* (b) *its equivalent circuit where* $R_3 = R_3'R_3''/(R_3' + R_3'')$ *and* $R_4 = R_4'R_4''/(R_4' + R_4'')$. *It is assumed that* C_1 *and* C_2 *are short circuits at the signal frequency.*

is not typical, since it has an even number of stages; such circuits have a tendency to oscillate. However, it may be used as a good example for illustrating the techniques that have been developed. We shall assume that the coupling capacitors C_1 and C_2 act as short circuits at the signal frequencies. The resulting equivalent circuit is shown in Fig. 3-40b. Choosing the mesh currents as shown, we may write the following equations:

$$\mathbf{E}_1 + \mu_2\mathbf{E}_{g2} = (R_1 + R_2 + r_{p2} + \mathbf{Z}_6)\mathbf{I}_1 + (r_{p2} + \mathbf{Z}_6)\mathbf{I}_2$$
$$\mu_2\mathbf{E}_{g2} = (r_{p2} + \mathbf{Z}_6)\mathbf{I}_1 + (r_{p2} + \mathbf{Z}_6 + R_4)\mathbf{I}_2 \qquad (3\text{-}138)$$
$$\mu_1\mathbf{E}_{g1} = (r_{p1} + \mathbf{Z}_5 + R_3)\mathbf{I}_3$$

The grid voltages are given by

$$\mathbf{E}_{g1} = \mathbf{E}_1 - R_1\mathbf{I}_1 - \mathbf{Z}_5\mathbf{I}_3$$
$$\mathbf{E}_{g2} = -R_3\mathbf{I}_3 - \mathbf{Z}_6(\mathbf{I}_1 + \mathbf{I}_2) \qquad (3\text{-}139)$$

We may eliminate two of the five unknown quantities by substituting Eqs. (3-139) into (3-138). *It should be emphasized that these substitutions should be made at this point, since this will considerably reduce the labor required to solve the equations.* The resulting equations are:

$$E_1 = [R_1 + R_2 + r_{p2} + (1 + \mu_2)Z_6]I_1$$
$$+ [r_{p2} + (1 + \mu_2)Z_6]I_2 + \mu_2 R_3 I_3$$

$$0 = [r_{p2} + (1 + \mu_2)Z_6]I_1 + [r_{p2} + (1 + \mu_2)Z_6 + R_4]I_2 \qquad (3\text{-}140)$$
$$+ \mu_2 R_3 I_3$$

$$\mu_1 E_1 = \mu_1 R_1 I_1 + 0 I_2 + [r_{p1} + (1 + \mu_1)Z_5 + R_3]I_3$$

Using standard determinant techniques to solve these equations for I_2 and then multiplying by $-R_4$ and dividing by E_1, we obtain the following expression for the voltage gain:

$$A_v = \frac{E_2}{E_1} = -R_4 \frac{\begin{vmatrix} R_1 + R_2 + r_{p2} + (1 + \mu_2)Z_6 & 1 & \mu_2 R_3 \\ r_{p2} + (1 + \mu_2)Z_6 & 0 & \mu_2 R_3 \\ \mu_1 R_1 & \mu_1 & r_{p1} + (1 + \mu_1)Z_5 + R_3 \end{vmatrix}}{\begin{vmatrix} R_1 + R_2 + r_{p2} + (1 + \mu_2)Z_6 & r_{p2} + (1 + \mu_2)Z_6 & \mu_2 R_3 \\ r_{p2} + (1 + \mu_2)Z_6 & r_{p2} + (1 + \mu_2)Z_6 + R_4 & \mu_2 R_3 \\ \mu_1 R_1 & 0 & r_{p1} + (1 + \mu_1)Z_5 + R_3 \end{vmatrix}}$$

$$(3\text{-}141)$$

The answer will be left in determinant form.

As a second example, let us compute the voltage gain of the two-stage transistor amplifier shown in Fig. 3-41a. Here we have a common-collector working into a common-emitter stage with feedback between the output and the input. To simplify the results, we shall assume that the capacitors C_1, C_2, and C_3 are short circuits at the signal frequency. Then, using the equivalent circuits of Figs. 3-36 and 3-35, we obtain the equivalent circuit of Fig. 3-41b. Several resistances have been combined here as indicated in the caption. In order to perform a nodal analysis, the voltage generators will be converted to current generators (see Fig. 3-41c). In addition, several of the impedances have been combined as indicated in the caption. Thus, we obtain the nodal equations

$$I_1 = (G_1 + G_5 + Y_6)E_1 - G_5 E_2 - \frac{h_{rc}}{h_{ic}} E_3$$

$$-h_{fe}I_{b2} = -G_5 E_1 + (G_5 + Y_9)E_2 - 0E_3 \qquad (3\text{-}142)$$

$$-h_{fc}I_{b1} = 0E_1 - \frac{h_{re}}{h_{ie}} E_2 + (Y_7 + Y_8)E_3$$

The base currents are given by

$$I_{b1} = Y_6 E_1 - \frac{h_{rc}}{h_{ic}} E_3$$

$$\qquad (3\text{-}143)$$

$$I_{b2} = -\frac{h_{re}}{h_{ie}} E_2 + Y_8 E_3$$

Equations (3-143) should be substituted into Eqs. (3-142). *The substitutions should be made at this time to reduce the work required to solve the problem.*

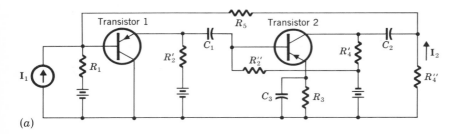

(a)

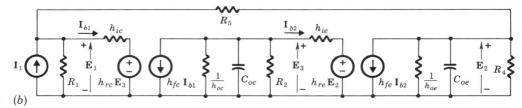

(b)

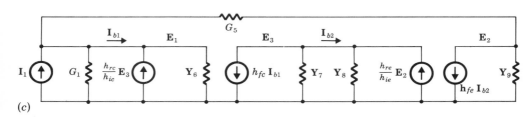

(c)

Fig. 3-41   (a) A two-stage transistor feedback amplifier; (b) its equivalent circuit where C_1, C_2, and C_3 are considered to be short circuits at the signal frequency; $R_2 = R_2' R_2'' / (R_2' + R_2'')$, and $R_4 = R_4' R_4'' / (R_4' + R_4'')$; (c) the equivalent circuit of (b) redrawn where $G_1 = 1/R_1$, $G_5 = 1/R_5$, $Y_6 = 1/h_{ic}$, $Y_7 = h_{oc} + j\omega C_{oc} + 1/R_2$, $Y_8 = 1/h_{ie}$, and $Y_9 = h_{oe} + j\omega C_{oe} + 1/R_4$.

Thus,

$$\mathbf{I}_1 = (G_1 + G_5 + Y_6)\mathbf{E}_1 - G_5\mathbf{E}_2 - \frac{h_{rc}}{h_{ic}}\mathbf{E}_3$$

$$0 = -G_5\mathbf{E}_1 + \left(G_5 + Y_9 - \frac{\mathbf{h}_{fe}h_{re}}{h_{ie}}\right)\mathbf{E}_2 + \mathbf{h}_{fe}Y_8\mathbf{E}_3 \qquad (3\text{-}144)$$

$$0 = \mathbf{h}_{fc}Y_6\mathbf{E}_1 - \frac{h_{re}}{h_{ie}}\mathbf{E}_2 + \left(Y_7 + Y_8 - \frac{\mathbf{h}_{fc}h_{rc}}{h_{ic}}\right)\mathbf{E}_3$$

To obtain the current gain $\mathbf{I}_2/\mathbf{I}_1$, solve Eqs. (3-144) for $\mathbf{E}_2$.   Then

$$\mathbf{K}_i = \frac{-\mathbf{E}_2}{\mathbf{I}_1 R_4''}$$

3-19 Linear equivalent circuits for multiterminal devices

The procedures of Secs. 3-3 and 3-4 can be extended to general active or passive devices having any number of terminals. For instance, consider the $(n + 1)$-terminal device shown in Fig. 3-42. The reference terminal is numbered zero. Thus, the number of terminal voltages is n. The current leaving the reference terminal is the sum of the currents entering the other terminals. Hence, we need only consider the other n terminal currents. The procedures used here are an extension of those of Sec. 3-3.

We shall first consider the case where the terminal voltages are the independent variables and the terminal currents are the dependent ones. Hence, we may write the following n equations:

$$i_k = f_k(e_1, e_2, \ldots , e_n) \qquad k = 1, 2, \ldots , n \tag{3-145}$$

These equations represent the low-frequency relationships (i.e., the static characteristics) of the device. The equivalent circuits derived from these equations will be valid at low frequencies. At higher frequencies, it may be necessary to modify them in essentially the same way as was done in Sec. 3-4.

Usually, for linear operation, it is the incremental variations around an operating point that are of interest. Therefore, as was done in Sec. 3-3, we shall consider the changes in the terminal currents at the particular operating point of the device. This requires the use of a multiple Taylor's series. We shall assume that the higher ordered terms in this series can be neglected as was done in Sec. 3-3. Then

$$\Delta i_k = \frac{\partial i_k}{\partial e_1} \Delta e_1 + \frac{\partial i_k}{\partial e_2} \Delta e_2 + \cdots + \frac{\partial i_k}{\partial e_n} \Delta e_n \qquad k = 1, 2, \ldots , n \tag{3-146}$$

The incremental changes in the terminal currents and voltages can be replaced by the alternating components of the terminal currents and volt-

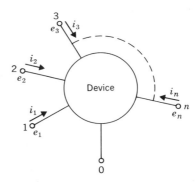

Fig. 3-42 The $(n + 1)$-terminal device. All voltages are measured with respect to the reference terminal 0.

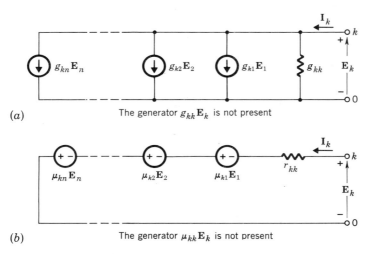

(a)   The generator $g_{kk}\mathbf{E}_k$ is not present

(b)   The generator $\mu_{kk}\mathbf{E}_k$ is not present

Fig. 3-43   Equivalent circuits between the k and reference terminals for the multiterminal device of Fig. 3-42, where the terminal voltages are the independent variables.   (a) The equivalent circuit using current generators; (b) the equivalent circuit using voltage generators.

ages.   Phasor notation will be used for these alternating components. Hence, we may write

$$\mathbf{I}_k = \frac{\partial i_k}{\partial e_1}\,\mathbf{E}_1 + \frac{\partial i_k}{\partial e_2}\,\mathbf{E}_2 + \cdots + \frac{\partial i_k}{\partial e_n}\,\mathbf{E}_n \qquad k = 1, 2, \ldots, n \qquad (3\text{-}147)$$

Let us make the following substitutions:

$$g_{kj} = \frac{\partial i_k}{\partial e_j} \qquad\qquad (3\text{-}148)$$

When $k = j$, g_{kk} represents a dynamic conductance.   When $k \neq j$, g_{kj} represents a transconductance.   Using this symbolism, we obtain

$$\mathbf{I}_k = g_{k1}\mathbf{E}_1 + g_{k2}\mathbf{E}_2 + \cdots + g_{kk}\mathbf{E}_k + \cdots + g_{kn}\mathbf{E}_n$$
$$k = 1, 2, \ldots, n \qquad (3\text{-}149)$$

For any given k, this equation may be represented by the equivalent circuit shown in Fig. 3-43a.   Note that no current generator is included for the term $g_{kk}\mathbf{E}_k$, since this term is taken into account by the conductance g_{kk}. This equivalent circuit represents the device only between the k and reference terminals.   Actually there are n such equivalent circuits, all of which share the same reference terminal.   Hence, a total equivalent circuit for the multiterminal device consists of n equivalent circuits of the type shown in Fig. 3-43a, *all* of which are connected *only* at the reference terminal.

We may obtain an alternative equivalent circuit using voltage generators as follows.   Rewriting Eq. (3-149), we have

$$\mathbf{E}_k = \frac{\mathbf{I}_k}{g_{kk}} - \frac{g_{k1}}{g_{kk}} \mathbf{E}_1 - \cdots - \frac{g_{k,k-1}}{g_{kk}} \mathbf{E}_{k-1} - \frac{g_{k,k+1}}{g_{kk}} \mathbf{E}_{k+1} - \cdots - \frac{g_{kn}}{g_{kk}} \mathbf{E}_n$$
$$k = 1, 2, \ldots, n \quad (3\text{-}150)$$

Using the symbolism

$$r_{kk} = \frac{1}{g_{kk}}$$

and

$$\mu_{kj} = \frac{g_{kj}}{g_{kk}} \qquad k \neq j$$

we may write Eq. (3-150) as

$$\mathbf{E}_k = r_{kk}\mathbf{I}_k - \mu_{k1}\mathbf{E}_1 - \cdots - \mu_{k,k-1}\mathbf{E}_{k-1} - \mu_{k,k+1}\mathbf{E}_{k+1}$$
$$- \cdots - \mu_{kn}\mathbf{E}_n \qquad k = 1, 2, \ldots, n \quad (3\text{-}151)$$

The resulting equivalent circuit for the device between the k and reference terminals is shown in Fig. 3-43b.   Note that there is no generator having the voltage $\mu_{kk}\mathbf{E}_k$.   There is, instead, the resistor r_{kk}.   As before, the complete equivalent circuit consists of n such circuits, *all* of which are connected *only* at the reference terminal.

The significance of these $\mu_{kj}(k \neq j)$ is that of a voltage-amplification factor.   Consider Eq. (3-146) under the condition that all terminal voltages except e_k and e_j are held constant.   In addition, assume that infinitesimally small changes are made in e_k and e_j, such that i_k remains constant.   Thus, we may write

$$di_k = \frac{\partial i_k}{\partial e_j} de_j + \frac{\partial i_k}{\partial e_k} de_k = 0 \qquad k \neq j \tag{3-152}$$

Hence

$$\frac{de_k}{de_j}\bigg|_{\substack{i_k,e_h \text{ const} \\ (h \neq j,k)}} = - \frac{\partial i_k/\partial e_j}{\partial i_k/\partial e_k} = - \frac{g_{kj}}{g_{kk}} = -\mu_{kj} \tag{3-153}$$

Thus μ_{kj} is the negative of the ratio of the infinitesimal change in e_k to that change in e_j required to keep i_k constant while all other terminal voltages are held fixed.   This is precisely the significance of the amplification factor μ for a vacuum-tube triode where, in this case, k represents the plate, j represents the control grid, and the cathode is the reference terminal.

The previous analysis is also applicable when the terminal currents are the independent variables and the terminal voltages are the dependent ones.

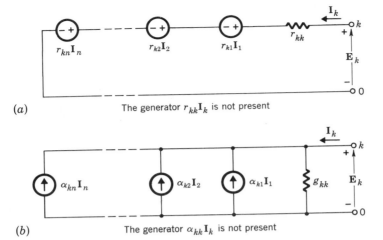

(a)   The generator $r_{kk}I_k$ is not present

(b)   The generator $\alpha_{kk}I_k$ is not present

Fig. 3-44   Equivalent circuits between the k and reference terminals for the multiterminal device of Fig. 3-42, where the terminal currents are the independent variables. (a) The equivalent circuit using voltage generators; (b) the equivalent circuit using current generators.

We start with the functional relations

$$e_k = F_k(i_1, i_2, \ldots, i_n) \qquad k = 1, 2, \ldots, n \tag{3-154}$$

Proceeding as before, we obtain

$$\mathbf{E}_k = r_{k1}\mathbf{I}_1 + r_{k2}\mathbf{I}_2 + \cdots + r_{kk}\mathbf{I}_k \cdots + r_{kn}\mathbf{I}_n$$
$$k = 1, 2, \ldots, n \tag{3-155}$$

where

$$r_{kj} = \frac{\partial e_k}{\partial i_j} \tag{3-156}$$

When $k = j$, r_{kk} is a *dynamic resistance;* when $k \neq j$, r_{kj} is a *transresistance.* The resulting equivalent circuit is shown in Fig. 3-44a, where a voltage generator for the term $r_{kk}\mathbf{I}_k$ does not appear. The equivalent circuit for the entire device consists of n such circuits, all connected together at the reference terminal.

The equivalent circuit between the k and reference terminals with current generators can be obtained by rearranging Eq. (3-155) as follows:

$$\mathbf{I}_k = g_{kk}\mathbf{E}_k - \alpha_{k1}\mathbf{I}_1 - \cdots - \alpha_{k,k-1}\mathbf{I}_{k-1} - \alpha_{k,k+1}\mathbf{I}_{k+1} - \cdots$$
$$- \alpha_{kn}\mathbf{I}_n \qquad k = 1, 2, \ldots, n \tag{3-157}$$

where

$$g_{kk} = \frac{1}{r_{kk}} \qquad\qquad\qquad (3\text{-}158)$$

and

$$\alpha_{kj} = \frac{r_{kj}}{r_{kk}} \qquad k \neq j \qquad\qquad (3\text{-}159)$$

The resulting equivalent circuit between the k and reference terminals is shown in Fig. 3-44b; the equivalent circuit for the entire device is obtained as before. α_{kj} is the negative of the ratio of an infinitesimal change in i_k to that change in i_j required to keep e_k constant while all other terminal currents are held fixed.

As an example of the use of these general equivalent circuits, consider the vacuum-tube-pentode amplifier shown in Fig. 3-45a. Previously, we have neglected the effects of any variation in the potential between the screen grid and cathode. This led to the simple equivalent circuit of Fig. 3-14, which is the commonly used one. Here we shall not make this

Fig. 3-45   (a) *A simple vacuum-tube-pentode amplifier;* (b) *its complete equivalent circuit.*

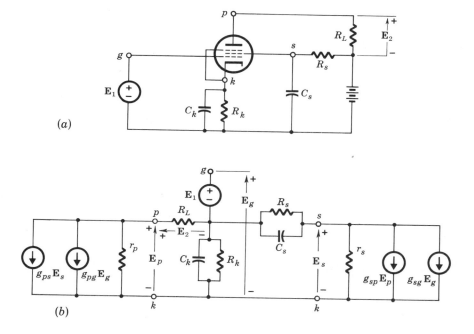

assumption for the equivalent circuit of Fig. 3-45, which is obtained by connecting the equivalent circuits between the plate and cathode and between the screen grid and cathode not only at the reference terminal but also through the external circuitry.   Here, as in the simple case, we have presumed that the control grid is always at some negative potential with respect to the cathode.   Because of this, the control grid current is zero and the equivalent circuit for the vacuum tube between the control grid and cathode is an open circuit, at low frequencies.   Note that the suppressor grid is connected to the cathode and, hence, there is no variation in the potential between the suppressor grid and the cathode.   Thus, the suppressor-grid potential does not affect the operation of any of the other electrodes and it is not included in the equivalent circuit.

REFERENCES

[1] Texas Instruments, Inc., "Transistor Circuit Design," pp. 96–97, McGraw-Hill Book Company, New York, 1963.
[2] L. P. Hunter, "Handbook of Semiconductor Electronics," 2d ed., sec. 11-1, McGraw-Hill Book Company, New York, 1962.
[3] W. R. Ferris, Input Resistance of Vacuum Tubes as Ultrahigh Frequency Amplifiers, *Proc. IRE*, vol. 24, pp. 82–105, January, 1936.
[4] J. M. Early, Design Theory of Junction Transistors, *Bell System Tech. J.*, vol. 32, pp. 1271–1312, November, 1953.

BIBLIOGRAPHY

Chirlian, P. M., and A. H. Zemanian: "Electronics," chap. 11, McGraw-Hill Book Company, New York, 1961.
Greiner, R. A.: "Semiconductor Devices and Applications," chap. 12, McGraw-Hill Book Company, New York, 1961.
Hunter, L. P.: "Handbook of Semiconductor Electronics," 2nd ed., pp. 11-5 to 11-35, 12-2 to 12-23, McGraw-Hill Book Company, New York, 1962.
Pritchard, R. L.: "Electric-network Representation of Transistors: A Survey, *IRE Trans. Circuit Theory*, vol. CT-3, pp. 5–21, March, 1956.

PROBLEMS

3-1. Obtain the open-circuit impedance parameters of the networks shown in Fig. 3-46.   Note that in Fig. 3-46c the generator shown is a dependent one (i.e., its voltage depends upon a current in the network) and, hence, its effect should be included when the open-circuit impedance parameters are computed.

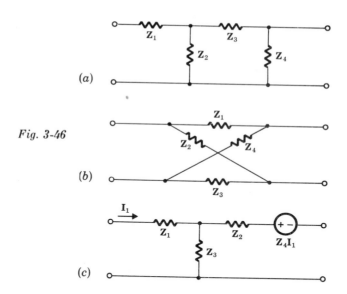

Fig. 3-46

(a)

(b)

(c)

3-2. Obtain the short-circuit admittance parameters of the networks of Fig. 3-46. Work with the networks directly.

3-3. Obtain the hybrid parameters for the networks of Fig. 3-46. Work with the networks directly.

3-4. Derive a set of equations which expresses the open-circuit impedance parameters in terms of the short-circuit admittance parameters.

3-5. Derive a set of equations which expresses the short-circuit admittance parameters in terms of the hybrid parameters.

3-6. Derive a set of equations which expresses the hybrid parameters in terms of the open-circuit impedance parameters.

3-7. A network is characterized by the following open-circuit impedance-parameter matrix:

$$\begin{bmatrix} 10 & 5 \\ 5 & 15 \end{bmatrix}$$

Determine three equivalent circuits which possess this matrix. Is it necessary that the equivalent circuit of this network have a voltage or a current generator?

3-8. Repeat Prob. 3-7 using an open-circuit impedance-parameter matrix which is

$$\begin{bmatrix} 10 & 5 \\ 4 & 15 \end{bmatrix}$$

3-9. A network is characterized by the following short-circuit admittance-parameter matrix:

$$\begin{bmatrix} 10 & -5 \\ -5 & 15 \end{bmatrix}$$

Determine three equivalent circuits which possess this matrix. Is it necessary that the equivalent circuit of this network possess a voltage or a current generator?

3-10. Repeat Prob. 3-9, using the following short-circuit admittance-parameter matrix:

$$\begin{bmatrix} 10 & -5 \\ -4 & 15 \end{bmatrix}$$

3-11. Obtain an equivalent circuit whose hybrid matrix is given by

$$\begin{bmatrix} 10 & -5 \\ -4 & 15 \end{bmatrix}$$

In the following problems where a plot of gain versus frequency is called for, semilog paper should be used and the frequency should be plotted against the log scale.

3-12. Plot the voltage gain of the amplifier shown in Fig. 3-47 for frequencies from 10 to 100,000 cps. Assume that the capacitor C_c is a short circuit at all signal frequencies.

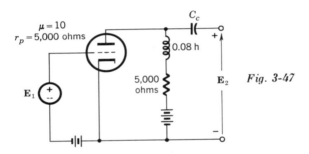

Fig. 3-47

3-13. Plot the voltage gain of the amplifier shown in Fig. 3-48 for frequencies from 1 to 10,000 cps. Assume that the reactance of the capacitor C_c is zero in this frequency range.

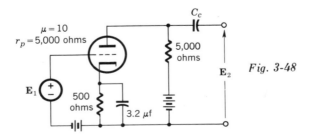

Fig. 3-48

3-14. Plot the voltage gain of the amplifier shown in Fig. 3-49 for frequencies from 1 to 10,000 cps. Assume that the reactance of the capacitor C_s is zero in this frequency range.

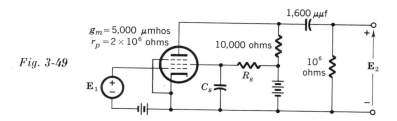

Fig. 3-49

3-15. Compute the voltage gain of the amplifier shown in Fig. 3-50. Assume that the reactances of C_1, C_c, and C_s are zero at the signal frequency. Also, assume that the value of g_m is known and $r_p \gg R_3$.

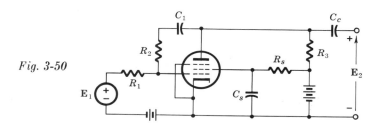

Fig. 3-50

3-16. Compute the voltage gain of the amplifier shown in Fig. 3-51. Assume that the reactances of C_1 and C_c are zero at the signal frequency.

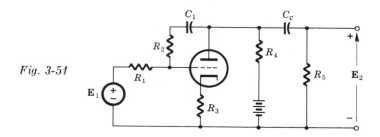

Fig. 3-51

3-17. Compute the voltage gain of the vacuum-tube amplifier shown in Fig. 3-52. What is the maximum value that the voltage gain can attain?

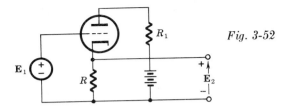

Fig. 3-52

3-18. Calculate the input impedance Z_i and the output impedance Z_o for the vacuum-tube amplifier shown in Fig. 3-53.   Assume that the reactance of C_c is zero at all frequencies of interest.

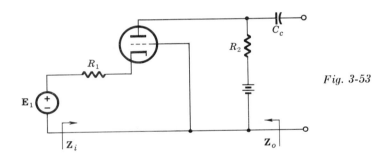

Fig. 3-53

3-19. A transistor, whose equivalent circuit is illustrated in Fig. 3-20a, is found to have the following parameter values: $r'_e = 30$ ohms, $r'_c = 1.2 \times 10^6$ ohm, $\mu = 4 \times 10^{-5}$ and $\alpha = 0.98$.   Compute the value of α in the equivalent circuit of Fig. 3-20b, if $r''_b = 100$ ohms.   Comment on the accuracy of the approximation $\alpha \approx \alpha'$ in this case.   Assume that r''_e and r''_c are zero.

3-20. Compute the h parameters for the transistor of Prob. 3-19.

3-21. A transistor has the following common-base h parameters: $h_{ib} = 40$ ohms, $h_{rb} = 4 \times 10^{-4}$ ohm, $h_{fb} = -0.98$, and $h_{ob} = 0.50 \times 10^{-6}$ mho. Compute the common-emitter and common-collector h parameters.   Use exact expressions.

3-22. For the transistor of Prob. 3-21, comment on the accuracy of the approximate expressions of Eqs. (3-64) and (3-65).

3-23. The transistor whose h parameters are given in Prob. 3-21 is connected into the elementary common-base amplifier circuit of Fig. 3-24 where $R_s = 1,000$ ohms and $R_L = 1,000$ ohms.   Compute the following quantities: K_i, A_i, A_v, R_i, R_o, K_p, A_p, K_T, K_{AP}, $K_{AP,\max}$.   Also consider that the input current source is replaced by a voltage source.   Then compute K_v and A_v.

3-24. Repeat Prob. 3-23, but now assume that the transistor is connected into the elementary common-emitter amplifier circuit of Fig. 3-25.

3-25. Repeat Prob. 3-23, but now assume that the transistor is connected into the elementary common-collector amplifier circuit of Fig. 3-26 where $R_s = 20,000$ ohms and $R_L = 500$ ohms.

3-26. Compute the current gain $\mathbf{K}_i$ for the amplifier of Prob. 3-25, but now assume that $R_s = 1,000$ ohms and $R_L = 1,000$ ohms. Compare this result with that of Probs. 3-25, 3-24, and 3-23.

3-27. Discuss the relative merits of the elementary common-base, common-emitter, and common-collector transistor amplifiers.

3-28. Compute the current gain $\mathbf{I}_2/\mathbf{I}_1$ and the voltage gain $\mathbf{E}_2/\mathbf{E}_1$ for the transistor amplifier shown in Fig. 3-54, where $h_{ie} = 2,000$ ohms, $h_{re} = 6 \times 10^{-4}$, $h_{fe} = 50$, and $h_{oe} = 25 \times 10^{-6}$ mho.

3-29. Repeat Prob. 3-28, but consider Fig. 3-54 to be modified by placing a capacitor which acts as a short circuit at the signal frequencies between points a and b.

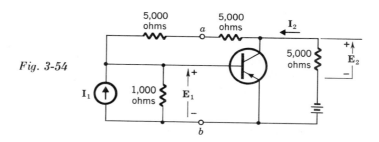

Fig. 3-54

3-30. Plot the current gain $\mathbf{I}_2/\mathbf{I}_1$ for the transistor amplifier shown in Fig. 3-55 for frequencies from 1 to 10,000 cps. Assume that C_1 acts as a short circuit at the signal frequencies. The h parameters for the transistor are: $h_{ie} = 2,000$ ohms, $h_{re} = 6 \times 10^{-4}$, $h_{fe} = 50$, and $h_{oe} = 25 \times 10^{-6}$ mho.

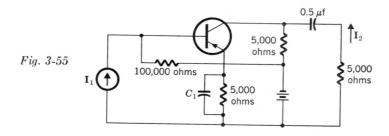

Fig. 3-55

3-31. Repeat Prob. 3-30, but now assume that $C_1 = 2 \ \mu\text{f}$.

3-32. Repeat Prob. 3-31 but now double the sizes of all capacitors.

3-33. Compute the current gain $\mathbf{I}_2/\mathbf{I}_1$ for the transistor amplifier shown in Fig. 3-56.

3-34. Repeat Prob. 3-33, but now assume that capacitors whose reactances are zero at the signal frequency have been connected between points *ab* and *bc*. Compare the relations obtained in this problem with those calculated in Prob. 3-33.

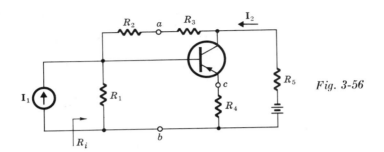

Fig. 3-56

3-35. Compute the input resistance R_i of the circuit shown in Fig. 3-56.

3-36. For the vacuum-tube-triode amplifier shown in Fig. 3-28a, $C_{gk} = 2\ \mu\mu\text{f}$, $C_{gp} = 2\ \mu\mu\text{f}$, and $C_{pk} = 2\ \mu\mu\text{f}$. Assume that $\mathbf{Z}_L$ is such that the voltage gain of this circuit is -50. Compute the effective input capacitance of this amplifier.

3-37. For the vacuum-tube-pentode amplifier of Fig. 3-29a, $C_{gk} = 2\ \mu\mu\text{f}$, $C_{gg2} = 2\ \mu\mu\text{f}$, $C_{gp} = 0.002\ \mu\mu\text{f}$, $C_{g2p} = 2\ \mu\mu\text{f}$, and $C_{pk} = 2\ \mu\mu\text{f}$. Assume that $\mathbf{Z}_L$ is such that the voltage gain of the circuit is -50 and that the reactances of C_k and C_s are zero at the signal frequency. Compute the effective input capacitance of this amplifier. Compare this answer with the result of Prob. 3-36. The capacitances between the cathode and any electrode include the capacitance between the electrode and the suppressor grid.

3-38. Plot a curve of voltage gain versus frequency for the amplifier shown in Fig. 3-57. Use frequencies from 1 to 100,000 cps. Assume that the reactances of C_k and C_c are zero at all signal frequencies. The parameters of the vacuum tube are $\mu = 100$ and $r_p = 200,000$ ohms.

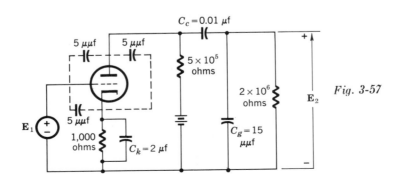

Fig. 3-57

3-39. Repeat Prob. 3-38, assuming that all capacitances are halved.

3-40. Repeat Prob. 3-38, but now assume that the voltage generator E_1 has an internal resistance of 100,000 ohms.

3-41. Derive an expression for the input admittance and voltage gain of the vacuum-tube amplifier shown in Fig. 3-57 that is valid for all frequencies. Assume that $\mu = 100$ and $r_p = 200,000$ ohms.

3-42. Repeat Prob. 3-41 but neglect the grid-to-plate capacitance. This would usually be the case when a vacuum-tube pentode is used.

3-43. For the vacuum-tube-triode cathode-follower amplifier of Fig. 3-30, $C_{gk} = 2\ \mu\mu f$, $C_{gp} = 2\ \mu\mu f$, and $C_{pk} = 2\ \mu\mu f$. Assume that R_L is such that the voltage gain E_2/E_1 of this circuit is 0.90. Compute an expression for the input admittance of this amplifier. Find a parallel RC network that has the same input admittance.

3-44. Repeat Prob. 3-43 for the pentode cathode-follower circuit of Fig. 3-18 where $C_{gk} = 2\ \mu\mu f$, $C_{gg2} = 2\ \mu\mu f$, $C_{pk} = 2\ \mu\mu f$, $C_{pg2} = 2\ \mu\mu f$, and $C_{gp} = 0.02\ \mu\mu f$. Assume that the voltage gain E_2/E_1 is 0.99, $R_g = 10^6$ ohms, and that C, C_k, and C_s are short circuits at the signal frequency. The capacitance between any electrode and the suppressor grid is included in the capacitance between that electrode and the cathode.

3-45. Derive expressions for the voltage gain and input admittance of the cathode-follower circuit of Fig. 3-18 that is valid at all frequencies. Do not neglect the interelectrode capacitance but consider that C, C_k, and C_s are short circuits.

3-46. The transconductance of the vacuum-tube pentode shown in Fig. 3-32 is 6,000 μmhos and the total capacitance C_t between the control grid and the cathode plus all the electrodes connected to the cathode is 10 $\mu\mu f$. The cathode-lead inductance L_k is 0.03 μh. Compute the input admittance of this vacuum tube at a frequency of 100 Mc/sec.

3-47. The input conductance of a certain vacuum-tube-pentode amplifier at a frequency of 100 Mc/sec is found to be 0.5×10^{-5} mho. A calculation of the input conductance due to cathode-lead inductance yields 0.25×10^{-5} mho. Assuming that the remaining component of conductance is due to transit-time effects, compute the transit time of the electrons. The transconductance of the vacuum-tube pentode is 8,000 μmhos and the constant k of Eq. (3-118) is 4.

3-48. The low frequency h parameters of the transistor of Fig. 3-58 are: $h_{ib} = 40$ ohms, $h_{rb} = 4 \times 10^{-4}$ ohm, $h_{fb} = -0.98$, $h_{ob} = 0.5 \times 10^{-6}$. In addition, $\omega_\alpha = 1.2 \times 10^6$ cps, and $C_{ob} = 30\ \mu\mu f$. Plot curves of the current gain I_2/I_1 and the voltage gain E_2/E_1 for frequencies from 10,000 to 10^7 cps.

Fig. 3-58

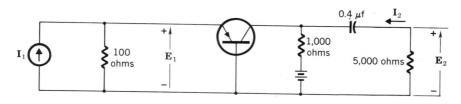

3-49. The transistor of Prob. 3-48 is connected into the circuit of Fig. 3-59. Plot curves of current gain I_2/I_1 for frequencies from 10,000 to 10^7 cps. Assume that C_1 is a short circuit at all frequencies of interest.

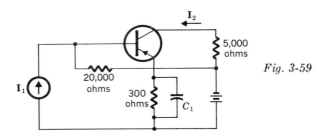

Fig. 3-59

3-50. The transistor of Prob. 3-48 is connected into the circuit of Fig. 3-26, where $R_s = 10,000$ ohms and $R_L = 500$ ohms. Plot curves of current gain I_2/I_1 for frequencies from 10,000 to 10^7 cps.

3-51. Compute the current gain I_2/I_1, the voltage gain E_2/E_1, the input impedance, and the output impedance of the circuit of Fig. 3-60. Use the equivalent circuit of Fig. 3-34.

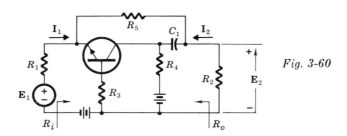

Fig. 3-60

3-52. A *p-n-p* junction transistor is connected into the circuit of Fig. 3-59. The parameters of the transistor are given by $r_{bb'} = 300$ ohms, $r_{b'e} = 5,700$ ohms, $r_{b'c} = 3.3 \times 10^6$ ohms, $r_{ce} = 800,000$ ohms, $C_{b'e} = 1,000\ \mu\mu f$, $C_{b'c} = 36\ \mu\mu f$, and $g_m = 5,500\ \mu$mhos. Plot a curve of current gain I_2/I_1 for frequencies from 10,000 to 10^7 cps. Assume that C_1 acts as a short circuit at all signal frequencies. Use the equivalent circuit of Fig. 3-37.

3-53. Determine the composite voltage gain $K_v = E_2/E_s$ of the tunnel-diode amplifier of Fig. 3-39a. Take the reactances of C_1 and L_1 into account and use the complete equivalent circuit of Fig. 3-38.

3-54. Compute the voltage gain, the input resistance, and the output resistance for the circuit of Fig. 3-61. Assume that C_1, C_2, C_3, and C_4 act as short circuits at the signal frequencies and that any stray capacitances can be neglected.

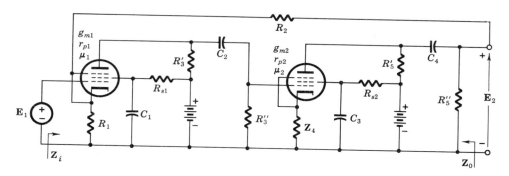

Fig. 3-61

3-55. Repeat Prob. 3-54, but now take the stray capacitances into account. Note that in this case, the amplification becomes complex and the input and output impedances (rather than resistances) must be found.

3-56. Compute the current gain I_2/I_1, the input impedance Z_i, and the output impedance Z_o for the transistor circuit of Fig. 3-62. Assume that the reactances C_1, C_2, C_3, and C_4 are zero at the signal frequencies. Use low-frequency h-parameter equivalent circuits for the transistors.

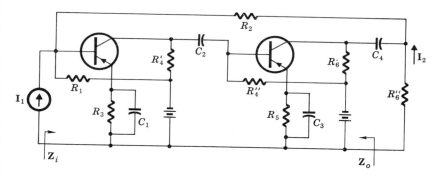

Fig. 3-62

3-57. Repeat Prob. 3-56 using the high-frequency h-parameter equivalent circuits.

3-58. For the vacuum-tube-pentode amplifier shown in Fig. 3-45a, $R_k = 50$ ohms, $R_s = 100,000$ ohms, $R_L = 10,000$ ohms, $g_{pg} = 9,000\ \mu$mhos, $g_{ps} = 1,000\ \mu$mhos, $r_p = 2 \times 10^6$ ohms, $g_{sp} = 500\ \mu$mhos, $g_{sg} = 9,000\ \mu$mhos, and $r_s = 10,000$ ohms. Compute the voltage gain E_2/E_1 of this amplifier under each of the following conditions:

    a. C_k acts as a short circuit; C_s acts as a short circuit

    b. C_k acts as a short circuit; C_s acts as an open circuit

    c. C_k acts as an open circuit; C_s acts as a short circuit

    d. C_k acts as an open circuit; C_s acts as an open circuit.

Piecewise-linear Equivalent Circuits of Electronic Devices

4

The equivalent circuits developed thus far have been linear ones that represent a good approximation to the characteristic curves of the device only over a restricted region.   In this chapter we shall develop nonlinear equivalent circuits which approximately represent the device over any arbitrarily large region of its static characteristics.   It should be emphasized that the use of these equivalent circuits does not replace the linear and graphical techniques of the two preceding chapters; instead, it augments them.   Nonlinear equivalent circuits are useful in such applications as pulse circuits and

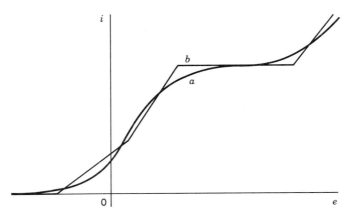

Fig. 4-1   *A piecewise-linear approximation.   Curve a is the nonlinear characteristic and curve b is the approximation.*

wave-shaping circuits.   Also, they provide further insight into the behavior of electronic devices.

Nonlinear equivalent circuits will be developed by approximating the static characteristics with confluent straight-line segments.   Such an approximation to a nonlinear curve is called a *piecewise-linear* one and is illustrated in Fig. 4-1.

4-1   Building blocks for piecewise-linear circuits

Our purpose in this section will be to demonstrate how a network having a given piecewise-linear characteristic can be synthesized, using resistors, ideal rectifiers, and generators.   These are the only elements that will be used in constructing the basic building blocks of piecewise-linear circuits.

The symbol and the current-voltage characteristic of the *ideal rectifier* are illustrated in Fig. 4-2.   The ideal rectifier acts as a short circuit when a forward voltage is applied and as an open circuit when a reverse voltage is applied.   The arrowhead in its symbol indicates the "forward direction." The ideal rectifier is a lossless device, since it cannot consume power.   Its characteristic consists of a semi-infinite line segment of zero slope and

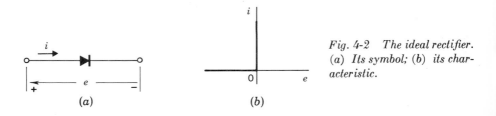

Fig. 4-2   *The ideal rectifier. (a) Its symbol; (b) its characteristic.*

(a)   (b)

another semi-infinite line segment of infinite slope. The point of intersection between the two line segments (in this case, the origin) is called
the *break point*.

In order to obtain a characteristic whose slope is not infinite in the
region where the ideal rectifier conducts, we may add a resistance in series
with the ideal rectifier. The resulting "building block" and its characteristic are shown in Fig. 4-3*a*. When the ideal rectifier is conducting,
this acts simply as the resistance R. Hence, the slope of the characteristic
for the forward direction is simply $1/R$.

Fig. 4-3   *Elementary building blocks of piecewise-linear circuits.*

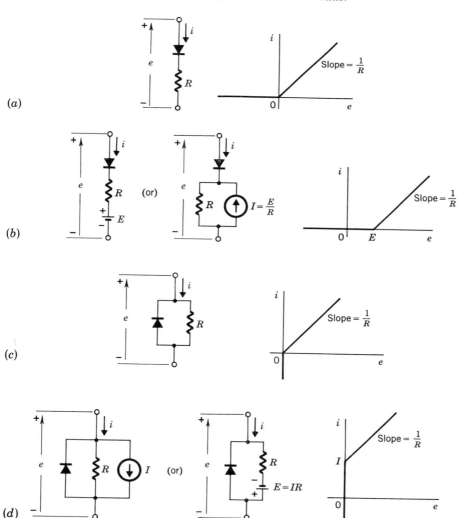

We shall require building blocks whose break points do not lie at the origin.   The break point may be shifted horizontally if a voltage source is connected in series with the building block.   The resulting circuit is indicated in the first diagram of Fig. 4-3*b*.   For the polarity indicated, the ideal rectifier will not conduct until the applied voltage *e* exceeds *E* volts.   Thus, the break point has been shifted to the right.   If the polarity of the voltage source is reversed, the break point will be shifted to the left.   The second diagram of Fig. 4-3*b* is the same building block with the voltage

Fig. 4-4   Modifications in the polarities of the elementary building blocks.

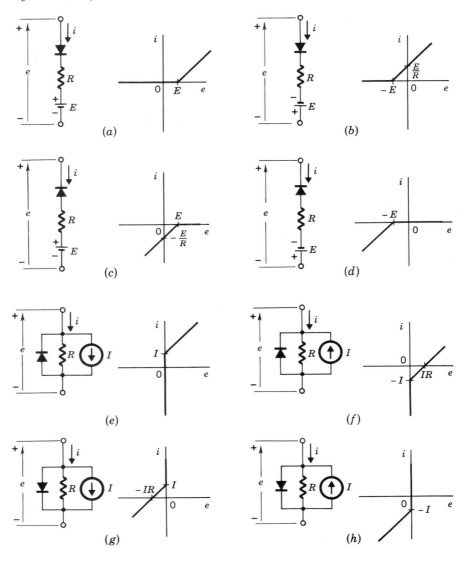

source and the series resistor replaced by a current source in shunt with the resistor.

The building blocks of Fig. 4-3a and b represent either a positive finite resistance or an infinite resistance, depending upon whether or not the ideal rectifier is conducting. We shall now consider building blocks that represent either a positive finite resistance or zero resistance. The simplest such building block is indicated in Fig. 4-3c. When the direction of the impressed current is opposite the direction indicated, this current will be through the ideal rectifier and the building block will act as a short circuit. When its direction is the same as that indicated, the ideal rectifier will act as an open circuit and the building block will appear as the resistance R. Hence, the characteristic curve is as shown, with its break point at the origin. Once again, it is desirable to shift the position of the break point. A vertical shift may be accomplished by including a current source as shown in the first diagram of Fig. 4-3d. For the polarities indicated, if the impressed current i is negative, all the current, including the source current I, will be through the ideal rectifier. The voltage e will be zero in this case, since the ideal rectifier acts as a short circuit. If the impressed current i is positive but smaller than I, the net current through the ideal rectifier will be, in its forward direction, $I - i$. Hence, the ideal rectifier will still act as a short circuit and the voltage e will be zero. If i is increased in the positive direction still further until it equals I, the net current through the rectifier will be zero. Any further positive increase in i must result in a current $i - I$ through the resistor R, since the ideal rectifier cannot carry current in the reverse direction and will act as an open circuit. Thus, for $i > I$, the characteristic has a slope of $1/R$, as is indicated in Fig. 4-3d. The second diagram of this figure represents the same building block. In this case, the current source in shunt with the resistor R has been replaced by a voltage source in series with that resistor.

For these building blocks, simple modifications occur in the characteristics if changes are made in the polarities of the ideal rectifiers or the generators. Such modifications are indicated in Fig. 4-4. It should be noted that if R becomes zero, then a vertical line results in Fig. 4-4a to d for that portion of the characteristic where the ideal rectifier is conducting. When R becomes an open circuit, a horizontal line results in Fig. 4-4e to h for that portion of the characteristic where the ideal rectifier is not conducting.

4-2 Synthesis of piecewise-linear voltage-current characteristics

As an example of the use of the piecewise-linear building blocks, we shall first demonstrate how a general piecewise-linear resistance may be synthesized. Consider a resistance whose characteristic is shown in Fig. 4-5a. In general, several different procedures may be used to synthesize a network having this characteristic. The various procedures lead to different net-

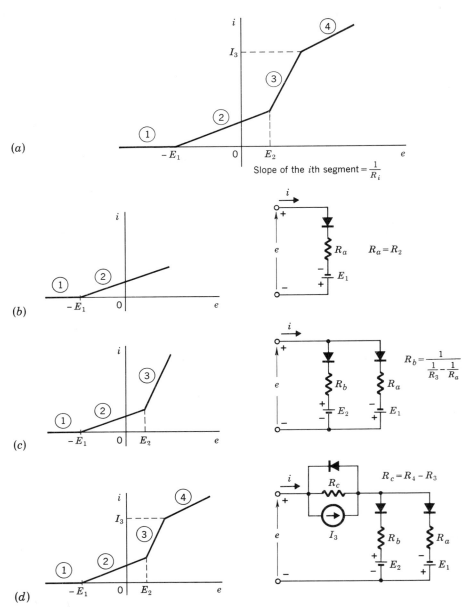

Fig. 4-5 The synthesis of a piecewise-linear resistance. (a) The piecewise-linear resistance; (b) the realization of the first segment; (c) the realization of the second segment; (d) the total resistance.

works, each of which has the same characteristic. We shall demonstrate one such technique here.

The general method is to realize each segment of the characteristic, proceding from left to right and adding a building block at each step. Figure 4-5b shows the first step, in which the first two segments are realized by a building block of the type shown in Fig. 4-4b. The next segment has a larger slope; hence a smaller resistance is required in this range. This may be accomplished by adding a resistance in parallel with the previous resistance. In other words, a building block of the form shown in Fig. 4-4a is used. Its break point is at the voltage $e = E_2$. The value of R_b is obtained by equating the resistance of the parallel combination of R_a and R_b to the reciprocal of the slope of the third segment. Note that the break point for this second building block is shifted off the abscissa by the amount of current in the first building block at the voltage $e = E_2$. Proceeding to the fourth segment, we see that the slope has decreased; hence, the resistance has increased. This means that resistance must be added in series with the previous total resistance. This may be accomplished by adding a building block of the form of Fig. 4-4e in series with the previous circuit, as is shown in Fig. 4-5d. The current generator has a value $i = I_3$. The

Fig. 4-6   Another example of the synthesis of a piecewise-linear resistance. (a) The piecewise-linear resistance; (b) its realization.

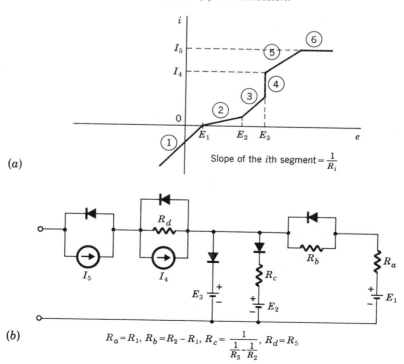

(a)

Slope of the ith segment $= \dfrac{1}{R_i}$

(b)

$$R_a = R_1, \ R_b = R_2 - R_1, \ R_c = \dfrac{1}{\dfrac{1}{R_3} - \dfrac{1}{R_2}}, \ R_d = R_5$$

value of R_c is such that R_c plus the reciprocal of the slope of the third segment is equal to the reciprocal of the slope of the fourth segment. The break point for this building block is shifted off the ordinate axis by the voltage across the previous circuit corresponding to $i = I_3$. This completes the synthesis.

A second synthesis is indicated in Fig. 4-6. In this case, the first segment has a finite nonzero slope and intersects the abscissa at E_1. This

Fig. 4-7 *A means of generating a family of current voltage characteristics from a single characteristic.* (a) *The characteristic;* (b) *the family generated by shifting in voltage;* (c) *the family generated by shifting in current.*

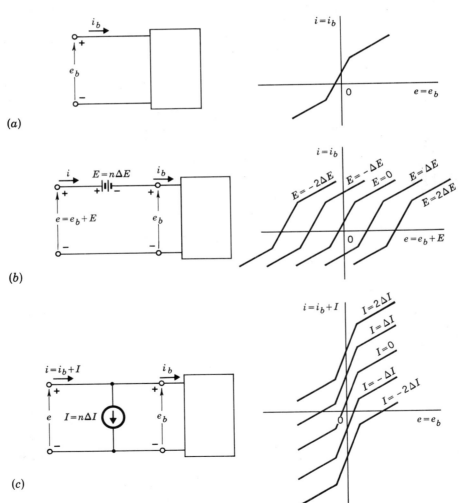

segment may be simply realized by the building block which comprises R_a in series with the voltage source E_1. The remainder of the analysis proceeds exactly as in the preceding example. *These synthesis procedures result in voltage-current characteristics which never decrease with increasing voltage if the resistances in all the building blocks are nonnegative.*

It is often desirable to generate a family of curves from a single curve. Such families of curves may be used to approximate the characteristics of vacuum tubes and transistors. Two techniques for obtaining these characteristics are illustrated in Fig. 4-7. Although a piecewise-linear characteristic has been used in this diagram, these techniques are applicable to any linear or nonlinear characteristic. Consider the device and its characteristic shown in Fig. 4-7a. If a voltage $E = n \Delta E$ is added in series with the device, as indicated in Fig. 4-7b, the characteristic will be shifted horizontally, as shown, because the applied potential e is the sum of the device's terminal voltage e_b and the series voltage E. In a similar fashion, current shifting can be obtained by including a current generator in shunt with the device, as shown in Fig. 4-7c. A combination of these procedures will shift the characteristic in any direction.

In the two examples of this section, the first break point fell on one of the axes. If this is not the case, these shifting techniques can be used to generate the actual characteristic. That is, the characteristic is presumed to be shifted either horizontally or vertically, so that the first break point lies on one of the axes, and then an appropriate building block is chosen for it. A voltage or current generator is then used to shift the characteristic back to its proper position. The remainder of the characteristic is synthesized as before.

4-3 Piecewise-linear circuit analysis

In this section, we shall demonstrate a technique for obtaining the static voltage-current characteristic of a circuit composed of the basic building blocks. Such circuits have characteristics that are linear between any two successive break points. No ideal rectifier changes its *state* (i.e., whether it acts as an open circuit or as a short circuit) throughout such a segment. If, for any given terminal condition, the states of the ideal rectifiers are known, then a simple linear analysis may be performed on the resulting network. The actual problem occurs in determining the states of the ideal rectifiers, or in determining the positions of the break points.

One general principle which we shall use to solve this problem is that, when an ideal rectifier is at its *critical point* (i.e., the point where it passes from its conducting to its nonconducting state or vice versa), the voltage across it and the current through it are both zero. This fact may be used to simplify the circuit. Analysis of the simpler circuit yields the corresponding break point in the overall characteristic. Once all the break points are determined, they may be connected by that set of straight-line segments

whose slopes never decrease with increasing voltage.   The two end segments
of the characteristic may be determined by calculating their slopes.

We shall illustrate these statements by analyzing the circuit of Fig.
4-8a.   First, let us determine the break point corresponding to the critical
point of the ideal rectifier D_1.   In this case, the voltage across D_1 and the
current through it must both be zero.   Hence, the voltage across the 2-ohm

Fig. 4-8   *An illustration of the analysis of a piecewise-linear circuit.   (a) The circuit;
(b) the degenerate circuit when D_1 is at its critical point; (c) the degenerate circuit when
D_2 is at its critical point; (d) the piecewise-linear characteristic.*

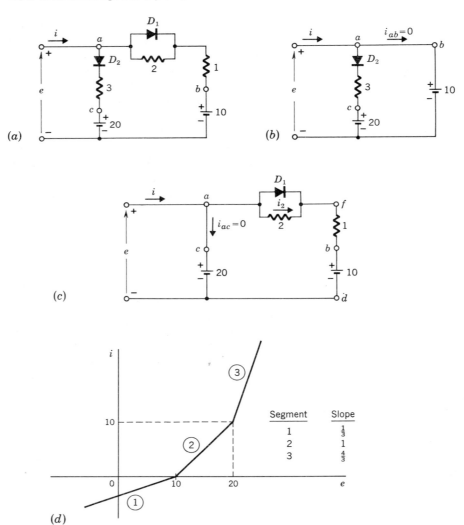

resistor is also zero, and so it draws no current. Consequently, the current through the 1-ohm resistor is also zero, resulting in no voltage drop from points a to b. Thus, the circuit may be redrawn as shown in Fig. 4-8b. From this degenerate circuit, we see that the ideal rectifier D_2 must act as an open circuit, since the net combination of batteries serves to reverse-bias it. Hence, the input current is $i = 0$ and the input voltage is $e = 10$ volts. These are the coordinates of one break point.

The second break point is determined by assuming that D_2 is at its critical point. Proceeding as before, we find that the voltage drop and the current between points a and c are zero, so the circuit degenerates into that of Fig. 4-8c. To determine the input current i, we must know the state of D_1. We shall use a trial-and-error procedure to determine this. Let us assume that D_1 is reverse-biased and, hence, an open circuit. Under this assumption, i_2 will be in the direction shown, because of the potentials established by the two batteries. However, the polarity of the resulting voltage drop across the 2-ohm resistor will forward-bias the ideal rectifier. Thus, our assumption is incorrect, and D_1 must act as a short circuit. Under this condition, the potential of 20 volts is impressed directly across the branch between point f and d. Hence, the input current is $i = 10$ amps. Thus, the coordinates of both break points have been determined. These break points are shown in Fig. 4-8d; since they are the only break points, a linear segment is drawn between them.

We shall now calculate the slopes of the two end segments. When the applied voltage e is greater than 20 volts, both D_1 and D_2 will conduct. Hence, the input resistance of the circuit with all generators replaced by their internal impedances is the resistance due to the 3- and 1-ohm resistors in parallel. Consequently, the slope of the third segment is $\frac{4}{3}$. On the other hand, when the impressed voltage e is less than 10 volts, both D_1 and D_2 are open circuits and the input resistance is 3 ohms. Thus, the slope of the first segment is $\frac{1}{3}$.

One important fact should be noted. In general, for circuits which have a large number of ideal rectifiers, the number of possible combinations of states for the ideal rectifiers, corresponding to the critical point of any single ideal rectifier, may be extremely large. Hence, the trial-and-error procedure for determining any break point can become so tedious that it becomes impractical unless a computer is used. Fortunately, many practical cases are sufficiently simple to allow the application of these techniques.

4-4 Piecewise-linear equivalent circuits for various types of diodes

In this and the subsequent sections, we shall develop piecewise-linear equivalent circuits for the commonly used electronic devices. We shall first consider the vacuum-tube diode whose characteristic is given by the dashed curves of Fig. 4-9. A commonly used simple approximation is shown in Fig. 4-9a, where the slope of the segment in the first quadrant

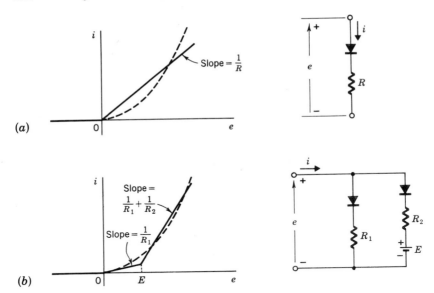

Fig. 4-9   Piecewise-linear equivalent circuits for the vacuum-tube diode.   The actual characteristic is shown by the dashed curve.   (a) The usual two-segment approximation; (b) a three-segment approximation.

is chosen to give an acceptable approximation over the region of operation. Usually, the corresponding equivalent circuit suffices for most applications. If more accuracy is required, a greater number of line segments may be used.   Figure 4-9b illustrates a case where three segments are used.

Some piecewise-linear equivalent circuits for the semiconductor diode are shown in Fig. 4-10.   The simple circuit shown in Fig. 4-10a, which assumes that the reverse resistance is an open circuit, is the one that is usually used.   The circuit of Fig. 4-10b takes the reverse resistance into account.   Figure 4-10c shows a more accurate equivalent circuit, which not only approximates the reverse resistance but also has additional break points and takes the reverse breakdown into account.   Because of its complexity, this equivalent circuit is rarely used.

A piecewise-linear equivalent circuit for the gas diode is shown in Fig. 4-11.   Since this characteristic has a region with a negative slope, an arbitrarily close approximation over this region cannot be obtained using equivalent circuits having only positive resistances.   Nevertheless, the equivalent circuit indicated is sufficiently accurate in nearly all practical cases.

All of these diodes are often approximated by the ideal rectifier of Fig. 4-2.   The error produced by such an approximation is frequently small enough to justify this simplification.

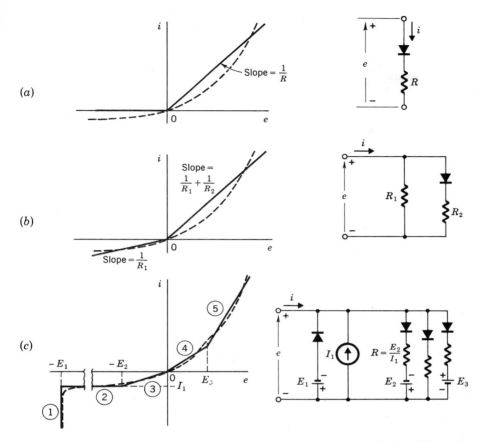

(a)

(b)

(c)

Fig. 4-10   *Piecewise-linear equivalent circuits for the semiconductor diode.   The scales of the negative axes are different from those of the positive axes to show the reverse characteristic.   (a) The usual two-segment approximation; (b) a two-segment approximation which takes the reverse characteristic into account; (c) a multisegment approximation that takes both the reverse characteristic and the reverse breakdown into account.*

Fig. 4-11   *(a) The voltage-current characteristic of a gas diode and its piecewise-linear approximation; (b) the piecewise-linear equivalent circuit.*

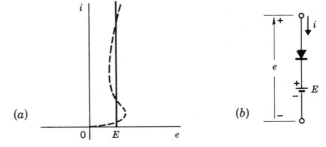

(a)

(b)

4-5   Piecewise-linear equivalent circuit of the vacuum-tube triode

A commonly used piecewise-linear approximation to the vacuum-tube-triode plate characteristics is shown in Fig. 4-12a.   Here the straight-line segments in the first quadrant are parallel and are equally spaced for equal increments in the grid voltage e_c.   The vacuum-tube triode is cut off in the other three quadrants.

The equivalent circuit, which produces this piecewise-linear approximation, is shown in Fig. 4-12b.   For the discussion of the operation of this equivalent circuit, it is simpler to consider, for the time being, that the ideal rectifier D_{p2} is not present.   Under this condition, the simple series circuit *pabk* yields the family of two-segment approximations shown in the first quadrant of Fig. 4-12a.   The purpose of the fixed battery potential E is to situate the break points of the two-segment approximations so as to better match the characteristic curves.   This battery is often omitted, in which case the break point for the piecewise-linear approximation corresponding to $e_c = 0$ is at the origin.

Fig. 4-12   (a) *Piecewise-linear approximation to the vacuum-tube-triode plate characteristics;* (b) *a piecewise-linear equivalent circuit for the vacuum-tube triode.*

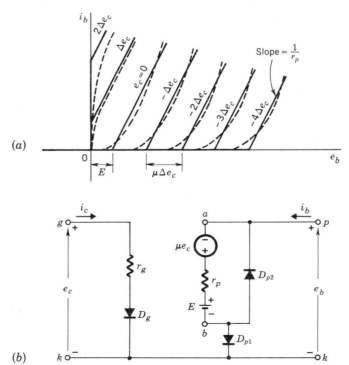

The generator μe_c serves to shift these curves horizontally, as shown. Under the assumption that D_{p2} is not present, the series circuit $pabk$ yields break points that lie on the negative e_b axis if e_c is positive and sufficiently large. This implies that these characteristics extend into the second quadrant and that the plate current i_b will not be zero for negative values of plate voltage e_b. Of course, vacuum-tube triodes do not operate in this way. The ideal rectifier D_{p2} is inserted as shown to prevent the voltage drop from point b to point a from ever becoming positive. Thus, if e_b is negative, the voltage drop from point k to point b must be positive, and the ideal rectifier D_{p1} will act as an open circuit. Thus, the plate current i_b will be zero for negative values of e_b.

The ideal rectifier D_{p2} will not affect the operation for positive values of e_b, since under these conditions it will always act as an open circuit. This can be seen from the following argument. If D_{p1} acts as a short circuit, then the positive voltage e_b appears across D_{p2}, thereby reverse-biasing it. On the other hand, if D_{p1} acts as an open circuit, the voltage drop from b to k must be negative. Summing the voltage drops around the loop $pabk$, we see that the voltage drop from a to b must be positive and, in fact, larger than e_b. Thus, D_{p2} will again be reverse-biased.

The ideal rectifier D_g and the resistor r_g are included to account approximately for the grid current when the grid is made positive with respect to the cathode.

Note that if the operation of the piecewise-linear equivalent circuit is so restricted that e_b and i_b are always positive and e_c is always negative, then the ideal rectifiers D_{p2} and D_g will act as open circuits, while D_{p1} will act as a short circuit. Moreover, if only alternating components of the voltages and currents are of interest, the battery E may be omitted. With these simplifications, the circuit of Fig. 4-12b assumes the usual form for the linear equivalent circuit of the vacuum-tube triode. *The component values in the linear and piecewise-linear equivalent circuits may differ greatly, since in the first case these values approximate the characteristics in the neighborhood of an operating point, whereas in the latter case they are average values for large-scale operations.*

4-6 Piecewise-linear equivalent circuit of the vacuum-tube pentode

Typical vacuum-tube-pentode plate characteristics and their piecewise-linear approximations are shown in Fig. 4-13a. It is assumed here that the approximately horizontal portions of these characteristics may be approximated by parallel straight-line segments which are equally spaced for equal increments in e_c. It is also assumed that the screen and suppressor grids are held at fixed potentials with respect to the cathode. The corresponding piecewise-linear equivalent circuit is shown in Fig. 4-13b. First, we shall establish that this circuit restricts the operation of the device to the first

quadrant and to the negative e_b axis.   The ideal rectifier D_{p1} will prevent
negative values of i_b.   Moreover, if e_b is negative and if D_{p1} is to conduct,
then the voltage drop from a to b must be negative and larger than e_b in
magnitude.   However, it is impossible to obtain a negative voltage drop
from a to b, since in that case the ideal rectifier D_{p2} will be forward-biased
and will act as a short circuit.   Thus, for a negative e_b, D_{p1} must act as an
open circuit and i_b will be zero.

We shall now discuss the shape of the piecewise-linear approximations
in the first quadrant.   Let us first consider the approximation for the case
where $e_c = 0$.   If e_b is positive, but small enough for i to be less than I,
the ideal rectifier D_{p2} will act as a short circuit.   Since D_{p1} must act as a
short circuit under this condition, the equivalent circuit between the output
terminals appears as the parallel combination of the conductances $g - g_p$
and g_p.   Hence, the operation is along the line whose slope is g.   As e_b is
increased, i will increase until it reaches the value I.   The action of D_{p2}
prevents i from increasing any further.   Thus, any further increase in e_b
only increases the current flowing through g_p.   Hence, the slope of the
remaining segment is g_p.   Note that this break point occurs at $i = I$ and

Fig. 4-13   (a) A piecewise-linear approximation for the vacuum-tube-pentode
plate characteristics; (b) a piecewise-linear equivalent circuit for the vacuum-tube
pentode.

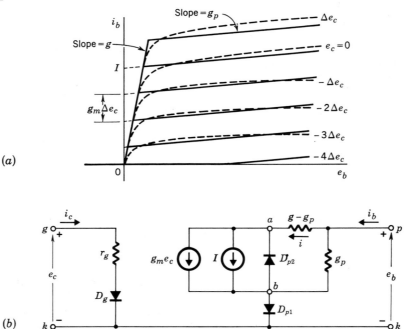

that the corresponding value of the plate current is

$$i_b = \frac{g}{g - g_p} I \qquad (4\text{-}1)$$

The intersection of the extension of the last segment with the ordinate axis occurs at the value I.

If the value of e_c is not zero, the value of the total current generator is $g_m e_c + I$. This value should replace I in the discussion of the preceding paragraph. Hence, we see that the current generator $g_m e_c$ serves to shift vertically only the last segment of the piecewise-linear curve. Values of e_c that are negative and sufficiently large will tend to make i_b negative. However, the ideal rectifier D_{p1} prevents this.

The grid circuit is approximated in the same way as it was for the vacuum-tube triode.

4-7 Piecewise-linear equivalent circuits for the transistor

Typical sets of common-base static output and input characteristics for a p-n-p transistor are shown in Fig. 4-14. These diagrams have been so drawn that the first quadrant represents positive values of current and voltage. This was not always the case when we previously discussed such static characteristics. Drawing the diagrams in this fashion will facilitate the development of the piecewise-linear equivalent circuits although it is not conventional. The piecewise-linear characteristics that we shall use are drawn dashed on these characteristics. The actual output characteristics of Fig. 4-14b are almost linear and equally spaced for $i_E \geqq 0$ and $e_{CB} \leqq 0$. Thus, the piecewise-linear approximation lies on the curves in the quadrant. We shall approximate the curves for $e_{CB} \geqq 0$ by the i_C axis. The variation of the input characteristics with e_{CB} will also be ignored as is shown by the dashed curve of Fig. 4-14c. Thus, the piecewise-linear equivalent circuit has the form shown in Fig. 4-15. The parameter h_{fb} is negative. A very simple equivalent circuit results if it is assumed that h_{ib}, h_{ob}, and E are zero. Some accuracy is lost in this case. However, the results of an analysis using such a circuit are often satisfactory.

If greater accuracy than that provided by the equivalent circuit of Fig. 4-15 is desired, then the equivalent circuit of Fig. 4-16 can be used. The addition of the conductance $g - h_{ob}$ plays essentially the same role here as does the conductance $g - g_p$ of Fig. 4-13. The curves to the right of the break point will no longer be vertical, but will have a slope of g. The break points will occur at

$$i_C = \frac{g h_{fb} i_E}{g - h_{ob}} \qquad \qquad \cdot (4\text{-}2)$$

The generator $h_{rb} e_{CB}$ has been included in the input side to account for the variation of the input characteristic with E_{CB}. The break point now lies

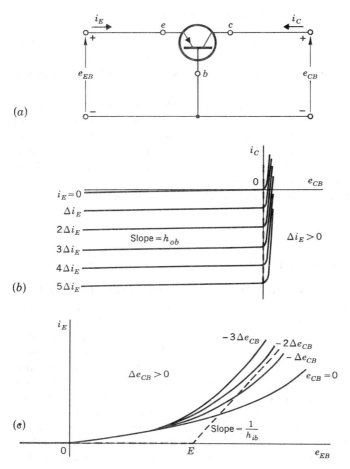

(a)

(b)

(c)

Fig. 4-14 (a) A p-n-p common-base transistor; (b) the common-base output characteristics, with the piecewise-linear approximation shown dashed; (c) the common-base input characteristics with the piecewise-linear approximation shown dashed.

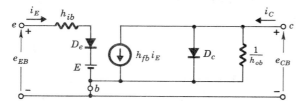

Fig. 4-15 A common-base piecewise-linear equivalent circuit for the p-n-p transistor. Note that h_{fb} is negative.

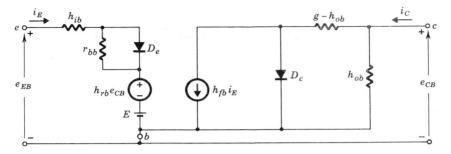

Fig. 4-16   A more complex form of the common-base piecewise-linear equivalent circuit for the p-n-p transistor.   Note that h_{ob} and g are conductances and that h_{fb} is negative.

at $E + h_{rb}e_{CB}$.   (For normal operation, e_{CB} is negative.)   Since the emitter-base junction has a finite back resistance, the resistance r_{bb} has been placed in shunt with the diode.

Typical common-emitter characteristics for the *p-n-p* transistor are given in Fig. 4-17.   A piecewise-linear approximation has been shown dashed.   A typical circuit that produces the piecewise-linear characteristics is given in Fig. 4-18.   Note that if i_B is made somewhat positive (for normal operation, it is negative), the transistor will *essentially* be cut off for much of the region of operation.   The diode D_{c2} is shunted by the resistance r_{bc} since a small collector current can exist even if the transistor is "cut off." This small current is not shown in Fig. 4-17.

The input circuit is essentially that of Fig. 4-16 with the polarities reversed.   If the collector-base junction becomes forward-biased, a very large collector current will exist.   This circuit makes no provision for this. However, it can be accounted for by the diode D_{cb} (shown dashed).   Usually, it is not necessary to include this diode, since the collector-base voltage is maintained at a negative potential.

This equivalent circuit can be often simplified by omitting r_{be}, r_{bc}, and D_{cb}.   At times, the $h_{re}e_{CE}$ generator can be replaced by a short circuit.

If *n-p-n* transistors are used instead of *p-n-p* transistors, the piecewise-linear equivalent circuits are the same except for a modification of the polarities of the voltages and the currents and the orientations of the diodes.

4-8   Piecewise-linear equivalent circuit for the tunnel diode

The current-voltage characteristic of the tunnel diode is of the form shown in Fig. 4-19*a*.   A fairly simple but useful piecewise-linear approximation of this characteristic is shown in Fig. 4-19*b*.   The corresponding piecewise-linear equivalent circuit is shown in Fig. 4-19*c*.   Since this characteristic has a portion with a negative slope, a negative resistance must be used to

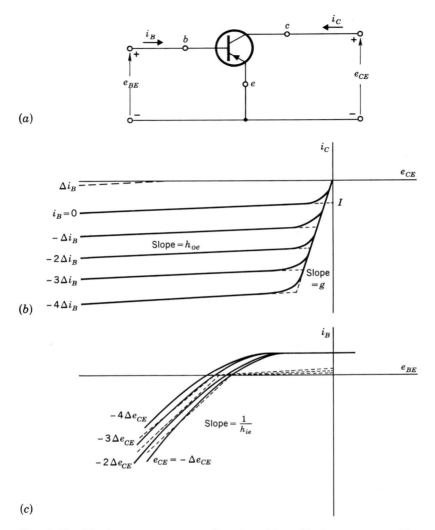

Fig. 4-17   (a) A p-n-p common-emitter transistor; (b) the common-emitter output characteristics with the piecewise-linear approximation shown dashed; (c) the common-base input characteristic with the piecewise-linear approximation shown dashed.

represent it.   This is in contrast to the previously developed piecewise-linear equivalent circuits.   In analyzing this circuit, the negative resistor $-R_2$ is treated exactly as a positive resistor would be.   If a current source whose value lies between I_1 and I_2 on Fig. 4-19b is impressed on this circuit, the resulting potential may take on any one of three possible values.   This implies instability, which is inherent in any tunnel diode.   Note that such instability does not occur if a voltage source is impressed.

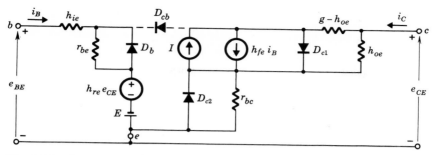

Fig. 4-18   A common-emitter piecewise-linear equivalent circuit for the transistor. Note that h_{ie}, r_{be}, and r_{bc} are resistances while h_{oe} and g are conductances.

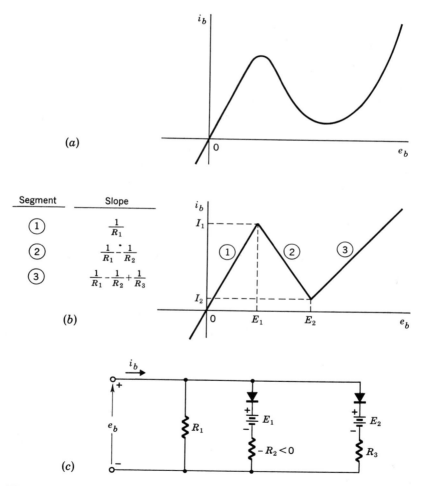

Fig. 4-19   (a) The current-voltage characteristic of the tunnel diode; (b) a three-segment piecewise-linear approximation to these characteristics; (c) a piecewise-linear equivalent circuit whose characteristics are given in (b).

4-9   Comparison of the parameters of piecewise-linear equivalent circuits with those of linear equivalent circuits

In some of the piecewise-linear equivalent circuits that have been developed, the symbolism is the same as that used in the linear equivalent circuits for the same device. For instance, Figs. 4-12 and 3-12 both have the parameters μ and r_p. In general, the parameters of the linear equivalent circuits represent different quantities than the corresponding parameters used in the piecewise-linear equivalent circuits. The parameters of the linear equivalent circuits are the slopes of characteristic curves at the operating *point*. The parameters of the piecewise-linear equivalent circuit represent an average of a slope over an operating *range*. Thus, these parameters cannot be interchanged without a loss of accuracy. Also, note that the form of the piecewise-linear equivalent circuit is often different from that of the linear equivalent circuit.

BIBLIOGRAPHY

Chirlian, P. M., and A. H. Zemanian: "Electronics," chap. 12, McGraw-Hill Book Company, New York, 1961.
Zimmermann, H. J., and S. J. Mason: "Electronic Circuit Theory," pp. 56–78, 171–174, 225–228, 304, John Wiley & Sons, Inc., New York, 1960.

PROBLEMS

4-1. Sketch the characteristic curves for the circuits of Fig. 4-4*a*, *b*, *c*, and *d* when all the resistances are replaced by short circuits.

4-2. Sketch the characteristic curves for the circuits of Fig. 4-4*e*, *f*, *g*, and *h* when all the resistances are replaced by open circuits.

4-3. Obtain a network that realizes the piecewise-linear characteristic shown in Fig. 4-20.

Fig. 4-20

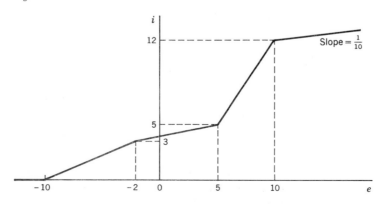

4-4. Obtain a network that realizes the piecewise-linear characteristic shown in Fig. 4-21.

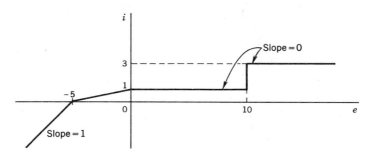

Fig. 4-21

4-5. Obtain a network that realizes the piecewise-linear characteristic shown in Fig. 4-22.

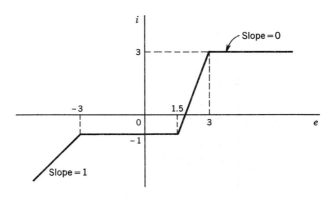

Fig. 4-22

4-6. Approximate the curve of Fig. 4-23 in a piecewise-linear fashion and derive a network that realizes this approximation.

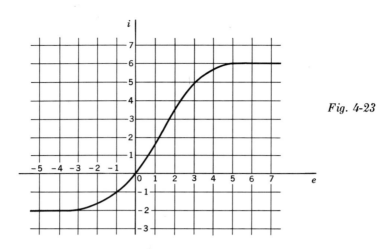

Fig. 4-23

4-7. Synthesize a network that produces the family of piecewise-linear characteristics shown in Fig. 4-24. Each curve is composed of four segments, one of which is horizontal and another vertical.

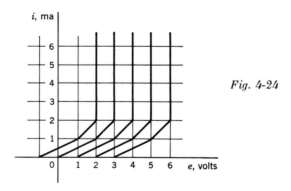

Fig. 4-24

4-8. Synthesize a network that produces the family of piecewise-linear curves shown in Fig. 4-25. Each curve is composed of three segments, one of which is vertical and another horizontal.

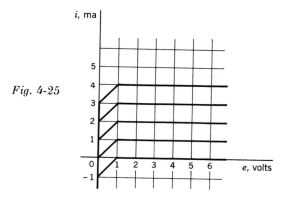

Fig. 4-25

4-9. Obtain a plot of i versus e for the piecewise-linear circuit of Fig. 4-26.

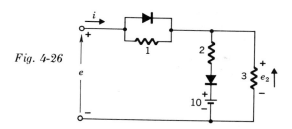

Fig. 4-26

4-10. Obtain a plot of i versus e for the piecewise-linear circuit of Fig. 4-27.

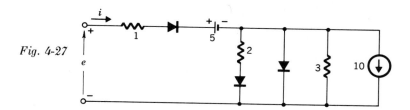

Fig. 4-27

4-11. Obtain a plot of e_2 versus e for the piecewise-linear circuit of Fig. 4-26.

4-12. Obtain a piecewise-linear equivalent circuit for the vacuum-tube-diode characteristic shown in Fig. 4-28, using only one ideal rectifier.   Then,

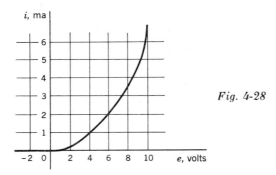

Fig. 4-28

using this equivalent circuit, calculate the operating point of this diode when
it is connected into the circuit of Fig. 4-29 and when $E = 10$ volts.   Repeat
this calculation for $E = 4$ volts.   Find the operating points by drawing load
lines on the characteristic curve.   Compare these results.

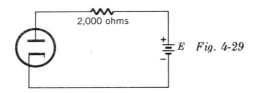

Fig. 4-29

4-13. Repeat Prob. 4-12, but now use a piecewise-linear circuit containing
two ideal rectifiers.   Compare these results with those of Prob. 4-12.

4-14. Sketch the i_b-versus-e_b characteristics of the piecewise-linear equivalent circuit for the vacuum-tube triode of Fig. 4-12b, if D_{p2} is replaced by an
open circuit.

4-15. Obtain a piecewise-linear equivalent circuit for the vacuum-tube
triode which approximates each characteristic curve with three straight-line
segments, rather than the two shown in Fig. 4-12a.

4-16. Determine the parameter values for the piecewise-linear equivalent
circuit of Fig. 4-12b for the 7027-A vacuum-tube triode.   Use this equivalent
circuit to determine the quiescent operating point when this tube is connected into the circuit of Fig. 4-30.   The plate characteristics of the triode

(connected) 7027-A vacuum tube are given in Fig. 1-20.   Compare this result with the value of the quiescent operating point obtained by a graphical analysis that uses a load line.

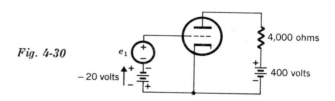

Fig. 4-30

4-17. Obtain the linear equivalent circuit for the 7027-A vacuum-tube triode which is valid for incremental changes about the graphically determined operating point obtained in Prob. 4-16.   Compare this circuit with the piecewise-linear equivalent circuit determined in Prob. 4-16.

4-18. Discuss how the form of the conventional linear equivalent circuit for the vacuum-tube pentode may be obtained from the piecewise-linear equivalent circuit of Fig. 4-13b.   Will the parameter values always be the same?

4-19. Determine the parameter values of the piecewise-linear equivalent circuit shown in Fig. 4-13b for the 6AU6 vacuum-tube pentode.   Use this equivalent circuit to obtain the operating point of the circuit shown in Fig. 4-31 and compare it to the value obtained graphically.   Assume that the screen grid-to-cathode voltage is 100 volts.   The plate characteristics of the 6AU6 vacuum-tube pentode are given in Fig. 1-27.

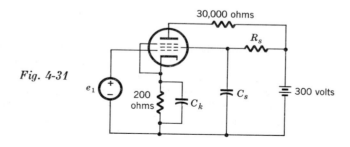

Fig. 4-31

4-20. Obtain piecewise-linear equivalent circuits for the *p-n-p* transistor whose characteristics are shown in Fig. 4-32, using first the circuit of Fig. 4-15 and then that of Fig. 4-16.

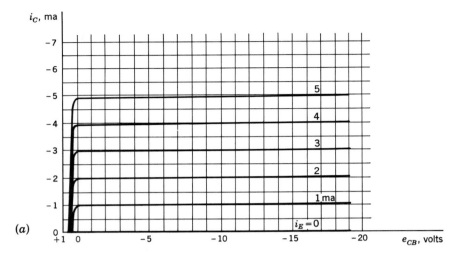

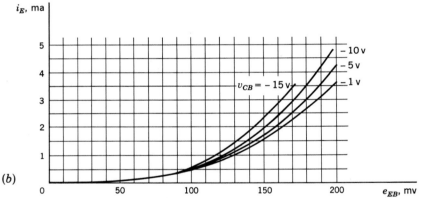

Fig. 4-32

4-21. Draw the input and output characteristics (i.e., i_B versus e_{BE} with e_{CE} as a parameter, and i_C versus e_{CE} with i_B as a parameter) for the piecewise-linear equivalent circuit of Fig. 4-18.

4-22. Use the piecewise-linear equivalent circuit of Fig. 4-15 to obtain expressions for all four coordinates of the quiescent operating point of the *p-n-p* transistor shown in Fig. 4-33. Note that E_{CC} is defined as negative.

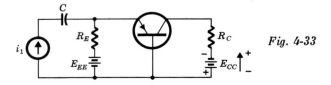

Fig. 4-33

4-23. Repeat Prob. 4-22, but now use the piecewise-linear equivalent circuit of Fig. 4-16.

4-24. Use the piecewise-linear equivalent circuit of Fig. 4-18 to obtain expressions for all four coordinates of the quiescent operating point of the *p-n-p* transistor of Fig. 4-34. Assume that $g - h_{oe}$ is a short circuit and r_{bc} and r_{be} are open circuits. Note that E_{CC} is defined as negative.

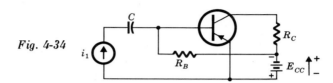

Fig. 4-34

4-25. Repeat Prob. 4-24 but do not neglect any elements.

4-26. Use the piecewise-linear equivalent circuit of Fig. 4-18 to obtain expressions for all four coordinates of the quiescent operating point of the *p-n-p* transistor shown in Fig. 4-35. Note that E_{CC} is defined as negative. Assume that $g - h_{oe}$ is a short circuit and that r_{be} and r_{bc} are open circuits.

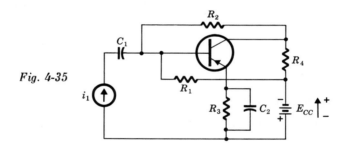

Fig. 4-35

4-27. Make a five-segment piecewise-linear approximation of the tunnel diode characteristic of Fig. 4-19a, and synthesize the corresponding piecewise-linear equivalent circuit, specifying all resistors in terms of the slopes of the segments.

Amplifier Fundamentals

5

One of the most important functions that vacuum tubes and transistors perform is that of amplification. That is, a small controlling signal is used to produce a larger signal of the same waveshape. In this chapter, we shall discuss amplifiers qualitatively and defer a discussion of their analysis and design to subsequent chapters.

5-1 Cascading of amplifiers

Vacuum-tube and transistor circuits can produce voltage, current, and power gains. In many instances, the gain of a single amplifier circuit is not sufficient, so amplifiers are cascaded. That is, the output of one amplifier is used to drive a succeeding one (see Fig. 5-1). The overall voltage and current gains of this device are given by

$$\mathbf{A}_v = \frac{\mathbf{E}_2}{\mathbf{E}_1} \tag{5-1}$$

$$\mathbf{A}_i = \frac{\mathbf{I}_2}{\mathbf{I}_1} \tag{5-2}$$

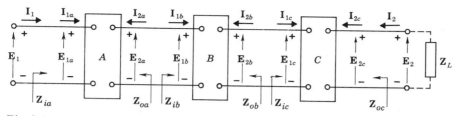

Fig. 5-1 A representation of a cascade of amplifier stages.

The overall power gain is given by

$$A_p = \frac{|E_2| \, |I_2| \cos \theta_2}{|E_1| \, |I_1| \cos \theta_1} \tag{5-3}$$

where θ_1 and θ_2 are the phase angles between $\mathbf{E}_1$ and $\mathbf{I}_1$ and between $\mathbf{E}_2$ and $\mathbf{I}_2$, respectively. The voltage and current amplification for the individual stages are given by

$$\mathbf{A}_{av} = \frac{\mathbf{E}_{2a}}{\mathbf{E}_{1a}} \qquad \mathbf{A}_{ai} = \frac{\mathbf{I}_{2a}}{\mathbf{I}_{1a}}$$

$$\mathbf{A}_{bv} = \frac{\mathbf{E}_{2b}}{\mathbf{E}_{1b}} \qquad \mathbf{A}_{bi} = \frac{\mathbf{I}_{2b}}{\mathbf{I}_{1b}} \tag{5-4}$$

$$\mathbf{A}_{cv} = \frac{\mathbf{E}_{2c}}{\mathbf{E}_{1c}} \qquad \mathbf{A}_{ci} = \frac{\mathbf{I}_{2c}}{\mathbf{I}_{1c}}$$

Making use of the relations

$$\mathbf{E}_1 = \mathbf{E}_{1a} \qquad \mathbf{E}_{2a} = \mathbf{E}_{1b} \qquad \mathbf{E}_{2b} = \mathbf{E}_{1c} \qquad \mathbf{E}_{2c} = \mathbf{E}_2$$

and

$$\mathbf{I}_1 = \mathbf{I}_{1a} \qquad \mathbf{I}_{2a} = -\mathbf{I}_{1b} \qquad \mathbf{I}_{2b} = -\mathbf{I}_{1c} \qquad \mathbf{I}_{2c} = \mathbf{I}_2 \tag{5-5}$$

we obtain

$$\mathbf{A}_v = \frac{\mathbf{E}_2}{\mathbf{E}_1} = \mathbf{A}_{av}\mathbf{A}_{bv}\mathbf{A}_{cv} \tag{5-6}$$

and

$$\mathbf{A}_i = \frac{\mathbf{I}_2}{\mathbf{I}_1} = \mathbf{A}_{ai}\mathbf{A}_{bi}\mathbf{A}_{ci} \tag{5-7}$$

In general, if we cascade n stages, we obtain

$$\mathbf{A}_v = \mathbf{A}_{1v}\mathbf{A}_{2v} \cdots \mathbf{A}_{nv} \tag{5-8}$$

$$\mathbf{A}_i = (-1)^{n+1}\mathbf{A}_{1i}\mathbf{A}_{2i} \cdots \mathbf{A}_{ni} \tag{5-9}$$

The factor $(-1)^{n+1}$ occurs in Eq. (5-9) because of the convention used in assigning the current.

The overall power gain is given by

$$A_p = |A_v| \, |A_i| \frac{\cos \theta_2}{\cos \theta_1} \tag{5-10}$$

If we define the power gain of an individual stage as the ratio of the power delivered to the next stage (or to the load) to the input power, then we have

$$A_p = A_{1p} A_{2p} \cdots A_{np} \tag{5-11}$$

Thus the overall voltage, current, and power gains are the products of the voltage gains, the current gains, and the power gains of the individual stages, respectively. Hence, extremely large gains can be obtained from amplifier stages that have only moderate gains.

5-2 Effect of input and output impedances on the gains of cascaded amplifier stages

In the discussion of the preceding section, we assumed that the gains of the amplifier stages were the actual operating gains. For instance, in Fig. 5-1, $\mathbf{A}_{av} = \mathbf{E}_{1a}/\mathbf{E}_{2a}$ represents the voltage gain of stage A *when it is terminated in the cascade of stages B and C and the load* $\mathbf{Z}_L$. In general, if the terminating impedance of stage A were changed, then the voltage gain would change. This also applies to current and power gains. Thus, when devices are cascaded, a knowledge of their input impedance is necessary if their operation is to be predicted. It is often tedious to determine the input impedance. For example, to determine $\mathbf{Z}_{ib}$, the input impedance of stage B, the terminating impedance of stage B must be known. This is given by $\mathbf{Z}_{ic}$, the input impedance of stage C. Thus, $\mathbf{Z}_{ic}$ must be calculated before $\mathbf{Z}_{ib}$ can be, and so forth. At times, there is isolation between the stages, so that the input impedance of one stage does not depend upon the termination of the succeeding stages. This greatly simplifies the calculations.

The output impedance of each amplifier stage is also important. Any amplifier can be characterized by Thévenin's theorem as a voltage generator in series with the output impedance. If the voltage source is replaced by a current source, then the amplifier can alternately be represented by a current generator in shunt with the output impedance (Norton's theorem). A convenient way of representing amplifiers is to assume that the input potential is 1 volt. Then, the voltage of the Thévenin's generator is equal to the open-circuit voltage gain. Such a representation is shown in Fig. 5-2a. Similarly, if an input current of 1 amp is assumed, the amplifier can be represented by the Norton's equivalent circuit of Fig. 5-2b. Note that Fig. 5-2a and b are not equivalent, since the amplifier inputs are different in each case. If the open-circuit voltage gain $\mathbf{A}_{v,oc}$ and the output impedance are known, then the voltage gain for any termination can be found. Similarly, the current gain can be found from $\mathbf{A}_{i,sc}$ and $\mathbf{Z}_o$. From Fig. 5-2a we see that if

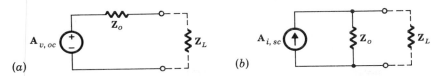

Fig. 5-2   (a) The Thévenin's equivalent circuit of an amplifier with a 1-volt input voltage. $A_{v,oc}$ is the voltage gain of the amplifier when the load impedance is an open circuit.   (b) The Norton's equivalent circuit of an amplifier with a 1-amp input current. $A_{i,sc}$ is the current gain of the amplifier when the load impedance is a short circuit.

$|Z_o| \ll |Z_L|$, the voltage gain will be approximately equal to $\mathbf{A}_{v,oc}$.   Similarly, using Fig. 5-2b, if $|Z_o| \gg |Z_L|$, the current gain is essentially given by $\mathbf{A}_{i,sc}$. Hence, if the impedance conditions are correct, the calculation of either the voltage gain or the current gain of an individual stage will depend only upon the parameters of that stage.

5-3   Coupling networks

Amplifier stages are not cascaded by just connecting the output of one stage to the input of the next.   This would be done if only signal considerations were involved.   However, the output bias voltage of an amplifier stage is usually quite different from the input bias voltage of the next amplifier stage, so more complex coupling techniques must be used.   For instance, in a vacuum-tube amplifier, the plate voltage may be several hundred volts positive, while the grid voltage is several volts negative.   We shall present the important amplifier coupling techniques in this section.   Quantitative discussions of the properties of these amplifiers will be given in Chap. 6.

Resistance-capacitance-coupled amplifiers

The direct bias voltage at the output of one stage can be isolated from the input to the next stage by placing a capacitor in series with the output as is shown in Fig. 5-3.   The coupling capacitors C_c act as open circuits for the direct bias voltages and prevent interaction of the output bias voltage of one stage with the input bias voltage of the next stage.   The value of C_c should be chosen so that it acts essentially as a short circuit at the signal frequencies. Actually we have oversimplified the problem somewhat.   When very low frequencies are used, C_c can no longer be considered to be a short circuit.   It acts as the series arm in a voltage divider and causes the amplification to decrease.   Although we have only illustrated the common-cathode vacuum-tube amplifier and the common-emitter transistor amplifier, the same coupling procedure can be used with other amplifier configurations.   Figure 5-4 illustrates this using the generalized device.   The elements of this coupling

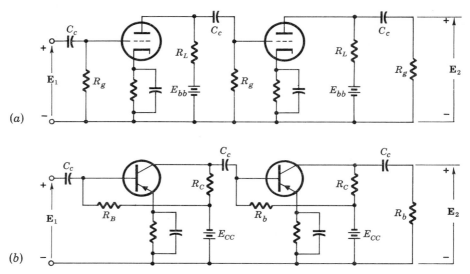

(a)

(b)

Fig. 5-3 Resistance-capacitance coupled amplifiers. (a) The common-cathode vacuum-tube amplifier; (b) the common-emitter transistor amplifier.

are resistances and capacitances, hence, the name resistance-capacitance coupling. This is often abbreviated as *RC* coupling.

Transformer-coupled amplifiers

A transformer performs the functions of a coupling network. That is, it transmits the alternating signal while "blocking" the direct bias voltage. A typical transformer-coupled amplifier is shown in Fig. 5-5. Transformers can be used as impedance-matching circuits. In addition, the direct current through their windings does not dissipate any power as it does in a load resistance. The ability of a transformer to step up the voltage or the current enables it to increase the voltage gain or the current gain of an amplifier. However, transformer coupling usually results in amplifiers that have poorer

Fig. 5-4 Resistance-capacitance coupled amplifier using the generalized device of Chap. 2. Point a is connected either to the common junction or to the power supply.

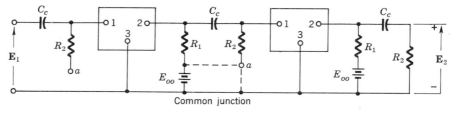

Common junction

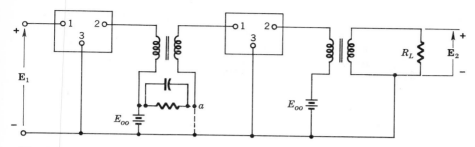

Fig. 5-5   A transformer-coupled amplifier.   Point a is connected either to the common junction or, through the RC network, to the power supply.

frequency responses and that are larger, heavier, and more expensive than *RC*-coupled amplifiers.

Direct-coupled amplifiers

An ideal coupling circuit is one that blocks the passage of direct voltages and currents but permits the passage of signal components.   Direct voltage is zero-frequency voltage and therefore these coupling circuits will not transmit zero-frequency signals.   Thus, the previously discussed coupling networks greatly attenuate signals that have extremely low-frequency com-

Fig. 5-6   Tuned amplifiers.   (a) Capacitor coupled; (b) mutual-inductance coupled.

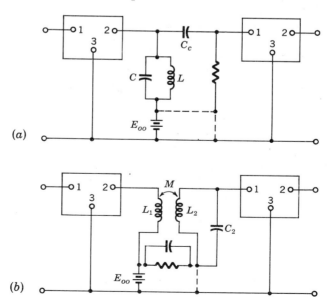

ponents.   One procedure that is used to amplify low-frequency signals is to connect the output of one stage directly to the input of the next one. Additional power supplies are then used to eliminate the effect of the unwanted bias voltages.   Such direct-coupled circuits will amplify all frequencies down to zero frequency.   However, there are many problems associated with direct-coupled amplifiers; hence they are only used where necessary.   These amplifiers are discussed in Sec. 6-27.

Tuned amplifiers

The amplifier interstages that have been discussed amplify a broad range of frequencies.   It is often desirable to amplify only a narrow range of frequencies and to reject all others.   Resonant circuits are usually used in such applications.   Fig. 5-6a is a simple tuned amplifier. C_c is a blocking capacitor that functions as it does in the RC-coupled amplifier of Figs. 5-3 and 5-4. The resonant circuit consisting of the inductor L and the capacitor C produces the frequency discrimination.   It presents a high impedance at the resonant frequency $1/(2\pi \sqrt{LC})$ and a low impedance at frequencies far removed from resonance.   The circuit of Fig. 5-6b also utilizes resonance. The two coils are coupled by mutual inductance and, hence, no blocking capacitor is required.

5-4   Decibel notation

Often it is desirable to express the power gain of a device in logarithmic form. This is true in audio devices, since the human ear functions logarithmically. If P_2 is the output power supplied to a load and P_1 is the input power, then the number of bels of power gain is given by

$$\text{No. of } b = \log_{10} \frac{P_2}{P_1} \tag{5-12}$$

The bel is usually too large a unit.   For this reason, the decibel, which is one-tenth of a bel, is usually used.   The number of decibels is given by

$$\text{No. of db} = 10 \log_{10} \frac{P_2}{P_1} \tag{5-13}$$

If the input impedance of the device is purely resistive and equal to R_1 and if the load impedance is purely resistive and equal to R_2, we have

$$\text{No. of db} = 10 \log_{10} \frac{|E_2|^2/R_2}{|E_1|^2/R_1} = 10 \log_{10} \frac{|I_2|^2 R_2}{|I_1|^2 R_1}$$

If $R_1 = R_2$ then we have

$$\text{No. of db} = 20 \log_{10} \left| \frac{E_2}{E_1} \right| = 20 \log_{10} \left| \frac{I_2}{I_1} \right| \tag{5-14}$$

Strictly speaking, the only time that Eq. (5-14) can be used is if the input and load resistances are equal. However, this relation is widely misused in that voltage ratios and current ratios are expressed in db even though $R_1 \neq R_2$. In such cases, the db voltage and db current ratios are not equal. It is permissible to use decibels in this way as long as it is understood that only a voltage ratio *or* a current ratio is expressed. The voltage, current, and power ratios will no longer be equal. If an amplifier has a voltage gain whose magnitude is A_v and a current gain whose magnitude is A_i, these can be expressed in db as

$$A_{v,\mathrm{db}} = 20 \log_{10} A_v \tag{5-15}$$
$$A_{i,\mathrm{db}} = 20 \log_{10} A_i \tag{5-16}$$

Note that $A_v \neq A_i$ and $A_{v,\mathrm{db}} \neq A_{i,\mathrm{db}}$. When amplifiers are cascaded, the overall gain is found by multiplying the gains of the individual stages. If the amplification of each stage is expressed in decibels, then the overall gain in decibels is found by adding the individual gains in decibels.

Although the decibel notation is a power ratio, at times it is modified to indicate an absolute level of power. In such cases, a standard reference level is chosen. For instance, the dbm is the number of decibels above one milliwatt and is given by

$$\text{No. of dbm} = 10 \log_{10} \frac{P}{10^{-3}} = 10 \log_{10} 10^3 P \tag{5-17}$$

where P is the power level in watts.

5-5   Classification of amplifiers

Many adjectives are used to describe amplifiers. For instance, the active device is usually specified (e.g., transistor amplifier or vacuum-tube amplifier). There are many other descriptive terms, and we shall discuss them here.

Voltage, current, and power amplifiers

Usually, an amplifier is designed to amplify either voltage, current, or power. For instance, if vacuum-tube amplifiers are cascaded, the function of each of the stages, except the last, is to provide a voltage that drives the next stage. Thus, these stages are called *voltage amplifiers* even though their current and power gains are large (and might be even larger than their voltage gain). Similarly, when transistor amplifiers are cascaded, all the stages but the last could be called *current amplifiers*. When the function of the amplifier is to supply power to a load, such as a loudspeaker, then it is classified as a *power amplifier*.

Small-signal and large-signal amplifiers

If an amplifier is operated such that linear analysis can be used, then it is called a small-signal amplifier.   If the operation is over such a large region of the static characteristics, so that graphical-analysis techniques are required, then it is called a large-signal amplifier.   Note that this classification depends upon the linearity of operation, not on any arbitrary signal level.

Classification according to operating frequency

Amplifiers are designed to amplify specific ranges of frequency.   For instance, an amplifier used in a sound system amplifies frequencies in the audible range (i.e., 20 to 20,000 cps).   Such an amplifier is called an *audio amplifier*.

The information in a standard television picture contains frequencies up to 4.5 Mc/sec.   An amplifier designed to amplify such signals is called a *video amplifier*.   Actually, the term "video amplifier" is applied to any *broad-band amplifier* whose frequency response is considerably greater than that of an audio amplifier.

Certain amplifiers are designed to pass a certain range of frequencies and to reject others.   Two such amplifiers are shown in Fig. 5-6.   These amplifiers utilize tuned circuits and are called *tuned amplifiers*.   These can be contrasted with audio and video amplifiers, which are designed to work over relatively broad ranges of frequency and do not use tuned circuits as such.   Hence they are called *untuned amplifiers*.

Class A, B, and C amplifiers

When an alternating signal is applied to an electronic device (e.g., vacuum tube or transistor) the instantaneous operating point will vary.   If the biasing voltage and the amplitude of the signal are such that the output current is never zero, then this is said to be *class A operation*.   (In the examples in Chap. 2, the operation was class A.)   If we consider the generalized circuit of Fig. 5-7, where the input bias is $X_{ii} = -4\Delta x$ and the signal is $x_1 = 2\Delta x \sin \omega t$, the operation will be class A.   If the input signal increases to $x_1 = 4\Delta x \sin \omega t$, then i_o will be zero for those times when $x_1 < -3\Delta x$. This will then not be class A operation.

If we change the quiescent input bias to $-7\Delta x$, the quiescent operating point will shift from point Q_1 to point Q_2.   The current i_o will only be nonzero when x_1 is positive, which is for one-half the cycle.   This is called *class B operation*.   If current is nonzero for more than one-half cycle but less than a full cycle, then the operation is called *class AB*.   For instance, if we return the quiescent operating point to Q_1 and apply a signal $x_1 = 4\Delta x \sin \omega t$, the operation will be class AB.

When output current is nonzero for substantially less than one half-cycle, then we have *class C* operation.   If the quiescent input bias is $X_{ii} = -10\Delta x$

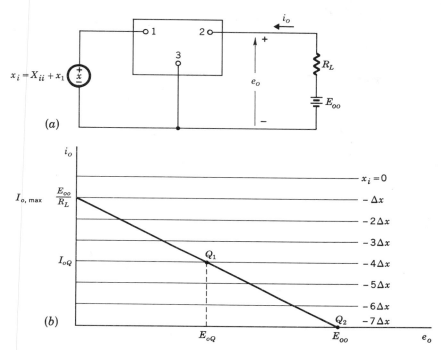

Figure 5-7   *(a) A simple amplifier circuit; (b) idealized characteristics for the generalized device and the load line for the amplifier.*

and $x_1 = 6\Delta x \sin \omega t$, then i_o will be nonzero only when $x_1 > 3\Delta x$. This will be class C operation. Note that when $x_i < -7\Delta x$, $i_o = 0$. Hence the curve labeled $-7\Delta x$ in Fig. 5-7b actually represents all the curves for values of input bias equal to or less than $-7\Delta x$.

Vacuum tubes are often operated so that the grid is maintained at a negative potential. Therefore, the grid current is zero. This is called *type 1* operation, and the subscript 1 can be added to the class of operation to indicate this (e.g., class A_1 operation). If there is grid current, then this is called *type 2* operation, and the subscript 2 can be added (e.g., class AB_2 operation).

5-6   Efficiency of ideal amplifiers

In Sec. 2-9 we discussed the output-circuit efficiency of generalized amplifiers. Let us now compute the maximum efficiency that an amplifier can have. It should be emphasized here that these calculations involve idealized characteristics and, thus, the efficiencies are much larger than in actual practice. The output-circuit efficiency is given by

$$\eta_2 = \frac{\text{a-c output power}}{\text{power supplied by power supply}} \times 100 = \frac{P_2}{P_{oo}} \times 100$$

Let us now consider the amplifier of Fig. 5-7, restricting the operation to class A. There is no distortion, so $P_{oo} = E_{oo}I_{oQ}$. The power P_{oo} is independent of the signal level. Hence, to obtain maximum efficiency, we use the largest signal which does not cause distortion. For the operating point shown, we have [see Eq. (2-40)]

$$\eta_{2,\max} = \frac{(E_{oo} - 0)(I_{o,\max} - 0)}{8E_{oo}I_{oQ}} \times 100$$

But $I_{o,\max} = 2I_{oQ}$; therefore

$$\eta_{2,\max} = 25\%\tag{5-18}$$

This efficiency is quite low. One reason is that the direct current I_{oQ} is through R_L and dissipates power in it. The use of the transformer-coupled circuit of Fig. 5-8a eliminates this problem. The load line in Fig. 5-8b is drawn with the assumption that the transformer is ideal. In order to obtain the largest possible output the operating point and R_L are adjusted so that

Fig. 5-8   (a) A simple transformer-coupled amplifier; (b) idealized characteristics for the generalized device and the load line for the amplifier. The slope of the load line is $-(n_1/n_2)^2 R_L$. The dashed load line is for class B operation.

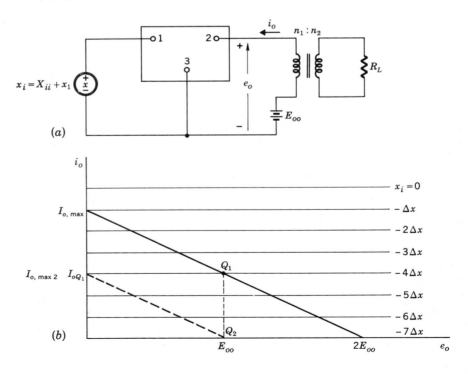

$E_{o,\max} = 2E_{oo}$. Then the efficiency is given by

$$\eta_{2,\max} = \frac{(I_{o,\max} - 0)(2E_{oo} - 0)}{8E_{oo}I_{oQ}}$$

Therefore

$$\eta_{2,\max} = 50\% \qquad\qquad\qquad (5\text{-}19)$$

This is a considerable improvement, but the efficiency is still quite low. So far we have only permitted class A operation. If this restriction is removed, the efficiency can be greatly increased. Let us now assume that the operation is class B. That is, for the circuit of Fig. 5-8, the quiescent input bias is shifted from $-4\Delta x$ to $-7\Delta x$. Note that if no signal is present, then $i_o = 0$ and $P_{oo} = 0$. We shall again assume maximum signal swing without distortion so that $x_1 = 6\Delta x \sin \omega t$. In this case

$$i_o = \begin{cases} I_{o;\max,2} \sin \omega t & \text{for } 0 \leqslant \omega t \leqslant \pi \\ 0 & \text{for } \pi \leqslant \omega t \leqslant 2\pi \end{cases}$$

Then $P_{oo} = E_{oo}I_{oA}$ where

$$I_{oA} = \frac{1}{2\pi} \int_0^{2\pi} i_o \, d\omega t$$

$$I_{oA} = \frac{I_{o;\max,2}}{\pi}$$

The instantaneous sinusoidal current is nonzero for only one half-cycle. Thus,

$$\eta_2 = \frac{(E_{oo} - 0)(I_{o;\max,2} - 0)(1/4)}{E_{oo}I_{o;\max,2}/\pi} \times 100$$

$$\eta_{2,\max} = \frac{\pi}{4} \times 100 = 78.5\% \qquad\qquad (5\text{-}20)$$

If we use class C operation, the maximum efficiency will be increased still further. In fact, it is theoretically possible to approach 100 percent efficiency. If class A operation is not used, then the signal will be distorted, since the output current will be zero for a portion of the cycle. This does not mean that we are always restricted to class A operation. In Chap. 7 we shall see that this distortion can be eliminated for class AB and for class B operation. In Chap. 8 we shall see how class C amplifiers can be utilized.

The calculations made in this section involved idealized characteristics. If characteristics of actual devices are used, the swing in output voltage and current has to be limited to prevent excessive distortion. Thus, the maximum efficiencies given here are high. For instance, in actual practice with vacuum tubes, the actual efficiencies may only be one-half of the predicted values. Larger swings are usually possible with transistors, and the efficiencies are closer to the maximum values. For class B and C operation, the reduction in efficiency is not as great. Class B efficiencies of 50 percent or more can be obtained readily. For class C operation, it is possible to obtain efficiencies of 85 to 90 percent or more. These calculations are based on sinusoidal signals. If other waveforms are used, the efficiencies can be higher. For instance, with class A operation, the circuit of Fig. 5-8a can have efficiencies that approach 100 percent if the input signal is a square wave. However, in most linear applications, the results obtained with sinusoids are typical.

5-7 Distortion

The output waveform of an ideal amplifier should be an exact reproduction of the input waveform multiplied by a constant. In an actual amplifier the output waveform will differ to some extent from that of the input. Such a difference in waveforms is termed *distortion*. There are two basic causes of distortion. One is the nonlinearity of the active element and is termed *non-linear distortion*. This was discussed in Secs. 2-10 and 2-11. The other is the variation of the parameters of the amplifier with frequency and is called *frequency distortion*. To illustrate, let us assume that a square wave, such as that shown in Fig. 5-9a, is applied to an amplifier. A Fourier analysis of this waveform yields

$$e_i(t) = \frac{4}{\pi} (\cos t - \tfrac{1}{3} \cos 3t + \tfrac{1}{5} \cos 5t - \tfrac{1}{7} \cos 7t + \cdots) \qquad (5\text{-}21)$$

If this signal were amplified by an ideal amplifier of voltage gain A, the output would be

$$e_o(t) = \frac{4A}{\pi} (\cos t - \tfrac{1}{3} \cos 3t + \tfrac{1}{5} \cos 5t - \tfrac{1}{7} \cos 7t + \cdots) \qquad (5\text{-}22)$$

If the amplification of all the frequencies is not the same, then the output and input waveforms will differ. The amplification is a complex number. Its magnitude is the magnitude, or amplitude, of the amplification; its phase angle is the phase shift of the amplifier. If there is to be no distortion, then

1. The magnitude of the amplification must not vary over the range of the input frequencies.
2. The phase shift over the range of input frequencies must be 0 or $\pm n\pi$, where n is an integer; or it must vary linearly with frequency such that the phase shift is given by $-k\omega$, where k is a positive constant.

Conditions (1) and (2) must be met if there is to be no frequency distortion. Distortion due to (1) is called *amplitude distortion;* that due to (2) is termed *phase distortion*. Typical effects of these distortions are shown in Fig. 5-9b and c.

If the magnitude of the amplification varies with frequency, then the relative magnitudes of the harmonics will vary with respect to each other. This will change the shape of the output waveform.

If the phase shift is zero degrees, then the phases of the various harmonics are undisturbed. Shifting the phase by an integral multiple of π radians is equivalent to multiplying the output by ± 1; this may produce a phase reversal but not distortion. The only other kind of phase characteristic that does not lead to distortion is one that just delays the signal in time. For instance, if $e_o(t) = e_i(t - \tau)$, that is, if the output is delayed by τ seconds, then

$$e_o(t) = \frac{4}{\pi} [\cos (t - \tau) - \tfrac{1}{3} \cos 3(t - \tau) + \tfrac{1}{5} \cos 5 (t - \tau) - \cdots]$$

or

$$e_o(t) = \frac{4}{\pi} [\cos (t - \tau) - \tfrac{1}{3} \cos (3t - 3\tau) + \tfrac{1}{5} \cos (5t - 5\tau) - \cdots]$$

$$(5\text{-}23)$$

In this case the phase shift $-k\omega = -\tau\omega$. Any other phase shift changes the phase angles among the various harmonics and leads to distortion.

Although we have discussed amplitude and phase distortion separately, they are related. In fact, very often, it is possible to calculate one from the knowledge of the other.

One means of rating the frequency distortion of an amplifier is to compare

Fig. 5-9   (a) A square wave; (b) and (c) typical effects of frequency distortion.

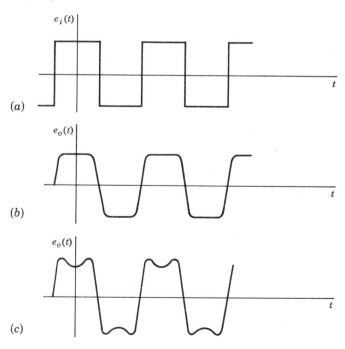

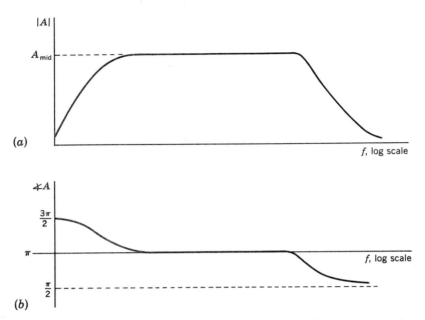

Fig. 5-10 (a) *A typical plot of the magnitude of amplification versus frequency;* (b) *a typical plot of the phase shift of an amplifier versus frequency. The frequency is plotted on a log scale so that the high- and low-frequency regions can be adequately displayed.*

an input square wave (or other standard waveform) with the output waveform. This is called the *transient response* of the amplifier and will be discussed further in Chap. 6. Another means of rating the amplifier is to plot the magnitude and phase of the amplifier versus frequency. Such plots are given in Fig. 5-10a and b. Since the frequency content of the input signal is usually known, these curves provide a means of determining the frequency distortion.

Very often there is a region where the magnitude of amplification remains essentially constant. Such a region is shown in Fig. 5-10a. The value of this amplification is designated A_{mid}. It is often convenient to normalize the curve by plotting $|A/A_{mid}|$ versus frequency. Such a graph is shown in Fig. 5-11a. This can be done since the amplitude distortion depends only upon the difference among the amplifications at the frequencies of interest and not upon the absolute values of the amplification at any one frequency. Thus, if the ordinate of Fig. 5-10a is divided by a constant, no information concerning frequency distortion is lost. A_{mid} is a convenient constant to divide by, since the response in the flat midband region becomes unity, and the relative response at other frequencies can be read off the graph. The *bandwidth* is defined as the useful range of frequencies of the amplifier. For instance, if the amplifier is to be used to amplify signals for an accurate voltmeter, the bandwidth might contain those frequencies where $0.95 \leqslant |A/A_{\mathrm{mid}}| \leqslant 1$. Such a bandwidth lies between f_{1a} and f_{2a} of Fig. 5-11a. On the other hand, for a less precise application, the bandwidth might lie between f_{1b} and f_{2b} where $0.5 \leqslant |A/A_{\mathrm{mid}}| \leqslant 1$. *Thus, for any specific device, the bandwidth depends upon the application for which it is to be used.* If such specific information is not present then the bandwidth is usually considered to be those frequencies between f_1 and f_2 where $0.707 = 1/\sqrt{2} \leqslant |A/A_{\mathrm{mid}}| \leqslant 1$. This is called *half-power bandwidth* and the frequencies f_1 and f_2 are called the *lower half-power frequency* and the *upper half-power frequency,* respectively. Note that if the output voltage falls off by $1/\sqrt{2}$, then the power delivered to a fixed resistance is halved.

Since the ear is a logarithmic device, the relative response of audio amplifiers is often plotted on a decibel basis. That is, we plot

$$\left| \frac{A}{A_{\mathrm{mid}}} \right|_{\mathrm{db}} = 20 \log_{10} \left| \frac{A}{A_{\mathrm{mid}}} \right| \tag{5-24}$$

Such a plot is shown in Fig. 5-11b. On a decibel basis, $1/\sqrt{2}$ corresponds to -3.0103 db ≈ -3 db. For this reason, the half-power frequencies are often called the *3-db frequencies.* In many applications, plots of frequency response in decibels versus frequency on a log scale approach a straight line.

Fig. 5-11 (a) *The normalized frequency response of an amplifier;* (b) *the normalized response plotted on a decibel basis.*

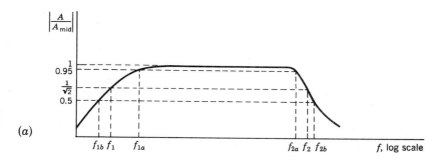

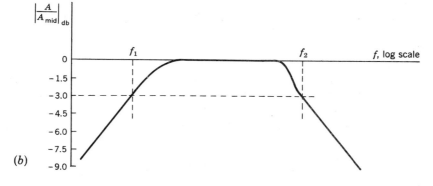

The logarithmic nature of the decibel allows both large and small amplitude variations to be displayed on the same set of axes.   For these reasons, plots of response in decibels are often used in applications other than audio amplifiers.

BIBLIOGRAPHY

Seely, S.: "Electron-tube Circuits," 2d ed., chap. 3, McGraw-Hill Book Company, New York, 1958.

PROBLEMS

5-1. Three identical amplifiers are cascaded as shown in Fig. 5-1.   The voltage gains of stages A and B are each -10 and the voltage gain of stage C is -5.   The current gains of stages A and B are each $+5$ while the current gain of stage C is $+15$.   Compute the voltage and current gains of the overall amplifier.

5-2. If the input impedance and the load impedance of the amplifier of Prob. 5-1 are purely resistive, what is the overall power gain?

5-3. Each one of the amplifiers of Fig. 5-1 has the following characteristics: open-circuit voltage gain -20; input impedance 1,000 ohms, independent of load impedance; output impedance 500 ohms, independent of input impedance. If $Z_L = 700$ ohms, compute the voltage, current, and power gains of the overall amplifier.   Repeat this problem, but now assume that the open-circuit voltage gain is unknown and that the short-circuit current gain is 40.

5-4. Repeat Prob. 5-3, but now assume that the load impedance is $100 + j1,000$ ohms.

5-5. An amplifier is to be made up of a cascade of amplifiers of the first type specified in Prob. 5-3.   The overall voltage gain is to have a magnitude of at least 10,000 and the load impedance is to be 100 ohms.   What is the minimum number of stages in cascade that can produce the required amplification?

5-6. The input impedance of a certain amplifier is 1,000 ohms.   Its load impedance is also 1,000 ohms.   The voltage gain of the amplifier is 20. Express the voltage gain, the current gain, and the power gain in decibels.

5-7. Repeat Prob. 5-6, but now assume that the load impedance is 2,000 ohms.   Assume that the input impedance and the voltage amplification do not change.   Explain why the gains in decibels do not equal each other.

5-8. The voltage gain of each amplifier in a cascade is 30 db.   There are five amplifiers in the cascade.   What is the voltage gain of the overall amplifier in decibels?   What is the numerical voltage gain of the amplifier?

5-9. The amplifier of Fig. 5-7a is operated such that $X_{ii} = -5\Delta x$.   If the operation is to be class A, what is the maximum signal that can be applied? Repeat this problem for the amplifier of Fig. 5-8a.

5-10. A generalized device has the characteristics shown in Fig. 5-12. The device is to be operated class A in the circuit of Fig. 5-8a.   What is the maximum output power that can be obtained if there is to be no distortion?   Use a power supply voltage $E_{oo} = 250$ volts.   Also determine the value of a-c load resistance, the output-circuit efficiency, the coordinates of the quiescent operating point, and the alternating input signal for operation at maximum efficiency. Assume that the characteristics extend linearly above $e_o = 300$ volts.

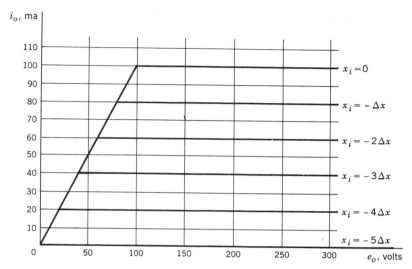

Fig. 5-12

5-11. Plot one period of the voltage of Eq. (5-21) using the first three terms in the Fourier series. Now assume that this waveform is applied to an amplifier with the following amplification:

$$A = \frac{10}{1 + j\omega}$$

Plot the output waveform.

5-12. An amplifier has a response such that

$$\frac{A}{A_{mid}} = \frac{1}{1 + j\omega/10,000} = \frac{1}{\sqrt{1 + (\omega/10,000)^2}} \quad \bigg/ - \tan^{-1} \frac{\omega}{10,000}$$

Plot the amplitude and phase response of this amplifier on semilog paper for frequencies from 100 to 100,000 cps. Find the upper half-power frequency. Find the frequency where the phase shift is $-45°$. Find the frequency where $|A/A_{mid}| = 0.9$.

5-13. An amplifier has a response such that

$$\frac{A}{A_{mid}} = \left(\frac{1}{1 - j10/\omega}\right)\left(\frac{1}{1 + j\omega/10,000}\right)$$

Plot the amplitude and phase response of this amplifier on semilog paper for frequencies from 1 to 100,000 cps. Find the upper and lower half-power frequencies. What approximations can be made in this problem?

5-14. Repeat Prob. 5-13, but now plot the amplitude response of the amplifier in decibels.

Class A
Small-signal
Amplifiers

Ideally the interstage networks that couple amplifier stages would pass the signal frequencies without attenuation and prevent the interaction of the bias voltages. Actually these networks do attenuate the signals, and this attenuation varies with frequency. The electronic devices themselves function differently at different frequencies. Thus, amplifiers will have responses that are functions of frequency.

In this chapter we shall determine the frequency response of commonly used amplifiers, and also consider amplifiers whose response is deliberately made to vary with frequency. We shall assume that the operation is class A and that the signal levels are small enough so that the operation is linear.

6-1 Frequency response of the RC-coupled common-cathode vacuum-tube amplifier

Resistance-capacitance coupling is a simple, inexpensive technique for cascading amplifier stages. It is used extensively for moderately broadband

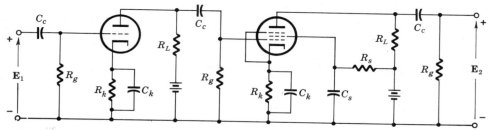

Fig. 6-1 RC-coupled common-cathode vacuum-tube amplifier stages. For purposes of illustration, a triode stage is cascaded with a pentode stage.

amplifiers. In Fig. 6-1, an RC-coupled common-cathode triode stage is shown coupled to an RC-coupled common-cathode pentode amplifier. When the frequency response of these amplifiers is to be determined, the interelectrode capacitances of the vacuum tubes must be considered as well as the elements of the coupling network. For the time being we shall assume that the bypass capacitors C_k and C_s are short circuits at the signal frequencies. The elements that will be considered in a single-stage triode amplifier are shown in Fig. 6-2. The capacitor C_o represents the plate-to-cathode capacitance C_{pk} plus any wiring capacitance between the leads to the plate and to the cathode. The stray capacitance between C_c and the lead connected to the cathode is included here also. The capacitor C_i represents the input capacitance of the next stage plus any stray wiring capacitance beyond C_c. In a vacuum-tube triode, C_i can be very much greater than the grid-to-cathode capacitance C_{gk}, because of the Miller effect (see Sec. 3-12). In Fig. 6-1, the next stage is a pentode and the Miller effect can be ignored. Actually, the input impedance of the vacuum tube is not purely capacitive. This is shown by Eqs. (3-103), (3-104), and (3-106). In most cases, however, accurate results are obtained if we consider that the input impedance is capacitive. C_c is the *coupling capacitor*. This is somewhat different from the others in that it is placed there deliberately. It is usually very much larger than C_o or C_i. An exact analysis of this amplifier would show that the output voltage would not be zero

Fig. 6-2 A representation of an RC-coupled amplifier showing only those elements that will be used in the calculation of the frequency response.

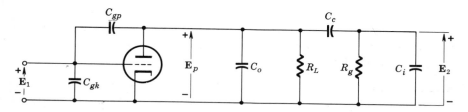

even if the μ and g_m of the tube were reduced to zero, because of the direct transmission of the signal through C_{gp}. This direct-transmission voltage can be neglected in most cases, since it is usually 1,000 or more times smaller than the voltage due to the amplification of the tube. We can then often neglect the presence of C_{gp} *provided that we compensate for it* in the following ways: (1) the capacitance C_{gp} cannot be ignored when C_i is computed, (2) the capacitance C_o tends to load down the output at high frequencies and, thus, reduce the gain. The component of the plate current through C_o is given by $j\omega C_o \mathbf{E}_p$. Similarly, the component of the plate current through C_{gp} is

$$j\omega C_{gp}(\mathbf{E}_p - \mathbf{E}_1) = j\omega C_{gp}\mathbf{E}_p\left(1 - \frac{\mathbf{E}_1}{\mathbf{E}_p}\right)$$

Because of the amplification $|E_p| \gg |E_1|$. Hence, the component of the plate current through C_{gp} is approximately $j\omega C_{gp}\mathbf{E}_p$. We can increase C_o by C_{gp} to account for the effect of C_{gp}. Thus, if we use C_{gp} in the computation of C_i, and if we increase C_o by C_{gp}, we can, to a high degree of accuracy, neglect C_{gp} otherwise. The symbol C_o will be considered to include C_{gp} henceforth.

If, in the pentode circuit of Fig. 6-1, we assume that the bypass capacitors C_k and C_s are short circuits, the representation of Fig. 6-2 becomes a valid one. Note that R_s is short-circuited and that the screen and suppressor grids are connected to the cathode. The capacitance C_o now represents the output capacitance of the pentode plus the wiring capacitance up to C_c. This capacitance should be increased by C_{gp} as it was in the case of the triode. However, in pentodes, C_{gp} is usually so small that it can be neglected. The output capacitance of a pentode is given by the sum of the capacitances between the plate and each of the cathode, the screen grid, and the suppressor grid:

$$C_{\text{out}} = C_{pk} + C_{pg2} + C_{pg3} \tag{6-1}$$

Similarly, the input capacitance of a pentode is the capacitance between the control grid and each of the cathode, the screen grid, and the suppressor grid:

$$C_{\text{in}} = C_{gk} + C_{gg2} + C_{gg3} \tag{6-2}$$

Fig. 6-3 *An equivalent circuit of the amplifier of Fig. 6-2. The modifications discussed in the text have been incorporated.*

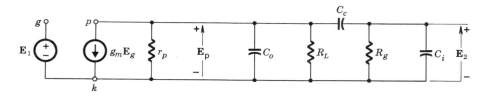

Note that the input and output capacitances of the pentode are computed as though the cathode, the screen grid, and the suppressor grid were all one electrode. The capacitor C_i is the sum of C_{in} for the next stage plus any wiring capacitance beyond C_c. Actually, the Miller effect should be considered in computing C_i, but C_{gp} is so small for pentodes that it can usually be neglected. The equivalent circuit of the amplifier of Fig. 6-2, subject to the modifications that we have discussed, is given in Fig. 6-3. Note that the capacitance C_{gk} has been neglected. This will affect the gain of a preceding stage, but not that of this one. Noting that $\mathbf{E}_g = \mathbf{E}_1$, we can write the following nodal equations:

$$-g_m\mathbf{E}_1 = \left[\frac{1}{r_p} + \frac{1}{R_L} + j\omega(C_o + C_c)\right]\mathbf{E}_p - j\omega\,C_c\mathbf{E}_2$$

$$0 = -j\omega C_c\mathbf{E}_p + \left[\frac{1}{R_g} + j\omega(C_i + C_c)\right]\mathbf{E}_2 \tag{6-3}$$

Solving for the voltage gain $\mathbf{A}_v = \mathbf{E}_2/\mathbf{E}_1$, we obtain

$$\mathbf{A}_v = \frac{-j\omega C_c g_m}{[1/r_p + 1/R_L + j\omega(C_o + C_c)][1/R_g + j\omega(C_i + C_c)] + \omega^2 C_c^2} \tag{6-4}$$

This expression can be simplified. However, we shall not do so, since we shall obtain much simpler expressions subsequently. The voltage gain $\mathbf{A}_v$ is a complex number that varies with frequency. A typical plot of the magnitude and phase of $\mathbf{A}_v$ versus frequency is shown in Fig. 6-4. The magnitude of the response is zero at zero frequency. It then rises to the value of $A_{v,\text{mid}}$ as the frequency increases. It remains essentially at this value as the frequency further increases and then finally begins to decrease. It falls off to zero as the frequency approaches infinity. In a similar way, the phase shift is 270° at zero frequency, decreases to 180°, remains essentially constant over a wide range of frequencies, and finally approaches 90°. Let us consider the reasons for this response. In the midband region, where $|A_v| \approx A_{v,\text{mid}}$ and $\measuredangle A \approx 180°$, the reactance of the coupling capacitor is very much smaller than the resistance of R_g; the reactances of the shunt capacitors C_o and C_i are very much greater than the resistance of the parallel combination of R_L, r_p, and R_g. Here, C_c can be approximated by a short circuit, and C_i and C_o can be approximated by open circuits. Thus, there is no variation of $\mathbf{A}_v$ with frequency. As the frequency is increased, the reactance of C_c decreases so that it still can be considered to be a short circuit. The reactances of C_o and C_i also decrease and can no longer be neglected, since they reduce the load impedance of the amplifier. As the load impedance decreases, the output voltage falls off and the phase shift departs from 180°. At frequencies below the midband range, the capacitors C_o and C_i can again be neglected, but now C_c can no longer be considered to be a short circuit. It acts as the series arm in a voltage divider and causes

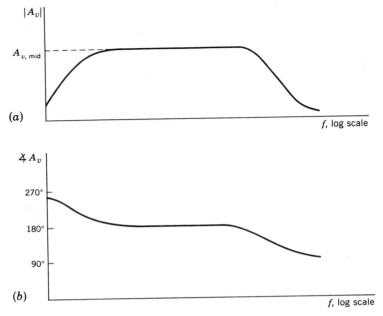

Fig. 6-4   *A plot of the frequency response of an RC-coupled amplifier.*
(a) The amplitude response; (b) the phase response.

the gain to fall off. In the preceding discussion, we have assumed that there are three well-defined regions. Actually, this need not be true. We can make C_c very small or add shunt capacitance to make C_o or C_i very large. Then there will be no range of frequencies where the capacitors can be ignored. There would then be no region of constant amplification. This would not be a practical amplifier. Actually, C_o and C_i represent stray capacitances and lie in the range 5 to 30 $\mu\mu$f. C_c is a coupling capacitor which is deliberately placed in the circuit; its range is usually between 0.01 and 0.5 μf. Thus, C_c may be 100,000 times as large as C_o or C_i. It is relatively easy to obtain a region of flat response. If we have an amplifier with a well-defined midband region, then it is valid to neglect C_o and C_i at low and mid-frequencies and to consider C_c to be a short circuit at mid and high frequencies.

Mid-frequency region

The modified form of Fig. 6-3 that is valid in the mid-frequency range is given in Fig. 6-5a. Let R_{sh} be the total resistance shunting the current generator. That is, R_{sh} is the parallel combination of r_p, R_L, and R_g.

$$\frac{1}{R_{sh}} = \frac{1}{r_p} + \frac{1}{R_L} + \frac{1}{R_g} = \frac{r_p R_L + r_p R_g + R_L R_g}{r_p R_L R_g} \tag{6-5}$$

Then

$$A_{v,\text{mid}} = -g_m R_{sh} = g_m R_{sh} \quad \underline{/180°} \tag{6-6}$$

High-frequency region

The equivalent circuit that is valid at high frequencies is given in Fig. 6-5b. Let C_{sh} be the total shunting capacitance

$$C_{sh} = C_o + C_i \tag{6-7}$$

Then

$$A_{v,\text{high}} = \frac{-g_m R_{sh}}{1 + j\omega R_{sh} C_{sh}} \tag{6-8}$$

We are often interested in the relative response of the amplifier (see Sec. 5-7).

$$\frac{A_{v,\text{high}}}{A_{v,\text{mid}}} = \frac{1}{1 + j\omega R_{sh} C_{sh}} \tag{6-9}$$

It is often convenient to express this relationship in terms of a constant

Fig. 6-5 (a) The mid-frequency equivalent circuit of an RC-coupled amplifier; (b) the high-frequency equivalent circuit; and (c) the low-frequency equivalent circuit.

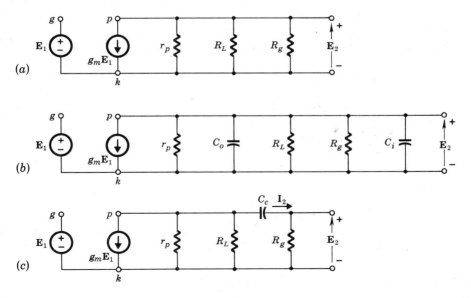

that is more general than a specific R_{sh} and C_{sh}.   To do this we let

$$\omega_2 = \frac{1}{R_{sh}C_{sh}}$$

or   (6-10)

$$f_2 = \frac{1}{2\pi R_{sh}C_{sh}}$$

Then

$$\frac{\mathbf{A}_{v,\text{high}}}{\mathbf{A}_{v,\text{mid}}} = \frac{1}{1 + j(f/f_2)} = \frac{1}{\sqrt{1 + (f/f_2)^2}} \qquad \underline{/-\tan^{-1}(f/f_2)} \qquad (6\text{-}11)$$

The significance of this equation will be discussed after we consider the low-frequency response.

Low-frequency region

The equivalent circuit for this region is shown in Fig. 6-5c.   The current I_2 is

$$\mathbf{I}_2 = \frac{-g_m\mathbf{E}_1 r_p R_L/(r_p + R_L)}{[r_p R_L/(r_p + R_L)] + R_g - j/\omega C_c}$$

Let

$$R_{\text{low}} = R_g + \frac{r_p R_L}{r_p + R_L} \qquad (6\text{-}12)$$

Note that R_{low} represents R_g in series with the parallel combination of r_p and R_L.   Then, since $\mathbf{A}_{v,\text{low}} = \mathbf{I}_2 R_g/\mathbf{E}_1$ and $R_{sh} = r_p R_L R_g/R_{\text{low}}(r_p + R_L)$, we have

$$\mathbf{A}_{v,\text{low}} = \frac{-g_m R_{sh}}{1 - j(1/\omega C_c R_{\text{low}})} \qquad (6\text{-}13)$$

If we let

$$\omega_1 = \frac{1}{C_c R_{\text{low}}}$$

or   (6-14)

$$f_1 = \frac{1}{2\pi C_c R_{\text{low}}}$$

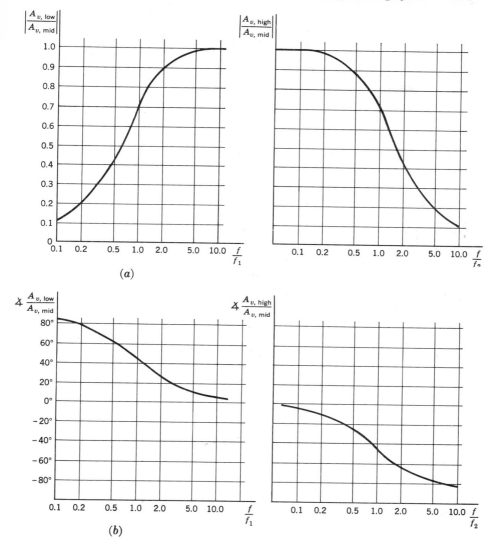

Fig. 6-6   (*a*) *The normalized amplitude response of an RC-coupled common-cathode vacuum-tube amplifier;* (*b*) *the normalized phase response.*

Then

$$\frac{\mathbf{A}_{v,\text{low}}}{\mathbf{A}_{v,\text{mid}}} = \frac{1}{1 - j(f_1/f)} = \frac{1}{\sqrt{1 + (f_1/f)^2}} \qquad \underline{/\tan^{-1}(f_1/f)} \qquad (6\text{-}15)$$

Figure 6-6 is a plot of amplitude and the phase of $\mathbf{A}_{v,\text{low}}/\mathbf{A}_{v,\text{mid}}$ and $\mathbf{A}_{v,\text{high}}/\mathbf{A}_{v,\text{mid}}$. The values of f_1 and f_2 correspond to the lower and upper half-power frequencies, respectively. The phase angles at f_1 and f_2 are $+45°$ and $-45°$, respectively. Note that these phase angles represent departures from the midband phase angle of 180°. In the midband region and at higher frequencies $A_{low}/A_{mid} \approx 1$, while in the midband region and at lower frequencies $A_{high}/A_{mid} \approx 1$. Thus, an approximate expression for the normalized gain that is valid at all frequencies is

$$\frac{A}{A_{mid}} = \frac{1}{[1 - j(f_1/f)][1 + j(f/f_2)]} \tag{6-16}$$

If the upper and lower half-power frequencies are known, then the frequency response of any *RC*-coupled amplifier is determined. That is, insofar as the frequency response is concerned, only f_1 and f_2 need be known but not any of the circuit elements. The approximations made here depend upon having a well-defined mid-frequency region. This will occur if $f_2 \gg f_1$. If the approximate response given by Eqs. (6-11) and (6-15) or by Eq. (6-16) is compared with the actual response given by Eq. (6-4), it is found[1] that the error in the amplitude will be less than 0.5 percent if $f_2 \geqslant 100f_1$. If $f_2 \geqslant 25f_1$, then the error in the amplitude will be less than 2 percent. If f_2 is not at least $10f_1$, the approximations should not be used. Actually, these requirements are not very stringent. Even poor audio amplifiers (for example, $f_1 = 50$ cps and $f_2 = 5{,}000$ cps) are such that $f_2 = 100f_1$. Actually, in most practical cases, $f_2 \gg 100f_1$.

Logarithmic plots of $|A_v/A_{mid}|$ are quite useful (see Sec. 5-7).

$$\left|\frac{A_{v,high}}{A_{v,mid}}\right|_{db} = 20 \log_{10} \frac{1}{\sqrt{1 + (f/f_2)^2}}$$

Thus,

$$\left|\frac{A_{v,high}}{A_{v,mid}}\right|_{db} = -10 \log_{10}\left[1 + \left(\frac{f}{f_2}\right)^2\right] \tag{6-17}$$

Let us consider the asymptotes of this response. If $f/f_2 \ll 1$,

$$\left|\frac{A_{v,low}}{A_{v,mid}}\right|_{db} = 0 \tag{6-18}$$

and if $f/f_2 \gg 1$,

$$\left|\frac{A_{v,high}}{A_{v,mid}}\right|_{db} = -20 \log_{10} \frac{f}{f_2} \tag{6-19}$$

If Eqs. (6-18) and (6-19) are plotted to a $\log_{10}(f/f_2)$ frequency scale, they will be straight lines. These asymptotes, as well as the actual curve, are shown in Fig. 6-7. Let us determine the slope of the asymptotic response. A band of frequencies from f_a to f_b is called an *octave* if $f_b = 2f_a$. If $f_b = 10f_a$

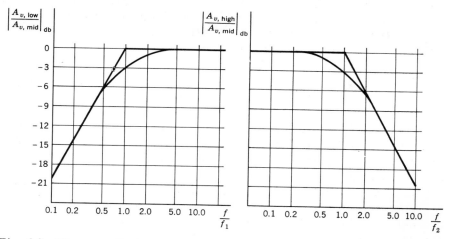

Fig. 6-7 *The normalized amplitude response of an RC-coupled common-cathode vacuum-tube amplifier plotted on a decibel basis.*

then the frequency band is called a *decade*. $\text{Log}_{10} 2 \approx 0.3$ and $\log_{10} 10 = 1$. Thus, the asymptotic slope is -6 db/octave or, equivalently, -20 db/decade. We can make an equivalent set of statements for the low-frequency response.

$$\left| \frac{A_{v,\text{low}}}{A_{v,\text{mid}}} \right|_{\text{db}} = -10 \log_{10} \left[1 + \left(\frac{f_1}{f} \right)^2 \right] \tag{6-20}$$

If $f_1/f \ll 1$,

$$\left| \frac{A_{v,\text{low}}}{A_{v,\text{mid}}} \right|_{\text{db}} = 0 \tag{6-21}$$

If $f_1/f \gg 1$,

$$\left| \frac{A_{v,\text{low}}}{A_{v,\text{mid}}} \right|_{\text{db}} = -20 \log_{10} \left(\frac{f_1}{f} \right) \tag{6-22}$$

A plot of this is also given in Fig. 6-7. The fact that the asymptotes can be drawn quite easily, and that the curve is fairly well approximated by them, makes the decibel plot convenient to use.

6-2   Factors affecting the frequency response of *RC*-coupled vacuum-tube amplifiers

The amplification of an *RC*-coupled vacuum-tube amplifier is completely specified if we know $A_{v,\text{mid}} = -g_m R_{sh}$, $f_1 = 1/(2\pi R_{\text{low}} C_c)$, and $f_2 = 1/(2\pi R_{sh} C_{sh})$.

The overall bandwidth of the amplifier is increased by increasing f_2 and by decreasing f_1. Let us consider what is involved in doing this. In order to decrease f_1, we must increase R_{low} or C_c. The resistance R_{low} consists of R_g in series with the parallel combination of R_L and r_p. The size of R_L is limited by high-frequency considerations, as we shall see, and by the fact that it is in series with the power supply. R_L is usually very much less than R_g. Thus,

$$R_{low} \approx R_g \tag{6-23}$$

R_g can be made as large as grid-leak considerations permit (see Sec. 2-2). If we wish to reduce f_1 any further, then C_c must be increased. In theory, C_c can be made as large as desired. In practice, the size of C_c is limited. If C_c is larger than 0.5 to 1.0 $\mu\mu$f, it becomes large and expensive. The increased physical size not only increases the dimensions of the amplifier, but also increases C_{sh}. This is because C_c possesses stray capacitance to the metallic chassis, which is usually at the same potential as the cathode at high frequencies. Thus, if the physical size of C_c is too great, the high-frequency response will suffer. (Note that the value of C_c itself does not affect the high-frequency response; rather it is the stray capacitance between it and the chassis.) *Electrolytic capacitors* combine large capacitance with small size. Unfortunately, they are not suitable for use as coupling capacitors in vacuum-tube circuits, since their leakage resistance is too low in comparison with R_g. Their leakage resistance also tends to fluctuate. The lowest value of f_1 that is obtained with an RC-coupled amplifier is usually in the vicinity of 1 cps. If lower values of f_1 are required, then other coupling techniques should be used.

In order to increase the value of f_2 we must decrease R_{sh} and C_{sh}. The shunt capacitance can be minimized by choosing tubes with small interelectrode capacitances. If values of f_2 greater than 50 kc/sec are desired, then pentodes should be used, since the Miller effect precludes the use of triodes. Careful wiring, with short leads, will tend to reduce the wiring capacitance. However, there is a certain minimum value below which C_{sh} cannot be reduced. To increase f_2 further, we must decrease R_{sh}. The upper half-power frequency can be made as large as desired in this case, but reducing R_{sh} reduces the magnitude of the midband gain, $g_m R_{sh}$. Thus, in effect, we can trade gain for high-frequency bandwidth. The product of the *midband gain and high-frequency bandwidth*, or, more simply, the *gain-bandwidth product* can be obtained from Eqs. (6-6) and (6-10).

$$|A_{v,\text{mid}}|f_2 = \frac{g_m}{2\pi C_{sh}} \tag{6-24}$$

Thus, the product of the midband gain and f_2 is a constant. It is desirable to make this constant as large as possible. When identical pentode stages are cascaded, $C_{sh} = C_{\text{out}} + C_{\text{in}} + C_w$ where C_w is the stray wiring capacitance.

Thus, $C_{out} + C_{in}$ represents the vacuum tube's contribution to the shunt capacitance. The quantity $g_m/2\pi(C_{out} + C_{in})$ is a figure of merit that indicates the ability of the pentode to function as a high-frequency amplifier. A good figure of merit for a pentode is 150 Mc/sec. We can adjust the mid-band gain and f_2 by varying R_{sh}, which consists of r_p, R_L, and R_g in parallel. Usually R_g is made as large as possible because of low-frequency considerations. The plate resistance r_p is usually quite large and cannot be easily changed in any event. Usually in pentode amplifiers $r_p \gg R_L$ and $R_g \gg R_L$ so that

$$R_{sh} \approx R_L \tag{6-25}$$

6-3   Frequency response of the RC-coupled common-emitter transistor amplifier

A cascade of common-emitter RC-coupled transistor amplifiers is shown in Fig. 6-8. We shall obtain the frequency response for a typical stage of this amplifier. For the time being, let us assume that the emitter bypass capacitor C_E is a short circuit at all frequencies of interest. The h-parameter equivalent circuit for a typical stage is given in Fig. 6-9. We have assumed that the simplified common-emitter h parameters given by Eq. (3-131) can be used here. This assumption is valid except in the case of amplifiers with a very large high-frequency bandwidth. To compensate somewhat for the approximation, the capacitor C_i is added to the circuit. This accounts for shunting capacitance at the input to the next stage and also for stray wiring capacitance. We then assume that the remaining input impedance can be represented by a constant resistance R_i. We shall further discuss this assumption subsequently. The current gain is $\mathbf{A}_i = \mathbf{I}_2/\mathbf{I}_1$. Hence, the overall current gain of the amplifier will be the product of the current gains of each stage. We shall compute the current gain, since it is fundamental in transistors. Transistor action is current-controlled, and more insight can be gained if the transistor is considered on a current basis. (Computation of the voltage gain is quite similar and will be left as an exercise.)

Fig. 6-8   A cascade of RC-coupled common-emitter transistor amplifier stages.

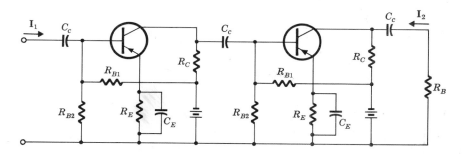

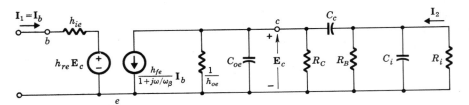

Fig. 6-9   The h-parameter equivalent circuit for one stage of the amplifier of Fig. 6-8. It is assumed that C_E is a short circuit.   Note that $R_B = R_{B1}R_{B2}/(R_{B1} + R_{B2})$; that is, R_B is the parallel combination of R_{B1} and R_{B2}.

As in the case of the *RC*-coupled vacuum-tube amplifier, practical *RC*-coupled transistor amplifiers will have well-defined mid-frequency, high-frequency, and low-frequency regions.   An equivalent circuit can be drawn for each of these regions.   These are shown in Fig. 6-10, where we have made use of the fact that $I_B = I_1$.

Mid-frequency region

The current gain $A_{i,\text{mid}} = I_2/I_1$ can be obtained from Fig. 6-10a by noting that $I_2 = -E_c/R_i$.   Then, if we let

$$\frac{1}{R_{sh}} = h_{oe} + \frac{1}{R_c} + \frac{1}{R_B} + \frac{1}{R_i} \tag{6-26}$$

we obtain

$$A_{i,\text{mid}} = \frac{h_{fe}R_{sh}}{R_i} \tag{6-27}$$

Note that R_{sh} is the parallel combination of the resistors $1/h_{oe}$, R_c, R_B, and R_i.   If $R_i \to 0$, then $R_{sh} \to R_i \to 0$ and $A_{i,\text{mid}} = h_{fe}$.

High-frequency region

The equivalent circuit of Fig. 6-10b can be analyzed in a manner similar to that of Fig. 6-10a.   The variation of h_{fe} with frequency, as well as the shunting effect of C_{oe} and C_i, must be included here.

$$A_{i,\text{high}} = \frac{h_{fe}}{1 + j\omega/\omega_\beta} \cdot \frac{R_{sh}}{1 + j\omega R_{sh}C_{sh}} \cdot \frac{1}{R_i}$$

where C_{sh} is the total shunt capacitance.

$$C_{sh} = C_{oe} + C_i \tag{6-28}$$

Thus

$$\frac{\mathbf{A}_{i,\text{high}}}{\mathbf{A}_{i,\text{mid}}} = \frac{1}{1 + j\omega/\omega_\beta} \cdot \frac{1}{1 + j\omega R_{sh}C_{sh}} \tag{6-29}$$

Let

$$\omega_2 = \frac{1}{R_{sh}C_{sh}}$$

or
$$\tag{6-30}$$

$$f_2 = \frac{1}{2\pi R_{sh}C_{sh}}$$

Then

$$\begin{aligned}\frac{\mathbf{A}_{i,\text{high}}}{\mathbf{A}_{i,\text{mid}}} &= \frac{1}{1 + jf/f_\beta} \cdot \frac{1}{1 + jf/f_2} \\ &= \frac{1}{\sqrt{1 + (f/f_\beta)^2}} \cdot \frac{1}{\sqrt{1 + (f/f_2)^2}} \quad \underline{/-\tan^{-1} f/f_\beta - \tan^{-1} f/f_2}\end{aligned} \tag{6-31}$$

Fig. 6-10   (a) *The mid-frequency;* (b) *high-frequency; and* (c) *low-frequency equivalent circuits for the amplifier of Fig. 6-9.*

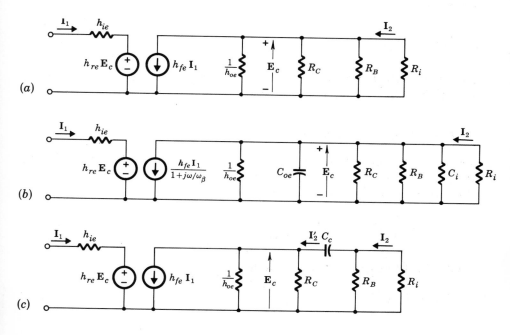

Low-frequency region

The equivalent circuit that is valid in the low-frequency region is given in Fig. 6-10c. We can write

$$\mathbf{A}_{i,\text{low}} = \frac{\mathbf{I}_2}{\mathbf{I}_1} = \frac{\mathbf{I}'_2}{\mathbf{I}_1}\frac{\mathbf{I}_2}{\mathbf{I}'_2}$$

Hence

$$\mathbf{A}_{i,\text{low}} = h_{fe} \cdot \frac{R_C/(1 + h_{oe}R_C)}{R_C/(1 + h_{oe}R_C) + R_BR_i/(R_B + R_i) + 1/j\omega C_c} \cdot \frac{R_B}{R_B + R_i}$$

Let

$$R_{\text{low}} = \frac{R_C}{1 + h_{oe}R_C} + \frac{R_BR_i}{R_B + R_i} \tag{6-32}$$

Thus

$$\mathbf{A}_{i,\text{low}} = \frac{h_{fe}R_BR_C}{R_C(R_B + R_i) + R_BR_i(1 + h_{oe}R_C)} \cdot \frac{1}{1 - j/\omega C_cR_{\text{low}}} \tag{6-33}$$

Then, rearranging, we obtain

$$\frac{\mathbf{A}_{i,\text{low}}}{\mathbf{A}_{i,\text{mid}}} = \frac{1}{1 - j/\omega C_cR_{\text{low}}} \tag{6-34}$$

Let

$$\omega_1 = \frac{1}{C_cR_{\text{low}}}$$

or   (6-35)

$$f_1 = \frac{1}{2\pi C_cR_{\text{low}}}$$

Therefore

$$\frac{\mathbf{A}_{i,\text{low}}}{\mathbf{A}_{i,\text{mid}}} = \frac{1}{1 - jf_1/f} = \frac{1}{\sqrt{1 + (f_1/f)^2}} \quad \underline{/\tan^{-1} f_1/f} \tag{6-36}$$

Equation (6-36) has the same form as Eq. (6-15), which gives the low-frequency response of the common-cathode vacuum-tube amplifier. Thus, the low-frequency plots of Fig. 6-6a and b apply here also. Again f_1 is the lower half-power frequency and the phase angle at this frequency is 45°.

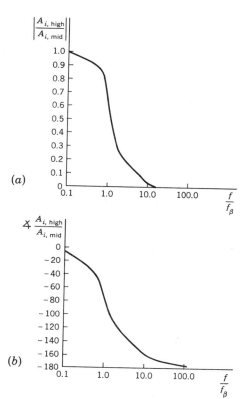

Fig. 6-11 (a) The normalized amplitude response curve of an RC-coupled transistor amplifier; (b) the normalized phase response curve. A value of $f_2 = 2f_\beta$ was chosen for this curve.

The high-frequency response given by Eq. (6-31) differs from the high-frequency response of the common-cathode vacuum-tube amplifier given by Eq. (6-11) in that there are two factors in the denominator. For this reason the high-frequency transistor response will fall off as $1/\omega^2$ rather than as $1/\omega$, and the phase shift of $\mathbf{A}_{i,\text{high}}/\mathbf{A}_{i,\text{mid}}$ will approach 180° as $\omega \to \infty$. A sketch of a typical high-frequency response is shown in Fig. 6-11. The half-power frequency occurs when

$$\frac{1}{\sqrt{1 + (f/f_\beta)^2}} \cdot \frac{1}{\sqrt{1 + (f/f_2)^2}} = \frac{1}{\sqrt{2}}$$

Solving, we obtain

$$f_{\frac{1}{2}} = \left\{ \frac{1}{2}\,(f_\beta{}^2 + f_2{}^2) \left[\sqrt{1 + \frac{4f_\beta{}^2 f_2{}^2}{(f_\beta{}^2 + f_2{}^2)^2}} - 1 \right] \right\}^{\frac{1}{2}} \tag{6-37}$$

The phase shift at this frequency can be found from the angle of Eq. (6-31). Figure 6-11 is a plot of $|A_{i,\text{high}}/A_{i,\text{mid}}|$ for $f_2 = 2f_\beta$. The abscissa is normalized with respect to f_β. Actually, we cannot draw a generalized curve as we have done for the common-cathode vacuum-tube amplifier, since the relation between f_2 and f_β is variable. A single equation that presents both the low- and high-frequency response is given by

$$\frac{\mathbf{A}_i}{\mathbf{A}_{i,\text{mid}}} = \frac{1}{1 - jf_1/f} \cdot \frac{1}{1 + jf/f_2} \cdot \frac{1}{1 + jf/f_\beta} \tag{6-38}$$

The accuracy of the equations developed in this section depends upon there being a well-defined midband region. In almost all practical amplifiers, this will be true. General statements about the magnitude of the error cannot be made, since the relationship between f_2 and f_β can vary. However, the statements concerning accuracy that were made in Sec. 6-1 are approximately correct, provided that the term f_2, in Sec. 6-1, is replaced by $f_{1/2}$.

As in the case of the vacuum tube, logarithmic plots of $|A_i/A_{i,\text{mid}}|$ are quite useful.

$$\left|\frac{A_{i,\text{high}}}{A_{i,\text{mid}}}\right|_{\text{db}} = -10 \log_{10}\left[1 + \left(\frac{f}{f_\beta}\right)^2\right]\left[1 + \left(\frac{f}{f_2}\right)^2\right] \tag{6-39}$$

Let us determine the asymptotes for this response
If $f_\beta \gg f$, and $f_2 \gg f$,

$$\left|\frac{A_{i,\text{high}}}{A_{i,\text{mid}}}\right|_{\text{db}} = 0 \tag{6-40}$$

If $f_\beta \ll f$, and $f_2 \gg f$,

$$\left|\frac{A_{i,\text{high}}}{A_{i,\text{mid}}}\right|_{\text{db}} = -20 \log_{10}\frac{f}{f_\beta} \tag{6-41}$$

If $f_2 \ll f$, and $f_\beta \gg f$,

$$\left|\frac{A_{i,\text{high}}}{A_{i,\text{mid}}}\right|_{\text{db}} = -20 \log_{10}\frac{f}{f_2} \tag{6-42}$$

If $f \gg f_\beta$ and $f \gg f_2$,

$$\left|\frac{A_{i,\text{high}}}{A_{i,\text{mid}}}\right|_{\text{db}} = -20 \log_{10}\frac{f}{f_\beta} - 20 \log_{10}\frac{f}{f_2} \tag{6-43}$$

Thus, the asymptotes will have the following slopes when plotted on a log frequency scale:

$$f < f_\beta \text{ and } f < f_2 \quad \text{slope} = 0 \text{ db/octave}$$

$$\left.\begin{array}{l} f > f_\beta \text{ and } f < f_2 \\ f > f_2 \text{ and } f < f_\beta \end{array}\right\} \quad \text{slope} = -6 \text{ db/octave} \quad (-20 \text{ db/decade}) \quad (6\text{-}44)$$

$$f > f_2 \text{ and } f > f_\beta \quad \text{slope} = -12 \text{ db/octave} \quad (-40 \text{ db/decade})$$

A plot of $|A_{i,\text{high}}/A_{i,\text{mid}}|_{\text{db}}$ is given in Fig. 6-12, where $f_2 = 10f_\beta$.

The normalized low-frequency response has the same form as that for the common-cathode vacuum-tube amplifier. Thus, Eqs. (6-20) to (6-22) apply here also. The low-frequency curve of Fig. 6-7 also can be used if the ordinate is labeled $|A_{i,\text{low}}/A_{i,\text{mid}}|_{\text{db}}$.

The convenience of the decibel plots can be especially appreciated in the case of the high-frequency response. Even though the equations are somewhat complex, the asymptotes can be drawn quite easily and the approximate curves can then be sketched. In general, if we are plotting a curve of the function

$$\frac{A}{A_\text{mid}} = \frac{1}{\sqrt{1 + (f/f_a)^2}} \cdot \frac{1}{\sqrt{1 + (f/f_b)^2}} \cdot \frac{1}{\sqrt{1 + (f/f_c)^2}} \cdots$$

$$f_a < f_b < f_c \cdots \quad (6\text{-}45)$$

Fig. 6-12 *The normalized amplitude response of an RC-coupled common-emitter transistor amplifier plotted on a decibel basis, $f_2 = 10f_\beta$.*

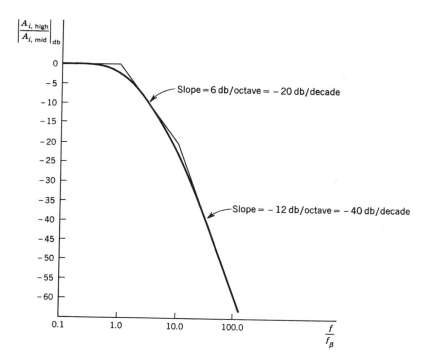

on a decibel basis, the slopes of the asymptotes will have the following values:

$$f_a < f < f_b \qquad \text{slope} = -6 \text{ db/octave} \qquad (-20 \text{ db/decade})$$
$$f_b < f < f_c \qquad \text{slope} = -12 \text{ db/octave} \qquad (-40 \text{ db/decade}) \qquad (6\text{-}46)$$
$$f_c < f \qquad \text{slope} = -18 \text{ db/octave} \qquad (-60 \text{ db/decade})$$

The frequencies f_a, f_b, f_c, . . . , where the slope of the asymptotes changes abruptly, are called the *break points*. If the break points are well separated, then the curve will differ from the asymptotes by 3 db at a break point.

We have assumed in this section that R_i, the input resistance of a common-emitter transistor amplifier, does not vary with frequency. Let us consider the validity of this assumption. From Eq. (3-85), the input impedance of a common-emitter transistor amplifier is given by

$$\mathbf{Z}_i = h_{ie} - \frac{\mathbf{h}_{fe}h_{re}\mathbf{Z}_L}{1 + h_{oe}\mathbf{Z}_L} \qquad (6\text{-}47)$$

At sufficiently high frequencies both $\mathbf{h}_{fe}$ and $\mathbf{Z}_L$ become zero. Thus,

$$\mathbf{Z}_{i,\text{high}} = h_{ie} \qquad (6\text{-}48)$$

At low frequencies, C_c approaches an open circuit and $\mathbf{Z}_L$ approaches R_C (see Fig. 6-10c).

$$Z_{i,\text{low}} = h_{ie} - \frac{h_{fe}h_{re}R_C}{1 + h_{oe}R_C} \qquad (6\text{-}49)$$

These represent two extremes in input resistances. Let us consider some typical values and see how much they actually differ. We shall assume that $h_{ie} = 2{,}000$ ohms, $h_{re} = 6 \times 10^{-4}$, $h_{fe} = 50$, and $h_{oe} = 25 \times 10^{-6}$ mho. Thus,

$$Z_{i,\text{high}} = R_{i,\text{high}} = 2{,}000 \text{ ohms}$$
$$Z_{i,\text{low}} = R_{i,\text{low}} = 2{,}000 - \frac{300 \times 10^{-4}R_C}{1 + 25 \times 10^{-6}R_C} \text{ ohms}$$

The value of R_C usually does not exceed 10,000 ohms. Then

$$Z_{i,\text{low}} = R_{i,\text{low}} = 1{,}760 \text{ ohms}$$

This does not represent a substantial change in resistance. Usually, smaller values of R_C are used, which results in a much smaller change in R_i. Note that R_i is calculated in the midband region where $Z_L = R_{sh}$. Then

$$R_{i,\text{low}} \leqslant R_i \leqslant R_{i,\text{high}}$$

Thus, for the figures used, the average change in R_i would be 6.5 percent. The input impedance will not be purely resistive at all frequencies. However, the magnitude of the reactive component usually can be ignored. In addition, C_i will somewhat account for its effect.

In this section we have used the h-parameter equivalent circuit that was derived from Eqs. (3-131). If we wish to operate at higher frequencies, then the h parameter of Eqs. (3-130) should be used. This will be done in Sec. 6-12. The common-base h-parameter equivalent circuit can also be used if more accuracy is desired.

6-4 Factors affecting the frequency response of RC-coupled common-emitter transistor amplifiers

The amplification of the RC-coupled common-emitter transistor amplifier is completely specified if $A_{i,\text{mid}} = h_{fe}R_{sh}/R_i$, $f_1 = 1/2\pi R_{\text{low}}C_c$, $f_2 = 1/2\pi R_{sh}C_{sh}$, and f_β are known. The overall bandwidth will increase if we decrease the lower half-power frequency f_1 and we increase the upper half-power frequency $f_{1/2}$. Let us consider what is involved in obtaining a required midband gain and high-frequency bandwidth.

The value of $h_{fe} = \beta_0$ depends upon the transistor itself. The larger β_0 is, the larger will be the midband gain. The term R_{sh}/R_i is the ratio of the parallel combination of $1/h_{oe}$, R_c, R_B, and R_i to R_i. If R_i is reduced, then R_{sh}/R_i increases and approaches unity as $R_i \to 0$. This increases $A_{i,\text{mid}}$. However, R_i often depends almost entirely upon the parameters of the transistor in the next stage and cannot be varied at will. If R_{sh} is varied without changing R_i, then $A_{i,\text{mid}}$ will vary directly with R_{sh}.

In order to decrease f_1 we must increase the size of R_{low} or C_c. The resistance R_{low} is made up of the parallel combination of $1/h_{oe}$ and R_C in series with the parallel combination of R_B and R_i. It is, of course, desirable to have $1/h_{oe}$, R_C, and R_B as large as possible. However, the size of R_C is limited, since the direct-bias current must pass through it. The value of R_B is determined from bias and stability considerations. Thus, R_{low} cannot be varied too readily. The principal way to lower f_1 is to increase C_c. In general, R_{low} for a common-emitter transistor is considerably less than it is for a vacuum tube. Thus, comparatively large values of C_c are required. The resistance levels in transistor circuits are relatively low. Hence, electrolytic capacitors can be used as the coupling capacitors, since their leakage resistance will be thousands of times greater than the bias impedances. This, and the fact that low voltages are encountered in transistor circuits, results in large capacitances with relatively small physical size. Note that the physical size of a capacitor varies directly with its rated working voltage.

High-frequency response depends upon f_β and f_2. The beta cutoff frequency f_β is a function of the transistor and does not vary with the circuit parameters. High-frequency response is improved as f_β is increased. Transistor manuals usually specify f_α. We then obtain f_β from Eq. (3-125). The frequency f_2 is given by $1/2\pi R_{sh}C_{sh}$. Most of C_{sh} is made up of C_{oe}. This is given by $C_{ob}/(1 - \alpha_0)$, where C_{ob} is the collector-base junction capacitance. The value of C_{ob}, as well as that of the α-cutoff frequency f_α, varies greatly with transistor type. Alloyed-junction transistors are low-frequency types.

Their α-cutoff frequencies are in the range of megacycles and C_{ob} is in the range of tens of $\mu\mu$f. In the drift transistor, the α-cutoff frequencies are in the range of tens of megacycles and the values of C_{ob} are of the order of several $\mu\mu$f. The value of f_2 can be increased by decreasing C_{sh} or R_{sh}. It is presumed that C_{sh} is kept small by the proper choice of a transistor and by careful wiring. Any further increase in f_2 must be accomplished by decreasing R_{sh}. If this is done by decreasing R_i, then the midband gain and f_2 will both increase. However, as we have seen, R_i cannot easily be varied. If R_{sh} is reduced without varying R_i (probably by reducing R_C), then $A_{i,\text{mid}}$ will decrease. From Eqs. (6-27) and (6-30), we have

$$A_{i,\text{mid}}f_2 = \frac{h_{fe}}{2\pi R_i C_{sh}} \tag{6-50}$$

Note that this product depends not only on the transistor parameters but also upon R_i. We can now trade midband gain for f_2. However, f_2 is not the only factor that affects the frequency response. From Fig. 6-12 we can see that if $f_2 \gg f_\beta$, then f_2 will have very little effect on the frequency response in the useful range of frequencies. Thus, too great an increase in f_2 only reduces the overall gain without effectively increasing the bandwidth.

6-5   Effect of impedance in cathode and screen-grid circuits

In the analysis of Sec. 6-1, we assumed that the cathode and screen-grid bypass capacitors had zero impedance at any signal frequencies. At low frequencies, the reactance of the capacitors increases and this assumption is not valid. The low-frequency response must, therefore, be modified. The case of the vacuum-tube triode will be considered first. A low-frequency equivalent circuit is given in Fig. 6-13. In general, $R_L \ll R_g$. Thus, $Z \approx R_L$. The voltage gain $\mathbf{A}'_{v,\text{low}} = \mathbf{E}'_2/\mathbf{E}'_1$ is then given by Eq. (3-42)

$$\mathbf{A}'_{v,\text{low}} = \frac{-\mu R_L}{r_p + R_L + \mathbf{Z}_k(1 + \mu)} \tag{6-51}$$

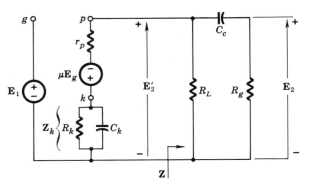

Fig. 6-13   A low-frequency equivalent circuit for the RC-coupled triode amplifier.

where

$$\mathbf{Z}_k = \frac{R_k}{1 + j\omega C_k R_k} \tag{6-52}$$

Then, substituting and rearranging, we obtain

$$\mathbf{A}'_{v,\text{low}} = \frac{-g_m r_p R_L}{r_p + R_L} \cdot \frac{1}{1 + \dfrac{R_k(1 + \mu)}{r_p + R_L}} \cdot \frac{1 + j\omega C_k R_k}{1 + \dfrac{j\omega C_k R_k}{1 + R_k(1 + \mu)/(r_p + R_L)}}$$

Since $R_g \gg R_L$, we can write

$$\frac{r_p R_L}{r_p + R_L} \approx R_{sh}$$

Therefore [see Eq. (6-6)]

$$\frac{\mathbf{A}'_{v,\text{low}}}{\mathbf{A}_{v,\text{mid}}} = \frac{1}{1 + \dfrac{R_k(1 + \mu)}{r_p + R_L}} \cdot \frac{1 + j\omega C_k R_k}{1 + \dfrac{j\omega C_k R_k}{1 + R_k(1 + \mu)/(r_p + R_L)}} \tag{6-53}$$

At sufficiently high frequencies $A'_{v,\text{low}}/A_{v,\text{mid}}$ approaches unity as it should, because C_k then acts as a short circuit. As the frequency decreases, $A'_{v,\text{low}}/A_{v,\text{mid}}$ decreases. Its minimum value is given by

$$\frac{\mathbf{A}'_{v,\text{low}}}{\mathbf{A}_{v,\text{mid}}}\bigg|_{\text{min}} = \frac{r_p + R_L}{r_p + R_L + R_k(1 + \mu)} \tag{6-54}$$

Notice that the unbypassed cathode impedance does not cause the gain to become zero. Let

$$f_{k1} = \frac{1}{2\pi C_k R_k} \tag{6-55}$$

and

$$f_{k2} = \frac{1 + R_k(1 + \mu)/(r_p + R_L)}{2\pi C_k R_k} \tag{6-56}$$

Note

$$f_{k2} > f_{k1}$$

Then

$$\frac{\mathbf{A}'_{v,\text{low}}}{\mathbf{A}_{v,\text{mid}}} = \frac{f_{k1}}{f_{k2}} \cdot \frac{1 + jf/f_{k1}}{1 + jf/f_{k2}} = \frac{f_{k1}}{f_{k2}} \sqrt{\frac{1 + (f/f_{k1})^2}{1 + (f/f_{k2})^2}} \quad \bigg/ \tan^{-1}\frac{f}{f_{k1}} - \tan^{-1}\frac{f}{f_{k2}} \tag{6-57}$$

Plots of the magnitude and phase of this expression are given in Fig. 6-14*a* and *b*. Note that there is a positive phase angle which approaches zero at sufficiently low or high frequencies.   On a decibel basis

$$\left| \frac{A'_{v,\text{low}}}{A_{v,\text{mid}}} \right|_{\text{db}} = -20 \log_{10} \frac{f_{k2}}{f_{k1}} + 10 \log_{10} \left[1 + \left(\frac{f}{f_{k1}} \right)^2 \right]$$
$$- 10 \log_{10} \left[1 + \left(\frac{f}{f_{k2}} \right)^2 \right] \quad (6\text{-}58)$$

A plot of this expression, with its asymptotes, is shown in Fig. 6-14c.   Again note that we can draw the asymptotes between the break points very simply.

Fig. 6-14   The low-frequency response of a vacuum-tube triode amplifier due to the cathode-bias circuit.   (a) The amplitude response;   (b) the phase response;   (c) the amplitude response plotted on a decibel basis.

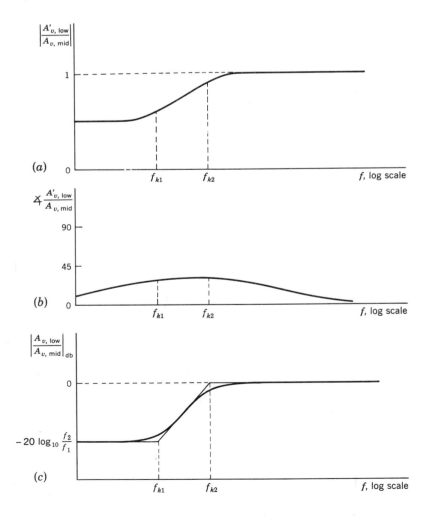

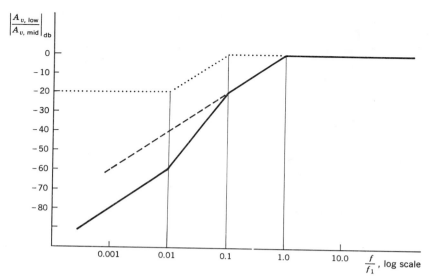

Fig. 6-15　Typical low-frequency response of an RC-coupled amplifier. The dashed curve is the response due to the coupling network alone and the dotted one is the response due to the cathode (or emitter) impedance alone. Only the asymptotes have been drawn.

To obtain the frequency response of the entire stage, we must include the effect of the coupling network. If $R_g \gg R_L$ we can assume that R_g and C_c have no effect on $\mathbf{E}_2'$ and that $\mathbf{E}_2/\mathbf{E}_2'$ is given by Eq. (6-15). The overall gain of the amplifier can be found by taking the product of Eqs. (6-15) and (6-57). Hence,

$$\frac{\mathbf{A}_{v,\text{low}}}{\mathbf{A}_{v,\text{mid}}} = \frac{f_{k1}}{f_{k2}} \cdot \frac{1 + jf/f_{k1}}{1 + jf/f_{k2}} \cdot \frac{1}{1 - jf_1/f} \tag{6-59}$$

A plot of $|A_{v,\text{low}}/A_{v,\text{mid}}|$ on a decibel basis is shown in Fig. 6-15.

The cathode-bias circuit causes the gain to fall off for frequencies near and between f_{k1} and f_{k2}. To improve the low-frequency response, f_{k1} and f_{k2} should be made small. Since the value of R_k is fixed by grid-bias considerations, C_k is used to adjust the frequency response. Values of C_k between 20 μf and 1,000 μf are usually required and electrolytic capacitors are used. Because of the small direct bias voltages, these capacitors occupy relatively small spaces. If C_k is reduced to zero, then f_{k1} and f_{k2} both approach infinity. There is no longer any variation of gain with frequency. However, the gain at all frequencies will be reduced by the factor given in Eq. (6-54). Sometimes this loss in gain is tolerated, because the frequency response is improved. Actually, C_k cannot be reduced to zero, because of stray capacitance across R_k. If C_k is to be ignored, then f_{k1}, which is calculated on the basis of the stray capacitance, must be somewhat higher than the highest input frequency.

When vacuum-tube pentodes are used, we must consider the effect not only of the cathode bias impedance but also of the impedance in the screen-grid circuit. The screen potential cannot be considered constant, and the more general form of the equivalent circuit of Sec. 3-19 must be used. The pentode circuit of Fig. 3-45 is the one that we shall analyze here. It is cumbersome, and we shall make some approximations[2,3] that simplify our results without creating a large error. These are:

1. The plate resistance r_p is very much larger than any resistance shunting it, so that we can consider r_p to be an open circuit.

2. The plate voltage is sufficiently high so that both the plate and screen currents are independent of the plate voltage. We can then write the approximate relation

$$\mathbf{I}_s = \delta \mathbf{I}_p \tag{6-60}$$

where δ is a constant.

3. $R_g \gg R_L$, so that the effective load resistance is R_L. Using these assumptions, the equivalent circuit of Fig. 3-45b becomes that of Fig. 6-16. The notation $g_m = g_{pg}$ has been used here. The voltage across R_L is given by

$$\mathbf{E}_2' = -\mathbf{I}_p R_L$$

and

$$\mathbf{I}_p = g_{ps}\mathbf{E}_s + g_m\mathbf{E}_g \tag{6-61}$$

Let

$$\mathbf{Z}_k = \frac{R_k}{1 + j\omega C_k R_k} \tag{6-62}$$

Fig. 6-16   An equivalent circuit for the vacuum-tube pentode, which can be used to account for the effects of the cathode and screen-grid bias circuits.

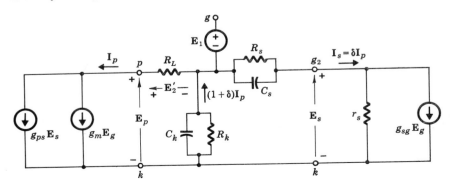

and

$$\mathbf{Z}_s = \frac{R_s}{1 + j\omega C_s R_s} \tag{6-63}$$

Then

$$\mathbf{E}_g = \mathbf{E}_1 - \mathbf{I}_p(1 + \delta)\mathbf{Z}_k$$

$$\mathbf{E}_s = -\mathbf{I}_p[\delta\mathbf{Z}_s + (1 + \delta)\mathbf{Z}_k]$$

Substituting in Eq. (6-61), and rearranging, we obtain

$$\mathbf{A}'_{v,\text{low}} = \frac{\mathbf{E}'_2}{\mathbf{E}_1} = \frac{-g_m R_L}{1 + (1 + \delta)(g_m + g_{ps})\mathbf{Z}_k + \delta g_{ps}\mathbf{Z}_s} \tag{6-64}$$

Since $R_L \gg R_g$ and $r_p = \infty$, we can write

$$R_L \approx R_{sh}$$

Let

$$f_{k1} = \frac{1}{2\pi R_k C_k} \tag{6-65}$$

$$f_{s1} = \frac{1}{2\pi R_s C_s} \tag{6-66}$$

Then

$$\frac{\mathbf{A}'_{v,\text{low}}}{\mathbf{A}_{v,\text{mid}}} = \frac{1}{1 + \dfrac{R_k(1 + \delta)(g_m + g_{ps})}{1 + jf/f_{k1}} + \dfrac{R_s \delta g_{ps}}{1 + jf/f_{s1}}} \tag{6-67}$$

At sufficiently high frequencies, $\mathbf{A}'_{v,\text{low}}/\mathbf{A}_{v,\text{mid}}$ becomes unity. Its minimum value is

$$\left|\frac{\mathbf{A}'_{v,\text{low}}}{\mathbf{A}_{v,\text{mid}}}\right|_{\min} = \frac{1}{1 + R_k(1 + \delta)(g_m + g_{ps}) + R_s \delta g_{ps}} \tag{6-68}$$

To simplify this expression, let

$$\gamma_k = R_k(1 + \delta)(g_m + g_{ps}) \tag{6-69}$$

$$\gamma_s = R_s \delta g_{ps} \tag{6-70}$$

Then

$$\frac{\mathbf{A}'_{v,\text{low}}}{\mathbf{A}_{v,\text{mid}}} = \frac{(1 + jf/f_{k1})(1 + jf/f_{s1})}{(1 + \gamma_k + \gamma_s)\left[1 + \dfrac{jf}{1 + \gamma_k + \gamma_s}\left(\dfrac{1 + \gamma_s}{f_{k1}} + \dfrac{1 + \gamma_k}{f_{s1}}\right) + \dfrac{(jf)^2}{(1 + \gamma_k + \gamma_s)f_{k1}f_{s1}}\right]} \tag{6-71}$$

The term in the bracket is a quadratic in the variable jf. It can always be factored into the form $(1 + jf/f_{k2})(1 + jf/f_{s2})$. Hence

$$\frac{\mathbf{A}'_{v,\text{low}}}{\mathbf{A}_{v,\text{mid}}} = \frac{1}{1 + \gamma_k + \gamma_s}\frac{(1 + jf/f_{k1})(1 + jf/f_{s1})}{(1 + jf/f_{k2})(1 + jf/f_{s2})} \tag{6-72}$$

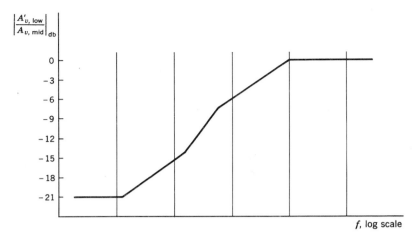

Fig. 6-17   A typical low-frequency amplitude response of a vacuum-tube-pentode amplifier due to the cathode and screen-bias circuits.   Each division on the frequency scale corresponds to an octave.   Only the asymptotes have been drawn.

Since $\mathbf{A}'_{v,\text{low}}/\mathbf{A}_{v,\text{mid}} \to 1$ as $f \to \infty$, we have

$$\frac{f_{k2}f_{s2}}{f_{k1}f_{s1}} = 1 + \gamma_k + \gamma_s \tag{6-73}$$

The frequencies f_{k2} and f_{s2} cannot be associated with the screen or cathode impedances in any simple fashion.   A typical plot in decibels of $|A'_{v,\text{low}}/A_{v,\text{mid}}|$ is given in Fig. 6-17.   As in the case of the triode, the overall low-frequency gain can be found by multiplying Eq. (6-72) by Eq. (6-15), thus

$$\frac{\mathbf{A}_{v,\text{low}}}{\mathbf{A}_{v,\text{mid}}} = \frac{1}{1 + \gamma_k + \gamma_s} \frac{(1 + jf/f_{k1})(1 + jf/f_{s1})}{(1 + jf/f_{k2})(1 + jf/f_{s2})} \frac{1}{1 - jf_1/f} \tag{6-74}$$

6-6   Effect of impedance in the emitter circuit

In the analysis of Sec. 6-3, we assumed that the stabilizing impedance, consisting of C_E in parallel with R_E, had zero impedance at all frequencies of interest.   Its effect will now be taken into account.   The equivalent circuit that will be used is shown in Fig. 6-18.   The conventional h-parameter equivalent circuit has been modified slightly by replacing the current generator with a voltage generator.   Then, writing mesh equations, and making use of the relation $\mathbf{E}_c = -(h_{fe}/h_{oe})\,\mathbf{I}_b + (1/h_{oe})\mathbf{I}_3$, we have

$$\mathbf{E}_1 = \left(h_{ie} + \mathbf{Z}_E - \frac{h_{re}h_{fe}}{h_{oe}}\right)\mathbf{I}_1 + \left(\mathbf{Z}_E + \frac{h_{re}}{h_{oe}}\right)\mathbf{I}_3 \tag{6-75}$$

$$0 = \left(\mathbf{Z}_E - \frac{h_{fe}}{h_{oe}}\right)\mathbf{I}_1 + \left(\mathbf{Z}_E + \frac{1}{h_{oe}} + \mathbf{Z}\right)\mathbf{I}_3 \tag{6-76}$$

where

$$\mathbf{Z}_E = \frac{R_E}{1 + j\omega R_E C_E} \qquad (6\text{-}77)$$

The effect that $\mathbf{Z}_E$ has on the current gain can be determined by considering the ratio $\mathbf{I}_3/\mathbf{I}_1$.

$$\frac{\mathbf{I}_3}{\mathbf{I}_1} = \frac{h_{fe} - h_{oe}\mathbf{Z}_E}{1 + h_{oe}\mathbf{Z} + h_{oe}\mathbf{Z}_E} \qquad (6\text{-}78)$$

Since R_E is usually no larger than several thousand ohms, $|h_{oe}\mathbf{Z}_E| \ll 1$. Equation (6-78) then becomes

$$\frac{\mathbf{I}_3}{\mathbf{I}_1} = \frac{h_{fe}}{1 + h_{oe}\mathbf{Z}}$$

This is independent of $\mathbf{Z}_E$. This seems to indicate that the emitter stabilizing impedance will not affect the gain of a cascade of amplifiers. However, it does, since the input impedance varies greatly with $\mathbf{Z}_E$. Thus, a change in $\mathbf{Z}_E$ in the next stage will vary $\mathbf{I}_2/\mathbf{I}_2'$ and, consequently, the current gain. It will be assumed that the input impedance $\mathbf{Z}_i$ of each stage in the cascade is identical, and that the impedance $\mathbf{Z}$ is purely resistive and equal to the parallel combination of R_C, R_B, and R_i. (Note R_i is the midband value of $\mathbf{Z}_i$.) The magnitude of $\mathbf{Z}$ can never be greater than R_c; thus, it will not increase greatly at low frequencies even though the impedance of C_c and $\mathbf{Z}_i$ will. Then, replacing $\mathbf{Z}$ by R, where

$$\frac{1}{R} = \frac{1}{R_C} + \frac{1}{R_B} + \frac{1}{R_i} \qquad (6\text{-}79)$$

and solving Eqs. (6-75) and (6-76), we obtain

$$\mathbf{Z}_i = \frac{h_{ie}(1 + h_{oe}R) - h_{re}h_{fe}R + \mathbf{Z}_E[1 + h_{oe}R + h_{ie}h_{oe} - h_{re}h_{fe} - h_{re} + h_{fe}]}{1 + h_{oe}R + h_{oe}\mathbf{Z}_E}$$

$$(6\text{-}80)$$

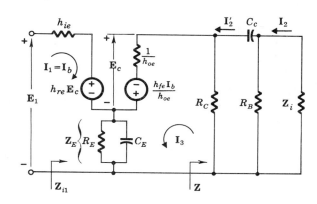

Fig. 6-18 A low-frequency equivalent circuit for the RC-coupled transistor amplifier.

Making use of the relation $1 + h_{oe}\mathbf{Z}_E \approx 1$, and Eq. (3-85), we have

$$\mathbf{Z}_i = R_i + \frac{\mathbf{Z}_E[1 + h_{oe}R + h_{ie}h_{oe} - h_{re}h_{fe} - h_{re} + h_{fe}]}{1 + h_{oe}R} \tag{6-81}$$

Using the inequalities of relation (3-62) and noting that $h_{fe} \gg 1 + h_{oe}R$, results in

$$\mathbf{Z}_i \approx R_i + \frac{\mathbf{Z}_E h_{fe}}{1 + h_{oe}R} \tag{6-82}$$

The current-divider ratio $\mathbf{I}_2/\mathbf{I}_2'$ is

$$\frac{\mathbf{I}_2}{\mathbf{I}_2'} = \frac{R_B}{R_B + \mathbf{Z}_i}$$

Then

$$\frac{\mathbf{I}_2}{\mathbf{I}_2'} = \frac{R_B}{R_B + R_i} \cdot \frac{1}{1 + \gamma_E} \cdot \frac{1 + jf/f_{e1}}{1 + jf/f_{e2}} \tag{6-83}$$

where

$$\gamma_E = \frac{R_E h_{fe}}{(1 + h_{oe}R)(R_B + R_i)} \tag{6-84}$$

$$f_{e1} = \frac{1}{2\pi R_E C_E} \tag{6-85}$$

$$f_{e2} = (1 + \gamma_E)f_{e1}$$

The magnitude of $\mathbf{I}_2'/\mathbf{I}_2$ varies between $R_B/(R_B + R_i)$, the midband value, and $R_B/[(R_B + R_i)(1 + \gamma_E)]$, the value at zero frequency. Plots of the magnitude and phase of $\mathbf{I}_2'/\mathbf{I}_2$ versus frequency will have the same shape as the curve of Fig. 6-14. To obtain the expression for the overall current gain, multiply Eq. (6-36) by

$$\frac{\mathbf{I}_2}{\mathbf{I}_2'} \frac{R_B + R_i}{R_B}$$

[Note that the factor $(R_B + R_i)/R_B$ has already been taken into account in Eq. (6-36).]

$$\frac{\mathbf{A}_{i,\text{low}}}{\mathbf{A}_{i,\text{mid}}} = \frac{1}{1 + \gamma_E} \cdot \frac{1 + jf/f_{e1}}{1 + jf/f_{e2}} \cdot \frac{1}{1 - jf_1/f} \tag{6-86}$$

This curve has the same shape as the low-frequency response of the vacuum-tube triode RC-coupled amplifier, with cathode bias. Thus, Fig. 6-15 applies here if the ordinate axis is labeled $|A_{i,\text{low}}/A_{i,\text{mid}}|_{\text{db}}$.

The capacitor C_E has the same effect on the response of the transistor amplifier as C_k does on the response of the triode amplifier. The discussion of C_k in Sec. 6-5 also applies to C_E. (Note that the stray capacitance across C_E is usually less than that across C_k.)

6-7   Input and output stages in a cascade of amplifiers

We have thus far considered the internal stages in a cascade of amplifiers. Let us now consider the input and output circuits. The output impedance of many amplifiers can be considered to be either a resistor or a parallel resistor-capacitor combination. In all of the amplifiers that have been considered, we have made provision for such a load (i.e., in the vacuum-tube amplifier, the load impedance could be represented by R_g and C_i; in the transistor amplifier it could be represented by R_i and C_i). Thus, we can directly apply the results of the previous sections to most output stages.

Insofar as the input stage is concerned, we need only find the voltage across it in the case of the vacuum tube, or the current into it in the case of the transistor. Once these quantities are known, the output of the first stage, which is the input to the next stage, can be found by multiplying by the amplification. To illustrate the calculation of the input quantities, consider Fig. 6-19a. The input voltage of the amplifier is given by

$$\mathbf{E}_1 = \frac{\mathbf{E}_s \mathbf{Z}_i}{R_s + \mathbf{Z}_i} \qquad\qquad (6\text{-}87)$$

Similarly, from Fig. 6-19b, the amplifier input current is given by

$$\mathbf{I}_1 = \frac{\mathbf{I}_s R_s}{R_s + \mathbf{Z}_i} \qquad\qquad (6\text{-}88)$$

A simple input circuit for an amplifier is shown in Fig. 6-20. Note that the input current is only considered to be the current in R_i. This is often the case in an actual amplifier. Then,

$$\frac{\mathbf{E}_1}{\mathbf{E}_s} = \frac{R_i}{R_s + R_i} \cdot \frac{1}{1 + jf/f_2} \qquad\qquad (6\text{-}89)$$

$$\frac{\mathbf{I}_1}{\mathbf{I}_s} = \frac{R_s}{R_s + R_i} \cdot \frac{1}{1 + jf/f_2} \qquad\qquad (6\text{-}90)$$

Fig. 6-19   Representations of the input to (a) a voltage amplifier and (b) a current amplifier.

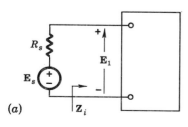
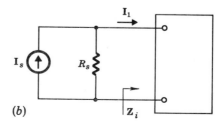

(a)   (b)

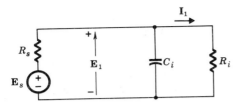

Fig. 6-20   A simple amplifier input.

where

$$f_2 = \frac{R_s + R_i}{2\pi C_i R_s R_i} \tag{6-91}$$

and

$$\mathbf{I}_s = \frac{\mathbf{E}_s}{R_s} \tag{6-92}$$

6-8   Bandwidth of cascaded amplifier stages

The gain of an amplifier is the product of the gains of its individual stages. If RC-coupled amplifiers are cascaded, the bandwidth of the overall amplifier will be less than that of any one stage. For instance, let us consider an amplifier whose high-frequency response is given by

$$\frac{\mathbf{A}_{\text{high}}}{\mathbf{A}_{\text{mid}}} = \frac{1}{1 + jf/f_2} = \frac{1}{\sqrt{1 + (f/f_2)^2}} \quad \underline{/-\tan^{-1} f/f_2} \tag{6-93}$$

If n of these are cascaded, then for the entire amplifier

$$\frac{\mathbf{A}_{T,\text{high}}}{\mathbf{A}_{T,\text{mid}}} = \frac{1}{(1 + jf/f_2)^n} = \frac{1}{[1 + (f/f_2)^2]^{n/2}} \quad \underline{/-n \tan^{-1} f/f_2} \tag{6-94}$$

On a decibel basis

$$\left| \frac{A_{T,\text{high}}}{A_{T,\text{mid}}} \right|_{\text{db}} = -10n \log_{10}\left[1 + \left(\frac{f}{f_2}\right)^2 \right] \tag{6-95}$$

Comparing this with Eqs. (6-17) to (6-19), we see that the break point of the asymptotes is f_2 and the asymptotic slope is $-6n$ db/octave or $-20n$ db/decade. The phase shift of the overall amplifier is just n times the phase shift of an individual stage. A plot of $|A_{T,\text{high}}/A_{T,\text{mid}}|_{\text{db}}$ is given in Fig. 6-21. The half-power bandwidth of the amplifier f_{2T} decreases with the number of stages and is found by solving the following equation

$$[1 + (f_{2T}/f_2)^2]^{n/2} = \sqrt{2}$$

Thus

$$f_{2T} = f_2 \sqrt{2^{1/n} - 1} \tag{6-96}$$

Values of f_{2T}/f_2 are given in Table 6-1.[4]

Table 6-1*

n	f_{2T}/f_2
1	1.00
2	0.64
3	0.51
4	0.44
5	0.39
6	0.35
7	0.32
8	0.30
9	0.28

*By permission from G. E. Valley, Jr., and H. Wallman, "Vacuum Tube Amplifiers," copyright 1948, McGraw-Hill Book Company.

Although high-frequency-response curves have been drawn, these results are directly applicable to the low-frequency response of cascaded amplifiers.

These results can be applied to the high-frequency response of vacuum tubes and to the low-frequency response of vacuum tubes and transistors. However, the high-frequency gain of the transistor which is given by Eq. (6-31) is of a different form from Eq. (6-93). If $f_\beta = f_2$, then the results of this section can be used, except that now

$$n = 2 \times \text{number of stages}$$

On the other hand, if $f_\beta \gg f_2$, or $f_2 \gg f_\beta$, then the response due to the factor $1/(1 + jf/f_\beta)$, or $1/(1 + jf/f_2)$, can usually be ignored over the operating-frequency range. In this case, Eq. (6-96) and Table 6-1 can be used.

Fig. 6-21 Plots of the amplitude response of one-stage, two-stage, and three-stage amplifiers.

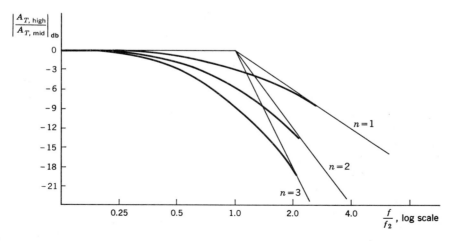

When identical amplifier stages are cascaded, the overall bandwidth is reduced. On the other hand, if the gain-bandwidth product of each stage is constant and the midband gain of the overall amplifier is kept constant (independent of the number of stages), then an increase in the number of stages may actually increase the bandwidth. For instance, let us assume for an amplifier characterized by Eq. (6-93) that $|A_{\text{mid}}|f_2 = 100 \times 10^6$ cps. A single-stage amplifier with a midband gain of 100 will have an upper half-power frequency of 1 Mc/sec. If we desire the same midband gain, we can cascade two stages, each with a midband gain of 10. The half-power frequency of each stage will then be 10 Mc/sec and the half-power frequency of the cascade will be 6.4 Mc/sec (see Table 6-1). Thus, the overall bandwidth has been increased. As the number of stages is increased (with constant total midband gain), f_{2T} will increase and then start to decrease. There is an optimum number of stages to use for maximum bandwidth. It can be shown that the maximum bandwidth occurs when the gain per stage is approximately equal to

$$\sqrt{\varepsilon} = \sqrt{2.7183} = 1.649 \qquad \text{or} \qquad 4.34 \text{ db}$$

The previous discussion assumed that the gain-bandwidth product is a constant. Actually, there are many situations where bandwidth cannot be interchanged with gain, and in such cases, an increase in the number of stages will reduce the bandwidth. For instance, the low-frequency bandwidth of either the vacuum-tube or the transistor amplifier and the "beta cutoff frequency" f_β of a transistor are independent of the midband gain. On the other hand, the factor f_2, given by Eq. (6-10) for the vacuum tube and by Eq. (6-30) for the transistor, does vary inversely with midband gain, and the previous discussion does apply. These principles will be illustrated when the design of an RC-coupled amplifier is discussed in the next section.

6-9 Design of RC-coupled amplifiers

To illustrate the ideas of the previous sections, we shall design both a vacuum-tube and a transistor RC-coupled amplifier.

The vacuum-tube amplifier

The amplifier is to have the following specifications: There is to be a well-defined midband region with $|A_{v,\text{mid}}| = 400$, $|A_{v,\text{high}}/A_{v,\text{mid}}| \geqslant 0.95$ at 10^5 cps, $|A_{v,\text{low}}/A_{v,\text{mid}}| \geqslant 1/\sqrt{2} = 0.707$ at 20 cps, and the amplifier is to have the minimum number of stages. Assume that a vacuum-tube pentode with the following characteristics will be used: $g_m = 5,000$ μmhos, $g_{ps} = 1,000$ μmhos, $r_p \geqslant 2 \times 10^6$ ohms, $R_{g,\text{max}} = 10^6$ ohms, $C_{\text{in}} = 8$ $\mu\mu$f, and $C_{\text{out}} = 6$ $\mu\mu$f, when the coordinates of the operating point are $E_{bQ} = 300$ volts, $I_{bQ} = 20$ ma, $E_{c2Q} = 250$ volts, $I_{c2Q} = 1$ ma, and $E_{cQ} = -5$ volts. It will also be assumed that the stray wiring capacitance is 6 $\mu\mu$f.

A cut-and-try procedure will be used to determine if the required $|A_{v,\text{mid}}|$ and f_2 can be achieved with this vacuum tube. The gain-bandwidth product for one stage is given by $|A_{v,\text{mid}}|f_2 = g_m/2\pi C_{sh} = 39.8 \times 10^6$ cps. Try one stage. Thus, $|A_{v,\text{mid}}| = 400$ and $f_2 = 99,500$ cps. Therefore, at 100,000 cps $|A_{v,\text{high}}/A_{v,\text{mid}}| < 0.707 < 0.95$. Hence, the amplification cannot be achieved with one stage. Next try two stages. The gain for each stage is $|A_{v,\text{mid}}| = \sqrt{400} = 20$. Therefore, $f_2 = 1.99 \times 10^6$, and for the total amplifier

$$\left| \frac{A_{vT,\text{high}}}{A_{v,\text{mid}}} \right| = \frac{1}{1 + (f/f_2)^2}$$

Then, at a frequency of 100,000 cps

$$\left| \frac{A_{vT,\text{high}}}{A_{vT,\text{mid}}} \right| = \frac{1}{1 + (1/19.9)^2} = 0.997 > 0.95$$

Thus, we can use two stages. A complete amplifier is shown in Fig. 6-22. The load resistance is labeled R_g. From Eq. (6-6), we have

$$R_{sh} = \frac{|A_{v,\text{mid}}|}{g_m} = \frac{20}{5,000} \times 10^6 = 4,000 \text{ ohms}$$

Since $R_g = 10^6$ (we shall use the maximum value of R_g to keep the size of C_c small) and $r_p \geq 2 \times 10^6$ ohms

$$R_L \approx R_{sh} = 4,000 \text{ ohms}$$

Before considering the low-frequency response of the amplifier, let us compute the values of the remaining resistances and the power-supply voltage. This voltage E_{bb} is connected between the points labeled B^+ and B^- in

Fig. 6-22   _The two-stage RC-coupled vacuum-tube amplifier._

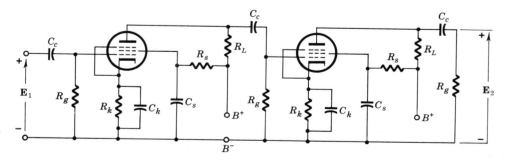

Fig. 6-22

$$E_{bb} = I_{bQ}R_L + E_{bQ} - E_{cQ} = 80 + 300 + 5 = 385 \text{ volts}$$

$$R_k = \frac{-E_{cQ}}{I_{bQ} + I_{c2Q}} = \frac{5}{21 \times 10^{-3}} = 238 \text{ ohms}$$

$$R_s = \frac{E_{bb} - E_{c2Q} + E_{cQ}}{I_{c2Q}} = \frac{385 - 250 - 5}{1 \times 10^{-3}} = 130,000 \text{ ohms}$$

Now, let us compute the low-frequency response. There are two amplifier stages; in addition, a coupling network consisting of an R_g and C_c is placed in the input circuit. This can be considered to be a third stage. Since $R_g \gg R_L$, $R_{\text{low}} = R_g$. Then, for the three-stage R_g-C_c circuit, assuming equal coupling capacitors

$$\left| \frac{A_{vT,\text{low}}}{A_{vT,\text{mid}}} \right| = \left(\frac{1}{\sqrt{1 + (f_1/f)^2}} \right)^3$$

where $f_1 = 1/2\pi C_c R_{\text{low}}$. For the time being, neglect the effect of the cathode and screen-grid impedances. Then, at 20 cps

$$\left[\frac{1}{1 + (f_1/20)^2} \right]^{3/2} = \frac{1}{\sqrt{2}}$$

Solving, we obtain $f_1 = 10.2$. Hence,

$$C_c = \frac{1}{2\pi f_1 R_{\text{low}}} = \frac{1}{2\pi(10.2) \times 10^6} = 0.0156 \ \mu\text{f}$$

This design does not allow for any loss in gain due to the cathode or screen-grid bias impedances. We shall increase the size of C_c so that some additional loss can be tolerated. Let us try a value of $C_k = 0.03 \ \mu\text{f}$, which yields $f_1 = 5.31$ cps. Then, at 20 cps

$$\left| \frac{A_{vT,\text{low}}}{A_{vT,\text{mid}}} \right| = \frac{1}{[1 + (5.31/20)^2]^{3/2}} = 0.903$$

The allowable loss due to the cathode and screen-grid impedances is given by

$$\left| \frac{A'_{vT,\text{low}}}{A_{vT,\text{mid}}} \right| = \frac{0.707}{0.903} = 0.783$$

Since there are two stages, the allowable loss per stage is $\sqrt{0.783} = 0.885$. Then, using Eqs. (6-60) to (6-70) we have

$$\delta = \frac{I_{c2Q}}{I_{bQ}} = \frac{1}{20} = 0.05$$

$$\gamma_k = R_k(1 + \delta)(g_m + g_{ps}) = 238(1.05)(6,000 \times 10^{-6}) = 1.5$$

$$\gamma_s = R_s \, \delta g_{ps} = (130,000)(0.05)(1,000 \times 10^{-6}) = 6.5$$

Then, at 20 cps

$$\left| \frac{A'_{v,\text{low}}}{A_{v,\text{mid}}} \right| = 0.885 = \left| \frac{1}{1 + \dfrac{1.5}{1 + j20/f_{k1}} + \dfrac{6.5}{1 + j20/f_{s1}}} \right|$$

The values of C_k and C_s are given by

$$C_k = \frac{1}{2\pi R_k f_{k1}} = \frac{1}{2\pi \times 238 f_{k1}} = \frac{669}{f_{k1}} \quad \mu\text{f}$$

$$C_s = \frac{1}{2\pi R_s f_{s1}} = \frac{1}{2\pi \times 130{,}000 f_{s1}} = \frac{1.23}{f_{s1}} \quad \mu\text{f}$$

As a first trial, the loss due to either the cathode-bias circuit or the screen-grid-bias circuit will be ignored. Since the value of C_k will be larger than C_s, we shall ignore the screen-grid circuit at the start. Then,

$$0.885 = \frac{1}{|1 + 1.5/(1 + j20/f_{k1})|}$$

Solving for f_{k1}, we obtain $f_{k1} = 4.72$ cps. Let us use $f_{k1} = 4$ cps so that provision is made for loss due to the screen-grid-bias circuit. Then, at 20 cps

$$0.885 = \frac{1}{\left| 1 + \dfrac{1.5}{1 + j5} + \dfrac{6.5}{1 + j20/f_{s1}} \right|}$$

We shall assume that $20/f_{s1} \gg 1$ so that $1 + j20/f_{s1} \approx j20/f_{s1}$. This will be verified. Then, making the approximations and solving for f_{s1}, we obtain $f_{s1} = 0.338$ cps. Thus, we have

$$C_k = 167.3 \ \mu\text{f}$$

$$C_s = 3.64 \ \mu\text{f}$$

The value of C_k is somewhat large, but is quite acceptable if electrolytic capacitors are used. The values of C_k and/or C_s can be decreased somewhat if C_c is increased, since this will decrease the allowed value of $|A'_{v,\text{low}}/A_{v,\text{mid}}|$. The design of the vacuum-tube amplifier is now complete. In summary, $R_L = 4{,}000$ ohms, $R_g = 10^6$ ohms, $R_k = 238$ ohms, $R_s = 130{,}000$ ohms, $C_c = 167.3 \ \mu\text{f}$, and $C_s = 3.64 \ \mu\text{f}$.

The values of the resistors and capacitors that are calculated may not be the same as those which are commonly manufactured. In the case of the capacitors, the next larger size can be chosen. The standard resistor values that are closest to the calculated ones should be selected. These values should be checked to verify that the operating point and the frequency response are not varied beyond allowable limits.

Transistor amplifier

The amplifier is to have the following specifications: There is to be a well-defined midband region; the magnitude of the current gain in the midband region is to be equal to or greater than 42, $|A_{i,\mathrm{high}}/A_{i,\mathrm{mid}}| \geqslant 0.96$ at 10^5 cps, $|A_{i,\mathrm{low}}/A_{i,\mathrm{mid}}| \geqslant 1/\sqrt{2} = 0.707$ at 20 cps; the minimum number of amplifier stages is to be used; and the stability factor of any stage is to be equal to or less than 5. The load impedance is 1,500 ohms, and the internal impedance of the input current generator is 10,000 ohms.

We shall assume that the transistor has the following characteristics: $h_{ie} = 1,500$ ohms, $h_{re} = 300 \times 10^{-6}$, $h_{fe} = 100$, $h_{oe} = 50 \times 10^{-6}$ mho, $f_\alpha = 202 \times 10^6$ cps ($f_\beta = 2 \times 10^6$ cps), and $C_{ob} = 4.90$ μμf ($C_{oe} = 495$ μμf). Assume that there are 5 μμf of stray wiring capacitance. The coordinates of the operating point are $I_{CQ} = -6$ma, $I_{BQ} = -100$ μamp, $E_{CQ} = -5$ volts, and $E_{BQ} \approx 0$ volts.

A typical amplifier is shown in Fig. 6-23. Two stages have been drawn, although at the present time we do not know the number of stages that are needed. It will be more convenient to work with the ratio $\mathbf{I}_2/\mathbf{I}_1$ rather than with $\mathbf{I}_2/\mathbf{I}_s$ in the mid- and high-frequency regions. To do this, we must know the ratio $\mathbf{I}_1/\mathbf{I}_s$. At mid- and high frequencies, this is

$$\frac{\mathbf{I}_1}{\mathbf{I}_s} = \frac{R'_s}{R'_s + R_i}$$

Where $R'_s = R_s R_B/(R_s + R_B)$, $R_B = R_{B1}R_{B2}/(R_{B1} + R_{B2})$, and R_i is the input resistance between the base and the common terminal. At low frequencies this ratio falls off, because of the presence of C_{ci}, R_E, and C_E. We can obtain a trial value for R_B by considering the stability factor $S = dI_C/dI_{CO}$. From Eq. (2-23), we obtain

$$S = \frac{1}{1 - \alpha R_B/(R_B + R_E)} = \frac{1}{1 - [\beta/(\beta + 1)][R_B/(R_B + R_E)]}$$

Let us try $R_E = 1,000$ ohms. Too large a value of R_E will result in too large a power supply voltage. If R_E is too small, then R_B will be small and will shunt the input signal.

$$S = \frac{1}{1 - (100/101)[R_B/(R_B + 1,000)]} = 5$$

Fig. 6-23   The two-stage RC-coupled transistor amplifier.

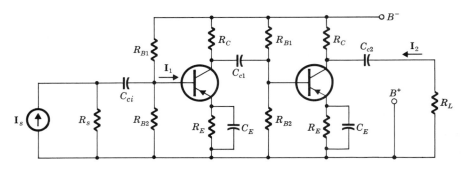

Solving for R_B, we obtain

$$R_B = 4,208 \text{ ohms}$$

If more than one stage is necessary, then we shall use this value for R_B also (if it proves to be suitable). Since R_B consists of R_{B1} in parallel with R_{B2}, it corresponds to the R_B that was discussed in Sec. 6-3. We do not know the input impedance of the amplifier, since the value of R_C is not known. However, R_i can be approximated. From Eq. (3-85)

$$R_i = h_{ie} - \frac{h_{re}h_{fe}R_{sh}}{1 + h_{oe}R_{sh}}$$

Substituting, we have

$$R_i = 1,500 - \frac{3 \times 10^{-2}R_{sh}}{1 + 50 \times 10^{-6}R_{sh}}$$

The second term will, in general, be quite small, so we can approximate R_i by 1,500 ohms. We shall verify this approximation subsequently. Then, substituting, we obtain $I_1/I_s = 0.664$. Thus

$$|A_{iT,\text{mid}}| = \left|\frac{I_2}{I_1}\right| = \frac{42}{0.664} = 63.3$$

We shall use the value $A_{iT,\text{mid}} = 64$. Note that the subscript T will be added to indicate a quantity for the entire amplifier, differentiating the symbol from one which applies to a single stage.

The high-frequency response will determine the number of stages that are to be used. There will be some stray wiring capacitance across the input of the amplifier. However, its effect can usually be neglected in comparison with the effects of C_{oe} and f_β. Let us try to see if the specifications can be achieved with one stage. Then, from Eq. (6-27), $R_{sh} = A_{i,\text{mid}}R_i/h_{fe}$. The resistance R_i represents the input resistance of the next stage. Since we assume that there is only one stage, $R_i = 1,500$, which is the load resistance. Thus, $R_{sh} = 960$ ohms. Then, from Eq. (6-30), $f_2 = 1/(2\pi R_{sh}C_{sh}) = 332,000$ cps, where $C_{sh} = C_{oe} + C_w = 500 \ \mu\mu\text{f}$. From Eq. (6-31), we have

$$\left|\frac{A_{i,\text{high}}}{A_{i,\text{mid}}}\right| = \frac{1}{\sqrt{1 + (f/f_\beta)^2}} \cdot \frac{1}{\sqrt{1 + (f/f_2)^2}}$$

Thus

$$\left|\frac{A_{i,\text{high}}}{A_{i,\text{mid}}}\right|_{f = 10^5} = \frac{1}{\sqrt{1 + \left(\dfrac{100}{2,000}\right)^2}} \cdot \frac{1}{\sqrt{1 + \left(\dfrac{100}{332}\right)^2}}$$

$$= (0.9876)(0.9575) = 0.946 < 0.96$$

Thus, we cannot obtain the desired frequency response using only one stage. Note that the first term is not a function of $A_{i,\text{mid}}$, and it cannot be adjusted by reducing $A_{i,\text{mid}}$.   Now, let us try two stages.   Then $A_{i,\text{mid}} = \sqrt{64} = 8$. Since $R_i \approx 1{,}500$ ohms

$$R_{sh} = \frac{8 \times 1{,}500}{100} = 120 \text{ ohms}$$

If we solve for R_i using this value of R_{sh}, we obtain $R_i = 1{,}496.4 \approx 1{,}500$ ohms.   Thus, our assumption that $R_i = 1{,}500$ ohms is justified.   Using this value of R_{sh}, we have $f_2 = 2.65$ Mc/sec.   Then the response of the amplifier at 100,000 cps is

$$\left| \frac{A_{iT,\text{high}}}{A_{iT,\text{mid}}} \right|_{f=100{,}000} = (0.9876)^2 \frac{1}{1 + (1/26.5)^2} = 0.973 > 0.96$$

Thus, the design can be met with two stages.   We can now determine the unknown resistances in the circuit.   For the first stage,

$$\frac{1}{R_{sh}} = h_{oe} + \frac{1}{R_C} + \frac{1}{R_B} + \frac{1}{R_i}$$

Substituting, and solving for R_C, we obtain

$$R_C = 135 \text{ ohms}$$

For the second stage, R_B is missing.   The value of R_C is then given by $1/R_C = 1/R_{sh} - h_{oe} - 1/R_i$; hence, $R_C = 131$ ohms.   If we use $R_C = 135$ ohms, the change in frequency response will be negligible.   Hence, for simplicity, we shall do so.   Since R_C is 135 ohms, the shunting effect of R_B is very small.   Therefore, we need not use a value of R_E greater than 1,000 ohms.   *Actually, R_C is much smaller than is typical.*   However, the numbers were deliberately chosen in this way to demonstrate how gain and bandwidth can be manipulated in a transistor.   The power supply voltage E_{CC} is connected between the points B^- and B^+, where

$$E_{CC} = I_{CQ}R_C + E_{CQ} + (I_{BQ} + I_{CQ})R_E = -11.91 \text{ volts}$$

The minus sign indicates that the terminal marked B^- is negative.   Since the base-to-emitter quiescent voltage can be neglected, we can combine Eqs. (2-8) to (2-10) and obtain

$$E_{CC} = I_{BQ}R_{B1} + (I_{BQ} + I_{CQ})R_E R_{B1}/R_B$$

Substituting and solving for R_{B1}, we have

$$R_{B1} = 7{,}684 \text{ ohms}$$

Then

$$R_{B2} = 9{,}305 \text{ ohms}$$

The low-frequency design will now be obtained.   We shall, for the time being, neglect the effect of the emitter stabilizing impedance.   There are three coupling capacitors; thus, there are effectively three stages. The subscripts i, 1, and 2 will be used to differentiate among these three stages. Then, proceeding as in Sec. 6-3, we have

$$R_{\text{low},1} = \frac{R_C}{1 + h_{oe}R_C} + \frac{R_B R_i}{R_B + R_i}$$

$$R_{\text{low},2} = \frac{R_C}{1 + h_{oe}R_C} + 1{,}500$$

$$R_{\text{low},i} = R_s + \frac{R_B R_i}{R_B + R_i}$$

Substituting, we obtain

$$R_{\text{low},1} = 1{,}240 \text{ ohms}$$

$$R_{\text{low},2} = 1{,}634 \text{ ohms}$$

$$R_{\text{low},i} = 11{,}106 \text{ ohms}$$

The low-frequency response is then given by

$$\left| \frac{A_{iT,\text{low}}}{A_{iT,\text{mid}}} \right| = \frac{1}{\sqrt{1 + (f_{11}/f)^2}} \cdot \frac{1}{\sqrt{1 + (f_{12}/f)^2}} \cdot \frac{1}{\sqrt{1 + (f_{1i}/f)^2}}$$

where

$$f_{11} = \frac{1}{2\pi R_{\text{low},1} C_{c1}}$$

$$f_{12} = \frac{1}{2\pi R_{\text{low},2} C_{c2}}$$

$$f_{1i} = \frac{1}{2\pi R_{\text{low},i} C_{ci}}$$

We shall adjust C_{c2} and C_{ci} so that $f_{11} = f_{12} = f_{1i} = f_1$.

There are instances when it is not desirable to make the three break points equal. However, we shall do so here to simplify the problem. (Since $R_{\text{low},i}$ is considerably greater than $R_{\text{low},1}$ and $R_{\text{low},2}$, an alternative procedure would be to make f_{1i} very much less than f_{11} and f_{12}. In this case, over much of the low-frequency range, the low-frequency behavior would be of the form $1/[\sqrt{1 + (f_{11}/f)^2} \sqrt{1 + (f_{12}/f)^2}]$.) Then, with equal break points, $C_{c2} = (R_{\text{low},1}/R_{\text{low},2})C_{c1} = 0.759C_{c1}$, $C_{ci} = (R_{\text{low},1}/R_{\text{low},i})C_{c1} = 0.112C_{c1}$. Then

$$\left| \frac{A_{iT,\text{low}}}{A_{iT,\text{mid}}} \right| = \frac{1}{[1 + (f_1/f)^2]^{3/2}}$$

and, at 20 cps, $[1 + (f_1/20)^2]^{3/2} = \sqrt{2}$. Solving for f_1, we obtain $f_1 = 10.2$ cps. Then, $C_{c1} = 1/2\pi R_{\text{low},1}f_1 = 12.6$ μf. In computing this value, the emitter stabilizing impedance is ignored. A larger value of C_{c1} should be used to account for the loss due to C_E and R_E. Let us use $C_{c1} = 20$ μf as a trial. Then $f_1 = 6.42$ cps and at 20 cps the response due to the coupling capacitors is given by

$$\frac{1}{[1 + (6.42/20)^2]^{3/2}} = 0.863$$

The allowable loss due to the two emitter lead impedances at 20 cps is then

$$\left| \frac{A'_{iT,\text{low}}}{A_{iT,\text{mid}}} \right| = \frac{0.707}{0.863} = 0.819$$

The allowable loss per stage is $|A'_{i,\text{low}}/A_{i,\text{mid}}| = \sqrt{0.819} = 0.905$. Then, using Eqs. (6-84) to (6-86), we obtain

$$\gamma_E = \frac{R_E h_{fe}}{(1 + h_{oe}R)(R_B + R_i)}$$

where

$$\frac{1}{R} = \frac{1}{R_C} + \frac{1}{R_B} + \frac{1}{R_i}$$

For the second stage, R_B is omitted from this relation. However, this does not greatly change R. In addition, γ_E is almost independent of R. Thus, we shall use the same γ_E for both stages. Hence $\gamma_E = 17.4$. Then

$$\left| \frac{A'_{i,\text{low}}}{A_{i,\text{mid}}} \right| = \frac{1}{1 + \gamma_E} \left| \frac{1 + jf/f_{e1}}{1 + jf/(1 + \gamma_E)f_{e1}} \right|$$

At 20 cps

$$\sqrt{0.819} = \frac{1}{18.4} \sqrt{\frac{1 + (20/f_{e1})^2}{1 + (1.087/f_{e1})^2}}$$

Thus, $f_{e1} = 0.511$ cps $= 1/2\pi R_E C_E$, and, therefore, $C_E = 312$ μf. This value, although large, is not unacceptable. In fact, if a tantalum electrolytic capacitor is used, it will occupy a fairly small volume. If the sizes of the coupling capacitors are increased, then the emitter bypass capacitors can be reduced somewhat. However, it is probably not advisable to do so, since the leakage resistance of a capacitor usually decreases as the capacitance increases. The emitter bypass capacitors are shunted by small resistances and their leakage resistance can be ignored. However, the coupling capacitors must have a relatively high leakage resistance. Thus, it is desirable to keep their capacitance relatively small. Hence, the trial value of 20 μf for C_{c1} will be used. Therefore

$$C_{c2} = 15.2 \text{ μf} \qquad \text{and} \qquad C_{ci} = 2.24 \text{ μf}$$

The design is now complete.   To summarize: $E_{CC} = -11.91$ volts, $R_C = 135$ ohms, $R_{B1} = 7{,}684$ ohms, $R_{B2} = 9{,}305$ ohms, $R_E = 1{,}000$ ohms, $C_{c1} = 20$ μf, $C_{c2} = 15.2$ μf, $C_{ci} = 2.24$ μf, and $C_E = 312$ μf.   As in the case of the vacuum-tube amplifier, these values are usually adjusted to ones that are commercially available.

In both the vacuum-tube amplifier and the transistor amplifier, the high-frequency response was better (broader) than the specifications, while the midband gain just met specifications.   In such cases, the shunting resistors can be increased somewhat so that both the midband gain and the high-frequency response exceed specifications.

6-10   Low- and high-frequency compensation with RC networks

The frequency response of an RC-coupled amplifier can be improved if a *compensating network* is added to the coupling network.   In general, compensating networks are RC networks or utilize resonance phenomena and contain inductance, in addition to resistance and capacitance.   We shall consider the RC compensating networks in this section and the others in the next two.

Low-frequency compensation

Low-frequency-compensated RC-coupled vacuum-tube and transistor amplifiers are shown in Fig. 6-24a and b, respectively.   An equivalent circuit that is valid for both of these amplifiers is shown in Fig. 6-24c.   The bypass capacitors C_k, C_s, and C_E are assumed to be short circuits at the signal frequencies.   Their effect can be accounted for by using the procedures of Secs. 6-5 and 6-6.   We can treat vacuum-tube and transistor amplifiers simultaneously throughout much of this analysis.   *However, because of differences in the impedance levels of the two circuits, there will be some differences in the approximations that can be made.*   The parameters of the equivalent circuit are related to the parameters of the amplifiers by the substitutions of Table 6-2.

The following assumptions will be made: The impedance $\mathbf{Z}$ is such that $r \gg |Z|$, so r can be considered to be an open circuit; and that $R_d \gg 1/\omega C_d$

Table 6-2

Equivalent circuit	*Vacuum-tube amplifier*	*Transistor amplifier*
r	r_p	$1/h_{oe}$
R_1	R_L	R_C
R_2	R_g	$R_B R_i/(R_B + R_i)$
$\mathbf{I}$	$g_m \mathbf{E}_1$	$h_{fe}\mathbf{I}_1$

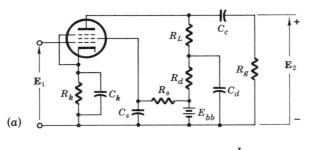

(a)

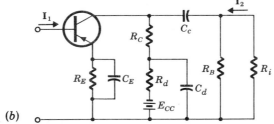

(b)

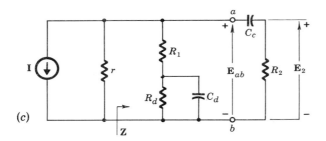

(c)

Fig. 6-24 *Low-frequency-compensated RC-coupled amplifiers. (a) Common-cathode vacuum-tube amplifier; (b) common-emitter transistor amplifier; (c) an equivalent circuit that is valid for both. The bypass capacitors C_k, C_s, and C_E are assumed to be short circuits.*

at all frequencies of interest, so R_d can be neglected. An analysis of this amplifier then yields

$$\frac{\mathbf{E}_2}{\mathbf{I}} = -\frac{(R_1 + 1/j\omega C_d)R_2}{R_1 + 1/j\omega C_d + R_2 + 1/j\omega C_c} \tag{6-97}$$

The input voltage and current of the vacuum tube and the transistor circuits both equal $\mathbf{I}$ multiplied by a constant that is independent of frequency. The output voltage is $\mathbf{E}_2$, and the output current, for the transistor circuit, is $-\mathbf{E}_2/R_i$. Thus, the frequency response of both the voltage gain and the current gain is given by Eq. (6-97). Manipulating this equation, we obtain

$$\frac{\mathbf{E}_2}{\mathbf{I}} = \frac{R_2}{1 + [(1 + j\omega R_2 C_c)/(1 + j\omega R_1 C_d)][C_d/C_c]} \tag{6-98}$$

If

$$R_2 C_c = R_1 C_d \tag{6-99}$$

$$\frac{\mathbf{E}_2}{\mathbf{I}} = \frac{R_2}{1 + C_d/C_c} = \frac{R_1 R_2}{R_1 + R_2} \tag{6-100}$$

Eq. (6-100) indicates that the frequency response is a constant, independent of frequency. However, C_c becomes an open circuit at zero frequency; hence the gain should fall off. This discrepancy results because the approximations that were made are not valid at extremely low frequencies. For instance, at sufficiently low frequencies, $1/\omega C_d > R_d$, not $R_d \gg 1/\omega C_d$. However, we can always choose R_1 small enough and R_d large enough so that the approximations are valid down to the lowest frequency of interest.

The midband equivalent circuit is that of Fig. 6-24c with C_c and C_d replaced by short circuits. As R_1 is decreased, R_{sh} [see Eqs. (6-5), (6-6), (6-26), and (6-27)] will be reduced and consequently the magnitude of the midband gain will decrease. The direct current from the power supply is through R_d; increasing R_d increases the power-supply voltage. Thus, as the low-frequency response is extended, the magnitude of the midband gain will decrease and the required power-supply voltage will increase. There are many instances when R_L or R_C are small because of considerations involving the frequency response (see Sec. 6-9). If C_d and R_d are added to the circuit such that Eq. (6-99) is satisfied and the approximations are met, then the low-frequency response may be improved without affecting $|A_{\text{mid}}|$. The exact improvements in the low-frequency response can then be found by exactly analyzing the complete circuit of Fig. 6-24c. However, the following approximate analysis will at times prove useful. Assume that

$$R_2 + \frac{1}{j\omega C_c} \gg R_1 + \frac{R_d}{1 + j\omega C_d R_d} \tag{6-101}$$

and

$$r \gg |Z| \tag{6-102}$$

Note that both of these approximations can be valid down to zero frequency. The second of these relations allows us to ignore the effect of r, while the first indicates that the voltage $\mathbf{E}_{ab}$ is given approximately by

$$\mathbf{E}_{ab} \approx \mathbf{I}\left(R_1 + \frac{R_d}{1 + j\omega R_d C_d}\right) \tag{6-103}$$

Then, solving for $\mathbf{E}_2$, we obtain

$$\frac{\mathbf{E}_2}{\mathbf{I}} = \frac{R_1[1 + (R_1 + R_d)/j\omega C_d R_1 R_d]}{(1 + 1/j\omega C_d R_d)(1 + 1/j\omega C_c R_2)}$$

If $R_2 \gg R_1$, then $R_2 = R_{\text{low}}$ [see Eqs. (6-12) and (6-32)], so that $f_1 = 1/2\pi C_c R_2$ is the lower half-power frequency of the amplifier without compensation. In addition, let

$$f_3 = \frac{1}{2\pi C_d R_d} \tag{6-104}$$

and

$$f_4 = \frac{R_1 + R_d}{2\pi C_d R_1 R_d} \tag{6-105}$$

Making use of the fact that $\mathbf{E}_2/\mathbf{I} \approx R_1$ in the midband region, we can write

$$\frac{\mathbf{A}_{\text{low}}}{\mathbf{A}_{\text{mid}}} = \frac{1 - jf_4/f}{(1 - jf_3/f)(1 - jf_1/f)} \tag{6-106}$$

Let

$$R_1' = \frac{R_1 R_d}{R_1 + R_d} \tag{6-107}$$

If $R_1' C_d = R_2 C_c$, then $f_1 = f_4$ and

$$\frac{\mathbf{A}_{\text{low}}}{\mathbf{A}_{\text{mid}}} = \frac{1}{1 - jf_3/f} \tag{6-108}$$

This has the same form as that of the low-frequency response of the uncompensated amplifier, except that f_1 has been replaced by f_3. If we are to achieve any improvement through compensation, $f_3 < f_1$. Since $R_d > R_1'$, then $f_1 = f_4 > f_3$ and some improvement will always be obtained. If $r \gg R_1$ and $R_1 \ll R_2$, there will usually be values of R_d for which R_d is considerably greater than R_1' and for which the relations (6-101) and (6-102) will be met. Then there can be substantial improvement in the low-frequency response.

At the start of this section we mentioned that the differences in impedance levels in the vacuum-tube and transistor circuits produced differences in the operation of these circuits. We shall consider these now. In the vacuum-tube-pentode amplifier, in general, $r_p \gg R_L$ and $R_g \gg R_L$. Thus, relations (6-101) and (6-102) can be easily satisfied. In the transistor amplifier, we cannot, in general, state that $R_i \gg R_C$, so the approximate solution of Eq. (6-106) may be of limited use in transistor amplifiers. However, the compensation procedure itself is quite useful.

If $R_1' C_d = R_2 C_c$ and $R_1' \ll R_2$, then $C_d \gg C_c$. The size of C_c is usually limited by its leakage resistance and by its stray capacitance to the common lead. The capacitor C_d is not limited in these ways; hence it can usually be made very much larger than C_c.

We have assumed that $f_4 = f_1$. If the value of f_4 is adjusted so that $f_4 > f_1$, then the frequency response will actually rise before it starts to fall off. This is sometimes done to account for the effects of cathode bias impedance, screen-grid bias impedance, or emitter bias impedance. This procedure also will partially compensate for a coupling network in another amplifier stage.

In a multistage amplifier, all of the stages usually use the same power supply. Since the impedance of the power supply cannot be zero, some components of the signal will appear across the power-supply terminals. This can result in undesirable signal feedback. The circuit consisting of R_d and C_d will attenuate any alternating voltage across the power-supply terminals and thus tend to prevent the output of one amplifier stage from being coupled back into another one. For this reason, the network consisting of R_d and C_d is called a *decoupling filter*. The decoupling filter also will tend to reduce the effect of any power-line frequency components that may be present in the output of the power supply.

High frequency compensation

Consider the circuit of Fig. 6-25, which could represent the equivalent circuit of either a vacuum-tube or a transistor amplifier. Solving for $\mathbf{I}_2/\mathbf{I}$, we obtain

$$\frac{\mathbf{I}_2}{\mathbf{I}} = \frac{r(1 + j\omega C_1 R_1)}{(r + R_1 + R_2)[1 + j\omega C_1 R_1(r + R_2)/(r + R_1 + R_2)]} \tag{6-109}$$

In the low- and mid-frequency regions, the capacitor C_1 can be considered to be an open circuit. Thus, for both the voltage gain and the current gain

$$\frac{\mathbf{A}_{\text{high}}}{\mathbf{A}_{\text{mid}}} = \frac{1 + jf/f_5}{1 + jf/f_6} \tag{6-110}$$

where

$$f_5 = \frac{1}{2\pi C_1 R_1} \tag{6-111}$$

and

$$f_6 = \frac{r + R_1 + R_2}{2\pi C_1 R_1(r + R_2)} \tag{6-112}$$

A typical plot of $|A_{\text{high}}/A_{\text{mid}}|_{\text{db}}$ is shown in Fig. 6-26. The asymptotic slope between f_5 and f_6 is 6 db/octave or 20 db/decade. The response in the high-frequency region is greater than the response in the mid-frequency region. Actually, when the compensating network consisting of the parallel combination of R_1 and C_1 is placed into the circuit, the midband gain is reduced while the high-frequency gain is unaffected.

Suppose that the current generator $\mathbf{I}$ is frequency-dependent, as it would be in the case of a transistor; then Eq. (6-110) becomes

$$\frac{\mathbf{A}_{\text{high}}}{\mathbf{A}_{\text{mid}}} = \frac{1}{1 + jf/f_\beta} \cdot \frac{1 + jf/f_5}{1 + jf/f_6} \tag{6-113}$$

Then, if the circuit parameters are adjusted so that $f_5 = f_\beta$, we have

$$\frac{\mathbf{A}_{\text{high}}}{\mathbf{A}_{\text{mid}}} = \frac{1}{1 + jf/f_6} \tag{6-114}$$

The upper half-power frequency has been increased from f_β to f_6 and the

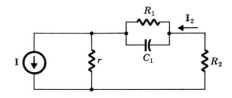

Fig. 6-25   An equivalent circuit of a high-frequency RC-compensating network.

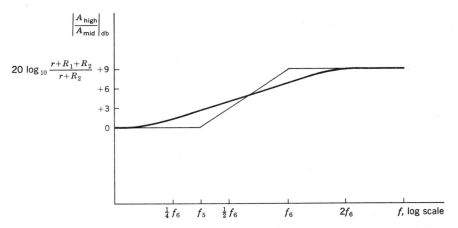

Fig 6-26   The amplitude response of the RC-compensating network of Fig. 6-25.

midband gain has been reduced by the factor $f_5/f_6 = f_\beta/f_6$. Thus, the gain-bandwidth product remains constant. This compensating network allows us to trade midband gain for f_β in a transistor amplifier. Thus, we can apply the techniques of Sec. 6-9 to compensate for too low a value of f_β.

This compensating network could partially offset the effect of the shunting capacitance. However, these results can be more easily obtained by reducing R_{sh}. In addition, we shall see in the next sections that the addition of inductance will permit us to compensate for C_{sh} somewhat without sacrificing midband gain. If shunt capacitances are present, then the results of the previous analysis are only approximate.

6-11 High-frequency compensation with shunt-peaked networks

A compensating network that reduces the effects of the shunting capacitance C_{sh} on the high-frequency response without lowering the midband gain is shown in Fig. 6-27. This circuit is called a *shunt-peaked network*, since the combination of either R_L or R_C in series with the inductance L forms a very low Q coil that is in parallel with C_{sh}. Compensation of this type is usually only needed for relatively broadband amplifiers. Consequently, these amplifiers are also called *shunt-peaked video amplifiers*. At low- and mid-frequencies, $R_1 \gg \omega L$ for the usual values of inductance, and the response of the amplifier is independent of L. An equivalent circuit that is valid in the high-frequency region is given in Fig. 6-27c. It can be used for both the vacuum-tube amplifier and the transistor amplifier, provided the substitutions of Table 6-2 of Sec. 6-10 are used. For the transistor,

$$\mathbf{I} = \mathbf{h}_{fe}\mathbf{I}_1 = \frac{h_{fe}\mathbf{I}_1}{1 + j\omega/\omega_\beta}$$

The capacitor C_{sh} represents the total shunting capacitance and is defined by Eqs. (6-7) or (6-28). In analyzing this circuit, we shall assume that

$$r \gg R_1 + j\omega L \qquad\qquad (6\text{-}115)$$

and

$$R_2 \gg R_1 + j\omega L \qquad\qquad (6\text{-}116)$$

for frequencies from zero to several times the upper half-power frequency of the uncompensated amplifier. These assumptions are usually quite good in the case of the vacuum tube. In transistor amplifiers they may not be valid. However, we have seen in Sec. 6-9 that there are instances when $R_C \ll R_i$ and $R_C \ll 1/h_{oe}$. Then the relations (6-115) and (6-116) will be valid. Shunt peaking is used to reduce the effects of C_{sh}. However, it is often of little use in compensating for the variations of $\mathbf{h}_{fe}$ with frequency. In the next section we shall analyze the transistor amplifier using a method that does not require the assumptions of this section and that also accounts for the variation of $\mathbf{h}_{fe}$ with frequency. In addition, we shall use the more exact form of the h-parameter equivalent circuit given by Eqs. (3-130). The analysis of the present section applies to vacuum-tube-pentode amplifiers

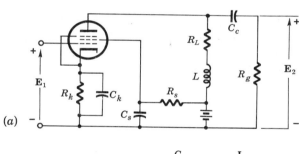

Fig. 6-27 Shunt-peaked amplifiers. (a) A common-cathode vacuum-tube amplifier; (b) a common-emitter transistor amplifier; (c) a high-frequency equivalent circuit for both amplifiers.

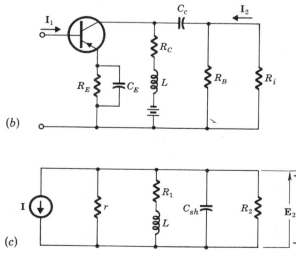

and to some transistor amplifiers. Vacuum-tube triodes are not used for video-frequency amplifiers because of the large Miller-effect capacitance.

If the inequalities of Eqs. (6-115) and (6-116) hold, we can then write

$$\frac{\mathbf{E}_2}{\mathbf{I}} = \frac{(R_1 + j\omega L)/j\omega C_{sh}}{R_1 + j(\omega L - 1/\omega C_{sh})} = \frac{R_1(1 + j\omega L/R_1)}{1 - \omega^2 L C_{sh} + j\omega R_1 C_{sh}} \tag{6-117}$$

For small values of ω, which would be encountered in the mid- and low-frequency regions, $\mathbf{E}_2/\mathbf{I} = R_1$. Thus, for both the voltage and the current gains, we have

$$\frac{\mathbf{A}_{\text{high}}}{\mathbf{A}_{\text{mid}}} = \frac{1 + j\omega L/R_1}{1 - \omega^2 L C_{sh} + j\omega R_1 C_{sh}} \tag{6-118}$$

This equation ignores the variation of $\mathbf{h}_{fe}$ with frequency in a transistor. We shall consider it subsequently.

The easiest way to obtain useful information from Eq. (6-118) is to plot its amplitude and phase angle versus frequency. Before doing this, we shall make some substitutions that present the results in a more general fashion. Let

$$f_2 = \frac{1}{2\pi R_1 C_{sh}} \tag{6-119}$$

Since $R_1 \ll R_2$ and $R_1 \ll r$, then $R_1 \approx R_{sh}$ [see Eqs. (6-5), (6-10), (6-26), and (6-30)] and f_2 is the upper half-power frequency of the uncompensated amplifier. The only other parameter that we need to know is the Q of the RL circuit at the frequency f_2. That is

$$Q_2 = \frac{2\pi f_2 L}{R_1} = \frac{\omega_2 L}{R_1} \tag{6-120}$$

Then, after substituting and manipulating, we obtain

$$\frac{\mathbf{A}_{\text{high}}}{\mathbf{A}_{\text{mid}}} = \frac{1 + jQ_2(f/f_2)}{1 - Q_2(f/f_2)^2 + j(f/f_2)} \tag{6-121}$$

or, equivalently

$$\left|\frac{A_{\text{high}}}{A_{\text{mid}}}\right| = \sqrt{\frac{1 + Q_2{}^2(f/f_2)^2}{[1 - Q_2(f/f_2)^2]^2 + (f/f_2)^2}} \tag{6-122}$$

and

$$\measuredangle \frac{A_{\text{high}}}{A_{\text{mid}}} = -\tan^{-1}\{(f/f_2)[1 - Q_2 + Q_2{}^2(f/f_2)^2]\} \tag{6-123}$$

A plot of $|A_{\text{high}}/A_{\text{mid}}|$ versus frequency, with Q_2 as a parameter, is given in Fig. 6-28.[5] When $Q_2 = 0$, the response is that of the uncompensated amplifier. As Q_2 increases, the bandwidth increases. $|A_{\text{high}}/A_{\text{mid}}|$ falls off essentially monotonically with frequency for values of Q_2 between 0 and 0.439. The curve for $Q_2 = 0.439$ has an extremely small rise. If abso-

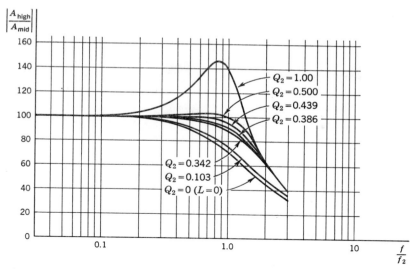

r̃ig. 6-28   *Curves of the amplitude response of the shunt-peaked amplifiers of Fig. 6-27.   (Adapted with permission from A. V. Bedford and G. L. Fredendall, Transient Response of Multistage Video-Frequency Amplifiers, Proc. IRE, vol. 27, pp. 277–284, 1939.)*

lutely no rise can be tolerated, $Q_2 = 0.414$ should be used.   For values of $Q_2 > 0.414$, the amplitude response rises and then falls.   The upper half-power frequency tends to increase as Q_2 increases.   However, if Q_2 is made too large, then the rise in the frequency response usually introduces a frequency distortion that is more severe than the one it corrects.   If a maximally flat frequency response is desired, then $Q_2 = 0.439$ is chosen.   The value of $Q_2 = 0.5$ is used at times, since this increases the upper half-power frequency without causing the gain to rise too much above the midband value.

The discussion of the previous paragraph pertains only to the amplitude response.   If phase distortion is considered, then other restrictions are placed on the value of Q_2.   For this circuit, phase distortion occurs when the phase shift of the amplifier does not vary linearly with frequency (see Sec. 5-7).   Thus, $\angle(A_{high}/A_{mid})/f$ should be constant.   If there is no phase distortion, then the time delay τ_d is given by [see Eq. (5-23)]

$$\tau_d = \frac{-\angle(A_{high}/A_{mid})}{\omega} \tag{6-124}$$

If τ_d is plotted, then departure from a constant is an indication of the amount of phase distortion.   Since we usually plot normalized frequency f/f_2, the expression for τ_d will be normalized in the following way

$$\tau_{dn} = -\frac{\omega_2}{\omega}\angle(A_{high}/A_{mid}) = -\frac{\angle(A_{high}/A_{mid})}{(f/f_2)} \tag{6-125}$$

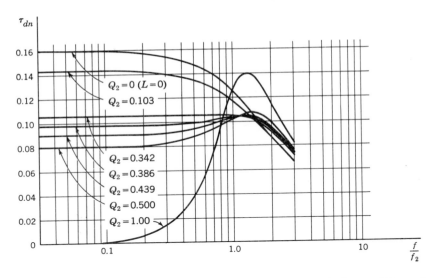

Fig. 6-29 Curves of the normalized relative time delay of the amplifiers of Fig. 6-27. The units of τ_{dn} are ω_2 sec. (Adapted with permission from A. V. Bedford and G. L. Fredendall, Transient Response of Multistage Video-Frequency Amplifiers, Proc. IRE, vol. 27, pp. 277–284, 1939.)

We shall call τ_{dn} the *normalized relative time delay;* it is plotted versus frequency, with Q_2 as a parameter, in Fig. 6-29.[5] As Q is increased from 0 to 0.342, the phase distortion, or the *delay distortion*, is reduced. The value of τ_{dn} decreases monotonically with frequency for these values of Q_2. If Q_2 is increased above 0.342, the delay distortion increases.

The optimum value of Q_2 depends upon the criterion used in choosing it. If amplitude distortion is the primary consideration, then a value of 0.439 to 0.5 might be used. If delay distortion is of utmost importance, then a value of 0.342 would be used. If both amplitude and delay distortion are weighted equally, then a value of Q_2 between 0.342 and 0.439 is usually used. We shall see that if transient response is considered, other criteria are used in choosing Q_2.

When amplifiers are cascaded, their amplitude responses are multiplied and their phase shifts are added. Thus, the relative response of a cascade of amplifiers can be obtained from Figs. 6-28 and 6-29. If a value of Q_2 is chosen such that the amplitude response is not monotonic and if identical stages are cascaded, then the nonmonotonicity will be exaggerated. Hence, if many stages are used, it is desirable to keep Q_2 less than 0.439 or 0.414.

In transistor amplifiers, high-frequency distortion is caused not only by the effect of C_{sh} but also by the variation of $\mathbf{h}_{fe}$ with frequency. The relative response can be obtained, in this case, by multiplying Eq. (6-121) by $1/(1 + jf/f_\beta)$. It is difficult to correct for this term using shunt peaking. There are instances when a rising response of Eq. (6-121) might partially compensate for a fall in the magnitude of $1/(1 + jf/f_\beta)$. However, such an occurrence is not general and would have to be found by a graphical cut-and-try procedure. In the next section, we shall consider more complex compensation techniques that may be used for the transistor.

6-12 A more general procedure for high-frequency compensation applied to the common-emitter transistor amplifier

Simple shunt peaking is of limited use in correcting the high-frequency response of cascaded common-emitter transistor amplifiers. A more versatile procedure, due to Gärtner,[6] will be presented here. We shall consider a cascade of amplifiers such as that shown in Fig. 6-30, where **Z** and **Y** are the compensating networks. Their forms shall be considered subsequently. Note that **Y** must be such that the bias voltage can be applied to the transistor. In addition, **Z** and **Y** should be such that the low- and mid-frequency performance of the amplifier is unaffected by the compensation. For increased accuracy at high frequencies, we shall use the h parameters of Eqs. (3-130) with slight modifications. In this type of amplifier cascade, $\mathbf{h}_{re}$ primarily affects the input admittance of the transistor. We shall consider $\mathbf{h}_{re} = 0$ and add a constant impedance $\mathbf{Z}_b$ to $\mathbf{h}_{ie}$ to account for it. The h parameters that will be used are

$$\mathbf{h}_{ie} = \frac{h_{ie}}{1 + j\omega/\omega_\beta} + \mathbf{Z}_b$$

$$\mathbf{h}_{re} = 0$$

$$\mathbf{h}_{fe} = \frac{h_{fe}}{1 + j\omega/\omega_\beta} \tag{6-126}$$

$$\mathbf{h}_{oe} = \frac{h_{oe}}{1 + j\omega/\omega_\beta} + j\omega \frac{C_{oe}}{1 + j\omega/\omega_\beta}$$

We shall assume that, in the low- and mid-frequency regions, $\mathbf{Z}_b$ is purely resistive and equal to R_b.

Fig. 6-30 A cascade of compensated common-emitter transistor amplifiers.

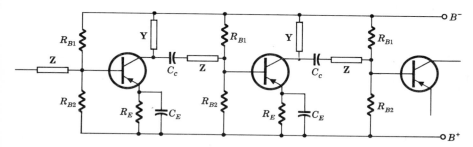

The high-frequency equivalent circuit for one stage of the amplifier is shown in Fig. 6-31, where it has been assumed that C_E and C_c are short circuits and that $R_B = R_{B1}R_{B2}/(R_{B1} + R_{B2})$ is very large in comparison with the input admittance of the next transistor amplifier stage. This approximation is usually quite good. The capacitance C_w represents any stray wiring capacitance. It will simplify the analysis if we determine a new set of h parameters that include $\mathbf{Z}$, $\mathbf{Y}$, and C_w. From the equivalent circuit, we then obtain

$$
\begin{aligned}
\mathbf{h}'_{ie} &= \mathbf{h}_{ie} + \mathbf{Z} \\
\mathbf{h}'_{re} &= 0 \\
\mathbf{h}'_{fe} &= \mathbf{h}_{fe} \\
\mathbf{h}'_{oe} &= \mathbf{h}_{oe} + \mathbf{Y} + j\omega C_w
\end{aligned}
\tag{6-127}
$$

The input impedance $\mathbf{Z}_i$ of any stage is given by

$$
\mathbf{Z}_i = \mathbf{h}'_{ie} = \mathbf{h}_{ie} + \mathbf{Z}
\tag{6-128}
$$

Then, using Eq. (3-78), we have

$$
\mathbf{A}_{i,\text{high}} = \frac{\mathbf{I}_2}{\mathbf{I}_1} = \frac{\mathbf{h}'_{fe}}{1 + \mathbf{h}'_{oe}\mathbf{Z}_i}
\tag{6-129}
$$

Substituting Eqs. (6-126) to (6-128) into Eq. (6-129), we obtain

$$
\mathbf{A}_{i,\text{high}} =
$$

$$
\frac{h_{fe}}{1 + \dfrac{j\omega}{\omega_\beta} + \left[h_{oe} + j\omega C_{oe} + (\mathbf{Y} + j\omega C_w)\left(1 + \dfrac{j\omega}{\omega_\beta}\right) \right]\left(\dfrac{h_{ie}}{1 + j\omega/\omega_\beta} + \mathbf{Z}_b + \mathbf{Z} \right)}
\tag{6-130}
$$

If $\mathbf{Z}$ and $\mathbf{Y}$ are left as general terms, then the task of optimizing this expression becomes difficult. To simplify the procedure somewhat, we shall assume a simple form for both $\mathbf{Z}$ and $\mathbf{Y}$. However, the procedure presented here is general and can be used with more complex impedances. Assume that

Fig. 6-31 A high-frequency equivalent circuit of one stage of the amplifier of Fig. 6-30.

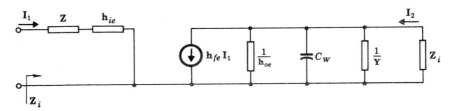

Y has the same form as it does in the shunt-peaked amplifier (a resistance in series with an inductance).

$$\mathbf{Y} = \frac{1}{R_1 + j\omega L_1} \tag{6-131}$$

To make the network as simple as possible, we choose **Z** to be just an inductance.

$$\mathbf{Z} = j\omega L_2 \tag{6-132}$$

Substituting in Eq. (6-130) and noting that in the mid-frequency region

$$A_{i,\text{mid}} = \frac{h_{fe}}{1 + (h_{oe} + 1/R_1)(h_{ie} + R_b)} \tag{6-133}$$

we have

$$\frac{A_{i,\text{high}}}{A_{i,\text{mid}}} = \frac{1 + (h_{oe} + 1/R_1)(h_{ie} + R_b)}{1 + j\dfrac{\omega}{\omega_\beta} + \left[h_{oe} + j\omega C_{oe} + \dfrac{1}{1 + j\omega/\omega_\beta}\left(j\omega C_w \right.\right.} \tag{6-134}$$
$$\left.\left. + \dfrac{1}{R_1 + j\omega L_1} \right)\right]\left[h_{ie}\left(1 + j\dfrac{\omega}{\omega_\beta}\right) + \mathbf{Z}_b + j\omega L_2 \right]$$

This equation is too complex to obtain any useful design relations, and there are too many variables to permit plotting a set of universal curves as was done for the shunt-peaked amplifier. Instead, the following procedure can be used.

For a particular transistor, h_{ie}, h_{fe}, h_{oe}, R_b, C_{oe}, and ω_β will be known constants, and a value of C_w can be assumed. Substitute them in Eqs. (6-133) and (6-134). Now choose the highest frequency of interest, f_o. At this frequency, the design specifications will permit $|A_{i,\text{high}}/A_{i,\text{mid}}|$ to be some fraction of unity. Call this fraction δ. Thus in Eq. (6-134)

$$\delta = \left| \frac{A_{i,\text{high}}}{A_{i,\text{mid}}} \right|_{f=f_0} \tag{6-135}$$

and from Eq. (6-133)

$$\frac{1}{R_1} = \frac{h_{fe}/A_{i,\text{mid}} - 1}{h_{ie} + R_b} - h_{oe} \tag{6-136}$$

Equation (6-136) does not uniquely determine R_1, since $A_{i,\text{mid}}$ is the mid-band current gain per stage and depends upon the number of stages. Start by trying one stage. Substitute the value of R_1 into Eq. (6-135). This yields an equation that relates L_1 to L_2. Curves of $|A_{i,\text{high}}/A_{i,\text{mid}}|$ should be plotted to determine the optimum values of L_1 and L_2. The shape of the resulting frequency response must be suitable (e.g., there should not be large peaks and the magnitude of the normalized response should not be less than δ in the frequency range for any frequencies less than f_0). The design is then complete. It is assumed that R_1, L_1, and L_2 are real positive constants.

If R_1 is negative, then the required gain per stage is too large. This can be corrected by using more stages or by obtaining a transistor with a larger value of h_{fe}. At any frequency, the magnitude of the current gain can be no greater than the magnitude of the short-circuit current gain $\mathbf{h}_{fe}$. Thus, the value of δ must be chosen such that

$$\delta \leqslant \frac{1}{[1 + (f_o/f_\beta)^2]^{\frac{1}{2}}} \tag{6-137}$$

Even if relation (6-137) is satisfied, the values of L_1 or L_2 could be imaginary or negative. Even if they are real and positive, the shape of the response may be unacceptable. In such cases, more stages should be tried, since this reduces the value of R_1 and may reduce the effect of C_{sh}. As the number of stages increases, the requirements on the frequency response of any one stage also increase. If Eq. (6-135) is valid for any one stage, and if n stages are used, we have

$$\delta_n = \delta^{1/n}$$

Now δ_n is used in Eq. (6-135) and must satisfy relation (6-137). Hence, this compensation procedure may not always work, and a new transistor with a higher f_β and/or a higher h_{fe}, and/or a lower C_{oe}, should be used.

This procedure did not consider the phase shift at all. Once the final form of the response is attained, the phase distortion should be checked to see if it is excessive. An alternative procedure would be to replace Eq. (6-135) with an equation for the phase shift.

Procedures of this type can be extended to more complex coupling networks. The algebraic manipulations become more difficult as the complexity of the network is increased. Such complex coupling networks are used in both vacuum-tube and transistor circuits where they provide some improvement over the simple shunt-peaked circuits.

The technique outlined in this section is general and can be applied to an equivalent circuit for which no approximations are made. For instance, all four h parameters and the input impedance (which is assumed independent of any variables) can be measured as functions of frequency. These can then be substituted into Eq. (6-129) to obtain an equation similar to Eq. (6-134). The procedure then follows in the same way as has been indicated.

6-13 Poles and zeros

We have thus far characterized frequency response by the behavior of the amplitude response and the phase shift as a function of ω. In this section we shall consider a different approach. For the circuits that we have considered, the only frequency-dependent parameters that were encountered are inductance, capacitance, and the variation of α with frequency. In all these cases, the term ω never appears by itself but is always multiplied by $j = \sqrt{-1}$. For instance, in the case of an inductance,

$$\mathbf{Z}_L = j\omega L \qquad \text{and} \qquad \mathbf{Y}_L = \frac{1}{j\omega L}$$

for a capacitance

$$\mathbf{Z}_C = \frac{1}{j\omega C} \qquad \text{and} \qquad \mathbf{Y}_C = j\omega C$$

and for a transistor

$$\boldsymbol{\alpha} = \frac{\alpha_0}{1 + j\omega/\omega_\alpha} \qquad \boldsymbol{\beta} = \frac{\beta_0}{1 + j\omega/\omega_\beta} \qquad \mathbf{h}_{fe} = \frac{h_{fe}}{1 + j\omega/\omega_\beta} \qquad \text{etc.}$$

The response of networks containing these elements will be made up of the algebraic combinations of terms of this type. Thus whenever ω appears in such networks, it will be multiplied by j. Hence, we can always make the substitution

$$p = j\omega \tag{6-138}$$

and eliminate all the $j\omega$ terms. Then, for an inductance

$$\mathbf{Z}_L = pL \qquad \mathbf{Y}_L = \frac{1}{pL} \tag{6-139}$$

for a capacitance

$$\mathbf{Z}_C = \frac{1}{pC} \qquad \mathbf{Y}_C = pC \tag{6-140}$$

and, for the transistor

$$\boldsymbol{\alpha} = \frac{\alpha_0}{1 + p/\omega_\alpha} \qquad \boldsymbol{\beta} = \frac{\beta_0}{1 + p/\omega_\beta} \qquad \mathbf{h}_{fe} = \frac{h_{fe}}{1 + p/\omega_\beta} \qquad \text{etc.} \tag{6-141}$$

The solution of the mesh or nodal equations of a network can always be expressed as the ratio of two determinants. After they are expanded and any fractions are cleared, the solution will be in the form of the ratio of two polynomials in the variable p. For instance, Eq. (6-11) can be written as

$$\frac{\mathbf{A}_{v,\text{high}}}{\mathbf{A}_{v,\text{mid}}} = \frac{1}{1 + p/\omega_2} \tag{6-142}$$

and Eq. (6-121) becomes

$$\frac{\mathbf{A}_{\text{high}}}{\mathbf{A}_{\text{mid}}} = \frac{1 + (Q_2/\omega_2)p}{1 + (1/\omega_2)p + (Q_2/\omega_2^2)p^2} \tag{6-143}$$

The general form of the response of a network can be written as

$$\mathbf{A}(p) = \frac{a_n p^n + a_{n-1}p^{n-1} + \cdots + a_1 p + a_0}{b_m p^m + b_{m-1}p^{m-1} + \cdots + b_1 p + b_0} \tag{6-144}$$

The p in the parentheses indicates that **A** *is a function of the variable p.* In addition, the a_i, $i = 1, 2, \ldots , n$, and the b_k, $k = 1, 2, \ldots , m$, are real numbers that are independent of frequency and that depend only upon the parameters of the network (i.e., the resistance, inductance, capacitance, transconductance, low-frequency short-circuit current gain, etc.). We can always express a polynomial in terms of its roots and a constant multiplier. Thus,

$$\mathbf{A}(p) = K \frac{(p - p_1)(p - p_3) \cdots (p - p_{2n-1})}{(p - p_2)(p - p_4) \cdots (p - p_{2m})} \tag{6-145}$$

Note that the roots of the numerator are given odd-numbered subscripts, while the roots of the denominator have even-numbered subscripts. The roots are constants which depend only upon the parameters of the network. They need not necessarily be real numbers; they can be imaginary or complex. Since the coefficients of Eq. (6-144) are real, if the roots of the numerator or the denominator are complex or imaginary numbers, they must occur in conjugate pairs.

The frequency response of Eq. (6-145) does not depend upon the value of the constant multiplier and is completely specified if we know the location of the roots of the numerator and the denominator. The location of these roots can be marked on a two-dimensional plot. The axis of real numbers is labeled σ and is called the σ *axis.* The axis of imaginary numbers is labeled $j\omega$ and is called the $j\omega$ axis. Note that if p is replaced by $j\omega$, the expression for the frequency response results. Usually, the roots of the numerator are marked with circles, while the roots of the denominator are marked with $\times$'s. Such a plot is shown in Fig. 6-32. A polynomial is zero when it is evaluated at one of its roots. Thus, at a root of the numerator $|A|$ is zero. Therefore, the roots of the numerator are called *zeros.* At a root of the denominator $|A|$ will be infinite. These roots are called *poles.* A diagram such as that of Fig. 6-32 is called a *pole-zero diagram* or a *pole-zero plot.* The entire plane of the plot is called the *p-plane.* The $j\omega$ axis divides it into a *left*

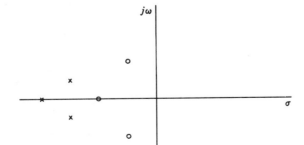

Fig. 6-32   A typical pole-zero diagram.

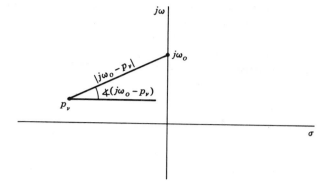

Fig. 6-33 A graphical construction that is useful in determining the frequency response.

half-plane and a *right half-plane.* We shall discuss the significance of these half-planes subsequently.

In order to obtain the frequency response we replace p by $j\omega$, so that for Eq. (6-145)

$$\mathbf{A}(j\omega) = K \frac{(j\omega - p_1)(j\omega - p_3) \cdots (j\omega - p_{2n-1})}{(j\omega - p_2)(j\omega - p_4) \cdots (j\omega - p_m)} \tag{6-146}$$

Thus

$$|A(j\omega)| = K \frac{|j\omega - p_1|\,|j\omega - p_3| \cdots |j\omega - p_{2n-1}|}{|j\omega - p_2|\,|j\omega - p_4| \cdots |j\omega - p_{2m}|} \tag{6-147}$$

and

$$\begin{aligned}
\angle A(j\omega) = {} & \angle(j\omega - p_1) + \angle(j\omega - p_3) + \cdots + \angle(j\omega - p_{2n-1}) \\
& - [\angle(j\omega - p_2) + \angle(j\omega - p_4) + \cdots \\
& \qquad\qquad\qquad\qquad\qquad\quad + \angle(j\omega - p_{2m})] \quad (6\text{-}148)
\end{aligned}$$

If the pole-zero plot is available, these magnitudes and angles can be calculated by means of the very simple graphical construction of Fig. 6-33. The frequency ω_o represents any one frequency, and p_ν represents either a pole or a zero. The length of the vector drawn from p_ν to $j\omega_o$ is $|j\omega_o - p_\nu|$ and its angle is $\angle(j\omega_o - p_\nu)$. To obtain the frequency response at any frequency ω_o, draw vectors from all the poles and zeros to the point $j\omega_o$. The lengths of the vectors and their phase angles are then measured. The amplitude response is obtained by multiplying the lengths of all the vectors from the zeros and then dividing this product by the product of the lengths of all the vectors from the poles. The phase shift is equal to the sum of the angles of all the vectors drawn from the zeros minus the sum of the angles of all the vectors drawn from the poles.

If a pole or a zero is very close to the $j\omega$ axis, then as ω_o passes along the axis near the pole the length of the vector $j\omega_o - p_\nu$ and its angle will change quite rapidly. If p_ν is very far from $j\omega_o$, then the magnitude and angle of the vector will vary only slightly as ω_o varies. Thus, the response at any frequency ω_o is determined primarily by the poles and zeros near $j\omega_o$. At times the poles and zeros that are the furthest from $j\omega_o$ can be neglected.

Note that there may be multiple poles and zeros. That is, some of the roots of the numerator and/or the denominator may be multiple. These can be indicated by multiple circles or x's on the pole-zero plot. The above discussion holds for multiple poles and zeros. Each pole or zero is counted in accordance with its multiplicity.

Let us now consider the pole-zero diagram of some of the amplifiers that we have considered. A typical low-frequency response is of the form

$$\frac{A_{low}}{A_{mid}} = \frac{1}{1 + \omega_1/p} = \frac{p}{p + \omega_1} \tag{6-149}$$

Its pole-zero pattern is given in Fig. 6-34a. The zero at the origin causes the gain to be zero at zero frequency. As ω_o increases, the lengths of the vectors drawn from the pole and from the zero increase and approach each other so that at mid- and high frequencies the gain approaches unity.

The high-frequency response of the transistor is given by Eq. (6-31) as

$$\frac{A_{i,high}}{A_{i,low}} = \frac{1}{1 + p/\omega_\beta} \cdot \frac{1}{1 + p/\omega_2} = \frac{\omega_\beta \omega_2}{(p + \omega_\beta)(p + \omega_2)} \tag{6-150}$$

The pole-zero plot is shown in Fig. 6-34b. The response in the low- and mid-frequency regions is essentially constant and the phase angle is zero, because at these frequencies the lengths of the vectors drawn from the poles at $-\omega_\beta$ and $-\omega_2$ to the $j\omega$ axis remain almost constant at the lengths ω_β and ω_2, respectively, and their phase angles are almost zero. In the high-frequency region the lengths of the vectors and their phase angles increase as ω_β increases. Figure 6-34a and b are not drawn to the same scale. In general, ω_2 or ω_β is usually 100 or more times ω_1.

An unbypassed bias impedance will produce a response of the form

$$\frac{A}{A_{mid}} = \frac{p + \omega_3}{p + \omega_4} \tag{6-151}$$

Its pole-zero plot is shown in Fig. 6-34c. At low frequencies, such as ω_{o1}, the vector drawn from the pole is much longer than the vector drawn from the zero. This results in diminished response. At higher frequencies, such as ω_{o2}, the length and angle of both vectors approach each other and the response approaches unity.

Figure 6-34d shows the pole-zero diagrams for a low-frequency-compensated amplifier. From Eq. (6-106), we have

$$\frac{A_{low}}{A_{mid}} = \frac{p(p + \omega_4)}{(p + \omega_3)(p + \omega_1)} \tag{6-152}$$

When the network is adjusted so that the $f_4 = f_1$, the zero cancels the pole, so that the pole-zero diagram then has the same form as that of Fig. 6-34a. Since $\omega_3 < \omega_1$, the frequency response will be improved.

Let us now obtain the pole-zero diagram of the shunt-peaked amplifier.

From Eq. (6-121) we have

$$\frac{A_{\text{high}}}{A_{\text{mid}}} = \frac{\omega_2(p + \omega_2/Q_2)}{p^2 + (\omega_2/Q_2)p + \omega_2^2/Q_2} \qquad (6\text{-}153)$$

The roots of the denominator are given by

$$p_2,\ p_4 = -\frac{\omega_2}{2Q_2} \pm \sqrt{\frac{\omega_2^2}{4Q_2}\left(\frac{1}{Q_2} - 4\right)} \qquad (6\text{-}154)$$

If $Q_2 < \frac{1}{4}$, then the roots will be real and lie on the negative σ axis on either side of the point $-\omega_2/2Q_2$, as shown in Fig. 6-34e. As Q_2 increases, the

Fig. 6-34 *Pole-zero diagrams for typical amplifiers.* (a) *Low frequency;* (b) *high frequency (transistor);* (c) *unbypassed bias lead;* (d) *low-frequency compensation;* (e) *shunt peaking with $Q < 0.25$; and* (f) *shunt peaking with $Q > 0.25$.*

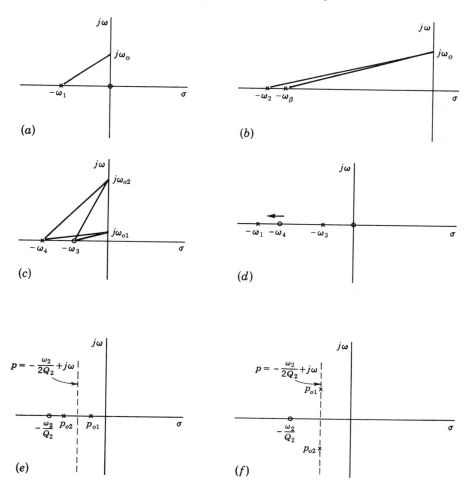

poles move along the σ axis toward the point $-\omega_2/2Q_2$. When $Q_2 = \frac{1}{4}$, there is a double pole at $-\omega_2/2Q_2$. As Q_2 increases further, the poles become complex and move along the vertical line whose equation is

$$p = \frac{-\omega_2}{2Q_2} + j\omega$$

(see Fig. 6-34f). At first glance, it may appear that the nonmonotonicity in the amplitude or the phase response could be related to the fact that the poles do not lie on the negative σ axis. However, this is not a *simple* function of the location of the poles and zeros.

6-14 Transient response

The ultimate reason for considering the frequency response of an amplifier is to determine the amount of distortion of the output signal (see Sec. 5-7). That is, the frequency response can be utilized to determine the output as a function of time in response to an arbitrary input. The two signals can then be compared. The response of an amplifier as a function of time is called the *transient response*. In this section we shall consider distortion on a transient basis and relate it to the frequency distortion.

An irregular input signal applied to a network will produce an irregular output signal. It is then difficult, unless tedious measurements are made, to estimate the distortion. On the other hand, if a regular input signal is applied, any distortion in the output waveform will be readily discernible. An input signal that is commonly used for such testing is the *unit step*. This is symbolically represented by $u(t)$ and is given by

$$u(t) = \begin{cases} 1 & t > 0 \\ 0 & t < 0 \end{cases} \tag{6-155}$$

Figure 6-35 illustrates such a function. The response of a network to a voltage or current whose waveform is $u(t)$ is called the *unit-step response*. We shall illustrate this with the circuit of Fig. 6-36a, which is a simple form of the high-frequency equivalent circuits of Secs. 6-1 and 6-3. For the vacuum tube, $k = g_m$ and the input is a unit step of voltage. For the transistor, $k = h_{fe}$ and the input is a unit step of current. The variation

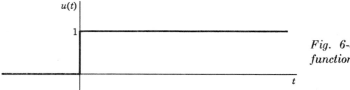

Fig. 6-35   The unit-step function.

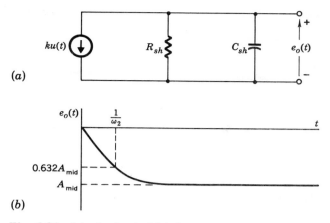

Fig. 6-36 (a) A simple high-frequency equivalent circuit with a unit step input; (b) its unit-step response.

of h_{fe} with frequency is neglected here. The differential equation for this circuit is

$$k = \frac{1}{R_{sh}} e_o + C_{sh} \frac{de_o}{dt} \qquad (6\text{-}156)$$

Solving, and assuming that there is no initial stored charge, we obtain

$$e_o(t) = -kR_{sh}(1 - e^{-t/R_{sh}C_{sh}}) \qquad (6\text{-}157)$$

but $-kR_{sh} = A_{\mathrm{mid}}$ and $\omega_2 = 1/R_{sh}C_{sh}$. Thus,

$$e_o(t) = A_{\mathrm{mid}}(1 - e^{-t\omega_2}) \qquad (6\text{-}158)$$

This voltage is illustrated in Fig. 6-36b. The t in the parentheses indicates that e_o is a function of time. The waveform approaches a steady magnitude of $|A_{\mathrm{mid}}|$ and the time constant is $1/\omega_2$, the reciprocal of the upper half-power angular frequency. To normalize, we often plot the output divided by A_{mid}. This will be denoted by the symbol $b(t)$. Hence,

$$b(t) = 1 - e^{-t\omega_2} \qquad (6\text{-}159)$$

This waveform is shown in Fig. 6-37. Its departure from the unit step can be seen immediately. As f_2 increases $b(t)$ rises more rapidly and better approximates the unit step.

Let us now investigate the effects of a coupling capacitor upon the unit-step response. Consider the circuit of Fig. 6-38a. The differential equation is

$$kR_1 = (R_1 + R_2)i + \frac{1}{C_c} \int i \, dt$$

and

$$e_o = -iR_2$$

Thus

$$e_o(t) = -kR_{sh}e^{-t/R_{low}C_c} \qquad (6\text{-}160)$$

Where, using notation of Secs. 6-1 and 6-3

$$R_{sh} = \frac{R_1 R_2}{R_1 + R_2} \qquad \text{and} \qquad R_{low} = R_1 + R_2$$

Thus, in normalized form

$$b(t) = e^{-t\omega_1} \qquad (6\text{-}161)$$

This is illustrated in Fig. 6-38b. The response does not appear to be very much like a unit step. However, as f_1 decreases to zero, the 0.368 point moves out toward infinite time and $b(t)$ does approach $u(t)$. The lower half-power frequency f_1 should be small enough so that $b(t)$ is close to unity for all times of interest. This will be discussed subsequently in terms of sag. We shall consider the complete frequency range by combining the circuits of Figs. 6-36a and 6-38a. This is shown in Fig. 6-39a. Let

$$\frac{1}{R_{sh}} = \frac{1}{R_1} + \frac{1}{R_2}$$

and $C_{sh} = C_1 + C_2$. If $f_2 = 1/2\pi R_{sh}C_{sh} \gg f_1 = 1/2\pi R_{low}C_c$, then an approximate analysis yields the waveform shown in Fig. 6-39b. If there is a well-defined midband region, then the response will essentially rise to unity, remain there for a time, and then fall off. Note that there is a break in the time axis. Actually, even with this break, Fig. 6-39b is not too representative, because the time constant of the exponential decay is very much greater

Fig. 6-37   The normalized unit-step response of the amplifier of Fig. 6-36a.

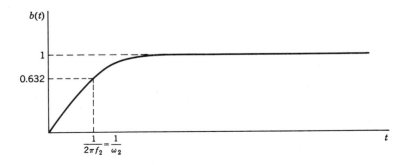

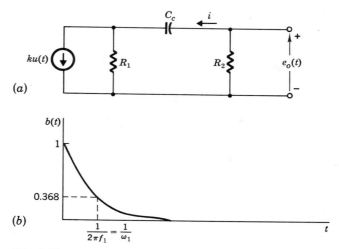

Fig. 6-38   *(a)*   *A simple low-frequency equivalent circuit; (b)*
its normalized unit step response.

than that of the exponential rise. Figure 6-39*b* is actually a combination
of Figs. 6-37 and 6-38*b*. The response of Fig. 6-37 usually takes place in
the first hundredth of an inch or so of the time axis of Fig. 6-38*b*. If there
is not a well-defined midband region, then there will not be a flat region of
the unit-step-response curve.

In most practical amplifiers, the midband region is well defined and the
buildup and the decay of the unit-step response can be considered separately.

Fig 6-39   *(a)*   *A simple equivalent circuit with both low- and high-frequency response;*
(b) its unit-step response.

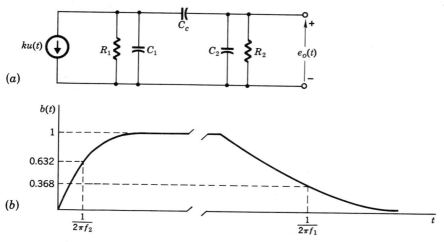

Often, in such cases, it is possible to obtain some simple numbers, or figures of merit, that can be used to rate the transient response.

Rise of the unit-step response

Consider the unit-step response of Fig. 6-37. One criterion of the distortion is the length of time it takes for the response to rise to unity. Often, as it is in Fig. 6-37, this time is infinite. Thus, the time it takes for the response to reach a value somewhat less than 1 is more representative. Nine-tenths is the value that is usually chosen. There is one other factor that must be considered. A network may introduce a time delay without producing distortion. For instance, if $A/A_{mid} = 1/-k\omega$, then the output will be a faithful reproduction of the input, but it will be delayed by k seconds. This time should not be "charged" against the response of the network. Often it is considered that the response has not started until it has reached 10 percent of its final value. Hence, a criterion for the speed of the response is defined as

$$\tau_r = \text{time for } b(t) \text{ to reach } 0.9 - \text{time for } b(t) \text{ to reach } 0.1 \qquad (6\text{-}162)$$

This is called the 10–90 *percent rise time* or simply the *rise time*. It is indicated on the unit-step response of Fig. 6-40. This unit-step response is typical of many networks. Notice that the response does not asymptotically approach unity, but actually overshoots and then approaches unity in a damped oscillatory fashion. The ratio of the maximum value of $b(t)$ to unity (the final value) is called the *overshoot*. We shall indicate it by δ_o. The 10–90 percent rise time and the overshoot are two important figures of merit for the rising portion of the unit-step response. Of course, they do not convey all of the information about $b(t)$, since two numbers cannot completely characterize a general curve. In certain computer applications the total speed of response is important. In such cases any delay time should

Fig. 6-40   A typical unit-step response illustrating the 10-90 percent rise time and the overshoot.

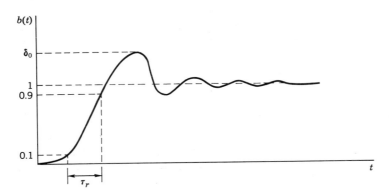

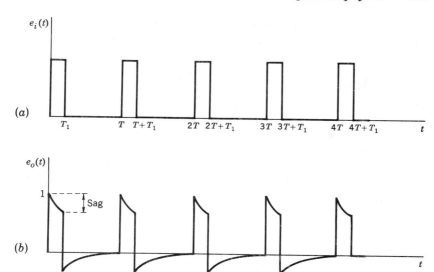

Fig. 6-41 (a) *A train of pulses;* (b) *the effect of the low-frequency response on the pulse train.*

be charged against the rise time of the amplifier. The 0–90 percent rise time could be considered in such cases.

The response of an amplifier to a train of pulses is an important criterion of its transient response. For instance, in a television amplifier, this indicates the amount of resolution in the picture, since it indicates how rapidly the image can be switched from black to white. It is also of importance in a radar amplifier, since the location of a pulse in time is an indication of the distance of the object sighted upon. A pulse train and some typical responses are shown in Fig. 5-9. In terms of the examples, if the rise time is too long, (1) the television picture cannot go rapidly from black to white and will have a blurred gray area between; (2) a radar pulse that does not have a well-defined leading edge cannot be fixed accurately in time, and, thus, the radar will not give accurate information about range. In general, τ_r should be considerably less than the width of the pulse. The overshoot is somewhat more important in the television image since it will distort the signal. It can be tolerated in the radar pulse if it is not so severe that it prevents successive pulses from being identified.

Decay of the unit-step response

Consider the curve of Fig. 6-38b. One way of rating it would be to determine the time it takes for the response to fall to 90 percent of its initial value. The longer this *fall time*, the better the response. The pulse response is usually used to obtain a figure of merit for the decay. For instance, if the input to the network of Fig. 6-38a is a train of pulses such as that shown in Fig. 6-41a, the response will be that given in Fig. 6-41b. For convenience, we have assumed that the period T is long enough so that the response becomes almost zero between pulses. We would ideally have the top of each pulse horizontal. Thus, the amount that it falls off is a criterion of the distortion. If the pulses are normalized so that the maximum height is unity, then the *sag* is equal to 1 minus the magnitude of $e_o(t)$ at the end of the pulse. In general, as the pulse becomes longer, the sag increases. Conversely, if there is a maximum sag that will be tolerated, the lower half-power frequency must decrease as the pulse length increases [see Eq. (6-161)]. The top of the pulse need not be just a simple exponential decay. For instance, in certain cases of low-frequency compensation, the response may actually rise before it falls off. In such cases, an overshoot can be spoken of in the decay.

6-15   Relation of the pole-zero diagrams to transient response

The response of a network to an applied signal is characterized by a differential equation. There are operational methods for solving such equations. These relate the pole-zero diagram to the response of the network. This process is too lengthy to be considered at this time, but some results of such an analysis will be given in this section. Networks of the type that we are considering are characterized by *linear integral-differential equations with constant coefficients*. When an operational method called the *Laplace transform* is used to solve these equations, the operations of differentiation and integration with respect to time become multiplication and division by a new variable. We shall denote this variable by the letter p. The integral-differential equation then becomes algebraic, and its solution is called the *response of the network in transformed form*. A function of time can be *transformed* into a function of p. Conversely, a function of p can be *inverse-transformed* into a function of time. In transformed form, the output of an amplifier in response to an arbitrary input is equal to the transformed form of the amplification times the transform of the input. For a great many networks, the transformed form of the amplification can be obtained from the frequency response if $j\omega$ is replaced by p. We shall present, without proof, some functions of time and their Laplace transforms in Table 6-3. It is assumed that these functions of time are zero for $t < 0$.

We shall state some general facts about the Laplace transform. The transient response is characterized by the location of the poles. For instance, a pair of simple poles on the $j\omega$ axis at $p = \pm j\omega_o$ gives rise to sines and/or cosines of frequency ω_o. A pole at the origin transforms into the unit step. Any pole in the left half-plane will transform into a function of time multiplied by a decaying exponential. A damped exponential falls off quite rapidly with time, so that any response whose transform is a pole, or a pair of poles in the left half-plane, will approach zero as t approaches

Table 6-3   **The Laplace transform of some simple functions**

$f(t)$	$F(p)$
$u(t)$	$\dfrac{1}{p}$
$\sin \omega_o t$	$\dfrac{\omega_o}{p^2 + \omega_o{}^2} = \dfrac{\omega_o}{(p + j\omega_o)(p - j\omega_o)}$
$\cos \omega_o t$	$\dfrac{p}{p^2 + \omega_o{}^2} = \dfrac{p}{(p + j\omega_o)(p - j\omega_o)}$
$e^{-at} \sin \omega_o t$	$\dfrac{\omega_o}{(p + a)^2 + \omega_o{}^2} = \dfrac{\omega_o}{(p + a + j\omega_o)(p + a - j\omega_o)}$
$e^{-at} \cos \omega_o t$	$\dfrac{p + a}{(p + a)^2 + \omega_o{}^2} = \dfrac{p + a}{(p + a + j\omega_o)(p + a - j\omega_o)}$
e^{-at}	$\dfrac{1}{p + a}$
e^{+at}	$\dfrac{1}{p - a}$

infinity. Similarly, poles in the right half-plane will have a transform that is multiplied by an increasing exponential, so that the poles in the right half-plane lead to unstable circuits wherein the response builds up with time. A simple pole on the σ axis produces an exponential rise or decay. A pair of simple poles not on the σ axis will lead to a sinusoid multiplied by the factor e^{-at} if the poles are in the left half-plane and to a sinusoid multiplied by e^{+at} if the poles are in the right half-plane. It is assumed that a is a real positive constant.

The ratio of two polynomials can be expanded in a series so that each term in the series contains only one pole. For instance

$$\frac{p}{(p + 1)(p + 2)} = \frac{-1}{p + 1} + \frac{2}{p + 2} \tag{6-163}$$

The function of time whose transform is given by Eq. (6-163) is

$$f(t) = -e^{-t} + 2e^{-2t}$$

Thus, we can determine the type of time functions that are present in the output signal simply by inspecting the pole-zero plot of the amplifier.

In all of this discussion nothing was mentioned about the zeros. The location of the zeros determines the relative magnitudes of the various time functions and the phase angle of any sinusoids. The zeros do not determine what components are present. (If a zero and a pole occur at the same point then the zero will cancel the pole and its transform will not appear in the output.)

Now let us use the Laplace transform to obtain the transient response of an amplifier to an arbitrary input waveform. The Laplace transform of the output waveform is obtained by multiplying the transformed form of the gain by the transform of the input waveform. It is often desirable to normalize the response by dividing it by the constant value $\mathbf{A}_{\text{mid}}$. For instance, let us calculate $b(t)$, the normalized unit-step response. Its Laplace transform $\mathbf{B}(p)$ is given by

$$\mathbf{B}(p) = \frac{1}{p} \frac{\mathbf{A}(p)}{\mathbf{A}_{\text{mid}}} \tag{6-164}$$

As an example, let us obtain the unit-step response of the amplifier of Fig. 6-38a. From Eq. (6-149), we have

$$\frac{\mathbf{A}(p)}{\mathbf{A}_{\text{mid}}} = \frac{p}{p + \omega_1}$$

Then, using Eq. (6-164)

$$\mathbf{B}(p) = \frac{1}{p} \cdot \frac{p}{p + \omega_1} = \frac{1}{p + \omega_1}$$

and $b(t) = e^{-\omega_1 t}$. This is verified by Eq. (6-161). The output does not have a unit step as one of its components, since the pole at $p = 0$ is canceled by the zero there.

Let us now consider the unit-step response of the shunt-peaked amplifier of Sec. 6-11. The normalized gain in transformed form is given by Eq. (6-153). The transform of the unit-step response is then

$$\mathbf{B}(p) = \frac{\omega_2(p + \omega_2/Q_2)}{p[p^2 + (\omega_2/Q_2)p + \omega_2^2/Q_2]} \tag{6-165}$$

The form of $b(t)$ is relatively complex and can be best discussed if the values are plotted. This is done in Fig. 6-42.[5] The rise time of the unit-step response decreases as Q_2 is increased. However, if $Q_2 > 0.25$, an overshoot develops. This can be explained in terms of the pole-zero diagram which is given in Fig. 6-34e and f, except that a pole must be added at the origin. If $Q_2 < 0.25$, the response will consist of the sum of decaying exponentials, since the poles lie on the σ axis. If $Q_2 > 0.25$ the poles become complex and, consequently, the output will contain damped sinusoids. This is the reason for the change in the character of the response when Q_2 exceeds 0.25. The rise time decreases as the overshoot increases. This happens in a great many networks. A compromise must usually be made between rise time and overshoot. If no overshoot is allowed, then, for the shunt-peaked amplifier, the critically damped case of $Q_2 = 0.25$ is used. This value is less than those discussed in Sec. 6-11, where the amplitude distortion or the phase distortion was considered. Thus, we can see that there is no *simple* interrelation among the three types of response. If a value of $Q_2 = 0.342$ is used, the rise time will be decreased and the overshoot will still be quite small; the frequency and phase distortion will also be reduced.

The rise time and overshoot of a single stage are not of prime importance, but the rise time and overshoot of the overall amplifier are. Unfortunately,

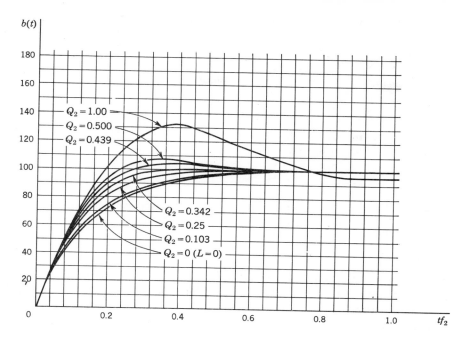

Fig. 6-42 Curves of the normalized unit-step response of the amplifiers of Fig. 6-27. (Adapted with permission from A. V. Bedford and G. L. Fredendall, Transient Response of Multistage Video-Frequency Amplifiers, Proc. IRE, vol. 27, pp. 277–284, 1939.)

the rise time and overshoot of the cascade cannot be determined from a knowledge of just the rise time and overshoot of the individual stages. However, there are some *approximate* rules that work quite well in most cases when the transform of the amplification does not have zeros in the right half-plane.[7] These rules are:

1. If there are n stages, with rise times $\tau_{r1}, \tau_{r2}, \ldots, \tau_{rn}$, and all of the stages are free of overshoot, then the overall rise time is

$$\tau_{rT} \approx \sqrt{\tau_{r1}{}^2 + \tau_{r2}{}^2 + \cdots + \tau_{rn}{}^2} \tag{6-166}$$

If n identical stages are used

$$\tau_{rT} \approx \tau_{r1} \sqrt{n} \tag{6-167}$$

If the overshoot per stage is very small (less than 1 or 2 percent) then Eqs. (6-166) and (6-167) are still valid. The overshoot of the overall amplifier will not increase as the number of stages is increased.

2. If the overshoot is about 5 to 10 percent per stage and there are n identical stages, the overshoot of the cascade will be

$$\delta_{oT} = \sqrt{n}\, \delta_o \tag{6-168}$$

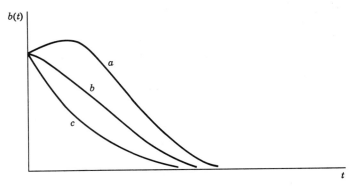

Fig. 6-43   The unit-step response of the low-frequency-compensated amplifier.   (a) $\omega_4 > \omega_1$; (b) $\omega_4 = \omega_1$; and (c) $\omega_4 < \omega_1$.   It is assumed that $\omega_3 < \omega_1$.

where δ_o is the overshoot of one stage.   In such cases, the rise time increases at a slower rate than is indicated by Eqs. (6-166) and (6-167).

The transform of the unit-step response of the low-frequency-compensated amplifier whose response is given by Eq. (6-106) is

$$\mathbf{B}(p) = \frac{p + \omega_4}{(p + \omega_3)(p + \omega_1)} = \frac{\omega_4 - \omega_3}{\omega_1 - \omega_3}\frac{1}{p + \omega_3} + \frac{\omega_4 - \omega_1}{\omega_3 - \omega_1}\frac{1}{p + \omega_1} \qquad (6\text{-}169)$$

From Eqs. (6-104) and (6-105) we have $\omega_4 > \omega_3$.   The unit-step response is given by

$$b(t) = \frac{1}{\omega_1 - \omega_3}[(\omega_4 - \omega_3)e^{-\omega_3 t} - (\omega_4 - \omega_1)e^{-\omega_1 t}] \qquad (6\text{-}170)$$

There are three general forms that the unit-step response will take.   (We shall assume that $\omega_3 < \omega_1$.)   These are illustrated in Fig. 6-43.   If $\omega_1 < \omega_4$, the response actually overshoots before it falls off.   If $\omega_1 > \omega_4$, the rate of falloff increases.   By varying the value of ω_4 we can trade overshoot for sag.

6-16   Frequency response of common-plate, common-base, and common-collector amplifiers

With very slight modifications the analysis of the previous sections can be applied to the other amplifier configurations.   We shall not discuss the common-grid amplifier, since it is very rarely used as an RC-coupled amplifier.

The common-plate amplifier or cathode follower

An RC-coupled cathode-follower amplifier is shown in Fig. 6-44a.   Its equivalent circuit is given in Fig. 6-44b, where we have assumed that the capacitors

C_k and C_s are short circuits at all frequencies of interest. Since the gain of the cathode follower is usually close to unity, the effect of R_{gi} can, in general, be neglected. The effect of the first coupling capacitor C_{c1} is not included in the gain of this stage. We shall consider it subsequently. The capacitance C_o is given by

$$C_o = C_{\text{out}} + C_w + C_{hk} \tag{6-171}$$

where C_{out} is defined by Eq. (6-1), C_w represents half of the stray wiring capacitance, and C_{hk} is the capacitance between the cathode and the heater of the vacuum tube. It is assumed that the heater is at the potential of the common lead. The resistor R_g is the grid-leak resistance of the next stage, and C_i is the sum of the remainder of the wiring capacitance plus the input capacitance of the next stage. Let us replace the circuit to the left of terminals ab by its Norton's equivalent circuit. Since $\mathbf{E}_2' = 0$ under short-circuit conditions, we have

$$\mathbf{I}_{sc} = g_m \mathbf{E}_1$$

Fig. 6-44   *(a) A common-plate RC-coupled vacuum-tube amplifier; (b) its equivalent circuit where* $\dfrac{1}{R_L} = \dfrac{1}{R_L{}'} + \dfrac{1}{R_s}$; *(c) a modified form of the equivalent circuit.*

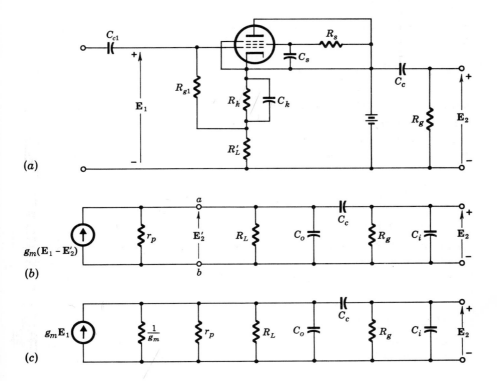

The open-circuit voltage is

$$\mathbf{E}_{oc} = \frac{g_m\mathbf{E}_1}{g_m + 1/r_p}$$

Thus, the equivalent circuit can be redrawn as in Fig. 6-44c. This is essentially the same as Fig. 6-3, which is the equivalent circuit for the common-cathode RC-coupled amplifier. The only differences are that the resistance $1/g_m$ is placed in parallel with r_p and the polarity of the current generator has been reversed. We can thus use all the results of Sec. 6-1 if we use new values for R_{sh} and R_{low}. These are given by

$$\frac{1}{R'_{sh}} = g_m + \frac{1}{r_p} + \frac{1}{R_L} + \frac{1}{R_g} \tag{6-172}$$

and

$$R'_{\text{low}} = \frac{1}{g_m + 1/r_p + 1/R_L} + R_g \tag{6-173}$$

The midband gain will not have a phase reversal, so that

$$A_{v,\text{mid}} = g_mR'_{sh} \tag{6-174}$$

The value of R'_{sh} is always less than $1/g_m$. Hence, the midband gain is less than unity and the upper half-power frequency f_2 is quite high. The gain-bandwidth product for a cathode-follower amplifier is still $g_m/2\pi C_{sh}$, however.

The input resistance of the cathode follower is usually many times the value of R_{g1}. If the ratio of E'_2/E_1 is equal to d, then the input resistance is $R_{g1}/(1 - d)$ (see Sec. 3-13). Usually d is very close to unity. Thus, the lower half-power frequency of the input circuit, consisting of C_{c1} and the input resistance, is given by $(1 - d)/2\pi R_{g1}C_{c1}$. This half-power frequency may be many times less than that of the other amplifier stages. Note that the terminating resistance R_g is usually the grid-leak resistance of a common-cathode amplifier. Cathode followers are not cascaded, since their voltage gains are less than unity.

The common-base transistor amplifier

A common-base transistor amplifier and its equivalent circuit are given in Fig. 6-45. The equivalent circuit is the same as that for the common-emitter amplifier shown in Fig. 6-9, except that the second subscript e has been replaced by b and ω_β has been replaced by ω_α. Thus, the results of the analysis of the common-emitter amplifier can be applied to the common-base amplifier by appropriately modifying the subscripts. Note that $h_{f\beta} = -\alpha_0$. Hence, for the common-base amplifier using junction transistors, the maximum current gain is less than unity. However, $\omega_\beta = (1 - \alpha_0)\omega_\alpha$ and $C_{oe} \approx C_{ob}/(1 - \alpha_0)$. Thus, the high-frequency response of the common-base circuit will be considerably greater than that of the common-emitter

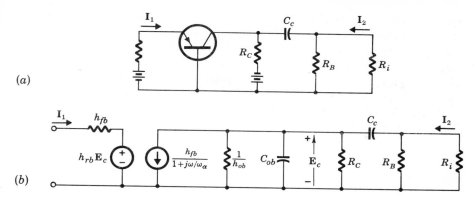

(a)

(b)

Fig. 6-45 (a) *A common-base RC-coupled transistor amplifier;* (b) *its equivalent circuit.*

amplifier.   As in the case of the cathode follower, common-base amplifiers are usually not cascaded but are used for special-purpose input or output stages.

The common-collector transistor amplifier

Figure 6-46 illustrates a common-collector transistor amplifier and its equivalent circuit.   The equivalent circuit of Fig. 3-36 has been used here. From Eqs. (3-61), (3-130), and (3-132), we have $h_{fc} = -(h_{fe} + 1)$, $h_{ic} = h_{ie}$, $h_{oc} = h_{oe}$ and $C_{oc} = C_{oe}$.   Thus, not only is the form of Fig. 6-46b the same as that of Fig. 6-9, but *most* of the values are *almost* equal.   The frequency response of the common-collector RC-coupled amplifier is essentially the

Fig. 6-46 (a) *A common-collector RC-coupled transistor amplifier;* (b) *its equivalent circuit.*

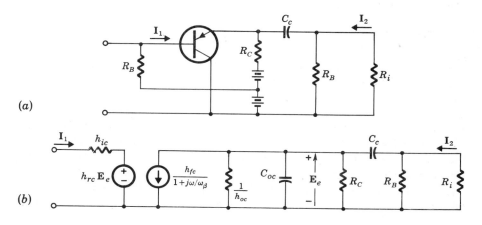

(a)

(b)

same as that of the common-emitter amplifier. The high input impedance of the common-collector amplifier does aid in lowering the half-power frequency of the input coupling network (i.e., the one containing C_{ci}). These amplifiers are usually not cascaded because of the high input impedance. Thus, the lower half-power frequency of the amplifier itself is unaffected by their high input impedance.

In Sec. 3-11 the relative merits of the three transistor amplifier configurations are considered.

6-17 The ideal transformer

In Sec. 5-3 we discussed the advantages and disadvantages of the transformer as a coupling network. Now, we shall develop the fundamental relations of the *ideal transformer*. In the next section practical transformers will be considered. A representation of an ideal transformer is shown in Fig. 6-47*a*. Two coils of wire are wound on a core that is assumed to be lossless and of zero reluctance. Thus, all of the flux set up by any turn of one coil links all the turns of both coils. It is also assumed that the wire possesses zero resistance. Since the same flux ϕ links both coils, we can write

$$e_1 = n_1 \frac{d\phi}{dt}$$

and

$$e_2 = n_2 \frac{d\phi}{dt}$$

Thus

$$\frac{e_1}{e_2} = \frac{n_1}{n_2} \tag{6-175}$$

The net magnetomotive force (mmf) around any closed loop is zero. Since the core is ideal, we have

$$n_1 i_1 + n_2 i_2 = 0 \tag{6-176}$$

so that

$$\frac{e_1}{e_2} = -\frac{i_2}{i_1} = \frac{n_1}{n_2} \tag{6-177}$$

A schematic representation for the ideal transformer is shown in Fig. 6-47*b*. The "dots" are used to indicate the polarity of the windings. If the current into one dotted terminal increases constantly, the other dotted terminal is the "positive end" of its coil.

Transformers can be used to transform impedance levels as well as voltage and current levels. In fact, this is one of their most important applica-

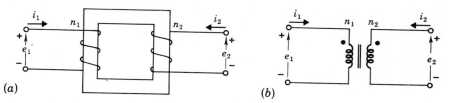

(a) (b)

Fig. 6-47   (a) An ideal transformer; (b) its schematic representation.

tions in amplifier work. Consider the circuit of Fig. 6-48. The input impedance is given by

$$Z_i = \frac{E_1}{I_1} = \frac{(n_1/n_2)E_2}{-(n_2/n_1)I_2}$$

Thus

$$Z_i = \left(\frac{n_1}{n_2}\right)^2 Z_L \tag{6-178}$$

Hence, the impedance transformation ratio is the square of the turns ratio.

6-18 Equivalent circuits for actual transformers

The ideal transformer introduces no frequency distortion. However, the frequency response of an actual transformer is far from perfect. In order to obtain the frequency characteristics of a practical transformer, we must obtain its equivalent circuit. This circuit is only approximate, as are all equivalent circuits. It represents a compromise between accuracy and a reasonable number of elements. The equivalent circuit that we shall use here is shown in Fig. 6-49a. It contains an ideal transformer whose turns ratio is the same as that of the actual transformer, plus other elements which cause the circuit to perform in essentially the same way as the actual transformer does. Equation (6-176) indicates that $I_1 = 0$ if $I_2 = 0$. A transformer with an open-circuited secondary is just an inductance. Hence, if $I_1 = 0$, then this inductance must be infinite. The shunt *magnetizing inductance* L_m is added to account for the fact that the primary inductance is finite. The power dissipated by R_c is approximately equal to the eddy-current and hysteresis losses in the core. The less the core loss, the greater

Fig. 6-48   A circuit illustrating the imped-ance-transforming properties of the ideal transformer.

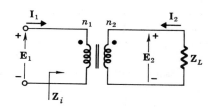

is the value of R_c.   Both the primary and secondary coils set up flux that link their own turns but not those of each other.   Such flux does not produce transformer action, but it does produce a voltage drop in each winding which is the same as the one that would be produced by an inductance in series with the transformer windings.   The *leakage inductances* L_p and L_s account for this voltage drop.   The resistances R_p and R_s are equal to the resistance of the primary and secondary windings.   As L_p, L_s, R_p, and R_s are decreased, the quality of the transformer is increased.   Any coil will possess capacitance between successive turns.   The capacitors C_p and C_s' take this into account.   For usual operation, one end of the primary and one end of the secondary windings are connected together as shown. C_{ps} represents the capacitive coupling between the windings.   It is desirable to have all the capacitances as small as possible.   A question can be raised as to whether or not these elements have been placed in the right position. For instance, why are L_p and L_s, but not C_p and C_s', placed adjacent to the transformer?   Actually, neither would be totally correct.   An exact equivalent circuit for the transformer would use distributed parameters (i.e., an infinite number of infinitesimal elements).   This circuit is just a useful approximation.

The capacitor C_{ps}, coupling the primary to the secondary, complicates the calculations.   It can be accounted for approximately by the following procedure.   The current through C_{ps} is given by

$$\mathbf{I}_{sp} = (\mathbf{E}_2 - \mathbf{E}_1)j\omega C_{ps}$$

If the drops in R_p, L_p, R_s, and L_s are neglected, we have

$$\mathbf{I}_{sp} = \mathbf{E}_2\left(1 \mp \frac{n_1}{n_2}\right)j\omega C_{ps} \tag{6-179}$$

Fig. 6-49   (a) An equivalent circuit for an actual transformer; (b) a modification that does not have the capacitive coupling between the primary and the secondary.

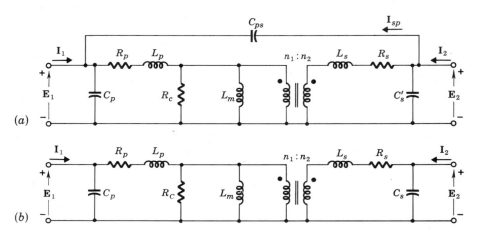

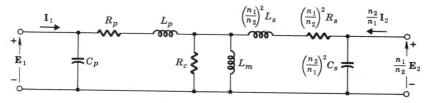

Fig. 6-50   The equivalent circuit of Fig. 6-49b referred to the primary side. Note that C_s is multiplied by n_2/n_1, since the impedance is inversely proportional to the capacitance.

where the upper sign is used if the dots are as shown.   We then partially account for C_{ps} by placing a capacitor $(1 \mp n_1/n_2)C_{ps}$ in shunt with C'_s so that it draws the same current $\mathbf{I}_{sp}$.   Such a circuit is shown in Fig. 6-49b, where

$$C_s = C'_s + \left(1 \mp \frac{n_1}{n_2}\right)C_{ps} \tag{6-180}$$

If $(1 \mp n_1/n_2)$ is negative, then the procedure should be modified so that a positive capacitance is added to C_p.   It should be stressed that either of these procedures only approximately accounts for C_{ps}.

If there is no coupling capacitance between the primary and secondary of the transformer, the circuit can be reduced still further.   We can eliminate the ideal transformer from the circuit of Fig. 6-49b by raising the impedance level of the secondary circuit by the amount $(n_1/n_2)^2$ as is indicated in Eq. (6-178).   The voltage and current levels are then transformed in accordance with Eq. (6-177).   Such a circuit, called an *equivalent circuit referred to the primary side*, is shown in Fig. 6-50.   Similarly, we can also obtain an equivalent circuit referred to the secondary side.

6-19   The transformer-coupled amplifier

The primary purpose for using transformer coupling is to impedance-match a fixed load to a vacuum tube or to a transistor.   Two typical circuits are shown in Fig. 6-51a and b.   Transformers can be used to produce a voltage or a current gain in circuits that normally do not provide it (e.g., the common-base transistor amplifier).   In most cases, transformer-coupled amplifiers have a poorer frequency response, are more costly, and are larger than *RC*-coupled amplifiers.   Thus, transformers are usually not used as interstage elements.   An exception to this is when good low-frequency response is not important (e.g., when short pulses are to be amplified).   Then, small and inexpensive transformers can be built and are used.   Fig. 6-51c shows such a circuit.

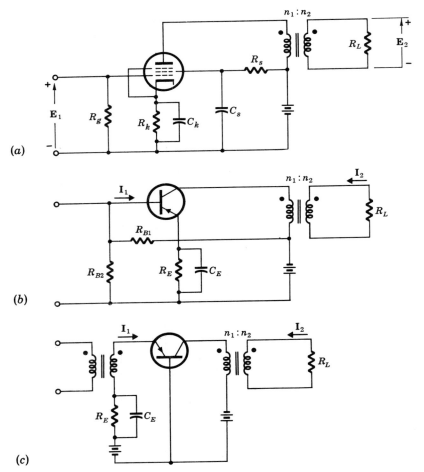

Fig. 6-51 *Transformer-coupled amplifiers.* (*a*) *Vacuum-tube pentode;* (*b*)
common-emitter transistor; and (*c*) *common-base transistor.*

Figure 6-52 shows an equivalent circuit that is valid if the active element
is either a common-cathode vacuum tube or any of the three transistor-
amplifier configurations and if the substitutions of Table 6-4 are made. We
have used the transformer equivalent circuit of Fig. 6-50 here.

Capacitor C_o represents the output capacitance of the active element
plus the capacitance C_p of the transformer. Similarly, the capacitor C_i represents the input capacitance of the load (transformed to the primary side)
plus the capacitor $(n_2/n_1)^2 C_s$ of the transformer. At all frequencies of
interest, the core-loss resistance R_o is usually very much larger than the
impedance in shunt with it, and it has been omitted from the equivalent
circuit. It has also been assumed that the impedance of any bypass capaci-

Table 6-4

Equivalent circuit	Vacuum tube	Transistor
r	r_p	$1/h_o$
$\mathbf{I}$	$g_m \mathbf{E}_1$	$h_f \mathbf{I}_1$

tors is zero.   Their effect can be taken into account by means of the procedure of Secs. 6-5 and 6-6.

A useful wideband transformer-coupled amplifier will have a well-defined midband region, where the response is almost independent of frequency. The gain will fall off at low and high frequencies.   At low frequencies the impedance of L_m becomes small, which causes the gain to fall off.   The series inductances L_p and $(n_1/n_2)^2 L_s$ are small, and their impedance can be considered to be a short circuit at low and mid-frequencies.   The capacitors C_i and C_o can be considered to be open circuits at these frequencies.   At high frequencies, the effect of L_m can be ignored, since its impedance becomes quite large.   However, we can no longer ignore L_p, $(n_1/n_2)^2 L_s$, C_i, and C_o.   The three ranges will be considered separately.

The mid-frequency region

The mid-frequency equivalent circuit is shown in Fig. 6-53, where the current generator has been replaced by a voltage generator.   For convenience, we shall write the gain $\mathbf{A}_{\text{mid}} = \mathbf{I}_2/\mathbf{I}$.   To obtain the current gain of a transistor amplifier, this quantity must be multiplied by h_f.   The voltage gain of common-cathode vacuum-tube amplifier is obtained by multiplying $\mathbf{A}$ by $-g_m R_L$.   Thus,

$$\mathbf{A}_{\text{mid}} = \frac{n_1}{n_2} \frac{r}{r + R_p + (n_1/n_2)^2 (R_s + R_L)} \tag{6-181}$$

If the dots on the transformer winding are reversed, this should be multiplied by minus one.

Fig. 6-52   *An equivalent circuit for the transformer-coupled amplifier.*

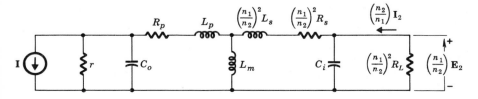

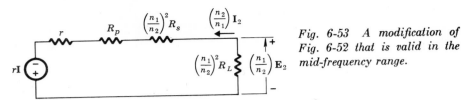

Fig. 6-53 *A modification of Fig. 6-52 that is valid in the mid-frequency range.*

The low-frequency region

An equivalent circuit that is valid in the low-frequency region is shown in Fig. 6-54. The mesh equations are

$$-r\mathbf{I} = (r + R_p + j\omega L_m)\mathbf{I}_a + j\omega L_m \frac{n_2}{n_1}\mathbf{I}_2$$

$$0 = j\omega L_m \mathbf{I}_a + \left[\left(\frac{n_1}{n_2}\right)^2 (R_s + R_L) + j\omega L_m\right]\frac{n_2}{n_1}\mathbf{I}_2$$

Solving and dividing by $\mathbf{A}_{mid}$, we obtain

$$\frac{\mathbf{A}_{low}}{\mathbf{A}_{mid}} = \frac{1}{1 + R_{lowT}/j\omega L_m} \tag{6-182}$$

where

$$R_{lowT} = \frac{(r + R_p)[(n_1/n_2)^2(R_s + R_L)]}{r + R_p + (n_1/n_2)^2(R_s + R_L)} \tag{6-183}$$

Let

$$\omega_1 = \frac{R_{lowT}}{L_m} \quad \text{and} \quad f_1 = \frac{R_{lowT}}{2\pi L_m} \tag{6-184}$$

Then

$$\frac{\mathbf{A}_{low}}{\mathbf{A}_{mid}} = \frac{1}{1 - jf_1/f} \tag{6-185}$$

This is exactly the same as the expression for the low-frequency response of the RC-coupled amplifier [see Eqs. (6-15) and (6-36)]. Hence, a plot of the low-frequency response of the transformer-coupled amplifier is given by the low-frequency portion of the curves of Figs. 6-6 and 6-7.

Let us see what is involved in obtaining a low value of f_1. As R_{lowT} is reduced, f_1 decreases. The resistance R_{lowT} is the parallel combination of $(r + R_p)$ and $(n_1/n_2)^2(R_s + R_L)$. In a good transformer, $R_p \ll r$ and

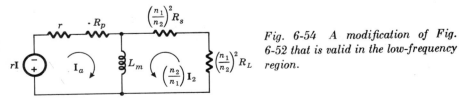

Fig. 6-54 *A modification of Fig. 6-52 that is valid in the low-frequency region.*

$R_s \ll R_L$. Thus, $R_{\text{low}T}$ is essentially $(n_1/n_2)^2 R_L$ in parallel with r. The value of $(n_1/n_2)^2 R_L$ can be reduced somewhat, but the design requirements often fix its value. The magnitude of r cannot be varied at will, since it represents r_p or $1/h_{oe}$. However, a resistance can be placed in shunt with the vacuum tube or the transistor to reduce the value of r. If it is decreased too much, A_{mid} will fall off. Thus, if we are to have a good low-frequency response without reducing the value of A_{mid}, the value of L_m must be high. The cores of transformers are made of ferromagnetic material. This causes both the coupling between the coils and the value of L_m to be high. However, such cores can become saturated and lose their effectiveness. The direct flux, which is set up by the direct-bias current through the primary winding, can cause such saturation. To prevent this, the core must contain a relatively large amount of iron, which makes the transformer large, heavy, and expensive. There are some circuits where the saturation due to the direct current is not present. In such cases, the transformer can be smaller. These circuits will be discussed in the next chapter. In order to obtain good low-frequency response with vacuum-tube pentodes, they are chosen so that their plate resistance is not too high or their outputs are shunted by resistors.

The high-frequency region

The high-frequency equivalent circuit for the transformer-coupled amplifier is shown in Fig. 6-55. The complete solution of this circuit is quite complex. We shall eventually obtain it; however, let us start by making some approximations that are often valid. Usually, low-frequency considerations keep r small, so that we often have

$$r \ll \frac{1}{\omega C_o} \tag{6-186}$$

over all frequencies of interest. The effect of C_o can then be ignored. Writing two current-divider ratios and clearing fractions, we obtain

$$A_{\text{high}} = \frac{(n_1/n_2)r}{(n_1/n_2)^2 R_L + [1 + j\omega C_i (n_1/n_2)^2 R_L]\{r + R_p + (n_1/n_2)^2 R_s + j\omega[L_p + (n_1/n_2)^2 L_s]\}} \tag{6-187}$$

Fig. 6-55   *The high-frequency equivalent circuit for the amplifier of Fig. 6-52.*

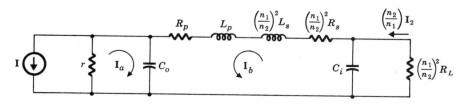

Then

$$\frac{\mathbf{A}_{\text{high}}}{\mathbf{A}_{\text{mid}}} = \frac{1}{1 - \dfrac{\omega^2 C_i L_T (n_1/n_2)^2 R_L}{R_T} + j\omega \dfrac{L_T + C_i R_{Ta}(n_1/n_2)^2 R_L}{R_T}} \tag{6-188}$$

where

$$R_T = r + R_p + \left(\frac{n_1}{n_2}\right)^2 (R_s + R_L) \tag{6-189}$$

$$R_{Ta} = r + R_p + \left(\frac{n_1}{n_2}\right)^2 R_s \tag{6-190}$$

and

$$L_T = L_p + \left(\frac{n_1}{n_2}\right)^2 L_s \tag{6-191}$$

There are many circumstances when the value of $(n_1/n_2)^2 R_L$ is quite small; at other times it is extremely large. For instance, if R_L represents a loudspeaker, its resistance may be only several ohms and $(n_1/n_2)^2 R_L$ may be only several thousand ohms. Let us assume that, at all frequencies of interest,

$$\left(\frac{n_1}{n_2}\right)^2 R_L \ll \frac{1}{\omega C_i} \tag{6-192}$$

We can then neglect C_i so that Eq. (6-188) becomes

$$\frac{\mathbf{A}_{\text{high}}}{\mathbf{A}_{\text{mid}}} = \frac{1}{1 + j\omega L_T/R_T} \tag{6-193}$$

Let

$$f_2 = R_T/2\pi L_T \tag{6-194}$$

then

$$\frac{\mathbf{A}_{\text{high}}}{\mathbf{A}_{\text{mid}}} = \frac{1}{1 + jf/f_2} \tag{6-195}$$

In the case of the transistor, we ignored the factor of $1/(1 + j\omega/\omega_\beta)$ for the common-emitter or common-collector amplifier and $1/(1 + j\omega/\omega_a)$ for the common-base amplifier. Usually, $f_\beta \gg f_2$, so that this can be done. If not, then this factor should be included in Eq. (6-195). The response has the same form as the RC-coupled amplifier, and the high-frequency portion of Figs. 6-6 and 6-7 can represent it. If the variation of $\mathbf{h}_f$ with frequency is included, then the response will be of the form of Figs. 6-11 and 6-12. The upper half-power frequency is increased by increasing R_T or by reducing L_T. Usually, $R_T \approx r + (n_1/n_2)^2 R_L$. The value of R_L is usually fixed. A change in (n_1/n_2) will also change L_T and, thus, may not achieve any significant improvement. The value of r cannot be made too large, because of low-frequency considerations. If good high-frequency response is desired, the *equivalent leakage inductance* L_T must be kept small. This is done by careful winding on high-quality cores. In general, it is more difficult to achieve broadband response with a transformer-coupled amplifier than it is with an *RC*-coupled amplifier.

Now let us consider an additional approximation which can be used when $(n_1/n_2)^2 R_L$ is quite large. (This occurs when common-cathode vacuum-tube amplifiers or common-collector transistor amplifiers are cascaded.) We shall assume that

$$\left(\frac{n_1}{n_2}\right)^2 R_L \gg R_{Ta} \tag{6-196}$$

so that

$$R_T \approx \left(\frac{n_1}{n_2}\right)^2 R_L$$

In addition, we shall assume that

$$\left(\frac{n_1}{n_2}\right)^2 R_L R_{Ta} C_i \gg L_T \tag{6-197}$$

Thus, Eq. (6-188) becomes

$$\frac{\mathbf{A}_{\text{high}}}{\mathbf{A}_{\text{mid}}} = \frac{1}{1 - \omega^2 C_i L_T + j\omega C_i R_{Ta}}$$

In order to obtain a set of general curves, we shall introduce the following terminology:

$$\omega_0 = \frac{1}{\sqrt{C_i L_T}} \qquad f_0 = \frac{1}{2\pi \sqrt{C_i L_T}} \tag{6-198}$$

$$Q_0 = \frac{\omega_0 L_T}{R_{Ta}} = \frac{1}{R_{Ta}\omega_0 C_i} \tag{6-199}$$

Then, substituting, we obtain

$$\frac{\mathbf{A}_{\text{high}}}{\mathbf{A}_{\text{mid}}} = \frac{1}{1 - (f/f_0)^2 + j(f/f_0)(1/Q_0)} \tag{6-200}$$

Curves of $|A_{\text{high}}/A_{\text{mid}}|$ and $\measuredangle(A_{\text{high}}/A_{\text{mid}})$ are given in Fig. 6-56.[8] Note that these curves are not normalized with respect to f_2 but with respect to f_0, which is the resonant frequency of L_T and C_i. Thus, the high-frequency bandwidth is increased if the leakage inductance and the stray capacitance are reduced. In transformed form Eq. (6-200) is

$$\frac{\mathbf{A}_{\text{high}}}{\mathbf{A}_{\text{mid}}} = \frac{\omega_0^2}{p^2 + (\omega_0/Q_0)p + \omega_0^2} \tag{6-201}$$

The poles of this network occur at

$$p_{2,4} = -\frac{\omega_0}{2Q_0} \pm \frac{\omega_0}{2Q_0}\sqrt{1 - 4Q_0^2} \tag{6-202}$$

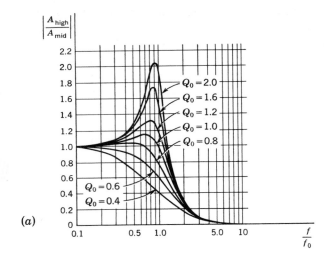

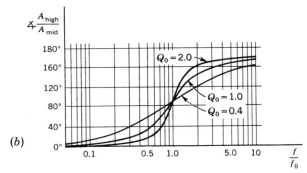

Fig. 6-56 Frequency response of the transformer-coupled amplifier assuming that $r \ll 1/\omega c_0$, $R_T \approx (n_1/n_2)^2 R_L$, and $(n_1/n_2)^2 R_L R_{Ta} C_i \gg L_T$. (a) Amplitude response and; (b) phase response.[8] (By permission from F. E. Terman, "Radio Engineers' Handbook," copyright 1943, McGraw-Hill Book Company.)

As Q_0 is increased the rise time decreases. However, if $Q_0 > \frac{1}{2}$, the unit-step response will overshoot.

If the inequality of relation (6-197) does not hold, but all the other assumptions are valid, we can still use all of the above results if we redefine Q_0 as

$$Q_0 = \frac{R_T}{\omega_0[L_T + C_i R_{Ta}(n_1/n_2)^2 R_L]}$$

We have thus far obtained the high-frequency response subject to the assumption, among others, that $r \ll 1/\omega C_0$. This assumption is usually valid for common-cathode vacuum-tube amplifiers. However, it is not always valid when transistors are used. If the current generator of Fig. 6-55 is replaced by a voltage generator, a mesh analysis yields

$$-\mathbf{I}r = \left(r + \frac{1}{j\omega C_o}\right)\mathbf{I}_a + \frac{1}{j\omega C_o}\mathbf{I}_b \qquad (6\text{-}203)$$

$$0 = \frac{1}{j\omega C_o}\mathbf{I}_a + \left(R_a + j\omega L_T + \frac{1}{j\omega C_o} + \frac{R_L'}{1 + j\omega R_L' C_i}\right)\mathbf{I}_b$$

where

$$R_a = R_p + \left(\frac{n_1}{n_2}\right)^2 R_s \qquad (6\text{-}204)$$

and

$$R_L' = \left(\frac{n_1}{n_2}\right)^2 R_L \qquad (6\text{-}205)$$

Then

$$(n_2/n_1)\mathbf{I}_2 = \frac{\mathbf{I}_b}{1 + j\omega R_L' C_i}$$

Solving and manipulating, we obtain

$$\frac{\mathbf{A}_{\text{high}}}{\mathbf{A}_{\text{mid}}} =$$

$$\frac{1}{1 + \dfrac{j\omega}{R_T}\{(R_a + j\omega L_T)[rC_0(1 + j\omega R_L' C_i) + R_L' C_i] + R_L' r(C_i + C_o) + L_T\}}$$

$$(6\text{-}206)$$

This is quite complex and there are too many variables to conveniently plot a set of curves. In general, a frequency response that has a form somewhat similar to that of Fig. 6-56 will be obtained. The denominator of Eq. (6-206) is a cubic equation in the variable $p = j\omega$. General solutions to cubic equations do exist. However, the form is so involved that numerical procedures are usually used to solve them. One pole of Eq. (6-206) will always lie on the negative σ axis. The other two may lie on the negative σ axis or in the left half-plane. If these roots are off the σ axis, then the unit-step response will overshoot. Again, to increase the bandwidth, the leakage inductance and the stray capacitance should be reduced.

6-20 Tuned amplifiers—the parallel resonant circuit

Thus far, we have concerned ourselves with obtaining amplifiers with as broad a bandwidth as possible. We shall now consider amplifiers that would, ideally, amplify a certain range of frequencies and reject all others. One application of such a circuit would be in radio receivers, which amplify the signals received from one station but reject the signals from all other

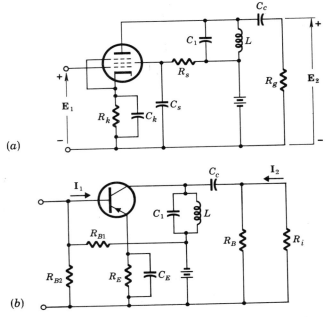

Fig. 6-57 RC-coupled single-tuned amplifiers. (a) *Common-cathode vacuum-tube amplifier; and* (b) *common-emitter transistor amplifier.*

stations.   These amplifiers are called *tuned amplifiers* or *bandpass amplifiers*. They use tuned circuits of varying complexity.   Two typical ones are shown in Fig. 6-57.   Before considering them, we shall analyze the simple parallel-resonant circuit shown in Fig. 6-58.   Circuits of this type are useful in a frequency range of from tens of kilocycles per second to several hundred megacycles per second, and, for these frequencies, the losses in the capacitor can often be neglected.   The impedance is given by

$$\mathbf{Z} = \frac{(1/j\omega C)(R + j\omega L)}{R + j(\omega L - 1/\omega C)}$$

Manipulating, we have

$$\mathbf{Z} = \frac{(L/C)(1 - jR/\omega L)}{R[1 + j(\omega L/R)(1 - 1/\omega^2 LC)]} \tag{6-207}$$

To generalize, let

$$\omega_0 = \frac{1}{\sqrt{LC}} \qquad f_0 = \frac{1}{2\pi \sqrt{LC}} \tag{6-208}$$

and

$$Q_0 = \frac{\omega_0 L}{R} = \frac{1}{\omega_0 RC} = \frac{1}{R}\sqrt{\frac{L}{C}} \tag{6-209}$$

Substituting, we obtain

$$\mathbf{Z} = \frac{Q_0{}^2R[1 - j(f_0/f)(1/Q_0)]}{1 + jQ_0[(f/f_0) - (f_0/f)]} = \frac{Q_0{}^2R[(f/f_0) - j(1/Q_0)]}{(f/f_0) + jQ_0[(f^2/f_0{}^2) - 1]} \tag{6-210}$$

For most tuned amplifiers, $Q_0 > 10$. In fact, very often, $Q_0 > 100$, so that the second term in the denominator is important. Even though Eq. (6-210) is exact, erroneous results may be obtained when values of f are substituted, unless many significant figures are used. *In general, large errors can be obtained when two nearly equal numbers are subtracted.* To eliminate the need for extreme accuracy, we shall introduce a new normalized frequency variable δ. Let

$$\delta = \frac{f - f_0}{f_0} \tag{6-211}$$

Substituting, we obtain

$$\mathbf{Z} = \frac{Q_0{}^2R[1 + \delta - j(1/Q_0)]}{1 + \delta + jQ_0\delta(\delta + 2)} \tag{6-212}$$

Note that the difference between two nearly equal numbers no longer appears. If $Q \gg 1$, we can approximate Eq. (6-212) by

$$\mathbf{Z} = \frac{Q_0{}^2R}{1 + jQ_0\delta(\delta + 2)/(\delta + 1)} \tag{6-213}$$

Under these conditions, the maximum magnitude of the impedance occurs when $f = f_0$ or $\delta = 0$.

$$Z_{\max} = Q_0{}^2R = (\omega_0L)Q_0 = R_0 \tag{6-214}$$

In normalized form

$$\frac{\mathbf{Z}}{R_0} = \frac{1}{1 + jQ_0\delta(\delta + 2)/(\delta + 1)} \tag{6-215}$$

A plot of the magnitude of this expression for various values of Q_0 is given in Fig. 6-59. Such a plot is called a *resonance curve*. Notice that it becomes sharper as Q_0 is increased. The circuit is said to become more *selective* as the width of the resonance curve decreases. We shall develop tuned amplifiers whose amplification varies with frequency in the same way that Fig.

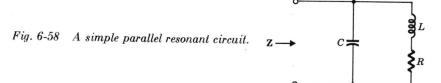

Fig. 6-58 A simple parallel resonant circuit.

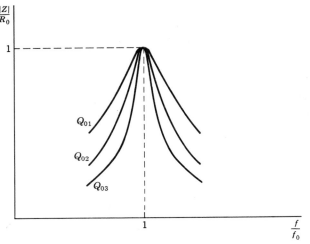

Fig. 6-59 Typical curves of the normalized impedance of a parallel resonant circuit. $Q_{03} > Q_{02} > Q_{01}$.

6-59 does. Let us define the bandwidth B of a parallel resonant circuit, such that

$$B = f_2 - f_1 \tag{6-216}$$

where

$$f_2 = \text{upper frequency where } \left| \frac{Z}{Q_0^2 R} \right| = \frac{1}{\sqrt{2}} \tag{6-217}$$

$$f_1 = \text{lower frequency where } \left| \frac{Z}{Q_0^2 R} \right| = \frac{1}{\sqrt{2}} \tag{6-218}$$

If $Q_0 \gg 1$, the magnitude of Eq. (6-210) becomes

$$\left| \frac{Z}{R_0} \right| = \frac{1}{|1 + jQ_0(f/f_0 - f_0/f)|} = \frac{1}{\sqrt{1 + Q_0^2(f/f_0 - f_0/f)^2}} \tag{6-219}$$

The magnitude of the impedance function is an even function of frequency. That is, the response for negative f is the same as that for positive f. (The phase angle is an odd function of frequency.) In obtaining the values of f_1 and f_2, we must be careful to obtain the positive frequency values. Thus

$$Q_0 \left(\frac{f_2}{f_0} - \frac{f_0}{f_2} \right) = 1 \tag{6-220}$$

and

$$Q_0 \left(\frac{f_0}{f_1} - \frac{f_1}{f_0} \right) = 1 \tag{6-221}$$

Equating, and solving, we obtain

$$f_1 f_2 = f_0^2 \tag{6-222}$$

Substituting in Eq. (6-220), we have

$$B = f_2 - f_1 = \frac{f_0}{Q_0} \tag{6-223}$$

Thus, the frequencies f_1 and f_2 are spaced with *geometric symmetry* about f_0. In fact, the entire curve of Eq. (6-219) has geometric symmetry about f_0. In addition, the bandwidth $f_2 - f_1$ varies directly with f_0 and inversely with Q_0.

Let us now obtain expressions for f_1 and f_2. From Eqs. (6-222) and (6-223), we obtain

$$f_2{}^2 - f_2 \frac{f_0}{Q_0} - f_0{}^2 = 0$$

Solving for f_2, and using the positive value, we have

$$f_2 = \frac{f_0}{2Q_0} + \sqrt{f_0{}^2 \left(1 + \frac{1}{4Q_0{}^2}\right)} \tag{6-224}$$

Similarly

$$f_1 = -\frac{f_0}{2Q_0} + \sqrt{f_0{}^2 \left(1 + \frac{1}{4Q_0{}^2}\right)} \tag{6-225}$$

If $Q_0 \gg 1$, we can make some approximations that simplify these expressions. Expanding the square root of Eq. (6-224) in a power series, we obtain

$$f_2 = \frac{f_0}{2Q_0} + f_0 \left(1 + \frac{1}{8Q_0{}^2} + \cdots\right)$$

If $Q_0 \gg 1$, we can neglect all powers of Q_0 except the first. Hence,

$$f_2 \approx f_0 \left(1 + \frac{1}{2Q_0}\right)$$

In a similar way, Eq. (6-225) can be manipulated to obtain

$$f_1 \approx f_0 \left(1 - \frac{1}{2Q_0}\right)$$

For the high-Q case, f_0 and f_1 exhibit approximate *arithmetic symmetry* about f_0. In fact, if $Q_0 \gg 1$, then for frequencies that are not far from f_0, we can assume that the resonance curve has arithmetic symmetry about f_0. This often proves convenient.

6-21 Single-tuned *RC*-coupled amplifiers

The amplifiers of Fig. 6-57 have only one tuned circuit and use a coupling capacitor to prevent the bias voltages of succeeding stages from interacting.

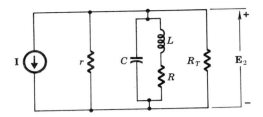

Fig. 6-60   An equivalent circuit for the single-tuned amplifier.

Thus, they are called *single-tuned RC-coupled amplifiers.* At the frequencies where such amplifiers are used, we can always assume that C_c, C_k, C_s, and C_E are short circuits. The bandwidths are usually narrow enough so that the variation of $\mathbf{h}_f$ with frequency can be ignored. The value of $\mathbf{h}_f$ obtained at $f = f_0$ should be used. An equivalent circuit that is valid for the common-cathode vacuum-tube amplifier and all three transistor amplifier configurations is shown in Fig. 6-60. The substitutions of Table 6-4, Sec. 6-19, should be used. In addition, $R_T = R_g$ for the vacuum tube, and it equals $R_B R_i/(R_B + R_i)$ for the transistor. The capacitor C represents the parallel combination of C_1 with the parasitic capacitances. These are the output capacitance of the active element, the wiring capacitance, and the input capacitance of the load. Then

$$\mathbf{E}_2 = \frac{-\mathbf{I}}{(1/r) + (1/\mathbf{Z}) + (1/R_T)}$$

where $\mathbf{Z}$ is given by Eq. (6-215). Substituting and manipulating, we have

$$\mathbf{E}_2 = \frac{-\mathbf{I}R_{sh}}{1 + jQ_0(R_{sh}/R_0)[\delta(\delta + 2)/(\delta + 1)]} \tag{6-226}$$

where

$$\frac{1}{R_{sh}} = \frac{1}{r} + \frac{1}{R_T} + \frac{1}{R_0} \tag{6-227}$$

Let us define an effective Q for this circuit

$$Q_{\text{eff}} = \frac{Q_0 R_{sh}}{R_0} \tag{6-228}$$

Since R_{sh} is the parallel combination of r, R_T, and R_0

$$Q_{\text{eff}} < Q_0 \tag{6-229}$$

Then, for a vacuum tube

$$\mathbf{A}_v = \frac{-g_m R_{sh}}{1 + jQ_{\text{eff}}\delta(\delta + 2)/(\delta + 1)} \tag{6-230}$$

At $f = f_0$, the gain is maximum and is

$$\mathbf{A}_{v0} = -g_m R_{sh} \tag{6-231}$$

The normalized response is given by

$$\frac{\mathbf{A}_v}{\mathbf{A}_{v0}} = \frac{1}{1 + jQ_{\text{eff}}\delta(\delta + 2)/(\delta + 1)} \tag{6-232}$$

This has exactly the same form as Eq. (6-215), except that Q_0 has been replaced by Q_{eff}, and thus, Fig. 6-59 is a plot of the normalized amplitude response of this amplifier. Hence, the half-power bandwidth is given by

$$B = \frac{f_0}{Q_{\text{eff}}} \tag{6-233}$$

At the half-power frequencies, the phase shift is $\pm 45°$. The gain-bandwidth product is

$$|A_{v0}|B = \frac{g_m R_{sh} f_0}{Q_{\text{eff}}} = \frac{g_m}{2\pi C} \tag{6-234}$$

This result is the same as that given by Eq. (6-24) for the simple RC-coupled amplifier.

For a transistor amplifier $\mathbf{I}_2 = -\mathbf{E}_2/R_i$. Thus,

$$\mathbf{A}_i = \frac{h_f R_{sh}/R_i}{1 + jQ_{\text{eff}}\delta(\delta + 2)/(\delta + 1)} \tag{6-235}$$

At $f = f_0$

$$A_{i0} = \frac{h_f R_{sh}}{R_i} \tag{6-236}$$

The normalized form of this expression is the same as Eq. (6-232). If R_i could be reduced to zero, then R_{sh} also approaches zero such that $R_{sh}/R_i = 1$. The current gain is then a maximum. However, Q_{eff} also will be zero and the circuit will not provide any selectivity. It is sometimes difficult to obtain the desired selectivity with transistor amplifiers because the value of R_i is too low. If Q_0 is increased, then Q_{eff} will also increase [see Eq. (6-228)], and the bandwidth will be reduced. To increase Q_0, the ratio of L to R must be increased. We can very roughly say that the size of an inductance increases with the square of the number of turns while its resistance increases linearly with the number of turns. Thus, Q_0 will increase if L is increased. However, the parasitic capacitance limits the minimum value of C and, hence, the maximum value of L is fixed by the relation $f_0 = 1/2\pi \sqrt{LC}$. Thus, we cannot always obtain the desired selectivity by increasing L. In the next section, we shall see that a low value of R_i need not prevent us from obtaining the desired selectivity.

We shall now demonstrate that, in general, it is desirable to use as large a value of L as possible. The gain-bandwidth product for the transistor amplifier is given by

$$A_{i0}B = \frac{h_f/R_i}{2\pi C} \tag{6-237}$$

From Eqs. (6-234) and (6-237) we can conclude that, for both the vacuum-tube and the transistor amplifiers, it is desirable to make C as small as possible. Thus, L should be made as large as possible. It is often desirable to vary $f_0 = 1/2\pi \sqrt{LC}$. This is done so that the amplifier can be tuned to different signals. Even if the amplifier is only to work at one frequency, there is always provision made to vary f_0 slightly, for purposes of adjustment. If L is made adjustable, usually by moving a low-loss ferromagnetic core into or out of it, then the capacitor C need only be the parasitic capacitance of the circuit. Hence the minimum value of C will always be used. If a variable capacitor is used to tune the circuit, then values of C that are larger than the parasitic capacitance will be required and the gain-bandwidth product will be reduced. In some frequency ranges, the losses due to the ferromagnetic core become very large. It is somewhat easier to construct a variable capacitor than a variable inductor. For these reasons, both variable-inductance and variable-capacitance tuned circuits are used.

When tuned amplifiers are cascaded, the overall amplification is the product of the responses of the individual stages. Thus, the midband gain increases and the bandwidth decreases. It can be shown that the decrease in half-power bandwidth as the number of stages increases is given by Eq. (6-96). Again, we see that the bandwidth of the simple RC-coupled amplifier and that of the single tuned amplifier are related. In the case of the tuned amplifier, the decrease in bandwidth may actually be desirable since it increases the selectivity of the circuit.

6-22   Impedance-level control in tuned amplifiers— tapped inductances

The input resistance of a transistor amplifier is often such that Q_{eff} is too small and the amplifier does not possess the required selectivity. In such cases, the effective input resistance of the transistor must be made to appear larger. An impedance-matching transformer placed between the output of the tuned circuit and the input to the transistor will accomplish this. In Fig. 6-61 we have so modified the equivalent circuit of Fig. 6-60. The input bias is supplied through the secondary of the transformer and the resistor

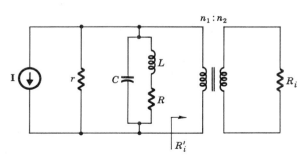

Fig. 6-61 A single-tuned circuit that uses a transformer as an impedance-matching device.

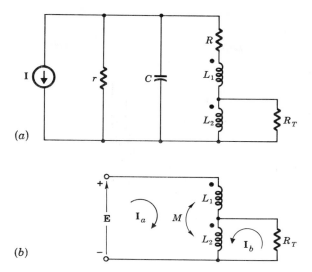

Fig. 6-62 (a) A single-tuned circuit that uses a tapped coil as an imped-ance-matching device; (b) a circuit used to calculate the input impedance of the coil.

R_B can be omitted. Thus, the resistor R_T has been replaced by R_i. Let us assume that the transformer is ideal. Then $R'_i = (n_1/n_2)^2 R_i$ can be adjusted to be any value that is desired.

There is an optimum turns ratio that will provide maximum current gain. If the load resistance is fixed, then the maximum power dissipation in the load and maximum load current occur simultaneously. (If the load resistance is varied, then maximum load current will occur when the load resistance is zero, but maximum power dissipation occurs when the load is matched to the generator resistance.) If R_0 represents the impedance of the tuned circuit at resonance, then maximum current gain occurs when

$$\left(\frac{n_1}{n_2}\right)^2 R_i = \frac{R_0 r}{R_0 + r}$$

$$\frac{n_1}{n_2}\bigg|_{\text{opt}} = \sqrt{\frac{R_0 r}{R_i(R_0 + r)}} \tag{6-238}$$

This equation is not as important as it may seem, since selectivity requirements often govern the choice of the impedance level rather than the current gain. In addition, we shall see in Sec. 6-26 that mismatch is at times deliberately introduced to prevent the circuit from oscillating.

The circuit of Fig. 6-61 is rarely used, because essentially the same effect can be achieved by using the circuit of Fig. 6-60 and tapping the coil. Such a circuit is shown in Fig. 6-62a. The input impedance of the coil will be obtained from the circuit of Fig. 6-62b. We have assumed that all the resistance of the coil is in series with L_1. Since L_2 is usually considerably less than L_1, the assumption is quite good. Then, from Fig. 6-62b, we have

$$\mathbf{E} = j\omega(L_1 + L_2 + 2M)\mathbf{I}_a + j\omega(M + L_2)\mathbf{I}_b$$
$$0 = j\omega(M + L_2)\mathbf{I}_a + (j\omega L_2 + R_T)\mathbf{I}_b$$

Solving for the impedance $Z_1 = E/I_a$ and noting that $L = L_1 + L_2 + 2M$, we obtain

$$Z_i = j\omega L + \frac{\omega^2(L_2 + M)^2}{R_T + j\omega L_2} \qquad (6\text{-}239)$$

For most applications the impedance of $\omega L_2 \ll R_T$, so that

$$Z_i = j\omega L + \frac{\omega^2(L_2 + M)^2}{R_T} \qquad (6\text{-}240)$$

This can be represented as an inductance L in series with a resistance $\omega^2(L_2 + M)^2/R_T$. The resistance varies with frequency. In general, the frequencies of interest are very close to ω_0, so that we can assume that the resistance does not change with frequency. Hence,

$$Z_i = j\omega L + \frac{\omega_0^2(L_2 + M)^2}{R_T} \qquad (6\text{-}241)$$

The reactive portion of the impedance must be left as a function of frequency, since it results in the difference of two nearly equal terms [see Eq. (6-207)]. The term $L_2 + M$ depends upon the position of the tap. Its minimum value is zero, so that the component of series resistance due to R_T can be made as small as desired. It is assumed that the resistance R of the coil is small enough so that the desired selectivity can then be obtained.

A tapped inductance is used in this example. Instead of this, we could use a tapped capacitor. That is, C could be replaced by two capacitors in series, with R_T connected between their junction and the common terminal. The results for this circuit are quite similar to those for the tapped inductance.

6-23 Mutual-inductance-coupled single-tuned circuits

Coupled coils are often used to produce an impedance transformation. Two such circuits are shown in Fig. 6-63. When mutual-inductance coupling is used, no coupling capacitor, grid-leak resistance, or shunting base-bias resistance is needed. Thus, these circuits are quite commonly used. The untuned winding is placed in the circuit of lowest impedance. Hence, Fig. 6-63a is typical of the equivalent circuits of common-emitter transistor amplifiers, while 6-63b is typical of common-cathode vacuum-tube amplifiers. Such circuits are also used to couple an antenna, which has a low impedance, to an amplifier. We shall analyze each of these circuits separately.

Tuned primary, untuned secondary

Proceeding as we did to obtain Eq. (6-239), the impedance Z_1 is given by

$$Z_1 = R_1 + j\omega L_1 + \frac{\omega^2 M^2}{R_2 + R_i + j\omega L_2}$$

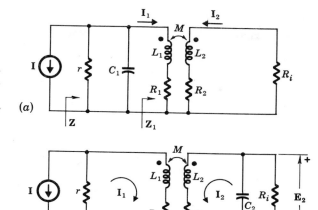

Fig. 6-63 Two single-tuned mutually inductive coupled circuits. (a) *Tuned primary, untuned secondary; and* (b) *untuned primary, tuned secondary.*

For most practical circuits, $R_2 + R_i \gg \omega L_2$ at all frequencies of interest. Also, as in the case of Eq. (6-241), we can consider the term $\omega^2 M^2$ to be a constant equal to $\omega_0^2 M^2$. Thus, we have

$$\mathbf{Z}_1 = R_1 + \frac{\omega_0^2 M^2}{R_2 + R_i} + j\omega L_1$$

where

$$\omega_0 = \frac{1}{\sqrt{L_1 C_1}} \tag{6-242}$$

Hence, $\mathbf{Z}_1$ appears as a constant resistance in series with an inductance. At ω_0 the Q of this circuit is given by

$$Q_1 = \frac{\omega_0 L_1}{R_1 + \omega_0^2 M^2/(R_2 + R_i)} \tag{6-243}$$

Then, using the results of Secs. 6-20 and 6-21

$$\mathbf{Z} = \frac{R_{sh}}{1 + jQ_{\text{eff},1}\, \delta(\delta + 2)/(\delta + 1)}$$

where

$$Q_{\text{eff},1} = \frac{Q_1 r}{r + Q_1 \omega_0 L_1} \tag{6-244}$$

and

$$R_{sh} = \frac{Q_1 \omega_0 L_1 r}{r + Q_1 \omega_0 L_1} \tag{6-245}$$

Then

$$\mathbf{I}_2 = \frac{j\omega M \mathbf{I}_1}{R_i + R_2 + j\omega L_2}$$

and

$$\mathbf{I}_1 = \mathbf{I}\,\frac{\mathbf{Z}}{\mathbf{Z}_1}$$

Thus, the current gain $\mathbf{I}_2/\mathbf{I}$ is given by

$$\mathbf{A}_i = \frac{j\omega M \mathbf{Z}}{(R_i + R_2 + j\omega L_2)\left(R_1 + \dfrac{\omega_0{}^2 M^2}{R_2 + R_i} + j\omega L_1\right)}$$

In general, the effective Q of the primary inductance will be large, so that $\omega L_1 \gg R_1 + \omega_0{}^2 M^2/(R_2 + R_i)$. In addition, $R_i + R_2 \gg \omega L_2$. Therefore,

$$\mathbf{A}_i \approx \frac{M R_{sh}/(R_i + R_2)L_1}{1 + jQ_{\text{eff},1}\,\delta(\delta + 2)/(\delta + 1)} \tag{6-246}$$

If Eq. (6-246) represents the gain of a transistor amplifier, then it should be multiplied by h_f. The gain at resonance is

$$\mathbf{A}_{i0} = \frac{M R_{sh}}{L_1(R_i + R_2)} = \frac{M\omega_0{}^2 L_1 r}{(R_i + R_2)[\omega_0{}^2 L_1{}^2 + R_1 r + \omega_0{}^2 M^2 r/(R_2 + R_i)]} \tag{6-247}$$

To obtain the value of M that gives the largest current gain, differentiate this with respect to M and set the derivative equal to zero.

$$M_{\text{opt}} = \frac{1}{\omega_0}\sqrt{\frac{(\omega_0{}^2 L_1{}^2 + R_1 r)(R_2 + R_i)}{r}} \tag{6-248}$$

Selectivity considerations often cause smaller values of M to be used. The normalized gain is

$$\frac{\mathbf{A}_i}{\mathbf{A}_{i0}} = \frac{1}{1 + jQ_{\text{eff},1}\,\delta(\delta + 2)/(\delta + 1)} \tag{6-249}$$

This has exactly the same form as Eq. (6-215) and, hence, the half-power bandwidth is

$$B = \frac{f_0}{Q_{\text{eff},1}} \tag{6-250}$$

If r is not large enough, then $Q_{\text{eff},1}$ will be too small. In addition, the output capacitance of the active element (transistor) may be quite large, which results in too small a value of L_1. Both of these effects can be reduced by connecting the output of the transistor to a tap on L_1.

Untuned primary, tuned secondary

The circuit of Fig. 6-63b is usually used with vacuum tubes and, thus, we can consider R_i to be an open circuit. Replacing the current generator by a voltage generator and writing mesh equations, we have

$$-r\mathbf{I} = (r_1 + j\omega L_1)\mathbf{I}_1 + j\omega M \mathbf{I}_2$$
$$0 = j\omega M \mathbf{I}_1 + \left[R_2 + j\left(\omega L_2 - \frac{1}{\omega C_2} \right) \right] \mathbf{I}_2 \tag{6-251}$$

where $r_1 = r + R_1$

Then

$$\mathbf{I}_2 = \frac{r\mathbf{I}j\omega M}{(r_1 + j\omega L_1)[R_2 + j(\omega L_2 - 1/\omega C_2)] + \omega^2 M^2}$$

For vacuum-tube pentodes, which are usually used in such circuits, $r_1 \gg \omega L_1$ for frequencies of interest. We can then write $r_1 + j\omega L_1 \approx r_1$. Special care should be taken when such approximations are made in resonant circuits to ensure that highly critical terms do not become inaccurate. The approximation is valid in this case.

Since $\mathbf{E}_2 = -\mathbf{I}_2/j\omega C_2$, we have

$$\frac{\mathbf{E}_2}{\mathbf{I}} = \frac{-Mr/C_2 r_1 R_2}{1 + \dfrac{\omega^2 M^2}{r_1 R_2} + j\dfrac{\omega L_2}{R_2}(1 - 1/\omega^2 L_2 C_2)} \tag{6-252}$$

As in the case of Eq. (6-241), we can approximate $1 + \omega^2 M^2/r_1 R_2$ by $1 + \omega_0{}^2 M^2/r_1 R_2$. In addition, we shall use the substitutions

$$\omega_0 = \frac{1}{\sqrt{L_2 C_2}} \qquad f_0 = \frac{1}{2\pi\sqrt{L_2 C_2}} \tag{6-253}$$

$$Q_2 = \frac{\omega_0 L_2}{R_2} \tag{6-254}$$

and

$$\delta = \frac{f - f_0}{f_0}$$

Then, proceeding as in Sec. 6-20, we obtain

$$\frac{\mathbf{E}_2}{\mathbf{I}} = \frac{-(Mr/C_2 r_1 R_2)/(1 + \omega_0{}^2 M^2/r_1 R_2)}{1 + j\dfrac{Q_2}{1 + \omega_0{}^2 M^2/r_1 R_2}\delta\dfrac{2 + \delta}{1 + \delta}}$$

If Fig. 6-63b is the equivalent circuit of a vacuum-tube amplifier, then $\mathbf{I} = g_m \mathbf{E}_1$ and $r = r_p$. Then, at ω_0, we have

$$\mathbf{A}_{v0} = \frac{-g_m M r_p/C_2 r_1 R_2}{1 + \omega_0{}^2 M^2/r_1 R_2} = \frac{-g_m \omega_0 M Q_2 r_p/r_1}{1 + \omega_0{}^2 M^2/r_1 R_2} \tag{6-255}$$

and

$$\frac{\mathbf{A}_v}{\mathbf{A}_{v0}} = \frac{1}{1 + jQ_{\text{eff},2}\delta(\delta + 2)/(\delta + 1)} \tag{6-256}$$

where

$$Q_{\text{eff},2} = \frac{Q_2}{1 + \omega_0^2 M^2/r_1 R_2} \qquad (6\text{-}257)$$

and the bandwidth is given by

$$B = \frac{f_0}{Q_{\text{eff},2}} \qquad (6\text{-}258)$$

If we maximize A_{v0} with respect to M, we obtain

$$M = \frac{1}{\omega_0}\sqrt{r_1 R_2} \qquad (6\text{-}259)$$

Often, when vacuum-tube pentodes are used, $r_p \gg R_1$ so that $r_1 \approx r_p$.   Thus

$$A_{v0} = -g_m \omega_0 M Q_{\text{eff},2} \qquad (6\text{-}260)$$

6-24 Double-tuned amplifiers

Amplifiers that use more than one tuned circuit have frequency-response characteristics that are more versatile than those we have considered.   An equivalent circuit for such an amplifier is shown in Fig. 6-64a.   The analysis of this circuit is quite tedious.   To obtain the results that can be easily used, we shall make some simplifying approximations.   If a resistor R is in parallel with an inductance L, the impedance of the combination is given by

$$\mathbf{Z} = \frac{j\omega L R}{R + j\omega L} = \frac{\omega^2 L^2 R + j\omega L R^2}{R^2 + \omega^2 L^2}$$

If $R \gg \omega L$ and if we work in a narrow range of frequencies, so that the fre-

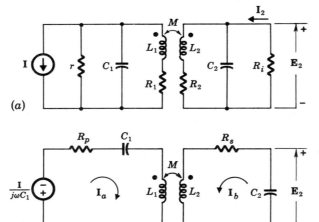

Fig. 6-64 (a) A double-tuned amplifier circuit; (b) an approximation of this circuit that will be used for analysis.

quency dependence of effective series resistance can be neglected, we can write

$$\mathbf{Z} \approx \frac{\omega_0^2 L^2}{R} + j\omega L \tag{6-261}$$

We shall assume that when the resistance of the coil itself is added to $\omega_0^2 L^2/R$ the total effective series resistance is obtained.

$$R_p = \frac{\omega_0^2 L_1^2}{r} + R_1 \tag{6-262}$$

and

$$R_s = \frac{\omega_0^2 L_2^2}{R_i} + R_2 \tag{6-263}$$

If the current generator shunted by C_1 is replaced by a voltage generator in series with C_1, the circuit of Fig. 6-64b results. Writing mesh equations, we obtain

$$\frac{-\mathbf{I}}{j\omega C_1} = \mathbf{Z}_p \mathbf{I}_a + j\omega M \mathbf{I}_b \tag{6-264}$$

$$0 = j\omega M \mathbf{I}_a + \mathbf{Z}_s \mathbf{I}_b$$

where

$$\mathbf{Z}_p = R_p \left[1 + j \frac{\omega L_1}{R_p} \left(1 - \frac{1}{\omega^2 L_1 C_1} \right) \right] \tag{6-265}$$

and

$$\mathbf{Z}_s = R_s \left[1 + j \frac{\omega L_2}{R_s} \left(1 - \frac{1}{\omega^2 L_2 C_2} \right) \right] \tag{6-266}$$

Let us assume that the primary and secondary circuits are adjusted so that

$$f_0 = \frac{1}{2\pi \sqrt{L_1 C_1}} = \frac{1}{2\pi \sqrt{L_2 C_2}} \tag{6-267}$$

Then let

$$Q_1 = \frac{\omega_0 L_1}{R_p} \tag{6-268}$$

and

$$Q_2 = \frac{\omega_0 L_2}{R_s} \tag{6-269}$$

Proceeding as in Sec. 6-20, we have

$$\mathbf{Z}_p = R_p \left[1 + jQ_1 \frac{\delta(\delta + 2)}{\delta + 1} \right]$$

$$\mathbf{Z}_s = R_s \left[1 + jQ_2 \frac{\delta(\delta + 2)}{\delta + 1} \right] \tag{6-270}$$

Usually $\delta = (f - f_0)/f_0 \ll 1$ so that $(\delta + 2)/(\delta + 1) \approx 2$. This approximation could have been made in the preceding sections.   However, there was no need to.   It is done here to simplify the relatively complex results. Thus,

$$\mathbf{Z}_p = R_p(1 + j2Q_1\delta) \tag{6-271}$$

$$\mathbf{Z}_s = R_s(1 + j2Q_2\delta) \tag{6-272}$$

Substitute these expressions into Eqs. (6-264) and solve for $\mathbf{E}_2/\mathbf{I}$.

$$\frac{\mathbf{E}_2}{\mathbf{I}} = \frac{-M/j\omega_0 C_1 C_2 R_p R_s}{1 - 4\delta^2 Q_1 Q_2 + j2\delta(Q_1 + Q_2) + \omega_0{}^2 M^2/R_p R_s}$$

where we have again assumed that $\omega M \approx \omega_0 M$ and $\omega C_2 \approx \omega_0 C_2$ over all frequencies of interest [see Eq. (6-241)].   Let

$$b = \frac{\omega_0 M}{\sqrt{R_p R_s}} \tag{6-273}$$

Then

$$\frac{\mathbf{E}_2}{\mathbf{I}} = \frac{-(1/j\omega_0{}^2 C_1 C_2 \sqrt{R_p R_s})[b/(1 + b^2)]}{1 - 4\delta^2 Q_1 Q_2/(1 + b^2) + j2\delta(Q_1 + Q_2)/(1 + b^2)} \tag{6-274}$$

If Fig. 6-64 represents the equivalent circuit of a vacuum tube, then Eq. (6-274) must be multiplied by g_m to obtain the voltage gain.   Similarly, for a transistor, the current gain is obtained by multiplying by $-h_f/R_i$.   Then, when $f = f_0$

$$\mathbf{A}_{v0} = \frac{-g_m}{j\omega_0{}^2 C_1 C_2 \sqrt{R_p R_s}} \cdot \frac{b}{b^2 + 1} \tag{6-275}$$

and

$$\mathbf{A}_{i0} = \frac{h_{fe}}{j\omega_0{}^2 C_1 C_2 R_i \sqrt{R_p R_s}} \cdot \frac{b}{b^2 + 1} \tag{6-276}$$

If either of these expressions is maximized with respect to b, we obtain

$$b_{\mathrm{opt}} = \pm 1 \tag{6-277}$$

$$M_{\mathrm{opt}} = \frac{\pm \sqrt{R_p R_s}}{\omega_0} \tag{6-278}$$

For convenience, we shall normalize with respect to the maximum gain at resonance $\mathbf{A}_{0,\max}$.

$$\frac{\mathbf{A}}{\mathbf{A}_{0,\max}} = \frac{2b/(b^2 + 1)}{1 - 4\delta^2 Q_1 Q_2/(1 + b^2) + j2\delta(Q_1 + Q_2)/(1 + b^2)} \tag{6-279}$$

A plot of $|A/A_{0,\max}|$ versus frequency for various values of b is shown in Fig. 6-65.   The case $Q_1 = Q_2$ has been plotted here.   For values of $b \leqslant 1$, the response resembles the usual resonance curve.   However, for $b > 1$, the shape changes considerably.   The maximum of the response no longer occurs at $f = f_0$, and the curve has two peaks.   We shall discuss the utility of this

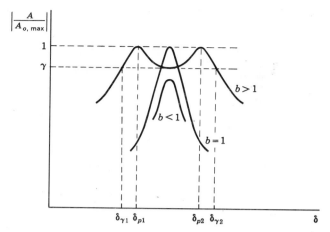

Fig. 6-65 *Resonance curves for the double-tuned amplifier. These curves are drawn for $Q_1 = Q_2$.*

type of response in the next section. To determine the frequencies where the peaks occur, set $(d/d\delta)|A/A_{0,\text{max}}| = 0$. Solving for δ, we obtain

$$\delta = 0$$

$$\delta_{p1,p2} = \pm \frac{1 + b^2}{2Q_1Q_2} \sqrt{\frac{Q_1Q_2}{1 + b^2} - \frac{(Q_1 + Q_2)^2}{2(1 + b^2)^2}} \tag{6-280}$$

If $Q_1Q_2/(1 + b^2) \leqslant (Q_1 + Q_2)^2/2(1 + b^2)^2$, the value of δ_{p1} and δ_{p2} are imaginary, there is only one peak in the response curve, and $\delta = 0$ is a maximum. However, if the inequality is reversed, then there will be a double hump and $\delta = 0$ will be a minimum. The critical value of b is given by

$$b_{\text{crit}} = \frac{1}{\sqrt{2}} \sqrt{\frac{Q_1}{Q_2} + \frac{Q_2}{Q_1}} \tag{6-281}$$

When $b > b_{\text{crit}}$, the double-humped response results.

Let us now consider that $Q_1 = Q_2 = Q_0$. Actually, we shall see that we can achieve this in most practical cases. Then

$$\delta_{p1,p2} = \frac{\pm 1}{2Q_0} \sqrt{b^2 - 1} \tag{6-282}$$

and $b_{\text{crit}} = 1$. The frequencies where the peaks occur can be found from the relation $f/f_0 = 1 + \delta$.

In Secs. 6-20 to 6-23 we determined the half-power bandwidth. In practice, the bandwidth is set by the design requirements. For instance, we could consider the bandwidth to be those frequencies where

$$\gamma \leqslant \left| \frac{A}{A_{0,\text{max}}} \right| \leqslant 1 \tag{6-283}$$

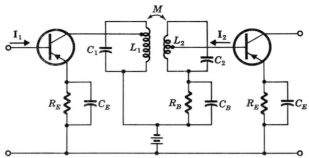

Fig. 6-66   A double-tuned transistor amplifier circuit using tapped coils.

γ is an arbitrary number less than one. In order to obtain the broadest bandwidth, for the double-humped curve, the minimum at $\delta = 0$ should be adjusted to be equal to γ. The bandwidth B_γ then lies between $\delta_{\gamma 1}$ and $\delta_{\gamma 2}$, as shown in Fig. 6-65. From Eq. (6-279) we have

$$\gamma = \frac{2b}{b^2 + 1} \tag{6-284}$$

Solve for b and choose the value greater than $b_{\text{crit}} = 1$.

$$b_\gamma = \frac{1}{\gamma} + \sqrt{\frac{1}{\gamma^2} - 1} \tag{6-285}$$

Note that $\gamma < 1$, so that b_γ is real. Then, setting the magnitude of Eq. (6-279) equal to $2b/(b^2 + 1)$ and solving for $\delta_{\gamma 1,\gamma 2}$, we obtain

$$\delta_{\gamma 1,\gamma 2} = \pm \frac{1}{\sqrt{2}\, Q_0} \sqrt{b^2 - 1} \tag{6-286}$$

If we compare this with Eq. (6-282), we see that

$$\delta_{\gamma 1} = \sqrt{2}\, \delta_{p1} \tag{6-287}$$
$$\delta_{\gamma 2} = \sqrt{2}\, \delta_{p2}$$

Then, using the relation $\delta = f/f_0 - 1$, we have

$$B_\gamma = \frac{\sqrt{2}}{Q_0} f_0 \sqrt{b^2 - 1} \tag{6-288}$$

The value of b can be related to the *coefficient of coupling* of the coils. This is defined by

$$k = \frac{M}{\sqrt{L_1 L_2}} \tag{6-289}$$

Manipulating Eq. (6-273), we obtain

$$b = k \sqrt{Q_1 Q_2} \tag{6-290}$$

The maximum value that the coefficient of coupling can have is unity. Thus,

$$b_{max} = \sqrt{Q_1 Q_2} \tag{6-291}$$

A procedure especially useful in transistor circuits, and which can be used to raise Q_1 and Q_2, is to tap the coils L_1 and L_2 and connect the load and the transistor to these taps. By properly adjusting the taps, the values of Q_1 and Q_2 can be made equal. A typical circuit utilizing these connections is shown in Fig. 6-66. The procedure of Sec. 6-22 can be used to calculate the impedances of this circuit.

6-25 More-complex tuned circuits—the design of bandpass amplifiers

An ideal bandpass amplifier would have a frequency characteristic like that shown in Fig. 6-67a. That is, the response should be constant for a specified range of frequencies and zero elsewhere. However, this characteristic cannot be realized in practice. Practical design specifications require that the response lie within the crosshatched area of Fig. 6-67b. The region between $f_{\rho 1}$ and $f_{\rho 2}$ is called the *pass band*. Here the normalized response

Fig. 6-67   (a) *The frequency response of an ideal bandpass amplifier; (b) design requirements for a practical bandpass amplifier. The response must lie within the crosshatched area.*

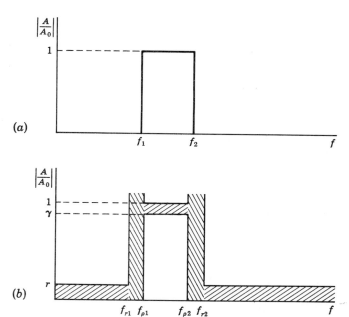

is held close to unity. $\gamma \leqslant |A/A_0| \leqslant 1$. The frequencies from zero to f_{r1} and from f_{r2} to ∞ constitute the *stop band*, where the normalized response must be less than a specified value r. The remaining frequencies, those between f_{r1} and $f_{\rho 1}$, and $f_{\rho 2}$ and f_{r2}, make up the *transition band*. No specific requirements are placed in this interval. However, it is assumed that $|A/A_0|$ falls from the pass-band value to the stop-band value in this region. In addition to the frequency requirements, the magnitude of A_0 will also be specified.

Let us consider how a simple single-tuned RC-coupled amplifier would be designed in view of these requirements. (Much of the discussion of Sec. 6-8 applies here.) Choose f_0 such that

$$f_0 = \sqrt{f_{\rho 1} f_{\rho 2}} \tag{6-292}$$

The minimum value of capacitance should be used to maximize the gain-bandwidth product. Equation (6-208) then determines L. The maximum Q that can be conveniently obtained should be used for Q_0. Try one stage. The required value of R_{sh} is found from A_0 using Eq. (6-231) or (6-236). If the actual value of R_{sh} calculated by Eq. (6-227) is greater than this value, shunt resistance should be placed across R_T. If the value calculated from Eq. (6-227) is too small, an impedance-matching technique must be used and/or Q_0 must be increased. We shall assume that the actual R_{sh} of Eq. (6-227) is equal to or greater than the required one. The value of Q_{eff} is obtained from Eq. (6-228) and the frequency response is then given by Eq. (6-232). The pass-band requirements are then checked at $f_{\rho 1}$ or $f_{\rho 2}$, and if they are met we proceed to the stop-band requirements. If they are not met, try additional stages and repeat the procedure until a broad enough pass band is obtained. It may not be possible to do this. In that case, a vacuum tube with a higher $g_m/2\pi C$ or a transistor with a higher $h_f/2\pi CR_i$ should be chosen. If the gain-bandwidth product is larger than required, then the gain of each amplifier stage should be increased, if possible, until the pass-band requirements are exactly obtained. This will improve the selectivity in the stop band. When the pass-band design is completed, the stop-band response should be checked. If $f_{r1} f_{r2} = f_0$, then, because of the geometric symmetry, the stop-band response need only be verified at either f_{r1} or f_{r2}. If $f_{r1} f_{r2} > f_0$, then check the response at f_{r1}, and if $f_{r1} f_{r2} < f_0$, check the response at f_{r2}. If the stop-band requirements are not met, increase the number of stages while adjusting their Q's so that the pass-band specifications are exactly realized. If too many stages are needed, it is possible that the pass-band specifications cannot be achieved. In such a case, a more-complex coupling network, or an active element that provides a higher gain-bandwidth product, is needed.

If r or R_T is too low to obtain the desired Q_{eff}, then an impedance-matching circuit, using either tapped coils or mutual inductance, should be used. There are additional degrees of freedom in this case, but the basic procedure is the same.

In general, double-tuned circuits are used when the design specifications are somewhat more severe. We shall assume that coils with equal Q's are used, to determine b_γ from γ. Establish the value of Q_0 from Eq. (6-288). Use the smallest values of capacitors that are feasible. These will determine the inductances. Then we can calculate the reflected resistance and the actual Q of the coils. Assume that the calculated Q_0 is less than the actual Q_0 given by Eq. (6-268) or (6-269). If this is so, then shunt resistance can be added to reduce the Q to the desired value. We assume here that the Q's of the primary and secondary can be made equal and that $b > 1$. In this case, the gain at the peaks of the response curve can be obtained from Eq. (6-275) or (6-276) with $b = 1$. Thus,

$$A_{v,\text{max}} = \frac{g_m Q_0{}^2 \sqrt{R_p R_s}}{2}$$

or

$$A_{i,\text{max}} = \frac{h_{fe} Q_0{}^2 \sqrt{R_p R_s}}{2 R_i}$$

If these gains are not sufficiently large, try two stages. In this case use a new value of γ which is the square root of the original γ. Continue to increase the number of stages until the pass-band requirements are met. This may not always be possible. In that case g_m or h_{fe}/R_i must be raised and/or the shunting capacitors reduced. The stop-band design then proceeds in essentially the same way that it does for the single-tuned amplifier. The use of tapped inductances can prove helpful here also, especially for transistor circuits.

The networks that we have considered are called *synchronously tuned*. That is, all the circuits are tuned to the same resonant frequency. If stringent design requirements are imposed (i.e., γ very close to unity, r very small, and the width of the transition bands quite narrow), it is possible that these procedures will not produce an acceptable circuit. In such cases, a more general procedure called *filter synthesis* is used to design the network. The resonant frequencies of the various tuned circuits may not all be the same when this general procedure is used. Such networks are called *stagger tuned*.

6-26 Neutralization

Thus far in our discussion of tuned amplifiers, we have neglected the fact that any coupling that allows an output signal to be "fed back" to the input circuit may cause the amplifier to oscillate. The phenomenon of oscillation is quite complex. We shall discuss it briefly here and defer a detailed discussion of it until Chap. 11. The oscillation can be analyzed by considering the input admittance of the active element. In Sec. 3-12 we saw that the input admittance of a common-cathode vacuum-tube triode amplifier

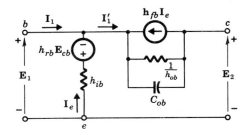

Fig. 6-68   An equivalent circuit of a common-emitter transistor amplifier.

whose voltage gain was $\mathbf{A}_v$ is given by

$$\mathbf{Y}_i = j\omega[C_{gk} + (1 - \mathbf{A}_v)C_{gp}] \tag{6-293}$$

For a pentode, C_{gk} is replaced by $C_{in} = C_{gk} + C_{gg2} + C_{gg3}$. Let us assume that the voltage gain $\mathbf{A}_v$ is a complex number such that

$$\mathbf{A}_v = A_R + jA_x \tag{6-294}$$

Then

$$\mathbf{Y}_i = \omega A_x C_{gp} + j\omega[C_{gk} + (1 - A_R)C_{gp}] \tag{6-295}$$

The first term is a shunt conductance, which can be positive or *negative*, depending upon the phase angle of the load impedance.

To obtain the input admittance of a common-emitter transistor amplifier, we shall use the common-base h-parameter equivalent circuit of Fig. 6-68. It will demonstrate the importance of C_{ob}. Then

$$\mathbf{E}_{cb} = \mathbf{E}_2 - \mathbf{E}_1 = \mathbf{E}_1(\mathbf{A}_v - 1)$$

where $\mathbf{A}_v = \mathbf{E}_2/\mathbf{E}_1$ is the voltage gain of the circuit. Then

$$\mathbf{I}_e = -\mathbf{E}_1 \frac{1 + h_{rb}(\mathbf{A}_v - 1)}{h_{ib}}$$

and

$$\mathbf{I}_1' = -h_{fb}\mathbf{I}_e + \mathbf{E}_1(1 - \mathbf{A}_v)(h_{ob} + j\omega C_{ob})$$

Solving for the input admittance, we obtain

$$\mathbf{Y}_i = \frac{(1 + h_{fb})[1 + h_{rb}(\mathbf{A}_v - 1)]}{h_{ib}} + (1 - \mathbf{A}_v)(h_{ob} + j\omega C_{ob}) \tag{6-296}$$

We usually operate at frequencies well below ω_α, where h_{fb} is essentially a real number independent of frequency. Then, writing $\mathbf{A}_v$ as in Eq. (6-294), we obtain

$$\mathbf{Y}_i = (1 + h_{fb})\frac{1 + h_{rb}(A_R - 1)}{h_{ib}} + h_{ob}(1 - A_R) + \omega C_{ob}A_x$$
$$+ j\left[(1 - A_R)\omega C_{ob} - A_x h_{ob} + \frac{(1 + h_{fb})h_{rb}A_x}{h_{ob}}\right] \tag{6-297}$$

The sum of the first two terms of the conductance, in general, is positive; but the third can be negative, which can result in a net negative conductance.

If we have a high-Q parallel resonant circuit, whose impedance is given by

$$Z_1 = \frac{R_0}{1 + jQ_0[(f/f_0) - (f_0/f)]}$$

and we shunt it by a negative resistance $-R$, the resulting impedance is

$$Z = \frac{R_0R/(R - R_0)}{1 + jQ_{\text{eff}}[(f/f_0) - (f_0/f)]} \tag{6-298}$$

where

$$Q_{\text{eff}} = Q_0R/(R - R_0) \tag{6-299}$$

In transformed form, this becomes

$$Z = \frac{p\omega_0R_0R/(R - R_0)Q_{\text{eff}}}{p^2 + (\omega_0/Q_{\text{eff}})p + \omega_0^2} \tag{6-300}$$

The poles of this expression occur at

$$p_{1,2} = \frac{-\omega_0}{2Q_{\text{eff}}} \pm j \frac{\omega_0}{2Q_{\text{eff}}} \sqrt{4Q_{\text{eff}}^2 - 1} \tag{6-301}$$

If $R < R_0$, then $Q_{\text{eff}} < 0$, the poles lie in the right half-plane, and the response of the amplifier will contain an exponentially increasing sinusoid. This is oscillation. (Any active element will saturate and, thus, the signal level will eventually stabilize.) To prevent oscillation, we must either make C_{gp} or C_{ob} very small or eliminate their effect. In the vacuum-tube pentode this is accomplished by actually reducing C_{gp} to extremely small values. For this reason, pentodes are used in most low-level tuned vacuum-tube amplifiers. However, vacuum-tube triodes are used at high power levels and for many low-noise applications, and tuned transistor amplifiers are used at all power levels. To eliminate the effects of the feedback capacitors C_{ob} or C_{gp}, another current which is equal to, but 180° out of phase with, the current through them, is introduced at the input terminal. Circuits which accomplish this are called *neutralizing circuits*. Several of them are illustrated in Fig. 6-69. In each case, the coil is center-tapped so that $E_1 = -E_2$. In the case of the vacuum tube, $C_N = C_{gp}$, and the net current fed back to the grid node is zero. In a transistor, the feedback impedance is somewhat more complex. Usually $C_N \approx C_{ob}$ provides neutralization. However, there are times when this value must be adjusted and a shunt resistor included. The circuits of Fig. 6-69 can be modified by using a tapped tuning capacitor, consisting of two capacitors in series, instead of the tapped inductance.

Neutralization often proves quite troublesome. An additional capacitor must be added to the circuit and its adjustment is critical. Also, C_N must be adjusted if f_0 is changed, because E_2 is not exactly equal to E_1 in an actual circuit, and the feedback impedance is complex in the case of a transistor.

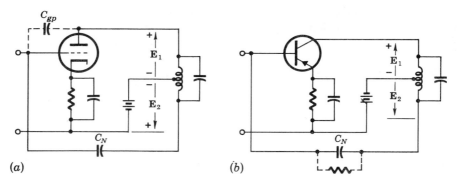

Fig. 6-69 (a) *A neutralized common-cathode vacuum-tube-triode amplifier;* (b) *a neutralized common-emitter transistor amplifier.*

In the case of vacuum tubes, we can always avoid the need for neutralization by using pentodes. It can be avoided in transistor amplifiers if the proper circuitry is used. If $R > R_0$ [see Eq. (6-301)], the circuit will not oscillate. Consider Fig. 6-62a with R_T a negative resistance. The magnitude of the apparent shunting negative resistance $-R$ can be made as large as desired by making L_2 small enough [see Eq. (6-241)]. Thus, transistor circuits which do not oscillate and which do not require a neutralizing circuit can be built using tapped coils. When the circuit is adjusted so that it is stable, (i.e., does not oscillate), the gain will be reduced somewhat. This is usually a small price to pay for the advantage of not needing a neutralizing capacitor.

It might appear as though the common-base transistor amplifier would not require neutralization. However, there is still feedback due to h_{rb}. Similar neutralizing circuits are used to eliminate its effect.

A common-grid vacuum-tube amplifier (see Fig. 3-19) does not require neutralization. The common grid shields the plate from the cathode and reduces the feedback effect greatly. Because of their low input impedance, common-grid circuits are not used too often. They are used, at times, as low-noise input stages of radio and television receivers.

6-27   Direct-coupled amplifiers

In Secs. 6-1 to 6-6, and 6-10, we discussed the low-frequency response of amplifiers and the means for extending this response. However, there are applications where signals of extremely low frequencies (on the order of fractions of a cycle per second or less) must be amplified. In such cases, RC-coupled amplifiers are not suitable. If the amplifier is not required to amplify very high frequencies, so that the effects of stray capacitance can be neglected, then the cathode, screen-grid, or emitter-bypass capacitance can be omitted. This will eliminate the dependence of the frequency response on these elements and also reduce the gain. However, a principal cause of the loss in gain at low frequencies is the coupling capacitor C_c. If it is short circuited, then the low-frequency response can become perfect. The bias voltages of the various circuits will then interact. For instance, if the grid of a vacuum tube is connected directly to the plate of one preceding it, a large positive direct voltage will be applied between the grid and the cathode. In the common-emitter transistor amplifier, if a base of one stage is connected directly to the collector of the preceding one, then too large a negative voltage will be applied between the base and the emitter. In both cases, improper operation will result. The use of two power supplies can correct this situation. Consider the vacuum-tube circuit of Fig. 6-70a. If R_1, R_2, and the negative power supply $-E_{cc}$ are adjusted properly, then the proper negative grid bias will result. Thus, this circuit eliminates the problem of bias interaction. The voltage divider, consisting of R_1 and R_2, will reduce the signal by the ratio $R_2/(R_1 + R_2)$. There are circuits which do not require this voltage divider. However, they are quite cumbersome in that they require many power supplies or power supplies with very high voltages. For this reason, they are seldom used. Figure 6-70b illustrates a direct-coupled transistor amplifier that operates on the same principles. The first vacuum tube uses a cathode-bias resistance. The successive stages do not require it because the power supply E_{cc} can be used to obtain the required negative bias. The emitter resistors are included in each transistor stage for stabilizing purposes. If the output resistances R_1' and R_2' are properly chosen, then the output can be made to be zero if the input signal is zero. The various voltages and currents can be found by an application of Kirchhoff's laws.

Fig. 6-70 Direct-coupled amplifiers. (a) *Common-cathode vacuum-tube amplifier; and* (b) *common-emitter transistor amplifier.*

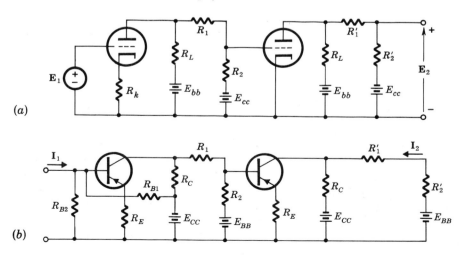

Although obtaining the correct bias voltages is a problem in direct-coupled amplifiers, it is a very minor one in comparison with the problem of operating-point stability. To illustrate this, let us consider a cascade of *RC*-coupled amplifiers, each with a voltage gain of 10. Because of temperature fluctuations and power-supply changes, the operating point of each stage will fluctuate very slowly. For instance, assume that the input bias voltage of the first stage fluctuates ± 0.1 volt over a period of several minutes. This would appear as a very low-frequency signal. However, the *RC*-coupled network would almost completely reject signals of such low frequency. Hence, there would be no harmful results. On the other hand, if the amplifier were direct-coupled, it could not distinguish between these bias-voltage shifts and low-frequency signals. Thus, the voltage of the second stage would shift by ∓ 1 volt, and that of the third stage by ± 10 volts, etc. Thus, minute variations in bias potentials can cause serious effects in direct-coupled amplifiers. The drift acts as a spurious input signal. Often, there is no convenient way of distinguishing between drift in bias voltages and a very low frequency signal. The smallest signal to be amplified should be much greater than the effective "drift signal" at the input. In severe cases of drift, operating-point shifts in the latter stages of the amplifier may result in very nonlinear operation or excessive dissipation. For these reasons the power-supply voltage should be well regulated. However, minute changes in power-supply voltage cannot be eliminated. In addition, much of the drift is caused by changes in the circuit elements themselves. These changes are due primarily to thermal effects and are especially troublesome in transistor circuits. One means of reducing these thermal effects is to include additional temperature-sensitive elements which compensate for changes in other circuit elements. For instance, consider the circuit of Fig. 6-71. The semiconductor diode and the transistor are mounted close together, so that each operates at essentially the same temperature. An increase in the temperature tends to increase the collector current of the transistor. However, the increase in temperature also decreases the resistance of the reverse-biased diode. This, in turn, will reduce the base current, which will reduce the collector current. Thus, the inclusion of the diode tends to reduce the thermal sensitivity of the circuit. The diode must be properly matched to the transistor. If its resistance does not change enough, then the collector cur-

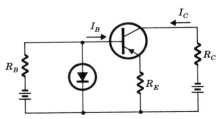

Fig. 6-71 *An illustration of the use of a semiconductor diode as a thermal-compensating element. Actually only one power supply is needed.*

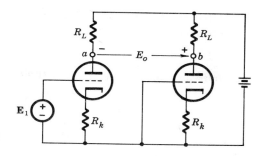

Fig. 6-72 Balanced amplifiers. (a) Common-cathode vacuum-tube amplifier; (b) common-emitter transistor amplifier.

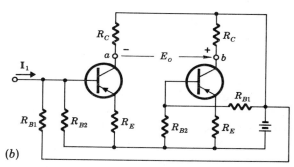

rent will rise with increasing temperature. If it changes too much, then the collector current can actually decrease with increasing temperature. It may prove difficult to match the diode and the transistor.

If we use two active elements in each stage instead of one, many of the effects of drift can actually be canceled. Consider the circuit of Fig. 6-72. This is called a *balanced amplifier*. Assume that the two vacuum tubes or the two transistors are identical. If the power-supply voltage shifts, then the plate or collector voltage of each active element will change equally. Thus, the output voltage E_o will be unaffected. Similarly, there will be no output voltage resulting from thermal drifts or any other changes *provided that the changes in both halves of the circuit are equal.* To accomplish this, the active elements should be picked so that they are as nearly identical as possible. In addition, they should be mounted very close together so that their temperatures will be equal. Succeeding stages of the amplifier are also balanced. Instead of connecting one grid or one base to the common lead, one is connected to point *a* while the other is connected to point *b*. An arrangement similar to that of Fig. 6-70 must be used to prevent bias interaction. The use of balanced amplifiers allows direct-coupled amplifiers to amplify much smaller signals. (The tendency for the operating points to drift is still present. However, this drift no longer appears as an output signal.)

One means of eliminating the problem of the drift of direct-coupled

amplifiers is to avoid using them.   This can be accomplished if we can obtain
a high-frequency voltage or current whose amplitude varies in accordance
with the low-frequency signal.   This high-frequency signal can then be
amplified by an ordinary RC-coupled amplifier.   Its amplitude will be an
amplified replica of the low-frequency signal, and an amplified signal can
be recovered from it.   Such processes, called *modulation and demodulation*,
will be considered in detail in Chap. 13.   We shall consider a very simple
circuit for accomplishing it here (see Fig. 6-73).   The switches sw_1 and sw_2
are mechanically driven switches which open and close synchronously.   A
typical rate for driving these switches is 60 cps.   If an input voltage e_1,
which is shown by the solid curve of Fig. 6-74, is applied to the system,
then the voltage e_1' will be of the form shown in the dotted curve (this
assumes that $R_1 \ll R_i$).   One-half of the input signal is removed.   For this
reason, this is called a *chopper amplifier*.   If information regarding the input
wave shift is not to be lost, then the frequency ω_a at which the switches
are driven must be much greater than the highest frequency of e_1, ω_b.   We
have obtained a higher frequency signal whose amplitude varies in accordance with the input signal.   If ω_a is the frequency at which the switches
are driven and if $1/\omega_a C_1 \ll R_i$, then input voltages or currents of the amplifier will have the same wave form as the dashed curve of Fig. 6-74, but
the direct component will be removed from them.   This alternating
signal then can be amplified by the RC-coupled amplifier.   The output
circuit removes the alternations from the output signal, so that e_2 has
the same form as e_1.   Since switch sw_2 is driven in synchronism with
sw_1, e_2' will only be of one polarity.   Its waveform will be essentially that
of the dashed curve of Fig. 6-74.   The capacitor C_2 will charge and discharge through R_2.   If $1/R_2 C_2 \ll \omega_a$, then the output voltage will not
be able to follow the on-off swings of e_2'.   Thus, the output will be smoothed
and e_2 will resemble the solid curve.   The output voltage should be able
to change rapidly enough to follow the changes in e_1.   Hence, $1/R_2 C_2$
should be considerably greater than the highest signal frequency ω_b.   Again,
we see that $\omega_a \gg \omega_b$.   In practice, ω_a must be at least 10 times ω_b if this
amplifier is to function properly.   Thus, if $f_a = 60$ cps, which is a fairly
rapid rate at which to drive a switch, then the usable upper frequency limit

Fig. 6-73   A chopper amplifier.

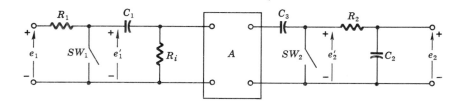

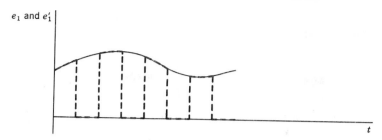

Fig. 6-74   Waveforms of a chopper amplifier.

of the amplifier is 6 cps. This is adequate for a great many instrumentation problems. However, the very limited high-frequency response does limit the usefulness of mechanical chopper amplifiers. (There are "chopper circuits" that use "electronic switches." These can be driven at higher frequencies.)

REFERENCES

[1] T. S. Gray, "Applied Electronics," 2d ed., pp. 520–521, John Wiley & Sons, Inc., New York, 1954.

[2] F. E. Terman, "Electronic and Radio Engineering," 4th ed., pp. 265–266, McGraw-Hill Book Company, New York, 1955.

[3] E. J. Angelo, Jr., "Electronic Circuits," pp. 310–313, McGraw-Hill Book Company, New York, 1958.

[4] G. E. Valley, Jr. and H. Wallman, "Vacuum Tube Amplifiers," McGraw-Hill Book Company, pp. 172–173, New York, 1948.

[5] A. V. Bedford and G. L. Fredendall, Transient Response of Multistage Video-frequency Amplifiers, *Proc. IRE*, vol. 27, pp. 277–284, 1939.

[6] W. W. Gärtner, "Transistors: Principles, Design, and Applications," chap. 15, D. Van Nostrand Company, Inc., Princeton, N.J., 1960.

[7] Valley and Wallman, *ibid.*, pp. 77–78.

[8] F. E. Terman, "Radio Engineers' Handbook," p. 372, McGraw-Hill Book Company, New York, 1943.

BIBLIOGRAPHY

Gärtner, W. W.: "Transistors: Principles, Design, and Applications," chaps. 12, 14, and 15, D. Van Nostrand Company, Inc., Princeton, N.J., 1960.

Pettit, J. M., and M. M. McWhorter: "Electronic Amplifier Circuits: Theory and Design," chaps. 3–5, 7, 9–11, McGraw-Hill Book Company, New York, 1961.

Valley, G. E., Jr., and H. Wallman: "Vacuum Tube Amplifiers," chaps. 2, 4, and 5, McGraw-Hill Book Company, New York, 1948.

PROBLEMS

6-1. Determine the voltage gain of the amplifier of Fig. 6-1. Make no approximations except that all bypass capacitors are short circuits at the signal frequencies. Do not neglect the interelectrode capacitances.

6-2. Compute the magnitude of the mid-frequency voltage gain, the upper and lower half-power frequencies, and plot the normalized frequency response (amplitude and phase) of the amplifier of Fig. 6-2. The vacuum tube has the following parameter values: $g_m = 5,000$ μmhos, $r_p = 10,000$ ohms, $C_{gp} = 6.0$ $\mu\mu$f, $C_{gk} = 6.0$ $\mu\mu$f, $C_{pk} = 3.0$ $\mu\mu$f. The circuit constants are $R_L = 10,000$ ohms, $C_c = 0.1$ μf, $R_g = 10^6$ ohms. Assume that the wiring capacitance is 5 $\mu\mu$f and that C_i is 10 $\mu\mu$f. Plot the low-frequency response and the high-frequency response separately. Use semilog paper.

6-3. Repeat Prob. 6-2, but now assume that C_i represents the input capacitance of an identical amplifier stage. For convenience, assume that the voltage gain of the second stage remains constant at the midband value. How would the results change if this assumption were not made?

6-4. An *RC*-coupled vacuum-tube-pentode amplifier has the equivalent circuit shown in Fig. 6-3. The parameters of the pentode are $g_m = 5,000$ μmhos, $r_p \geqslant 2 \times 10^6$ ohms, $C_{in} = 10$ $\mu\mu$f, $C_{out} = 10$ $\mu\mu$f, $C_{gp} = 0.001$ $\mu\mu$f. The circuit constants are $R_L = 5,000$ ohms, $R_g = 10^6$ ohms, and $C_c = 0.1$ μf. Assume that the wiring capacitance is 5 $\mu\mu$f, and that C_i is 10 $\mu\mu$f. Find the magnitude of the midband voltage gain, the upper and lower half-power frequencies, and plot the normalized frequency response (amplitude and phase) of the amplifier.

6-5. Repeat Prob. 6-4, but now assume that C_i represents the input capacitance of an identical amplifier stage. For convenience, assume that the voltage gain of the second stage remains constant at the midband value. Compare and discuss the answers of Probs. 6-2 to 6-5. Plot the low-frequency response and the high-frequency response separately. Use semilog paper.

6-6. Plot the normalized amplitude response of the amplifier of Prob. 6-4 in decibels.

6-7. If the plate resistance of the vacuum-tube pentode of Prob. 6-4 is exactly 2×10^6 ohms, what is the maximum magnitude that $A_{v,\text{mid}}$ can have? What is the upper half power-frequency that corresponds to this value of midband gain? What is the gain-bandwidth product of the amplifier?

6-8. Three identical amplifier stages, of the type given in Prob. 6-4, are cascaded. Determine the midband voltage gain of the overall amplifier and plot the normalized frequency response (amplitude, amplitude in db, and phase) of the amplifier.

6-9. Repeat Prob. 6-8, but now assume that the coupling capacitance and the parasitic capacitance of the last stage are halved.

6-10. Compute an exact expression for the current gain of the two-stage transistor amplifier of Fig. 6-8. Do not neglect the output capacitance of the transistor or the variation of $\mathbf{h}_{fe}$ with frequency. Assume that the capacitors C_E are short circuits at the signal frequency.

6-11. A transistor has the following parameter values: $h_{ie} = 5,000$ ohms, $h_{re} = 2 \times 10^{-4}$, $h_{fe} = 100$, $h_{oe} = 60 \times 10^{-6}$ mho, $C_{ob} = 3$ $\mu\mu$f, and $f_\alpha = 20 \times 10^6$ cps. It is used as the active element in an *RC*-coupled amplifier whose equivalent circuit is given in Fig. 6-9. The parameters of the circuit are $R_C =$ 10,000 ohms, $R_B = 50,000$ ohms, $R_i = 5,000$ ohms, and $C_c = 5$ μf. Assume that the stray wiring capacitance is 5 $\mu\mu f$ and that C_i is 10 $\mu\mu f$. Determine the midband current gain and plot the normalized frequency response (amplitude and phase), of the amplifier.

6-12. Repeat Prob. 6-11, but now assume that $h_{fe} = 50$. Discuss the reasons for the changes in the answers.

6-13. Plot the asymptotes of the normalized amplitude response in db for the amplifiers of Probs. 6-11 and 6-12.

6-14. Discuss the concept of a gain-bandwidth product in a transistor amplifier. Compare it with the gain-bandwidth product in a vacuum-tube amplifier.

6-15. An RC-coupled transistor amplifier is made up of three identical stages. The parameters of the transistor are: $h_{ie} = 5,000$ ohms, $h_{re} = 0$, $h_{fe} = 100$, $h_{oe} = 60 \times 10^{-6}$ mho, $C_{ob} = 3$ $\mu\mu f$, and $f_\alpha = 20 \times 10^6$ cps. The values of the circuit elements (see Fig. 6-9) are: $R_C = 10,000$ ohms, $R_B = 50,000$ ohms, $R_i = 5,000$ ohms. Assume that the stray wiring capacitance plus C_i is equal to 15 $\mu\mu f$. Determine the midband current gain of the amplifier. Plot the normalized frequency response (amplitude, amplitude in db, and phase) of the amplifier.

6-16. Repeat Prob. 6-15, but now assume that $h_{re} = 16 \times 10^{-4}$ and the load resistance for the last stage is $R_i = 5,000$ ohms (see Fig. 6-9). Do not assume that the input resistance of each stage is 5,000 ohms.

6-17. A vacuum-tube triode, whose equivalent circuit is given in Fig. 6-13, requires a quiescent grid bias of -5 volts and a quiescent plate current of 25 ma. The vacuum tube is operated such that $r_p = 10,000$ ohms and $\mu = 100$. The element values are $R_L = 10,000$ ohms and $R_g = 10^6$ ohms. Find a value for C_k such that $|A_v/A_{v,\text{mid}}| \geqslant 0.9$ at 20 cps. Consider only the effect of the cathode-bias impedance in this example. After the value of C_k is determined, plot the normalized frequency response (amplitude and phase) of the circuit.

6-18. A vacuum-tube pentode has the following parameter values: $g_m = 6,000$ μmhos, $g_{ps} = 1,500$ μmhos, $r_p \geqslant 2 \times 10^6$ ohms, and $\mathbf{I}_s = 0.1I_p$. It is operated in an amplifier whose equivalent circuit is given in Fig. 6-16, where $R_s = 100,000$ ohms, $R_k = 1,000$ ohms, $R_L = 10,000$ ohms, $C_k = 100$ μf, and $C_s = 2.0$ μf. Determine the low-frequency response of this amplifier due to the cathode- and screen-grid bias impedances. Plot the normalized frequency response (amplitude and phase) for this circuit.

6-19. A vacuum-tube pentode which is used in the amplifier of Fig. 6-16 is operated at the following operating point: $E_{bQ} = 300$ volts, $I_{bQ} = 10$ ma, $E_{cQ} = -9$ volts, $E_{c2Q} = 250$ volts, $I_{c2Q} = 1.5$ ma. At this operating point, the parameters of the vacuum tube are: $g_m = 6,000$ μmhos, $g_{ps} = 1,500$ μmhos, $r_p \geqslant 2 \times 10^{+6}$ ohm. The load resistance in the circuit is $R_L = 9,100$ ohms. Determine values for C_k and C_s such that $|A_v/A_{v,\text{mid}}| \geqslant 0.8$ at 50 cps. Consider only the effects of the cathode-bias impedance and the screen-grid bias impedance in this problem.

6-20. A transistor has these low-frequency parameters: $h_{ie} = 1,500$ ohms, $h_{re} = 300 \times 10^{-6}$, $h_{fe} = 100$, $h_{oe} = 50 \times 10^{-6}$ mho. It is operated in the circuit of Fig. 6-18 where $R_C = 2,000$ ohms, $R_B = 20,000$ ohms, the input impedance of the next stage $Z_i = 2,000$ ohms, $R_E = 1,000$ ohms, and $C_E =$

300 μf. The reactance of C_c is assumed to be zero. Will the emitter stabilizing impedance affect the gain $\mathbf{I}_2/\mathbf{I}_i$ to any great extent? Now, assume that the impedance $\mathbf{Z}_i$ is equal to $\mathbf{Z}_{i1}$ (where $\mathbf{Z}_{i1}$ is calculated when $\mathbf{Z}_i = 2,000$ ohms) and compute the current gain of the amplifier as a function of frequency. Plot the amplitude and phase response of this amplifier. What is the midband gain?

6-21. The element values of Fig. 6-20 are $R_s = 10,000$ ohms, $R_i = 20,000$ ohms, and $C_i = 200 \mu\mu$f. Determine the upper half-power frequency of the ratio $|E_1/E_s|$. Repeat this for the ratio $|I_1/E_s|$.

6-22. Three identical RC-coupled vacuum-tube amplifier stages are cascaded. The upper and lower half-power frequencies of the amplifier are 2 cps and 100,000 cps, respectively. What are the upper and lower half-power frequencies of the individual stages?

6-23. Prove this statement: If an amplifier is composed of n identical stages whose gain-bandwidth product is constant, then the maximum gain-bandwidth product of the overall amplifier occurs when the gain of each individual stage is approximately equal to 4.34 db. Hint: use the approximation $2^{1/n} - 1 \approx (\ln 2)/n$.

6-24. Design an RC-coupled voltage amplifier, using the minimum number of stages, that meets the following specifications: $|A_{\text{mid}}| \geqslant 64$; at a frequency of 10^6 cps, $|A/A_{\text{mid}}| \geqslant 0.9$; and at a frequency of 50 cps, $|A/A_{\text{mid}}| \geqslant 0.8$. The amplifier is to have a d-c blocking capacitor in its input stage. The load is a 10^6-ohm resistance shunted by 12 $\mu\mu$f. (See Fig. 6-22 for the form of the amplifier.) Use vacuum-tube pentodes with the following characteristics: $g_m = 8,000 \mu$mhos, $g_{ps} = 1,500 \mu$mhos, $r_p \geqslant 3 \times 10^6$ ohms, $R_{g.\text{max}} = 10^6$ ohms, $C_{\text{in}} = 12 \mu\mu$f, and $C_{\text{out}} = 8 \mu\mu$f. The coordinates of the operating point are $E_{bQ} = 350$ volts, $I_{bQ} = 30$ ma, $E_{c2Q} = 250$ volts, $I_{c2Q} = 2$ ma, and $E_{cQ} = -5$ volts. The wiring capacity is 5 $\mu\mu$f for any stage.

6-25. Consider the design of Prob. 6-24, but now assume that a new pentode is available with a g_m that is sufficiently high so that only one stage is needed. Determine this value of g_m.

6-26. Using the minimum number of stages, design an RC-coupled vacuum-tube amplifier that meets the following specifications: $|A_{\text{mid}}| \geqslant 20$, the lower and upper half-power frequencies are to be 20 cps and 20,000 cps, respectively. Cathode bias is to be used and the maximum power-supply voltage is to be 405 volts. A d-c blocking capacitor should be included in the input circuit. Use vacuum-tube triodes with the following specifications: $\mu = 20$, $r_p = 20,000$, $C_{gp} = 2 \mu\mu$f, $C_{gk} = 2 \mu\mu$f, and $C_{pk} = 1.5 \mu\mu$f. The coordinates of the operating point are $E_{bQ} = 300$ volts, $I_{bQ} = 10$ ma, and $E_{cQ} = -5$ volts. The maximum value at R_g is 10^6 ohms. The stray wiring capacitance is 5 $\mu\mu$f. The output load resistance is 10^6 ohms.

6-27. Design an RC-coupled transistor amplifier of the type shown in Fig. 6-23, using the following specifications: $|A_{i,\text{mid}}| = |I_s/I_2| \geqslant 49$; at a frequency of 0.5×10^6 cps, $|A_i/A_{i,\text{mid}}| \geqslant 0.8$; and at a frequency of 50 cps, $|A_i/A_{i,\text{mid}}| \geqslant 0.8$. The minimum number of amplifier stages are to be used and the stability factor of any stage is to be equal to or less than 7. The load impedance and the internal impedance of the input current generator are each 2,000 ohms. Use p-n-p transistors with the following characteristics: $h_{ie} = 2,000$ ohms, $h_{re} = 30 \times 10^{-6}$, $h_{fe} = 50$, $h_{oe} = 40 \times 10^{-6}$ mho, $C_{ob} = 4 \mu\mu$f, and $f_\alpha = 100 \times 10^6$ cps. The coordinates of the operating point are given by $I_{CQ} = -5$ ma, $I_{BQ} = -100$ μamps, $E_{CQ} = -6$ volts, and $E_{BQ} \approx$ 0 volts. Assume that the stray wiring capacitance can be neglected.

6-28. If the transistor of Prob. 6-27 were replaced by an *n-p-n* transistor, how would the design change?

6-29. Can the design of Prob. 6-27 be realized with only one transistor if the value of h_{fe} is increased? Prove your answer.

6-30. The amplifier of Fig. 6-24a has the following element values: $R_L = 10,000$ ohms, $R_d = 10,000$ ohms, $R_g = 10^6$ ohms, $C_c = 0.005$ μf, and $C_d = 1.0$ μf. The vacuum tube has the following parameter values: $g_m = 5,000$ μmhos, $r_p = 2 \times 10^6$ ohms. Assume that C_k and C_s are short circuits at the signal frequencies. Determine $A_{v,\text{mid}}$ and plot $|A_{v,\text{low}}/A_{v,\text{mid}}|$ for this amplifier. First use the approximate expression of Eq. (6-106) and then use exact calculations. Comment on the accuracy of the approximate relation in this case. If R_d is replaced by a short circuit, how do these results change?

6-31. Repeat Prob. 6-30, but now use a value of $C_d = 2.0$ μf and then use a value of $C_d = 0.5$ μf.

6-32. An *RC*-coupled vacuum-tube-pentode amplifier is to have a lower half-power frequency of 20 cps. The form of the circuit is to be that of Fig. 6-24a, where $R_L = 10,000$ ohms, $R_g = 10^6$ ohms, $g_m = 5,000$ μmhos, and $r_p \geqslant 2 \times 10^6$ ohms. The coordinates of the operating point are $E_{bQ} = 250$ volts, $I_{bQ} = 10$ ma, $E_{cQ} = -5$ volts, $E_{c2Q} = 250$ volts, and $I_{c2Q} = 1$ ma. If $R_d = 0$, what value of C_i is required to obtain the desired low-frequency response? Now use a coupling capacitor that is one-half of this value and find the value of R_d and C_d such that the low-frequency response remains unchanged. Compute the value of E_{bb}, R_s, and R_k for both cases. Assume that C_k and C_s are short circuits at all frequencies of interest.

6-33. The transistor of Fig. 6-24b has the following parameter values: $h_{ie} = 2,000$ ohms, $h_{re} = 300 \times 10^{-6}$, $h_{fe} = 50$, $h_{oe} = 10 \times 10^{-6}$ mho. The coordinates of the operating point are $E_{CQ} = -5$ volts, $I_{CQ} = -1$ ma, and $I_{BQ} = -100$ ma. The circuit elements are $R_E = 1,000$ ohms, $R_C = 1,000$ ohms, $R_d = 10,000$ ohms, $R_B = 10,000$ ohms, $R_i = 2,500$ ohms, $C_c = 1$ μf, and $C_d = 2$ μf. Plot the low-frequency current gain (magnitude and phase) using the approximate expression of Eq. (6-98) and then using an exact expression. Calculate the value of E_{CC}.

6-34. Repeat Prob. 6-33, but now use a value of $R_d = 100,000$ ohms.

6-35. Repeat Probs. 6-33 and 6-34, but change the value of C_d to 4 μf, and then repeat the calculations using a value of $C_d = 1$ μf.

6-36. For the amplifier of Prob. 6-33, consider that R_d and C_d are variable. The low-frequency response is to be constant, within approximately 10 percent, down to 10 cps. Determine the values of R_d, C_d, C_c, and E_{CC} if this design is to be realized. If $R_d = 0$, what value of C_c is required to make $|A_{i,\text{low}}/A_{i,\text{mid}}| = 0.9$ at 10 cps.

6-37. A single-stage *RC*-coupled amplifier of the type shown in Fig. 6-27a has the following element values: $R_L = 10,000$ ohms, $R_g = 10^6$ ohms, and $C_c = 0.01$ μf. The parameters of the vacuum-tube pentode are $g_m = 5,000$ μmhos, $r_p \geqslant 2 \times 10^6$ ohms, $C_{\text{out}} = 8$ $\mu\mu$f, $C_{\text{in}} = 10$ $\mu\mu$f. Assume that this is cascaded with an identical amplifier and that the wiring capacitance is 5 $\mu\mu$f. Find the upper half-power frequency of the one-stage amplifier if no shunt peaking is used. Then find a value of L which maximizes the upper half-power frequency and also keeps the amplitude response monotonic.

6-38. Repeat Prob. 6-37, but now assume that the amplitude response is allowed to rise 2 or 3 percent above the midband value.

6-39. Repeat Prob. 6-37, but now adjust the value of L for the minimum delay distortion.

6-40. Discuss how the equations of Sec. 6-12 would be modified if all the common-emitter h parameters of Eq. (3-130) were used.

6-41. Use the constructions of Fig. 6-33 to plot the amplitude and phase response of the shunt-peaked amplifier of Fig. 6-27a for values of $Q_2 = 1.00$, 0.439, 0.342, and 0.200. (The notation is that of Sec. 6-11.)

6-42. Determine the 10–90 percent rise time for the amplifier of Prob. 6-37 when no shunt peaking is used. Find a value of L that minimizes the 10–90 percent rise time without producing any overshoot. What is the 10–90 percent rise time in this case? Now repeat this calculation assuming that about 5 percent overshoot is allowed.

6-43. Compare and discuss the amplifiers of Probs. 6-37 to 6-39, and 6-42.

6-44. Plot the unit-step response of the amplifier of Probs. 6-30 and 6-31, when $C_d = 2.0\ \mu\text{f}$. (Assume that the approximate relations for low-frequency compensation can be used.)

6-45. The amplifiers of Probs. 6-30 and 6-31 are to amplify a rectangular pulse whose width is $\frac{1}{10}$ sec. Compute the sag. Assume that the pulse-repetition rate is very long.

6-46. Repeat Prob. 6-45, but now assume that the pulse width is $1/1,000$ sec.

6-47. An amplifier has a normalized gain in transformed form given by

$$\mathbf{A}(p) = 1 + \frac{0.1p(p + a)}{(p + a)^2 + \omega_0^2}$$

What is the unit-step response of this amplifier?

6-48. An amplifier has a normalized unit-step response that is given by
$$f(t) = 1 + 0.1e^{-0.2t} + 0.1e^{-0.3t}\cos 4t$$
Find the normalized amplification as a function of $j\omega$.

6-49. Determine the midband amplification, the lower and upper half-power frequencies, and plot the normalized frequency response (amplitude and phase) of the cathode-follower amplifier of Fig. 6-44a. The circuit elements have the following values: $R_L = 10,000$ ohms, $R_g = 10^6$ ohms, $R_{g1} = 10^6$ ohms, $R_k = 200$ ohms, $C_{c1} = 0.01\ \mu\text{f}$, and $C_{c2} = 0.1\ \mu\text{f}$. The parameters of the vacuum tube are $g_m = 5,000\ \mu\text{mhos}$, $r_p \geqslant 2 \times 10^6$ ohms, $C_{\text{out}} = 8\ \mu\mu\text{f}$, $C_{\text{in}} = 12\ \mu\mu\text{f}$, $C_{gp} = 0.001\ \mu\mu\text{f}$, and $C_{hk} = 10\ \mu\mu\text{f}$. Assume that C_k and C_s are short circuits at all frequencies of interest. In the low-frequency region, consider the effects of both coupling capacitors. The wiring capacity is $5\ \mu\mu\text{f}$ and the input capacitance of the next amplifier stage is $12\ \mu\mu\text{f}$.

6-50. Determine the midband amplification and plot the normalized frequency response (amplitude and phase) of the common-base transistor amplifier of Fig. 6-45a. The circuit elements have the following values: $R_C = 10,000$ ohms, $R_B = 1,500$ ohms, $R_i = 40$ ohms, and $C_c = 5\ \mu\text{f}$. The parameters of the transistor are $h_{ib} = 40$ ohms, $h_{rb} = 4 \times 10^{-6}$, $h_{fb} = -0.99$, $h_{ob} = 10^{-6}$ mho, $f_\alpha = 200 \times 10^6$ cps, and $C_{ob} = 5\ \mu\mu\text{f}$. Assume that the stray wiring capacitance plus the input capacitance of the next stage is $3\ \mu\mu\text{f}$.

6-51. Repeat Prob. 6-50 for the common-collector transistor amplifier of Fig. 6-46a. Use the same transistor. The circuit elements are $R_C = 10,000$ ohms, $R_B = 20,000$ ohms, $R_i = 5,000$ ohms, and $C_c = 5\ \mu\text{f}$. Assume that the stray capacitance plus the input capacitance of the next stage is $3\ \mu\mu\text{f}$.

6-52. Compute the input resistance of the ideal transformer shown in Fig. 6-75. The turns ratios are $n_1/n_2 = 10$, $n_1/n_3 = 5$.

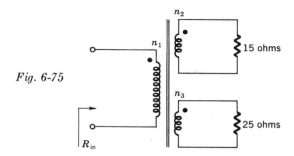

Fig. 6-75

6-53. The transformer-coupled amplifier whose equivalent circuit is shown in Fig. 6-52 has the following parameter values: $R_p = 500$ ohms, $R_s = 0.5$ ohm, $L_p = 0.025$ henry, $L_s = 15 \times 10^{-6}$ henry, $L_m = 30$ henrys, $n_1/n_2 = 40$, $r = 400$ ohms, and $R_L = 2$ ohms. The active element is a vacuum-tube pentode with $g_m = 5,000\,\mu$mhos, and $r_p = 5,000$ ohms. Compute the mid-frequency voltage gain and the upper and lower half-power frequencies for the amplifier. Assume that $1/\omega C_o \gg r$ and $1/\omega C_i \gg (n_1/n_2)^2 R_L$ for all frequencies of interest.

6-54. Repeat Prob. 6-53, but now assume that R_L is an open circuit and $C_i = 200\,\mu\mu$f. Plot the high-frequency response of this amplifier.

6-55. The transformer-coupled amplifier whose equivalent circuit is shown in Fig. 6-52 has the following parameter values: $R_p = 500$ ohms, $R_s = 1$ ohm, $L_p = 0.025$ henry, $L_s = 300 \times 10^{-6}$ henry, $C_o = 400\,\mu\mu$f, $C_i = 200\,\mu\mu$f, $L_m = 30$ henrys, $(n_1/n_2) = 9$, $R_L = 40$ ohms, and $r = 100,000$ ohms. If the active element is a common-base transistor where h_{fb} is -0.99 and where $h_{ob}^{-1} = r = 100,000$ ohms, compute the mid-frequency current gain and plot the frequency response of the amplifier.

6-56. For the parallel resonant circuit of Fig. 6-58, plot a curve of $|Z|/R_0$ versus δ and f/f_0 for values of $Q_0 = 10, 100, 1,000$. What are the half-power bandwidths in each of these cases? The notation of Sec. 6-20 is used in this problem.

6-57. The voltage gain of the single-tuned RC-coupled amplifier of Fig. 6-57a is to have a half-power bandwidth of exactly 10,000 cps, a center frequency of $f_0 = 500,000$ cps and as large a midband voltage gain as possible. The output capacitance of the pentode is $20\,\mu\mu$f. Assume that the input capacitance of the next stage is $20\,\mu\mu$f and the stray wiring capacitance is $10\,\mu\mu$f. For the pentode $g_m = 5,000\,\mu$mhos and $r_p = 2 \times 10^6$ ohms. The value of R_g is 2×10^6 ohms. Find the value of the inductance L. If L has a $Q_0 = 100$, what size resistance must be placed in parallel with R_g to obtain the desired bandwidth? What is the midband voltage gain? Assume that all bypass capacitors are short circuits at the signal frequencies.

6-58. The current gain of the single-tuned RC-coupled transistor amplifier of Fig. 6-57b is to have a half-power bandwidth of exactly 10,000 cps, a center frequency of $f_0 = 500,000$ cps, and as large a midband current gain as possible. Assume that $h_{ie} = 5,000$ ohms, $h_{fe} = 100$, $h_{re} \approx 0$, $h_{oe} = 10^{-6}$ mho, $\omega_\beta \gg$

0.5×10^6 cps, and $C_{oe} = 30 \mu\mu$f. The values of R_B and R_i are 50,000 and 5,000 ohms, respectively. The wiring capacitance is $20 \mu\mu$f. Neglect the input capacitance of the next stage. Find the value of the inductance L. If L has a $Q_0 = 100$, can the design be achieved with this circuit? Now add the ideal transformer as shown in Fig. 6-61. Determine the turns ratio necessary to obtain the required bandwidth. What is the current gain at $f = f_0$ in this case? Assume that all bypass capacitors are short circuits at the signal frequencies. Does the resistor R_B have to be used when the impedance-matching transformer is added to the circuit?

6-59. Repeat Prob. 6-58, but instead of the ideal transformer, use the tapped coil of Fig. 6-62. Find the values of $L = L_1 + L_2 + 2M$ and $L_2 + M$ and the current gain at $f = f_0$.

6-60. Repeat Prob. 6-58, but now assume that $h_{oe} = 10 \times 10^{-6}$ mho, and $C_{oe} = 300 \mu\mu$f. In this case, two impedance-matching transformers can be used. Place one between the transistor and the tuned circuit so that the transistor's output impedance appears to be the same as it was in Prob. 6-58. The second transformer is used as it was in Prob. 6-58. Determine the turns ratio of both transformers. What is the current gain at $f = f_0$?

6-61. Repeat Prob. 6-59, but now use the circuit of Fig. 6-76 with two capacitors, instead of the tapped inductor. Assume that $C_{oe} = 20 \mu\mu$f so that the total shunt capacitance can be made the same as that in Prob. 6-58. What effect does this reduction in C_{oe} produce?

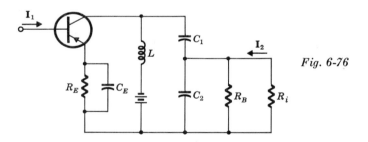

Fig. 6-76

6-62. Repeat Prob. 6-58, but now use the mutual-inductance-coupled circuit of Fig. 6-63a. Assume that the Q of the primary coil alone is 100, that $R_2 = 0$, and that R_B is not present in this circuit.

6-63. The double-tuned amplifier of Fig. 6-64a has the following parameter values: $C_1 = C_2 = 50 \mu\mu$f, the Q of the primary and secondary coils alone are each 100, $r = R_i = 10^6$ ohms. The resonant frequency is to be 500,000 cps and the bandwidth where $|A/A_0| \geq 0.8$ is to be 25,000 cps. Find the values of M, L_1, L_2 and any resistances that are to be placed across r and R_i to obtain the desired bandwidth. If the active element is a vacuum-tube pentode with $g_m = 5,000 \mu$mhos, what is the maximum voltage gain of the circuit? At what frequencies does this maximum voltage gain occur?

6-64. Repeat Prob. 6-63, but now assume that r and R_i are each 10,000 ohms. Use the circuit of Fig. 6-66 to bring the primary and secondary Q's up to the required value. In this case, if the active element is a transistor, with an $h_{fe} = 100$, what will be the magnitude of the maximum current gain? Assume that C_1 and C_2 are 50 $\mu\mu$f.

6-65. For the amplifier of Prob. 6-57, compute the normalized voltage gain at a bandwidth of 20,000 cps. The bandwidth is defined by $f_b - f_a = 20,000$ where $f_b f_a = f_0{}^2$. Then redesign the amplifier of Prob. 6-57 so that two stages are used. What is the normalized voltage gain at f_a and f_b in this case?

6-66. A direct-coupled amplifier has a voltage gain of 10^4. The power-supply voltage changes slightly, which causes the effective input voltage to increase by 0.001 volt. What will be the change in the direct-output voltage? If an *RC*-coupled amplifier were used, what would this change become?

Untuned Large-signal Amplifiers

When the signal levels present in an amplifier become so large that the non-linearity of the active elements can no longer be ignored, they are spoken of as *large signals*. Large-signal amplifiers are usually, but not always, power amplifiers (see Sec. 5-5). We shall consider the analysis and design of these amplifiers here. Much of the preliminary material that is necessary for this discussion has been presented in Chap. 2 and in Sec. 5-6. In this chapter, we shall consider untuned amplifiers that amplify a relatively broad range of frequencies. The generalized device notation of Sec. 2-7 will be used wherever it is possible.

7-1 Class A single-ended amplifiers

A typical *single-ended amplifier* is shown in Fig. 7-1. Transformer coupling has been illustrated, but this need not be the case. The term single-ended

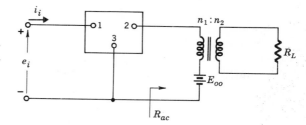

is used to differentiate this type from the push-pull amplifiers that will be discussed in Sec. 7-4.   To avoid excessive distortion, single-ended amplifiers are operated class A.   A typical set of output characteristics is shown in Fig. 7-2.   The quantity x_i is used to represent either the input voltage or the input current (but not both).   The labeling of the x_i parameter is typical of a transistor.   However, there is no loss of generality and all the results can be applied equally well to vacuum tubes.

If we assume that the distortion is quite small, then the procedures of Secs. 2-2, 2-3, and 2-8 can be used to determine the operating point and the a-c load line.   If the distortion is appreciable, then the procedures of Secs. 2-10 and 2-11 should be used.   The quantities that are of interest are P_2,

Fig. 7-2   *The output characteristics of a generalized device.   Relative scales have been used.   The quantity x_i represents either e_i or i_i.   The value of P_{oD} is chosen to be 49.*

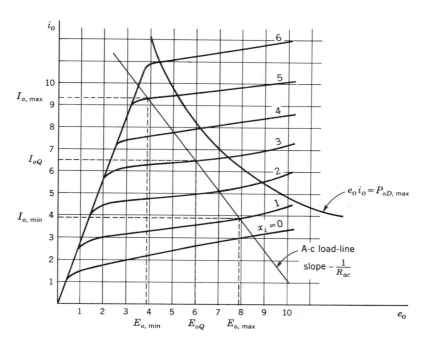

the signal power delivered to the load; the power P_{oo} supplied by the battery; the efficiency of the output circuit η_2; the power dissipated within the output of the device P_{oD}; the rms signal output voltage and current E_2 and I_2, respectively; the rms signal input voltage and/or current E_1 and I_1, respectively; and the distortion.   The procedure for calculating all these quantities when distortion is negligible is given in Sec. 2-9.   We shall summarize these procedures here using the quantities defined in Fig. 7-2, where it is assumed that coordinates of the quiescent operating point are: $E_{oQ} = 6$, $I_{oQ} = 6.5$, and $X_{iQ} = 3$.   (Relative values are used here.)   The input signal is given by $x_i = 2 \cos \omega t$.   If the transformer is ideal,

$$P_2 = \frac{(E_{o,\max} - E_{o,\min})(I_{o,\max} - I_{o,\min})}{8} \tag{7-1}$$

$$E_2 = \frac{E_{o,\max} - E_{o,\min}}{2\sqrt{2}} \tag{7-2}$$

$$I_2 = \frac{I_{o,\max} - I_{o,\min}}{2\sqrt{2}} \tag{7-3}$$

$$P_{oo} = E_{oo}I_{oQ} \tag{7-4}$$

$$\eta_2 = \frac{P_2}{P_{co}} \tag{7-5}$$

$$P_{oD} = P_{oo} - P_2 \tag{7-6}$$

If there is a resistance in series with the power supply the power dissipated in it should be subtracted from P_{oD} in Eq. (7-6).   A distortion analysis using the procedures of Secs. 2-10 and 2-11 should also be performed to determine the distortion and to see if Eqs. (7-1) to (7-6) are valid.   When the distortion is large, then Eqs. (7-1) to (7-6) should be modified.   If the output current is of the form

$$i_2 = I_{oA} + \sqrt{2}\,(I_{o1} \cos \omega t + I_{o2} \cos 2\omega t + I_{o3} \cos 3\omega t + \cdots) \tag{7-7}$$

we can write

$$P_2 = I_{o1}^2 R_{ac} \tag{7-8}$$

$$E_2 = I_{o1}R_{ac} \tag{7-9}$$

$$I_2 = I_{o1} \tag{7-10}$$

$$P_{oo} = E_{oo} \frac{1}{2\pi} \int_0^{2\pi} i_2 d(\omega t) \tag{7-11}$$

$$P_{oo} = E_{oo}I_{oA} \tag{7-12}$$

$$\eta_2 = \frac{P_2}{P_{oo}} \tag{7-13}$$

$$P_{oD} = P_{oo} - (I_{o1}^2 + I_{o2}^2 + \cdots)R_{ac} \tag{7-14}$$

If there is resistance in series with the power supply, the power dissipated in it should also be subtracted from P_{oo} to obtain P_{oD}.   Thus, a complete analysis of this amplifier can be performed. We must now consider how these results can be used in the design of an amplifier.

7-2   Design of class A single-ended amplifiers

The design of a power amplifier consists of choosing a device and determining the coordinates of the operating point, the value of R_{ac}, and the required input signal such that the desired output power is delivered to R_L, the distortion is equal to or less than a specified amount, and the device output dissipation is equal to or less than the rated value. The procedures for determining some of these quantities differ greatly for the vacuum-tube triode, for the vacuum-tube pentode or beam power tube, and for the transistor. In such cases, we shall have to consider their individual characteristics and not use the generalized device.

The maximum allowable device output dissipation $P_{oD,\max}$ (i.e., the plate dissipation in the vacuum tube, and the collector-junction dissipation in a transistor) is specified by the manufacturer. It represents the maximum *average* power that can be dissipated in the output circuit of the device. The actual value of P_{oD} is given by Eqs. (7-6) and (7-14) and depends upon the signal level. It decreases if the signal increases. There are usually times when signals are absent, so that the plate dissipation should be designed for quiescent conditions. That is,

$$E_{oQ}I_{oQ} \leqslant P_{oD,\max} \tag{7-15}$$

The equation

$$e_o i_o = P_{oD,\max} \tag{7-16}$$

plots as a hyperbola. Such a curve is shown in Fig. 7-2. The quiescent operating point should not be located above this curve if the device output dissipation is not to exceed the rated value. Now let us consider specific devices and see how the amplifier design proceeds.

The vacuum-tube triode

In order to determine a starting point in the choice of R_{ac}, we shall idealize the triode characteristics by assuming that they are linear as long as the plate current is not less than a specified value I_a. In Fig. 7-3 triode characteristics that are equally spaced and linear for $i_b > I_a$ have been drawn. When the grid is positively biased, grid current results, which often produces excessive distortion. For instance, consider the circuit of Fig. 7-4. If $e_s < |E_{cQ}|$, the net grid bias is negative and the full signal voltage appears between the grid and the cathode. (The capacitor C_k is assumed to be a short circuit at signal frequencies.) If $e_s > |E_{cQ}|$, grid current will result

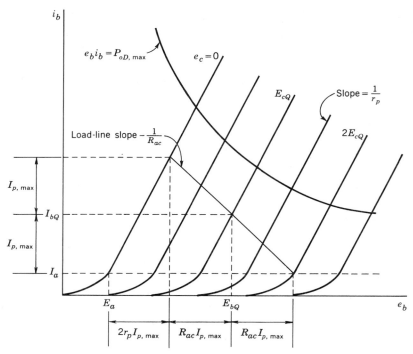

Fig. 7-3   Idealized output characteristics of a vacuum-tube triode.   Note that E_{cQ} is negative.

and there will be a voltage drop in R_s.   Thus, the positive peak of the sine wave will be flattened.   We shall restrict our operation such that

$$e_c \leqslant 0$$
$$i_b \geqslant I_a$$

(7-17)

A load line has been drawn on the output characteristics of Fig. 7-3.   To maximize the power delivered to R_{ac}, the signal level and grid bias are

Fig. 7-4   A vacuum-tube-triode power amplifier.

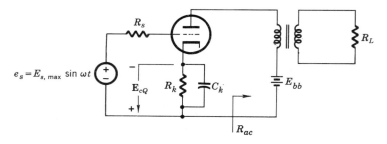

adjusted so that relations (7-17) are satisfied with the equal signs. The quiescent plate voltage is often specified because of power-supply considerations. The output power will be maximized with respect to R_{ac}, subject to the above restrictions. The various lengths that have been marked off in Fig. 7-3 are obtained by multiplying the peak signal current $I_{p,max}$ by the appropriate slopes. Then

$$E_{bQ} - E_a = I_{p,max}(2r_p + R_{ac})$$ (7-18)

$$P_2 = \frac{I_{p,max}^2}{2} R_{ac}$$ (7-19)

Thus

$$P_2 = \frac{(E_{bQ} - E_a)^2}{2(2r_p + R_{ac})^2} R_{ac}$$ (7-20)

Setting dP_2/dR_{ac} equal to zero and solving for R_{ac}, we obtain

$$R_{ac} = 2r_p$$ (7-21)

If we had chosen other constraints, a different relationship might have been obtained, since E_{bQ} might not be independent of R_L.

If a triode amplifier is operated at very low fixed signal levels, so that the operation is linear, and if R_{ac} is varied, then the maximum power output occurs when $R_L = r_p$. It is only when the nonlinearities of the device are considered and additional constraints are imposed that other results are obtained. Actual triode characteristics are nonlinear over their entire operating range with the nonlinearities increasing as i_b decreases. If the input signal and the operating point are held constant while R_{ac} is varied, the curve of P_2 versus R_{ac} will peak when $R_{ac} \approx r_p$ (if the distortion is not too large). However, if R_{ac} is increased further, then the distortion decreases. Typical curves of power output and percent harmonic distortion versus load resistance are shown in Fig. 7-5. Note that the distortion falls off

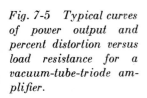

Fig. 7-5 Typical curves of power output and percent distortion versus load resistance for a vacuum-tube-triode amplifier.

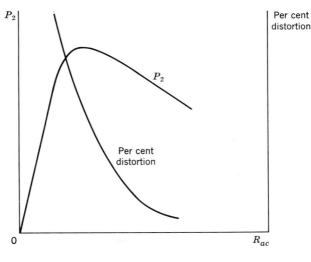

quite rapidly with increasing R_{ac}, but the curve of P_2 versus R_{ac} has a broad peak. If the value of $R_{ac} = 2r_p$ is chosen, P_2 is approximately 89 percent of the maximum value while the distortion decreases considerably. If we set $R_{ac} = 2r_p$ and then increase the input signal level, the output power can be increased to more than the value obtained when $R_{ac} = r_p$, but the distortion will be less.

Let us consider the design of a vacuum-tube-triode power amplifier. It is assumed that the following quantities are specified: the required output power P_2, the maximum allowable distortion, the quiescent plate voltage (if the transformer is good, this is approximately equal to $E_{bb} + E_{cQ}$), and the maximum plate dissipation.

1. For various triodes, determine I_a, E_a, and the average value of r_p. Then use Eq. (7-20), with $R_{ac} = 2r_p$, to determine the triode to be used. Remember that this is very approximate, since I_a and r_p really cannot be accurately specified and Eq. (7-20) is an approximation.

2. Determine $I_{p,\max}$ from the equation

$$I_{p,\max} = \sqrt{\frac{2P_2}{R_{ac}}}$$

Use a value of P_2 that is slightly greater than the required value.

3. Then,

$$I_{bQ} = I_a + I_{p,\max}$$

Since E_{bQ} is specified, the coordinates of the operating point are now determined. Verify that they lie below the grid-bias hyperbola.

4. Compute the actual power output and the distortion. If P_2 is large enough and the distortion and the plate dissipation are small enough, the design is complete and the required input signal can be determined. It must be emphasized that this procedure is very approximate and yields only a first trial for the design. It may be necessary to vary R_{ac}. Increasing R_{ac} will reduce the distortion; reducing R_{ac} will increase P_2. The operating point can also be shifted to vary P_2, the distortion, or the plate dissipation. If the design cannot be achieved, then try a larger tube (i.e., one with greater i_b for the same e_b and e_c; it will also have a greater allowable plate dissipation). Equations (7-18) to (7-21) were derived on the basis of a constant value of r_p in a linear region. In the actual triode, no such region exists. In addition, the design is based on an assumed value of I_a, but until the design is complete, the relationship between I_a and the distortion is unknown. Thus, it again must be stressed that this procedure is quite approximate.

The vacuum-tube pentode

Typical characteristics for a vacuum-tube pentode are shown in Fig. 7-6. There are severe nonlinearities in the region of the knees of the curves and the curves become crowded together for large negative grid voltages. Load lines have been drawn for several values of R_{ac}. The operation will be restricted to negative grid voltages. Thus, the input signal is assumed to be $e_g = -E_{cQ} \cos \omega t$. Typical curves of power output and distortion versus R_{ac} are shown in Fig. 7-7. The distortion for the negative half of the current cycle is almost independent of R_{ac}. However, the clipping of the positive half-cycle varies directly with R_{ac}. The second-harmonic distortion becomes zero when the flattening of the positive and negative peaks is equal [see Eq. (2-53)]. Thus, the distortion is minimum for an optimum value of R_{ac}. If the load resistance is increased further, the distortion increases rapidly because of the increased clipping of the positive peak. If the operation were linear, the maximum output power would occur when $R_{ac} = r_p$ (which is smaller than the value that produces minimum distortion). However, for large signal levels, the clipping of the signal that occurs at small values of R_{ac} limits the output power. The maximum power output usually occurs at a value of R_{ac} that is very close to the one that produces minimum distortion.

If the required power output, the maximum allowable distortion, the quiescent plate voltage, and the maximum plate dissipation are specified, then an optimum value of R_{ac} can be found for any given operating point. Try various operating points, subject to the requirements on the plate dissipation and the plate voltage, until the output requirements are met. If

Fig. 7-6 *Typical output characteristics for a vacuum-tube pentode. Note that E_{cQ} is negative.*

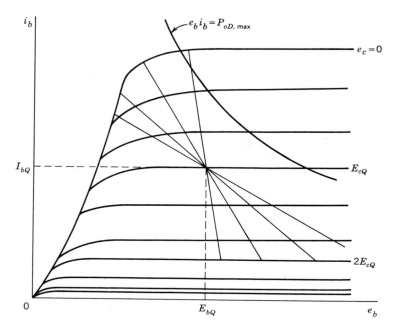

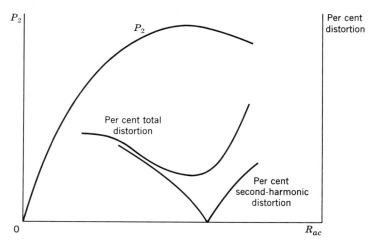

Fig. 7-7   Typical curves of power output and percent distortion for a vacuum-tube pentode or a beam power tube.

the design cannot be achieved, then the requirements on E_{bQ} may have to be relaxed or a larger tube used.

The class A amplifier has a maximum theoretical efficiency of 50 percent for both vacuum-tube triodes and pentodes. In practice, it may only be half of this value. Thus, the plate dissipation has a minimum value which is equal to P_2. Its probable value is closer to $3P_2$. This should be considered when the vacuum tube is chosen.

The transistor

A typical set of characteristics for the common-emitter transistor is shown in Fig. 7-8. There are several differences in the allowed operation of the vacuum tube and the transistor. The vacuum tube is often restricted to operation below the zero-grid-voltage curve. However, operation at large magnitudes of base current is permissible with the transistor. There is a maximum allowable base current, but the collector-junction dissipation often limits the operation before it is reached. In a vacuum tube, the efficiency is usually much less than the theoretical maximum. However, the knees of the transistor output characteristics are very close to the axis of ordinates. Thus, large signal levels can be attained, and the efficiency of operation can be very close to the theoretical maximum value of 50 percent. Thus, the allowable collector-junction dissipation need be only slightly greater than the required power output.

Even if the actual collector-junction dissipation is less than that specified by the manufacturer, the transistor may still be overheated. This is because its temperature depends not only upon the power dissipated in it, but also upon the means provided for removing the resultant heat. (Procedures for cooling transistors are discussed in detail in Sec. 7-8.) The rated power dissipation assumes that certain cooling procedures are used and that the ambient temperature is below a specified value. If these assumptions are not valid, then the transistor may be damaged by overheating even though the power dissipation is less than the rated value. The results of Sec. 7-8 can be used to determine the maximum allowable power dissipation in such cases.

Since the input circuit of the transistor also introduces distortion, the analysis of Sec. 2-11 should be used. The distortion is a function of the impedance of the preceding stage. At times, if this impedance is the proper value, the total distortion is minimized, since the distortion due to the input characteristics can tend to cancel the distortion due to the output characteristics. Resistance is sometimes placed in series or shunt with the input to achieve this optimum condition.

If the required power output, the maximum allowable distortion, and the quiescent collector voltage are specified, then the following design procedure can be used to obtain the required circuit. Choose a transistor with a collector dissipation somewhat greater than the required power output. Pick an operating point with the required E_{CQ}, close to (but below) the allowable dissipation hyperbola, choose a load line, and check the output quantities. The signal component of the base current should be chosen to

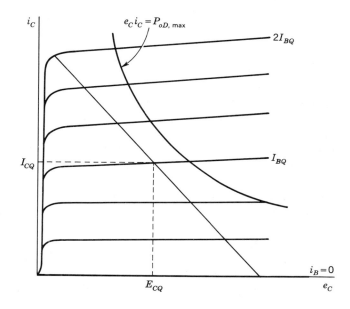

Fig. 7-8   Typical output characteristics for a common-emitter transistor. (It has been assumed that the transistor is cut off when $i_B = 0$. Actually this occurs when $i_B \approx -I_{C0}$.)

cause i_B to vary between $i_B \approx 0$ and $i_B \approx 2I_{BQ}$. If high efficiency is desired, the load line should be drawn into the knees of the curves as shown. The distortion can be reduced somewhat at the expense of efficiency by reducing R_{ac}. Again, a cut-and-try procedure should be used once the first operating point is located. If the design cannot be achieved, then a transistor with a larger rated output dissipation should be chosen.

For both the vacuum tube and the transistor, we have shown the operating point below the device output dissipation curve (see Figs. 7-3, 7-6, and 7-8). It may not be necessary to leave a safety factor here. Manufacturers sometimes specify maximum ratings as the maximum permissible value, in which case some safety factor should be allowed for. On the other hand, if a maximum design value is specified, no additional safety factor is needed in most cases. The device output dissipation should not be made any larger than is necessary, so that the efficiency will be as large as possible. However, the device should be chosen so that the output dissipation is close to the maximum rated value. This may eliminate the need for a larger and more expensive device.

In addition to the device output dissipation, a maximum output voltage rating is usually specified. In the transistor, it is limited by collector-junction breakdown. In a vacuum tube, it may be limited by arc over between electrodes. At maximum signal levels the maximum output voltage is somewhat less than twice the power-supply voltage. In the transistor, the collector voltage can almost swing down to zero, because of the location and shape of the knees of the static output characteristic. Hence, the maximum collector voltage will be approximately $2E_{CC}$. It should be verified that these voltages do not exceed rated values. Maximum current ratings may also be specified. The amplifier should be designed so that these ratings are not exceeded.

7-3   Parallel operation

If two identical generalized devices are connected in parallel (i.e., terminals 1 connected to each other, terminals 2 connected to each other, and terminals 3 connected to each other), the characteristics of the resultant device can be obtained from those of the original by doubling all current scales, including those of the input parameter, while holding all voltage scales constant.

If two devices whose output characteristics are given in Fig. 7-2 are paralleled, if the new device is operated so that the value of R_{ac} is one-half of the value used for one device, and if the quiescent input current is doubled, then the locus of operation will be that shown in Fig. 7-2 (with the current scales doubled). Thus, the output power will be doubled while the distortion remains constant. The allowable device output dissipation also will be doubled. Parallel operation can be used to increase power output without increasing distortion. However, there are two reasons why this is not often done. First, if the two devices are not exactly the same, then the power dissipated within them will not be equal. Hence, even if the two parallel devices are nominally the same, one may actually have a considerably greater power dissipation than the other. Thus, if the devices are to be used at, or near, their rated dissipation, they must be carefully matched. This often proves inconvenient. Second, there is another circuit, which also uses two devices, that offers greater advantages. We shall discuss it next.

7-4 Push-pull amplifiers

A commonly used power amplifier configuration is shown in Fig. 7-9. This circuit provides all the advantages of parallel operation and more. It is assumed that both generalized devices are identical and that their input signals differ by 180°. Thus, when the output current of one device increases, the other decreases. This is called a *push-pull* amplifier. It has several advantages which we shall illustrate with the following discussion.

If the input signal to device 1 is $x_{11} = X_{1,\text{max}} \cos \omega t$, then the output current i_{o1} will be of the form

$$i_{o1} = i_{o1}(\omega t) = I_{oA} + \sqrt{2}\,(I_{o1} \cos \omega t + I_{o2} \cos 2\omega t + I_{o3} \cos 3\,\omega t \\ + I_{o4} \cos 4\omega t + \cdot\cdot\cdot) \quad (7\text{-}22)$$

Since the input signals are 180° out of phase, $x_{12} = X_{1,\text{max}} \cos (\omega t + \pi)$ and we have

$$i_{o2} = i_{o1}(\omega t + \pi) = I_{oA} + \sqrt{2}\,[I_{o1} \cos (\omega t + \pi) + I_{o2} \cos 2(\omega t + \pi) \\ + I_{o3} \cos 3(\omega t + \pi) + I_{o4} \cos 4(\omega t + \pi) + \cdot\cdot\cdot] \quad (7\text{-}23)$$

The load current and the flux in the core of the transformer are pro-

Fig. 7-9 A push-pull amplifier.

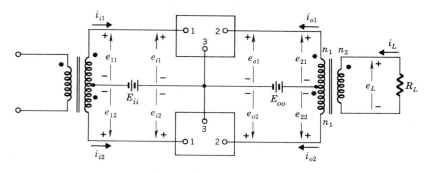

portional to

$$i_{oT} = i_{o1} - i_{o2} \tag{7-24}$$

Substituting, and using the relation $\cos (x + n\pi) = (-1)^n \cos x$, we obtain

$$i_{oT} = 2\sqrt{2} \, (I_{o1} \cos \omega t + I_{o3} \cos 3\omega t + I_{o5} \cos 5\omega t + \cdot \cdot \cdot) \tag{7-25}$$

All of the even harmonics have been canceled. This is an important advantage of the push-pull circuit. A second advantage is that there is no direct flux that tends to saturate the core of the transformer (see Sec. 6-19). It can then contain much less ferromagnetic material. Output transformers for push-pull circuits are lighter, smaller, and less expensive than transformers of comparable quality that are used in single-ended circuits.

The turns ratio of the transformer is $2n_1/n_2$. The effective resistance R_{dd}, viewed across the primary winding, is

$$R_{dd} = 4 \left(\frac{n_1}{n_2} \right)^2 R_L \tag{7-26}$$

Therefore, each device has an a-c load resistance of

$$\frac{R_{dd}}{2} = 2 \left(\frac{n_1}{n_2} \right)^2 R_L \tag{7-27}$$

Note that if one device were made inoperative by opening the lead to its terminal 2, the remaining device would effectively be connected to a transformer whose turns ratio is n_1/n_2, and its a-c load resistance would be $(n_1/n_2)^2 R_L$. The reason for the apparent discrepancy is that when both devices operate, they interact with each other through the transformer. For instance, i_{o1} sets up a flux that affects e_{22}. The flux that links each half of the secondary is ideally the same. Thus

$$e_{21} = -e_{22} \tag{7-28}$$

Since the devices are not necessarily linear, this would not be the case if the transformer were replaced by two resistors. Equation (7-28) is said to come about because of *transformer action*. Since this occurs in a common winding it is also called *autotransformer action*.

A single cathode-bias resistance will provide grid bias for both vacuum tubes of a push-pull amplifier as shown in Fig. 7-10a. The current through the resistor R_k is

$$i_{o1} + i_{o2} = 2I_{oA} + 2\sqrt{2} \, (I_{o2} \cos 2\omega t + I_{o4} \cos 4\omega t + \cdot \cdot \cdot) \tag{7-29}$$

No (fundamental) component of current of frequency ω is through R_k. Thus, in theory, there is no reason to bypass it. However, in practice, a bypass capacitor is usually used, because two identical vacuum tubes can

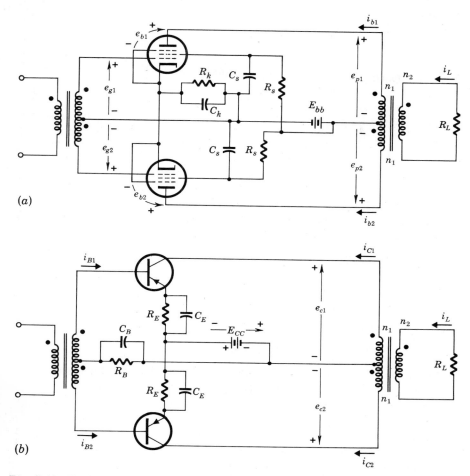

F'g. 7-10 *Push-pull amplifiers.* (a) *Common-cathode vacuum-tube pentode, and* (b) *common-emitter transistor.*

never be found. Thus, $i_{o2}(\omega t)$ is not exactly equal to $i_{o1}(\omega t + \pi)$ and there will not be exact cancellation of the fundamental.

An emitter resistance is not used to obtain bias, but to stabilize the collector current (see Sec. 2-5). The voltage across it should only depend upon the collector current of one transistor, since it cannot be assumed that the same instabilities will develop in each transistor. Thus, separate emitter resistors, as shown in Fig. 7-10b, are used, and they are bypassed. The resistor R_B limits the direct base current. It is bypassed so that it does not affect the signal current.

A cathode-bias resistance tends to stabilize vacuum-tube operation. If the plate current decreases, so will the voltage drop across R_k, which tends to increase the plate current. Since balance is quite important in push-pull circuits, this extra stability is desirable. Thus, vacuum-tube circuits, at times, use two separate cathode-bias impedances.

7-5   The composite device

To completely determine the output of a push-pull amplifier, a graphical analysis should be performed. We shall do this by replacing the two active elements by a single *composite device* which produces the same load current i_L as does the push-pull circuit. From Fig. 7-9 and Eq. (7-24), we have

$$i_L = \frac{n_1}{n_2}(i_{o1} - i_{o2}) = \frac{n_1}{n_2} i_{oT} \tag{7-30}$$

Thus, the composite device shown in Fig. 7-11 works into a transformer of turns ratio n_1/n_2, and has an output current equal to i_{oT}. The quantity x_i will be used to represent either e_i or i_i. We shall neglect the distortion due to the input circuit. Its effect will be considered subsequently. The output current of a device is a function of its output voltage and its input current or voltage. Thus (see Fig. 7-9)

$$i_{o1} = f(x_{i1}, e_{o1}) \tag{7-31}$$
$$i_{o2} = f(x_{i2}, e_{o2})$$

The two functions are the same, since the two devices are identical. Neglecting any direct-voltage drop in the transformer, we have

$$e_{o1} = E_{oo} + e_{21} \tag{7-32}$$
$$e_{o2} = E_{oo} + e_{22} \tag{7-33}$$

Then, using Eq. (7-28) and substituting, we obtain

$$e_{o2} = 2E_{oo} - e_{o1} \tag{7-34}$$

Note that this equation is a result of the autotransformer action. If there are bypassed cathode-bias resistances or emitter-stabilizing resistances, then the value of E_{oo} should be reduced by an amount equal to the voltage drop across them. (This voltage drop is a function of I_{oA} and can vary with

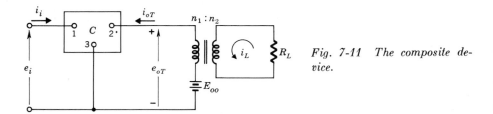

Fig. 7-11   The composite device.

signal level.) The input quantity x_i is the sum of the signal and the direct bias.

$$x_{i1} = X_{ii} + x_{11} \tag{7-35}$$

$$x_{i2} = X_{ii} + x_{12} \tag{7-36}$$

We assume that the input signals x_{11} and x_{12} are 180° out of phase. Then

$$x_{i2} = X_{ii} - x_{i1} \tag{7-37}$$

Substituting Eqs. (7-31) to (7-37) and (7-28) into Eq. (7-24), we obtain

$$i_{oT} = f(X_{ii} + x_{11}, E_{oo} + e_{21}) - f(X_{ii} - x_{11}, E_{oo} - e_{21}) \tag{7-38}$$

$$i_{oT} = f(X_{ii} + x_{11}, e_{o1}) - f(X_{ii} - x_{11}, 2E_{oo} - e_{o1}) \tag{7-39}$$

Equation (7-38) or (7-39) is an expression for the static characteristic output curves of the composite device. To construct them, we require the static output characteristics of an individual device and the location of two of the coordinates of the operating point. The *composite output characteristic* is a plot of i_{oT} versus $e_{oT} = e_{o1}$, with the input *signal* x_{11} as a parameter. Figure 7-12 illustrates the construction of two such curves for $x_{11} = 0$ and -1. The procedure used is: specify values for X_{ii} and E_{oo}, then subtract the individual curves for $X_{ii} + x_{11}$ and $X_{ii} - x_{11}$ from each other as indicated in Eq. (7-39). To conveniently do this, line up the abscissas of two characteristics so that zero, of one, corresponds to $2E_{oo}$, of the other, as is shown in Fig. 7-12. The E_{oo} points are then adjacent to each other. The two curves can be directly subtracted on a point-by-point basis. If this is repeated for other values of x_{11}, the entire composite characteristic can be obtained. Figure 7-13 illustrates such a set of composite characteristics. Since $i_L = (n_1/n_2)i_{oT}$, the effective load resistance for the composite device is

$$R_{ac} = \left(\frac{n_1}{n_2}\right)^2 R_L \tag{7-40}$$

so that the slope of the load line is $-(n_1/n_2)^2 R_L$. If no signal is present, $i_{oT} = 0$ and $e_{o1} = e_{oT} = E_{oo}$. Thus, the abscissa intercept of the load line is E_{oo}. The intersection of the load line with the appropriate composite characteristic curve yields the instantaneous value of i_{oT}, just as it would on a set of ordinary output characteristics. Thus, the usual distortion and power-output calculations can be made. The locus of the output of the composite device lies along the a-c load line. The locus of operation of the individual devices is found by reversing the construction procedure. That is, at a point where R_{ac} intersects a composite curve, project straight up and down until the device characteristics that were used to construct the composite curve are intersected. These points are the instantaneous operating points of devices 1 and 2. The locus of operation of both devices is shown

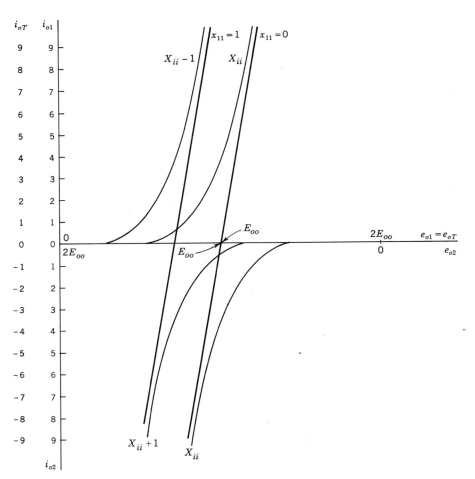

Fig. 7-12   An illustration of the construction of the composite-device output characteristics.

in Fig. 7-13.   It is *not* a straight line, since the load that each individual device "sees" is not a simple resistance, due to autotransformer action.

Thus far, the distortion due to the input characteristics has been neglected. It is quite important to consider it for transistors and also for vacuum tubes if there is grid current.   Once the locus of operation of the individual device is known, we can obtain a plot of x_i versus e_o.   The procedure of Sec. 2-11 can then be applied directly to the individual devices to determine their input voltage and current.   If the advantages of push-pull operation are to be obtained, x_{11} must equal $-x_{12}$.   If this is not the case (because of distortion), then the input circuit should be adjusted to make it essentially true.   We shall consider this in Sec. 7-9.

We have thus far used generalized-device characteristics that resemble those of the vacuum-tube triode. Since even harmonics predominate here, the composite-device characteristics are very linear. If the device characteristics resembled those of a pentode, or a transistor, a set of curves similar to those of Fig. 7-14 would result. Note that there is more nonlinearity of the composite characteristics, since the devices themselves produce a substantial amount of odd-harmonic distortion.

The upper and lower portions of these curves are symmetric, so that only the upper half of the composite characteristics need be constructed and the information can be obtained from one set of output characteristics.

Fig. 7-13 *Composite output characteristics of two devices operating, at a specific operating point, in push-pull.*

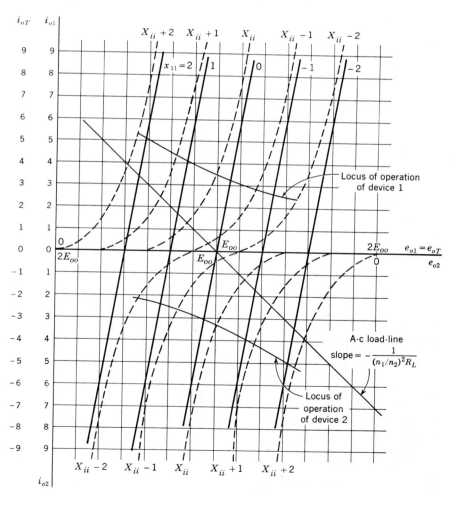

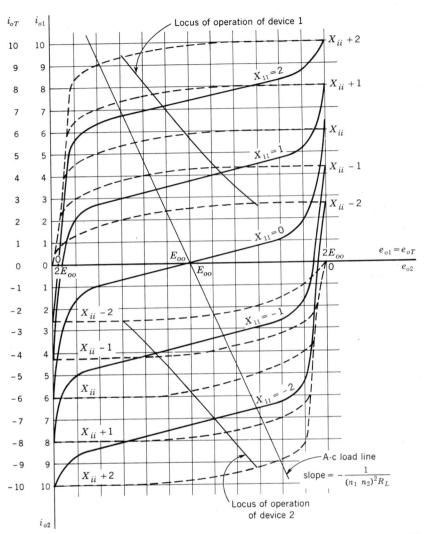

Fig. 7-14 Composite output characteristics of two devices operating, at a specific operating point, in push-pull.

7-6 Class AB and class B push-pull operation

In Sec. 5-6, we saw that the output-circuit efficiency would be increased if the operation were shifted from class A to class AB or B. Single-ended amplifiers are restricted to class A operation because of the excessive distortion that results in any other mode of operation. This is not the case when push-pull amplifiers are used. In class B operation, each device will conduct for an alternate half-cycle and the output waveform need not be distorted. Such operation is represented in Fig. 7-15. In actual circuits, true class B operation, where there is output current for exactly one-half of the cycle, is not used, because excessive distortion can result. In class B operation, at any time, one device always has zero output current, so that the composite characteristic is composed of the individual device characteristics with no subtraction performed. Both the vacuum tube and the transistor have characteristics that are quite nonlinear near cutoff. If a small signal is applied, the operation will be entirely in this region and the distortion will be very high. [For class A operation, the subtractive process linearizes this highly curved region near cutoff (see Fig. 7-13).] This effect can best be seen by considering the *transfer characteristics* of the composite device. This is a plot of output current versus x_i with e_{oT} as a parameter. The same variables are plotted here as in the output characteristics and the construction is similar. Figure 7-16a shows one composite transfer characteristic curve for $e_{o1} = e_{o2} = e_{oT} = E_{oo}$ and $x_{11} = 0$. The input bias X_{ii} is adjusted for exact class B operation. The composite characteristic is quite nonlinear. One means of avoiding much of the distortion is to operate so that the currents i_{o1} and i_{o2} are not zero for somewhat more than one half-

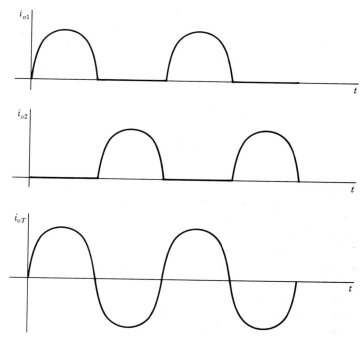

Fig. 7-15 Curves of individual-device output currents i_{o1} and i_{o2} and composite-device output current i_{oT}, in an ideal class B push-pull amplifier.

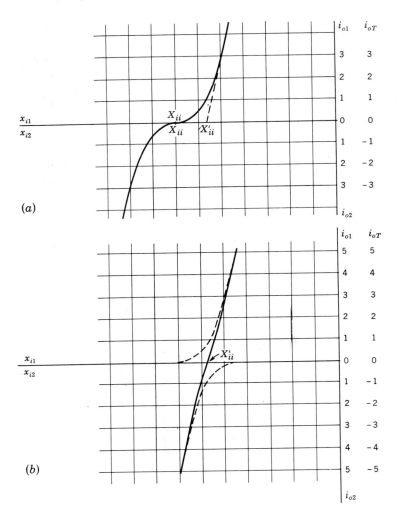

Fig. 7-16   Composite transfer characteristics.   (a) Biased at exact cutoff; and (b) biased at projected cutoff.

cycle.   The value of X_{ii} is usually obtained by assuming that the curve continues straight down as shown by the dotted line of Fig. 7-16a.   This is called the *projected curve* and the bias X'_{ii} is called the *projected cutoff bias.* Figure 7-16 shows a composite characteristic drawn using the projected cutoff bias X'_{ii}.   (When composite transfer curves are constructed, the abscissa axes are lined up so that the direct-bias points coincide.)   Note that most of the nonlinearity is gone.   To avoid the distortion of Fig. 7-16a, which is called *crossover distortion*, class B amplifiers are usually operated at projected cutoff bias.   This is not true class B operation; it is actually class AB

operation.   It is sometimes called class B, but class ABB might be a better
name.   A typical set of class AB output characteristics is shown in Fig. 7-17.
Notice that over most of the region of operation, the characteristics are those
of the individual devices, themselves, as it would be in class B operation.
The composite-device characteristics are so similar to those of the individual devices that it is often unnecessary to draw the composite-device
characteristics.   If the input bias is shifted so that the operation proceeds
from class A to class ABB, the distortion and efficiency will, in general,
increase.

Fig. 7-17   *Composite output characteristics for two devices operating class AB.*

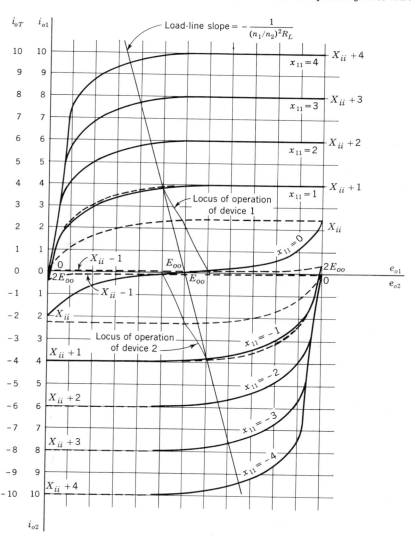

7-7 Design of push-pull amplifiers

The design of a push-pull amplifier is considerably different from that of a single-ended amplifier. For instance, a class A vacuum-tube-triode push-pull amplifier is usually so linear that the maximum-power-transfer theorem can be used in determining the effective load resistance, and Eq. (7-21) is not used. The internal resistance r_{pd} of the composite device is given by the reciprocal of the slope of the composite output characteristic. Thus, for maximum output power

$$\frac{n_1}{n_2} = \sqrt{\frac{r_{pd}}{R_L}} \tag{7-41}$$

For vacuum-tube pentodes operating class A, at maximum signal level, the curve of power output versus load resistance peaks at a value of load resistance considerably less than that predicted by the maximum-power-transfer theorem. If the load resistance is increased further, severe clipping of the signal results and the power output is limited. The distortion curve does not exhibit a minimum, such as that shown in Fig. 7-7, since the even harmonics are cancelled by the push-pull circuit.

If vacuum-tube pentodes are operated class B or class ABB, a minimum in the distortion curve does result at an optimum value of load resistance $R_{ac,\text{opt}}$. For values of load resistance that are less than the optimum value, $(\frac{1}{6})(I_{o,\text{max}} - I_{o,\text{min}}) > (\frac{1}{3})(I_{o\alpha} - I_{o\beta})$ [see Eq. (2-54)]. This is due to the crowding of the class ABB composite characteristics at low signal levels. As the load resistance is increased, the locus of operation crosses the knees of the characteristic curves (see Figs. 7-14 and 7-17), which reduces $I_{o,\text{max}} - I_{o,\text{min}}$ in relation to $I_{o\alpha} - I_{o\beta}$. A minimum in the third-harmonic distortion results at some optimum value of load resistance $R_{ac,\text{opt}}$. There is not exact cancellation of the harmonic, since Eq. (2-54) is only approximate. The higher harmonics, such as the fifth and seventh, probably cannot be neglected in this case. However, the total harmonic distortion will have a minimum value when $R_{ac,\text{opt}}$ is used. The power output tends to peak at a value of load resistance near $R_{ac,\text{opt}}$ for the same reason that it does in class A operation. Class AB operation lies between class A and Class B operation. Thus, the distortion curve may or may not have a minimum. However, if the load resistance is increased above the value that yields maximum power output, the distortion increases greatly.

The statements concerning power output can also be applied to transistors. However, the shape of their static characteristics is such that the minimum in the distortion does not result.

The design is complicated by the fact that the composite characteristics cannot be drawn until the operating point is fixed and vice versa. If E_{oQ} is specified, then an input bias value can be picked and a first trial design obtained. Experience will aid in the choosing of the operating point. The fact that the distortion, available power output, and efficiency increase as the operation moves closer to class AB can be used here. This assumes that the input signal is increased as the operation shifts toward class AB.

There may be distortion due to nonlinearities in the input circuit. These occur in the transistor, and in the vacuum tube if there is grid current. The driver stage (Sec. 7-9) should be designed to minimize this distortion.

The individual device output dissipation P_{oD} is just half of the output dissipation of the composite device P_{oCD}. Thus,

$$P_{oD} = \frac{1}{2} P_{oCD}$$

where

$$P_{oCD} = P_{oo} - P_2 \tag{7-42}$$

The power dissipated in any resistance in series with the power supply should be subtracted from P_{oCD}. The dissipation is usually determined for quiescent operation. However, the devices themselves may operate quite nonlinearly. In this case, P_{oo} may increase with signal level, and graphical means should be used to determine P_{oCD} at the maximum signal level. Hence, the greater of

$$P_{oCD} = 2E_{oQ}I_{oQ} \tag{7-43}$$

and

$$P_{oCD} = 2E_{oo}I_{oA} - P_{2T} \tag{7-44}$$

should be used [see Eqs. (7-12) and (7-14)]. Note that I_{oQ} and I_{oA} are the quiescent and average output currents of the individual devices and P_{2T} is the total output power of the fundamental and all the harmonics.

If a vacuum tube is operated class B or class ABB, then there is very little plate current during quiescent operation. If a cathode resistance were used to obtain bias, its value would be excessive, so fixed bias is usually used instead.

For class ABB operation, the specified quiescent output voltage and projected cutoff bias determine the operating point. The characteristics can then be drawn. For vacuum-tube pentodes or transistors they will resemble Fig. 7-17. The knees of the curves limit the value of $(n_1/n_2)^2 R_L$. In this type of operation, E_{oo} supplies very little power until a signal is applied. (For this reason this circuit is very often used in battery-operated transistor amplifiers.) Equation (7-44) is used to calculate the device output dissipation. If the currents are sinusoidal, then I_{oA} can be obtained by the analysis of Sec. 5-6. If the peak signal current in each device is $I_{o,\max}$,

$$I_{oA} = \frac{2I_{o,\max}}{\pi}$$

$$P_2 = \frac{1}{2} I_{o,\max}^2 \left(\frac{n_1}{n_2}\right)^2 R_L$$

and

$$P_{oCD} = \frac{2I_{o,\max}E_{oo}}{\pi} - \frac{1}{2} I_{o,\max}^2 \left(\frac{n_1}{n_2}\right)^2 R_L \qquad (7\text{-}45)$$

If there is distortion, or if the input signal is not a sine wave, then Eq. (7-45) is no longer valid. However, it is often sufficiently accurate for design purposes, since the device output dissipation is usually less for nonsinusoidal signals. If there is a great deal of distortion, then I_{oA} can be found by using Eq. (2-51). The power supplied by the power supply is then $2E_{oo}I_{oA}$ and $P_{oCD} = 2E_{oo}I_{oA} - P_{2T}$.

7-8   Thermal effects

The maximum device output dissipation is specified to limit the operating temperature of the device. The device can be cooled with forced air or, at very high power levels, with water. Transistors are not usually operated at power levels that warrant water cooling. Thermal conduction and radiation are usually used to cool them. At high power levels, the transistor is placed in contact with a large piece of metal called a *heatsink* to increase the heat flow to the surrounding area. The temperature problem is more critical in transistors than in vacuum tubes, because transistors are damaged at lower temperatures and because the transistor currents can vary greatly with temperature. We shall consider the thermal aspects of a transistor connected to a heatsink.

In order to make temperature calculations, we shall introduce the concept of a *thermal resistance* θ. If a power of P_J watts is dissipated in a junction, and if the ambient temperature (i.e., the temperature of the surroundings) is T_A, then the temperature of the junction is

$$T_J = T_A + P_J\theta_T \qquad (7\text{-}46)$$

where θ_T is the thermal resistance (in degrees centigrade per watt) between the region and the ambient surroundings. Thermal resistance is analogous to electrical resistance. In a transistor, there are several thermal resistances that must be considered. These are diagrammatically illustrated in Fig. 7-18. There is resistance θ_J between the junction itself and the case of the transistor. The resistance θ_I occurs between the case and the heatsink. The heatsink itself possesses some thermal resistance θ_H. Finally, heat leaves the heatsink through the parallel resistances θ_R and θ_C, which are due to radiation and conduction, respectively. The function of the heatsink is to reduce the values of θ_R and θ_C. Figure 7-18 is actually oversimplified. Conduction and radiation take place from all parts of the system and the temperature varies over the surface of the elements. Thus, an exact thermal network would require an infinite number of elements. However, the results obtained with Fig. 7-18 are usually accurate enough to be used in design calculations. The value of θ_J depends upon the construction of the transistor. Typical values for power transistors range from 0.2 to 2.0 °C/watt. A thin mica spacer is often used to electrically insulate the transistor from the heatsink. The spacer introduces a resistance of approximately[1] 25.4°C/(watt)(cm²) for each millimeter of thickness. The thermal resistance of the heatsink θ_H depends upon the thermal resistivity of the material. Typical values[1] are $\rho = 0.26$°C (cm)/(watt) for copper, $\rho = 0.443$°C (cm)/(watt) for pure aluminum, and $\rho = 0.66$°C (cm)/(watt) for commercial aluminum. Thermal resistance is calculated from resistivity in the same way that electrical resistance is. For instance, the thermal resistance between the inner and outer edges of an annular circle of inner radius r_1, outer radius r_2, and thickness d, is[1]

$$\theta_H = \frac{2.3\rho}{2\pi d} \log_{10} \frac{r_2}{r_1} \tag{7-47}$$

If the ring is a heatsink, the actual value of θ_H is quite difficult to obtain, since heat flows from it at all points. Equation (7-47) gives a value that is somewhat high.

The largest resistances in the system are often those between the heatsink and the ambient temperature. They vary with the cross-sectional area of the heatsink and its position. An empirical formula[1] for the conduction resistance θ_C is

$$\theta_C = \frac{2,900}{A} \left(\frac{L}{T_H - T_A} \right)^{0.25} \text{°C/watt} \tag{7-48}$$

where A is the total surface area of the plate in cm² and T is the temperature in degrees Kelvin. Usually A includes the area of both sides. The dimension L is the length in the vertical direction. The resistance θ_C increases with L, since the cooling air rises along the heatsink. For horizontal plates, use L = area of one surface/(length + width). Note that L can

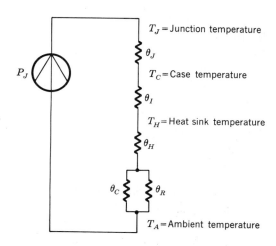

Fig. 7-18   A simplified thermal network for a transistor.

T_J = Junction temperature

θ_J

T_C = Case temperature

θ_I

T_H = Heat sink temperature

θ_H

θ_C θ_R

T_A = Ambient temperature

be fairly large for horizontal plates, since the convection from the lower surface is quite small. If forced-air cooling is used, this resistance can be reduced by a factor of $\frac{1}{4}$ or more.

The radiation resistance can be expressed by the relation[1]

$$\theta_R = \frac{1.78 \times 10^{11}}{\epsilon A} \cdot \frac{T_H - T_A}{T_H{}^4 - T_A{}^4} \qquad °C/\text{watt} \tag{7-49}$$

where ϵ represents the *emissivity*, A is the area in square centimeters and T is the temperature in degrees *Kelvin*. Some typical values[1] of ϵ are: ideal black body, 1; dull black paint or lacquer, 0.96; polished copper, 0.03; polished aluminum, 0.09. Thus, the importance of using dull black radiators can be seen. It should be emphasized that the formulas given here are empirical and are not exact.

Equations (7-48) and (7-49) are functions of the surface temperature of the heatsink. If the temperature varies from point to point, then these equations cannot be used. If the thermal conductivity of the heatsink is large enough, then this temperature variation can be neglected. If the maximum dimension from the transistor to the edge of the heatsink is less than 5 cm and the heatsink is made of copper that is thicker than 0.2 cm, or aluminum that is thicker than 0.32 cm, the heatsink temperature can be assumed to be constant.

In order to design a heatsink, the values of θ_J and θ_I should be determined. The temperature T_H can then be calculated using the relation

$$T_H = T_J - P_J(\theta_J + \theta_I) \tag{7-50}$$

The total heatsink resistance $\theta_H + \dfrac{\theta_C \theta_R}{\theta_C + \theta_R}$ can then be found from Eq. (7-46) and the heatsink designed. If P_J is too large, then the resistance of $\theta_J + \theta_I$ may cause T_J to become excessive even if the heatsink resistance is zero. However, if rated dissipation values are not exceeded, this usually will not occur.

The value of thermal resistance calculated from Eq. (7-46) may not be satisfactory because of thermal runaway (see Sec. 2-4). That is, we have assumed that P_J is constant, whereas it is actually a function of T_J. If P_J is independent of T_J, then, from Eq. (7-46) (the derivatives reciprocal is)

$$\frac{dP_J}{dT_J} = \frac{1}{\theta_T} \tag{7-51}$$

On the other hand, if at the operating temperature

$$\frac{dP_J}{dT_J} > \frac{1}{\theta_T} \tag{7-52}$$

then the power increases with T_J and instability *may* occur. In any event, the power and the temperature will tend to increase above the design value. Let us consider the significance of relation (7-52) for class A amplifiers. The power P_J is the product $E_{CQ}I_{CQ}$. If the quiescent collector voltage is constant, then P_J varies directly with the collector current I_C. On the other hand, if I_C is constant, P_J will actually decrease as T_J increases, since the collector voltage will decrease. Thus, thermal runaway is usually no problem in RC-coupled amplifiers where the large series resistance tends to keep the value of I_{CQ} constant. Let us assume the worst possible case, where the collector voltage is constant at E_{CQ}. Then, for stability [see Eq. (7-52)]

$$E_{CQ}\frac{dI_{CQ}}{dT_J} \leqslant \frac{1}{\theta_T} \tag{7-53}$$

Let us write

$$\frac{dI_{CQ}}{dT_J} = \frac{dI_{CQ}}{dI_{C0}}\frac{dI_{C0}}{dT_J} \tag{7-54}$$

where I_{C0} is the reverse collector saturation current. But the stability factor (see Sec. 2-4) is $S = dI_C/dI_{C0}$. Substituting and manipulating in Eq. (7-53), we obtain

$$S\theta_T E_{CQ}\frac{dI_{C0}}{dT_J} \leqslant 1 \tag{7-55}$$

The quantity dI_{C0}/dT_J is temperature-dependent and should be determined at the operating temperature of the transistor. Relation (7-55) thus imposes an upper limit of S, θ_T, and E_{CQ}, which ensures stability.

Each of the thermal resistances of Fig. 7-18 is actually shunted by thermal capacitance. They take into account the fact that if P_J is changed, the various temperatures in the circuit do not change instantaneously, but take a finite time to reach equilibrium. This often proves useful, since it allows the instantaneous power (but not the average power) to be greater than the maximum rated power. The duty cycle in such cases must be much shorter than the thermal time constants so that excessive heating does not occur during a portion of the cycle.

7-9 Phase-inverter circuits

The push-pull amplifier requires two input signals 180° out of phase with each other. These are called *balanced* signals, whereas the usual single-ended systems are *unbalanced*. We have made the transition from an unbalanced system to a balanced one by means of an input transformer (see Figs. 7-9 and 7-10). Circuits called *phase inverters* can be used to replace the input transformer. Two such circuits are shown in Figs. 7-19a and b. Their operation is similar and we shall discuss them simultaneously. The upper RC-coupled amplifier is conventional and it produces a 180° phase shift in voltage. A portion of the signal across R_g or R_{B2} is tapped off and used to drive the lower RC-coupled amplifier. Thus, the driving signals for

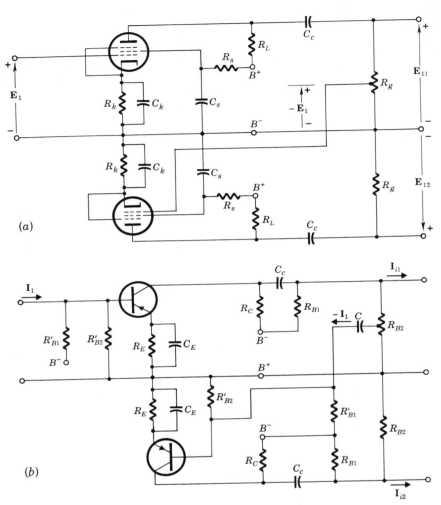

Fig. 7-19   Basic phase-inverter circuits using (a) Common-cathode vacuum-tube pentode amplifier; and (b) common-emitter transistor amplifier.

the upper and lower amplifiers are 180° out of phase.   If the position of the tap is adjusted so that the magnitudes of these driving signals are equal, then the desired balanced output signal will be obtained (if loading of the output circuits is neglected).   The transistor phase inverter is the more complex of the two because it must supply a direct-bias current as well as a signal to the push-pull amplifier.   This accounts for the two resistances R_{B1} and R_{B2}.   The capacitor C is a d-c blocking capacitor and should be large enough to be ignored at signal frequencies.

If the parameters of the devices change (possibly due to aging), the output signals may no longer be equal in magnitude. The location of the tap should be adjusted periodically in critical applications. Two circuits that tend to compensate for changes in the device parameters are shown in Fig. 7-20. The voltage drop across R_k or R_E is in phase with the input voltage. Thus, the input of the lower amplifier will be 180° out of phase with the input of the upper amplifier. If the two output signals are to be equal in magnitude, then

$$E_a = (\tfrac{1}{2})E_1 \tag{7-56}$$

This is a condition that never can be exactly achieved, so that the gain of the lower amplifier may have to be somewhat larger than that of the upper one. This circuit tends to be self-balancing. If the gain of the upper stage decreases (increases), then so will the signal applied to the lower circuit, which will tend to decrease (increase) its output. If the gain of the lower stage decreases (increases), the voltage E_a will increase (decrease) and tend

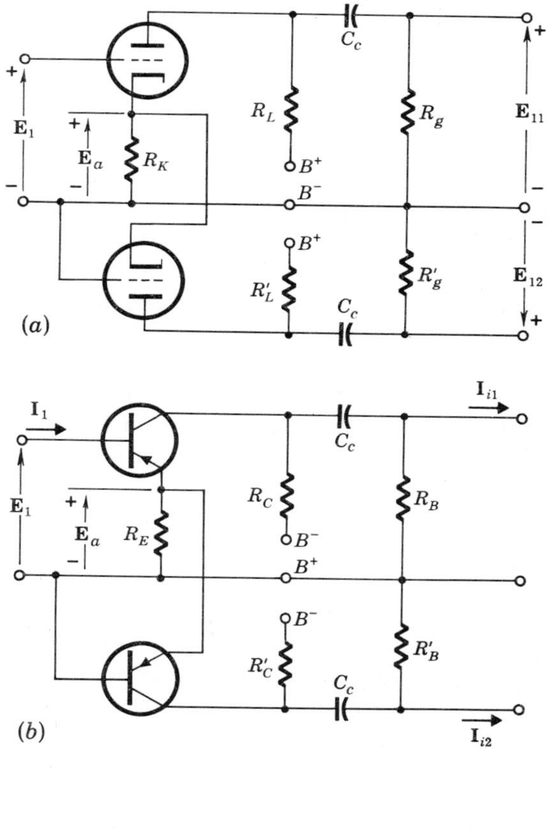

Fig. 7-20 (a) Cathode-coupled vacuum-tube phase inverter; (b) emitter-coupled transistor phase inverter. For simplicity, the biasing circuits have been omitted.

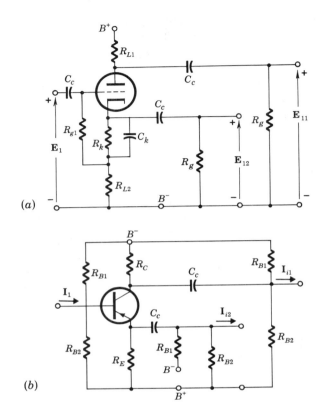

Fig. 7-21 (a) Vacuum-tube split-load phase inverter; and (b) transistor split-load phase inverter.

to offset this effect.   The phase inverters of Fig. 7-19 compensate for changes in the gain of the upper stages but not the lower ones.

Two very simple phase-inverter circuits, called *split-load* phase inverters, each of which uses only one device, are shown in Fig. 7-21.   One circuit is essentially a common-cathode or common-emitter amplifier, while the other is a common-collector or a common-plate amplifier.   In the vacuum-tube circuit, the current through R_{g1} usually can be ignored, so the output voltages will be equal in magnitude and 180° out of phase if $R_{L1} = R_{L2}$.   Since the maximum voltage gain of a cathode follower is unity, the voltages E_{11} and E_{12} cannot be greater than E_1.   Thus, this phase inverter provides no gain, which is one of its disadvantages.   Since the emitter current of a transistor is somewhat greater than the collector current, R_E must be less than R_C. The current gain of this circuit can be substantially in excess of unity.   The primary disadvantage of both these circuits is that the output impedances of the upper and lower circuits are not equal, so that an unbalance can result when the load is connected.   This is especially true when nonlinearities in the push-pull input circuit are taken into account.

One fact that we have ignored is the frequency response of these amplifiers.   The methods of Chap. 6 can be used to perform any necessary analyses.   If the amplifiers of the phase inverters introduce phase shift, then the two output signals will no longer be 180° out of phase.   Thus, they should always be operated well within the midband region.

In addition to causing distortion, the nonlinearity of the input circuit of a push-pull amplifier may cause the input signals to be no longer equal in magnitude and 180° out of phase.   In vacuum tubes which are operated so that there is no grid current there is no problem.   However, at times, the input signal is increased to increase the output power and efficiency, and the grids become positive for a portion of the cycle.   Consider Fig. 7-22a. When tube 1 conducts, current will be through R_{s1} and a voltage drop will result.   Then e_{11} will be clipped on the positive peak.   Similarly, e_{12} will be clipped on its positive peak.   (The two positive peaks do not occur simultaneously.)   To eliminate this effect, both R_{s1} and R_{s2} must be zero. If they are very much less than the minimum value of R_i, then the clipping will be negligible.   Typical values of R_i range from essentially an open circuit for negative grid bias to several thousand ohms for positive grid bias.   The phase inverter should be designed so that its output imped- ance is substantially less than the minimum value.   In addition, substantial power may be dissipated in the grids.   For both of these reasons, if there is grid current, the phase inverter may have to be designed as a power amplifier.

There is base current in a transistor at all times and the input charac- teristics are nonlinear.   A representative input circuit is shown in Fig. 7-22b. These nonlinearities will cause the input signals to be distorted and to be

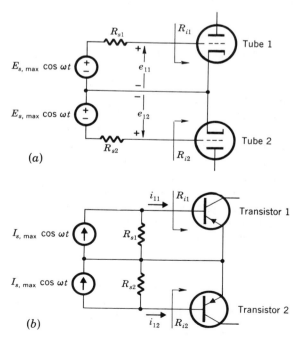

Fig. 7-22   Representations of the input circuits of push-pull amplifiers.   (a) Common- cathode vacuum-tube ampli- fier; and (b) common-emitter transistor amplifier.

(a)

(b)

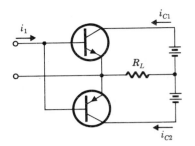

Fig. 7-23. A push-pull common-emitter complementary symmetry transistor amplifier. The input biasing circuits have been omitted.

unequal in magnitude and 180° out of phase. The input characteristic can be linearized by placing a resistance in series with the base. This series resistance will tend to limit the base current and thus reduce the gain. If the values of R_s can be increased, the base currents will exhibit less distortion. If $R_s \gg R_i$, the distortion can be neglected.

7-10 Transistors with complementary symmetry

A *p-n-p* transistor and an *n-p-n* transistor chosen to have characteristics which are the same except that the *polarities of the voltages and currents are reversed* can be used to construct a push-pull amplifier without an output transformer or phase inverter. Figure 7-23 illustrates the basic idea of such a circuit. If the base current divides equally between the two transistors, they will effectively be driven by signals 180° out of phase. The load current is equal to $i_{C1} + i_{C2}$ and the alternating components of the collector voltages are equal in magnitude and 180° out of phase. Thus, all the conditions for true push-pull operation have been achieved. The primary advantage of this circuit is that no output transformer is required. The output transformer is ordinarily used not only to achieve proper push-pull operation, but also to match the load impedance to the amplifier. If the transformer is required for this reason, then it is probably easier to pick identical *p-n-p* (or *n-p-n*) transistors and use a conventional circuit than to try to match a pair of *p-n-p* and *n-p-n* transistors.

One disadvantage of the amplifier of Fig. 7-23 is that the power supply is not connected to the common lead. If a common-collector complementary-symmetric push-pull circuit is used, this difficulty can be avoided. The output impedance of the common-collector amplifier is considerably less than that of the common-emitter amplifier. This may prove helpful if the load is a low impedance.

REFERENCES

1 "Thermal Resistance as Applied to Transistors," Tung-Sol Electric, Inc., Application Note 2-62, July 5, 1962.

BIBLIOGRAPHY

Gärtner, W. W.: "Transistors: Principles, Design, and Applications," chap. 13, D. Van Nostrand Company, Inc., Princeton, N.J., 1960.

Gray, T. S.: "Applied Electronics," 2d ed., pp. 460–476, 530–533, 609–619, John Wiley & Sons, Inc., New York, 1954.

Greiner, R. A.: "Semiconductor Devices and Applications," chap. 14, McGraw-Hill Book Company, New York, 1961.

PROBLEMS

In the following problems, the type 7027-A beam power tube will be used. It can also be used as a triode by connecting the screen grid to the plate. The ratings of this vacuum tube are $E_{b,\max} = 600$ volts, $E_{g2,\max} = 500$ volts, maximum plate dissipation = 35 watts, maximum screen-grid dissipation = 5 watts. The heater requires a voltage of 6.3 volts rms, and a current of 0.9 amp rms. The output characteristics for the pentode are given in Fig. 7-24. Note that some screen-grid characteristics are included in this characteristic. The output characteristics for the triode connection are given in Fig. 7-25. In the triode connection, the $E_{g2,\max}$ rating limits the plate voltage.

We shall also use the type 2N301 *p-n-p* transistor. Ratings of this transistor are $|E_{C,\max}| = 40$ volts, peak collector current = 3 amps., $|I_{CQ,\max}| = 1.5$ amps., maximum collector dissipation = 11 watts, maximum case temperature = 85°, thermal resistance between collector and case 1°C/watt. The common-emitter output characteristics are given in Fig. 7-26 and the common-emitter input characteristics are given in Fig. 7-27.

Assume that all bypass and coupling capacitors are short circuits at all signal frequencies.

7-1. A triode-connected type 7027-A vacuum tube is connected into the circuit of Fig. 7-28. The coordinates of the quiescent operating point are $E_{bQ} = 350$ volts and $E_{cQ} = -30$ volts. The value of R_L is 16 ohms and the turns ratio $n_1/n_2 = 14.2$. The input signal is $e_g = 30 \cos \omega t$ volts. Compute the power output, plate circuit efficiency, plate dissipation under quiescent conditions and under maximum signal conditions, the power-supply voltage E_{bb}, and the value of R_k. Compute the percent second, third, fourth, and total harmonic distortion. What is the efficiency of operation if the heater power and the power dissipated in R_k are taken into account?

7-2. Repeat Prob. 7-1, but now use a value of $R_L = 8$ ohms.

7-3. A type 7027-A beam power tube is connected into the circuit of Fig. 7-29. The coordinates of the quiescent operating point are $E_{bQ} = 300$ volts, $E_{cQ} = -15$ volts, $E_{c2Q} = 300$ volts. The load resistance is 16 ohms, the transformer turns ratio $n_1/n_2 = 11.2$, and the input signal is $15 \cos \omega t$ volts. Compute the power output, plate current efficiency, plate dissipation under quiescent conditions and under maximum signal conditions, the power-supply voltage E_{bb}, the value of R_k and the value of R_s (zero is an acceptable value). Compute the percent second, third, fourth, and total harmonic distortion. What is the efficiency of operation if the heater power, the power dis-

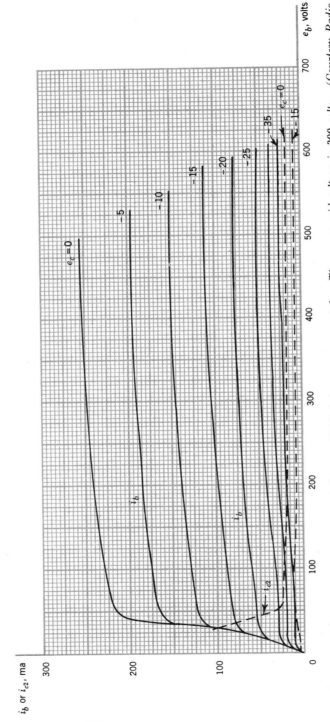

i_b or i_{c2}, ma

e_b, volts

Fig. 7-24   Static output characteristics of the type 7027-A beam power pentode.   The screen-grid voltage is 300 volts.   (Courtesy Radio Corporation of America.)

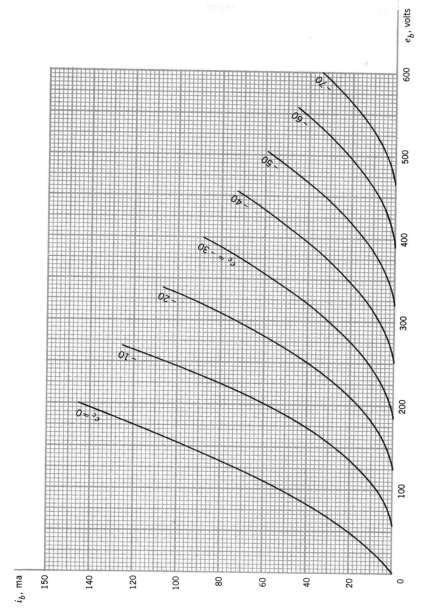

Fig. 7-25   Static output characteristics of the triode-connected type 7027-A.   (Courtesy Radio Corporation of America.)

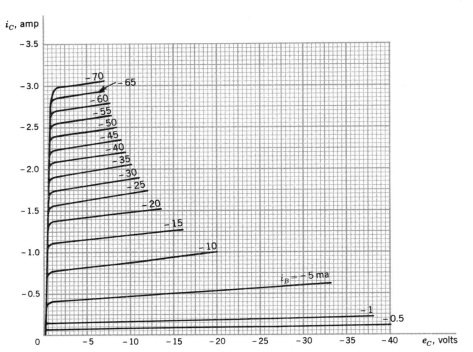

*Fig. 7-26   Static output characteristics of the type 2N301 p-n-p (common-emitter)
transistor.   (Courtesy Radio Corporation of America.)*

sipated in R_k and R_s, and the screen-grid dissipation are taken into account?
Hint: all the power, except the heater power, is supplied by the battery.

7-4. Repeat Prob. 7-3, but now use a turns ratio of $n_1/n_2 = 15.4$.

7-5. Repeat Prob. 7-3, but now use a value of $E_{cQ} = -10$, and $e_g =
10 \cos \omega t$.   Why would this circuit not be used?

7-6. A 2N301 transistor is connected into the circuit of Fig. 7-30.   The
coordinates of the quiescent operating point are $E_{CQ} = -5$ volts, $I_{BQ} =
-20$ ma.   The values of the circuit elements are $R_E = 1$ ohm, $R_L = 4$ ohms,
and $n_1/n_2 = 0.89$.   If the base signal current $i_b = 10 \cos \omega t$ ma, compute the
power output, collector-circuit efficiency, overall efficiency (i.e., output
power/P_{oo}), collector-junction dissipation under quiescent conditions and
under maximum signal conditions, and the percent second, third, fourth,
and total harmonic distortion.   What is the value of E_{CC}?   If $\alpha = 0.985$ and
the stability factor is to be less than 15, compute the values of R_{B1} and R_{B2}.
What is the current i_1 in this case?   Is it sinusoidal?

7-7. Repeat Prob. 7-6, but now assume that $i_b = 19.5 \cos \omega t$ ma.

7-8. Repeat Prob. 7-6, but now assume that $i_1 = 19.5 \cos \omega t$ ma.   Now
use a value of i_1 so that the peak-to-peak swing of i_b is 40 ma.   Do not neglect
the input circuit distortion.   Assume that the operating point is the same
and that R_B, the parallel combination of R_{B1} and R_{B2}, is 20 ohms.   Repeat
all the calculations for $R_B = 1000$ ohms.   Neglect any changes in the operating point.

7-9. Design a single-ended amplifier using a triode-connected 7027-A vacuum tube that meets the following specifications: $P_2 = 1.6$ watts, $E_{bQ} = 300$ volts, $R_L = 4$ ohms, and total harmonic distortion equal to or less than 10 percent. The design should be of the form of Fig. 7-28. The values of E_{bb}, n_1/n_2, R_k, and e_g should be specified and the ratings should not be exceeded. (Note that the maximum screen-grid voltage limits the maximum plate voltage here.)

7-10. Design a single-ended amplifier using a 7027-A beam power tube that meets the following specifications: $P_2 = 10$ watts, $E_{bQ} = 300$ volts, $E_{c2Q} = 300$ volts, $R_L = 16$ ohms, and the total harmonic distortion less than 10 percent. The design should be of the form of Fig. 7-29. The values of R_k, R_s, n_1/n_2, E_{bb}, and e_g should be specified (zero is an acceptable value of R_s). The tube ratings should not be exceeded.

7-11. Design a single-ended amplifier, using a 2N301 transistor, that meets the following specifications: $E_{CT} = -12$ volts, $P_2 = 4.5$ watts, $R_L = 4$ ohms, stability factor less than 5, and total harmonic distortion less than 15 percent. The circuit should be of the form of Fig. 7-30. The values of E_{CC}, R_E, R_{B1}, R_{B2}, n_1/n_2, and i_b should be specified. Now assume that the ideal current generator i_b is replaced by one whose internal impedance is R_B (the parallel combination of R_{B1} and R_{B2}) and repeat the problem. What should be the value of i_1?

Fig. 7-27 Static input characteristics of the type 2N301 p-n-p (common-emitter) transistor. (Courtesy Radio Corporation of America.)

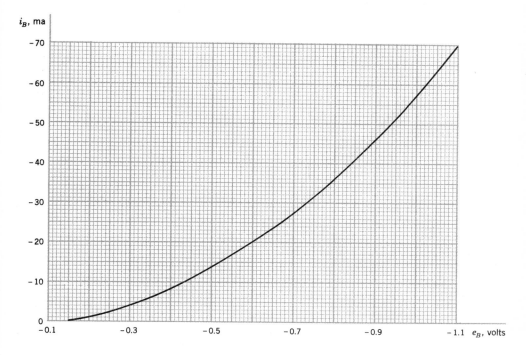

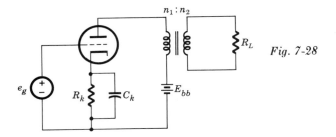

Fig. 7-28

7-12. Modify the design of Prob. 7-10 by connecting two type 7027-A vacuum tubes in parallel so that the power output is doubled without increasing the distortion.

7-13. Modify the design of Prob. 7-11 by connecting two type 2N301 transistors in parallel so that the power output is doubled without increasing the distortion.

7-14. A pair of triode-connected type 7027-A vacuum tubes are connected into the push-pull circuit of Fig. 7-10a (the circuit is modified so that triodes can be used), where $E_{bb} = 380$ volts and direct voltage drop across R_k is 30 volts. Obtain the composite characteristics of this device. Plot curves P_2 and percent second, third, and total harmonic distortion versus $R_{pp} = R_{dd} = 4(n_1/n_2)^2 R_L$. Use the maximum signal voltage that can be applied without causing grid current or causing the ratings to be exceeded. What should the value of R_k be?

7-15. A pair of type 7027-A vacuum-tube pentodes are connected into the push-pull circuit of Fig. 7-10a, where $E_{bb} = 315$ volts, $E_{c2Q} = 300$ volts, and $E_{cQ} = -15$ volts. Obtain the composite characteristics of this device. Plot curves of P_2 and percent second, third, and total harmonic distortion versus $R_{pp} = R_{dd} = 4(n_1/n_2)^2 R_L$. Use the maximum signal voltage that can be applied without causing grid current or causing the ratings to be exceeded. What should the value of R_k be?

7-16. A pair of 2N301 transistors are connected into the push-pull circuit of Fig. 7-10b, where $E_{CC} = -6$ volts, the voltage drop across R_E is 1 volt, and R_B is adjusted so that the quiescent base current of each transistor is 25 ma. Obtain the composite characteristic of this device. Plot curves of P_2 and

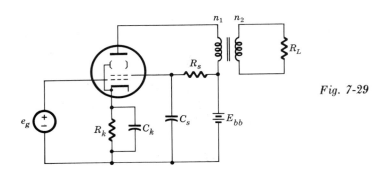

Fig. 7-29

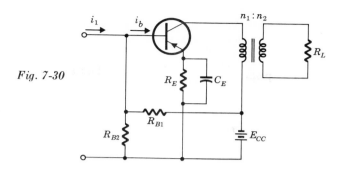

Fig. 7-30

percent second, third, and total harmonic distortion versus $R_{cc} = R_{dd} = 4(n_1/n_2)^2 R_L$. Use the maximum signal current that can be applied without causing the instantaneous magnitude of the base current to exceed 45 ma. What is the value of R_E? Now assume that two resistors are used to obtain base current for each transistor. (See Fig. 7-30.) Find values of R_{B1} and R_{B2} such that the stability factors of each device are less than 5. Ignore the input circuit distortion. Repeat this problem, but now do not let the instantaneous magnitude of the base current exceed 65 ma. Assume that $I_C = 0$ if $I_B = 0$.

7-17. Design a push-pull amplifier using a pair of triode-connected 7027-A vacuum tubes. (Modify Fig. 7-10a.) The quiescent plate voltage of each tube is to be approximately 300 volts, $R_L = 4$ ohms, the total harmonic distortion is to be equal to or less than 2.5 percent, the grid current is to be zero, and the operation is to be class A. The power output is to be 6.5 watts. Determine E_{cQ}, R_k, n_1/n_2, the plate-circuit efficiency, and e_{g1} for this amplifier.

7-18. Design a push-pull amplifier using a pair of 7027-A vacuum tubes. The quiescent plate voltage of each tube is to be 300 volts, $E_{c2Q} = 300$ volts, $R_L = 4$ ohms, the total harmonic distortion is to be equal to or less than 1.5 percent, the grid current is to be zero, and the operation is to be class A. The power output is to be 22 watts. Find E_{cQ}, R_k, n_1/n_2, the plate-circuit efficiency, and e_g for this amplifier (see Fig. 7-10a). Assume that the curve for $e_c = -40$ volts lies along the 15-ma ordinate for $e_b > 200$ volts.

7-19. Design a push-pull amplifier using a pair of 2N301 transistors. The average collector voltage of each transistor is to be -5 volts, $R_L = 4$ ohms, and the total harmonic distortion is to be equal to or less than 7 percent; the operation is to be class A, and the stability factor is to be less than or equal to 8. The power output is to be 4 watts. Find the values of I_{BQ}, E_{CC}, R_E, R_{B1}, R_{B2}, and the collector-circuit efficiency, and i_B. (Neglect input-circuit distortion.)

7-20. Design a push-pull amplifier using type 7027-A vacuum tubes with $E_{bQ} = 400$ volts, $E_{c2Q} = 300$ volts, and $R_L = 16$ ohms, and the total harmonic distortion less than 2.5 percent. The power output should be 20 watts. The operation should be class AB and the grid current should be zero. All the elements of the circuit, the plate-circuit efficiency, and the input signal should be specified (see Fig. 7-10a). The plate-circuit efficiency should be as large as possible.

7-21. Design a push-pull amplifier using type 7027-A vacuum tubes with

$E_{bQ} = 300$ volts, $E_{c2Q} = 300$ volts, and $R_L = 4$ ohms. The operation is to be class ABB. Use the projected cutoff method to obtain the grid bias. Assume that the curve of i_b for $e_c = -40$ volts lies along the 10-ma ordinate and that $i_b = 0$ if $e_c < -40$ volts. Distortion should be considered when this bias is obtained. (Note that the transfer characteristics can be obtained from the plate characteristics.) The total harmonic distortion is to be less than 10 percent. (The distortion should also be checked using a small signal.) The grid current is to be zero and the ratings of the vacuum tube are not to be exceeded. The output power is to be 22 watts. Specify all of the elements of the circuit (see Fig. 7-10a), η_2, and the input signal.

7-22. Design a push-pull amplifier using type 2N301 transistors with $E_{CQ} \approx -12$ volts, $R_L = 4$ ohms, $P_2 = 8$ watts, and the total harmonic distortion less than 10 per cent. The operation can be either class A or class AB. All the elements of the circuit and the input signal should be specified (see Fig. 7-10b). Neglect input-circuit distortion.

7-23. Design a push-pull amplifier using type 2N301 transistors with $E_{CQ} = -10$ volts, and $R_L = 4$ ohms. The operation is to be class ABB. Use the projected cutoff method to determine the bias. Distortion should be considered when this bias is obtained. (Determine the transfer characteristics from those which are specified.) The total harmonic distortion is to be less than 12 percent and the ratings of the transistor are not to be exceeded. The output power is to be 20 watts. Specify all the elements of the circuit and the input signal (see Fig. 7-10b). Neglect the input-circuit distortion. Then determine the input signal if $R_B = R_{B1}R_{B2}/(R_{B1} + R_{B2}) = 10$ ohms. Assume that $R_E = 0$ in all these calculations. (Check distortion at small-signal levels also.)

7-24. The collector-base junction of a 2N301 transistor is to operate at a temperature of 85°C when it is dissipating 10 watts. The ambient temperature is 20°C. It is to be insulated from the heatsink by a mica spacer 0.05 mm thick. The effective area of the transistor case in contact with the mica is 5 cm². What must be the effective resistance of the heatsink $\theta_H + \theta_R\theta_C/(\theta_R + \theta_C)$? Note that the internal thermal resistance of the transistor is given in the specifications.

7-25. Design the heatsink required in Prob. 7-24. Assume that it is made of a metal with a very high thermal conductivity, so that $\theta_H \approx 0$ and its surface temperature is constant. Also assume that it is lacquered a dull black.

7-26. The transistor of Prob. 7-24 is to be operated at a value of $E_{CQ} = -5$ volts and at a temperature of 85°C, $dI_{CO}/dT_J = 0.01$. What is the maximum value that the stability factor may have if the operation is to be stable? Assume that the collector voltage is independent of the collector current.

7-27. For the phase inverters of Fig. 7-19a, compute the percentage of R_g that is to be tapped if perfect phase inversion is to result. Assume that the upper and lower circuits are identical. The answers should be in terms of the circuit elements and the parameters of the vacuum tubes.

7-28. Repeat Prob. 7-27, for the percentage of R_{B2} that is to be tapped in the circuit of Fig. 7-19b. The answer should be in terms of the circuit elements and the h parameters of the transistors. The input impedance of each half of the push-pull amplifier is R_i. To simplify the analysis assume that $h_{rc} = 0$.

7-29. The phase inverter of Fig. 7-20a is such that the two vacuum tubes are identical. If $R = R_L R_g/(R_L + R_g)$ and $R' = R'_L R'_g/(R'_L + R'_g)$, what relation must exist among R, R', R_k, and the parameters of the vacuum tubes if phase inversion is to be ideal?

7-30. Repeat Prob. 7-29 for the circuit of Fig. 7-20b. Here, let $R = R_C R_B/(R_C + R_B)$ and $R' = R'_C R'_B/(R'_C + R'_B)$. The answer should be in terms of R, R', R_E, and the h parameters of the transistors. Assume that R_B and R'_B include the input resistance of the next stage. To simplify the analysis assume that $h_{re} = 0$.

7-31. Compute the output impedance of both outputs of the phase inverters of Fig. 7-21a. The answers should be in terms of the circuit elements and the parameters of the vacuum tubes.

7-32. Repeat Prob. 7-31 for the phase inverters of Fig. 7-21b. The answers should be in terms of the circuit elements and the h parameters of the transistors.

Tuned Large-signal Amplifiers

The maximum output-circuit efficiency of an amplifier increases as the operation is shifted from class A to class B (see Sec. 5-6). If class C operation is used, the maximum theoretical output-circuit efficiency can approach 100 percent. The untuned power amplifiers of Chap. 7 were not operated class C, since excessive (harmonic) distortion would have resulted. However, if an amplifier is only to provide gain at a single frequency, or over a narrow band of frequencies, tuned circuits, which reject the unwanted harmonics, can be used. Highly efficient operation is then possible. These amplifiers are usually used as the output stages in radio transmitters. The output power often exceeds 50,000 watts and the efficiency is of prime importance. The operation of these amplifiers is nonlinear, and hence they are called large-signal amplifiers. Since they are tuned and operate at radio frequencies, they are also called *tuned radio-frequency power amplifiers.*

8-1   General discussion of class B and class C operation

Let us consider some typical tuned power amplifiers. Figure 8-1 illustrates two simple vacuum-tube and transistor amplifiers. To simplify the diagrams, the emitter-stabilizing circuit and the neutralizing networks (see Sec. 6-26) have been omitted. Battery bias is shown; other methods of bias will be discussed in Sec. 8-6. A common-emitter transistor amplifier is illustrated; however, common-base circuits are also often used. Much of the analysis of the various amplifier configurations is the same, so we shall base our discussion on the generalized device shown in Fig. 8-2. It will be assumed that the effective Q of the resonant circuit is high enough so that e_o consists only of the direct voltage and the fundamental component of the signal. That is, the tuned circuit effectively eliminates the harmonics (see Secs. 6-20 and 6-21). We also assume that the input quantity (e.g., the grid voltage for a vacuum tube, or the base current for a common-emitter transistor) is sinusoidal. The capacitors C_{c1}, C_c, and C_B are considered to be short circuits at the signal frequency. Figure 8-3a illustrates typical

Fig. 8-1   Simplified forms of tuned power amplifiers.   (a) A common-cathode vacuum-tube-triode amplifier; (b) a common-emitter-transistor amplifier.   Neutralization networks have been omitted from both of these amplifiers.

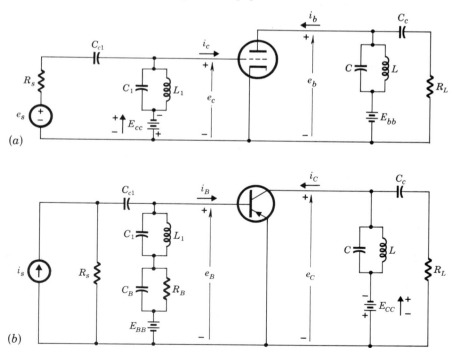

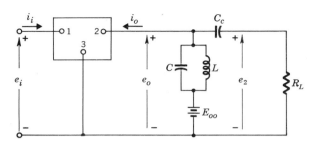

Fig. 8-2 A generalized-device representation of a tuned power amplifier.

curves of output voltage and current for a tuned class C amplifier. Note that the ωt axis has been labeled so that the voltage is a cosine wave. A typical input voltage and current are shown in Fig. 8-3b. If the device is a vacuum tube, then x_i would represent the grid voltage and y_i the grid current. Although the output voltage is sinusoidal, the output current is very distorted. It is not zero for only a portion of a cycle; even then, it is not a sinusoid. If the device output dissipation P_{oD} were zero, then the output circuit efficiency would be 100 percent. The instantaneous power dissipated within the output circuit of the device is

$$p_{oD} = e_o i_o \tag{8-1}$$

so

$$P_{oD} = \frac{1}{2\pi} \int_{-\pi}^{\pi} p_{oD}\, d(\omega t) \tag{8-2}$$

but $i_o = 0$ unless $\theta_1 \leqslant \omega t \leqslant \theta_2$, so

$$P_{oD} = \frac{1}{2\pi} \int_{\theta_1}^{\theta_2} p_{oD}\, d\omega t \tag{8-3}$$

We shall define the conduction angle θ_c as

$$\theta_c = \theta_2 - \theta_1 \tag{8-4}$$

where θ_1 is measured in negative degrees or radians from zero. The power supplied by the battery is

$$P_{oo} = \frac{1}{2\pi} \int_{\theta_1}^{\theta_2} i_o E_{oo}\, d\omega t = \frac{E_{oo}}{2\pi} \int_{\theta_1}^{\theta_2} i_o\, d\omega t \tag{8-5}$$

and the output power is

$$P_2 = \frac{E_2{}^2}{R_{ac}} \tag{8-6}$$

where

$$E_2 = \frac{E_{2,\max}}{\sqrt{2}} \tag{8-7}$$

(see Fig. 8-3a).

The output circuit efficiency is given by

$$\eta_2 = \frac{P_2}{P_{oo}} = \frac{P_{oo} - P_{oD}}{P_{oo}} \tag{8-8}$$

If θ_c is small enough (ideally zero), we can consider that e_o is constant for values of $\theta_1 \leqslant \omega t \leqslant \theta_2$, so that Eq. (8-3) becomes

$$P_{oD} \approx \frac{E_{o,\min}}{2\pi} \int_{\theta_1}^{\theta_2} i_o \, d\omega t \tag{8-9}$$

Then, substituting Eqs. (8-5) and (8-9) into Eq. (8-8), we obtain

$$\eta_2 = 1 - \frac{E_{o,\min}}{E_{oo}} \tag{8-10}$$

If the output circuit is properly adjusted, $E_{o,\min}$ can approach zero. Thus, η_2 can approach 100 percent as θ_c approaches zero. The efficiency is always less than 100 percent, since $E_{o,\min}$ and θ_c are always greater than zero. From

Fig. 8-3   (a) *Typical curves of output voltage and current for a tuned class C amplifier;* (b) *typical curves of input voltage and current.*

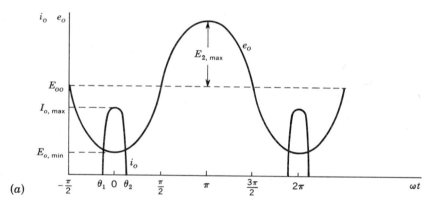

(a)

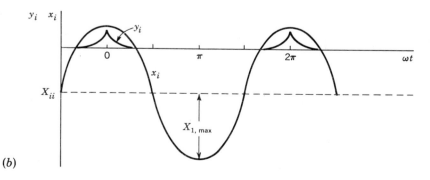

(b)

the law of conservation of energy, we can write

$$P_2 \lessgtr P_{oo} = E_{oo} \int_{\theta_1}^{\theta_2} i_o \, d\omega t \qquad (8\text{-}11)$$

Thus, as $\theta_2 - \theta_1$ decreases, $I_{o,\text{max}}$ must increase if the output power is not to decrease. The peak current of electronic devices is limited and, hence, the minimum value of θ_c is limited. However, efficiencies of 85 percent or higher are possible.

In order to obtain the quantities of interest, the instantaneous value of i_o must be found and integrated. We shall consider a procedure for doing this in the next section.

We have assumed that the parallel resonant circuit is tuned to the frequency of the input signal. However, if it is tuned to an integral multiple of this frequency instead, then the output will approximately be a sinusoid at the frequency to which the resonant circuit is tuned. This is true because i_o is very distorted and, hence, contains many harmonics of relatively large amplitude. Such circuits are called *frequency multipliers*. Their analysis is similar to that of the conventional amplifier. These circuits cannot be used to multiply the fundamental by an arbitrarily large number, since the amplitude of the higher harmonics falls off with increasing frequency.

8-2   Analysis of tuned class B and class C amplifiers

In the graphical analysis of Chap. 7, the load impedance was purely resistive, so that, with the exception of a phase reversal, the output voltage and current waveforms were the same. Thus, the plot of i_o versus e_o was a straight line (i.e., the a-c load line). For the tuned class B or class C amplifiers, the waveform of e_o does not resemble that of i_o (see Fig. 8-3). Hence, the locus of operation on the device output characteristics is not a straight line. Thus, any analysis using these characteristics would be quite tedious. However, by using an appropriate set of characteristics, we can obtain a locus of operation that is a straight line. Assume that, because of the resonant circuit, the output voltage is sinusoidal,

$$e_o = E_{oo} - \sqrt{2} \, E_2 \cos \omega t \qquad (8\text{-}12)$$

If we also assume that the device input consists of a sinusoidal signal superimposed upon a direct bias, we have

$$x_i = X_{ii} + \sqrt{2} \, X_1 \cos \omega t \qquad (8\text{-}13)$$

where, as is usually the case, x_i represents either the input voltage or the input current. Since e_o and x_i have the same waveforms, a plot of e_o versus x_i is a straight line. Therefore, instead of working with a plot of i_o versus e_o with x_i as a parameter, let us use a plot of x_i versus e_o with i_o as a parameter. These are called *constant-current characteristics* and a typical set is given in Fig. 8-4. The dashed curves represent an input quantity. For instance, in a vacuum tube, x_i would be grid voltage and y_i would be grid current. The curves resemble those for a vacuum-tube triode. If a vacuum-tube pentode is used, there would be another set of constant-current characteristics for the screen-grid current. (A typical set of transistor characteristics is given in Fig. 8-13.) The scales are given in normalized form. If high-power vacuum tubes are used, the voltage scale would be in kilovolts and the current scale in amperes. Transistors are not operated at very high-power

Fig. 8-4 Constant output current characteristics for a generalized device. Constant y_i curves are also shown. Note that the $i_o = 0$ curve actually is a boundary. All points below it represent $i_o = 0$.

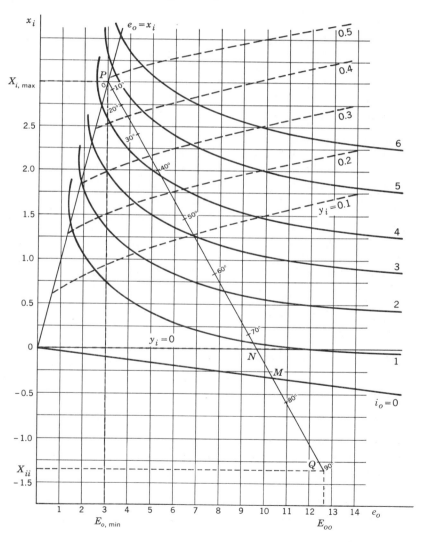

levels.   Transistor voltage scales would be in volts and the current scales in amperes or milliamperes.   The parametric equations for the locus of operation are given by Eqs. (8-12) and (8-13).   The locus is drawn between points P and Q in Fig. 8-4.   Actually, the locus should be twice this length and should be extended beyond point Q to another point called P', which is not shown on the diagram.   That is, as ωt varies from $-\pi/2$ to 0, to $\pi/2$, to π, to $3\pi/2$, the instantaneous operating point moves from point Q to P, to Q, to P', to Q, respectively.   However, since the operation is class B or C, the output current will be zero for operation along QP'; hence it is not drawn.

The voltages and currents are even functions of time, and thus, if the response for $0 \leqslant \omega t \leqslant \pi/2$ is known, then the response for $-\pi/2 \leqslant \omega t \leqslant 0$ is also known.   The locus from point Q to P is marked in lengths proportional to $\cos \omega t$ as indicated.   That is, each length is $\overline{PQ} \cos \omega t$, $\omega t = 0, 10°, 20°, 30°, \ldots, 90°$.   The point Q is the quiescent operating point.   Its coordinates are X_{ii} and E_{oo}.   Point P has the coordinates $X_{i,\max}$ and $E_{o,\min}$.   From Eqs. (8-12) and (8-13), we have

$$X_{i,\max} = X_{ii} + \sqrt{2}\, X_1 \tag{8-14}$$

$$E_{o,\min} = E_{oo} - \sqrt{2}\, E_2 \tag{8-15}$$

These values are unknown.   They depend not only upon the device, but also upon the resonant circuit.   Point P is often chosen as a design parameter. In Sec. 8-5, we shall discuss how this can be done.   For the time being, let us assume that it is known.   Once the points P and Q are determined, the locus can be drawn between them and marked in degrees.   Then, i_o and y_i as functions of ωt can be obtained by interpolating between the constant i_o and y_i curves, respectively.   The degree markings on the line $\overline{PQ}$ are used to do this.

If the output current is given by the Fourier series

$$i_o = I_{oA} + \sqrt{2}\, (I_{o1} \cos \omega t + I_{o2} \cos 2\omega t + \cdots) \tag{8-16}$$

then I_{oA} is the average value of i_o

$$I_{oA} = \frac{1}{2\pi} \int_{\theta_1}^{\theta_2} i_o \, d\omega t \tag{8-17}$$

Since i_o is an even function of time, we can write

$$I_{oA} = \frac{1}{\pi} \int_0^{\theta_2} i_o \, d\omega t \tag{8-18}$$

The fundamental component of plate current can be obtained from the relation

$$\sqrt{2}\, I_{o1} = \frac{2}{\pi} \int_0^{\theta_2} i_o \cos \omega t \, d\omega t \tag{8-19}$$

We do not have an analytic expression for i_o, so approximate techniques must be used to perform the desired integrations.   Consider the curve $f(\omega t)$ shown

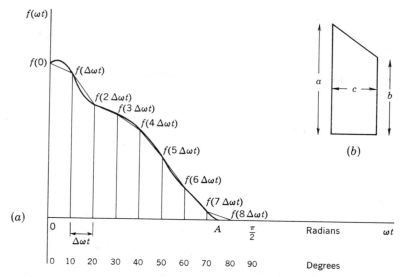

Fig. 8-5 (a) *An illustration of integration using trapezoidal approxima-tions;* (b) *a trapezoid.*

in Fig. 8-5a. We may approximate its integral from 0 to A by adding the area of the trapezoids obtained by connecting points on the curve by straight lines. Actually, for i_o and y_i, we do not have a smooth curve, but only a set of discrete points determined at distinct values of ωt. *Thus, a straight-line approximation is as good as any other.* The area of the trapezoid of Fig. 8-5b is $c(a + b)/2$. Thus, we can approximate the integral by

$$\int_0^{\pi/2} f(\omega t)\ d\omega t = \Delta\omega t \left\{ \frac{f(0) + f(\Delta\omega t)}{2} + \frac{f(\Delta\omega t) + f(2\,\Delta\omega t)}{2} \right.$$
$$\left. + \cdots + \frac{f[(n - 1)\,\Delta\omega t] + f(n\,\Delta\omega t)}{2} \right\}$$

where $\Delta\omega t = \pi/2n$ radians. Combining terms, we have

$$\int_0^{\pi/2} f(\omega t)\ d\omega t = \Delta\omega t \left\{ \frac{f(0)}{2} + f(\Delta\omega t) + f(2\,\Delta\omega t) \right.$$
$$\left. + \cdots + f[(n - 1)\,\Delta\omega t] + \frac{f(n\,\Delta\omega t)}{2} \right\} \quad (8\text{-}20)$$

If we chose $n = 9$, so that $\Delta\omega t = \pi/18$ radians, or $10°$, we obtain

$$\int_0^{\pi/2} f(\omega t)\ d\omega t = \frac{\pi}{18} \left[\frac{f(0°)}{2} + f(10°) + f(20°) \right.$$
$$\left. + \cdots + f(80°) + \frac{f(90°)}{2} \right] \quad (8\text{-}21)$$

Table 8-1

ϕ, deg	cos ϕ	$i_o(\phi)$	i_o cos (ϕ)	y_i	y_i cos ϕ
0	1.000				
10	0.985				
20	0.940				
30	0.866				
40	0.766				
50	0.643				
60	0.500				
70	0.342				
80	0.174				
90	0.000				

Thus, Eqs. (8-18) and (8-19) become, for 10° increments,

$$I_{oA} = \frac{1}{18}\left[\frac{i_o(0°)}{2} + i_o(10°) + i_o(20°) + \cdots + i_o(80°) + \frac{i_o(90°)}{2}\right] \quad (8\text{-}22)$$

and

$$\sqrt{2}\,I_{o1} = \frac{1}{9}\left[\frac{i_o(0°)}{2} + i_o(10°)\cos 10° + i_o(20°)\cos 20°\right.$$
$$\left. + \cdots + i_o(80°)\cos 80° + \frac{i_o(90°)\cos 90°}{2}\right] \quad (8\text{-}23)$$

If greater accuracy is desired, smaller increments can be used. We shall also be interested in obtaining the corresponding input quantities.

$$y_i = Y_{iA} + \sqrt{2}\,(Y_{i1}\cos \omega t + Y_{i2}\cos 2\omega t + \cdots) \quad (8\text{-}24)$$

Then, to obtain Y_{iA} and Y_{i1}, we can proceed exactly as in Eqs. (8-18), (8-19), (8-22), and (8-23) except that y_i is used instead of i_o. The simplest way of performing these calculations is to set up a table. A sample one is given here. The values of i_o and y_i are interpolated from the curve of Fig. 8-4 and are substituted into the first and third blank columns of the table. The second and fourth columns are then calculated. The values from the table are then substituted into Eqs. (8-22) and (8-23) or into modifications of them where i_o is replaced by y_i.

The other quantities that we shall need in our computations can be obtained directly from Fig. 8-4. The peak signal output voltage is given by $E_{oo} - E_{o,\min}$. Thus, if the output voltage is expressed by Eq. (8-12), then the rms value of the output signal voltage is given by

$$E_2 = \frac{E_{oo} - E_{o,\min}}{\sqrt{2}} \quad (8\text{-}25)$$

Similarly, the rms value of the signal component of x_i is

$$X_1 = \frac{X_{i,\max} - X_{ii}}{\sqrt{2}} \tag{8-26}$$

We are now in a position to calculate the quantities of interest. Assume that the resonant circuit is adjusted so that it appears as a pure resistance at the signal frequency. Then the output power is

$$P_2 = E_2 I_{o1} \tag{8-27}$$

The effective resistance of the output circuit is just the ratio of the fundamental component of the voltage to the current. Hence,

$$R_{ac} = \frac{E_2}{I_{o1}} \tag{8-28}$$

The power supplied by E_{oo} is

$$P_{oo} = E_{oo} I_{oA} \tag{8-29}$$

If we assume that the zero-frequency resistance of the inductance L is negligible, the device output dissipation is given by

$$P_{oD} = P_{oo} - P_2 \tag{8-30}$$

The output circuit efficiency is

$$\eta_2 = \frac{P_2}{P_{oo}} \tag{8-31}$$

The output quantities have now been obtained. At times, we are interested in similar input quantities. The average power dissipated in the input of the device is given by

$$P_{iD} = \frac{1}{2\pi} \int_0^{2\pi} x_i y_i \, d\omega t$$

If $x_i = X_{ii} + \sqrt{2}\, X_1 \cos \omega t$ and y_i is given in Eq. (8-24), we have

$$P_{iD} = \frac{1}{2\pi} \int_0^{2\pi} (X_{ii} + \sqrt{2}\, X_1 \cos \omega t)[Y_{iA} + \sqrt{2}\,(Y_{i1} \cos \omega t$$
$$Y_{i2} \cos 2\omega t + \cdots)]\, d\omega t$$

Solving, we obtain

$$P_{iD} = X_{ii} Y_{iA} + X_1 Y_{i1} \tag{8-32}$$

If a power supply X_{ii} is used to produce an input bias, then the power supplied by it will be

$$P_{ii} = X_{ii} Y_{iA} \tag{8-33}$$

This assumes that all the direct component of y_i passes through or appears across the power supply. Note that P_{ii} is often negative. That is, the power supply actually dissipates power. For instance, in the circuit of Fig. 8-1a the battery E_{cc} dissipates power when the grid draws current. The input generator (e.g., the generators e_s and i_s in Fig. 8-1) must supply any power that is absorbed by the power supply or in the input of the device.

The conduction angle θ_c can be obtained by noting where the $i_o = 0$ curve crosses the locus of operation. This is point M in Fig. 8-4. Thus,

$$\theta_c = 2 \cos^{-1} \frac{\overline{MQ}}{\overline{PQ}} \tag{8-34}$$

In this case, $\theta_c = 152.8°$. The factor of 2 is used, since the output current is an even function of time (see Fig. 8-3a). Similarly, we can define

$$\theta_y = 2 \cos^{-1} \frac{\overline{NQ}}{\overline{PQ}} \tag{8-35}$$

as an input conduction angle. If transistors are used and y_i represents a voltage, it becomes meaningless to speak of a conduction angle θ_y.

When vacuum-tube pentodes are used, the screen-grid dissipation is given by $E_{c2} I_{c2A}$ where I_{c2A} is found by the same type of graphical procedure that we have discussed. The screen-grid voltage contains only a direct component because of the bypass capacitor.

8-3   The resonant circuit

The function of the resonant circuit in a tuned amplifier is to provide the correct load impedance to the amplifier, to reject the unwanted harmonics, and to couple the power to the load. The first two functions can be studied using the techniques of Secs. 6-20 to 6-25. The resonant circuits in tuned power amplifiers are sometimes called *tank circuits*. Such a circuit is shown in Fig. 8-6a. Its efficiency is

$$\eta = \frac{I_L{}^2 R_L}{I_L{}^2 R_L + I_a{}^2 R} \tag{8-36}$$

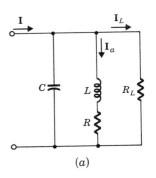

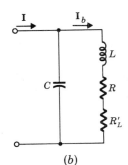

Fig. 8-6   (a) A simple output network; (b) an equivalent circuit.

(a)   (b)

where we have neglected the losses in the capacitors. The analysis is considerably simplified if we use the equivalent circuit of Fig. 8-6b, where

$$R_L' = \frac{\omega_0^2 L^2}{R_L} \tag{8-37}$$

This assumes that $R_L \gg \omega_0 L$ and is derived as is Eq. (6-261). It is also assumed that the capacitor is adjusted to resonance at ω_0, the frequency of operation. Then the efficiency will be

$$\eta = \frac{I_b^2 R_L'}{I_b^2(R + R_L')} = \frac{R_L'}{R + R_L'} \tag{8-38}$$

Let Q_0 be the Q of the coil itself at resonance

$$Q_0 = \frac{\omega_0 L}{R} \tag{8-39}$$

and Q_{eff} is the Q of the coil shunted by R_L

$$Q_{\text{eff}} = \frac{\omega_0 L}{R + R_L'} \tag{8-40}$$

These definitions are compatible with those of Secs. 6-20 and 6-21. Then, substituting in Eq. (8-38), we obtain

$$\eta = \frac{1/Q_{\text{eff}} - 1/Q_0}{1/Q_{\text{eff}}} = 1 - \frac{Q_{\text{eff}}}{Q_0} \tag{8-41}$$

Thus, if the efficiency of the tank circuit is to be high, $Q_0 \gg Q_{\text{eff}}$. If R_L can be varied, then Q_{eff} can be made as small as desired. The value of Q_0 is usually several hundred. The circuit is usually adjusted so that Q_{eff} ranges between 10 and 20. The efficiency of the tank circuit is then 90 percent or more. The selectivity is a function of Q_{eff}. However, the only frequencies that must be rejected are harmonics of ω_0 which are far removed from ω_0. Even at low values of Q_{eff}, the harmonic rejection can be quite good, so the assumption of Sec. 8-2, that the device output voltage e_o is sinusoidal, is justified. If this amplifier is to be the output stage of a commercial radio transmitter, then the radiation of unwanted frequencies must be kept to a minimum, and additional filtering often is added to the circuit. The efficiency of this filter also must be considered.

We have assumed that the value of R_L can be varied. Usually it is fixed by the design requirements. The tank circuit of Fig. 8-7a is often used to provide a means of controlling the effective value of R_L. We shall assume that $R_L \gg \omega_0 L_2$. Then, proceeding as in Sec. 6-23, we obtain the equivalent circuit of Fig. 8-7b. The power dissipated in R_2 and R_L is

$$P' = I_a^2 \frac{(\omega_0 M)^2}{R_2 + R_L} \tag{8-42}$$

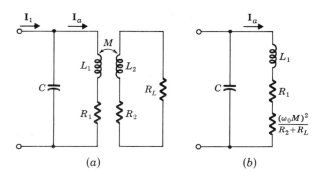

Fig. 8-7   (a) A mutual-inductance-coupled output network; (b) an equivalent circuit.

The power dissipated in R_L can be obtained by multiplying Eq. (8-42) by $R_L/(R_2 + R_L)$.   Thus, the efficiency of operation is

$$\eta = \frac{(\omega_0 M)^2/(R_2 + R_L)}{R_1 + (\omega_0 M)^2/(R_2 + R_L)} \cdot \frac{R_L}{R_2 + R_L} \tag{8-43}$$

Defining

$$Q_{01} = \frac{\omega_0 L_1}{R_1} \tag{8-44}$$

$$Q_{\text{eff},1} = \frac{\omega_0 L_1}{R_1 + (\omega_0 M)^2/(R_2 + R_L)} \tag{8-45}$$

$$Q_{02} = \frac{\omega_0 L_2}{R_2} \tag{8-46}$$

$$Q_{\text{eff},2} = \frac{\omega_0 L_2}{R_2 + R_L} \tag{8-47}$$

and substituting into Eq. (8-43) yields

$$\eta = \left(1 - \frac{Q_{\text{eff},1}}{Q_{01}}\right)\left(1 - \frac{Q_{\text{eff},2}}{Q_{02}}\right) \tag{8-48}$$

To obtain high efficiencies, the coupled resistance must be much greater than the primary resistance and R_L must be much greater than R_2.   As in the case of the simple coil of Fig. 8-6, the Q_{01} will usually be several hundred and $Q_{\text{eff},1}$ will be between 10 and 20.   The load resistance is usually such that Q_{02} is 50 (or more) times $Q_{\text{eff},2}$.   The efficiencies obtainable with the mutual-inductance-coupled circuit compare quite favorably with those of Fig. 8-6. Efficiencies of 90 percent or higher are obtainable.   The selectivity of this tuned circuit is given by the relations of Sec. 6-23.

If the impedances in transistor circuits are too small, then tapped coils can be used to obtain the desired selectivity (see Secs. 6-22 and 6-23).

We have assumed that the circuits of Figs. 8-6 and 8-7 are adjusted for resonance.   This is usually accomplished by varying C, since air-core coils are used to keep the losses low.   The proper value of C must be determined. This can be done by measuring the power delivered to R_L.   However, this requires the use of radio-frequency measuring equipment.   A simpler technique is to measure I_{oA}, the average value of i_o (see Fig. 8-3). This can be done by placing a simple d'Arsonval ammeter in series with the power-supply lead to the tank circuit. From Fig. 8-3 we can see that the voltage e_o is a minimum between θ_1 and θ_2. If the tank circuit is detuned, the output signal voltage will decrease and e_o will increase for those times that $i_o \neq 0$. This will increase i_o. Thus, the capacitor C is adjusted for a *minimum* in I_{oA}. This is an approximate adjustment, but it is usually accurate enough.

8-4   Effects of input-circuit distortion on class B and class C amplifiers

We have thus far neglected the effects of input-circuit distortion in the analyses. If such distortion is present, it cannot be assumed that x_i varies sinusoidally [see Eq. (8-13)], so that the locus of operation is no longer a straight line as is shown in Fig. 8-4. We shall modify the procedure to take input distortion into account. Two typical input circuits are shown in Fig. 8-8. The generators e_s and i_s are the cosinusoidal input generators, and E_{ss} and I_{ss} are bias generators. The voltages and currents e_b and i_b are of the form

$$x_b = X_{ss} + x_s = X_{ss} + \sqrt{2}\,X_s \cos \omega_0 t \tag{8-49}$$

Thus, the locus of operation on a plot of x_b versus e_o will be a straight line. It is desirable to alter the characteristics of Fig. 8-4 so that the ordinate is expressed in terms of x_b instead of x_i. Before we do this, let us consider the approximations that will be made. If the impedance $\mathbf{Z}$ contains inductances and capacitances, then a nonlinear differential equation must be solved to obtain e_o and i_o. Usually, tuned circuits, adjusted to be a pure resistance at the frequency ω_0, are used. We shall assume that $\mathbf{Z}$ is constant at this value and is equal to R. We also assume that the impedance is constant

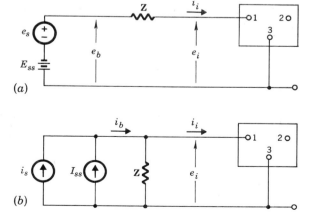

Fig. 8-8 Generalized input circuits. (a) Voltage source; and (b) current source.

down to zero frequency. This is usually not the case. The generator X_{ss} may have to be adjusted to obtain the proper bias. Let us assume that in Fig. 8-4, x_i represents a voltage and y_i represents a current. Then, for each constant-y_i curve, we can write

$$e_b = Ri_i + e_i \tag{8-50}$$

The constant-i_i curves can now be plotted on an e_b, e_o set of axes. Thus, if we used the same scales as in Fig. 8-4, the constant-i_i curves would be shifted upward by an amount equal to Ri_i. Similarly, if x_i represents a current and y_i a voltage, we have

$$i_b = Ge_i + i_i \tag{8-51}$$

where $G = 1/R$.

We must now plot the constant-output-current characteristics of the x_b, e_o axes. The procedure of Sec. 2-11 can be used. To obtain x_b in terms of x_i, the dynamic characteristic of Fig. 2-20b must be drawn. This requires a knowledge of the locus of operation, which cannot be found until x_b is known in terms of x_i. As a first trial, assume that the straight line $\overline{PQ}$ is the locus of operation (see Fig. 8-4). The dynamic input characteristic is then drawn and x_b is obtained in terms of x_i. The characteristics of Fig. 8-4 can then be replotted on an x_b versus e_o axis. The locus of operation on these curves will be a straight line. The actual locus of operation is now known and the assumed dynamic input characteristic can be checked. If it is severely in error, draw a new one using the new locus of operation. Repeat the procedure until the assumed dynamic input characteristic agrees with the calculated one. Once the new characteristics are drawn, the analysis proceeds essentially as in Sec. 8-2. When the device input quantities are computed, the value of x_i and not of x_b should be used. The results of this analysis are only approximate and should be treated as such. However, they are often accurate enough to check the feasibility of a design and to estimate the operating conditions. If the generator impedance is changed, a new set of characteristics must be drawn.

If x_i represents an input voltage and if the output impedance of the circuit that drives the power amplifier is very much less than the input impedance of the power amplifier, then the input-circuit distortion can be ignored. On the other hand, if x_i represents an input current, then for undistorted operation, the output impedance of the driving stage should be very much greater than the input impedance of the power amplifier. Thus, the design of the driver amplifier can do much to eliminate the need for the approximate analysis of this section.

8-5   Design of class B and class C amplifiers

We shall assume in this discussion that the stage preceding the amplifier is designed so that the input circuit distortion can be neglected. If this is not the case, then the characteristics of the device should be modified in accordance with Sec. 8-4. We shall begin with a discussion of vacuum-tube-triode amplifiers. These results will be extended to the beam power tube, the vacuum-tube tetrode, the vacuum-tube pentode, and the transistor.

Vacuum-tube triode

The design of the amplifier consists of the proper choice of the points P and Q of Fig. 8-4. The location of point P depends to a great extent upon the variation of plate current with grid bias. To obtain high efficiency, the grid is always driven positive to obtain large swings in output voltage and current. As the grid voltage is increased from the cutoff value, the total current from the cathode increases steadily. However, as the grid becomes positive, some of it is diverted to the grid. If the grid voltage is increased sufficiently, it will begin to take a larger and larger proportion of the cathode current. As the grid voltage is increased above the plate voltage, the plate current does not usually increase and, eventually, will decrease. Point P should be chosen so that $E_{o,\min} \geqq X_{i,\max}$, that is, $E_{b,\min} \geqq E_{c,\max}$. A line whose equation is $e_o = x_i$ ($e_b = e_c$) is often drawn on the constant-current characteristic, and point P is chosen to lie on it. Such a line is shown in Fig. 8-4. Often, to limit the grid current, the grid voltage is not allowed to become equal to the plate voltage. The point P is then made to lie on a line $e_o = kx_i$ ($e_b = ke_c$). The value of k usually lies between 1 and 2. The intersection of this line and the constant-i_o curve that represents the desired peak output current determines the location of point P. The peak values of grid voltage and grid current should be checked to see if they have been exceeded.

The location of point Q requires that E_{oo} and X_{ii} be specified. The peak output voltage is given by $E_{oo} - E_{o,\min}$. Thus, the peak tube voltage is

$$E_{o,\max} = 2E_{oo} - E_{o,\min} \qquad (8\text{-}52)$$

This should not exceed rated values. The voltage $E_{o,\min}$ is known, because point P is fixed. Thus, a value of E_{oo} can be chosen. The first trial of $E_{o,\max}$ should be somewhat less than the rated value. The value of X_{ii} (E_{CQ}) must now be picked. The $i_o = 0$ curve is used here. If class B operation is desired, then the intersection of the $i_o = 0$ curve with a vertical line drawn through E_{oo} determines the bias X_{iiB}. If class C operation is desired, then a more negative grid voltage should be used. Ordinarily, values of X_{ii} are chosen so that the conduction angle lies between 120 and 150 degrees.[1] Note that the maximum magnitude of the grid voltage occurs when the signal becomes negative and is equal to

$$X_{i,\min} = 2X_{ii} - X_{i,\max} \qquad (8\text{-}53)$$

This should not exceed the peak negative-grid-voltage rating of the vacuum tube. The driver amplifier will have to supply the power dissipated by the grid and the bias circuit. Thus, the grid swing may be limited, so the driver stage will not have to supply large amounts of power. This will affect not only the value of X_{ii}, but also the position of point P. In general, if the maximum value of i_o remains constant, the driving power decreases as $E_{o,\min}$ increases. Once the values of P and Q are chosen, the load power and the input and output dissipation of the device can be determined. If the required power output is obtained without exceeding any ratings, the design is complete. The design can be modified in the following ways if it is unsatisfactory. The output-circuit efficiency can be increased and the dissipation decreased by reducing the conduction angle θ_c and/or $E_{o,\min}$. However, the output power is also decreased if θ_c is decreased, unless the peak output current is increased. Increasing the plate voltage will increase the output power and plate dissipation. If the design is still unsatisfactory, a larger tube will be required. Once the design is complete, the effective resistance of the tank circuit can be obtained from Eq. (8-28). The tank circuit can then be designed using the results of Secs. 6-20 to 6-25 and 8-3. The power dissipated in the tank must be considered in the design.

Vacuum-tube tetrodes and pentodes; beam power tubes

The analyses and designs of circuits using these tubes are similar to those of the vacuum-tube triode. The constant-current characteristics include an additional set of constant screen-grid current characteristics. The screen-grid input power is analyzed in the same way as the control-grid input power is, except that the screen-grid voltage is usually constant, so that its dissipation is the product of the direct screen-grid voltage and the average screen-grid current. The screen-grid voltage is usually chosen to be considerably larger than the maximum control-grid voltage. This limits the control-grid current. Consequently, tetrodes, pentodes, and beam power tubes require less grid-driving power than do vacuum-tube triodes. If a pentode is not used, then the minimum plate voltage must be equal to or greater than the screen-grid voltage. Otherwise, the plate current falls off and the screen-grid current rises greatly because of secondary emission effects. This increases screen dissipation and reduces output power.

Transistor amplifers

The constant-current characteristics of a common-emitter transistor (i_B versus e_C; see Fig. 8-13) are quite horizontal and linear, except at knees which occur at very small values of collector voltage. The operation can be restricted to lie just above this value of e_C. This determines the value of $E_{o,\min}$. (Note: for a p-n-p transistor, the scales of Fig. 8-4 would be negative.) The point P can be chosen at any value of x_i that does not exceed peak base- and collector-current ratings or base-voltage ratings. The driving power, supplied by the preceding stage, increases as $|I_{B,\max}|$ increases. The remainder of the design, including the choice of point Q, is similar to that of the vacuum-tube triode.

8-6   Input bias in class B and class C amplifiers

In vacuum tubes, grid bias is usually not obtained by means of a cathode resistance in class B or class C amplifiers, because the plate current is zero for at least one half-cycle. A separate negative power supply can be used to obtain the bias. However, this is often undesirable. If the grid is driven positive, so that there is grid current, we can obtain the negative bias by means of the circuit of Fig. 8-9a. The grid and cathode of the vacuum tube can be considered to be a vacuum-tube diode. When e_g is positive, the capacitor is charged with the polarity shown. Since grid current can be only in the direction indicated, the capacitor can discharge only through R. The capacitor will not discharge completely, and there will always be a voltage across it which produces a negative grid bias. The average value of this voltage is the direct-grid bias. If R were an open circuit, the capacitor would charge to a voltage of $E_{g,\text{max}}$. Thereafter, e would remain constant at that value. This would provide too much grid bias, since the grid would never again be driven positive. However, R is not an open circuit, and it can be adjusted to obtain the proper grid bias. To design this circuit, compute the Fourier series for the grid current given by Eq. (8-24)

$$i_c = I_{cA} + \sqrt{2}\,(I_{c1} \cos \omega t + I_{c2} \cos 2\omega t + \cdots) \tag{8-54}$$

All of the direct current passes through R; hence,

$$R = \frac{-E_{cQ}}{I_{cA}} \tag{8-55}$$

The value of the capacitor C should be chosen large enough so that it is effectively a short circuit at the signal frequencies.

One advantage of grid-leak bias is that if the value of e_g changes *slightly*, the direct grid bias changes in a way that tends to keep the amplifier operation constant. For instance, if $E_{g,\text{max}}$ is reduced, the value of E_{cQ} becomes

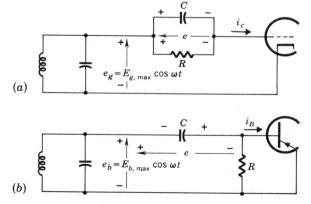

Fig. 8-9 (a) A vacuum-tube grid-leak bias circuit; (b) a transistor input-bias circuit.

less negative. This also is a disadvantage of the circuit. If the exciting signal e_g should become zero (which is a large change), the grid bias also would become zero. This results in large values of plate current and usually causes the plate-dissipation rating to be greatly exceeded. A circuit breaker is sometimes placed in series with the power supply to prevent this. A cathode-bias circuit (R_k shunted by C_k) is at times included. It is designed so that it does not provide substantial bias if the operation is normal. However, should the excitation fail and the plate current increase, the voltage drop across R_k would provide sufficient negative bias to prevent the plate current from becoming excessive.

Cathode bias can be used with class C vacuum-tube amplifiers, even though the plate current is zero for substantial portions of the time, if a large enough bypass capacitor is used. However, a large value of R_k would be required to obtain the bias, and it would have to be in series with the power supply. Thus, cathode bias would be expensive and inefficient.

The two power supplies in the transistor circuit of Fig. 8-1b are not required if the circuit of Fig. 8-9b is used. The operation there is essentially the same as that of Fig. 8-9a. In the case of the transistor, the emitter-base junction performs the same function that the cathode-grid diode does in the vacuum tube. Thus, when e_b is negative, the capacitor C will be charged negatively, as is shown. When e_b becomes less negative than e, the net base-emitter voltage will be positive and the transistor will be cut off. The charge can then leak off the capacitor C through both the high impedance of the transistor and the resistor R. Similar to the case of the vacuum tube, the direct bias can be controlled by varying R.

The circuit of Fig. 8-9b would function in essentially the same way if the resistor R were placed across the capacitor. Then Fig. 8-9a and b would have the same form. Conversely, the resistor R of Fig. 8-9a could be placed across the grid-cathode leads. In the arrangement of Fig. 8-9a, very little signal voltage will appear across the bias resistor. Hence, the circuit of Fig. 8-9a will require less signal power than the circuit of Fig. 8-9b. In Fig. 8-9b, no direct current passes through the signal source. This can be an advantage at times. The circuits of Fig. 8-9a and b are used with either vacuum-tube or transistor circuits. However, the circuit of Fig. 8-9a is more common.

8-7   Neutralization

The neutralization of radio-frequency power amplifiers is essentially the same as the neutralization of small-signal radio-frequency amplifiers, so the discussions and circuits of Sec. 6-26 apply here also. If an amplifier is designed to operate at only one frequency, neutralization usually does not provide too much trouble; hence, radio-frequency power amplifiers are often neutralized vacuum-tube triodes. Vacuum-tube tetrodes and pentodes and

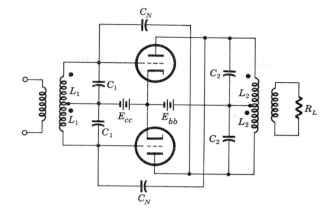

Fig. 8-10 A tuned push-pull vacuum-tube triode amplifier. (A single tuning capacitor can also be used.)

beam power amplifiers rarely require neutralization. Even so, triodes are very often used as high-power amplifiers, because they do not have screen-grid dissipation.

The neutralizing capacitor (see Fig. 6-69) is connected between the input and the output of the amplifier. The difference of potential there may be of the order of tens of kilovolts or more. The capacitor must be able to withstand this voltage without breaking down. Of course, breakdown voltages should be considered whenever components are chosen.

8-8   Push-pull class B and class C amplifiers

Radio-frequency push-pull power amplifiers are constructed in a manner similar to the push-pull circuit of Figs. 7-9 and 7-10 except that the ferromagnetic-core transformers are replaced by tuned circuits. A typical vacuum-tube-triode amplifier is shown in Fig. 8-10. The capacitors C_N are for neutralizing purposes. Since one tube is always cut off, it might appear that the output could be analyzed by considering each tube separately. However, this is not the case, since the two circuits interact in the tank circuit. The amount of this interaction depends upon the coefficient of coupling between the two coils L_2 and also upon the circuit elements. It manifests itself in a change in the effective load impedance.

REFERENCES

[1] F. E. Terman, "Electronic and Radio Engineering," 4th ed., p. 464, McGraw-Hill Book Company, New York, 1955.

BIBLIOGRAPHY

Alley, C. L., and K. W. Atwood, "Electronic Engineering," chap. 12, John Wiley & Sons, Inc., New York, 1962.

Gray, T. S.: "Applied Electronics," 2d ed., pp. 629–652, John Wiley & Sons, Inc., New York, 1954.

Terman, F. E.: "Electronic and Radio Engineering," 4th ed., chap. 13, McGraw-Hill Book Company, New York, 1955.

PROBLEMS

The following problems shall use the two vacuum tubes and the transistor whose characteristics and ratings are supplied. (The ratings have been adjusted for illustrative purposes.)

Type 5671 *vacuum-tube triode.* The ratings of this vacuum tube are: maximum plate voltage 30,000 volts, maximum negative grid voltage −5,000 volts, plate dissipation 25 kilowatts, peak cathode current 50 amp, grid dissipation 2,500 watts. The heater voltage is 11 volts rms, and the heater current is 285 amp rms. The constant-current characteristics are supplied in Fig. 8-11.

Type 6166 *beam power tube.* The ratings of this vacuum tube are: maximum plate voltage 14,000 volts, maximum direct screen-grid voltage 2,000 volts, maximum negative control-grid voltage −2,400 volts, plate dissipation 10 kilowatts, screen-grid dissipation 400 watts, control-grid dissipation 100 watts. The rated filament voltage is 5 volts rms and the filament current is 181 amp rms. The constant-current characteristics are given in Fig. 8-12*a* and *b*. To avoid confusion, the constant plate-current curves are on one characteristic and the constant control- and screen-grid curves are on the other.

Type 2*N*301 *transistor.* The ratings of this transistor are: maximum (negative) collector voltage −40 volts, maximum (negative) base-emitter voltage −20 volts, maximum (negative) collector current −3 amp, collector dissipation 11 watts. An idealized set of constant-collector current and constant base-voltage characteristics are given in Fig. 8-13.

8-1. A type 5671 vacuum-tube triode is connected into the circuit of Fig. 8-1*a*. The values of the voltages are $E_{bb} = 12,500$ volts, $E_{cc} = -1,250$ volts, $e_s = 1,800 \cos \omega t$ volts. The operation is such that the peak plate current is 18 amp. Determine the average values of i_b and i_c, the rms values of the fundamental components of i_b and i_c, the plate dissipation, the grid dissipation, the conduction angle, the plate-circuit efficiency, the effective load resistance, and the power output. Are any ratings exceeded? Assume that $R_s = 0$. What is the efficiency if all the power dissipated in the tube and in the circuit is considered?

8-2. Repeat Prob. 8-1, but now assume that $E_{cc} = -1,000$ volts and that the peak plate current is 30 amp.

8-3. A type 6166 beam power tube is connected into the circuit of Fig. 8-1*a*. The screen grid is connected in the usual way. The values of the circuit voltages are $E_{bb} = 5,000$ volts, $E_{c2Q} = 1,200$ volts, $E_{cc} = -300$ volts,

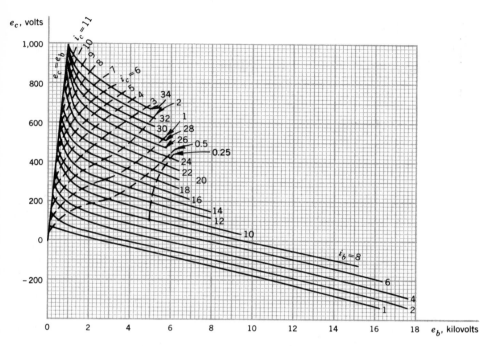

Fig. 8-11   The constant-current characteristics of the type 5671 vacuum-tube triode.
(Courtesy Radio Corporation of America.)   Assume that $i_b = 0$ if $e_b < -40e_c$, where
e_c is negative.

$e_g = 500 \cos \omega t$ volts. The peak tube current is 8 amp. Determine the power output; the average values of i_b, i_{c2}, and i_c; the rms values of the fundamental components of i_b and i_c; the plate dissipation; the screen-grid dissipation; the control-grid dissipation; the conduction angle; and the effective load resistance. Are any ratings exceeded? What should the value of the screen-grid resistance be? Assume that the generator resistance $R_s = 0$.

8-4. Repeat Prob. 8-3, but now assume that $e_g = 600 \cos \omega t$ volts and that the peak tube current is 12 amp.

8-5. A 2N301 transistor is connected into the circuit of Fig. 8-1*b*. The values of R_B and E_{BB} are such that the base current will be zero if $i_s > -20$ ma. Assume that the base current is $i_B = i_s + 20$ ma if $i_s < -20$ ma and $i_B = 0$ if $i_s > -20$ ma. This assumes that i_B cannot be positive (or, equivalently, $I_{CO} = 0$) and that there is no signal current in i_s. The value of E_{CC} is -25 volts and $i_s = 55 \cos \omega t$ ma. Assume that R_s is an open circuit and that C_B acts as a short circuit at the signal frequency. The operation is to be such that the peak collector current is -2 amp. Determine the output power, the average values of i_C and e_B, the rms values of the fundamental components of i_C and e_B, the collector junction dissipation, the emitter junction dissipation, and the effective load resistance. Are any ratings exceeded?

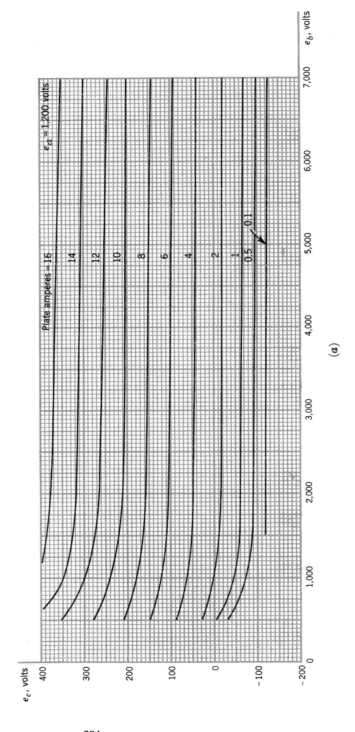

(a)

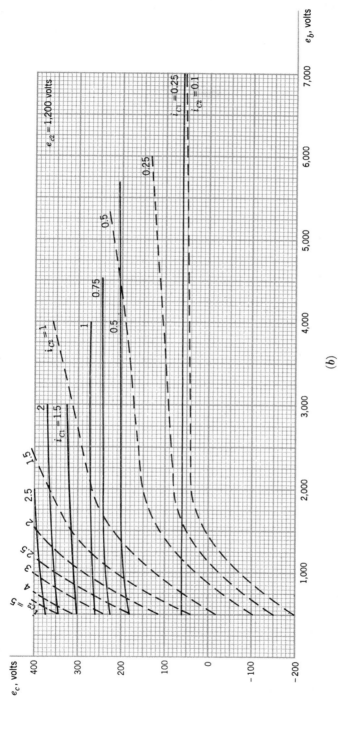

Fig. 8-12 The constant-current characteristics of the type 6166 beam power tube. (Courtesy Radio Corporation of America.) (a) Constant plate-current curves. Assume that $i_b = 0$ if $e_c < -150$ volts. (b) Constant control-grid and screen-grid current curves. Assume that $i_{c2} = 0$ if $e_c < -150$ volts.

385

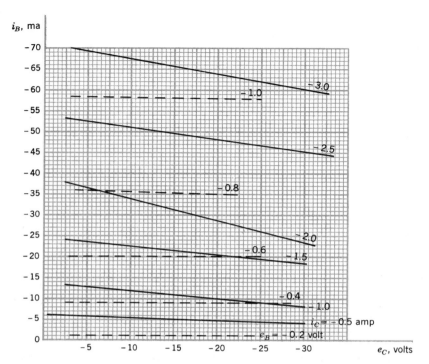

Fig. 8-13 Idealized constant collector-current and constant base-voltage curves for a 2N301 transistor in the common-emitter configuration. Assume that $i_C = 0$ if $i_B = 0$.

8-6. The tank circuit of Fig. 8-6a is to operate at a frequency of 10 Mc/sec. The capacitor C is 50 $\mu\mu$f. The Q of the coil alone is 300. If the efficiency of the tank circuit is to be greater than 90 percent, what is the maximum value of R_L?

8-7. The tank circuit of Fig. 8-7a is to operate at a frequency of 10 Mc/sec. The capacitor C is 50 $\mu\mu$f and the Q of L_1 alone is 300. $R_L = 50$ ohms. Assume that $R_2 \ll R_L$. The efficiency of the tank circuit is to be 90 percent or more. Compute the minimum value of the mutual inductance. If the coefficient of coupling between the two coils is 0.8 ($k = M/\sqrt{L_1 L_2}$), what is the minimum value of L_2?

8-8. The input resistance of the tank circuit of Fig. 8-7a is to be 4,000 ohms at 10 Mc/sec. The value of R_L is 50 ohms and the efficiency of the tank circuit is to be equal to or greater than 90 percent. The Q of L_1 alone is 300. Design the tank circuit. Neglect R_2. Assume that the coefficient of coupling of the coils is 0.8 ($k = M/\sqrt{L_1 L_2}$).

8-9. Repeat Prob. 8-8, but now assume that $R_2 = 2$ ohms.

8-10. Consider the design of Prob. 8-8, but now assume that $C \geqslant 500$ $\mu\mu$f. What is the maximum efficiency that can be obtained?

8-11. Design a class C amplifier using a type 5671 vacuum-tube triode to meet the following specifications: $E_{bb} = 15,000$ volts, output power 36,000 watts, and R_L = 50 ohms. Determine the values of E_{cc}, e_g, the power supplied by e_g, and the elements of the tank circuit. R_s = 0 (see Fig. 8-1*a*). The tank circuit of Fig. 8-7*a* is to be used. Assume that the Q of the primary coil alone is 300, R_2 = 1 ohm, and the minimum value of C is 50 $\mu\mu$f. The frequency of operation is 10 Mc/sec. Verify that no ratings have been exceeded. What is the conduction angle?

8-12. Redesign the amplifier of Prob. 8-11 to obtain the maximum output power without exceeding ratings.

8-13. Design a class C amplifier using a type 6166 beam power tube to meet the following specifications: E_{bb} = 6,500 volts, E_{c2Q} = 1,200 volts, output power 11,000 watts, and R_L = 50 ohms. Use the tank circuit of Fig. 8-7*a*. Assume that it has an efficiency of 90 percent. Determine the values of E_{cc}, e_g, and the power supplied by e_g. R_s = 0 (see Fig. 8-1*a*). What is the conduction angle? Verify that no ratings have been exceeded.

8-14. Redesign the amplifier of Prob. 8-13 to obtain the maximum output power without exceeding ratings.

8-15. Design a class C amplifier using a type 2N301 transistor that is to meet the following specifications: E_{CC} = −15 volts, output power 7 watts, and R_L = 50 ohms. Assume that R_s is an open circuit (see Fig. 8-1*b*), that $i_B = i_s + I_o$ when $i_s < -I_o$, and that $i_B = 0$ when $i_s > -I_o$ (see Prob. 8-5 and Fig. 8-1). Determine I_o, i_s, and the power supplied by i_s. Use the tank circuit of Fig. 8-7 and assume that it is ideal.

8-16. Redesign the amplifier of Prob. 8-15 to obtain the maximum output power without exceeding ratings.

8-17. Assume that the amplifier of Prob. 8-1 obtains its grid bias by means of a grid-leak circuit. If e_s were to become zero, what would the plate current and plate dissipation become? Assume that the tank circuit has zero resistance for direct current.

Introduction to Signal-flow Graphs

In this chapter, we shall introduce a diagrammatic procedure for representing and evaluating a set of linear simultaneous equations, such as those found in linear amplifier problems. These representations are called *signal-flow graphs*, or *signal-flow diagrams*.[1,2] They help in the study of general network configurations as well as in the solution of specific network problems. The signal-flow graph will be introduced here with some simple techniques for its construction and analysis. The bibliography at the end of this chapter contains much additional reference material.

9-1 Definition of a signal-flow graph and its relation to a block diagram

Many times in the discussion of amplifiers it is convenient to reduce their representations to *block diagrams*. That is, the amplifier is represented

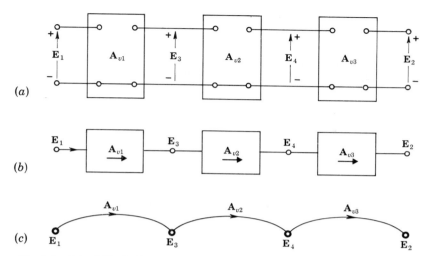

Fig. 9-1   (*a*) *A block-diagram representation of a cascade of voltage amplifiers;* (*b*) *a simplified block-diagram representation; and* (*c*) *a signal-flow-graph representation.*

simply by a set of blocks which are labeled with specific gains.   For instance, consider the cascade of three amplifier stages shown in Fig. 9-1*a*.   The voltage gains of the three stages are A_{v1}, A_{v2}, and A_{v3}, when they are connected as shown.   Thus, the overall voltage gain is

$$A_v = \frac{E_2}{E_1} = A_{v1}A_{v2}A_{v3} \qquad (9\text{-}1)$$

A_{v1}, A_{v2}, and A_{v3} could be any of the appropriate gain expressions of Chap. 6. The blocks could also represent more complex amplifier stages.   Block diagrams are thus a convenient method of representing the performance of a complex amplifier without obscuring the details with a large number of circuit elements.   There is no need to draw the two wires.   For instance, the block diagram of Fig. 9-1*b* conveys the same information as Fig. 9-1*a*.   The arrows indicate the direction of the transmission of the signal.   For instance

$$E_3 = A_{v1}E_1 \qquad (9\text{-}2)$$

but

$$E_1 \neq A_{v1}E_3 \qquad (9\text{-}3)$$

For convenience, block diagrams should be as simple as is possible.   Figure 9-1*c* conveys all the information of Fig. 9-1*a* or *b* in an abbreviated form. This representation is called a signal-flow graph.   A block diagram of a more complex amplifier structure is shown in Fig. 9-2*a*.   This is called a *feedback amplifier*, since a portion of the output signal is fed back to the input.   These amplifiers will be discussed in great detail in the next chapter.

The plus sign in the circle of Fig. 9-2a is called a *summing point*, wherein the output voltage (or current) is the sum of the applied voltages (or currents). The voltages are all indicated in the diagram. The signal-flow-graph representation is shown in Fig. 9-2b. In each case

$$\mathbf{E}_2 = \mathbf{A}_v(\mathbf{E}_1 + \beta\mathbf{E}_2)$$

or

$$\frac{\mathbf{E}_2}{\mathbf{E}_1} = \frac{\mathbf{A}_v}{1 - \mathbf{A}_v\beta} \tag{9-4}$$

The significance of this relation will be discussed in the next chapter.

Thus far we have presented some simple signal-flow graphs. Let us now formalize the representation so that procedures for evaluating complex networks can be developed. We shall use the signal-flow diagram of Fig. 9-3 in this discussion. The small circles are called *nodes*. These are given *node values* that represent the variables of the system. For instance, y_0, x_1, x_2, and x_3 could represent voltages and/or currents. The signal-flow graph can be used to represent any set of simultaneous equations; hence, the node values can represent any set of variables. The line segments are called *branches*. They are given a direction by the arrows and are sometimes called *directed branches*. Each branch is assigned a value a_{ij} called the *branch gain*, or the *branch transmittance*. The *output end of a branch* is the end of the branch towards which the arrow points. The *input end of a branch* is the other end. The *signal transmission* along a branch is defined as the product of the node value at the input end of a branch times the branch transmittance. A branch is said to *enter*, or to be *incident* on, a node if it is connected to the node and its arrow points towards the node. It is said to *leave* the node if it is connected to the node and its arrow points away from the node.

To write the equations of a signal-flow graph, we use the following rule: *Any node value is equal to the sum of all the signal transmissions of all the*

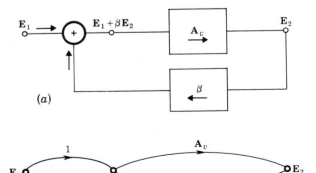

(a)

(b)

Fig. 9-2   A simple feed-back amplifier.   (a) Block-diagram representation; and (b) signal-flow-graph representation.

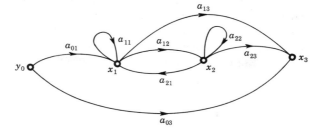

Fig. 9-3 A signal-flow graph.

branches incident on the node. For instance, in Fig. 9-3

$$x_1 = a_{01}y_0 + a_{11}x_1 + a_{21}x_2 + 0x_3$$
$$x_2 = 0y_0 + a_{12}x_1 + a_{22}x_2 + 0x_3 \qquad (9\text{-}5)$$
$$x_3 = a_{03}y_0 + a_{13}x_1 + a_{23}x_2 + 0x_3$$

Note that a branch, such as a_{11} or a_{22}, can be connected from a node to itself. However, it is treated as any other branch.

If no branches enter a node, then that node is called a *source node*, or simply a *source*. Node y_0 is a source. It represents an independent variable. If the signal-flow graph represents a set of network equations, then the source nodes represent the independent driving generators. If a node has no branches leaving it, then it is called a *sink node* or simply a *sink*. Node x_3 of Fig. 9-3 is a sink.

Equations (9-5) represent a set of linear simultaneous equations. To obtain a form that can be readily solved by determinants, they should be rearranged as follows

$$-a_{01}y_0 = (a_{11} - 1)x_1 + a_{21}x_2 + 0x_3$$
$$0 = a_{21}x_1 + (a_{22} - 1)x_2 + 0x_3 \qquad (9\text{-}6)$$
$$-a_{03}y_0 = a_{13}x_1 + a_{23}x_2 - x_3$$

The quantity y_0 is considered to be known. In this way, a set of simultaneous equations can be written for any signal-flow graph, and all variables can be obtained in terms of the driving function and the branch transmittances.

9-2   Method for obtaining a signal-flow graph from a set of simultaneous equations

In the last section it was demonstrated that a set of simultaneous equations could be written for a signal-flow graph. Let us now consider the inverse procedure and obtain the signal-flow graph that represents a set of simultaneous equations.   For instance, consider

$$y_1 = b_{11}x_1 + b_{12}x_2 + b_{13}x_3$$
$$y_2 = b_{21}x_1 + b_{22}x_2 + b_{23}x_3 \qquad (9\text{-}7)$$
$$y_3 = b_{31}x_1 + b_{32}x_2 + b_{33}x_3$$

We would like to convert this into the form of Eqs. (9-5).   This can be done quite simply by adding x_1 to each side of the first equation, x_2 to each side of the second equation, etc., and by bringing the known quantities over to the right-hand side.   Thus,

$$x_1 = -y_1 + (b_{11} + 1)x_1 + b_{12}x_2 + b_{13}x_3$$
$$x_2 = -y_2 + b_{21}x_1 + (b_{22} + 1)x_2 + b_{23}x_3 \qquad (9\text{-}8)$$
$$x_3 = -y_3 + b_{31}x_1 + b_{32}x_2 + (b_{33} + 1)x_3$$

The signal-flow graph can now be drawn.   The node values are y_1, y_2, y_3, x_1, x_2, and x_3.   The coefficients on the right-hand side of the first equation yield the branch transmittance of the branches incident on node x_1.   Similarly, the second equation yields the branch transmittances of the branches incident on node x_2, etc.   Thus, the signal-flow graph for the set of simultaneous equations of Eqs. (9-7) is given in Fig. 9-4.   There are three independent quantities y_1, y_2, and y_3 and thus three source nodes.   (Note that the order of the subscripts of the branch transmittances of Fig. 9-4 is different from that of Fig. 9-3.)   In amplifier theory, there is usually only one independent generator y_0 and we can write

$$y_1 = k_1y_0$$
$$y_2 = k_2y_0 \qquad (9\text{-}9)$$
$$y_3 = k_3y_0$$

In this case, the three nodes y_1, y_2, and y_3 can be replaced by a single node y_0 as shown in Fig. 9-5.   We have demonstrated these techniques with a

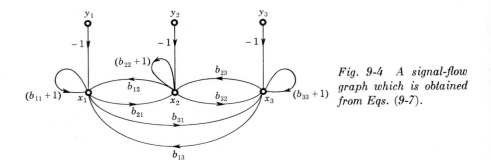

Fig. 9-4   *A signal-flow graph which is obtained from Eqs. (9-7).*

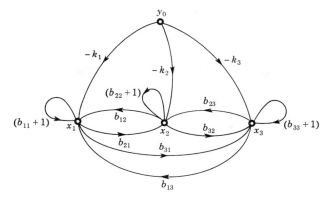

Fig. 9-5 *A modification of Fig. 9-4 which can be used when there is only one independent generator.*

set of third-order simultaneous equations. However, the same procedures would be used for simultaneous equations of any order.

9-3 Some elementary simplifications of signal-flow graphs

In this section we shall consider some techniques of simplifying a signal-flow graph without altering the relations among any of the variables. We shall use a set of signal-flow-graph equations similar to Eqs. (9-5) in our discussion:

$$x_1 = a_{01}y_0 + a_{11}x_1 + a_{21}x_2 + \cdots + a_{n1}x_n$$
$$x_2 = a_{02}y_0 + a_{12}x_1 + a_{22}x_2 + \cdots + a_{n2}x_n$$
$$\cdots \cdots \cdots \cdots \cdots \cdots \cdots \cdots \cdots \cdots \cdots \cdots \cdots \cdots$$
$$x_n = a_{0n}y_0 + a_{1n}x_1 + a_{2n}x_2 + \cdots + a_{nn}x_n$$

$$(9\text{-}10)$$

where it is assumed that there is only one independent source, y_0. (Note that this assumption is not necessary to obtain the results of this section.) The branches incident on a node affect only the equation for that node (for example, a_{02}, a_{12}, a_{22} $\cdots$ a_{n2} are the only branches that affect the value of x_2). Thus, we can make the following simplifications, which are illustrated in Fig. 9-6:

Combination of two parallel branches

If two or more branches are connected from node x_i to node x_j and *all* are incident on x_j, then they can be replaced by a single branch whose transmittance is the sum of the transmittances of the individual branches. For instance, in Fig. 9-6a this is true since $a_{ij1}x_i + a_{ij2}x_i = (a_{ij1} + a_{ij2})x_i$ and the transmittances a_{ij1} and a_{ij2} only appear in the equation for x_j [see Eqs. (9-10)]. Note that the branch from node x_j to node x_i is not included here.

Elimination of a self-loop

A branch that starts and ends on the same node is called a *self-loop*. For instance, branches a_{11} and a_{22} of Fig. 9-3 are self-loops. We shall see in the next section that it is often desirable to have a signal-flow graph that does not contain such loops. They can be eliminated without altering any of the variables by the following procedure. Consider Eqs. (9-10); solve the jth equation for x_j by bringing the $a_{jj}x_j$ term to the left-hand side. Thus,

$$x_j = \frac{a_{0j}}{1 - a_{jj}} y_{01} + \frac{a_{1j}}{1 - a_{jj}} x_1 + \cdots + \frac{a_{j-1,j}}{1 - a_{jj}} x_{j-1}$$
$$+ 0x_j + \frac{a_{j+1,j}}{1 - a_{jj}} x_{j+1} + \cdots + \frac{a_{nj}}{1 - a_{jj}} x_n \quad (9\text{-}11)$$

where we have assumed that

$$a_{jj} \neq 1 \tag{9-12}$$

Equation (9-11) could replace the equation for x_j in Eqs. (9-10). This would still represent a valid set of equations for all the variables even though the signal-flow graph has been changed. (Note that the jth equation has only been rearranged.) However, x_j no longer has a self-loop, since the coefficient of x_j on the right-hand side of the equation is now zero. *Only those branches of the signal-flow graph that are incident on x_j will be changed.* They will be multiplied by $1/(1 - a_{jj})$. All the other branches are unchanged. Thus, the equivalency indicated in Fig. 9-6b is valid. By repeating this procedure at each node in turn, all the self-loops can be eliminated. This procedure breaks down if $a_{jj} = 1$, since $1/(1 - a_{jj})$ becomes infinite. In the type of network that we shall consider, this is not usually a problem. Consider Eqs. (9-7) and (9-8). If $a_{jj} = 1$, then $b_{jj} = 0$. If Eqs. (9-7) represent a set of mesh or nodal equations, then b_{jj} represents the sum of the impedances around a mesh or the sum of all the admittances connected to a node. In most practical problems, these are not zero. In the next section, a procedure that may cause some of the a_{jj}'s to become equal to unity will be considered. However, we shall see that this will cause no problem in any practical case.

Node splitting

There are times when it is convenient to represent all nodes as sources or sinks. This can be done simply by splitting each node into two nodes, one with all the incident branches and the other with the remaining branches. This has been done in the portion of the flow graph of Fig. 9-6c. In the second diagram, the node x_j has been split into two nodes, both with the same variable. Thus Eqs. (9-10) will be unaffected by the splitting of the

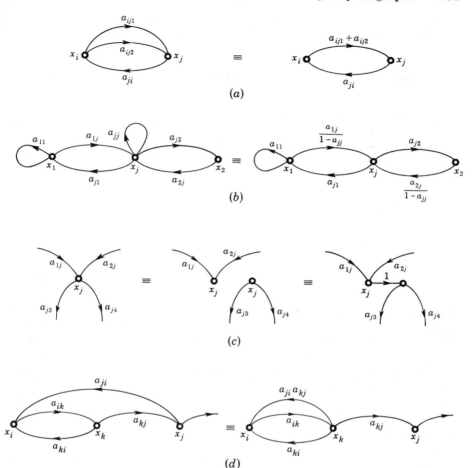

Fig. 9-6   *Techniques for the modification of signal-flow graphs which do not change the values of any of the variables.*   *(a) Elimination of parallel branches; (b) elimination of self-loops; (c) node splitting; and (d) shift of the input end of a branch.*

node. The value of x_j remains unchanged because the branches incident upon it are unchanged. The signal transmission from node x_j is unchanged, since we have made the value of the second node equal to x_j. The third network of Fig. 9-6c accomplishes this by means of a branch of unity transmittance.

Shift of the input end of a branch

If the input end of a branch is shifted from one node to another and this does not change the *product* of its branch transmittance and input-node value, then the node values of the signal-flow graph will be unchanged. In

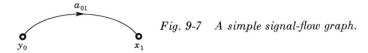

Fig. 9-7   A simple signal-flow graph.

general, this procedure will require changing the branch transmittance. Consider Fig. 9-6d.   The signal transmission along one branch incident on node x_i is $a_{ji}x_j$.   However, $x_j = a_{kj}x_k$.   Thus, we can shift the input end of the branch to x_k provided that the branch transmittance is changed to $a_{ji}a_{kj}$. In both cases the signal transmission is $a_{ji}x_j = a_{ji}a_{kj}x_k$.   If another branch were incident on node x_j, then we could not express x_j in terms of x_k alone and this procedure could not be used.   Note that the two branches incident on node x_i can be combined by the procedure of Fig. 9-6a.

9-4   Reduction of signal-flow graphs

In most amplifier applications, the output voltage or current in response to an input signal is to be determined.   Hence only one of the unknowns in a set of mesh or nodal equations need be found.   Similarly, when signal-flow graphs are considered, we wish to calculate only one of the node values in terms of the independent generators.   Assume that there is only one independent generator, so that a signal-flow graph similar to that of Fig. 9-5 results.   If the signal-flow graph consisted of only two nodes and one branch as shown in Fig. 9-7, then the desired solution could be obtained by inspection.

$$x_1 = a_{01}y_0 \tag{9-13}$$

The procedure to be developed next will eliminate a node of a dependent variable from the signal-flow graph without changing the value of any of the other variables.   Successive applications of this procedure will produce a signal-flow graph of the form of Fig. 9-7, and the problem will be solved. We shall assume that the node to be removed does not have a self-loop. If it does, it can be eliminated by the procedure of Sec. 9-3.

The procedure for eliminating a node is called *node pulling* and can be done as follows.   Choose the equation for the node in question from the signal-flow graph equations [Eqs. (9-10)].   If node x_j is to be eliminated, write

$$x_j = a_{0j}y_{01} + a_{1j}x_1 + \cdots + a_{j-1,j}x_{j-1} + 0x_j + a_{j+1,j}x_{j+1}$$
$$+ \cdots + a_{nj}x_n \tag{9-14}$$

Now use this equation to eliminate x_j from all the other equations.   For instance, for $h \neq j$

$$x_h = a_{0h}y_0 + a_{1h}x_1 + a_{2h}x_2 + \cdots + a_{jh}x_j + \cdots + a_{nh}x_n \tag{9-15}$$

or

$$x_h = a_{0h}y_0 + \sum_{k=1}^{n} a_{kh}x_k \tag{9-16}$$

Substituting Eq. (9-14), we obtain

$$x_h = (a_{0h} + a_{0j}a_{jh})y_0 + \sum_{\substack{k=1 \\ k \neq j}}^{n} (a_{kh} + a_{kj}a_{jh})x_k \tag{9-17}$$

If we repeat this operation for $h = 1, 2, \ldots, j-1, j+1, \ldots n$, then the variable x_j will be eliminated from the equations and a new signal-flow graph can be drawn with one less node.

Let us determine the significance of Eq. (9-17). Consider the transmittance from node x_r to node x_h. The original transmittance a_{rh} is still present, but the transmittance $a_{rj}a_{jh}$ has been added. This can be considered to be the transmittance from node x_r to node x_h through node x_j. For instance, consider the simple signal-flow graph of Fig. 9-8a. The node x_2 can be eliminated simply by adding $a_{12}a_{23}$ to the transmittance of the branch from node 1 to node 3 (see Fig. 9-8b). In general, a node is eliminated by replacing it by branches which supply the branch transmittances of all possible transmission paths through the node. A transmission path through a node consists of one branch entering and one branch leaving the node. A signal-flow graph more complex than the previous one is shown in Fig. 9-8c. The resultant signal-flow graph with node x_2 eliminated is shown in Fig. 9-8d. Although the node that is removed cannot have a self-loop, all of the other nodes can. In fact, self-loops can be created by this procedure. The node-pulling technique can be applied to each node in turn. Of course, any self-loops must be eliminated by the procedure of Sec. 9-3 before this can be done. If any of the transmittances of a self-loop are unity, then that procedure will not work. (Node pulling can cause unity self-loops.) Two things can be done in this case. The first is to eliminate other nodes, if possible. This may change the value of the self-loop. The second is to rearrange the original simultaneous equations by renumbering the variables and rearranging the equations. It can be shown[3] that if the original system of simul-

Fig. 9-8   (a) A simple three-node signal-flow graph; (b) the equivalent signal-flow graph with one node eliminated; (c) a more complex signal-flow graph; and (d) the elimination of node x_2 of this signal-flow graph.

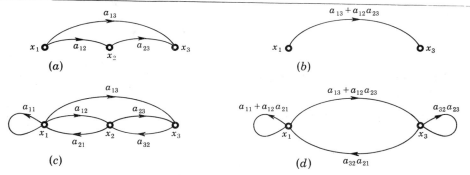

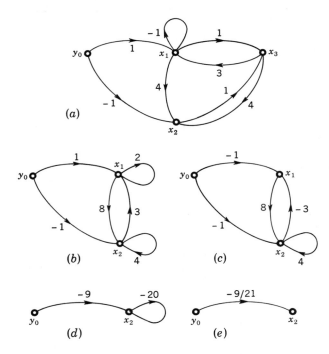

Fig. 9-9   An illustration of the reduction of a signal-flow graph. (a) The signal-flow graph; (b) node x_3 removed; (c) the self-loop of node x_1 removed; (d) node x_1 removed; and (e) the self-loop of node x_2 removed.

taneous equations is linearly independent, then the branch transmissions of the self-loops always can be made not equal to unity by such a procedure.

Now let us consider an example of node pulling. We wish to obtain x_2 in terms of y_0 and the branch transmittances for the signal-flow graph of Fig. 9-9a. Since node x_3 has no self-loop, it is eliminated first. This is shown in Fig. 9-9b, where 1×3 is added to the self-loop of node x_1, 1×4 is added to the branch transmittance from node x_1 to x_2, 1×3 is added to the branch transmittance from node x_2 to x_1, and a self-loop of transmittance 1×4 is added to node x_2. The self-loop at node x_1 is removed in Fig. 9-9c by multiplying the transmission of all the branches incident on node x_1 by $1/(1 - 2) = -1$. Node x_1 is eliminated in Fig. 9-9d. Finally, to solve the problem, the self-loop is eliminated from node x_2. The reduced network is shown in Fig. 9-9e, and the solution is

$$x_2 = -(\tfrac{9}{21})y_0 \tag{9-18}$$

Thus, it can be seen that signal-flow graphs provide a systematic means of representing and solving electric network problems.

REFERENCES

[1] S. J. Mason, Feedback Theory: Some Properties of Signal Flow Graphs, *Proc. IRE*, vol. 41, pp. 1144–1156, 1953.

[2] S. J. Mason, Feedback Theory: Further Properties of Signal Flow Graphs, *Proc. IRE*, vol. 44, pp. 920–926, 1956.
[3] S. Seshu and N. Balabanian, "Linear Network Analysis," p. 415, John Wiley & Sons, Inc., New York, 1959.

BIBLIOGRAPHY

Mason, S. J.: Feedback Theory: Some Properties of Signal Flow Graphs, *Proc. IRE*, vol. 41, pp. 1144–1156, 1953.

Mason, S. J.: Feedback Theory: Further Properties of Signal Flow Graphs, *Proc. IRE*, vol. 44, pp. 920–926, 1956.

Mason, S. J., and H. J. Zimmerman: "Electronic Circuits, Signals, and Systems," chaps. 4 and 5, John Wiley & Sons, Inc., New York, 1960.

Peskin, E.: "Transient and Steady State Analysis of Electric Networks," chap. 8, D. Van Nostrand Company, Inc., Princeton, N.J., 1961.

Seshu, S., and N. Balabanian: "Linear Network Analysis," pp. 407–425, John Wiley & Sons, Inc., New York, 1959.

Truxal, J. G.: "Automatic Feedback Control System Synthesis," pp. 88–113, McGraw-Hill Book Company, New York, 1955.

PROBLEMS

9-1. Obtain the signal-flow graph which represents the equations.

$$x_1 = y_0 + 2x_1 + 3x_2 + x_3$$
$$x_2 = 2y_0 + x_1 + 7x_2 + 9x_3$$
$$x_3 = -y_0 - x_1 - x_2 + 4x_3$$

9-2. Obtain a set of equations which characterize the signal-flow graph of Fig. 9-10. The equations should be in a form suitable for solution by determinants. Assume that y_0 is known.

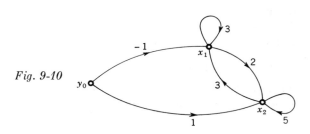

Fig. 9-10

9-3. Repeat Prob. 9-2 for the signal-flow graph of Fig. 9-11.

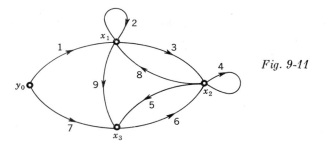

Fig. 9-11

9-4. Obtain a signal-flow graph which represents the linear simultaneous equations

$$y_0 = 3x_1 + 2x_2$$
$$-2y_0 = 2x_1 + x_2$$

9-5. Obtain a signal-flow graph which represents the linear simultaneous equations

$$y_0 = x_1 + x_2 + x_3$$
$$0 = x_1 - 2x_2 + x_3$$
$$-y_0 = x_1 + x_2 - 3x_3$$

9-6. Eliminate all the parallel branches from the signal-flow graph of Fig. 9-12.

9-7. Eliminate all the self-loops from the signal-flow graph of Fig. 9-12.

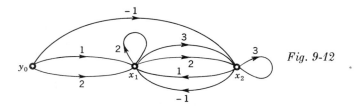

Fig. 9-12

9-8. Repeat Prob. 9-7 for the signal-flow graph of Fig. 9-11.

9-9. Use signal-flow-graph reduction techniques to solve the simultaneous equations of Prob. 9-5 for x_2.   Assume that y_0 is known.

9-10. Use node-pulling techniques to obtain x_2 in terms of y_0 for the signal-flow graph of Fig. 9-10.

9-11. Repeat Prob. 9-10, but now assume that the branch transmittance between node y_0 and node x_1 is $+1$.

9-12. Repeat Prob. 9-10 for the signal-flow graph of Fig. 9-11.

Feedback Amplifiers

![chapter number 10]

If a signal at the output of any stage of an amplifier affects its earlier stages, then the complete circuit is called a *feedback amplifier*. The process of returning the signal to an earlier stage is called *feedback*. We have thus far considered the disadvantages of feedback in such things as the Miller effect in vacuum-tube-triode and transistor amplifiers. However, there are many times when feedback is deliberately introduced and substantial benefits result. In fact, many amplifier applications depend upon feedback for their success. For example, feedback can reduce nonlinear distortion and some undesirable signals and can eliminate much of the variation of gain caused by changes in the parameters of vacuum tubes or transistors. In this chapter we shall use signal-flow graphs to study the general concepts of feedback. In addition, we shall develop techniques for analyzing specific feedback amplifiers. Equivalent circuits will be used here.

10-1. Basic principles of feedback amplifiers

A typical feedback amplifier is characterized by the signal-flow diagram of Fig. 10-1. The variables X_1, X_2, and X_3 can represent voltages and/or

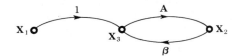

Fig. 10-1 A signal-flow-graph representation of a simple feedback amplifier.

currents. (A block diagram of this type of feedback system is shown in Fig. 9-2a.) X_1 represents the input signal; X_2 represents the output signal. The gain of the amplifier without feedback is A, and β represents the fraction of the output signal that is returned to the input. (Note that the conventional notation is conflicting; β as used in this chapter is *not* the short-circuit current gain of the common-emitter transistor amplifier.) Thus, the signal at the input of the amplifier is

$$X_3 = X_1 + \beta X_2 \tag{10-1}$$

In addition,

$$X_2 = AX_3 \tag{10-2}$$

Eliminating X_3, we obtain

$$X_2 = X_1 \frac{A}{1 - A\beta} \tag{10-3}$$

We shall define the gain K of the amplifier in the usual way as X_2/X_1. Hence,

$$K = \frac{A}{1 - A\beta} \tag{10-4}$$

Note that there are two gains to be considered. A is the gain of the amplifier alone without feedback, while K is the gain of the entire feedback amplifier. Many times, the feedback network, which we shall call the β *network*, is simply a resistive voltage or current divider. In this case, β will be a real positive number. For much of the useful frequency range, A may be a real negative number. Let us consider Eq. (10-4), assuming that we have such an amplifier. If

$$|A\beta| \gg 1 \tag{10-5}$$

then we can approximate K as

$$K \approx -\frac{1}{\beta} \tag{10-6}$$

If β is a purely resistive network, then the gain of the amplifier seems to be constant, independent of all the parameters of the active elements (e.g., the vacuum tubes or the transistors) and independent of frequency. This would be ideal in that there would be no frequency distortion or nonlinear distortion. (Nonlinear distortion can be considered to be a variation of the parameters of the active elements with signal level.) Also the gain would not change as the active elements aged.   However, the amplifier is not completely free of distortion or variation in gain, since Eq. (10-6) is only approximate.   In addition, if $|A|$ falls off for any reason such as the presence of frequency distortion or because of aging of the active elements, then the inequality of relation (10-5) may no longer be valid so that Eq. (10-6) may no longer apply. However, in a well-designed feedback amplifier, the dependence of the amplification upon the characteristics of the active elements can be greatly reduced. We shall study all of these effects in great detail subsequently.

If $\mathbf{A}$ is a real negative number, β is a real positive number, and $-A\beta \gg 1$, then $-A \gg 1/\beta$.   Thus, the introduction of this type of feedback reduces the overall gain of the amplifier [see Eq. (10-6)].   For this reason, a feedback amplifier may have more stages than a nonfeedback amplifier that has the same gain.   Usually, this is a small price to pay for the advantages of feedback.   The type of feedback that we have been discussing is called *negative feedback*, because the signal $\mathbf{X}_2\beta$ is 180° out of phase with the input signal $\mathbf{X}_1$.   Thus, $\mathbf{X}_3$, the signal at the input to the amplifier portion of the feedback amplifier, is actually the difference between two signals.   This can be seen from Eq. (10-1).   In general, $|\mathbf{X}_1| > |\mathbf{X}_2\beta|$.   We can now physically see why the gain of the feedback amplifier can be almost independent of $\mathbf{A}$. Suppose that $|A|$ increases, then $|X_3|$ will decrease, because the signal subtracted from $\mathbf{X}_1$ will increase.   This tends to counteract the effect of the increase in $|A|$ and to stabilize the gain.

Let us now consider a somewhat different amplifier.   Assume that both $\mathbf{A}$ and β are real positive numbers and that $A\beta < 1$.   Then, Eq. (10-4) shows that $|K| > |A|$.   Thus, we have actually increased the gain by the introduction of feedback.   This is called *positive feedback*, since the signal $\mathbf{X}_2\beta$ is in phase with $\mathbf{X}_1$.   At first glance, positive feedback may appear to be quite attractive, since it results in an increased gain.   However, it is very rarely used in amplifiers for two reasons.   First, the advantages gained when negative feedback is used become disadvantages.   That is, the distortion and the dependence of the gain of the amplifier upon the parameters of the active elements are greater than they are in the nonfeedback case.   Second, positive-feedback amplifiers have a tendency to oscillate, which renders them useless as amplifiers.

In the discussion of negative and positive feedback, we neglected the variation of the phase shift of $\mathbf{A}$ or β with frequency.   Because of this, true negative or positive feedback amplifiers do not exist.   In fact, the feedback can be negative at some frequencies and positive at others.   We shall discuss this in greater detail when Nyquist plots are considered.

Feedback can be classified as *voltage feedback* or *current feedback*.   In voltage feedback, the signal fed back (which can be either a voltage or a current) is proportional to the output voltage.   In current feedback, the signal fed back is proportional to the output current.   If voltage-negative feedback is used, the output voltage of the amplifier tends to become independent of the value of $\mathbf{A}$, while current-negative feedback tends to stabilize the value of the output current.

The effects that have been presented qualitatively here will be discussed quantitatively in subsequent sections.

10-2   Analysis of some very simple feedback amplifiers

Before proceeding with a general discussion of feedback amplifiers, let us study some very simple ones. Consider the vacuum-tube amplifier of Fig. 10-2. Equation (10-4) will be used here to obtain the amplification. We will assume that the capacitor C_k is a short circuit at the signal frequency. The gain without feedback is that which would be obtained if the wire from a to b were broken and the dotted connection were made. In this case

$$\mathbf{A} = \frac{\mathbf{E}_2}{\mathbf{E}_3} = -g_m R_{sh} \tag{10-7}$$

where

$$R_{sh} = \frac{r_p(R_1 + R_2)}{r_p + R_1 + R_2} \tag{10-8}$$

This is a voltage-feedback amplifier, since $\mathbf{E}_3 = \mathbf{E}_1 + \mathbf{E}_2 R_2/(R_1 + R_2)$. The value of β is defined in Eq. (10-1). Thus

$$\beta = \frac{R_2}{R_1 + R_2} \tag{10-9}$$

Hence, using Eq. (10-4)

$$\mathbf{K} = \mathbf{E}_2/\mathbf{E}_1 = \frac{-g_m R_{sh}}{1 + g_m R_{sh} R_2/(R_1 + R_2)} \tag{10-10}$$

If

$$g_m R_{sh} R_2/(R_1 + R_2) \gg 1 \tag{10-11}$$

then

$$\mathbf{K} \approx -\frac{R_1 + R_2}{R_2} \tag{10-12}$$

This agrees with the discussion of Sec. 10-1. This example seems to indicate that Eq. (10-4) will be quite useful in the analysis of specific amplifier circuits. *Actually, this is not the case. In all but the simplest amplifier cir-*

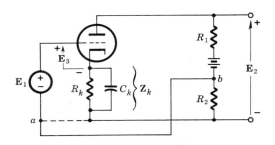

Fig. 10-2 A simple vacuum-tube feedback amplifier.

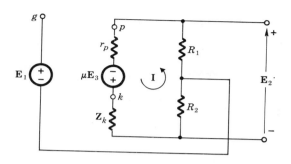

Fig. 10-3 An equivalent circuit for the amplifier of Fig. 10-2.

cuits, $\mathbf{A}/(1 - \mathbf{A}\beta)$ *cannot be used to obtain expressions for the gain.* For instance, if $\mathbf{A} = 0$ because the g_m of the tube becomes zero, then Eq. (10-4) predicts that $\mathbf{K} = 0$. However, if there is *direct transmission* between the input and output (through a feedback network) the gain $\mathbf{K}$ will not become zero even if $\mathbf{A}$ does. A direct transmission path would occur in Fig. 10-2 if the grid-to-plate capacitance were considered. Let us consider another case where this example breaks down. If C_k is not considered to be a short circuit, then there will be an additional feedback term. That is, the voltage drop across $\mathbf{Z}_k = R_k/(1 + j\omega C_k R_k)$ will affect $\mathbf{E}_3$. To obtain the gain of this circuit, we shall use the equivalent circuit of Fig. 10-3.

$$\mathbf{E}_g = \mathbf{E}_3 = \mathbf{E}_1 - \mathbf{I}(R_2 + \mathbf{Z}_k) \tag{10-13}$$

$$\mu \mathbf{E}_3 = \mathbf{I}(r_p + \mathbf{Z}_k + R_1 + R_2) \tag{10-14}$$

and

$$\mathbf{E}_2 = -\mathbf{I}(R_1 + R_2)$$

Then, solving, we obtain

$$\mathbf{K} = \frac{-\mu(R_1 + R_2)}{r_p + \mathbf{Z}_k + R_1 + R_2 + \mu(\mathbf{Z}_k + R_2)} \tag{10-15}$$

Manipulating, we have

$$\mathbf{K} = \frac{-\mu(R_1 + R_2)/(r_p + \mathbf{Z}_k + R_1 + R_2)}{1 + \mu(\mathbf{Z}_k + R_2)/(r_p + \mathbf{Z}_k + R_1 + R_2)} \tag{10-16}$$

If

$$\mu(\mathbf{Z}_k + R_2)/(r_p + \mathbf{Z}_k + R_1 + R_2) \gg 1$$

$$\mathbf{K} \approx - \frac{R_1 + R_2}{\mathbf{Z}_k + R_2} \tag{10-17}$$

Note that Eq. (10-16) has been put in the form of $\mathbf{A}/(1 - \mathbf{A}\beta)$. However, until the problem was solved, we did not know what to call $\mathbf{A}$ or β. For instance, why should β be defined as $(\mathbf{Z}_k + R_2)/(R_1 + R_2)$? In an example as simple as this, reasons for choosing $\mathbf{A}$ and β as indicated by Eq. (10-16) might be found *once the answer is known.* In more complex feedback amplifiers, even this cannot be done. This will be illustrated further in Sec. 10-7. In general, equivalent-circuit analysis is the proper procedure to use to obtain the gain of a feedback amplifier. If the gain expression is put in the form $\mathbf{G}/(1 - \mathbf{GB})$, then this is of the form of Eq. (10-4); hence, the discussions of Sec. 10-1 may apply. For instance, if $\mathbf{GB}$ is real and negative and $|GB| \gg 1$, then

$$\mathbf{K} \approx \frac{1}{\mathbf{B}} \tag{10-18}$$

If $\mathbf{B}$ is independent of the parameters of the active elements, we still obtain the advantages of feedback.

In summary, the relation $\mathbf{A}/(1 - \mathbf{A\beta})$ is very useful in studying the general concepts of a feedback amplifier. However, it is of only limited use in obtaining the gain of an actual feedback amplifier. If the actual gain can be put in the form $\mathbf{G}/(1 - \mathbf{GB})$ it may prove quite helpful to the understanding of the feedback amplifier.

The amplifier of Fig. 10-3 uses both voltage and current feedback. The voltage feedback results from the voltage drop across R_2, while the current feedback is due to the voltage drop across $\mathbf{Z}_k$. Since $\mathbf{Z}_k$ and R_2 are in series, it may appear strange that two different kinds of feedback result. To explain this, assume that $\mathbf{Z}_k$ is purely resistive and that a load resistance is placed across the output terminals. This will tend to decrease $\mathbf{E}_2$ and to increase $\mathbf{I}$, which in turn will decrease the feedback voltage across R_2 and increase the feedback voltage across $\mathbf{Z}_k$. The first of these effects tends to

Fig. 10-4   (a) A simple current-feedback common-emitter transistor amplifier; (b) its equivalent circuit.

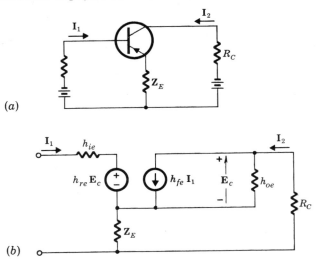

increase $\mathbf{E}_2$ and $\mathbf{I}$, while the second tends to decrease them. Thus, R_2 produces voltage feedback, since its presence tends to stabilize the output voltage. On the other hand, the presence of $\mathbf{Z}_k$ tends to stabilize $\mathbf{I}$ and, therefore, introduces current feedback.

A simple transistor amplifier with current feedback is shown, with its equivalent circuit, in Fig. 10-4. The gain of this amplifier is given by Eq. (6-78). Thus,

$$\mathbf{K}_i = \frac{h_{fe} - h_{oe}\mathbf{Z}_E}{1 + h_{oe}R_c + h_{oe}\mathbf{Z}_E} \tag{10-19}$$

Note that even if h_{fe} becomes zero, there will be output because of the $h_{oe}\mathbf{Z}_E$ term. In general, the factor $h_{re}\mathbf{E}_c$ will introduce feedback in a transistor amplifier. In this simple case it did not appear, because we assumed that $\mathbf{I}_1$ was specified.

10-3   Effect of feedback on nonlinear distortion and noise— importance of open-loop gain, return ratio, and return difference

Nonlinear distortion results in the production of harmonic or intermodulation terms (see Sec. 2-10). Thus, we can represent distortion by a linear system with an additional generator that produces these distortion signals. Such a circuit is shown in Fig. 10-5. Usually the nonlinear distortion occurs in the output stages where the signal swings are larger. For this reason, we have split the $\mathbf{A}$ branch into two branches, $\mathbf{A}_1$ and $\mathbf{A}_2$, and injected the distortion signal at their junction.

Extraneous signals called *noise*, which can prove quite troublesome, are often introduced at some point in the amplifier. For instance, the power supply may not produce a pure direct voltage. It may have components of the power-line frequency (usually 60 cps and its harmonics) present in its output. This will act just as a signal voltage and will appear in the output signal. The active elements themselves produce random fluctuations in signal level, and this also will result in an output noise. In some cases, noise can completely obscure the signal. The signal $\mathbf{X}_d$ can be considered to be a noise signal as well as a distortion signal.

The output signal $\mathbf{X}_2$ for the amplifier of Fig. 10-5 can be found by suc-

Fig. 10-5 The signal-flow graph of a feedback amplifier with a distortion or noise signal applied to one of the intermediate stages.

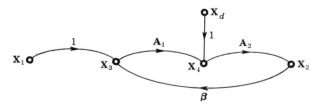

cessively eliminating nodes. This is shown in Fig. 10-6. Thus, we have

$$\mathbf{X_2} = \mathbf{X}_{2s} + \mathbf{X}_{2d} = \frac{\mathbf{A_1A_2X_1}}{1 - \mathbf{A_1A_2\beta}} + \frac{\mathbf{A_2X}_d}{1 - \mathbf{A_1A_2\beta}} \tag{10-20}$$

Let us now consider the advantage gained by using feedback. If the β branch were not present in Fig. 10-5, the output would be

$$\mathbf{X'_2} = \mathbf{X'}_{2s} + \mathbf{X'}_{2d} = \mathbf{A_1A_2X'_1} + \mathbf{A_2X'}_d \tag{10-21}$$

where the primes indicate the nonfeedback case. It is the ratio of the distortion or noise to the signal that is of importance, not their absolute values. We shall denote this ratio by **D**. In the feedback case,

$$\mathbf{D} = \frac{\mathbf{X}_d}{\mathbf{X_1}} \frac{1}{\mathbf{A_1}} \tag{10-22}$$

and in the nonfeedback case,

$$\mathbf{D'} = \frac{\mathbf{X'}_d}{\mathbf{X'_1}} \frac{1}{\mathbf{A_1}} \tag{10-23}$$

These ratios are complex numbers. It is their magnitude in which we are interested. It appears as though no advantage is gained by using feedback. However, this is often not the case. The value of the output signal is usually specified (e.g., the output voltage, current, or power). The signal swings of the last stage, hence, the distortion signal $\mathbf{X}_d$, are then fixed,

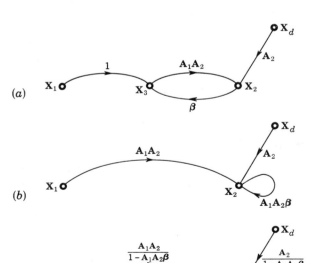

Fig. 10-6 Solution of Fig. 10-5 for x_2. (a) Elimination of node x_4; (b) elimination of node x_3; (c) elimination of the self-loop of node x_2.

whether or not feedback is used.　Hence,

$$\mathbf{X}_{2s} = \mathbf{X}_{2s}'$$ (10-24)

and

$$\mathbf{X}_d = \mathbf{X}_d'$$

Thus, the input signals must be different in the feedback and in the non-feedback cases.　Substituting Eqs. (10-20) and (10-21) into Eq. (10-24), we have

$$\frac{\mathbf{X}_1\mathbf{A}_1\mathbf{A}_2}{1 - \mathbf{A}_1\mathbf{A}_2\beta} = \mathbf{X}_1'\mathbf{A}_1\mathbf{A}_2$$

Hence,

$$\mathbf{X}_1 = \mathbf{X}_1'(1 - \mathbf{A}_1\mathbf{A}_2\beta)$$ (10-25)

Substituting, and taking the ratio of Eqs. (10-22) and (10-23), we obtain

$$\frac{\mathbf{D}}{\mathbf{D}'} = \frac{1}{1 - \mathbf{A}_1\mathbf{A}_2\beta}$$ (10-26)

Therefore, if the input signal can be increased to compensate for the loss in gain due to feedback, the distortion and noise can be reduced by the factor $1/(1 - \mathbf{A}_1\mathbf{A}_2\beta)$.　In a good negative-feedback amplifier, the magnitude of $1 - \mathbf{A}_1\mathbf{A}_2\beta$ might be 100 or more, so that amplifiers with very low distortion can be built.　In fact, if power amplifiers are to have harmonic distortion of less than 1 per cent, it is impractical to build them without using feedback.

The input signal must be increased when feedback is used.　If this cannot be done, then additional amplification may be needed.　This can be in the form of a preamplifier that precedes the feedback amplifier.　The distortion will be quite small here, since the signal levels will be low.　The entire feedback amplifier can be designed to give the required gain, in which case the feedback amplifier would probably have more stages than the non-feedback amplifier.　We shall discuss the design of feedback amplifiers in Sec. 10-12.

If $\mathbf{X}_d$ represents a noise signal, then the discussion is complicated somewhat.　In general, if the signal level can be raised, feedback will reduce the effects of noise just as it reduces the distortion.　However, there are circumstances when the input-signal level is fixed, and the interfering noise is produced in the first amplifier stage.　In this case, the input signal level cannot be increased unless it is amplified.　The amplification will increase the noise level equally.　Then, the ratio of $|D/D'|$ will be unity, and no advantage is gained by using feedback.

The reduction of noise and distortion that can be obtained by the use of feedback is given by the magnitude of Eq. (10-26).　If the feedback is negative, then $\mathbf{A}_1\mathbf{A}_2\beta$ will be a real negative number.　When its magnitude is large, then $1/|1 - \mathbf{A}_1\mathbf{A}_2\beta|$ will be small and the distortion will be greatly reduced.　If positive feedback is used, then $\mathbf{A}_1\mathbf{A}_2\beta$ will be a real positive

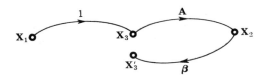

number.   In most circumstances with positive feedback, $|A_1 A_2 \beta|$ must be less than 1 if oscillation is not to occur.   In these cases, $1/|1 - A_1 A_2 \beta|$ will be greater than unity, and the distortion will be increased, if the output signal is kept constant.

The quantity $A_1 A_2 \beta$ is called the *open-loop gain* of the feedback amplifier. Consider Fig. 10-7.   This is the signal-flow graph of the feedback amplifier of Fig. 10-1, except that the β branch has been removed from node X_3, so that the feedback loop has been broken.   Let us compute the gain X_3'/X_3.

$$\frac{X_3'}{X_3} = A\beta \qquad (10\text{-}27)$$

Thus, the open-loop gain for the simple feedback amplifiers that we have been considering is obtained by breaking the feedback loop, and taking the ratio of a signal applied at the input of the β circuit to the signal returned to the output of the β circuit.   For this reason, the negative of the open-loop gain is called the *return ratio*.   The quantity that is often of interest is $1 - A\beta$.   If a unit signal is applied ($X_3 = 1$), then $X_3' = A\beta$, so that $1 - A\beta$ is the difference between the applied signal and the returned signal.   Hence, $1 - A\beta$ is called the *return difference*.   This is a measure of the advantage gained when feedback is used.

10-4   Effect of feedback on the sensitivity of the gain of an amplifier to changes in parameter values

If the parameters of the active elements of an amplifier vary, then the gain of the amplifier will change.   For the transistor, the parameter variations are usually due to changes in either the temperature or the power-supply voltage.   On the other hand, for the vacuum tube, they are often due to aging or changes in the power-supply voltage.   Many electronic instruments require amplifiers with a very constant gain.   The use of feedback can make the gain of an amplifier almost insensitive to changes in the parameters of the active elements.   The gain of a feedback amplifier is given by Eq. (10-4) as

$$K = \frac{A}{1 - A\beta}$$

Now let us assume that A changes by an amount ΔA.   Then K will change by an amount ΔK. Thus,

$$K + \Delta K = \frac{A + \Delta A}{1 - (A + \Delta A)\beta} \tag{10-28}$$

Then

$$\Delta K = \frac{A + \Delta A}{1 - (A + \Delta A)\beta} - \frac{A}{1 - A\beta} \tag{10-29}$$

Usually, it is not the actual change that we are interested in, but the fractional change. Then, dividing Eq. (10-29) by Eq. (10-4) and rearranging, we obtain

$$\frac{\Delta K}{K} = \frac{\Delta A/A}{1 - (A + \Delta A)\beta} \tag{10-30}$$

The quantity $\Delta A/A$ represents the fractional change in the amplification without feedback. Hence, the fractional change in the gain has been reduced by the return difference of the feedback amplifier computed *after* the change in A has occurred. If negative feedback is used and $(A + \Delta A)\beta$ is a large negative number, then a considerable improvement in the sensitivity to parameter value changes is obtained by using feedback. If ΔA results because of aging, then eventually $|(A + \Delta A)\beta|$ will become small and the advantages of feedback will be lost. Feedback amplifiers should be checked from time to time to see that this has not occurred. (Note that $|A|$ can decrease greatly while $|K|$ does not, and, hence, the amplifier can have sufficient gain but yet not function properly.)

Differences, rather than derivatives, were used in the analysis of this section, so that the results would be accurate for large changes in A and not just for infinitesimal ones.

10-5 Effect of feedback on frequency response

Let us now consider the effect of feedback on the frequency distortion of a simple amplifier. We shall assume that the gain formula of Eq. (10-4) can be used, and that

$$A = -\frac{A_{mid}}{1 + jf/f_2} \tag{10-31}$$

Then

$$K = \frac{-A_{mid}}{1 + A_{mid}\beta} \cdot \frac{1}{1 + jf/f_2(1 + A_{mid}\beta)} \tag{10-32}$$

It is assumed that A_{mid} and β are real positive numbers. The half-power bandwidth has been increased by a factor $1 + A_{mid}\beta$ while the gain has been reduced by the same factor. The gain-bandwidth product has not changed. It might appear that no advantage has been gained by using feedback. However, the use of feedback allows gain to be traded for bandwidth where it might not have been convenient to do so, such as in the case of the variation of h_f with frequency in a transistor. In addition, if feedback is used to improve the frequency response, it will also provide the advantages discussed in Secs. 10-3 and 10-4. If the frequency response of the amplifier is more complex than that given by Eq. (10-31), then a gain-bandwidth trade using feedback may prove more advantageous than other types of gain-bandwidth trades.

If feedback is used to achieve any of the advantages discussed in Secs. 10-3 and 10-4, then it becomes somewhat academic to speak of its greatly improving the frequency response. This is because the open-loop gain must be high to obtain the advantages of feedback. Hence, in a well-designed feedback amplifier, $|A\beta|$, and, as a consequence, $|A|$, should not fall off over any frequencies of interest. Since the use of feedback does increase the bandwidth, a good feedback amplifier usually has a bandwidth much greater than that required by the bandwidth of the input signals. For instance, a high-quality audio amplifier should have a frequency response that is essentially flat for frequencies from 20 to 20,000 cps. However, the frequency response of a feedback amplifier that is designed to amplify these signals may be essentially flat for frequencies from 2 to 200,000 cps.

10-6   Effect of feedback on impedance levels

Feedback can have a profound effect on the output impedance of an amplifier. We shall use the representation discussed in Sec. 5-2, where an amplifier was represented by its Thévenin's or Norton's equivalent circuit to determine the output impedance. Two typical amplifier representations are shown in Fig. 10-8. Note that $A_{v,oc}$ and $A_{i,sc}$ are open-circuit and short-circuit amplifications respectively, and *do not change* if Z_L changes. The output impedance Z_o accounts for changes in gain with load impedance. We shall assume that feedback is added to these amplifiers and see how the output impedance

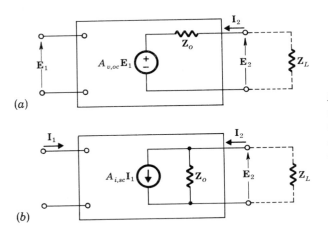

(a)

(b)

Fig. 10-8 (a) A Thévenin's equivalent circuit of a voltage amplifier; (b) a Norton's equivalent circuit of a current amplifier.

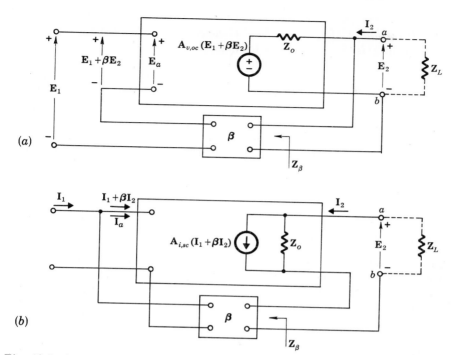

Fig. 10-9 (a) *An ideal voltage-feedback amplifier;* (b) *an ideal current-feedback amplifier.*

is changed. Consider the voltage-feedback amplifier of Fig. 10-9a. Assume that the β circuit is ideal so that $\mathbf{E}_a = \mathbf{E}_1 + \beta \mathbf{E}_2$ and $\mathbf{Z}_\beta$ is infinite. Then we can compute the effective output impedance using the relation (from Thévenin's theorem) $\mathbf{Z}_{o,vfb} = -\mathbf{E}_{oc}/\mathbf{I}_{sc}$. (The subscript *vfb* stands for voltage feedback.) Under open-circuit conditions, the gain of the amplifier is given by Eq. (10-4). Then

$$\mathbf{E}_{2oc} = \frac{\mathbf{A}_{v,oc}\mathbf{E}_1}{1 - \mathbf{A}_{v,oc}\beta} \tag{10-33}$$

If a short circuit is placed across terminals *ab*, then $\mathbf{E}_2 = 0$, so that the feedback voltage has been eliminated, and

$$\mathbf{I}_{2sc} = -\frac{\mathbf{A}_{v,oc}\mathbf{E}_1}{\mathbf{Z}_o} \tag{10-34}$$

Thus

$$\mathbf{Z}_{o,vfb} = \frac{\mathbf{Z}_o}{1 - \mathbf{A}_{v,oc}\beta} \tag{10-35}$$

If negative feedback is used, the output impedance is reduced by the *return difference under open-circuit conditions*. (Note that this is the maximum return difference for a voltage-feedback amplifier.)

Now consider the current-feedback amplifier of Fig. 10-9b. We shall again assume that the β circuit is ideal, so that $\mathbf{I}_a = \mathbf{I}_1 + \beta\mathbf{I}_2$ and $\mathbf{Z}_\beta = 0$. Then, when a short circuit is placed across terminals ab

$$\mathbf{I}_{2sc} = \mathbf{I}_1 \frac{\mathbf{A}_{i,sc}}{1 - \mathbf{A}_{i,sc}\beta} \tag{10-36}$$

Under open-circuit conditions, $\mathbf{I}_2 = 0$ and the feedback current becomes zero. Thus,

$$\mathbf{E}_{2oc} = -\mathbf{A}_{i,sc}\mathbf{I}_1\mathbf{Z}_o \tag{10-37}$$

Hence

$$\mathbf{Z}_{o,ifb} = \mathbf{Z}_o(1 - \mathbf{A}_{i,sc}\beta) \tag{10-38}$$

When negative-current feedback is used, the output impedance is multiplied by the *return difference under short circuit conditions*. (Note that this is the maximum return difference for a current-feedback amplifier.)

If $\mathbf{Z}_o$ is the output impedance of a device and $\mathbf{Z}_L$ is the load impedance, and $|\mathbf{Z}_o| \ll |\mathbf{Z}_L|$, then the output voltage will be almost independent of $\mathbf{Z}_L$. On the other hand, if $|\mathbf{Z}_o| \gg |\mathbf{Z}_L|$, then the output current will be almost independent of $\mathbf{Z}_L$. Thus, it is to be expected that voltage feedback will reduce the output impedance, whereas current feedback will increase it.

We have computed the output impedance here. However, Eqs. (10-35) and (10-38) apply to the impedance viewed into any two terminals of a feedback amplifier, provided that $\mathbf{Z}_o$ is the impedance without feedback (but with no other circuit changes), and that the current feedback becomes zero when the terminals are open-circuited, and that the voltage feedback becomes zero when the terminals are short-circuited.

10-7   Calculation of the gain of feedback amplifiers

Equivalent circuits will be used to analyze feedback amplifiers. Thus, there is really nothing new involved and the procedures that we have been using can now be applied to feedback amplifiers. Two feedback amplifiers will be analyzed in this section to illustrate some useful techniques.

Consider the three-stage vacuum-tube voltage-feedback amplifier shown in Fig. 10-10a. The voltage gain from the grid of the first tube to the grid of the third tube $\mathbf{A}_{v1} = \mathbf{E}_3/\mathbf{E}_1$ is just the voltage gain of a two-stage RC-coupled voltage amplifier. Thus, the procedures of Chap. 6 can be used to analyze it. Note the feedback *does not* affect the ratio $\mathbf{E}_3/\mathbf{E}_1$, although it does affect the value of $\mathbf{E}_1$. The gain, $\mathbf{A}_{v1}$, should include the effects of the parasitic capacitances even though they have not been drawn in Fig. 10-10a. The equivalent circuit for the complete amplifier is shown in Fig. 10-10b. The first two stages of the amplifier are accounted for by the $\mathbf{A}_{v1}\mathbf{E}_1$ term, which appears in the equivalent circuit of the third vacuum tube. The capacitances C_1 and C_2 represent the input and the output capacitances of the amplifier, respectively. To simplify the analysis, we shall assume that, in the last stage, the coupling capacitor C, the cathode bypass capacitor C_{k2}, and the screen-grid bypass capacitor C_{s2} are short circuits at the signal frequency. The analysis would be essentially the same if we did not do this, but some of the concepts would be obscured by unnecessary detail. The conductance G_2 represents the parallel combination of R_2', R_2'' and the plate resistance of the third vacuum tube.

Before we analyze the vacuum-tube amplifier, let us consider the transistor amplifier of Fig. 10-11a. Its equivalent circuit is shown in Fig. 10-11b. The effects of the first two stages have been accounted for by the expression $\mathbf{A}_{i1}\mathbf{I}_1$. The current gain $\mathbf{A}_{i1}$ can be found by the methods of Chap. 6. As we discussed in Sec. 6-6, the emitter impedance primarily affects the current entering the transistor stage. If the emitter impedance of the third stage is considered when $\mathbf{A}_{i1}$ is calculated, we can, to a high degree of accuracy, ignore it otherwise. This has been done in Fig. 10-11b. We have also assumed that the last coupling capacitor C is a short circuit. The conductance G_2 represents the parallel combination of R_2', R_2'', and $1/h_{oe}$ for the last stage. The admittance $\mathbf{Y}_i$ represents the input admittance of the first amplifier stage (including R_{B1} and R_{B2}). The feedback will affect the values of $\mathbf{E}_1$ and $\mathbf{I}_1$ but not their ratio, so that $\mathbf{Y}_i$ is calculated as though the feedback loop were not present. (It does act as a load upon the last stage, but this effect is negligible here.) Equations (6-80) to (6-82) can be used for this purpose. (The feedback does affect the impedance seen at termi-

Fig. 10-10 (a) A three-stage vacuum-tube voltage-feedback amplifier; (b) an equivalent circuit for this amplifier which uses the approximations and substitutions discussed in the text. Note that the input generator has been replaced by Norton's theorem.

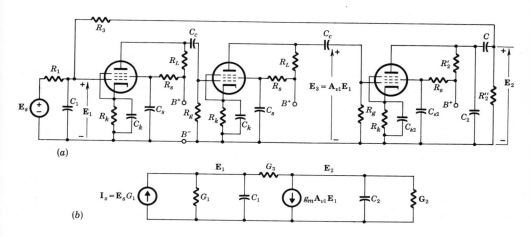

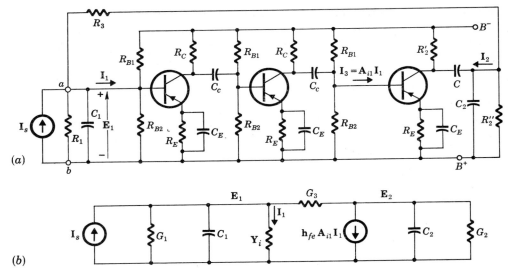

Fig. 10-11 (a) *A three-stage transistor voltage-feedback amplifier;* (b) *an equivalent circuit for the amplifier which uses the approximations and substitutions discussed in the text.*

nals ab by the external generator $\mathbf{I}_s$, since it affects the value of $\mathbf{E}_1$.) The equivalent circuits of Figs. 10-10b and 10-11b are the same except for the $g_m\mathbf{A}_{v1}\mathbf{E}_1$ and the $\mathbf{h}_{fe}\mathbf{A}_{i1}\mathbf{I}_1$ terms. (Assume that $\mathbf{Y}_i = 0$ in the vacuum-tube case.) In the transistor circuit,

$$\mathbf{I}_1 = \mathbf{E}_1\mathbf{Y}_i \qquad (10\text{-}39)$$

Now let us use the substitutions

$$\mathbf{A} = g_m\mathbf{A}_{v1} \qquad (10\text{-}40)$$

for the vacuum-tube amplifier, and

$$\mathbf{A} = \mathbf{h}_{fe}\mathbf{A}_{i1}\mathbf{Y}_i \qquad (10\text{-}41)$$

for the transistor amplifier. If Eqs. (10-39) to (10-41) are substituted, then the equivalent circuits of Figs. 10-10b and 10-11b become identical. The following nodal analysis is applicable to both amplifiers.

$$\mathbf{I}_s = (G_1 + G_3 + j\omega C_1 + \mathbf{Y}_i)\mathbf{E}_1 - G_3\mathbf{E}_2 \qquad (10\text{-}42)$$
$$0 = (\mathbf{A} - G_3)\mathbf{E}_1 + (G_2 + G_3 + j\omega C_2)\mathbf{E}_2 \qquad (10\text{-}43)$$

Solving for $\mathbf{E}_2/\mathbf{I}_s$, we obtain

$$\frac{\mathbf{E}_2}{\mathbf{I}_s} = \frac{-(\mathbf{A} - G_3)}{(G_1 + G_3 + \mathbf{Y}_i + j\omega C_1)(G_2 + G_3 + j\omega C_2) + G_3(\mathbf{A} - G_3)} \qquad (10\text{-}44)$$

To obtain the voltage gain of the vacuum-tube amplifier, multiply Eq. (10-44) by G_1 and substitute Eq. (10-40). To obtain the current gain of the transistor amplifier, multiply Eq. (10-44) by $-G_2''$ and substitute Eq. (10-41). Thus, the gain of both amplifiers has been obtained.

In order to interpret Eq. (10-44) more easily, we shall make some approximations. The conductance G_3 is usually very much less than unity, while $\mathbf{A}$ is essentially a gain very much greater than unity. We shall approximate $\mathbf{A} - G_3$ by $\mathbf{A}$. This is equivalent to ignoring the direct transmission through the resistance R_3. Making the approximation and manipulating Eq. (10-44), we obtain

$$\frac{\mathbf{E}_2}{\mathbf{I}_s} = \frac{-\mathbf{A}/[(G_1 + G_3 + j\omega C_1 + \mathbf{Y}_i)(G_2 + G_3 + j\omega C_2)]}{1 + \mathbf{A}G_3/[(G_1 + G_3 + \mathbf{Y}_i + j\omega C_1)(G_2 + G_3 + j\omega C_2)]} \qquad (10\text{-}45)$$

If

$$|\mathbf{A}G_3/[(G_1 + G_3 + \mathbf{Y}_i + j\omega C_1)(G_2 + G_3 + j\omega C_2)]| \gg 1 \qquad (10\text{-}46)$$

we have

$$\frac{\mathbf{E}_2}{\mathbf{I}_s} \approx -\frac{1}{G_3} \qquad (10\text{-}47)$$

Thus, the voltage gain of the vacuum-tube amplifier is approximately

$$\mathbf{K}_v \approx -\frac{G_1}{G_3} \qquad (10\text{-}48)$$

while the current gain of the transistor amplifier is approximately

$$\mathbf{K}_i \approx \frac{G_2''}{G_3} \qquad (10\text{-}49)$$

Thus, the gain of both these amplifiers can be made essentially independent of the parameters of the active elements over a band of frequencies. Note that the inequality of relation (10-46) will not be valid at all frequencies. At very low frequencies, $\mathbf{A}$ falls off because of the effects of the coupling and bypass capacitors. At high frequencies, $\mathbf{A}$ falls off because of parasitic capacitance and the variation of $\mathbf{h}_{fe}$ with frequency. In addition, the $j\omega C_1$ and $j\omega C_2$ terms cause the left-hand side of relation (10-46) to become small at high frequencies.

Let us interpret Eq. (10-46). We shall break up the product on the left-hand side and consider each term separately. $G_3/(G_1 + G_3 + j\omega C_1 + \mathbf{Y}_i)$ is the voltage-divider ratio $\mathbf{E}_1/\mathbf{E}_2$ if the generator $\mathbf{I}_s$ is replaced by an open circuit. This is what could be called $\boldsymbol{\beta}$. Note that the gain *does not* approach $1/\boldsymbol{\beta}$. The quantity $\mathbf{A}/(G_2 + G_3 + j\omega C_2)$ is a measure of the gain from the grid of the first vacuum tube, or the base of the first transistor, to the output. Note that it does not take into account the fact that the $\boldsymbol{\beta}$ circuit can load down the output. Thus, we can roughly say that $\mathbf{A}G_3/[(G_1 + G_3 + j\omega C_1 + \mathbf{Y}_i)(G_2 + G_3 + j\omega C_2)]$ is the open-loop gain of the amplifier. This discussion tends to substantiate the fact that the relation $\mathbf{A}/(1 - \mathbf{A}\beta)$ can be used to study the general principles of feedback amplifiers, but this relation cannot be used to compute the gain of specific ones.

10-8 Oscillation in feedback amplifiers

Whenever a feedback amplifier is constructed, there is always a danger that it will be *unstable*. That is, that it may oscillate. Consider the feedback amplifier of Fig. 10-7. If the open-loop gain is equal to $+1$ at some frequency, then a signal of that frequency, originating at any point in the feedback loop, will be returned to the same point with an equal magnitude. Thus, this signal will persist indefinitely, and oscillation will result. (Note that signals of all frequencies are always present because of random fluctuation in currents and voltages.) A question that can be asked is, if the phase angle of the open-loop gain is zero, and if its magnitude is greater than one, then will such a persistent signal build up? The answer is that it often will. *However, there are circumstances when it will not.* Oscillation is a complex phenomenon that can best be understood from a mathematical study rather than from simple physical arguments.

Before proceeding with this mathematical discussion, let us consider why oscillation is so undesirable. It can produce an interfering signal that will obscure the desired one. The "howl" that is often heard in public address systems is typical of this. Oscillation in an amplifier is harmful even if it does not obscure the signal (e.g., an audio amplifier may oscillate at the inaudible frequency of 100,000 cps), because the oscillation builds up until the amplifier is driven into highly nonlinear regions where it cannot function properly. Of course, there are instances when a circuit is designed to generate a signal. In such cases, an oscillator is built deliberately. Such circuits will be discussed in Chap. 11.

To analyze the stability of an amplifier, we shall consider the transformed form of the gain. This subject was introduced in Secs. 6-13 to 6-15. In particular, we are interested in the location of the poles of the transformed gain function $\mathbf{K}(p)$. As we have seen in Sec. 6-15, if these poles lie in the left half-plane, the transient response of the amplifier will decay exponentially. On the other hand, if the poles lie in the right half-plane, then the transient response will consist of terms which build up exponentially; consequently, oscillation will result. If the poles lie exactly on the $j\omega$ axis, then the response will consist of sinusoids which build up with time if the poles are not simple (of the first order). If the $j\omega$-axis poles are of the first order, then the transient response will contain a sinusoid which neither builds up nor decays. This condition is the borderline case of oscillation. It is unsuitable in an amplifier since, once excited, these sinusoids will persist. In addition, any slight change in any of the parameters of the amplifier may shift the poles into the right half-plane. Thus, we shall say that a feedback amplifier is *stable* if *all* of its poles lie in the left half-plane, and that it is *unstable* if *any* of its poles lie on the $j\omega$ axis or in the right half-plane. If an amplifier oscillates, then the output signal does not build up indefinitely. In actual amplifiers, the voltages and currents are limited by cutoff and saturation phenomena in the active elements.

To determine if a feedback amplifier is stable, we need only obtain the gain (as was done in Sec. 10-7), replace $j\omega$ by p, and then clear fractions so that the gain with feedback $\mathbf{K}(p)$ is expressed as the ratio of two polynomials in p. (It is assumed that any common factors in the numerator and denominator are canceled.) The denominator polynomial is then examined to see if it has any roots on the $j\omega$ axis or in the right half-plane. If it does not, then the amplifier is stable. The most straightforward manner of determining the location of the roots of a polynomial is to factor it. However, the polynomials encountered in feedback amplifiers are, ordinarily, of fairly high degree, and factoring will usually require an extremely tedious cut-and-try procedure. We do not need to know the location of the poles of the gain function, but only whether they lie on the $j\omega$ axis or in the right half-plane. Fortunately, there are several procedures that will supply this information without factoring the polynomial. These shall be considered in the next sections.

10-9   Routh-Hurwitz tests for the location of the roots of a polynomial

The Hurwitz test is a simple procedure to determine if a polynomial has roots in the right half-plane or on the $j\omega$ axis. It will be stated without proof. Consider a polynomial $\mathbf{D}(p)$, which has no roots at $p = 0$.

$$\mathbf{D}(p) = p^k + d_{k-1}p^{k+1} + \cdots + d_1p + d_0 \tag{10-50}$$

All of the coefficients $d_{k-1}, \ldots, d_1, d_0$ must be positive. If any are negative or zero, then the polynomial will have right half-plane roots and we need proceed no farther. An exception to this is if the polynomial contains only even (or only odd) powers. Then $\mathbf{D}(p)$ *may* have $j\omega$-axis roots instead of right half-plane roots. However, we consider this to be borderline instability. Thus, if any coefficients are nonpositive, we can state that the amplifier is not stable. If all the coefficients are positive, then the test must be applied. Break up $\mathbf{D}(p)$ into the sum of two polynomials.

$$\mathbf{D}(p) = \mathbf{m}(p) + \mathbf{n}(p) \tag{10-51}$$

where $\mathbf{m}(p)$ is an even polynomial (i.e., contains only even-powered terms, including the constant) and $\mathbf{n}(p)$ is an odd polynomial. Then, form the improper fraction.

$$\mathbf{\Phi} = \frac{\mathbf{m}(p)}{\mathbf{n}(p)} \tag{10-52}$$

$$\mathbf{\Phi} = \frac{\mathbf{n}(p)}{\mathbf{m}(p)} \tag{10-53}$$

Choose either Eq. (10-52) or (10-53) so that the highest power of the numerator is greater than the highest power of the denominator.   Let us assume that Eq. (10-52) is used.   The degree of $\mathbf{m}(p)$ is one greater than $\mathbf{n}(p)$. [Note that $\mathbf{m}(p)$ contains all of the even powers while $\mathbf{n}(p)$ contains all of the odd powers.]   Thus,

$$\Phi = a_1 p + \frac{\mathbf{R}_1(p)}{\mathbf{n}(p)} \tag{10-54}$$

The polynomial $\mathbf{R}_1(p)$ will be even and one degree less than $\mathbf{n}(p)$.   (This will be illustrated in the subsequent example.)   Then take the reciprocal of the remainder term

$$\frac{\mathbf{n}(p)}{\mathbf{R}_1(p)} = a_2 p + \frac{\mathbf{R}_2(p)}{\mathbf{R}_1(p)} \tag{10-55}$$

Continue this procedure with successive remainders.

$$\frac{\mathbf{R}_1(p)}{\mathbf{R}_2(p)} = a_3 p + \frac{\mathbf{R}_3(p)}{\mathbf{R}_2(p)} \tag{10-56}$$

The degrees of the numerator and the denominator of the remainder will decrease and the procedure will eventually terminate.   If any of the $a_1, a_2 \ldots$ are not positive, then $\mathbf{D}(p)$ will contain right half-plane roots. If all the $a_1, a_2, \ldots$ are positive, then $\mathbf{D}(p)$ will only contain left half-plane roots, except in a special case which will be discussed subsequently.   Let us consider some examples of this procedure.

$$\mathbf{D}(p) = p^4 + 6p^3 + 9p^2 + 12p + 4$$
$$\mathbf{m}(p) = p^4 + 9p^2 + 4$$
$$\mathbf{n}(p) = 6p^3 + 12p$$

The division can be set up in compact form.

$$
\begin{array}{r}
(\tfrac{1}{6})p \\
6p^3 + 12p\,\overline{\smash{\big)}\,p^4 + 9p^2 + 4} \\
\underline{p^4 + 2p^2} \hspace{2.5cm} (\tfrac{6}{7})p \\
7p^2 + 4\,\overline{\smash{\big)}\,6p^3 + 12p} \hspace{2cm} (\tfrac{49}{60})p\\
\underline{6p^3 + (\tfrac{24}{7})p} \hspace{1cm} \\
(\tfrac{60}{7})p\,\overline{\smash{\big)}\,7p^2 + 4}\\
\underline{7p^2} \hspace{2cm} (\tfrac{15}{7})p \\
4\,\overline{\smash{\big)}\,(\tfrac{60}{7})p} \\
\underline{(\tfrac{60}{7})p} \\
0
\end{array}
$$

The a's are $\tfrac{1}{6}$, $\tfrac{6}{7}$, $\tfrac{49}{60}$, $\tfrac{15}{7}$.   The polynomial $\mathbf{D}(p)$ has all its roots in the left half-plane.   If any of the a's had been negative, then the procedure could have been stopped, because it would have been known that $\mathbf{D}(p)$ had right half-plane roots.

If the original polynomial is such that $\mathbf{m}(p)$ and $\mathbf{n}(p)$ both have the same factor, then when the ratio $\mathbf{m}/\mathbf{n}$ or $\mathbf{n}/\mathbf{m}$ is formed, this factor will be lost. However, if the common factor is not canceled from $\mathbf{m}(p)$ and $\mathbf{n}(p)$, then it will be carried through the division and will appear as the last divisor. For instance, if

$$\mathbf{A}(p) = (p^2 + 1)(p^2 + 2p + 2) = p^4 + 2p^3 + 3p^2 + 2p + 2$$

then

$$\mathbf{m}(p) = p^4 + 3p^2 + 2 = (p^2 + 1)(p^2 + 2)$$
$$\mathbf{n}(p) = 2p^3 + 2p = (p^2 + 1)(2p)$$

$$
\begin{array}{r}
(\frac{1}{2})p \\
2p^3 + 2p \overline{\smash{\big)}\, p^4 + 3p^2 + 2} \\
\underline{p^4 + p^2} \qquad\qquad p \\
2p^2 + 2 \overline{\smash{\big)}\, 2p^3 + 2p} \\
\underline{2p^3 + 2p} \\
0
\end{array}
$$

Note that the test terminated prematurely (i.e., the last divisor is not a constant). We can then state that $2p^2 + 2$ is a factor of $\mathbf{A}(p)$, $\mathbf{m}(p)$, and $\mathbf{n}(p)$. The test proceeds as before, except that the common factor of $\mathbf{m}(p)$ and $\mathbf{n}(p)$ is not evaluated. The only factor that an even and an odd polynomial can have in common is an even polynomial (i.e., the product of two even polynomials is an even polynomial and the product of an even and an odd polynomial is an odd polynomial). Let us consider an even polynomial

$$\mathbf{E}(p) = p^{2k} + b_{k-1}p^{2(k-1)} + \cdots + b_1 p^2 + b_0 \qquad (10\text{-}57)$$

If p_0 is a root of such a polynomial, then $-p_0$ will also be a root. Hence, if $\mathbf{E}(p)$ has left half-plane roots, it must also have right half-plane roots. The only way that $\mathbf{E}(p)$ cannot have right half-plane roots is for all of its roots to lie on the $j\omega$ axis. This does not lead to a stable condition. Thus, we can state that, if a polynomial is to have all of its roots in the left half-plane, then all of the $a_1, a_2, \ldots$ in the Hurwitz test must be positive and the test must not terminate prematurely. A polynomial that has all of its roots in the left half-plane is called a *Hurwitz polynomial*.

The Routh test is another procedure to determine if the roots of a polynomial lie in the right half-plane. It is essentially the same as the Hurwitz test, except that an array is used in place of the long division. To perform this test, break the polynomial $\mathbf{D}(p)$ up into its even and odd parts as indicated in Eq. (10-51). Then

$$\mathbf{m}(p) = a_0 p^{2k} + a_1 p^{2k-2} + \cdots + a_k \qquad (10\text{-}58)$$
$$\mathbf{n}(p) = b_0 p^{2k-1} + \cdots + b_{k-1} p \qquad (10\text{-}59)$$

We have assumed that $\mathbf{m}(p)$ is of higher degree than $\mathbf{n}(p)$ and have formed the following array [if this is not the case, then the coefficients of $\mathbf{n}(p)$ will form the first row of the array]:

$$a_0 \quad a_1 \quad a_2 \ldots a_k$$
$$b_0 \quad b_1 \quad b_2 \ldots$$
$$c_0 \quad c_1 \ldots \qquad\qquad\qquad (10\text{-}60)$$
$$d_0 \quad d_1 \ldots$$
$$\cdots \cdots \cdots \cdots \cdots \cdots$$

The first two rows are obtained from Eqs. (10-58) and (10-59). The third row is obtained using the following relations:

$$c_0 = \frac{b_0 a_1 - a_0 b_1}{b_0}$$

$$c_1 = \frac{b_0 a_2 - a_0 b_2}{b_0}$$

$$c_2 = \frac{b_0 a_3 - a_0 b_3}{b_0} \qquad\qquad (10\text{-}61)$$

$$\cdot$$
$$\cdot$$
$$\cdot$$

In a similar way, any row is generated from the two preceding it. The operations of Eq. (10-61) are essentially those of long division. In fact, the third row contains the coefficients of the remainder of the first division of the Hurwitz test. Similarly, the fourth row contains the coefficients of the second remainder, and so on. Thus, this array will eventually terminate. The first column in the array is then examined. If any of the coefficients $a_0, b_0, c_0 \ldots$ are negative, then the polynomial $\mathbf{D}(p) = \mathbf{m}(p) + \mathbf{n}(p)$ will have right half-plane roots. The number of right half-plane roots is equal to the number of sign changes in the sequence $a_0, b_0, c_0, d_0, \ldots$. Multiple roots are counted as the order of their multiplicity (e.g., a double root is counted twice). Let us evaluate the previous example using the Routh procedure.

$$\mathbf{D}(p) = p^4 + 6p^3 + 9p^2 + 12p + 4$$

Then form the array

$$
\begin{array}{lll}
1 & 9 & 4 \\
6 & 12 & \\
7 & 4 & \\
60/7 & & \\
4 & & \\
0 & &
\end{array}
$$

All the coefficients of the first column are positive. Thus, there are no roots in the right half-plane. Note the similarity of this array and the long division of the first example. Since we are only interested in the signs of the coefficients, any row can be multiplied by a positive coefficient if this proves convenient.

If the Hurwitz test terminates prematurely, then the Routh test will also. The implications are the same in both cases.

The Hurwitz and Routh tests provide very simple means of determining whether or not an amplifier is stable. However, they do not provide any information as to how to stabilize an amplifier if it does oscillate, nor do they indicate any procedures for the successful design of feedback amplifiers. The Nyquist criterion, which will be discussed in the next section, will do all of this.

10-10 The Nyquist criterion for the stability of a feedback amplifier

In this section we shall discuss a test which will not only determine if an amplifier is stable, but will also indicate means for properly designing feedback amplifiers. This procedure is called the *Nyquist criterion*. We shall restrict ourselves to single-loop feedback systems. A single-loop amplifier is one in which there is only one feedback path. If the feedback loop is broken at *any* point, then all signal feedback will cease. For instance, the feedback amplifier of Fig. 10-1 is a single-loop system. We shall modify this diagram by splitting node X_3 as is shown in Fig. 10-12. This node splitting does not change the operation of the amplifier. Now let us break the feedback loop by removing the branch between node X_3' and X_3. The configuration of Fig. 10-7 results. The open-loop gain, denoted by $\mathbf{L}$, is given by

$$\mathbf{L}(j\omega) = \frac{\mathbf{X}_3'(j\omega)}{\mathbf{X}_3(j\omega)} \tag{10-62}$$

The return difference will be denoted by $\mathbf{F}(j\omega)$ and is

$$\mathbf{F}(j\omega) = 1 - \mathbf{L}(j\omega) \tag{10-63}$$

Note that we are expressing these quantities as functions of $j\omega$ rather than of p. The Nyquist criterion will involve a plot of $\mathbf{L}(j\omega)$ or $\mathbf{F}(j\omega)$ as a function of ω. We must plot both the magnitude and phase of $\mathbf{L}(j\omega)$. To do this, a polar plot shall be used. That is, evaluate $\mathbf{L}(j\omega)$ at a particular value of frequency ω_a. Then, using polar coordinates, plot the magnitude and phase angle of $\mathbf{L}(j\omega_a)$. Repeat this operation for all frequencies. The frequency scale does not show up in this polar plot. However, points on the

Fig. 10-12   A modification of the signal-flow diagram of the feedback amplifier of Fig. 10-1.

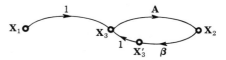

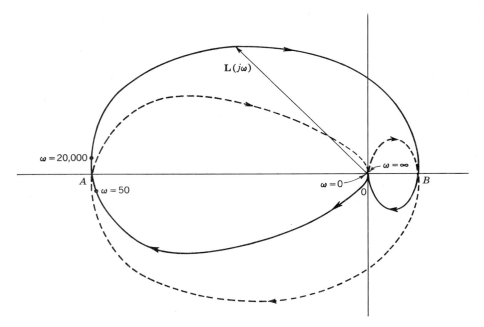

Fig. 10-13   A polar plot of the open-loop gain of a feedback amplifier.

graph can be marked to indicate the frequency, although this is usually not necessary.   A typical polar plot is shown in Fig. 10-13.   The vector $\mathbf{L}(j\omega)$ is drawn from the origin 0 to the curve.   The solid curve represents the polar plot.   The gain has been assumed to be zero at $\omega = 0$ and $\omega = \infty$. The arrows on the solid curve indicate the direction of increasing frequency. We have assumed a negative-feedback amplifier, so that the phase angle in the midband region is 180°.   (The phase angle has been assumed to be $-90°$ at $\omega = 0$ and at $\omega = \infty$.)   The dotted curve represents a plot of the conjugate of $\mathbf{L}(j\omega)$.   It is just a mirror image of the plot of $\mathbf{L}(j\omega)$.   The Nyquist criterion states the following.

Given a function $\mathbf{F}(p)$ which is equal to $\mathbf{N}(p)/\mathbf{D}(p)$ where $\mathbf{N}(p)$ and $\mathbf{D}(p)$ are polynomials in the complex variable p, and if a polar plot of $\mathbf{F}(j\omega)$ and its conjugate is made for all frequencies, then the number of times that the plot encircles the origin is equal to the number of right half-plane zeros of $\mathbf{F}(p)$ minus the number of right half-plane poles of $\mathbf{F}(p)$.

The word "encircles" should be clarified.   Consider a radius vector drawn from the origin to a point on the polar plot.   Now let this point trace out the curve corresponding to the following path.   Start at the point corresponding to $\omega = 0$ and increase ω to $\omega = \infty$, then return on the conjugate curve from $\omega = \infty$ to $\omega = 0$.   Such a path is shown by the arrows of Fig. 10-13.   Count the net number of *complete* revolutions that this vector makes when the complete contour is traced.   (Counterclockwise revolutions should be subtracted from clockwise ones.) This net number of revolutions is called the number of encirclements. As an example, consider Fig. 10-13a. (To avoid confusion assume that the plot is shifted slightly so that the points corresponding to $\omega = 0$ and $\omega = \infty$ lie to the left of the origin.) Then for frequencies between point O and A, the net rotation of the vector is zero. From A to B to O, there is one clockwise revolution; from O to B to A, there is another clockwise revolution; and finally, from A to O, there is no net rotation. Therefore, this function has two more zeros than poles in the right half-plane.

Let us now see how this criterion can be applied to feedback amplifiers. From Eq. (10-4), the gain of the feedback amplifier of Fig. 10-1 is

$$\mathbf{K}(p) = \frac{\mathbf{A}(p)}{1 - \mathbf{A}(p)\mathfrak{B}(p)} \tag{10-64}$$

But $\mathbf{A}(p)\mathfrak{B}(p)$ is just the open-loop gain. Thus, using Eq. (10-63), we have

$$\mathbf{K}(p) = \frac{\mathbf{A}(p)}{\mathbf{F}(p)} \tag{10-65}$$

Note that $\mathbf{A}(p)$ and $\mathbf{F}(p)$ are both ratios of two polynomials in p. The amplification $\mathbf{A}(p)$ is the gain of a nonfeedback amplifier, and will have all its poles in the left half-plane. Hence, if $\mathbf{K}(p)$ is to have right half-plane poles, then $\mathbf{F}(p)$ must have right half-plane zeros. [We shall assume that $\mathbf{A}(p)$ does not have right half-plane zeros that cancel the zeros of $\mathbf{F}(p)$.] Simple amplifier configurations do not produce right half-plane (or $j\omega$-axis) zeros. For instance, none of the interstage networks of Chap. 6 has right half-plane zeros. (If more-complex coupling networks are used, then such zeros may result.) The open-loop gain $\mathbf{L}(p)$ is the gain of a nonfeedback amplifier, and, hence, will not have right half-plane poles. Thus,

$$\mathbf{F}(p) = 1 - \mathbf{L}(p)$$

will not have right half-plane poles, since the only poles that it can have are those of $\mathbf{L}(p)$. That is, $\mathbf{F}(p)$ can only be infinite if $\mathbf{L}(p)$ is. However, $\mathbf{F}(p)$ can have right half-plane zeros even though $\mathbf{L}(p)$ does not.

For most simple amplifier structures, we can state that if $\mathbf{F}(p)$ has zeros in the right half-plane (or on the $j\omega$ axis), then the amplifier is unstable. If all the zeros of $\mathbf{F}(p)$ lie in the left half-plane, then the amplifier will be stable. Thus, to determine the stability of an amplifier, we need only make a polar plot of the return difference $\mathbf{F}(j\omega)$. If this encircles the origin, then the amplifier will be unstable. If it passes through the origin, then this is the borderline case of instability (i.e., poles on the $j\omega$ axis). It is slightly more convenient to obtain the open-loop gain than the return difference. From Eq. (10-63), we have

$$\mathbf{L}(j\omega) = 1 - \mathbf{F}(j\omega) \tag{10-66}$$

If $\mathbf{F}(j\omega) = 0$, then $\mathbf{L}(j\omega) = 1$. Thus, the previous criterion can be stated in the following way. If a simple feedback amplifier is to be stable, then the polar plot of $\mathbf{L}(j\omega)$ and its conjugate must not encircle or pass through the point $+1$. This point is called the *critical point* and is sometimes labeled (1,0). Consider that Fig. 10-13 contains such a plot. The amplifier will be stable if the length $\overline{OB}$ is less than unity; otherwise it will be unstable.

Let us now consider some practical procedures for obtaining the return difference. We shall illustrate these with the common-cathode vacuum-tube amplifier and the common-emitter transistor amplifier. The same basic procedure can be used for the other amplifier configurations. Consider that the vacuum tube of Fig. 10-14a is in a feedback loop. To measure the open-loop gain, "break" the lead to the grid and apply a generator $\mathbf{E}_3$ between grid and cathode. The returned voltage appears across the other side of the break and the cathode of the tube. Note that any impedance between the grid and the cathode, including the grid-to-cathode capacitance, is placed on the $\mathbf{E}_3'$ side of the circuit. When this measurement is made, any *independent* generators, other than $\mathbf{E}_3$ (e.g., the input generator), must be replaced by their internal impedances.

We have assumed that there is only one feedback loop present in the amplifier. However, in almost all cases, there are unavoidable local feedback loops around each amplifier stage. The grid-to-plate capacitance always constitutes a feedback loop. When vacuum-tube pentodes are used, this can usually be ignored. If vacuum-tube triodes are used for audio amplifiers, sufficient accuracy is often obtained if we consider that C_{gp} affects the input and output impedances (see Sec. 6-1) and neglect its effect as a feedback element. The cathode-bias impedance $\mathbf{Z}_k$ also produces feedback (see Fig. 10-15). Usually [see, for instance, Eq. (10-15)], the only action of this feedback is to make $\mathbf{Z}_k$ appear as an impedance $(1 + \mu)\mathbf{Z}_k$. In most circumstances, we can replace Fig. 10-15a by Fig. 10-15b in any *linear signal* analysis and thus eliminate the feedback due to $\mathbf{Z}_k$. In most practical cases,

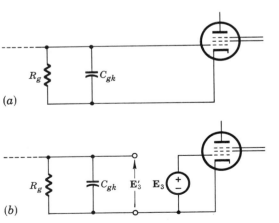

Fig. 10-14 (a) The grid circuit of a vacuum tube in a single-loop feedback amplifier; (b) the circuit to be used in computing the open-loop gain.

Fig. 10-15 (a) A vacuum tube
with a cathode-bias impedance;
(b) a modification of this circuit
that eliminates the local feedback
loop.

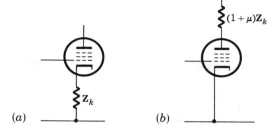

(a)   (b)

the effect of "local" feedback loops can be eliminated and the single-loop
procedures can be used.

Figure 10-16 will be used to illustrate the procedure for determining the
open-loop gain in a common-emitter transistor amplifier. The lead to the
base terminal is broken and a current generator I_3 is applied between the base
and the emitter. The input impedance of the transistor Z_i is placed external
to the transistor as shown in Fig. 10-16b. The current in it is I_3'. The
open-loop gain is I_3'/I_3. Any independent generators, except I_3, should be
replaced by their internal impedances. There is local feedback around each
transistor-amplifier stage. For instance, the reverse transfer-voltage ratio
h_r produces feedback through the $h_{re}E_c$ term. The emitter-stabilizing
impedance also introduces feedback (see Sec. 10-2). However, in both of
these cases, the primary effect is on Z_i. If Z_i is computed considering both
the emitter-stabilizing impedance and h_r and they are then both assumed to
be zero, sufficient accuracy usually results. Thus, the local feedback loops
can be eliminated from transistor-amplifier calculations.

When the feedback loop is broken, it is assumed that this is done in relation to signal frequencies, but that the operating point of the vacuum tubes
or transistors is not disturbed.

The Nyquist diagram can be used to establish a definition for positive
or negative feedback. If $|F(p)| > 1$, then the gain of the amplifier with

Fig. 10-16 (a) The base circuit of
a transistor in a single-loop feedback amplifier; (b) the circuit to be
used in computing the open-loop
gain. (Note that $I_b = I_3$.)

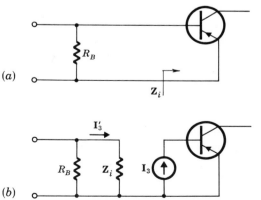

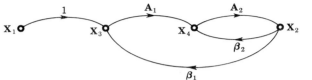

Fig. 10-17 The signal-flow diagram of a multiple-loop feedback amplifier.

feedback will be less than the gain without feedback. If $|F(p)| < 1$, then the introduction of feedback will increase the gain. In the Nyquist diagram $\mathbf{L}(j\omega) = 1 - \mathbf{F}(j\omega)$ is plotted. A circle of radius one whose center is at $+1$ is called the *circle of regeneration*. For those frequencies where the plot of $\mathbf{L}(j\omega)$ lies within this circle, the gain with feedback will be greater than the gain without feedback, and the feedback can be considered to be positive. For those frequencies where $\mathbf{L}(j\omega)$ lies outside of the circle of regeneration, the feedback is negative. Positive feedback is sometimes called *regenerative feedback* and negative feedback is sometimes called *degenerative feedback*.

The procedures that we have discussed apply to single-loop feedback amplifiers. If a multiple-loop feedback amplifier, such as that of Fig. 10-17, is used, then the Nyquist procedures must be modified. The procedure consists of opening all feedback loops and then closing successive ones, making polar plots and comparing them. The procedure will not be discussed here, but it is given in the first and fourth references of the bibliography. In any event, the procedures of Sec. 10-9 can be used to determine the stability of any feedback amplifier.

10-11   Absolute stability, conditional stability, gain margin, and phase margin

If the midband value of the open-loop gain is changed without affecting the frequency response, then only the size of the Nyquist diagram will vary. Let us determine how the stability is affected by such changes. Consider the plot of Fig. 10-18a. To simplify the diagram, we have assumed that the mid-frequency response extends down to zero frequency. A low-frequency response similar in shape to the dotted conjugate curve can be included. The length $\overline{OA}$ is the magnitude of the open-loop gain in the midband region. If $\overline{OB}$ is equal to or greater than 1, then the amplifier is unstable. Since the ratio $\overline{OB}/\overline{OA}$ is constant, the magnitude of $\overline{OA}$ is limited. Hence, the maximum value of the open-loop gain is limited. Now consider the Nyquist plot of Fig. 10-18b. No matter how large it becomes, the plot will always be to the left of the origin, and the critical point, $+1$, cannot be encircled. Thus, this amplifier will be stable, independent of the midband open-loop gain. Such amplifiers are called *absolutely stable*. It may seem as though all amplifiers should be constructed so that they are absolutely stable. However, this type of stability is usually only obtained with simple amplifiers which often do not provide enough gain.

Consider the Nyquist diagram of Fig. 10-18c. If $\overline{OC} < 1$, the amplifier will be stable. If the gain is increased so that $\overline{OC} \geqslant 1$ and $\overline{OB} \leqslant 1$, the amplifier will oscillate. However, if the gain is increased still further so that $\overline{OB} > 1$, the amplifier will again be stable. (See Sec. 10-10 for the definition of encirclement.) If an amplifier is stable, but can become unstable if the gain decreases, it is said to be *conditionally stable*. The advantage of conditional stability is that the midband open-loop gain $\overline{OA}$ can be made as large as desired. The interstage coupling network of these amplifiers must be fairly complex to obtain the desired Nyquist plot. For this reason, conditional stability is usually not used unless very large open-loop gains are required.

The most commonly used Nyquist plot resembles that of Fig. 10-18a. Let us consider some practical problems related to it. If $\overline{OB}$ is very close to unity, then any slight shift in power-supply voltage or element values might cause the amplifier to oscillate. To establish some design criteria, we shall assume that the open-loop gain is such that the phase shift decreases

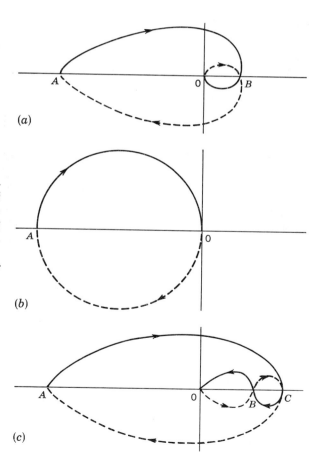

Fig. 10-18 *Nyquist diagrams. (a) Stable if $\overline{OB}$ < 1, unstable if $\overline{OB} \geqslant 1$; (b) absolutely stable; and (c) stable for $\overline{OC} < 1$, unstable if $\overline{OC} \geqslant 1$ and $\overline{OB} \leqslant 1$, conditionally stable if $\overline{OB} > 1$.*

(a)

(b)

(c)

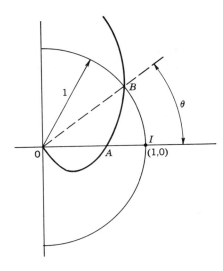

Fig. 10-19   An illustration of gain margin and phase margin.

(or increases) monotonically and the amplitude decreases monotonically as the frequency is increased above (or decreased below) the midband value. We can then state that the amplifier will be stable if the open-loop gain falls below unity before the phase shift becomes zero degrees, or that the amplifier will be stable if the phase shift has not become zero degrees when the open-loop gain falls off to unity.   Consider the portion of the Nyquist diagram shown in Fig. 10-19.   The circle is drawn with a radius of one and with its center at the origin.   The critical point (1,0) is marked on the diagram at point I.   The Nyquist plot intersects the unit circle at point B.   The phase angle at point B is θ degrees.   The angle θ is called the *phase margin*. When the phase angle is zero degrees, then the magnitude of the open-loop gain is $\overline{OA}$.   This is called the *gain margin*.   The gain margin is usually specified in decibels as follows:

$$GM|_{\text{db}} = -20 \log_{10} \overline{OA} \qquad (10\text{-}67)$$

If $GM|_{\text{db}}$ and θ are large, then there will be very little tendency for the amplifier to oscillate if the parameter values change.   These margins are just an indication of two points on a curve, and, consequently, do not completely specify it.   However, for the usual interstage networks, the specification of adequate gain and phase margins provides stable operation for most changes in parameter values.

If the gain margin and/or the phase margin is small, the open-loop gain may be very close to $+1$ at some frequencies.   This may cause the gain at these frequencies to become very large, thus producing an undesirable peak in the frequency response.   Adequate gain and phase margins may prevent this from occurring.

10-12   Design of feedback amplifiers

In this section, at first, we shall devote much of our attention to the high-frequency aspects of the design of feedback amplifiers (i.e., we shall assume that the mid-frequency range starts at zero frequency).   However, the low-frequency considerations are similar to the high-frequency ones and will be discussed subsequently.   We shall consider some simple expressions for the open-loop gain.   A single-stage amplifier could have an open-loop gain of the form

$$\mathbf{L}_1(j\omega) = -\frac{L_0}{1 + jf/f_2} \qquad (10\text{-}68)$$

A Nyquist plot of this expression is given in Fig. 10-20a.   Similarly, for

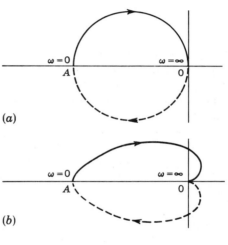

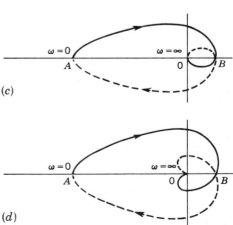

Fig. 10-20   *Nyquist diagrams for the open-loop gains given by (a) Eq. (10-68); (b) Eq. (10-69); (c) Eq. (10-70); and (d) Eq. (10-71).*

two, three, and four stages, we obtain

$$\mathbf{L}_2(j\omega) = -\frac{L_0}{(1 + jf/f_2)^2} \tag{10-69}$$

$$\mathbf{L}_3(j\omega) = -\frac{L_0}{(1 + jf/f_2)^3} \tag{10-70}$$

$$\mathbf{L}_4(j\omega) = -\frac{L_0}{(1 + jf/f_2)^4} \tag{10-71}$$

We have called the magnitude of the midband open-loop gain L_0 and assumed that the feedback is negative.   The Nyquist plots for Eqs. (10-69) to (10-71) are sketched in Figs. 10-20b, c, and d.   Let us now compare these four to determine the maximum magnitude of the midband open-loop gain L_0.   In each case, L_0 is equal to the length $\overline{OA}$.   The Nyquist diagram of Fig. 10-20a is absolutely stable.   Thus, in theory, the value of L_0 can be as large as desired.   In practice, a response of the form of Eq. (10-68) is only obtainable with a single-stage vacuum-tube amplifier, which usually does not supply sufficient gain.   The diagram of Fig. 10-20b is also absolutely stable. This type of response could be obtained from two identical vacuum-tube stages or from a single common-emitter transistor stage where $f_\beta = f_2$ [see Eq. (6-31)].   The single transistor stage usually does not provide sufficient gain. If common-cathode vacuum-tube amplifiers or common-emitter transistor amplifiers are used in a feedback amplifier, then an odd number of stages is usually used to obtain the desired 180° phase shift (negative feedback) in the midband region.   Note that the common-emitter transistor amplifiers have 180° phase shifts in their midband current gain.   The reason that expressions such as Eq. (6-27) do not have a minus sign is because of the convention used in assigning a direction to the output current.   Transformers can be used to obtain a 180° phase shift.   However, there are many instances when it is not desirable to use them.

The Nyquist diagram of Fig. 10-20c is the most practical that we have discussed thus far.   The amplifier will be stable if $\overline{OB} < 1$.   Rewriting Eq. (10-70), we obtain

$$\mathbf{L}_3(j\omega) = \frac{L_0}{[1 + (f/f_2)^2]^{3/2}} \qquad \underline{/180° - 3\tan^{-1}f/f_2} \tag{10-72}$$

The frequency which corresponds to point B will have a phase shift of zero degrees.   Thus,

$$180° - 3\tan^{-1}\frac{f_B}{f_2} = 0 \tag{10-73}$$

Solving, we obtain

$$\frac{f_B}{f_2} = \sqrt{3} \tag{10-74}$$

The magnitude of the gain at $f = f_B$ must be equal to or less than 1. Hence

$$\frac{L_0}{[1 + (f_B/f_2)^2]^{3/2}} \leqslant 1$$

Substituting Eq. (10-74), and solving, we have

$$L_0 \leqslant 8 \tag{10-75}$$

Thus, the maximum open-loop gain is 8 (or 18 db). This is usually not large enough for most practical cases. The assumption that all three stages have identical frequency responses limits the maximum value of L_0. This will be illustrated in a subsequent example.

The maximum open-loop gain for the Nyquist diagram of Fig. 10-20d can be obtained using the procedures of Eqs. (10-72) to (10-75). Note that $180° - 4 \tan^{-1} f_B/f_2 = 0$. Thus,

$$L_0 \leqslant 4 \tag{10-76}$$

Now let us consider the high-frequency design of a feedback amplifier. The design specifications are: the voltage gain in the midband region $K_0 = -50$; the open-loop gain in the midband region $L_0 = -100$; and the amplifier is to amplify frequencies up to 10,000 cps. We shall use the amplifier of Fig. 10-10a, which was analyzed in Sec. 10-7, and assume that the approximate expressions of Eqs. (10-45) to (10-49) are valid. Then, from Eq. (10-48),

$$\frac{G_1}{G_3} = \frac{R_3}{R_1} = 50 \tag{10-77}$$

The approximate expression for the open-loop gain is given by Eq. (10-46) as

$$\mathbf{L} = \frac{-g_m \mathbf{A}_{v1} G_3}{(G_1 + G_3 + j\omega C_1)(G_2 + G_3 + j\omega C_2)}$$

The gain of the first two amplifier stages can be written as

$$\mathbf{A}_{v1} = \frac{A_0}{(1 + jf/f_{21})(1 + jf/f_{22})}$$

The approximate gain of the third amplifier stage is

$$\frac{g_m}{G_2 + G_3 + j\omega C_2} = \frac{g_m/(G_2 + G_3)}{1 + jf/f_{23}}$$

where

$$f_{23} = \frac{G_2 + G_3}{2\pi C_2}$$

In addition,

$$\frac{G_3}{G_1 + G_3 + j\omega C_1} = \frac{G_3/(G_1 + G_3)}{1 + jf/f_{24}}$$

where

$$f_{24} = \frac{G_1 + G_3}{2\pi C_1} \tag{10-78}$$

The complete expression for the open loop gain is

$$\mathbf{L} = \frac{-L_0}{(1 + jf/f_{21})(1 + jf/f_{22})(1 + jf/f_{23})(1 + jf/f_{24})}$$

where

$$L_0 = \frac{g_m A_0 G_3}{(G_1 + G_3)(G_2 + G_3)}$$

If $f_{21} = f_{22} = f_{23} = f_{24}$, then the maximum value that L_0 can have is 4 [see Eq. (10-76)]. Thus, we cannot have all the half-power frequencies equal. For convenience, let us assume that

$$f_{21} = f_{22} = f_{2a} \qquad \text{and} \qquad f_{23} = f_{24} = f_{2b} \tag{10-79}$$

Thus

$$\mathbf{L} = \frac{-L_0}{(1 + jf/f_{2a})^2(1 + jf/f_{2b})^2}$$

For a moment, let us assume that f_{2b} is so much greater than f_{2a} that the second term in the denominator can be ignored. We shall determine the frequency f_c where the open-loop gain is 1. The specified value of L_0 is -100. Hence

$$\frac{100}{1 + (f_c/f_{2a})^2} = 1$$

Solving, we obtain

$$f_c = 9.95 f_{2a}$$

The phase angle of $\mathbf{L}$ at this frequency is given by $180° - 2 \tan^{-1} 9.95$.

$$\angle L(j\omega_c) = 11.5°$$

Since the amplifier is to work with frequencies of up to 10,000 cps, the open-loop gain should be essentially flat up to that frequency. Thus, let us choose $f_{2a} = 10 \times 10,000 = 100,000$ cps. (The magnitude of the open-loop gain will be approximately equal to 99 at a frequency of 10,000 cps.) Then $f_c = 0.995 \times 10^6$ cps. Now let us choose f_{2b} so that the phase margin is at least 5°. If $\angle[1/(1 + jf_c/f_{2b})^2] \leqslant 6.5°$, then this will be obtained. (Actually, the phase margin will be greater than 5° since $|1/(1 + jf_c/f_{2b})|$ will be slightly less than unity.) Then

$$\tan^{-1}\frac{f_c}{f_{2b}} = \frac{6.5°}{2} = 3.25°$$

so that $f_c/f_{2b} = 0.057$ and $f_{2b} = 17.46 \times 10^6$ cps. We have arbitrarily divided the half-power frequencies in Eqs. (10-79). Actually, all that is required is that two of the half-power frequencies be 100,000 cps and that the other two be 17.46×10^6 cps. Three of the half-power frequencies, f_{21}, f_{22}, and f_{23}, are half-power frequencies of the amplifier stages, while f_{24} is the half-power frequency of the β network. Both the gain of the amplifier stages and the resistance R_3 of the β network will decrease if their respective half-power frequencies increase. If R_1 and R_3 are too small, then they will load down the output circuit. In addition, R_1 may represent the internal impedance of the signal generator, and, hence, have a minimum value. As a compromise, we shall choose $f_{23} = f_{24} = 100,000$ cps and

$$f_{21} = f_{22} = 17.46 \times 10^6 \text{ cps}$$

To determine the value of R_1 and of R_3, let us assume that the input capacitor is 50 $\mu\mu$f. Then, substituting in Eqs. (10-77) and (10-78), we have $G_1/G_3 = 50$ and $(G_1 + G_3)/(2\pi \times 50 \times 10^{-12}) = 100,000$. Solving, we obtain $R_3 = 1.623 \times 10^6$ ohms and $R_1 = 32,460$ ohms. Since we wish a midband open-loop gain of -100 and the midband loss of the β network is $R_1/(R_1 + R_3) = \frac{1}{51}$, the required midband gain of the amplifier is 5,100. The methods of Chap. 6 are used in obtaining the amplifier design.

We have arbitrarily assumed that $f_{21} = f_{22}$ and $f_{23} = f_{24}$. If this is not done, then the half-power frequencies could be reduced somewhat. However, the amplifier design becomes more complex.

We have omitted the low-frequency design from this discussion. If we neglect the effect of the cathode and screen-grid bias impedance, then this design is essentially the same as the high-frequency design, except that there are only three RC-coupled stages rather than the four that were considered in the high-frequency case.

Actually, the effects of the cathode and screen-grid bias impedances must be considered. The results of Sec. 6-5 can be used here. The frequency response of these networks can be of help in obtaining the required design. In fact, the response of these networks is quite similar to that of the corrective networks that will be discussed in the next section.

The design procedure for transistors is similar to that for vacuum tubes. However, each amplifier stage introduces two frequency-dependent terms in the high-frequency response [see Eq. (6-31)]. This increases the complexity of the design. However, the principles that were discussed in this section can still be used.

10-13   Corrective networks

If the open-loop frequency response of a feedback amplifier is designed properly, then the midband magnitude of the open-loop gain can be made as large as desired. However, as was illustrated by the design of the last sec-

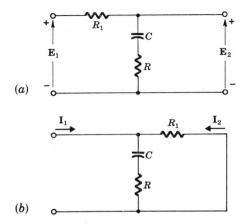

(a)

(b)

Fig. 10-21   *Phase-lag-compensating networks.   (a) Voltage type; (b) current type.*

tion, the upper (lower) half-power frequencies of the amplifier stages become quite high (low).   Thus, it may prove difficult to construct amplifiers with the required gain.   If networks could be devised that would cause the gain of an amplifier to fall off with increasing (or decreasing) frequency, but would not introduce any phase shift, then they would be ideal.   These could be used to reduce the magnitude of the open-loop gain below unity without causing its phase angle to approach zero degrees.   Unfortunately, amplitude and phase response are interrelated, so that we cannot obtain such ideal networks.   However, there are some networks that are not ideal, but which do prove quite helpful.   Consider the two networks drawn in Fig. 10-21a and b.   If we let $\mathbf{G} = \mathbf{E}_2/\mathbf{E}_1$ for the network of Fig. 10-21a and $\mathbf{G} = -\mathbf{I}_2/\mathbf{I}_1$ for the network of Fig. 10-21b, we have

$$\mathbf{G} = \frac{1 + jf/f_{2a}}{1 + jf/f_{2b}} \tag{10-80}$$

where

$$f_{2a} = \frac{1}{2\pi RC} \tag{10-81}$$

and

$$f_{2b} = \frac{1}{2\pi(R_1 + R)C} \tag{10-82}$$

This network does not reduce the frequency response to zero, but to f_{2b}/f_{2a} of its midband value.   Plots of the asymptotes of the amplitude response of this function and its phase shift are given in Fig. 10-22.   These networks are called *phase-lag networks*, since they produce a lagging phase angle.   As the frequency increases above $\sqrt{f_{2b}f_{2a}}$, the magnitude of the phase shift decreases toward zero.   Consider that two of these networks are used as interstage coupling networks and the corner frequencies of the first are f_{2a1} and f_{2b1}, while those of the second are f_{2a2} and f_{2b2}.   If f_{2b2} is considerably greater than f_{2a1}, then the loss in amplitude, at sufficiently high frequencies, will be the product of the losses of the individual sections, while the maximum phase shift will not be considerably greater than the maximum phase shift of one section.   These networks do not, by any means, eliminate the need for broadband amplifiers.   In practical cases, the frequency response of the phase-lag network is combined with the high-frequency response of the amplifier to obtain the desired overall response.

Compensating networks can be used to correct the low-frequency response.   Two such networks are shown in Fig. 10-23.   If $\mathbf{G} = \mathbf{E}_2/\mathbf{E}_1$ for the network of Fig. 10-23*a* and $\mathbf{G} = -\mathbf{I}_2/\mathbf{I}_1$ for the network of Fig. 10-23*b*, we have

$$\mathbf{G} = \frac{f_{1a}}{f_{1b}} \cdot \frac{1 + jf/f_{1a}}{1 + jf/f_{1b}} \tag{10-83}$$

where

$$f_{1a} = \frac{1}{2\pi RC} \tag{10-84}$$

$$f_{1b} = \frac{R_1 + R}{2\pi R_1 RC} \tag{10-85}$$

The response of this network is similar to that of the networks in Fig. 10-21,

Fig. 10-22   (*a*) *The asymptotes of amplitude response in db for the networks of Fig. 10-21; (b) the phase response of these networks.*

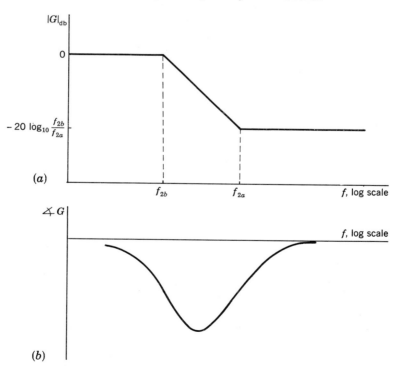

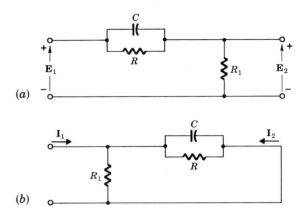

Fig. 10-23   Phase-lead-compensating   networks.   (a) Voltage type;   (b)   current type.

except that the amplitude response falls off with decreasing frequency and the phase angle leads instead of lags.   (The reason for the difference is that in these networks $f_{1b} > f_{1a}$.)   This is called the *phase-lead network*.   Its application in the low-frequency region is similar to that of the phase-lag network in the high-frequency region.

The cathode or screen-grid bias impedances and the emitter-stabilizing impedance (see Secs. 6-5 and 6-6) produce a frequency response that is essentially the same as that of the phase-lead network.   Thus, these impedances can serve the same function as the frequency-corrective network.

10-14   Operational amplifiers

Feedback can be used to obtain electronic devices that perform mathematical operations.   These devices are called *operational amplifiers*.   One applica-

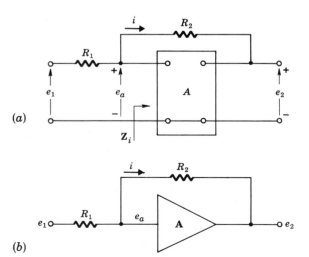

Fig. 10-24   (a) An operational amplifier that multiplies by a constant;   (b) a simplified representation of this amplifier.

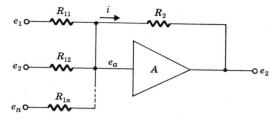

Fig. 10-25 An electronic circuit that performs the mathematical operation of addition and multiplication by a constant.

tion of them is in analog computers, where an electric circuit is set up such that its response is the solution of a differential equation. In this section, we shall develop amplifiers that can be used to solve linear integral-differential equations.

Multiplication by a constant; addition and subtraction

Consider the block diagram of the amplifier of Fig. 10-24a. We shall assume that the amplifier is ideal in that Z_i is infinite and $e_2/e_a = A$. Then, the current i must be through R_1 as well as R_2. Hence

$$i = \frac{e_1 - e_a}{R_1} = \frac{e_a - e_2}{R_2} \tag{10-86}$$

but

$$e_a = \frac{e_2}{A} \tag{10-87}$$

Substituting, we obtain

$$\frac{e_2}{R_2}\left[1 - \frac{1}{A}\left(1 + \frac{R_2}{R_1}\right)\right] = -\frac{e_1}{R_1} \tag{10-88}$$

If the voltage gain is sufficiently high so that

$$1 \gg \left|\frac{1}{A}\left(1 + \frac{R_2}{R_1}\right)\right| \tag{10-89}$$

then we can approximate e_2 by

$$e_2 = -\frac{R_2}{R_1}e_1 \tag{10-90}$$

Thus, we have achieved multiplication by a constant. The representation of Fig. 10-24b is the one that is usually used in analog computers.

Now consider the circuit of Fig. 10-25.

$$i = \frac{e_{11} - e_a}{R_{11}} + \frac{e_{12} - e_a}{R_{12}} + \cdots + \frac{e_{1n} - e_a}{R_{1n}} = \frac{e_a - e_2}{R_2}$$

Then, substituting Eq. (10-87), we obtain

$$\frac{e_2}{R_2}\left[1 - \frac{1}{A}\left(1 + \frac{R_2}{R_{11}} + \frac{R_2}{R_{12}} + \cdots + \frac{R_2}{R_{1n}}\right)\right]$$
$$= -\left[\frac{e_{11}}{R_{11}} + \frac{e_{12}}{R_{12}} + \cdots + \frac{e_{1n}}{R_{1n}}\right]$$

If

$$1 \gg \left|\frac{1}{A}\left(1 + \frac{R_2}{R_{11}} + \frac{R_2}{R_{12}} + \cdots + \frac{R_2}{R_{1n}}\right)\right| \tag{10-91}$$

then

$$e_2 = -R_2\left(\frac{e_{11}}{R_{11}} + \frac{e_{12}}{R_{12}} + \cdots + \frac{e_{1n}}{R_{1n}}\right) \tag{10-92}$$

Thus, we can multiply a number of voltages by arbitrary constants and add them. The constant multiplier can be adjusted by varying the input resistors. Note that the input circuits do not interact with each other.

These amplifiers introduce a minus sign. If this is not desired, then two amplifier stages should be cascaded. Two signals can be subtracted by multiplying them by -1 before they are added.

Differentiation

Consider the circuit of Fig. 10-26. We have

$$i = C\frac{d}{dt}(e_1 - e_a) = \frac{e_a - e_2}{R} \tag{10-93}$$

Then, substituting Eq. (10-87), we obtain

$$-C\frac{de_1}{dt} = \frac{e_2}{R} - \frac{1}{A}\left(\frac{e_2}{R} + C\frac{de_2}{dt}\right)$$

If

$$\left|\frac{e_2}{R}\right| \gg \left|\frac{1}{A}\left(\frac{e_2}{R} + C\frac{de_2}{dt}\right)\right| \tag{10-94}$$

then

$$e_2 = -RC\frac{de_1}{dt} \tag{10-95}$$

Thus, the output is proportional to the derivative of the input. The

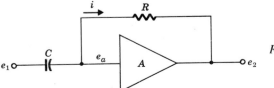

Fig. 10-26   A differentiator.

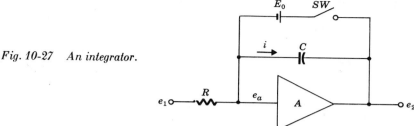

Fig. 10-27 An integrator.

inequality of relation (10-94) requires some comment.   There may be times when $de_2/dt \gg e_2$, and the inequality will not be valid no matter how large A is.   The value of A should be made large enough so that relation (10-94) is satisfied for almost all of the time and in practical cases (with bounded derivatives) is invalid only when e_2 is quite small.

Integration

Consider the circuit of Fig. 10-27.   For the time being, ignore the battery E_0. Then

$$i = \frac{e_1 - e_a}{R} = C \frac{d}{dt} (e_a - e_2) \tag{10-96}$$

Substitute Eq. (10-87):

$$C \frac{de_2}{dt} - \frac{1}{A} \left(\frac{e_2}{R} + C \frac{de_2}{dt} \right) = - \frac{e_1}{R}$$

If

$$\left| C \frac{de_2}{dt} \right| \gg \left| \frac{1}{A} \left(\frac{e_2}{R} + C \frac{de_2}{dt} \right) \right| \tag{10-97}$$

then

$$e_2 = - \frac{1}{RC} \int e_1 \, dt \tag{10-98}$$

This circuit provides a convenient means of establishing the initial value of a variable.   Assume that the switch *sw* of Fig. 10-26 is closed prior to $t = 0$ and is opened at $t = 0$.   Then, at $t = 0+$, just after the switch is opened, the voltage across the capacitor is E_0 and, thus,

$$e_{20} - e_{a0} = E_0$$

Substituting Eq. (10-87) and assuming that $1 \gg |1/A|$, we have

$$e_{20} = E_0 \tag{10-99}$$

Thus, the battery and switch are a simple means of establishing the initial value of a variable.

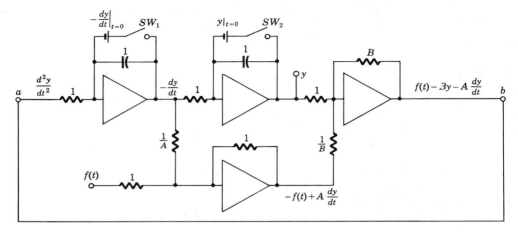

Fig. 10-28   A circuit for the solution of the differential equation of Eq. (10-100). The values of resistance and capacitance are given in megohms and μf, respectively.

To illustrate the use of these operational amplifiers, let us solve a simple differential equation.

$$\frac{d^2y}{dt^2} + A\frac{dy}{dt} + By = f(t) \tag{10-100}$$

Rewrite this equation as

$$\frac{d^2y}{dt^2} = -A\frac{dy}{dt} - By + f(t) \tag{10-101}$$

Consider the circuit of Fig. 10-28.   For the time being, assume that the connection between points a and b is broken and that a generator equal to the unknown d^2y/dt^2 is available and connected to point a.   The analog computer should provide a means for generating the driving function $f(t)$.   Then the voltages will be as marked on the diagram.   Using Eq. (10-101), we see that the voltage at point b equals d^2y/dt^2.   If the d^2y/dt^2 generator is removed and points a and b are connected as shown, then, since an equilibrium must be established, the circuit voltages will be the required ones. The unknown y can be obtained from the terminal so marked.   The voltages equal to d^2y/dt^2 and $-dy/dt$ can also be obtained from the appropriate terminals.

The initial values of y and dy/dt are established by means of the appropriate batteries.   At $t = 0$, switches sw_1 and sw_2 are opened and $f(t)$ is applied.   Note that writing the differential equation in the form of Eq. (10-101) allows us to use integrating circuits and, thus, to conveniently establish initial values.

We have worked with voltage amplifiers in this section.   We could have proceeded on a dual basis and used current amplifiers.

BIBLIOGRAPHY

Bode, H. W. "Network Analysis and Feedback Amplifier Design," chap. 7, D. Van Nostrand Company, Inc., Princeton, N.J., 1945.   (A difficult graduate-level book.)

Gray, T. S.: "Applied Electronics," pp. 570–600, John Wiley & Sons, Inc., New York, 1954.

Millman, J.: "Vacuum-tube and Semiconductor Electronics," chap. 17, McGraw-Hill Book Company, New York, 1958.

Truxal, J. G.: "Automatic Feedback Control System Synthesis," pp. 143–159, McGraw-Hill Book Company, New York, 1955.

PROBLEMS

10-1. A feedback amplifier has a gain that is given by Eq. (10-4).   If $A = -20$ and $\beta = 0.1$, comment on the accuracy of Eq. (10-6).   Repeat this problem for values of A equal to -100 and $-1,000$.

10-2. The gain of a feedback amplifier is given by Eq. (10-4) where $A = -9$ and $\beta = 0.1$.   If $|A|$ increases by 10 percent, what will the percentage change in K be?

10-3. Repeat Prob. 10-2, but now use values of $A = -1,000$ and $A = +9$.

10-4. Obtain an exact expression for the voltage gain of the amplifier of Fig. 10-29.   The answer should be in terms of the parameters of the vacuum tubes and the circuit elements.   Assume that the reactance of C is zero at the signal frequency.

10-5. Obtain an exact expression for the current gain of the amplifier of Fig. 10-30.   The answer should be in terms of the low-frequency h parameters of the transistor and the circuit elements.   Assume that the reactance of C is zero at the signal frequency.

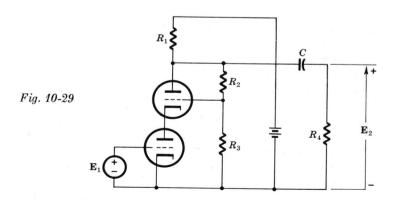

Fig. 10-29

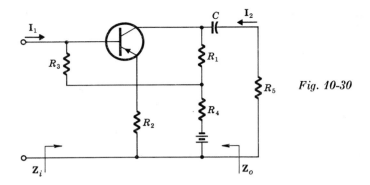

Fig. 10-30

10-6. Compare the ratio of the distortion to the signal X_{2d}/X_{2s} for the feedback amplifier of Fig. 10-31. Use the following three cases: $\beta_1 = 0$ and $\beta_2 = 0$; $\beta_1 = 0$ and $\beta_2 = \beta_2$; $\beta_1 = \beta_1$ and $\beta_2 = \beta_2$. Assume that the input signal X_1 can be varied so that X_{2s} remains constant.

10-7. Repeat Prob. 10-6, but now assume that X_1 is constant.

10-8. If, for the amplifier of Fig. 10-17, $K = X_2/X_1$ and A_1 changes by an amount ΔA_1, what will the fractional change $\Delta K/K$ be?

10-9. Repeat Prob. 10-8 for a fractional change ΔA_2 in A_2.

10-10. A feedback amplifier is such that its gain expression is given by Eq. (10-4). If $A = -A_0/[(1 + jf/f_a)(1 + jf/f_b)]$, how does the midband-gain–half-power-bandwidth product vary with β?

10-11. Compute the output impedance of the amplifier of Fig. 10-2. Assume that C_k is a short circuit.

10-12. Repeat Prob. 10-11, but now do not assume that C_k is a short circuit.

10-13. Compute an expression for the input impedance Z_i of the amplifier of Fig. 10-30.

10-14. Compute an expression for the output impedance Z_o of the amplifier of Fig. 10-30. Assume that the impedance of the input generator is infinite.

10-15. Compute the voltage gain of the amplifier of Fig. 10-10a, as was done in Sec. 10-7, but do not consider that the coupling capacitor C is a short circuit.

Fig. 10-31

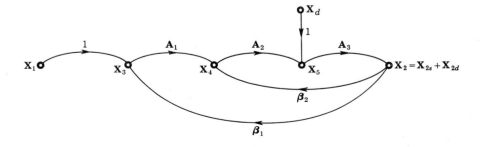

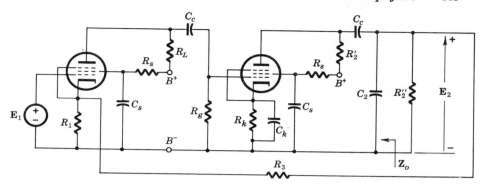

Fig. 10-32

10-16. Compute the current gain of the amplifier of Fig. 10-11*a*, as was done in Sec. 10-7, but do not assume that the coupling capacitor C is a short circuit.

10-17. Compute the voltage gain E_2/E_1 of the amplifier of Fig. 10-32. Neglect the effect of all coupling, bypass, and parasitic capacitors.

10-18. Repeat Prob. 10-17, but do not neglect the coupling, bypass, and parasitic capacitors.

10-19. Compute the ouput impedance Z_o of the amplifier of Fig. 10-32. Neglect the effects of the coupling, bypass, and parasitic capacitors.

10-20. Compute the current gain I_2/I_1 of the amplifier of Fig. 10-33. Assume that all coupling and bypass capacitors are short circuits and that high-frequency effects can be ignored.

10-21. Repeat Prob. 10-20, but do not consider that the coupling and bypass capacitors are short circuits or that the high-frequency effects can be ignored.

10-22. Compute the input and output impedances for the amplifier of Fig. 10-33. Use the assumptions of Prob. 10-20.

Fig. 10-33

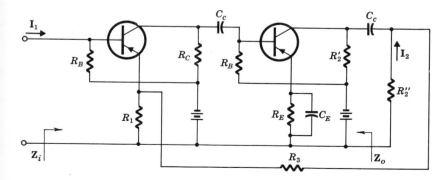

10-23. The following polynomials are the denominator polynomials of the transformed form of the gain expression of a feedback amplifier. There are no common factors in the numerators. Use the Hurwitz test to determine which amplifiers are stable.

a. $p^3 + 5p^2 + 8p + 6$
b. $p^3 - 4p^2 + 9p + 7$
c. $p^3 + 9p + 2$
d. $p^4 + 2p^3 + 3p^2 + 2p + 2$
e. $p^4 + p^3 + p^2 + 12p + 6$

10-24. Repeat Prob. 10-23, but now use the Routh procedure.

10-25. The open-loop gain of a feedback amplifier is given by $-6/(1 + jf/10,000)^3$. Draw the Nyquist diagram for this amplifier. Is it stable?

10-26. Repeat Prob. 10-25 for an open-loop gain of $-3/[(1 + jf/10,000)^4 (1 + j10/f)^3]$.

10-27. Repeat Prob. 10-25 for an open-loop gain of $-6/(1 + jf/10,000)^4$.

10-28. A feedback amplifier has an open-loop gain of $-8/(1 + jf/f_2)^4$. Will this amplifier be stable for any finite and nonzero value of f_2?

10-29. Obtain exact expression for the open-loop gain of the amplifier of Fig. 10-10a. Assume that all bypass capacitors are short circuits. Neglect any parasitic capacitances that are not shown.

10-30. Repeat Prob. 10-29 for the amplifier of Fig. 10-11a. Neglect any high-frequency effects.

10-31. Determine the gain and phase margins for the amplifier of Prob. 10-25.

10-32. Repeat Prob. 10-31 for the amplifier of Prob. 10-26. Note that there are actually two sets of gain and phase margins, one for the high frequencies and one for the low frequencies.

10-33. The low-frequency response of the open-loop gain of a feedback amplifier is given by $-100/[(1 + jf_a/f)(1 + jf_b/f)(1 + jf_c/f)]$ and the amplifier is to work with frequencies down to 20 cps. The magnitude of the open-loop gain is not to be less than 75 over the useful range of frequencies. Design the amplifier, in regard to the low-frequency response, so that it will be stable and have, at least, a 10° phase margin.

10-34. The current gain of a single transistor amplifier stage is $A_i = A_0/[(1 + jf/f_2)(1 + jf/10^8)]$. Three of these are to be used in a "single loop" feedback amplifier whose open-loop gain is $-A_{i1}A_{i2}A_{i3}\beta$. The midband open-loop gain is to have a magnitude of at least 100 and $\beta = \frac{1}{50}$. Design the amplifier. The maximum value of the product of A_0f_2 is equal to 50×10^6. The three stages are not to be identical. Design the amplifier so that it is stable. There should be a 5° phase margin. (Assume that A_0f_2 can be made less than 50×10^6 if desired.) The frequencies f_2 need not be equal for each stage.

10-35. The open-loop gain of a feedback amplifier is $100/[(1 - jf_a/f)(1 - jf_b/f)^2(1 + jf/f_c)^2(1 + jf/f_d)^2]$. What relations must exist among f_a, f_b, f_c, and f_d if this amplifier is to be stable? Assume that f_a and f_b are both very much less than f_c and f_d.

10-36. Discuss how a cathode-bias impedance or an emitter-stabilizing impedance can be used in the design of a feedback amplifier.

10-37. Set up a circuit which can be used to solve the following differential equation:

$$\frac{d^3y}{dt^3} + 3\frac{d^2y}{dt^2} - 5\frac{dy}{dt} + 6y = f(t)$$

where

$$y\Big|_{t=0} = 0 \qquad \frac{dy}{dt}\Big|_{t=0} = -3 \qquad \text{and} \qquad \frac{d^2y}{dt^2}\Big|_{t=0} = 7$$

Assume that a generator whose output voltage is equal to $f(t)$ is available.

10-38. Repeat Prob. 10-37, but now assume that $f(t) = e^{-3t} \sin 2t$ and that no such generator is available. [*Hint:* set up a differential equation whose solution is $f(t)$.]

Sinusoidal Oscillators

Very often such electronic devices as receivers, transmitters, and a great variety of electronic test equipment must generate a sinusoid of specified frequency. To obtain these signals, an oscillator is built. That is, we deliberately construct an unstable feedback amplifier. The basis for much of the analysis of oscillator circuits has been developed in the last chapter. However, simplifications and modifications can be made for the usual oscillator circuits. These will be discussed in this chapter.

11-1 Criteria for oscillation

The criteria for the stability of feedback amplifiers, which were discussed in Secs. 10-9 and 10-10, can also be applied to determine if a circuit will oscillate. For instance, if a feedback circuit has the Nyquist plot of Fig. 10-18a, we can state that it will oscillate if the gain is such that $\overline{OB} > 1$. In general, if the open-loop gain of a feedback amplifier is equal to $L_a/\underline{0}$ at some frequency ω_a, and $L_a > 1$, we *cannot* state that the amplifier will oscillate (see Fig. 10-18c). However, if we restrict ourselves to relatively simple circuits, where the amplitude response decreases monotonically and the phase

Fig. 11-1 The generalized linear device to be used in the study of oscillation.

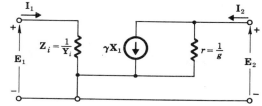

angle increases or decreases monotonically as we depart from a midband region, then Nyquist diagrams such as those of Fig. 10-20 result. *In such cases, we can state that a device will oscillate if the magnitude of its open-loop gain is greater than 1 when its phase angle is zero.* Most oscillator circuits fit into this category; thus, the criterion for their oscillation is quite simple. As a corollary, if there is oscillation for one value of gain, then increasing the magnitude of the open-loop gain (without changing the frequency response) will not cause the oscillation to cease. In order that our analysis can apply to both vacuum tubes and transistors, we shall use the generalized active element of Fig. 11-1. The impedance Z_i is the input impedance of the active element. In a common-cathode vacuum tube, it could include the input capacitance. However, it is often convenient to treat the interelectrode capacitances as external elements. For the transistor, Z_i represents the input impedance. This impedance depends upon the load impedance of the transistor. However, there are a great many circumstances when h_r can be ignored, in which case Z_i would be equal to h_i [see Eq. (3-85)]. In the common-cathode vacuum tube $\gamma = g_m$ and $r = r_p$; for the transistor, $\gamma = h_f$ and $r = 1/h_o$. The output capacitance will be included as an external element. We shall now consider two procedures to determine if a simple structure will oscillate.

Infinite gain

An oscillator may be thought of as an amplifier with zero input signal. Then, if there is to be an output, the gain must be infinite. Consider the typical oscillator structure shown in Fig. 11-2. In order to write the nodal equation for this circuit, we must know if X_1 corresponds to a voltage or to a current. To keep the results general, we shall define a new variable γ_1 such that $\gamma_1 = \gamma$ if $X_1 = E_1$, and $\gamma_1 = \gamma/Z_i$ if $X_1 = I_1$. Thus, we can

Fig. 11-2 A basic oscillator structure.

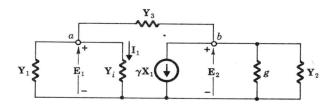

replace γX_i by $\gamma_1 E_1$ for both types of circuits.   The nodal equations then are

$$0 = (Y_1 + Y_i + Y_3)E_1 - Y_3 E_2 \tag{11-1}$$

$$0 = (\gamma_1 - Y_3)E_1 + (Y_3 + Y_2 + g)E_2 \tag{11-2}$$

The solution for E_2 in determinant form is

$$E_2 = \frac{\begin{vmatrix} Y_1 + Y_i + Y_3 & 0 \\ \gamma_1 - Y_3 & 0 \end{vmatrix}}{\begin{vmatrix} Y_1 + Y_i + Y_3 & -Y_3 \\ \gamma_1 - Y_3 & Y_3 + Y_2 + g \end{vmatrix}} \tag{11-3}$$

The numerator determinant is zero.   If there is to be any output, the denominator determinant must also be zero.   Hence,

$$\gamma_1 = -\frac{(Y_1 + Y_i)(Y_2 + Y_3 + g) + Y_3(Y_2 + g)}{Y_3} \tag{11-4}$$

This equation is not as simple as it may seem.   The right-hand side is usually a complex number which is a function of frequency.   Thus,

$$\gamma_1 = G(\omega) + jB(\omega) \tag{11-5}$$

If γ_1 is a real number, then the criteria for oscillation become

$$\gamma_1 = G(\omega) \tag{11-6}$$

$$B(\omega) = 0 \tag{11-7}$$

In general, there is only one value of ω, called ω_0, that will satisfy Eq. (11-7); thus, this equation is used to determine the frequency of oscillation.   This value can then be substituted into Eq. (11-6).   Thus, for the simple Nyquist plots that we have been considering,

$$\gamma_1 \gtrless G(\omega_0) \tag{11-8}$$

is the condition that must be imposed upon the active element if oscillation is to occur.   We shall see examples of this procedure in the next section.

The h parameters of a transistor are complex functions of frequency. Thus, it may not always be possible to consider that γ_1 is a real number. However, the basic procedure is the same.

Zero impedance, negative resistance

Another procedure for determining the criterion for oscillation of a simple structure is to establish a loop with zero impedance for some value of ω.   A sinusoidal current can then persist indefinitely in this loop.   For instance, consider the basic oscillator structure of Fig. 11-2.   We wish to determine the impedance looking into terminals ab when Y_3 is removed.   A simple analysis yields

$$Z_{ab} = \frac{1}{Y_1 + Y_i} + \frac{1}{g + Y_2} + \frac{\gamma_1}{(Y_1 + Y_i)(g + Y_2)} \tag{11-9}$$

If

$$\frac{1}{Y_3} + Z_{ab} = 0 \tag{11-10}$$

for some value of ω, then there will be oscillation. Substituting Eq. (11-9) into Eq. (11-10), we obtain

$$\gamma_1 = -\frac{(Y_1 + Y_i)(Y_2 + Y_3 + g) + Y_3(Y_2 + g)}{Y_3} \tag{11-11}$$

Thus, the criterion for oscillation is the same as Eq. (11-4) and the discussion following it holds here also. Note that the impedance around any loop could have been set equal to zero to determine this criterion.

To obtain some physical insight into this procedure, let us examine a specific example. Assume that $Y_i = 0$, $g = 0$, γ_1 is a real number, and that Y_1 and Y_2 represent capacitance admittances. Thus,

$$Y_1 = j\omega C_1$$
$$Y_2 = j\omega C_2$$

Substitution in Eq. (11-9) yields

$$Z_{ab} = -\frac{\gamma_1}{\omega^2 C_1 C_2} + \frac{1}{j\omega C_1} + \frac{1}{j\omega C_2}$$

This represents the series connection of two capacitors C_1 and C_2, and a *negative* resistance $-\gamma_1/\omega^2 C_1 C_2$. Now let us assume that Y_3 represents an inductance with a series resistance.

$$\frac{1}{Y_3} = R + j\omega L$$

Then, substituting in Eq. (11-10) and using Eqs. (11-5) to (11-8), we obtain the criterion for oscillation.

$$\gamma_1 \geqslant \omega^2 C_1 C_2 R$$
$$\omega_0 = \frac{1}{\sqrt{LC_1 C_2/(C_1 + C_2)}}$$

Thus, we can consider that oscillation results when there is a negative resistance of proper magnitude to offset the losses of the circuit elements.

Both procedures presented in this section are equivalent to setting the open-loop gain equal to unity.

11-2   Typical radio-frequency oscillator circuits

Some representative oscillator circuits are shown in Fig. 11-3.   In Fig. 11-3*a*
and *b*, the feedback takes place between the coupled coils.   There are modifications of this circuit wherein the input circuit is tuned or where both input
and output circuits are tuned.   The oscillators of Fig. 11-3*c* and *d* are called

*Fig. 11-3   Some basic radio-frequency oscillator circuits.   (a) and (b) tuned output;
(c) and (d) Colpitts; (e) and (f) Hartley.*

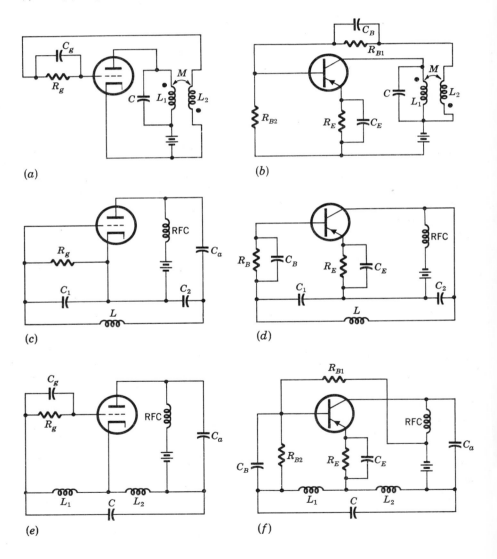

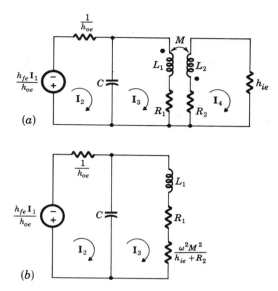

Fig. 11-4 (a) An equivalent-circuit representation of the oscillator of Fig. 11-4b; (b) a modification of this circuit.

Colpitts oscillators. The tuned circuit consists of the two capacitors C_1 and C_2 and the inductor L. The counterpart of this circuit is the Hartley oscillator, which is shown in Fig. 11-3e and f. Here the tuned circuits consist of the inductors L_1 and L_2, and the capacitor C. Some of these circuits use an inductor labeled RFC (radio frequency choke). It is designed so that it is essentially an open circuit at the frequency of operation. The elements R_g, C_g, R_B, R_{B1}, R_{B2}, C_B, R_E, C_E, and C_a are included for bias purposes. In these circuits, the operation is often quite nonlinear. The tuned circuits are used to reject any unwanted harmonics. Linear and nonlinear operation of oscillators is discussed in Sec. 11-4. We have illustrated the transistor circuits in the common-emitter configuration. Common-base and common-collector circuits can also be used, and their circuits are similar.

Let us demonstrate how the criterion for oscillation developed in the last section can be applied to these circuits. For instance, let us apply the infinite-gain procedure to Fig. 11-3b. We shall assume that C_B and C_E are short circuits at the signal frequency and that R_{B2} can be considered to be an open circuit. Then, using the approximate equivalent circuit discussed in Sec. 11-1, we obtain the equivalent circuit of Fig. 11-4, where a voltage generator is used instead of a current generator. We shall assume that h_{ie}, h_{oe}, and h_{fe} are real numbers and that $h_{ie} + R_2 \gg \omega L_2$, and $h_{ie} + R_2 \gg \omega M$. Then, since $I_4 = I_1$,

$$I_1 = -\frac{j\omega M I_3}{h_{ie} + R_2}$$

The circuit of Fig. 11-4b can be obtained using the procedure of Sec. 6-23.

Then

$$0 = \left(\frac{1}{h_{oe}} - \frac{j}{\omega C}\right) \mathbf{I}_2 - j\left[-\frac{1}{\omega C} + \frac{h_{fe}\omega M}{h_{oe}(h_{ie} + R_2)}\right] \mathbf{I}_3$$

$$0 = +\frac{j}{\omega C} \mathbf{I}_2 + \left[R_1 + \frac{\omega^2 M^2}{h_{ie} + R_2} + j\left(\omega L_1 - \frac{1}{\omega C}\right)\right] \mathbf{I}_3$$

Setting the real and imaginary parts of the determinant of the equations equal to zero, we obtain

$$R_1 + \frac{\omega^2 M^2}{h_{ie} + R_2} + \frac{h_{oe}L_1}{C} - \frac{h_{fe}M}{C(h_{ie} + R_2)} = 0 \tag{11-12}$$

and

$$\omega^2 L_1 C - \frac{\omega^2 M^2 h_{oe}}{h_{ie} + R_2} - 1 - R_1 h_{oe} = 0 \tag{11-13}$$

Solving Eq. (11-13) for ω^2, we obtain, for the frequency of oscillation,

$$\omega_0 = \sqrt{\frac{1 + R_1 h_{oe}}{L_1 C - M h_{oe}/(h_{ie} + R_2)}} \tag{11-14}$$

Then

$$h_{fe} \geqslant \left[\frac{C(h_{ie} + R_2)}{M}\right]\left(R_1 + \frac{\omega_0^2 M^2}{h_{ie} + R_2} + \frac{h_{oe}L_1}{C}\right) \tag{11-15}$$

This gives the minimum value of h_{fe} that can be used if the circuit is to oscillate. Note that the frequency of oscillation depends upon the parameters of the circuit and the transistor as well as on the resonant circuit.

Now let us analyze the circuit of Fig. 11-3c. We shall assume that $1/\omega C_1 \ll R_g$ and that the RFC acts as an open circuit at the signal frequency. Thus, the equivalent circuit for this oscillator is given in Fig. 11-2. The criterion for oscillation for this circuit is Eq. (11-4) where $\gamma_1 = g_m$, $g = 1/r_p$, $\mathbf{Y}_1 = j\omega C_1$, $\mathbf{Y}_2 = j\omega C_2$, $\mathbf{Y}_3 = 1/(R + j\omega L)$, and $\mathbf{Y}_i = 0$. Note that we have included a resistance in series with the coil and assumed that the capacitors are lossless. This is usually justified in practice. Then, substituting in Eq. (11-4) or (11-11), and setting the real and imaginary parts equal to zero, we obtain

$$\omega_0 = \sqrt{\frac{C_1 + C_2}{C_1 C_2 L} + \frac{R}{C_2 L r_p}} \tag{11-16}$$

$$g_m \geqslant \omega_0^2 C_1 C_2 R + \frac{\omega_0^2 L C_1 - 1}{r_p} \tag{11-17}$$

The two circuits that we have analyzed in this section are typical of many radio-frequency oscillator circuits.

11-3   The *RC* oscillator

The frequency range of the oscillators that were discussed in the last section is the same as that of the transistor or the vacuum tube.   However, at low frequencies the resonant circuit elements become vary large.   In Sec. 10-12, it was demonstrated that a simple three-stage *RC*-coupled amplifier with identical stages would oscillate if the magnitude of the midband open-loop gain were greater than 8.   This provides a simple means of obtaining a low-frequency oscillator without using large resonant circuits.   Consider the circuits shown in Fig. 11-5.   They are, effectively, three-stage *RC*-coupled amplifiers with only one active element.   If fewer than three *RC* sections are used, these circuits will not oscillate.   This can be seen from a study of the Nyquist plots of Fig. 10-20.   The procedure of Sec. 11-1 can be used to determine the frequency of oscillation and the criterion for oscillation. These structures are sometimes called *phase shift* oscillators because of the phase shifts introduced by the *RC* circuits.   (Note that all oscillator circuits have elements that introduce phase shift.)   These *RC* oscillators have no tuned circuits to reject harmonics; thus, the operation should be linear to prevent excessive distortion.   In the next section, we shall discuss linear and nonlinear operation of oscillators.

There are more-complex *RC*-circuit oscillators that are used.   These use bridge structures in their feedback networks.   The principles of analysis of Sec. 11-1 can be applied to these also.

Fig. 11-5   RC phase-shift oscillators.   (a) A common-cathode vacuum tube is the active element; and (b) a common-emitter transistor is the active element.   (The third R also acts as a bias element.)

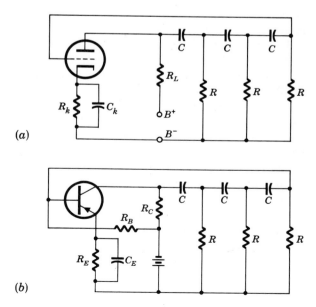

(a)

(b)

11-4   Linear and nonlinear operation of oscillators

In an oscillator, the amplitude of the oscillation builds up until an equilibrium condition is reached. If this amplitude is small, then the operation can be quite linear, and the output will be a sinusoid with a relatively small amount of distortion. On the other hand, if the amplitude of oscillation is very large, then the output may be very distorted.   Linearity of operation is related to the efficiency of operation, just as it is in amplifiers. If an oscillator operates class C, then its efficiency and distortion will be considerably higher than if the operation is class A. Many times, oscillators are designed to supply high power, and, in such cases, class C operation is often used. Tuned circuits are often used to reject harmonics.

If the active elements of the oscillator circuits were really linear, then the amplitude of the oscillation would build up indefinitely. All active elements have cutoff and saturation regions which limit the amplitude of the oscillation. For instance, in a transistor, the collector current effectively becomes zero when the emitter current is zero; in a vacuum tube, the plate current is essentially zero if the grid voltage is negative enough. The vacuum-tube pentode and the transistor have knees in their output characteristics where the curves crowd together. This represents a saturation region. As the instantaneous operating point moves into the highly nonlinear region, the effective gain of the active element decreases. For instance, consider the phase-shift oscillator of Fig. 11-5. If the open-loop gain is adjusted so that it is just slightly higher than the minimum value required for oscillation, then the oscillation will not proceed far into the nonlinear region. On the other hand, if the magnitude of the open-loop gain is increased greatly, then the amplitude of oscillation will be considerably larger and the output will be distorted. It may appear as though the magnitude of the open-loop gain should be the minimum that produces oscillation. However, any slight reduction in gain, which could be caused by aging of the elements or by a change in power-supply voltage, would then cause the oscillation to cease. There are several procedures that will yield linear operation and a certainty of oscillation. One is to use a nonlinear resistance which varies in such a way that it reduces the open-loop gain as the amplitude of oscillation increases. For instance, if Y_3 in Fig. 11-2 is a conductance whose value decreases with the current through it, then the open-loop gain would fall off as the signal level increased. An ordinary tungsten-filament lamp is often used for these purposes.

If very linear operation is desired, then the procedure illustrated in Fig. 11-6 can be used. The signal output of the oscillator is amplified and then applied to a simple diode rectifier circuit. A direct voltage will appear across C_g. It will have the indicated polarity so that E will be negative. This acts as a negative grid bias for the amplifier. Increasing the negative grid bias will reduce the open-loop gain. Thus, the amplitude of the oscillation will decrease as A_v increases and can be made quite small. This is called an

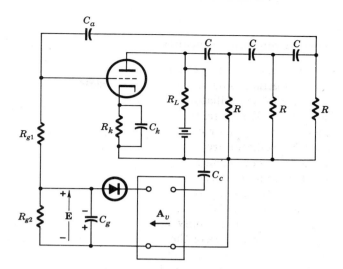

Fig. 11-6 An amplitude-stabilized oscillator. C_a and C_c are blocking capacitors. $(C_a R_{g1} \gg CR)$

amplitude-stabilized oscillator circuit. Although a vacuum-tube circuit is illustrated, the same basic procedure can be applied to transistors. Note that the amplitude-stabilizing circuit introduces a feedback loop of its own. Care should be taken that this does not cause extraneous oscillation. This is usually of a very low frequency and causes the amplitude of the output signal to vary periodically.

Let us now consider how input bias is obtained for a class C oscillator. In the case of the vacuum-tube oscillator, grid-leak bias is often used. The discussion of Sec. 8-6 applies here. Initially, the grid bias will be zero and the transconductance will be quite high. Thus, the oscillation will build up. This will increase the negative grid bias and, thus, reduce the transconductance. Hence, the amplitude of oscillation will be limited.

In the case of the transistor, the problem is somewhat different. If the bias circuits of Fig. 8-9 were used, there would be, initially, zero base current. Hence, the transistor would almost be cut off and oscillation probably would not build up. Thus, transistor oscillator circuits are usually constructed so that there is a negative direct base-current bias produced by the power supply. The circuits of Fig. 11-3b, d, and f illustrate this. Bias circuits similar to those of Fig. 8-9 can be added to the circuit (see Fig. 11-3b and d). This circuit will tend to produce a positive base-current bias as oscillation builds up and thus will limit the amplitude of oscillation.

The device nonlinearities as well as the grid or base bias will limit the amplitude of oscillation in both vacuum-tube and transistor oscillators. These nonlinearities should be considered in any circuit where the amplitude of oscillation is large.

11-5   Frequency stability

The frequency of operation of an oscillator circuit will not remain constant, but will drift.   The magnitude of these drifts is a measure of the frequency stability of an oscillator.   In many applications, a shift of 1 or 2 percent is tolerable.   However, there are many other times when the frequency must be held to extremely close tolerances.   For instance, it is not uncommon to specify oscillator frequencies plus or minus several cycles per megacycle. In fact, specifications are often much more restrictive.   For the time being, let us assume that the operation of the oscillator is linear and examine the causes of the frequency drift.   The frequencies of oscillation of two representative RF oscillator circuits are given by Eqs. (11-14) and (11-16).   Note that ω_0 depends not only upon the elements of the tuned circuit but also upon the parameters of the active element and the resistances of the circuit. The parameters of the active element vary with bias voltages, temperature, and age.   Thus, it is desirable to minimize their effects.   For instance, in Eq. (11-16), it would be desirable to make the ratio R/r_pLC_2 as small as possible.   In addition, the power-supply voltages should be stabilized so that they do not introduce a source of parameter change.

The frequency of oscillation primarily depends upon the elements of the resonant circuit.   For instance, if r_p is sufficiently large, then Eq. (11-16) can be approximated by

$$\omega_0 = \sqrt{\frac{C_1 + C_2}{C_1 C_2 L}} \tag{11-18}$$

Thus, these elements should not vary.   Temperature fluctuations will change the dimensions of the elements and cause ω_0 to shift.   This may sound quite trivial, but remember that we are dealing with changes on the order of parts per million or less.   The resonant circuits are often put into temperature-controlled ovens to maintain their stability.   The capacitance of the active elements also appears in the expression for ω_0.   To be specific, let us discuss the Colpitts-oscillator circuits of Fig. 11-3c and d.   The capacitors C_1 and C_2 consist not only of the capacitance shown, but also of the grid-to-cathode and plate-to-cathode capacitance of the vacuum tube or the effective capacitance between the emitter and base and between the emitter and collector of the transistor.   In the transistor, these capacitances fluctuate with voltage.   In the vacuum tube, any changes in operating temperature will change C_{gk} and C_{pk}.   If possible, the effect of these fluctuations should be minimized.   To simplify our discussion, let us assume that the series combination of C_1 and C_2 is replaced by a capacitor C such that

$$C = \frac{C_1 C_2}{C_1 + C_2} \tag{11-19}$$

and that the capacitances of the active element change such that the per-

Fig. 11-7 The resonant circuit of a Clapp oscillator.

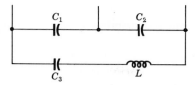

centage change in both C_1 and C_2 is the same. Let us call ΔC the net change in C. We shall compute the change in ω_0^2. (For convenience, we shall work with ω_0^2 rather than with ω_0.) From Eq. (11-18)

$$\Delta\omega_0^2 = \frac{1}{L(C + \Delta C)} - \frac{1}{LC} \tag{11-20}$$

$$\Delta\omega_0^2 = -\frac{L\,\Delta C}{LC(LC + L\,\Delta C)}$$

In general, $C \gg \Delta C$, so that this can be approximated by

$$\frac{\Delta\omega_0^2}{\omega_0^2} = -\frac{\Delta C}{C} \tag{11-21}$$

If ΔC is a change due to the active element, then it will be independent of the external capacitances. Thus, if C_1 and C_2 and, thus, C, are made larger, the frequency shift will decrease. This requires that L be decreased, if ω_0 is not to change. If we replace the tuned circuit of the Colpitts oscillator by the one shown in Fig. 11-7, then the stability can be increased. The oscillator is now called a *Clapp (or series-tuned) oscillator*. In the Colpitts oscillator, one limitation on the maximum value of C is the minimum value of L that can conveniently be used. However, in this circuit, C_1 and C_2 can be made as large as desired, since the effective capacitance of the circuit is given by

$$C_{\text{eff}} = \frac{C_3 C}{C_3 + C} \tag{11-22}$$

where C is defined by Eq. (11-19). (We shall see that the choice of capacitance is complicated by the requirements for oscillation.) If we assume that the changes in capacitance are all due to the active element, then only C will change. Thus,

$$\Delta C_{\text{eff}} = \frac{C_3(C + \Delta C)}{C_3 + C + \Delta C} - \frac{C_3 C}{C_3 + C} \tag{11-23}$$

Then, if these terms are placed over a common denominator and *then* it is assumed that $\Delta C \ll C$, we obtain

$$\frac{\Delta C_{\text{eff}}}{C_{\text{eff}}} = \frac{\Delta C}{C}\frac{C_{\text{eff}}}{C} \tag{11-24}$$

The value of C can be much greater for the Clapp oscillator than for the

Colpitts oscillator and C_{eff}/C can be very much less than 1. Thus, the frequency stability of the Clapp circuit can be much greater than that of the Colpitts oscillator. If the capacitors C_1 and C_2 could be made arbitrarily large, then ω_0 could be made insensitive to changes in the active-element capacitance. However, the criterion for oscillation limits the maximum values of C_1 and of C_2. For instance, in a vacuum-tube circuit, Eq. (11-17) places limits upon $C_1 C_2$.

In either the Colpitts or the Clapp circuit, the values of C_1 and C_2 need not be equal. If one of the capacitances of the active element tends to vary more than the other, then the larger capacitance should be placed across it. For instance, in the transistor circuit, C_2 is usually larger than C_1. If exceptional frequency stability is not required, then the Colpitts circuit is used, since it is simpler.

Thus far, we have ignored nonlinear effects in our discussion of stability. In general, the parameters of the active element will vary with the nonlinearities. As a consequence, ω_0 will be sensitive to them. Since the nonlinearities change with shifts in the operating point, linear oscillators have less frequency drift than nonlinear ones.

11-6   Crystal oscillators

If an oscillator is to operate at only one frequency, then exceptional stability can be obtained by using *piezoelectric crystals*. These crystals, which are often made of quartz, will deform if a voltage is applied to their opposite faces. Conversely, if they are deformed, a voltage will appear across their opposite faces. The symbol for a crystal and its equivalent electric circuit are shown in Fig. 11-8. The crystal acts as a resonant electric circuit of very high Q. Its resonant frequency is essentially the mechanical resonant frequency of the crystal, which is exceptionally stable. Because of the parameter values and the high effective Q, a crystal oscillator can be designed so that the shape of the Nyquist plot depends mainly upon the equivalent circuit of the crystal. Thus, the frequency of oscillation is essentially determined by the resonant frequency of the crystal. To further improve their stability, crystals are often placed in temperature-controlled ovens. Crystals can be used to replace the resonant circuits in many oscillator configurations. A typical crystal oscillator called the *Pierce oscillator* is shown in

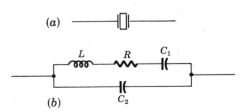

Fig. 11-8 (a) *The symbol for a piezoelectric crystal;* (b) *its equivalent circuit.*

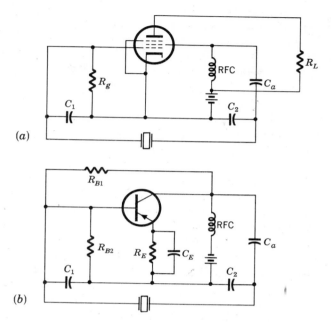

*Fig. 11-9 Pierce crystal oscillators. (a) Electron-cou-
pled vacuum-tube oscillator; (b) transistor oscillator.*

Fig. 11-9. It is essentially a Colpitts oscillator with the inductance replaced
by the crystal. In the vacuum-tube circuit, the capacitors C_1 and C_2 are
usually not external elements but are the interelectrode capacitances.

The output of an oscillator may be taken across the resonant circuit.
However, changes in output impedance will vary the resonant frequency.
To prevent this, a buffer amplifier can be placed between the oscillator and
the load. When vacuum-tube tetrodes or pentodes are used, another
arrangement is often effective. The screen grid is used as the "plate" of
the oscillator, and the output is taken from the plate. Thus, the load is
decoupled from the oscillator circuit. This is called an *electron-coupled
oscillator* (see Fig. 11-9a).

11-7   Design of an oscillator circuit with a specified amplitude of oscillation

Let us consider the design of transistor and vacuum-tube oscillator circuits.
The transistor oscillator will be considered first. Specifications: Frequency
of oscillation is to be $f_0 = 10^7/2\pi$ cps ($\omega_0 = 10^7$ radians/sec), amplitude
of oscillation should be such that the operation is quite linear; a Colpitts
oscillator circuit is to be used.

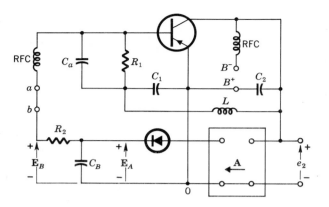

Fig. 11-10   An amplitude-stabilized Colpitts transistor oscillator.

We shall use a transistor with the following characteristics: $h_{ie} = 2,000$ ohms, $h_{fe} = 51$, $h_{re} \approx 0$, $h_{oe} = 50 \times 10^{-6}$ mho. The junction capacitances are $C_{in} = C_{out} = 2$ $\mu\mu$f. To obtain these characteristics, the following operating point is used: $E_{CQ} = -10$ volts, $I_{CQ} = -5.0$ ma, $I_{BQ} = -100$ μa and $E_{BQ} \approx 0$ volts. In addition, we shall assume that h_{fe} falls off as I_{BQ} increases in a positive manner, so that $h_{fe} = 100$ if $I_{BQ} = -200$ μa and $h_{fe} \approx 0$ if $I_{BQ} = +2$ μa.

The amplitude-stabilized oscillator of Fig. 11-10 will be used. Equation (11-4) will be used to determine the criterion for oscillation. It will be assumed that the capacitances C_1 and C_2 are lossless and that the RFC acts as an open circuit. Thus, in Eq. (11-4), $\gamma_1 = h_{fe}/h_{ie}$, $\mathbf{Y}_1 = j\omega C_1$, $\mathbf{Y}_2 = j\omega C_2$, $\mathbf{Y}_i = 1/h_{ie}$, $\mathbf{Y}_3 = 1/(R + j\omega L)$, and $g = h_{oe}$. The inductance has been assumed to have a series resistance R. Substituting in Eq. (11-4) and rearranging, we obtain

$$\omega_0 = \sqrt{\frac{C_1 + C_2}{LC_1C_2} + \frac{h_{oe}R}{LC_2} + \frac{Lh_{oe} + C_2R}{h_{ie}LC_1C_2}} \qquad (11\text{-}25)$$

and

$$\frac{h_{fe}}{h_{ie}} \geqslant \omega_0{}^2 C_1 C_2 R + \frac{\omega_0{}^2 LC_2 - h_{oe}R - 1}{h_{ie}} + h_{oe}(\omega_0{}^2 LC_1 - 1) \qquad (11\text{-}26)$$

To simplify the analysis, choose $C_1 = C_2 = C$. Assume that

$$\omega_0 \approx \sqrt{\frac{C_1 + C_2}{LC_1C_2}} = \sqrt{\frac{2}{LC}}$$

This assumption must be subsequently verified. Then, substituting in Eq. (11-26), we obtain,

$$\frac{h_{fe}}{h_{ie}} \geqslant \omega_0{}^2 C^2 R + \frac{1 - h_{oe}R}{h_{ie}} + h_{oe} \qquad (11\text{-}27)$$

In general, $1 \gg h_{oe}R$, so that we can neglect the $h_{oe}R$ term. Actually, this approximation is on the safe side, since it causes the requirements for oscillation to become more stringent. The resistance of the coil can be expressed in terms of its Q at resonance: $R = \omega_0 L/Q_0 = 2/(Q_0\omega_0 C)$. Substituting in Eq. (11-27) and solving for C, we obtain

$$C \leqslant \left(\frac{h_{fe} - 1}{h_{ie}} - h_{oe}\right)\frac{Q_0}{2\omega_0} \tag{11-28}$$

This value represents the minimum value that $C_1 = C_2 = C$ can have if the circuit is to oscillate. Let us assume that $Q_0 = 10$.

$C \leqslant 12{,}475 \ \mu\mu f$

To obtain the best possible stability, the largest value of C should be used. Since h_{fe} can become considerably greater than 51, this relation can be used with the equals sign. However, to obtain a practical value, we shall use

$C_1 = C_2 = 12{,}000 \ \mu\mu f$

Note that C_1 and C_2 are effectively in shunt with the input and output capacitances of the transistor. Thus, the actual capacitances that are placed in the circuit should be 11,998 $\mu\mu f$. This very small change can often be ignored. Actually, some means of adjusting the frequency (by varying L or C) is usually included so that the desired frequency can be obtained precisely. The value of inductance can be found by using the relation $\omega_0 \approx \sqrt{2/LC}$. Solving this yields 1.667 μh. This is a relatively small inductance, although it is readily obtainable. If it is desirable to use a larger inductance, then the value of C should be reduced. However, we shall use the specified value. Thus,

$L = 1.667 \ \mu h$

Since $Q_0 = 10$, the resistance of the coil is 1.667 ohms. Let us now substitute into Eq. (11-25) to see if the approximation $\omega_0 \approx \sqrt{2/LC}$ is justified. This substitution yields

$\omega_0 = \sqrt{10^{14}(1.00046)} = 1.00023 \times 10^7 \approx 10^7$

Thus, the assumption is justified.

Now consider the design of the amplitude-stabilizing circuit. The specified amplitude of oscillation will depend upon the nonlinearities of the characteristics of the transistor. Let us assume that these are such that the operation will be linear enough if $E_{2,\text{max}} \leqslant 0.05$ volts, where

$e_2 = E_{2,\text{max}} \sin \omega_0 t$

The required base-current bias is $I_{BQ} = -100 \ \mu a$. The base current depends upon the voltage E_B, which in turn depends upon the power-supply voltage E_{CC} and the direct voltage E_A that appears across C_B. Applying Thévenin's theorem between terminal b and the reference terminal, we obtain the effective bias circuit which consists of a voltage E_T in series with a resistance R_T where

$$E_T = \frac{E_A R_1 + E_{CC} R_2}{R_1 + R_2} \tag{11-29}$$

and

$$R_T = \frac{R_1 R_2}{R_1 + R_2} \tag{11-30}$$

It has been assumed that the direct voltage E_A, of the polarity indicated, appears across C_B. The direct base-current bias is given by $I_{BQ} = E_T/R_T$. Let us assume that $R_1 = R_2 = 30,000$ ohms. Then $R_T = 15,000$ ohms and to obtain the proper base current $E_T = -1.5$ volts. Since $E_{CQ} = -10$ volts, let us set the power-supply voltage E_{CC} equal to -10 volts. Then, substituting in Eq. (11-29), we obtain

$$E_A = 7 \text{ volts}$$

If the capacitance C_B is chosen large enough so that the time constant $C_B R_T$ is very much larger than the period of the alternating voltage applied to the input of the diode, then E_A will be equal to the peak value of this alternating voltage. Thus,

$$E_A = |A| E_{2,\max}$$

Hence

$$|A| = 140$$

To obtain a value of C_B set $C_B \times 15,000 \gg \dfrac{1}{10^7}$. A typical value is

$$C_B = 0.01 \ \mu f$$

Note if the Q of the circuit is greater than 10, then oscillation can occur at a lower value of h_{fe}. This will mean that the amplitude of oscillation will increase. To prevent this, either C or the gain of the amplifier can be increased.

A bias-stabilizing impedance R_E in parallel with C_E can be placed in series with the emitter lead. In this case, the magnitude of E_{CC} and of E_T should be increased by an amount equal to the direct voltage drop across R_E. The capacitance should be large enough so that $h_{fe}/\omega_0 C_E \ll h_{ie}$ [see Eq. (6-82)].

The value of C_a should be large enough so that it acts as a short circuit in comparison with h_{ie}. Thus, $C_a \gg 1/\omega_0 h_{ie}$. A typical value is

$$C_a = 0.01 \ \mu f$$

One fact that has been ignored thus far is that the feedback loop of the amplitude-stabilization circuit may cause instability. This usually manifests itself in a slow periodic variation in the bias current I_B, which, in turn, causes the magnitude of e_2 to vary periodically. To determine if such oscillation results, the feedback loop should be broken between points a and b. The open-loop gain can then be obtained by considering that a current generator is applied between point a and the reference terminal 0. The

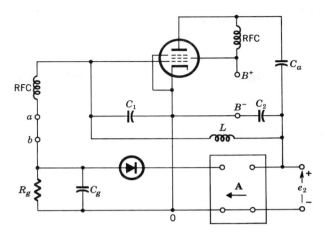

Fig. 11-11 An amplitude-stabilized Colpitts vacuum-tube oscillator.

ratio of the returned current (i.e., the current in an impedance equal to the transistor circuit's input impedance, which is placed between point b and the reference terminal) to the generator current yields the open-loop gain. A Nyquist plot then is used to determine the stability of the amplifier. The Nyquist plot can be varied by changing R_1, R_2, C_B, or the frequency response of the voltage amplification $\mathbf{A}$. In general, $\mathbf{A}$ will be a tuned amplifier. Even though it is only required to amplify signals of frequency ω_0, it may have to be a broadband amplifier. The basic principles of the design of Sec. 10-12 can be applied to stabilize this system. Care must be taken because the amplifier $\mathbf{A}$ is a bandpass system that operates about the frequency ω_0, while the applied signal generator and the output voltage across C_B will only contain relatively low-frequency components.

Now let us consider the design of the oscillator using a vacuum tube. Since many of the details are identical, we shall omit some of the explanatory statements. A vacuum-tube pentode with the following characteristics will be used: $g_m = 5,000$ μmhos, $r_p \geqslant 10^6$ ohms, $C_{\text{in}} = C_{\text{out}} = 10$ $\mu\mu$f. To obtain these characteristics, the following operating point is used: $E_{bQ} = 300$ volts, $E_{cQ} = -5$ volts, $E_{c2Q} = 300$ volts. In addition, we shall assume that the transconductance falls off as the negative grid bias is increased, so that $g_m = 100$ μmhos when $E_{cQ} = -10$ volts and $g_m = 10,000$ μmhos when $E_{cQ} = -0.1$ volt.

The oscillator circuit is shown in Fig. 11-11. We shall again assume that the capacitances are lossless and that R is the resistance of the inductance. To simplify the analysis, we shall choose $C_1 = C_2 = C$ so that $\omega_0 \approx \sqrt{2/LC}$. Thus, substituting in Eq. (11-17), we obtain

$$g_m \geqslant \omega_0{}^2 C^2 R + \frac{1}{r_p} \qquad (11\text{-}31)$$

Solving for C and writing R in terms of Q_0, we obtain

$$C \leqslant \frac{Q_0}{2\omega_0}\left(g_m - \frac{1}{r_p}\right)$$

If $Q_0 = 10$, then

$$C \leqslant 2499.5 \; \mu\mu\text{f}$$

This value should include C_{in} and C_{out} of the pentode. The frequency of oscillation is given by Eq. (11-16). Substituting and solving for L, we obtain

$$L = \frac{2}{C\omega_0{}^2[1 - 1/(r_p Q_0 C \omega_0)]}$$

Hence

$$L = 8 \; \mu\text{h}$$

Now let us consider the amplitude-stabilizing circuit. If

$$e_2 = E_{2,\text{max}} \sin \omega t$$

then the grid bias will be equal to

$$E_c = -|A| E_{2,\text{max}}$$

The required grid bias is -5 volts. Let us assume that the operation will be linear enough if $E_{2,\text{max}} \leqslant 0.05$ volts. Hence, $|A| = 100$.

The value of R_g should be chosen as large as possible. It is limited by the maximum grid-leak resistance rating of the vacuum-tube pentode. A value of $R_g = 10^6$ ohms is typical. The value of C_g then should satisfy the inequality $R_g C_g \gg 1/\omega_0$ or $C_g \gg 10^{-13}$. A typical value is $C_g = 100 \; \mu\mu\text{f}$. The value of C_a should be chosen so that $\omega_0 C_a \gg 1/r_p$ and $C_a \gg C_{\text{out}}$ (of the pentode). A typical value is $C_a = 1,000 \; \mu\mu\text{f}$.

Since the plate and screen-grid voltages are both 300 volts, the power-supply voltage should be 300 volts.

The stabilization of the bias feedback loop proceeds in the same way as in the transistor circuit. The Nyquist diagram is obtained on a voltage basis in this case. That is, the feedback loop is broken between points a and b. A voltage generator is placed between point a and the reference terminal. The returned voltage is that between point b and the reference terminal.

BIBLIOGRAPHY

Greiner, R. A.: "Semiconductor Devices and Applications," chap. 17, McGraw-Hill Book Company, New York, 1961.

Millman, J.: "Vacuum-tube and Semiconductor Electronics," chap. 18, McGraw-Hill Book Company, New York, 1958.

Terman, F. E.: "Electronic and Radio Engineering," chap. 14, McGraw-Hill Book Company, New York, 1955.

PROBLEMS

11-1. Derive the criterion for oscillation given by Eq. (11-4), using the fact that the open-loop gain must equal $+1$.

11-2. Obtain the minimum value of g_m that the vacuum tube of Fig. 11-3a can have if there is to be oscillation. Assume that each inductance has a resistance in series with it and that any bypass capacitors are short circuits. Determine the frequency of oscillation. The answers should be in terms of the parameters of the vacuum tube and the circuit elements.

11-3. Repeat Prob. 11-2 for the circuit of Fig. 11-3e. Assume that the RFC is an open circuit.

11-4. Derive the minimum value of h_{fe} that the transistor of Fig. 11-3d can have if there is to be oscillation. Assume that each inductance has a resistance in series with it, that any bypass capacitors are short circuits, and that the RFC is an open circuit. Also assume that the h parameters of the transistor are real numbers. Determine the frequency of oscillation. The answers should be in terms of the h parameters of the transistor and the circuit elements. Now assume that $\mathbf{h}_{fe} = h_{fe}/(1 + j\omega/\omega_\beta)$ and repeat the problem. What is the maximum frequency at which oscillation can be maintained?

11-5. Repeat Prob. 11-4 for the circuit of Fig. 11-3f.

11-6. Determine the criterion for oscillation and the frequency of oscillation for the circuit of Fig. 11-5a. The answer should be in terms of the parameters of the vacuum tube and the circuit elements. Assume that C_k is a short circuit at all frequencies of interest.

11-7. Design a phase-shift oscillator circuit using a transistor. Determine the criterion for oscillation and the frequency of oscillation for this circuit. Assume that C_E is a short circuit at all frequencies of interest.

11-8. Determine the criterion for oscillation for both the vacuum tube and the transistor Clapp oscillator. Assume that $\omega C_2 \gg 1/r_p$ and that $\omega C_2 \gg h_{oe}$.

11-9. Compare the frequency drift of the Hartley, Colpitts, and Clapp oscillator circuits to changes in the capacitance of the active elements. Assume that the total inductance is constant in all three circuits.

11-10. Relate the frequency stability of the vacuum-tube Clapp oscillator to the transconductance of the vacuum tube, the inductance, and the resistance of the inductance. Assume that the plate resistance of the vacuum tube is infinite and that the frequency drift is due to changes in interelectrode capacitances of the vacuum tube.

11-11. Determine the criterion for oscillation and the frequency of oscillation of the circuits of Fig. 11-9. Use the equivalent circuit of Fig. 11-8b for the crystal. What does the frequency of oscillation become as R approaches zero?

Pulse, Switching, and Digital Circuits

12

Many electronic devices, such as digital computers, function on the basis of the presence or absence of a signal. The active elements (e.g., transistors, diodes, and vacuum tubes) are operated as switches. In fact, they take over operations that were performed by relays in earlier devices. In digital computers, the active elements are switched from an on to an off state or vice versa and, in so doing, generate signals which perform mathematical operations. Electronic devices are also used as switches in many electronic instruments. For instance, they are used as time-base generators in oscilloscopes. The circuits that are used in these cases are different from those designed as linear amplifiers. We shall present some of their fundamentals here. In Secs. 12-1 and 12-2 we shall discuss the transient response of general switching devices. In subsequent sections, we shall introduce some fundamental switching circuits. Additional details of the subject of pulse, switching, and digital circuits are given in the references cited in the bibliography at the end of the chapter.

12-1   Operation of vacuum tubes and transistors as switches—piecewise-linear analysis

In many applications, we are interested in whether or not a signal is present. Actually, there may be two signal levels, corresponding to whether or not the device is "on" or "off," and we may wish to know which level is present at any given time and to be able to switch rapidly from one level to the other. In such cases, the active element often is driven to cutoff so that it acts essentially as an open circuit or it is driven into a saturation region where it acts essentially as a short circuit. The active elements are driven between these extreme limits (rather than using them as linear amplifiers with low-level pulses) in order to improve reliability. The characteristics of active elements vary from device to device, with time, and with the operating point. If these circuits are to reliably distinguish between the on and off levels, then these levels should be greatly separated. Actually, at times, we go one step further and overdrive the electronic device. We shall illustrate these concepts using Fig. 12-1, which will also define the *saturation and cutoff regions.* Some of these statements will subsequently be modified for the transistor.

Fig. 12-1   An illustration of the cutoff, active, and saturation regions.

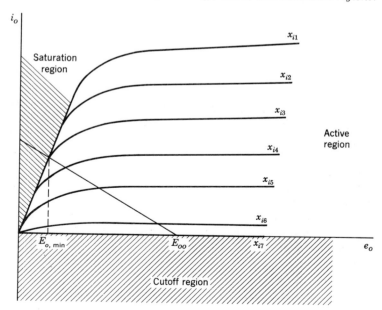

For a vacuum tube, x_{i1} would correspond to zero bias while x_{i7} would be a sufficiently large negative grid bias to cut off the plate current. For a common-emitter transistor, x_{i7} would approximately correspond to $-I_{c0}$. Now consider the load line. If the input signal swings the bias from x_{i3} to x_{i7}, then the output voltage will vary from E_{oo} to $E_{o,\min}$. However, if the input signal is increased, then the output will be unchanged. Thus, for reliable operation, the input signal swing could be somewhat greater than $x_{i7} - x_{i3}$. The region between the cutoff and saturation regions is called the *active region*. Note that the terms cutoff and saturation regions do not really refer to the crosshatched area of Fig. 12-1, since the operating point never enters them. Actually, the saturation region is the line where all the characteristics crowd together. For instance, the operating point corresponding to $E_{o,\min}$ actually lies on the curve for x_{i1}, x_{i2}, and x_{i3}. In a similar way, the cutoff region is the abscissa axis and corresponds to x_{i7}, x_{i8}, x_{i9}, ...

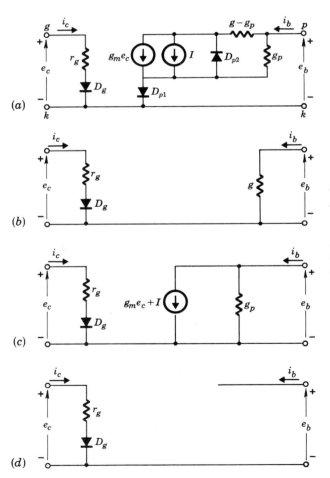

F i g . 1 2 - 2 (a) T h e piecewise-linear equivalent circuit for the vacuum-tube pentode; (b) the saturation-region equivalent circuit; (c) the active-region equivalent circuit; and (d) the cutoff-region equivalent circuit.

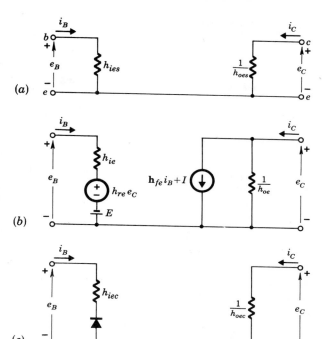

Fig. 12-3 Piecewise-linear equivalent circuits for the common-emitter transistor. (a) Saturation region; (b) active region; and (c) cutoff region.

We are often interested in the transient response of these amplifiers. Linear equivalent circuits cannot be used because of the large swings into highly nonlinear regions. However, piecewise-linear equivalent circuits are quite useful. To use the piecewise-linear equivalent circuit, the characteristics in the active region are linearized. Such a procedure is illustrated in Fig. 4-13 for the vacuum-tube pentode. The equivalent circuit is redrawn in Fig. 12-2. The details of this equivalent circuit are explained in Sec. 4-6. The equivalent circuits of Fig. 12-2b, c, and d are valid in the saturation, active, and cutoff regions, respectively. The analysis of Chap. 4 can be used to determine when each equivalent circuit should be used. Sometimes it is simpler to inspect the characteristics to determine when the operation shifts from one region to the other. If the pentode is operated so that the grid is always biased negatively, then we can assume that D_g is an open circuit. In a similar fashion, equivalent circuits for the common-emitter transistor that are valid in each of the three regions can be obtained from Fig. 4-18. These are shown in Fig. 12-3 where we have substituted for the parameters of Fig. 4-18. We have neglected any interaction between the input and the output circuits in the saturation and cutoff regions, which considerably simplifies the form of these circuits. The diode shown in Fig. 12-3c conducts for base current in the normal direction. It should be reversed for the *n-p-n* transistor. At times the diode can be replaced by a short circuit in an analysis procedure. The large value of h_{iec} accounts for the junction

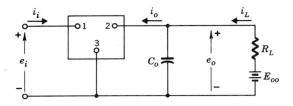

Fig. 12-4 *A generalized-device pulse amplifier.*

impedance. For both the vacuum tube and the transistor, the output impedance in the cutoff region is very high, while in the saturation region it is very low and can often be considered a short circuit. Now consider the generalized device of Fig. 12-4. The characteristics of this device are shown in Fig. 12-5. We shall assume that the input parameter is instantaneously varied from x_{i5} to x_{i1}. Because of the shunting capacitance C_o, the output voltage cannot change instantaneously. Thus, the locus of operation will not be along the load line. However, the endpoints of the operation, after transients have died away, will be on the load line. Let us define a voltage $E_{o,\text{crit}}$ as the value of e_o at the breakpoint of the x_{i1} curve. Now assume that the power-supply voltage is $E_{oo1} > E_{o,\text{crit}}$. When x_i is switched, the operating point will instantaneously shift to point a and, then, in a finite time, move to points b, c, and d. For those times when the operation is between points a and b, the active equivalent circuit is used. When the operation is between points b and d, the saturation equivalent circuit should be used. On the other hand, if we shift E_{oo} to $E_{oo2} < E_{o,\text{crit}}$, then the locus

Fig. 12-5 *Generalized piecewise-linear-device output characteristics showing the locus of operation in response to an input pulse when output capacitance is present.*

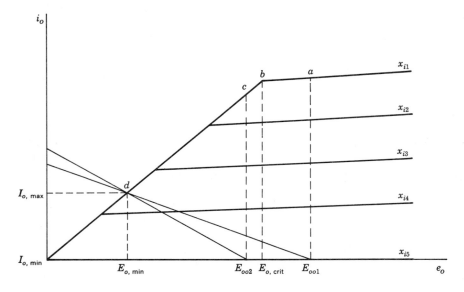

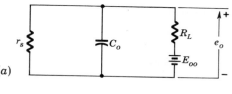

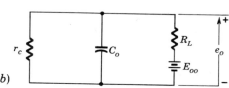

Fig. 12-6 (a) The saturation equivalent circuit of the generalized device of Fig. 12-4; (b) the cutoff equivalent circuit for this device.

of operation is along the line *cd* and the saturation equivalent circuit should always be used. In this circuit, the current i_o changes instantaneously with time. However, the load current does not.

$$i_L = \frac{E_{oo} - e_0}{R_L} \tag{12-1}$$

Note that i_o is not an external current, since some of the capacitance is associated with the active device. Finally, note that $E_{o,\text{crit}}$ does not just depend upon the generalized device; it is a function of the "maximum" value of x_i.

Now let us compute the pulse response of the generalized device of Fig. 12-4. (This analysis is actually oversimplified for the transistor. It will be extended in the next section.) We shall assume that $E_{oo} < E_{o,\text{crit}}$. Let $1/h_{oes}$ and $1/g = r_s$. Also let $1/h_{oec}$ and the open-circuit output of the vacuum tube be represented by r_c. The equivalent circuits for the operation are shown in Fig. 12-6a and b. Let us assume that a step is applied to the input so that operation is switched from the cutoff to the saturation regions. That is, using Fig. 12-5,

$$x_i = \begin{cases} x_{i5} & \text{for } t < 0 \\ x_{i1} & \text{for } t > 0 \end{cases} \tag{12-2}$$

Then, from Fig. 12-6b, at $t = 0$,

$$e_o(0) = E_c = E_{oo} \frac{r_c}{r_c + R_L} \tag{12-3}$$

Thus, using Fig. 12-6a, the final value of the response is given by

$$e_o(\infty) = E_s = E_{oo} \frac{r_s}{r_s + R_L} \tag{12-4}$$

Thus, the transient response is

$$e_o(t) = E_s - (E_s - E_c)e^{-t/R_{sh,s}C_o} \tag{12-5}$$

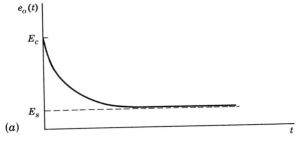

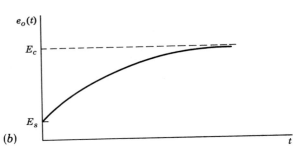

Fig. 12-7 The step response of a pulse amplifier. (a) The response when the active device is switched from cutoff to saturation; (b) the response when the active device is switched from saturation to cutoff.

where

$$R_{sh,s} = r_s R_L / (r_s + R_L) \tag{12-6}$$

This waveform is shown in Fig. 12-7a. The time constant is $R_{sh,s} C_o$.

Now let us consider that the device has been operating in the saturation region and, at $t = 0$, it is switched to the cutoff region. That is,

$$x_i = \begin{cases} x_{i1} & \text{for } t < 0 \\ x_{i5} & \text{for } t > 0 \end{cases} \tag{12-7}$$

Then, standard transient-analysis techniques yield

$$e_o(t) = E_c - (E_c - E_s)e^{-t/R_{sh,c}C_o} \tag{12-8}$$

where

$$R_{sh,c} = \frac{r_c R_L}{r_c + R_L} \tag{12-9}$$

This waveform is shown in Fig. 12-7b. Its time constant is $R_{sh,c} C_o$. Note that the time constants of the buildup and decay are considerably different, since $r_c \gg r_s$ for most electronic devices. In an ideal case, $r_s = 0$ and $r_c = \infty$. Then, Eq. (12-5) becomes,

$$e_o(t) = 0 \tag{12-10}$$

and Eq. (12-7) becomes,

$$e_o(t) = E_{oo}(1 - e^{-t/R_L C_o}) \tag{12-11}$$

The previous analysis has been quite simple because the active region was not used. If it is, then the segment of the output characteristic that is used will not pass through the origin. Hence, the device cannot be treated as a simple resistance but can be represented as a resistance in shunt with a current generator. Its current is equal to the ordinate intercept of the segment in question. The preceding analysis will be valid if the initial or final values are taken from the intercept of the segment and the load line. It will be necessary to extend the segment in those cases where the operation passes from the active to the saturation region. In such cases, two steps will have to be used to obtain the transient response. That is, one equation will apply for $e_o > E_{o,crit}$ and another for $e_o < E_{o,crit}$.

The response to a pulse is a combination of Eqs. (12-5) and (12-8). This assumes that the pulse width is long enough so that one transient dies away before the other starts. A typical input pulse and its response are given in Fig. 12-8. If a number of stages are cascaded, the pulse response will deteriorate (e.g., the rise time will increase) for the reasons presented in Sec. 6-15. In computer circuits, the speed at which a mathematical operation can be performed depends upon the total time that it takes for it to respond to a pulse. This includes any delay time. Now consider that x_i

Fig. 12-8 *Typical pulse response.* (a) *Input pulse;* (b) *output pulse.*

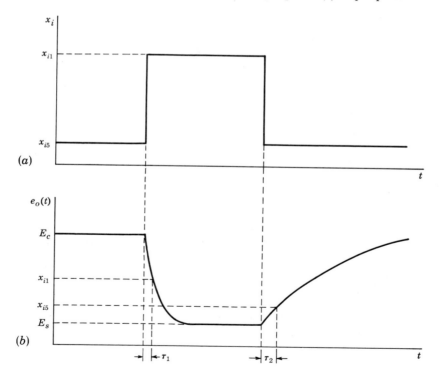

represents a voltage and that $e_o(t)$ is used to drive another stage.   If $E_c = x_{i1}$ and $E_s = x_{i5}$, then no delay time is added.   (This assumes that the device leaves the saturation region if $x_i > x_{i1}$.)   However, if

$$E_{o,\text{max}} - E_{o,\text{min}} = E_c - E_s > x_{i1} - x_{i5}$$

then there will be periods of time when no response occurs in the next stage. For instance, if x_{i1} and x_{i5} are as indicated in Fig. 12-8b, then τ_1 and τ_2 will be such delay times as far as the next stage is concerned.   This discussion applies primarily to the vacuum tube.   Factors relating to the transistor will be given in the next section.

12-2   Switching in a transistor—the effect of charge storage

When a transistor is switched from saturation to cutoff, or vice versa, the results are considerably different from those of linear operation.   Let us consider a common-emitter p-n-p transistor and assume that the base current is pulsed with a nonideal current generator.   The current generator is

Fig. 12-9   The switching response of a transistor.

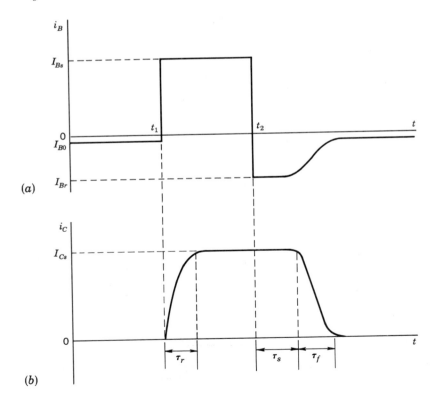

(a)

(b)

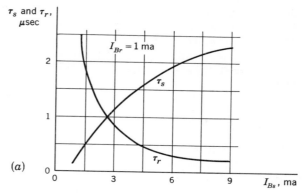

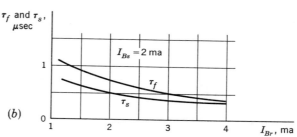

Fig. 12-10 (a) Switching rise time and storage time versus I_{Bs} for the 2N383 transistor; (b) fall time and storage time versus I_{Br} for this transistor. (Courtesy Tung-Sol Electric, Inc.)

such that, in the cutoff region, it tends to drive the base current in a direction reverse to its normal direction (i.e., positive for a *p-n-p* transistor). The curves are plotted in Fig. 12-9. For a *p-n-p* transistor, the ordinates are plotted so that the upper axis is negative. The reverse base current I_{B0} is approximately equal to $-I_{C0}$ and can be represented as the reverse saturation current of the reverse-biased diode (see Fig. 12-3c). Now, let us assume that at $t = t_1$ the base current is switched to a value that will produce saturation. The collector current will rise to its saturation value as shown. This will not occur in zero time. This effect is due to the time required to modify both the depletion region of the collector junction and the charge distribution in the base. The quantity τ_r is called the *switching rise time*, and it represents the time required for this collector saturation to become established. Actually, this does not take place in a finite amount of time, so that τ_r should represent the time for i_C to reach a substantial proportion of its final value (e.g., 90 percent). If the base current is increased, then I_{Cs} will not change substantially. However, the switching processes will be speeded up and τ_r will be reduced. A typical curve of τ_r versus I_{Bs} is shown in Fig. 12-10a.

There is a charge, stored in the base region, which increases as I_{Bs} is increased. At time t_2 the base-current generator is reversed. The base current also reverses, and drops to the value I_{Br}. This is greater in magnitude than I_{B0} and is due to the charges being swept out of the base. (It can be considered that a capacitance is in parallel with the base junction diode of Fig. 12-3c.)   Thus, the base current exponentially decreases back to the saturation value I_{B0}.   If I_{Bs} is greater than the value required to produce saturation, then there will be an excess charge stored in the base.   The collector current will remain essentially constant until this *excess stored charge* is removed.   Thus, the collector current persists beyond t_2 until time $t_2 + \tau_s$. The *storage time* τ_s is the time required for the excess charge to be removed from the base region.   Increases in I_{Bs} will increase the excess stored charge and, hence, increase τ_s.   A typical curve of τ_s versus I_{Bs} is shown in Fig. 12-10a.   If I_{Br} is increased, the excess charge will be removed at a faster rate and τ_s will be reduced.   A typical plot of τ_s versus I_{Br} is shown in Fig. 12-10b.   The presence of a storage time depends upon excess charge storage in the base region and only occurs when the transistor is driven into saturation.

The time required for i_C to fall essentially to its cutoff value is called the *switching fall time* and is denoted by τ_f.   This is the time required for the charge density in the base region to return to its cutoff value.   It does not include the storage time.   If I_{Br} is increased, the charge density in the base region will reduce at a more rapid rate and τ_f will be reduced.   A typical plot of τ_f versus I_{Br} is shown in Fig. 12-10b.   The time $\tau_f + \tau_s$ is the total time required to turn the transistor off.

If I_{Bs} is increased, τ_r will be reduced but τ_s will be increased.   Often I_{Bs} is made somewhat larger than necessary; this reduces τ_r.   Then increasing the base drive increases I_{Br} and, hence, reduces τ_s.   Fortunately, this also reduces τ_f.   Note that the statements made at the end of the last section concerning overdriving the active element must be modified in the case of the transistor.

12-3   Multivibrators

In this section we shall consider an oscillator which can be used to generate a continuous train of pulses.   It is called a *multivibrator*.   Two such circuits are shown in Fig. 12-11.   The operation of both of these circuits is similar, and they will be described simultaneously.   When we speak of an increase in the voltage or current, it will refer to the magnitude of the voltage or current.   The waveforms of T_a are given in Fig. 12-12.   (They are actually the waveforms for a vacuum tube, but those for the transistor are similar.)   The waveforms of T_b differ from those of T_a by one half-cycle. Assume that T_a and T_b are both conducting equally, but that some random fluctuation increases the output current of T_a.   This will decrease e_{oa}.   The voltage across C_1 and C_2 cannot change instantaneously.   Thus, the grid or base voltage of T_b will decrease.   This will increase e_{ob}.   The grid or base voltage of T_a will increase and, hence, its output current will increase further. This process will continue until T_b is cut off.   At this time, T_a should be saturated.   If the active elements could respond instantaneously and there were no parasitic capacitance, then this process would take place in zero time.   If T_a is a vacuum tube, then its grid may be driven positive.   How-

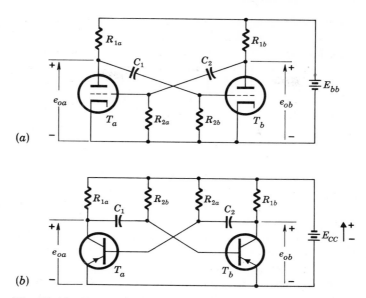

Fig. 12-11 *Free-running multivibrators.* (*a*) *Vacuum-tube circuit;* (*b*) *transistor circuit.*

ever, once there is grid current, a very low-resistance discharge path is supplied to C_2 and the bias drops to zero very quickly.

The capacitor C_1 will discharge so that, eventually, T_b will no longer be cut off. As its current increases, e_{ob} decreases, which tends to drive T_a towards cutoff. The procedure outlined above repeats itself until T_b is saturated and T_a is cut off, whereupon the cycle starts again. The rate of oscillation depends upon the discharge of the capacitors C_1 and C_2. For the vacuum tube, if the effective plate resistance of the active element in the saturation region is r_s, and if we define

$$R'_{2a} = R_{2a} + \frac{r_s R_{1b}}{r_s + R_{1b}}$$

and

$$R'_{2b} = R_{2b} + \frac{r_s R_{1a}}{r_s + R_{1a}}$$

then the time constant for one half-cycle is $R'_{2b}C_1$, while the time constant for the other half-cycle is $R'_{2a}C_2$. For the transistor,

$$R'_{2a} = \frac{R_{2a}h_{iec}}{R_{2a} + h_{iec}} + \frac{R_{1b}}{1 + h_{oes}R_{1b}}$$

and

$$R'_{2b} = \frac{R_{2b}h_{iec}}{R_{2b} + h_{iec}} + \frac{R_{1a}}{1 + h_{oes}R_{1a}}$$

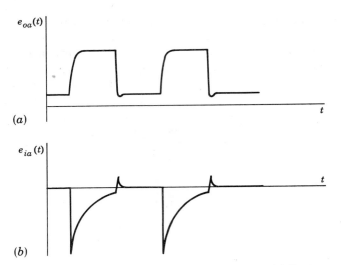

Fig. 12-12 Waveforms in a free-running multivibrator.
(a) Output voltage; (b) input voltage.

(see Fig. 12-3).   The buildup and decay times of e_{oa} or e_{ob} depend upon the concepts discussed in Secs. 12-1 and 12-2.   In a good multivibrator, these times will be small in comparison to a cycle.   The slight "wiggle" at the start of each cycle of Fig. 12-12 is due to the effects of grid current in the vacuum tube.

It is possible for both T_a and T_b to become saturated when their circuits are turned on, in which case no oscillatory action will take place.   More complex circuitry is sometimes used to ensure that oscillations will start.

If an external signal is applied to the grid or base of the cutoff device such that it drives it from the cutoff region, the cycle will be initiated.   This often proves convenient, since it allows the multivibrator to be synchronized by an external signal.   For instance, suppose that the multivibrator is adjusted to oscillate at a frequency just slower than that of a signal applied to one grid or base.   The cycles will be initiated each time the signal drives the device from the cutoff region and the multivibrator will run in exact synchronism with the signal.   If the period of the input signal is approximately an integral multiple or submultiple of the frequency of the multivibrator, it will also synchronize it.   In this case, the frequency of the multivibrator will be an exact harmonic or subharmonic of the applied signal.   This circuit is called a *free-running multivibrator*, since it is not necessary to apply an external signal to obtain operation.

12-4   Bistable multivibrators—counter circuits

If the coupling capacitors of the free-running multivibrator are replaced by direct coupling, very different operation results.   Consider the circuits of

Fig. 12-13. We shall again describe both circuits simultaneously. The magnitudes of the voltages will be discussed here. Assume that T_a and T_b are conducting equally, but that some disturbance increases the output current of T_a. The voltage e_{oa} will decrease and the input bias of T_b will be driven towards cutoff. This will increase e_{ob} and further increase the output current of T_a. This process will continue until T_b is cut off and T_a is saturated as in the case of the free-running multivibrator. However, the circuits are direct coupled; hence, this condition will be maintained indefinitely. Now suppose that a pulse whose polarity tends to drive the device towards cutoff is applied to both grids or to both bases. Since T_b is cut off, the pulse applied to it will have no effect. However, if the pulse applied to T_a is sufficiently large to drive it from the saturation region, then e_{oa} will rise. If this rise is sufficiently large, it will increase the output current of T_b and decrease e_{ob}. This will further decrease the current through T_a and increase e_{oa}. This will repeat itself until T_b is saturated and T_a is cut off. Thus, this circuit will change its state whenever the proper input pulse is applied. (Pulses which tend to saturate the devices can also change the state.)

Now let us consider the circuit of Fig. 12-14, which provides such triggering action, and consider some of its applications. It consists basically of the circuit of Fig. 12-13b. The diodes D_a and D_b are called *steering diodes*.

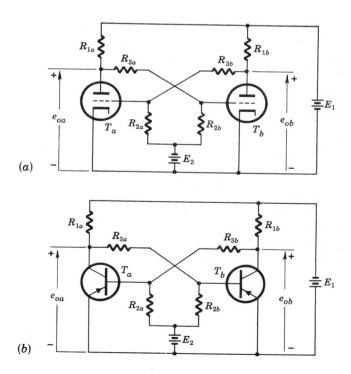

Fig. 12-13   *Bistable multivibrators.*   (a) *Vacuum-tube circuit;* (b) *transistor circuit.*

(a)

(b)

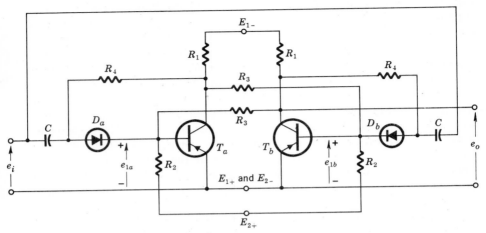

Fig. 12-14   A basic counter circuit.

They cause the triggering pulse to be applied to the proper transistor. If this were not done, a cutoff pulse would be applied to the bases of both transistors. This would waste energy and tend to interfere with proper triggering. Let us consider that T_a is cut off and T_b is saturated. Then D_a will be reverse-biased, since its anode essentially will be at the large negative potential of the collector of T_a and its cathode will be at the positive potential of the base of T_a. On the other hand, if the transistors are ideal, then D_b will act as a short circuit, since the collector voltage of T_b is zero, while the base of T_b will be at a negative potential. (In an actual circuit, the collector voltage will not be zero so that D_b may be *slightly* reverse-biased.) Thus, if a positive pulse is applied at e_i, D_a will prevent it from being applied to the base of T_a while D_b will allow it to be applied to the base of T_b. In general, a positive pulse will always be applied to the base of the cut-off transistor. The diodes also perform another function. *They prevent a negative pulse from affecting either transistor*, since they can only conduct in one direction.

Now let us assume that the input voltage e_i is the train of pulses shown in Fig. 12-15a. If this voltage were applied to a series circuit consisting of C and R_2 alone, then the fictitious voltage e_1 across R_2 would have the form shown in Fig. 12-15b. Actually, neither e_{1a} nor e_{1b} has this waveform. The diodes will eliminate all negative pulses and alternate positive pulses. That is, e_{1a} and e_{1b} will only consist of positive pulses; when one is positive, the other will be zero because of steering action. In general, the waveform will not even have the shape of e_1, because the base and collector currents will affect e_{1a} and e_{1b}. However, positive pulses will be present at the base of the saturated transistor, if e_i has the waveform of Fig. 12-15a.

Now let us assume that T_a is cut off and that T_b is saturated. When e_1 has a positive pulse, it will be applied as e_{1b} to the base of T_b. Then T_b will become cut off and T_a will be saturated. The next positive pulses in e_1 will saturate T_b and cut off T_a. In this way, successive positive pulses of e_1 will change the state of the circuit. (Note that the RC input circuit provides positive and negative pulses even if the input pulses are of only one polarity. In addition, the RC circuit and the diodes prevent the input pulses from interfering with switching action once the cycle has been initiated.) If we consider that T_b is ideal, then its collector voltage is zero when it conducts and will be a negative value when it is cut off. This voltage is the output voltage e_o. It is shown plotted in Fig. 12-15c. Transients have been neglected here. Since the state only changes on successive positive pulses, the frequency of e_o will be one-half of that of e_i. For this reason, this is called a *scale-of-two circuit*. If e_o becomes the input of another scale-of-two circuit, then its output will have a frequency that is one-quarter of the input frequency, and so on.

Frequency scaling is a useful application of these circuits, but a far more important one is counting pulses. Consider that some indication is placed in the collector circuit of T_b to show when it is cut off, and that a great many circuits of the form of Fig. 12-14 are cascaded. Assume that all the T_b's

Fig. 12-15 Some typical waveforms for the circuit of Fig. 12-14. (a) The input voltage; (b) the idealized voltage e_1; and (c) the output voltage, neglecting transients.

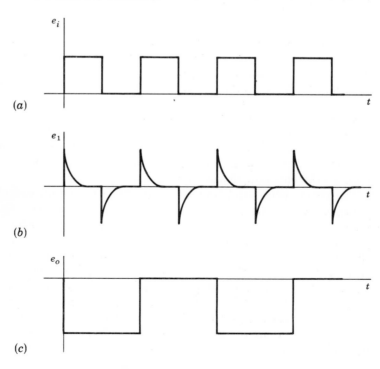

are initially conducting. We shall use the notation that a transistor is on if it is saturated and off if it is cut off. In addition, T_{a1} and T_{b1} will be the transistors of the first counter; T_{a2} and T_{b2} will be the transistors of the second counter, etc. The leading edge of each pulse of e_i will produce a positive pulse of e_1. The first such pulse will switch T_{a1} on and switch T_{b1} off. This produces a negative-going pulse in e_o which will not affect the next counter. The polarity of the output of the RC circuit will depend upon the derivative of the input voltage (see Sec. 12-6). The leading edge of the next pulse of e_i will switch T_{a1} off and T_{b1} on. This will produce a positive-going pulse that activates the next counter, and turns T_{b2} off. In a similar way, the leading edge of each of the input pulses will activate the first counter. Every second input pulse will activate the second counter; every fourth pulse will activate the third counter, etc. If all the T_b's are on at the start, then the following table can be used to determine the number of pulses.

Table 12-1

No. of pulses	T_b cut off			
0	none			
1	T_{b1}			
2		T_{b2}		
3	T_{b1}	T_{b2}		
4			T_{b3}	
5	T_{b1}		T_{b3}	
6		T_{b2}	T_{b3}	
7	T_{b1}	T_{b2}	T_{b3}	
8				T_{b4}

These counters operate in the *binary number system*. If there are n counters, then $2^n - 1$ pulses can be counted. Thus, circuits can be constructed that will count large numbers of pulses. Some means should be provided to reset the counter. One means of doing this is to apply a momentary cutoff bias onto all the bases of transistors T_a.

In vacuum-tube and transistor circuits, if the cutoff collector voltage is sufficiently high, a simple means of indicating if an active element is cut off is a neon bulb in series with a resistance. This is connected from plate to cathode or collector to emitter. If the device is cut off, the potential across the bulb will be high and it will glow. If the device is saturated, the bulb will be dark. The current drawn by these bulbs is not large enough to disturb the circuit operation. One of the most important applications of counter circuits is in digital computers. In this case, the outputs from the various counters are used in the solution of the desired problem.

The counter circuits that we have presented are very basic and they are usually modified. For instance, capacitors are often placed across the resistances R_{3a} and R_{3b} in Fig. 12-13 to speed the operation. Transistor counters are often operated so that they do not actually enter the saturation region; this eliminates the problem of storage time. In digital computers, an exceptionally large number of operations are usually carried out, and speed of operation is quite important. Thus, it is desirable to have counters that respond quite rapidly.

12-5 Logic circuits

Digital-computer circuits operate between saturation and cutoff levels. Let us call the saturation level 1 and the cutoff level 0. Thus, a counter circuit will count the number of times that the level switches from 1 to 0, or vice versa. In order to function, a digital computer must perform certain logical operations on these 1 or 0 signals. We shall consider several of these.

The AND circuit

It is often desirable to build up a circuit called an AND circuit that will have an output of 1 if all of several input circuits have outputs equal to 1. However, if *any* of the input circuits has an output of 0, then the output of the AND circuit should be zero. For instance, if there are three inputs A, B, and C, then the output of the AND circuit is 1 if A *and* B *and* C are 1. In order to demonstrate circuitry, let us assume that 1 corresponds to a negative voltage and 0 is zero volts. (Thus, 1 will saturate a *p-n-p* transistor and 0 will cut it off.) The logical AND operation can be performed by the circuit of Fig. 12-16. Assume that when e_a, e_b, or e_c represents 1, it will be slightly greater than E. If e_a, e_b, and e_c are all 1, then all three diodes will be cut off and $e_o = E$. Thus, the output is a 1. On the other hand, if e_a, e_b, or e_c is zero, then the diode in series with it will conduct and e_o will, effectively, be zero. Thus, the circuit performs the desired function.

The OR circuit

An OR circuit is one which produces an output if *any* of its inputs is 1. That is, its output is 1 if e_a, *or* e_b, *or* e_c is 1. Such a circuit is shown in Fig.

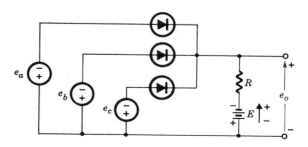

Fig. 12-16 An AND circuit.

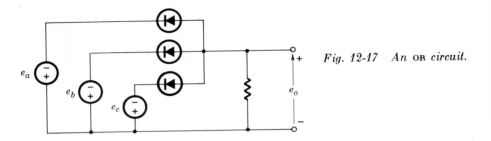

Fig. 12-17   An OR *circuit.*

12-17.   If any generator is 1, then its diode will conduct; otherwise it will not. Thus, if any generator is 1, it will be directly connected to the output and the output will be 1.

The NEGATE *circuit*

This is a circuit that will convert a 1 to a 0 and vice versa.   This can be done very simply with a common-emitter transistor amplifier such as that shown in Fig. 12-18.   If e_i is 0, then the transistor will be cut off and e_o will be a large negative value and, hence, 1.   If e_i is 1, then the transistor will saturate and e_o will be a 0.

The NOR *circuit*

If several inputs are included in the circuit of Fig. 12-18, the circuit will perform the functions of an OR circuit cascaded with a negate circuit.   Hence, it is called a NOR circuit.   This is illustrated in Fig. 12-19.   If e_a, or e_b, or e_c is 1, then e_o will be 0.   If e_a, e_b, and e_c are all zero, then e_o will be 1.

The logic circuits presented in this section are representative of circuits of this type.   However, there are many variations.   For instance, the transistor circuits are usually altered so that they do not operate in the saturation region.   This eliminates storage-time effects.

12-6   Differentiating and integrating circuits

There are many applications where it is desirable to obtain a signal that is approximately the derivative of the input signal.   (This can be done with an operational amplifier.   However, if great accuracy is not desired, then

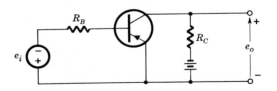

Fig. 12-18   A NEGATE *circuit.*

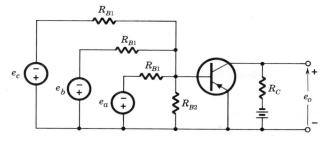

Fig. 12-19   A NOR *circuit.*

much simpler circuits can be used.) For instance, consider the counter circuit of Fig. 12-14. The waveforms for this circuit are shown in Fig. 12-15. If the voltage e_i consists of square positive pulses, then e_1 will contain both negative and positive spikes. If these negative spikes were not present, then the counter would not function properly. The input RC circuit approximately differentiates the input voltage e_i to obtain the voltage e_1. Consider the circuit of Fig. 12-20. Its differential equations are

$$e_i = \frac{1}{C} \int i \, dt + iR \tag{12-12}$$

and

$$e_o = iR \tag{12-13}$$

If the RC time constant is considerably smaller than the period of the input signals, then we can often state

$$\frac{1}{C} \int i \, dt \gg iR \tag{12-14}$$

This inequality is not always true no matter how small RC is. However, since the function of these circuits is only to obtain an *approximate* derivative, the accuracy is usually sufficient if RC is much smaller than one period.

If relation (12-14) is valid, we can state

$$i = C \frac{de_i}{dt} \tag{12-15}$$

Fig. 12-20   A *differentiating circuit.*

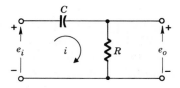

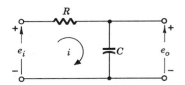

Fig. 12-21   An integrating circuit.

Substituting in Eq. (12-13), we obtain

$$e_o = RC \frac{de_i}{dt} \tag{12-16}$$

Typical input and output waveforms for this circuit are shown in Fig. 12-15a and b.

A circuit which will approximately integrate an input waveform is shown in Fig. 12-21.   Its differential equations are

$$e_i = Ri + \frac{1}{C} \int i \, dt \tag{12-17}$$

$$e_o = \frac{1}{C} \int i \, dt \tag{12-18}$$

If

$$Ri \gg \frac{1}{C} \int i \, dt \tag{12-19}$$

then

$$e_o = \frac{1}{RC} \int e_i \, dt \tag{12-20}$$

The approximation of relation (12-19) usually depends upon the fact that RC is much larger than the period of the input signal.

12-7   Clipping and clamping circuits

A circuit that limits the amplitude of an output signal is called a *clipping circuit*.   One application of such a circuit is in the generation of an approximate square wave from a sine-wave input.   Consider the circuit of Fig. 12-22.   If $E_b \leqq e_i \leqq E_a$, where E_b is a negative voltage, then neither diode will conduct and $e_o = e_i$.   If $e_i > E_a$, then D_a will conduct and act as a short circuit.   Thus, $e_o = E_a$.   If $e_i < E_b$, then D_b will conduct, and, thus, $e_o = E_b$. Figure 12-22b illustrates the behavior of this circuit.   If $E_a = -E_b$ and $e_1 = E_{1,\max} \sin \omega t$, where $E_{1,\max} \gg E_a$, then the output of this circuit will be a fairly good square wave.   The relative amplitude of the positive and negative peaks can be changed by varying E_a and E_b.

We have illustrated a clipping circuit that uses diodes.   These circuits are also built using vacuum tubes or transistors.   These are, essentially, amplifiers that are driven between saturation and cutoff.

Another application of clipping circuits is in devices that are required to respond to changes in a signal's frequency, but not in its amplitude. Frequency-modulation systems are an example of this. These will be discussed in Chap. 13.

It is often desirable to convert an alternating signal to one which is unidirectional without altering its waveform. A circuit which performs this operation is called a *clamping circuit* or a *d-c restorer*. A typical one is shown in Fig. 12-23a. Consider the input voltage shown in Fig. 12-23b. On the first negative cycle, the diode will conduct and the capacitor C will charge to the voltage $e = E_{i,\max}$, with the polarity shown. The capacitor can only discharge through the resistor R. If the product RC is much larger than the period of the signal, then e will remain essentially constant at $E_{i,\max}$. The output voltage will then be given by

$$e_o = E_{i,\max} + e_i \tag{12-21}$$

Thus, e_o will not be negative at any time. The output waveform of this circuit is shown in Fig. 12-23c. If $E_{i,\max}$ changes, the circuit will readjust itself so that the minimum voltage is zero. If $E_{i,\max}$ is decreased, then it may require many cycles for the capacitor to discharge before equilibrium conditions are established.

The preceding discussion assumes that the diode is ideal, and that $RC \to \infty$. In actual cases, this is not true, and e_o will be slightly negative at the negative peak of e_i. Often, the resistance R is omitted and the shunt

Fig. 12-22   (a) *A diode clipping circuit; (b) the waveforms in this circuit when a sinusoidal signal is applied.*

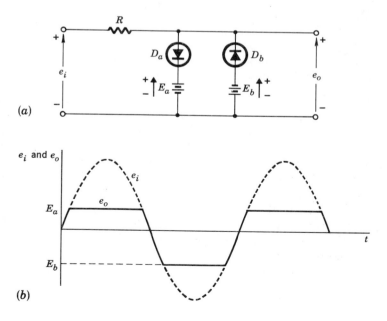

(a)

(b)

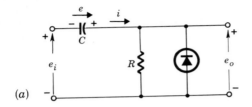

(a)

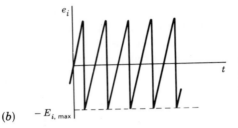

(b) $-E_{i,\,max}$

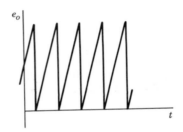

(c)

Fig. 12-23   (a) A diode clamping circuit; (b) an input waveform; (c) the
output waveform.

leakage resistance of the diode takes its place.   If R is made very large, then
the circuit will not respond quickly if the input signal is reduced.   This is
usually not a serious consequence.

Once an equilibrium condition is established, the charge lost by the
capacitor over any one cycle is equal to the charge gained by it over the
same cycle.   Thus,

$$\int_0^{2\pi} i\,d\omega t = 0 \tag{12-22}$$

If the time scale is adjusted so that e_o is positive for $0 < \omega t < \theta_1$ and e_o is
negative for $\theta_1 < \omega t < 2\pi$, then Eq. (12-22) becomes

$$\int_0^{\theta_1} i\,d\omega t = \int_{\theta_1}^{2\pi} i\,d\omega t$$

Let us assume that the diode has a forward resistance of r_f and a reverse
resistance of r_r.   Let

$$R_1 = \frac{r_r R}{r_r + R} \tag{12-23}$$

If $r_f \ll R$, then we can write,

$$\frac{1}{R_1} \int_0^{\theta_1} e_o \, d\omega t = \frac{1}{r_f} \int_{\theta_1}^{2\pi} e_o \, d\omega t \tag{12-24}$$

or

$$\frac{\int_{\theta_1}^{2\pi} e_o \, d\omega t}{\int_0^{\theta_1} e_o \, d\omega t} = \frac{r_f}{R_1} \tag{12-25}$$

Thus, the area under the negative e_o curve will decrease as r_f/R_1 decreases. In the limit, as this ratio approaches zero, e_o never becomes negative. If $r_f = 0$, there will be no time when e_o is negative. However, if R_1C is not sufficiently large, then the diode will conduct over a finite portion of the cycle and the waveform will be clipped and distorted. Thus, to obtain good nondistorted clamping action, $R_1 \gg r_f$ and R_1C must be much larger than one period.

BIBLIOGRAPHY

Greiner, R. A.: "Semiconductor Devices and Applications," chaps. 18–20, McGraw-Hill Book Company, New York, 1961.

Joyce, M. V., and K. K. Clarke: "Transistor Circuit Analysis," chaps. 10–15, Addison-Wesley Publishing Company, Inc., Reading, Mass., 1961.

Millman, J., and H. Taub: "Pulse and Digital Circuits," chaps. 4–18, McGraw-Hill Book Company, New York, 1956.

Pettit, J. M.: "Electronic Switching, Timing, and Pulse Circuits," chaps. 1–3, 5–8, McGraw-Hill Book Company, New York, 1959.

Ryder, J. D.: "Engineering Electronics," chap. 9, McGraw-Hill Book Company, New York, 1957.

PROBLEMS

12-1. The output capacitance of the generalized device of Fig. 12-4 is $20 \ \mu\mu f$. Its static output characteristics are given in Fig. 12-24. The circuit is operated such that $E_{oo} = 50$ volts and $R_L = 33,330$ ohms. The input bias is $x_i = -8$ for $t < 0$ and $x_i = 0$ for $t > 0$. Determine the step response of the amplifier.

12-2. Repeat Prob. 12-1, but now assume that $E_{oo} = 120$ volts.

12-3. Repeat Prob. 12-1, but now assume that $E_{oo} = 120$ volts and $R_L = 8,000$ ohms.

12-4. Repeat Prob. 12-1, but now assume that $x_i = 0$ for $t < 0$ and $x_i = -8$ for $t > 0$.

12-5. Repeat Prob. 12-4, but now assume that $E_{oo} = 120$ volts.

12-6. For the amplifier of Prob. 12-1, $x_i = -8$ for $t < 0$, $x_i = 0$ for $0 \leqslant t \leqslant 10^{-6}$ sec, and $x_i = -8$ for $t > 10^{-6}$ sec. Obtain and plot the transient response of the amplifier.

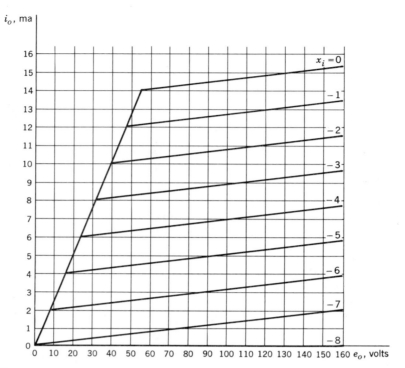

Fig. 12-24

12-7. Repeat Prob. 12-6, but now assume that $E_{oo} = 120$ volts.

12-8. A type 2N383 transistor, whose switching characteristics are given in Fig. 12-10, is to be pulsed from cutoff to saturation and then back to cutoff as shown in Fig. 12-9. It is desired that the sum of τ_r, τ_s, and τ_f be a minimum. Determine the value of I_{Bs} which allows this to be accomplished. Assume that $I_{Br} = 1$ ma. Only use values of current that are specified in the curves. Use the curves of Fig. 12-10.

12-9. The multivibrator of Fig. 12-11a has the following element values: $R_{1a} = R_{1b} = 10,000$ ohms, $R_{2a} = R_{2b} = 10^6$ ohms, $C_1 = C_2 = 0.01$ μf, $E_{bb} = 300$ volts. Assume that the vacuum tubes cut off when $e_c < -20$ volts and that the plate resistance of the triode is 1,000 ohms when it is saturated, and that it is an open circuit when the tube is cut off. Compute the frequency of operation of the multivibrator. Assume that the parasitic capacitances can be neglected, so that the tubes can instantaneously switch from saturation to cutoff.

12-10. The multivibrator of Fig. 12-11b has the following element values: $R_{1a} = R_{1b} = 1,000$ ohms, $R_{2a} = R_{2b} = 10^6$ ohms, $C_1 = C_2 = 0.01$ μf, and $E_{cc} = -30$ volts. The transistor parameters are (see Fig. 12-3) $h_{ies} = 500$ ohms, $h_{iec} = 10^6$ ohms, $h_{oes} = \frac{1}{10}$ mho, and $h_{oec} = 2 \times 10^{-6}$ mho. Assume that the transistor cuts off when its base-to-emitter voltage is 0 volts or higher. Compute the frequency of oscillation of the multivibrator. Assume

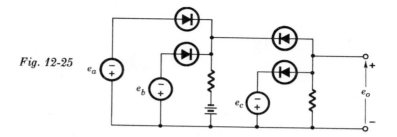

Fig. 12-25

that the transistors instantaneously switch from the cutoff to the saturation regions.

12-11. Design a counter circuit that will count up to 2,000 pulses. (Use block-diagram form.)

12-12. Discuss the operation of the logic circuit of Fig. 12-25.

12-13. For the circuit of Fig. 12-20, assume that e_i is a square wave with a period of 0.002 sec. Determine and plot e_o for the first cycle if $R = 10^6$ ohms and $C = 0.0001$ μf.

12-14. Repeat Prob. 12-13 if $C = 10$ $\mu\mu$f.

12-15. For the circuit of Fig. 12-21, assume that e_i is a square wave with a period of 0.001 sec. Determine e_o for the first cycle if $R = 10^6$ ohms and $C = 0.01$ μf.

12-16. Repeat Prob. 12-15 for $C = 1.0$ μf.

12-17. What is the output of the circuit of Fig. 12-26 if the input is given by Fig. 12-23*b* where $E_{i,\max} = 300$ volts. Assume that the diode is ideal, that RC is very long compared to the period of the signal, and that the positive and negative peaks of the signal are equal in magnitude.

12-18. Repeat Prob. 12-17, but assume that the diode is reversed.

12.19. Repeat Prob. 12-17, but assume that the polarity of the 100-volt battery is reversed.

12-20. Repeat Prob. 12-17, but now assume that the forward resistance of the diode is 100 ohms and its reverse resistance is 10^6 ohms, that $R = 10^9$ ohms, and that C is such that $0.5 \times 10^6 C$ is very much larger than one period of the input signal.

12-21. Discuss the changes that would occur in Prob. 12-17 if RC is not very long in comparison with the period of the input signal.

Fig. 12-26

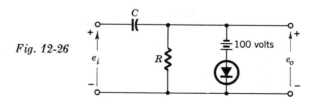

Modulation and Demodulation

13

A communications system is designed to convey information from one point to another. To accomplish this, a signal is made to vary in response to the information. Thus, a periodic signal, whether it be a sinusoid, a square wave, or any other waveform, does not transmit information. If the amplitude, frequency, or phase of a periodic signal is varied by intelligence, then a signal is obtained that can convey information. The process by which a function is made to vary in accordance with some specified intelligence is called *modulation*. The inverse process, that is, the recovering of the information from the signal, is called *demodulation* or *detection*. It is often inconvenient to transmit a signal directly. For instance, spoken messages carry for only a few feet. It is also difficult to transmit low-frequency electrical signals for any great distance. However, frequencies of 100 kc/sec or higher can be transmitted over great distances using electromagnetic waves. To take advantage of this, the modulation process often consists of varying the amplitude, frequency, or phase of a radio-frequency sinusoid. Modulation may take on other forms. For instance, telegraph signals can be considered

494

to be the modulation of a direct voltage. There are other modulation schemes where the amplitude, length, or position of pulses are varied.

13-1 Modulation of a sinusoid

The waveform that is most often modulated is the sinusoid. For instance, suppose that we have a signal

$$x(t) = A \cos (\omega_c t + \phi) \tag{13-1}$$

If A and ϕ are constants, then this signal is unmodulated and $x(t)$ is called the *carrier*. Its frequency is given by $f_c = \omega_c/2\pi$. Now let us assume that we wish to transmit some information $x_m(t)$. We can do this by varying A such that

$$A = A(t) = A_c + k_1 x_m(t) \tag{13-2}$$

and

$$x(t) = [A_c + k_1 x_m(t)] \cos (\omega_c t + \phi) \tag{13-3}$$

This process is called *amplitude modulation* since the amplitude of the carrier is varied. The information $x_m(t)$ is called the *modulating signal*. The quantity k_1 is a constant.

Let us see how the modulation could be applied to the frequency or phase of the carrier. The instantaneous phase angle of the cosinusoid of Eq. (13-1) is given by

$$\theta(t) = \omega_c t + \phi(t) \tag{13-4}$$

where we have assumed that ϕ could be a function of time. The instantaneous angular frequency ω_i is defined as the rate of change of the phase angle. Thus,

$$\omega_i = \frac{d\theta}{dt} \tag{13-5}$$

Thus, Eq. (13-4) yields

$$\omega_i = \omega_c + \frac{d\phi}{dt} \tag{13-6}$$

Note that if ϕ is a constant, then

$$\omega_i = \omega_c \tag{13-7}$$

which is the frequency of the unmodulated sinusoid. Now let us assume that we vary the instantaneous frequency in accordance with the modulating signal. That is,

$$\omega_i = \omega_c + k_2 x_m(t) \tag{13-8}$$

where k_2 is a constant.   Note that the instantaneous frequency varies with the *amplitude* of the modulating signal.   This is called *frequency modulation*. Equating Eqs. (13-6) and (13-8), we obtain

$$\phi(t) = k_2 \int x_m(t) \, dt \tag{13-9}$$

Thus

$$x(t) = A \cos [\omega_c t + k_2 \int x_m(t) \, dt] \tag{13-10}$$

If $\phi(t)$ is made to vary directly in accordance with the modulating signal, the process is called *phase modulation*.   In this case,

$$\phi(t) = k_3 x_m(t) \tag{13-11}$$

and

$$x(t) = A \cos [\omega_c t + k_3 x_m(t)] \tag{13-12}$$

In the following sections of this chapter, we shall consider these modulation systems in detail.

13-2   Amplitude modulation

Let us now consider amplitude modulation in detail.   To simplify the analysis, we shall, for the time being, assume that the modulating signal is a cosinusoid such that

$$x_m(t) = A_m \cos \omega_m t \tag{13-13}$$

This will be extended to more complex modulating signals subsequently. Substituting into Eq. (13-3), we obtain

$$x(t) = [A_c + k_1 A_m \cos \omega_m t] \cos \omega_c t \tag{13-14}$$

Thus

$$x(t) = A_c[1 + m \cos \omega_m t] \cos \omega_c t \tag{13-15}$$

where

$$m = \frac{k_1 A_m}{A_c} \tag{13-16}$$

The quantity m is called the *index of modulation*.   It is sometimes multiplied by 100 and called the *percent modulation*.   A plot of Eq. (13-15) is given in Fig. 13-1.   The curves marked *envelope of modulation* represent upper and lower limits on the value of $x(t)$.   The equation for the envelope of modulation is

$$\pm A_c(1 + m \cos \omega_m t)$$

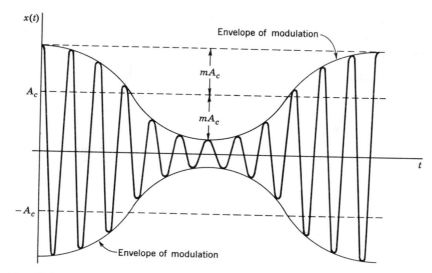

Fig. 13-1 An amplitude-modulated wave.

where the plus sign is used for the upper envelope and the minus sign is used for the lower one.   If $m = 1$, then $x(t)$ must be zero when $\omega_m t = \pi$, 3π, 5π, ...   If $m > 1$, then the expression for the upper (lower) envelope will become negative (positive) for some values of time.   Mathematically, this is acceptable and values of $m > 1$ can be used in Eq. (13-15).   However, most electronic devices are such that their output is zero for those values of time that $1 + m \cos \omega_m t < 0$.   Thus, if $m > 1$, the modulated signal $x(t)$ will be zero for some periods of time.   The envelope of $x(t)$ will no longer have the shape of the modulating signal and distortion will result.   This is analogous to cutting off the active elements in an audio amplifier.   (Even if the electronic devices do not introduce distortion, the envelope will not have the shape of the modulating signal if $m > 1$.)   To avoid excessive distortion, we shall assume that $0 \leqslant m \leqslant 1$.

Consider Eq. (13-15).   Using the trigonometric identity for the product of two cosines, we have

$$x(t) = A_c \cos \omega_c t + \frac{mA_c}{2} \cos (\omega_c + \omega_m)t + \frac{mA_c}{2} \cos (\omega_c - \omega_m)t \qquad (13\text{-}17)$$

Thus, we see that the modulation process produces additional frequency components above and below the carrier frequency.   These are called *sidebands* and differ from the carrier frequency by (plus or minus) the modulating frequency.   The carrier itself is *unaffected by the modulation*.   Its amplitude remains constant at the value A_c.   A plot called a *frequency spectrum* is sometimes made to indicate the relative magnitudes of the frequencies of a waveform.   Such a plot is shown in Fig. 13-2a.

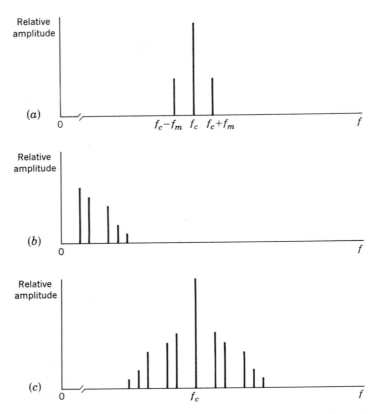

Fig. 13-2   (a) The frequency spectrum of an amplitude-modulated wave where the modulating frequency is a sinusoid; (b) the frequency spectrum of a modulating signal; (c) the frequency spectrum of an amplitude-modulated wave where the frequency spectrum of the modulating signal is given in (b).

Let us now consider that the waveform is not sinusoidal. Assume that $x_m(t)$ has the frequency spectrum shown in Fig. 13-2b. If this is used to amplitude-modulate a wave, then the resultant waveform will have the frequency spectrum shown in Fig. 13-2c. There is a pair of sidebands for each frequency of $x_m(t)$. The frequency scales of Fig. 13-2b and c are the same, and there is a break in the frequency axis of Fig. 13-2c.

Modulated signals are usually amplified by tuned amplifiers. For instance, in radio receivers, such amplifiers are necessary to reject unwanted signals. If the relative amplitudes or phase angles of the sidebands are changed, it is equivalent to altering the relative amplitudes or phase angles of the frequencies of the modulating signal. Thus, any tuned amplifier that is used to amplify the modulating signal can introduce frequency distortion in the same way that an *RC*-coupled amplifier can distort the modulating signal. A discussion of the frequency response of tuned amplifiers is given in Secs. 6-20 to 6-25. If amplitude modulation is desired with frequencies up to f_a, then any amplifier should have, essentially, a flat response for frequencies from $f_c - f_a$ to $f_c + f_a$.

Let us again consider that the carrier is modulated by a cosinusoid and obtain the relative power of the carrier and the sidebands. If $x(t)$ is either a voltage or a current, then the power will be proportional to the square of its rms value. Thus, P_c, the carrier power, will be proportional to $A_c{}^2/2$ while the total power contained in both sidebands will be proportional to $m^2 A_c{}^2/4$. Thus, the ratio of the power of both sidebands to the carrier power is

$$\frac{P_{sb}}{P_c} = \frac{m^2}{2} \tag{13-18}$$

If there is 100 percent modulation, then the sideband power will be one-half of the carrier power. This analysis is only true if there is a single sinusoid modulating the carrier. For instance, if the carrier is 100 percent modulated by a square wave, then the maximum amplitude will be $2A_o$ for half the time and zero for the other half of the time. Since the carrier power is unchanged by modulation,

$$\frac{P_{sb}}{P_c} = 1 \tag{13-19}$$

13-3 Amplitude-modulating circuits

The output stage of a high-power radio-frequency amplifier is usually operated class C (see Chap. 8). Its output in response to the input radio-frequency signal is quite nonlinear. Thus, if the driving signal of a class C amplifier is modulated, the output signal will be quite distorted (i.e., the envelopes of the input and output signals will not be the same). Thus, it is usually desirable to introduce the modulation in the final class C amplifier stage. We shall consider several techniques for accomplishing this. Another modulation technique will also be discussed.

Output-voltage-modulated class C amplifiers

Consider the class C radio-frequency amplifier of Fig. 8-2, which was analyzed in Sec. 8-2. If the power-supply voltage E_{oo} is varied while all the other quantities remain fixed, then the radio-frequency power delivered to the load P_2 and the rms radio-frequency output voltage E_2 will change. Thus, if E_{oo} is varied about its quiescent value, a modulated wave will result. The relationship between E_{oo} and E_2 is often quite linear, so that the modulation is satisfactory. Before proceeding further, let us consider some assumptions. Modulation results in the generation of sidebands. We shall

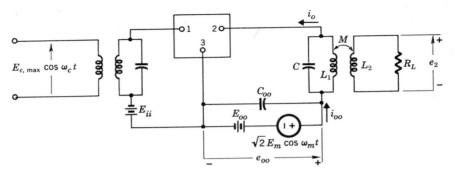

Fig. 13-3   An output-voltage-modulating circuit.

assume that the tuned output circuits of the class C amplifier have a frequency response that is constant for frequencies from the lowest sideband frequency to the highest sideband frequency. In general, responses of this type can be obtained, since $\omega_m \ll \omega_c$. We shall also assume that the impedance of the power supply is constant from zero frequency up to the highest modulating frequency.

We must now consider how the power-supply voltage can be varied in accordance with a modulating signal. A simple way of doing this is to place a generator which produces the modulating voltage in series with a direct power supply. Such a circuit is shown in Fig. 13-3. The instantaneous "power-supply voltage" is e_{oo}, and it is given by

$$e_{oo} = E_{oo} + \sqrt{2}\, E_m \cos \omega_m t \tag{13-20}$$

If the rms value of e_2 varies linearly with e_{oo}, then the output voltage of the amplifier will be of the form

$$e_2 = k(E_{oo} + \sqrt{2}\, E_m \cos \omega_m t) \cos \omega_c t \tag{13-21}$$

and we will have achieved amplitude modulation. Let us now consider the power supplied by the two generators of e_{oo}. The capacitor C_{oo} should be effectively a short circuit for the radio-frequency signals, but an open circuit for the modulating frequencies. Thus,

$$i_{oo} = I_{oA} + \sqrt{2}\, (I_{m1} \cos \omega_m t + I_{m2} \cos 2\omega_m t + \cdots) \tag{13-22}$$

Then, using Eq. (13-20), the power supplied by the power supply is

$$P_{oo} = E_{oo} I_{oA} \tag{13-23}$$

while the power supplied by the modulating generator is

$$P_m = E_m I_{m1} \tag{13-24}$$

If the effects of distortion are ignored, then I_{oA} will be independent of E_m, and, hence, the power supplied by the direct power supply is unchanged by modulation. In general, the output-circuit efficiency remains essentially constant as e_{oo} varies.[1] The carrier power remains constant independent of modulation [see Eq. (13-17)]. Thus, for both the modulated and the unmodulated cases,

$$P_c = P_{oo}\eta \tag{13-25}$$

where η is the output circuit efficiency. If P_{sb} is the total sideband power, then

$$P_{sb} + P_c = (P_{oo} + P_m)\eta \tag{13-26}$$

Thus

$$P_{sb} = P_m\eta \tag{13-27}$$

Thus, if the amplifier is 100 percent modulated by a sinusoid, the modulating generator supplies one-half of the power P_{oo}. The modulating generator usually is an audio power amplifier and can be designed using the methods of Chap. 7. An amplifier whose function is to supply a modulating voltage is called a *modulator*. A vacuum-tube output-modulated class C amplifier circuit is shown in Fig. 13-4. The audio amplifier is usually operated class B or class ABB for reasons of efficiency. This circuit is called a *plate-modulated class C amplifier*. The corresponding transistor circuit would be called a *collector-modulated class C amplifier*.

Fig. 13-4   A plate-modulated class C amplifier.

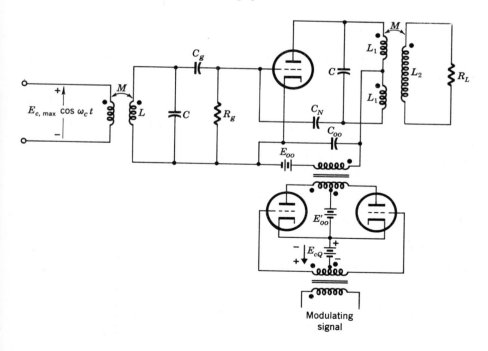

Modulating
signal

The device output dissipation increases when a modulating signal is applied. If we assume that the circuit elements are ideal, then we have

$$P_{sb} + P_c + P_{oD} = P_{oo} + P_m \tag{13-28}$$

That is, any power supplied by the direct power supply or by the modulator must be delivered to R_L as output power or be dissipated within the active element. Then, using Eq. (13-26), we have

$$P_{oD} = (P_c + P_{sb})\left(\frac{1}{\eta} - 1\right) \tag{13-29}$$

The output-circuit dissipation increases with modulation. For sinusoidal modulators, P_{sb} can be as much as one-half of P_c. Thus, the introduction of modulation can increase P_{oD} by a factor of 1.5. If the modulating signal is not a sinusoid, then the sideband power can be more than one-half of the carrier power and modulation can increase P_{oD} by more than the factor of 1.5. In the transmission of speech or music, 100 percent modulation is rarely achieved for long periods of time, so that the rated device output dissipation can be 1.5 times (or less) the value of P_{oD} with no modulation.

Plate modulation can be used with vacuum-tube tetrodes. However, if the plate voltage decreases below the suppressor-grid voltage, the plate current will decrease greatly because of secondary emission effects. This will result in excessive distortion and a loss of efficiency. If the plate voltage is restricted to values greater than the suppressor-grid voltage, the operation will be quite limited. At times, the suppressor-grid voltage, as well as the plate voltage, is varied by the modulating signal to eliminate these effects.

Input-voltage-modulated class C amplifiers

If the input bias (E_{ii} of Fig. 13-3) of a class C amplifier is varied, the output voltage E_2 will also vary. We can obtain modulation by modifying the circuit of Fig. 13-3 in the following way. Replace the modulating generator by a short circuit and reconnect it in series with E_{ii}. The power that the modulating generator must supply is thereby greatly reduced. The modulating amplifier can thus use smaller active elements and dissipate less power. However, this type of operation usually results in greatly reduced efficiency of the class C amplifier. In addition, the nonlinear distortion of the envelope is greater for input-circuit than for output-circuit modulation. Finally, it is somewhat more difficult to adjust the circuit when this type of modulation is used.[1] For these reasons, output-circuit modulation is much more common than input-circuit modulation.

Nonlinear modulation

If two signals of different frequencies are applied to a nonlinear element, modulation will result. For instance (see Sec. 2-10), consider a device with the transfer characteristic

$$x_0 = a_0 + a_1 x_i + a_2 x_i{}^2 \tag{13-30}$$

where x_i represents the input signal and x_o is the output signal. If

$$x_i = X_{ic,\max} \cos \omega_c t + X_{im,\max} \cos \omega_m t$$

then

$$x_o = a_0 + \frac{a_2}{2}(X^2_{ic,\max} + X^2_{im,\max}) + a_1(X_{ic,\max} \cos \omega_c t + X_{im,\max} \cos \omega_m t)$$

$$+ \frac{a_2}{2}(X^2_{ic,\max} \cos 2\omega_c t + X^2_{im,\max} \cos 2\omega_m t)$$

$$+ a_2 X_{ic,\max} X_{im,\max}[\cos(\omega_c + \omega_m)t + \cos(\omega_c - \omega_m)t] \tag{13-31}$$

If this signal is amplified by a tuned amplifier so that only those frequencies close to ω_c are passed, we obtain

$$x'_o = a_1 X_{ic,\max}\left[\cos \omega_c t + \frac{a_2 X_{im,\max}}{a_1} \cos(\omega_c + \omega_m)t\right.$$

$$\left. + \frac{a_2 X_{im,\max}}{a_1} \cos(\omega_c - \omega_m)t\right] \tag{13-32}$$

Thus, amplitude modulation has been achieved. This is called *square-law modulation* because of the form of Eq. (13-30). To obtain such a nonlinear characteristic, an amplifier is operated class A but is biased into a nonlinear region. The actual Taylor's-series expansion for x'_0 will contain cubic and higher terms. These will result in additional sideband frequencies and will produce harmonic distortion of the envelope. It is to reduce these effects that the active element is operated class A. Because of the limited efficiency that results, nonlinear modulation is only used in low-level applications.

13-4 Detection of amplitude-modulated signals

The intelligence contained in an amplitude-modulated wave must be converted to its original state if the system is to be of use (i.e., the output of the system should be a signal of the same waveform as that of the input). A circuit which recovers the modulating signal from a modulated wave is called a *detector*. We shall consider several techniques for the detection of amplitude-modulated signals in this section.

Linear detection

A simplified form of a very commonly used detector circuit is shown in Fig. 13-5. This is called a *linear-diode detector* since it utilizes either a vacuum-tube or a semiconductor diode. The term linear is used since it is assumed that the diode has a constant forward resistance and a constant reverse resistance, neither of which changes with signal level. Actually,

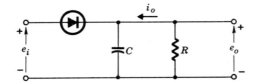

Fig. 13-5   A basic linear-diode detector circuit.

such a characteristic is not linear, since the forward and reverse resistances are not equal.   If elements that were linear in the strict sense were used, then detection would not result.   Let us assume that the waveform of e_i is given by the dashed curve of Fig. 13-6 and that the diode is ideal (i.e., its back resistance is infinite and its forward resistance is zero).   During the first cycle, e_o becomes the value shown by the solid curve.   The capacitor can only discharge through the resistor R.   We shall assume that the rate of decay of the voltage $e^{-t/RC}$ is considerably less than the maximum rate of falloff of the sinusoid of frequency ω_c.   Thus, at a time slightly later than the peak of the cycle $e_i < e_o$ and the diode will not conduct.   Hence, e_o will decay exponentially until the next cycle when the value of $e_i = e_o$.   The diode then acts as a short circuit, so that $e_o = e_i$ until a point slightly past the peak, and then the cycle repeats itself.   The resulting output voltage is shown in the solid curve of Fig. 13-6.   It has a jagged appearance.   If the carrier frequency is increased while the modulating frequency is held constant, then the time that the capacitor discharges will be reduced and the jaggedness of the curve will be lessened.   In Fig. 13-6, $\omega_c = 12 \, \omega_m$.   Usually, ω_c is 100 or more times ω_m so that the output voltage can follow the envelope of modulation quite closely.

Fig. 13-6   The input and output waveforms of Fig. 13-5.   (e_i is dashed.)

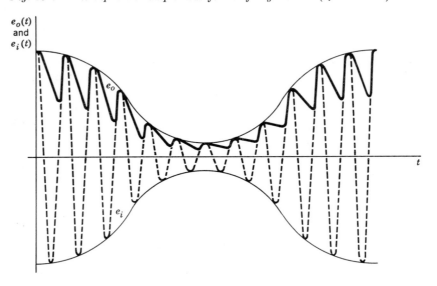

If the output voltage is not to be distorted, then the RC product must be properly chosen. For instance, if it is too small, then e_o will fall off too much between successive cycles of the carrier and the jagged result of Fig. 13-6 will result. To eliminate this effect,

$$RC \gg \frac{1}{\omega_c} \tag{13-33}$$

On the other hand, if RC is too large, then e_o will not be able to fall off fast enough to follow the envelope of the modulation. To prevent this from occurring

$$RC \ll \frac{1}{\omega_m} \tag{13-34}$$

where ω_m should be the highest frequency that is contained in the modulation. If relations (13-33) and (13-34) are to be compatible

$$\omega_c \gg \omega_m \tag{13-35}$$

This is usually the case and the circuit of Fig. 13-5 yields good results.

The output voltage of the circuit of Fig. 13-5 has a direct component which may interfere with the bias of the next amplifier stage. Resistance-capacitance coupling is often used to eliminate this. Such a circuit is shown in Fig. 13-7. The a-c and the d-c load impedances are now different. To analyze this circuit the *detection characteristic* of the diode must be obtained. This is a plot of demodulated output voltage versus demodulated output current with the carrier voltage as a parameter. To obtain this characteristic, the circuit of Fig. 13-5 can be used. An *unmodulated* carrier is applied. The direct output voltage and current e_o and i_o are measured for various values of R and plotted. It is assumed that the capacitor C is large enough so that relation (13-33) is satisfied. The peak carrier voltage is then changed and the procedure is repeated. A typical set of characteristics is shown in Fig. 13-8. (Note that $-i_o$ is plotted.) Now let us analyze the circuit of Fig. 13-7. We shall assume that the capacitor C_c is a short circuit at all frequencies of interest. The equation for the d-c load line is

$$i_o = -\frac{e_o}{R_1} \tag{13-36}$$

Fig. 13-7 A diode rectifier circuit with RC coupling.

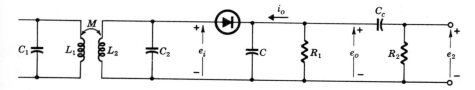

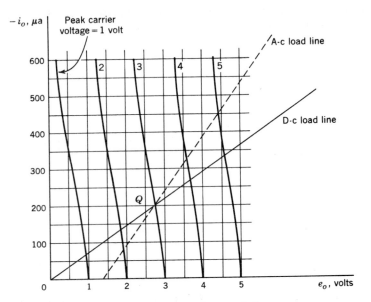

Fig. 13-8   A typical demodulation characteristic.

It is shown in Fig. 13-8.   The slope of the a-c load line is $-1/R_{ac}$ where

$$R_{ac} = \frac{R_1 R_2}{R_1 + R_2} \tag{13-37}$$

It is drawn through the quiescent operating point.   In this case, the quiescent operation results when the carrier is unmodulated.   For instance, if the peak unmodulated carrier voltage is 3 volts, then point Q is the quiescent operating point.   The a-c load line is shown dashed in Fig. 13-8.   The instantaneous value of e_o can be obtained from the intersection of the a-c load line with the characteristic curves.   (The peak carrier voltage varies with the modulation.)   Note that if the peak carrier voltage falls below 1.4 volts, the output will be clipped.   Thus, if excessive distortion is not to result, the maximum modulation index is limited.   The slopes of the a-c and d-c load lines are R_{ac} and $R_1 = R_{dc}$, respectively.   Thus, the maximum index of modulation that can be used without causing clipping is

$$m_{\max} = \frac{R_{ac}}{R_{dc}} \tag{13-38}$$

If this is to approach 100 percent, $R_{ac} \approx R_{dc}$.   To accomplish this in the circuit of Fig. 13-7, $R_2 \gg R_1$.

The input impedance of the detector circuit is of importance, since a tuned circuit usually precedes it (see Fig. 13-7).   Let us compute the input impedance, assuming that the diode is ideal and that relations (13-33) and

(13-34) are satisfied. The output voltage e_2 will then have the shape of the envelope of the modulation. If

$$e_i = E_{max} \cos \omega_c t$$

(that is, if the signal is unmodulated) then the output power will be

$$P_2 = \frac{E_{max}^2}{R_1}$$

(If R_1 is sufficiently large, then $e_o = E_{max}$.) Note that the output voltage is of zero frequency. Since the components are ideal, the input power is equal to the output power. If R_i is the effective input resistance, then

$$\frac{E_{max}^2}{R_1} = \frac{E_{max}^2}{2R_i}$$

Thus

$$R_i = \frac{R_1}{2} \tag{13-39}$$

If modulation is applied to the carrier, the effective input resistance will change, since the a-c and d-c load resistances are not equal. If $R_2 \gg R_1$ in Fig. 13-7, as it often is, then these resistances will be almost equal and Eq. (13-39) can be used to compute the input resistance. In general, the effective input resistance can be found by equating the input and output powers.

Another form of detection makes use of an ordinary amplifier that is biased class B. Its output consists of only the upper (or lower) half of the waveform of Fig. 13-1. The "average" value of this waveform can be considered to vary with the modulation. It will be of the same waveform as that of the envelope. If such a waveform is amplified by a circuit that rejects frequencies close to or greater than the carrier frequency, as well as ω_c, the output will have the same waveshape as the envelope. Thus, demodulation results. The primary disadvantage of this type of detection is that it tends to introduce distortion, because of the curvature of the characteristics of electronic devices near cutoff. However, the input resistance of this detector can be very high.

Nonlinear detection

A square-law circuit can be used for demodulation as well as for modulation. Consider that a square-law detector has the transfer characteristics given by Eq. (13-30) and that the input signal is the amplitude-modulated wave of Eq. (13-17). Assume that the output of the detector is passed through an amplifier that rejects all frequencies except those close to the modulating frequency. The output of this amplifier will then be

$$x_o(t) = a_2 A_c^2 m \left(\cos \omega_m t + \frac{m}{4} \cos 2\omega_m t \right) \tag{13-40}$$

Thus, detection has been achieved but $25m$ percent harmonic distortion has been introduced. If higher terms are included in the Taylor's series of Eq. (13-30), then still more distortion will result. If more than one modulating frequency is present, then other distortion terms will result. For these reasons, square-law detectors are used in applications where the amount of distortion is unimportant or where the value of m is kept small. One of the advantages of square-law detection is that it uses an amplifier circuit and, hence, produces gain. The input impedance of the detector can be quite high, also.

13-5   Frequency and phase modulation

In Sec. 13-1 we saw that intelligence can be transmitted by varying the instantaneous frequency of the signal. This is defined as frequency modulation and it is characterized by Eq. (13-10). Let us assume that the modulating signal is a cosinusoid given by

$$x_m(t) = X_{m,\max} \cos \omega_m t \tag{13-41}$$

Substitution in Eq. (13-10) yields

$$x(t) = A \cos\left(\omega_c t + \frac{k_2 X_{m,\max}}{\omega_m} \sin \omega_m t\right) \tag{13-42}$$

where we have assumed that the constant of integration is zero. The rate of variation of the instantaneous frequency is ω_m, and the amount of frequency deviation is proportional to $X_{m,\max}/\omega_m$. Thus, the instantaneous frequency variation can be kept within any limit desired simply by limiting $X_{m,\max}$. It was thought at one time that wideband signals could be transmitted over an extremely narrow bandwidth using frequency modulation. However, we shall see that this is *not* the case. Before proceeding with our discussion of frequency modulation, let us consider the phase-modulated signal of Eq. (13-12). Now let us assume that the modulating signal is a sinusoid given by

$$x_m(t) = X_{m,\max} \sin \omega_m t \tag{13-43}$$

Substituting in Eq. (13-12) yields

$$x(t) = A \cos\left(\omega_c t + k_3 X_{m,\max} \sin \omega_m t\right) \tag{13-44}$$

Equations (13-42) and (13-44) can be put into the same form. Thus, we can simultaneously analyze frequency modulation by a cosinusoid and phase modulation by a sinusoid using the following equation:

$$x(t) = A \cos\left(\omega_c t + m_F \sin \omega_m t\right) \tag{13-45}$$

where m_F is either the *frequency- or the phase-modulation index* and is given by

$$m_F = m_f = \frac{k_2 X_{m,\max}}{\omega_m} \tag{13-46}$$

for the frequency-modulation system and

$$m_F = m_f = k_3 X_{m,\text{max}} \tag{13-47}$$

for the phase-modulated system. Then, for both systems Eq. (13-45) is valid. Using the identity for the sum of the cosines of two angles, we obtain

$$x(t) = A[\cos \omega_c t \cos (m_F \sin \omega_m t) - \sin \omega_c t \sin (m_F \sin \omega_m t)] \tag{13-48}$$

Two other trigonometric identities that are needed are:

$$\cos (m_F \sin \omega_m t) = J_0(m_F) + 2J_2(m_F) \cos 2\omega_m t$$
$$+ 2J_4(m_F) \cos 4\omega_m t + \cdots \tag{13-49}$$

and

$$\sin (m_F \sin \omega_m t) = 2J_1(m_F) \sin \omega_m t + 2J_3(m_F) \sin 3\omega_m t + \cdots \tag{13-50}$$

where $J_0(m_F)$, $J_1(m_F)$, . . . , $J_k(m_F)$, . . . are Bessel's functions of the first kind of order k. The first six of these functions are given in Fig. 13-9. Substituting Eqs. (13-49) and (13-50) into Eq. (13-48) and manipulating, we obtain

$$x(t) = A\{J_0(m_F) \cos \omega_c t + J_1(m_F)[\cos (\omega_c + \omega_m)t - \cos (\omega_c - \omega_m)t]$$
$$+ J_2(m_F)[\cos (\omega_c + 2\omega_m)t + \cos (\omega_c - 2\omega_m)t] + \cdots\} \tag{13-51}$$

Thus, a carrier and an *infinite* set of sidebands result. The carrier amplitude is a function of the modulating signal. The frequency of the sidebands depends only upon the frequency of the modulating signal. If a transmission system is to be useful, it must have a limited bandwidth. Fortunately, in the case of frequency and phase modulation, the sidebands far removed from the carrier are usually small and can be neglected. Note that the higher order Bessel's functions remain close to zero for small values of m_F. An empirical rule[2] for determining the number of sideband pairs that are of importance is to use $m_F + 1$ pairs of sidebands if $m_F > 1$. This can be seen from an inspection of Fig. 13-9. The bandwidth required by a frequency- or phase-modulated system is equal to or greater than that required by an amplitude-modulated system where the modulating signals are the same.

One of the primary advantages of frequency or phase modulation over amplitude modulation is that the effects of interfering noise can easily be reduced in these systems. To study these effects, let us consider an unmodulated carrier and a sinusoidal noise signal at a frequency near the carrier frequency. The total signal is given by

$$x(t) = X_{c,\text{max}} \cos \omega_c t + X_{a,\text{max}} \cos (\omega_c + \omega_a)t \tag{13-52}$$

where X_a represents the noise. The instantaneous amplitude and phase of $x(t)$ can be determined from a phasor diagram such as that of Fig. 13-10. The phasor $\overline{OA}$ represents the carrier $X_{c,\text{max}} \cos \omega_c t$. Thus, the phasor $\overline{AB}$, representing the noise, must "rotate" at an angular frequency ω_a. The resultant phasor is $\overline{OB}$. The amplitude of $\overline{OB}$ will vary from $X_{c,\text{max}} + X_{a,\text{max}}$

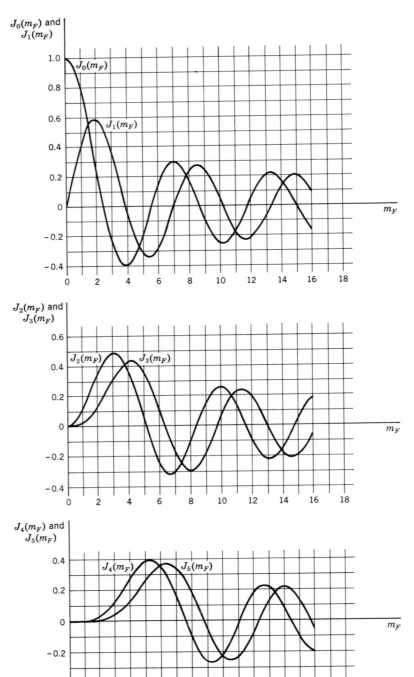

Fig. 13-9   Plots of Bessel's functions of the first kind.   (By permission from F. E. Terman, "Radio Engineers' Handbook," copyright 1943, McGraw-Hill Book Company, New York.)

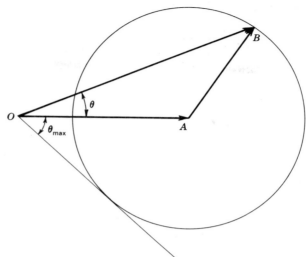

Fig. 13-10   A phasor diagram that can be used to calculate the effect of an interfering signal.

to $X_{c,\max} - X_{a,\max}$.   Hence, the index of amplitude modulation is given by $X_{a,\max}/X_{c,\max}$.   If we assume that the transmitter's output power is constant, then the ratio $X_{a,\max}/X_{c,\max}$ will be fixed.   The relative interference depends upon the ratio of the index of modulation of the noise to the index of modulation of a "signal."   In amplitude modulation, the index of modulation cannot be increased at will.   It must be adjusted so that the largest modulating signal will not result in more than 100 percent modulation.   Now let us consider the amount of frequency modulation produced by the noise.   The instantaneous value of the angle θ is given by

$$\theta = \tan^{-1} \frac{X_{a,\max} \sin \omega_a t}{X_{c,\max} + X_{a,\max} \cos \omega_a t} \tag{13-53}$$

The frequency-modulated signal will have the instantaneous frequency $\omega_c t + d\theta/dt$.   If this is compared with Eq. (13-45), we see that the amount of interference depends upon the relative magnitudes of $m_F \sin \omega_m t$ and $d\theta/dt$. In a frequency-modulated system, the value of m_F can be made as large as desired without introducing distortion or increasing the power of the transmitter.   Thus, if large values of m_F are used, the effects of interference can be made to be much less than those in a comparable amplitude-modulated system.   However, large values of m_F result in a relatively large number of important sidebands.   If small values of m_F are used (0.5 or less), the effective bandwidths of the frequency- or phase-modulation systems will be no greater than a corresponding amplitude-modulated system.   However, there will also be no improvement in noise performance.   In fact, the noise performance of the amplitude-modulated system may actually be better. On the other hand, if m_F is much greater than unity, the noise performance will be greatly improved, but the bandwidth required will be quite high.   In general, the relative noise reduction increases with bandwidth.

There are broadband noise-reducing systems that can be used with amplitude-modulated systems.   However, these are extremely complex.   Thus, frequency modulation is used for low-noise commercial broadcasting.

13-6   Frequency- and phase-modulating circuits

A very close relationship exists between frequency and phase modulation. The same circuits can be used to produce both if minor modifications are made.   Before considering actual modulating circuits, we shall demonstrate how a phase modulator can produce frequency modulation, and vice versa. If a circuit produces phase modulation, then Eqs. (13-10) and (13-12) demonstrate that it will also produce frequency modulation if the modulating signal is integrated before it is applied to the phase modulator.   Integrating circuits were discussed in Secs. 10-14 and 12-6.   A simple integrating circuit is shown in Fig. 12-21.   The output of these circuits is inversely proportional to frequency, which is in accordance with Eqs. (13-46) and (13-47).   In a similar way, phase modulation can be obtained from a frequency-modulation system if the modulating signal is differentiated.   Differentiating circuits are also discussed in Secs. 10-14 and 12-6.   Now let us consider some modulating circuits.

Variable-reactance circuits

The frequency of oscillation of all of the circuits of Fig. 11-3 are approximately equal to the resonant frequencies of their tank circuits.   Thus, if we could construct a capacitor or inductor whose reactance could be made to vary in accordance with a modulating signal, frequency modulation would be produced.   Consider the circuits of Fig. 13-11a and b.   Their equivalent circuit is given in Fig. 13-11c, where $k = g_m$, r_i is an open circuit, and $r_o = r_p$ for the vacuum tube circuit; and $k = h_{fe}/h_{ie}$, $r_i = h_{ie}$, and $r_o = h_{oe}^{-1}$ for the transistor circuit.   (We have assumed that $h_{re} = 0$.)   For the time being, high-frequency effects and parasitic capacitances will be ignored.   We have assumed that the bypass capacitors C_s, C_k, and C_E are short circuits and that the radio-frequency choke is an open circuit at the carrier frequency. Consider that the voltage generator $\mathbf{E}_m$ is replaced by a short circuit.   Then the output admittance is given by

$$\mathbf{Y}_0 = \frac{kR + 1}{R - j/\omega C} + \frac{1}{r_o} \tag{13-54}$$

when

$$R = \frac{R_1 r_i}{R_1 + r_i} \tag{13-55}$$

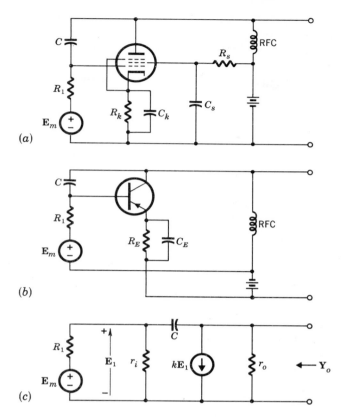

Fig. 13-11   (a) A reactance-tube modulator; (b) a reactance-transistor modulator (E_m is assumed to have zero resistance to direct current); (c) their equivalent circuit.

If

$$\frac{1}{\omega C} \gg R \qquad \text{and} \qquad kR \gg 1 \tag{13-56}$$

then

$$\mathbf{Y}_o = \frac{1}{r_o} + jkR\omega C \tag{13-57}$$

Thus, the output impedance is a resistance in shunt with a capacitance. If the g_m of the vacuum tube or the h_{fe} of the transistor could be varied, then the effective capacitance would also vary. Now consider that E_m is the modulating voltage. Its frequency ω_m is very much less than the carrier frequency. The magnitude of $1/\omega_m C$ will be very large and the reactance of the RFC will be small at ω_m. Thus, E_m will primarily affect only the input bias of the active element. This will change g_m and h_{fe} and, hence, the effective output capacitance. This circuit is called a *reactance modulator*. In

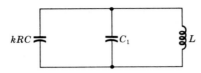

Fig. 13-12   An equivalent tank circuit where one of the capacitances is the output of a reactance modulator. Losses have been neglected.

use, it is connected in parallel with the capacitance of any of the tank circuits of Fig. 11-3. An equivalent tank circuit is shown in Fig. 13-12. Resistive elements have been neglected. The capacitor C_1 consists of any fixed capacitor plus the parasitic-output capacitance of the active element of Fig. 13-11. The resonant frequency is

$$\omega_0 = \frac{1}{\sqrt{L(C_1 + kRC)}}$$

If

$$kRC \gg C_1$$

then

$$\omega_0 \approx \frac{1}{\sqrt{kRCL}} \tag{13-58}$$

If the frequency modulation is to be without distortion, then $g_m^{-\frac{1}{2}}$ or $h_{fe}^{-\frac{1}{2}}$ should vary linearly with the modulating signal plus the direct bias. If kRC is not much greater than C_1, then g_m or h_{fe} should vary so that $1/\sqrt{1 + kRC/C_1}$ is a linear function of the modulation. Neither of these variations usually occurs. However, if the modulating signal is kept small, very little distortion usually results.

In the previous discussion, we have assumed that the $\mathbf{h}_{fe}$ of the transistor is a real number. If this is not the case, then the input admittance will not be a constant resistance in parallel with a capacitance. We have also assumed that the other parameters of the transistor do not vary with the modulating voltage.

A semiconductor diode can also be used in a variable-reactance modulator circuit. Consider the circuit of Fig. 13-13a. The direct voltage should be large enough so that the diode is always reverse-biased. The equivalent circuit is given in Fig. 13-13b. The capacitor C_j is the junction capacitance of the diode, and r_b is the back resistance of the diode. Let us assume that the capacitor C can be considered to be a short circuit at the carrier frequency. If the voltage e is constant, then the output admittance of this circuit, for frequencies at or near the carrier frequency, is

$$Y_o = \frac{1}{R} + j\omega C_j \tag{13-59}$$

where

$$R = \frac{R_1 r_b}{R_1 + r_b} \tag{13-60}$$

The junction capacitance varies with the potential across the depletion layer. This potential is approximately given by e. Then,

$$C_j \approx k_1 e^{-n} \tag{13-61}$$

where k_1 is a constant and n is a constant less than unity. If e varies in accordance with the modulating signal, then (since C is essentially an open circuit at ω_m) its primary effect is to vary C_j. Then

$$C_j = k_1(E_{ii} + e_m)^{-n} \tag{13-62}$$

Thus the resonant frequency is

$$\omega_0 = k_2 E_{ii}{}^{n/2}\left(1 + \frac{e_m}{E_{ii}}\right)^{n/2} \tag{13-63}$$

where k_2 is a constant. Expanding in a Taylor's series, we have, if

$$\frac{e_m}{E_{ii}} < 1$$

then

$$\omega_0 = k_2 E_{ii}{}^{n/2}\left[1 + \frac{ne_m}{2E_{ii}} + \frac{n}{4}\left(\frac{n}{2} - 1\right)\frac{e_m{}^2}{E_{ii}{}^2} + \cdots\right] \tag{13-64}$$

Thus, if the ratio e_m/E_{ii} is kept small, ω_0 will vary almost linearly with e_m and the distortion will be minimized.

In most reactance-modulator circuits, the frequency deviation must be kept small to avoid distortion. To increase the frequency deviation, the output of the frequency-modulated oscillator is applied to one or more stages of frequency multipliers (see Sec. 8-1). This will increase both the carrier frequency and the frequency deviation.

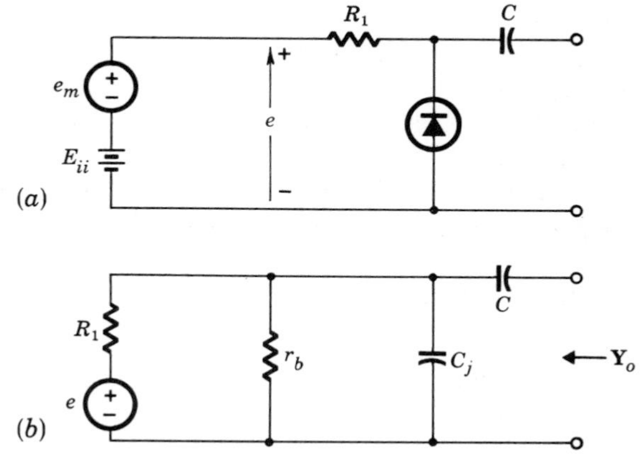

Fig. 13-13 (a) A react-ance diode modulator; (b) its equivalent circuit.

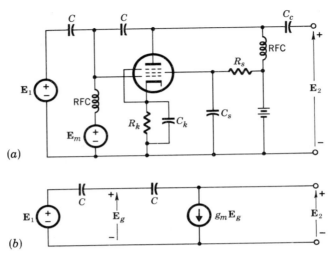

(a)

(b)

Fig. 13-14   (a) *A phase modulator;* (b) *its equivalent circuit.*

Phase-shifting circuits

We shall now discuss a circuit[3] that can be used to produce phase modulation. Consider the amplifier of Fig. 13-14. The voltage E_1 is assumed to be a sinusoidal generator whose frequency is ω_c. The voltage E_m is the modulating signal. We shall assume here, as we did for the reactance-modulator circuit, that E_m only affects the transconductance of the vacuum tube. An equivalent circuit for this amplifier is shown in Fig. 13-14b. It has been assumed that C_c, C_k, and C_s are short circuits and that the two radio-frequency chokes are open circuits at ω_c. The plate resistance has also been assumed to be an open circuit. The voltage gain E_2/E_1 of this circuit is

$$A_v = \frac{\omega C + jg_m}{\omega C - jg_m} = 1 \underline{/2 \tan^{-1} g_m/\omega C} \tag{13-65}$$

The magnitude of the voltage gain is independent of g_m and is equal to unity. The phase shift is a function of g_m and, hence, of the modulating voltage. Thus, phase modulation is produced. The phase angle does not vary linearly with g_m. In addition, the relation between the modulating signal and g_m is not linear. Sometimes these two nonlinearities can offset one another. In general, if the phase deviation is kept small, the distortion will be quite low. To obtain additional phase shift, several of these amplifiers are often cascaded with the same modulating signal applied to each amplifier. Usually, isolating amplifiers are placed between them. Frequency multipliers can also be used here.

The variable-reactance modulators are used to change the frequency of an oscillator. Consequently, a crystal oscillator cannot be used (see Sec.

11-6). In many commercial applications, crystal oscillators are required because of their frequency stability. The phase-shift circuit of Fig. 13-14 can be used in conjunction with a crystal oscillator, since the frequency of E_1 always remains constant.

13-7   Detection of frequency- and phase-modulated signals

The similarity of frequency and phase modulation allows similar circuits to be used in their detection. The converse of the methods discussed at the beginning of Sec. 13-6 can be used to convert one type of detector to the other. We shall consider some basic methods for detection here.

Slope detection

An ordinary amplitude-modulation detector of the type shown in Fig. 13-7 can be used to detect frequency modulation if the tuned circuit is properly adjusted. For instance, assume that the resonance curve of the tuned circuit is given by Fig. 13-15. If the circuit is tuned so that ω_1, and not ω_0, is the unmodulated carrier frequency, then e_i, the input voltage to the diode detector of Fig. 13-7, will vary as the frequency is changed and this circuit will demodulate a frequency-modulated signal. The circuit is called a *slope detector*. The slope of the resonance curve is not constant. As a consequence, this type of detector produces a great deal of distortion. It is not often used, except in systems where the frequency deviation is kept quite small. We shall now discuss detector circuits that can be used for large frequency deviations.

The discriminator circuit

Frequency-modulation detectors all produce a radio-frequency voltage whose amplitude varies with frequency. Amplitude-modulation detectors can then be used to obtain the demodulated output. Before we consider actual

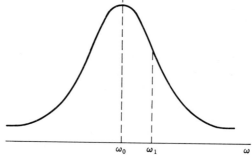

Fig. 13-15 A resonance curve which is used to illustrate slope detection.

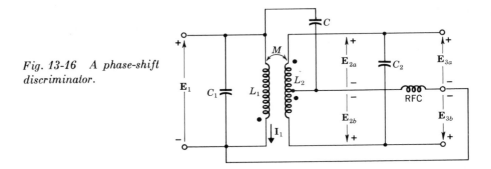

*Fig. 13-16   A phase-shift
discriminator.*

detector circuits, let us discuss the tuned circuit of Fig. 13-16.   The primary
and secondary circuits are each tuned to resonance at the carrier frequency ω_c.
We shall assume that the Q of the tuned circuits is such that the peak of the
resonance curve is essentially flat over the frequency deviation of the input
signal.   The capacitor C is considered to be a low impedance and the radio-
frequency choke a very high impedance at all input frequencies.   If the
impedance coupled into L_1 is much less than $\omega_c L_1$, we have

$$\mathbf{I}_1 = \frac{\mathbf{E}_1}{j\omega L_1} \tag{13-66}$$

At resonance, the secondary impedance is purely resistive and is equal to R.
Hence (consider that C_2 is composed of two equal capacitors in series),

$$\mathbf{E}_{2a} = \frac{jM E_1}{2\omega C_2 L_1 R} = \frac{j\omega L_2 M \mathbf{E}_1}{2L_1 R} \tag{13-67}$$

$$\mathbf{E}_{2b} = \frac{-jM E_1}{2\omega C_2 L_1 R} = -\frac{j\omega L_2 M \mathbf{E}_1}{2L_1 R} \tag{13-68}$$

Thus, at resonance, the phase angle of $\mathbf{E}_1$ differs from that of $\mathbf{E}_{2a}$ and $\mathbf{E}_{2b}$
by 90°.   Now consider the voltages $\mathbf{E}_{3a}$ and $\mathbf{E}_{3b}$.   These are given by

$$\mathbf{E}_{3a} = \mathbf{E}_1 + \mathbf{E}_{2a} \tag{13-69}$$

$$\mathbf{E}_{3b} = \mathbf{E}_1 + \mathbf{E}_{2b} \tag{13-70}$$

A phasor diagram illustrating these voltages is shown in Fig. 13-17a.   Now
let us assume that the input frequency shifts above ω_c.   The relative amplitude of the voltages will not change, because it is assumed that the resonance
curve is flat.   However, the phase angle is very sensitive to frequency shifts,
so the phasor diagram becomes that of Fig. 13-17b.   The magnitude of $\mathbf{E}_{3a}$
has been reduced while that of $\mathbf{E}_{3b}$ has increased.   Similarly, for frequencies
below ω_c we have the phasor diagram of Fig. 13-17c.   Now, the magnitude
of $\mathbf{E}_{3a}$ has increased while that of $\mathbf{E}_{3b}$ has decreased.   We have thus achieved

a circuit wherein the magnitude of the voltages varies with frequency. If we add two amplitude-modulation detectors to the circuit of Fig. 13-16, a frequency-modulation detector results. This is shown in Fig. 13-18. The output voltage of each of the detectors will be approximately equal to their peak input voltages, $|E_{3a,\max}|$ and $|E_{3b,\max}|$. The diodes are connected so that the output voltage e_o is the difference between the two output voltages: Thus,

$$e_o = |E_{3a,\max}| - |E_{3b,\max}| \tag{13-71}$$

This voltage will vary fairly linearly with frequency until the voltage falls off because of the resonance curve. A typical plot of e_o versus frequency is given in Fig. 13-19. This circuit is called a *Foster-Seeley discriminator*. (It has been assumed here that the resistors R are large enough so that the resonant circuit is not affected by the detector.)

If the amplitude of the input signal of a discriminator varies, then the amplitude of e_o will also vary. In Sec. 13-5 we discussed that one of the primary advantages of frequency modulation was its relative freedom from interference. However, if the detector responds to amplitude modulation,

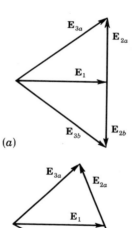

(a)

Fig. 13-17 Phasor diagrams for the phase-shift discriminator of Fig. 13-16. (a) $\omega = \omega_0$; (b) $\omega > \omega_0$; and (c) $\omega < \omega_0$.

(b)

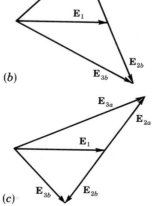

(c)

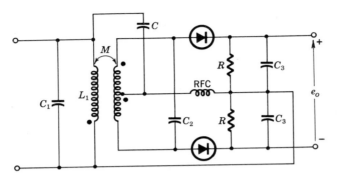

Fig. 13-18   A Foster-Seeley discriminator for the detection of frequency-modulated signals.

the advantages gained by using frequency modulation will be lost, since the interference will amplitude-modulate the signal.   To remove the amplitude modulation from the signal, a circuit called a *limiter* is used.   This performs the same function as the clipper circuits of Sec. 12-7.   In frequency-modulation receivers, the limiters are usually just amplifiers that are driven between their saturation and cutoff regions.   As a consequence, the peak value of the voltage will not vary, and the signal essentially will not be amplitude-modulated.   Of course, the limiter precedes the detector stage.

The ratio detector

If the Foster-Seeley discriminator circuit is modified somewhat, a circuit can be obtained that is relatively insensitive to variations in amplitude. Such a circuit is shown in Fig. 13-20.   Note that the connections of one of the diodes have been reversed.   For the time being, neglect the capacitor C_4.

Fig. 13-19   The output characteristic of a Foster-Seeley discriminator.

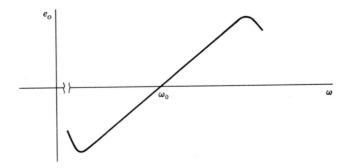

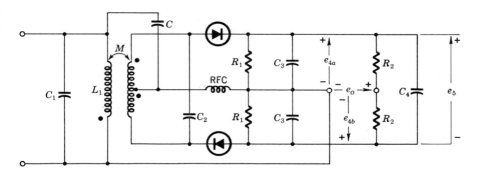

Fig. 13-20   A ratio detector.

Thus, Eq. (13-71) becomes

$$e_5 = e_{4a} - e_{4b} = |E_{3a,\max}| + |E_{3b,\max}| \tag{13-72}$$

where $\mathbf{E}_{3a}$ and $\mathbf{E}_{3b}$ are defined in Fig. 13-16.

The output is taken as shown.   Since the two resistors R_2 are equal, we have

$$e_o = e_{4a} - \frac{e_5}{2} \tag{13-73}$$

$$e_o = |E_{3a,\max}| - \frac{|E_{3a,\max}| + |E_{3b,\max}|}{2}$$

$$e_o = \frac{|E_{3a,\max}| - |E_{3b,\max}|}{2} \tag{13-74}$$

(It is assumed that the resistors are large enough so that they do not affect the resonant circuit.)   The voltage e_5 varies only slightly with changes in the instantaneous frequency, because increases in $|E_{3a,\max}|$ are accompanied by decreases in $|E_{3b,\max}|$, and vice versa (see Fig. 13-17).   Now let us consider the effect of C_4.   It is made quite large, so that the time constant R_2C_4 is much larger than the longest period encountered in the modulating signal (for example, 0.25 sec for an audio system).   Thus, e_5 will tend to remain constant as the frequency shifts because of modulation.   Hence, the sum of $|E_{3a,\max}|$ and $|E_{3b,\max}|$ is fixed.   However, as the instantaneous frequency changes, their *ratio* will vary essentially in accordance with Fig. 13-17.   The value of e_o given by Eq. (13-74) will be almost one-half of that produced by the Foster-Seeley discriminator.   (Note that $|E_{3a,\max}|$ and $|E_{3b,\max}|$ are changed somewhat because of the constraint that e_5 is constant.)   Now let us consider that noise amplitude-modulates the signal (at an audio rate). The sum of $|E_{3a,\max}|$ and $|E_{3b,\max}|$ is constant, and their ratio is fixed by the frequency deviation.   Hence, e_o will not vary with amplitude modulation. In actual circuits, there is some variation of e_5 with amplitude modulation, since the components are not ideal and since the time constant R_2C_4 is not infinitely long.   This circuit does tend to reject amplitude modulation quite well.   The discriminator tends to produce less distortion, however.

REFERENCES

[1] T. S. Gray, "Applied Electronics," 2d ed., pp. 710–714, John Wiley & Sons, Inc., New York, 1954.
[2] F. E. Terman, "Radio Engineers' Handbook," p. 579, McGraw-Hill Book Company, New York, 1943.
[3] S. M. Beleskas, Phase Modulation Circuit, *Proc. Nat. Electron. Conf.*, vol. 3, pp. 654–661, 1947.

BIBLIOGRAPHY

Gray, T. S.: "Applied Electronics," 2d ed., chap. 12, John Wiley & Sons, Inc., New York, 1954.
Ryder, J. D.: "Electronic Fundamentals and Applications," 2d ed.. chaps. 15 and 16, Prentice-Hall, Inc., Englewood Cliffs, New Jersey, 1959.
Terman, F. E.: "Electronic and Radio Engineering," 4th ed., chaps. 15–17, McGraw-Hill Book Company, New York, 1955.

PROBLEMS

13-1. A sinusoidal carrier of frequency ω_c is amplitude-modulated by a sinusoidal signal of frequency ω_m.   The index of modulation is 0.5.   Plot the resulting waveform and the frequency spectrum.   Determine the amount of power contained in the sidebands relative to the carrier power.

13-2. Repeat Prob. 13-1, but now assume that the index of modulation is 2.   How many pairs of sidebands are produced?   *Hint:* Find the Fourier series of the envelope.

13-3. Repeat Prob. 13-1, but now assume that the modulating signal is a square wave.

13-4. Repeat Prob. 13-2, but now assume that the modulating signal is a square wave.

13-5. For the amplifier of Prob. 8-1, determine and plot the magnitude of the output radio-frequency voltage if E_{bb} is varied from 5,000 to 15,000 volts. Assume that the peak plate current remains constant.   Discuss how this plot could be used in the design of an amplitude modulator.

13-6. Repeat Prob. 13-5, but do not assume that the peak plate current remains constant.   Use $R_{ac} = 1,960$ ohms.   Note: A cut-and-try procedure will be required.

13-7. For the amplifier of Prob. 8-1, determine and plot the magnitude of the output voltage if E_{cc} varies from $-1,000$ volts to $-1,700$ volts.   (A cut-and-try procedure will be required.)   Discuss how this plot could be used in the design of an amplitude modulator.

13-8. A square-law modulator has the characteristic

$$x_0(t) = 1.0x_i + 1.0x_i{}^2$$

If $x_i = 1 \sin \omega_c t + 1 \sin \omega_{m1} t + 0.5 \sin \omega_{m2} t$, what will the output signal be? If $x_0(t)$ is amplified by a circuit that rejects all signals except those close to ω_c, what will the output of this circuit be? Discuss any distortion that is produced.

13-9. Repeat Prob. 13-8, but now assume that the modulator has the characteristic

$$x_0(t) = 1.0x_i + 1.0x_i{}^2 + 0.5x_i{}^3 + 0.5x_i{}^4$$

13-10. A cosinusoidal carrier of frequency f_c is 50 percent modulated by a cosinusoid of frequency f_m. This is then detected by the circuit of Fig. 13-5. The time constant $RC = 1/\sqrt{f_m f_c}$. If $f_m = 10,000$ cps and $f_c = 20,000$ cps, sketch the output waveform. Assume that the diode is ideal.

13-11. Repeat Prob. 13-10, but now assume that $f_c = 10^6$ cps.

13-12. The diode of Fig. 13-7 has the detection characteristic of Fig. 13-8. The resistance of R_1 is 16,667 ohms and the peak voltage of the unmodulated carrier is 3 volts. What is the minimum value of R_2 that can be used if a 50 percent modulated signal is to be detected without clipping?

13-13. Repeat Prob. 13-12, but now assume that the peak unmodulated carrier voltage is 5 volts.

13-14. An amplitude-modulated wave consists of a carrier of frequency ω_c and two pairs of sidebands at frequencies $\omega_c + \omega_{m1}$, $\omega_c - \omega_{m1}$, $\omega_c + \omega_{m2}$ and $\omega_c - \omega_{m2}$. Assume that the carrier and all sidebands are cosinusoids and that the peak amplitude of the carrier is 1.0 while that of the sidebands is 0.5. This signal is applied to a square-law detector with the characteristic

$$x_0 = 1.0x_i + 1.0x_i{}^2$$

If x_0 is amplified by a circuit that rejects frequencies close to or greater than ω_c, what will the output be? Discuss any distortion produced.

13-15. Repeat Prob. 13-14, but now assume that the detector has the characteristic

$$x_0 = 1.0x_i + 1.0x_i{}^2 + 0.5x_i{}^3 + 0.5x_i{}^4$$

13-16. Discuss the instantaneous frequency variation of a sinusoid that is frequency-modulated by a square wave.

13-17. Repeat Prob. 13-16 for a sinusoid that is phase-modulated by a square wave. What practical limitation occurs here?

13-18. A frequency-, or phase-, modulated wave has the form given by Eq. (13-45). The value of m_F is 0.5. Plot a frequency spectrum showing the relative values of the carrier and the first five pairs of sidebands.

13-19. Repeat Prob. 13-18 for values of $m_F = 1$, 5, 9, and 10.

13-20. Repeat Prob. 13-18, but assume that the term $\cos \omega_m t$ of Eq. (13-41) is replaced by a square wave which is an even function of time and varies at a frequency ω_m. Assume that the square wave can be expressed by two terms of its Fourier series. The value of m_F obtained from the fundamental component is 1.0.

13-21. Repeat Prob. 13-20 for a value of $m_F = 3$.

13-22. The output capacitance of a reactance modulator is $k_1 C$. The quantity k_1 is a function of the modulating voltage and is given by

$$k_1 = 1 + e_m$$

This reactance tube is to be used to control the frequency of an oscillator, which is given by

$$\omega_0 = \frac{1}{\sqrt{k_1 C L}}$$

Expand the value of ω_0 in a power series. Assume that $e_m = E_{m,\max} \cos \omega_m t$. What is the maximum value of $E_{m,\max}$ that can be used if the second-harmonic component of the variation of ω_0 is to be less than 10 percent? To simplify the analysis assume that terms whose powers are greater than the second can be ignored.

13-23. The diode-reactance modulator of Fig. 13-13 is used to frequency-modulate an oscillator whose instantaneous frequency is given by Eq. (13-64). The value of $n = \frac{1}{2}$. Assume that $e_m = E_{m,\max} \cos \omega_m t$ and that all the terms not shown in Eq. (13-64) can be ignored. Compute the maximum value that $E_{m,\max}/E_{ii}$ can have if the second-harmonic distortion of the frequency deviation is to be less than 2 percent.

13-24. Compute the voltage gain of the phase modulator of Fig. 13-14a if the plate resistance is not considered to be infinite. What relation must there be among the vacuum-tube parameters and the circuit elements if the circuit is to be a good phase modulator?

13-25. Obtain a power-series expansion for the phase shift as a function of $g_m/\omega C$ for the phase modulator of Fig. 13-14a. Assume that Eq. (13-65) is valid.

13-26. Compute an analytical expression for $\mathbf{E}_{3a}$ and $\mathbf{E}_{3b}$ for the discriminator of Fig. 13-16. Assume that the inductances have series resistance associated with them.

13-27. Use the results of Prob. 13-26 to obtain an expression for the output voltage of the Foster-Seeley discriminator circuit of Fig. 13-18. Assume that the detector portion of the circuit is ideal and does not affect the resonant circuit.

13-28. Use the results of Prob. 13-26 to obtain an expression for the output voltage of the ratio detector of Fig. 13-20. Assume that the detector portion of the circuit is ideal and does not affect the resonant circuit.

Power
Supplies

14

The electronic devices discussed so far require direct voltage sources to establish bias voltages and currents. The voltages can be obtained from batteries, but this is often inconvenient. It would be desirable to obtain the direct-bias voltages from the commercial electric power lines. They usually supply an alternating voltage. Thus, circuits must be designed to convert the alternating voltage to a direct voltage of the proper value. Such circuits are called *power supplies*. The process of converting the alternating voltage and currents to pulsating direct current is called *rectification*. In addition, the pulsating direct current must be *filtered* so that the output voltage is essentially constant. We shall consider the rectifier circuit first and then analyze filter circuits.

14-1 Idealized diode characteristics

Rectification very often makes use of either a vacuum-tube or a semiconductor diode. A piecewise-linear equivalent circuit, for these elements, that we shall use is given in Fig. 14-1. The resistor r_b is the back resistance of the

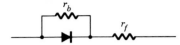

Fig. 14-1   The piecewise-linear equivalent circuit of a vacuum-tube or a semiconductor diode.

diode, while r_f is its forward resistance.   In almost all power-supply applications, the back resistance can be considered to be an open circuit.   The forward resistance of actual diodes is nonlinear.   However, for most power-supply applications, sufficient accuracy is obtained using the circuit of Fig. 14-1.   One exception is the gas diode, which has a practically constant voltage drop when it is conducting in the forward direction.   Its piecewise-linear equivalent circuit has a battery in place of r_f.

The symbol for an ideal diode and the solid-state diode is the same. To differentiate between the two, we shall omit the circle from the ideal diode.   Many circuits involving vacuum-tube or semiconductor diodes are identical, except for the heater connection of the vacuum tube.   For brevity, in these cases, we shall omit the vacuum-tube circuit.

14-2   The half-wave rectifier

A very simple rectifier circuit is shown in Fig. 14-2*a*.   The diode permits the current to be in only one direction.   Thus,

$$i = \begin{cases} \dfrac{E_{max}}{r_f + R_L} \sin \omega t = I_{max} \sin \omega t & 0 \leqslant \omega t \leqslant \pi \\ 0 & \pi \leqslant \omega t \leqslant 2\pi \end{cases} \tag{14-1}$$

This waveform is shown in Fig. 14-2*b*.   The direct current is the average value of this waveform.   Hence,

$$I_{L,dc} = \frac{I_{max}}{\pi} \tag{14-2}$$

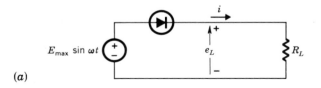

(a)

$E_{max} \sin \omega t$ e_L R_L

(b)

Fig. 14-2   (a)   A half-wave-rectifier circuit;   (b) its load current.

and the average value of the load voltage e_L is

$$E_{L,dc} = \frac{E_{max}R_L}{\pi(r_f + R_L)} = \frac{I_{max}R_L}{\pi} = \frac{E_{L,max}}{\pi} \tag{14-3}$$

Although this circuit produces a direct voltage across the load resistance, it would be unacceptable as a bias supply for many electronic devices, because the voltage e_L has alternating, as well as direct, components. These alternating components would act as spurious signals and mask the desired ones. For instance, in an audio amplifier, such a power supply would produce a loud *hum*. Filter circuits which eliminate this hum will be discussed in Secs. 14-4 to 14-9. A criterion that is often used to specify the amount of alternating voltage present in the output of a power supply is the *ripple factor* γ. This is defined as

$$\gamma = \frac{\text{rms value of alternating components of } e_L}{E_{L,dc}} = \frac{E_{L,ac}}{E_{L,dc}} \tag{14-4}$$

Many times, $E_{L,eff}$, the effective (rms) value of e_L, can be easily obtained ($E_{L,eff}$ has both alternating and direct components), so that it is convenient to obtain γ in terms of it. Consider the following. If

$$e_1 = e_2 + e_3 \tag{14-5}$$

where e_2 and e_3 are of *different* frequencies, then

$$E_{1,eff}^2 = E_{2,eff}^2 + E_{3,eff}^2 \tag{14-6}$$

Thus

$$E_{L,ac}^2 = E_{L,eff}^2 - E_{L,dc}^2 \tag{14-7}$$

and

$$\gamma = \sqrt{\left(\frac{E_{L,eff}}{E_{L,dc}}\right)^2 - 1} \tag{14-8}$$

If the load resistance has no reactive components, then load currents can replace the load voltages in these relations. Since the voltages and currents are half-sinusoids, their effective values are given by

$$E_{L,eff} = \frac{E_{L,max}}{2} \tag{14-9}$$

$$I_{L,eff} = \frac{I_{L,max}}{2} \tag{14-10}$$

Then, using Eqs. (14-3) and (14-8), we obtain

$$\gamma = \sqrt{\frac{\pi^2}{4} - 1} = 1.21 \tag{14-11}$$

This is quite large. For many electronic devices, γ must be much less than 0.001. This is why filtering is required.

The power dissipated within the diode is

$$P_{oD} = I_{L,\text{eff}}^2 r_f \tag{14-12}$$

It is often unnecessary to use (14-12) to obtain the dissipation, since manufacturers rate the diodes in terms of the direct load voltage and load current. We shall also see that the power-supply filter enters into the choice of the diode.

Another quantity of interest is the *efficiency of rectification*. This is defined as

$$\eta_r = \frac{\text{direct load power}}{\text{total input power}} \times 100 \tag{14-13}$$

For the half-wave rectifier, we have

$$\eta_r = \frac{I_{L,dc}^2 R_L}{I_{L,\text{eff}}^2 (r_f + R_L)} = \frac{4R_L}{\pi^2 (r_f + R_L)} \times 100 \tag{14-14}$$

Substituting, we obtain

$$\eta_r = \frac{40.5}{1 + r_f/R_L} \qquad \% \tag{14-15}$$

Thus, the maximum efficiency of rectification of the half-wave rectifier, without a filter, is 40.5 percent.

The maximum voltage that appears across the diode occurs when it is not conducting. This is called an inverse voltage. The maximum value of this voltage is the *peak inverse voltage*. For the circuit of Fig. 14-2, the peak inverse voltage is E_{max}. We shall subsequently see that the inclusion of a filter can markedly change this value.

The half-wave rectifier without a filter is not a very good power supply for most electronic devices. Before studying filters, we shall consider a circuit whose performance is considerably better than that of the half-wave rectifier.

14-3   The full-wave rectifier

Consider the circuit of Fig. 14-3a. It consists basically of two half-wave rectifiers with a common load resistance. Since e_1 and e_2 are 180° out of phase, each diode will conduct on alternate half-cycles. Thus, the load current of Fig. 14-3b results. This circuit is called a *full-wave rectifier*. Proceeding as in the last section, we obtain

$$i_L = \frac{E_{\text{max}}|\sin \omega t|}{r_f + R_L} = I_{L,\text{max}}|\sin \omega t| \tag{14-16}$$

$$e_L = \frac{E_{\text{max}} R_L |\sin \omega t|}{r_f + R_L} = E_{L,\text{max}}|\sin \omega t| \tag{14-17}$$

$$E_{L,dc} = \frac{2E_{L,\text{max}}}{\pi} \tag{14-18}$$

$$I_{L,dc} = \frac{2I_{L,\max}}{\pi} \tag{14-19}$$

$$E_{L,\text{eff}} = \frac{E_{L,\max}}{\sqrt{2}} \tag{14-20}$$

$$\gamma = \sqrt{\pi^2/8 - 1} = 0.48 \tag{14-21}$$

The power dissipated in each diode is

$$P_{oD} = \frac{I_{L,\text{eff}}^2 r_f}{2} \tag{14-22}$$

since the current in each diode is zero for one half-cycle. Note that for the same value of $I_{L,dc}$, the value of P_{oD}, for each diode, is one-quarter of that for the half-wave rectifier. The efficiency of rectification is given by

$$\eta_r = \frac{I_{L,dc}^2 R_L}{I_{L,\text{eff}}^2 (r_f + R_L)} \times 100 = \frac{8}{\pi^2} \cdot \frac{R_L}{r_f + R_L} \times 100 \tag{14-23}$$

Evaluating this, we have

$$\eta_r = \frac{81.1}{1 + r_f/R_L} \quad \% \tag{14-24}$$

When one diode is cut off, the other is essentially a short circuit. Thus, the peak inverse voltage is $2E_{\max}$.

The full-wave rectifier provides substantial improvement over the half-wave rectifier. It is more complex, in that two diodes and a transformer are

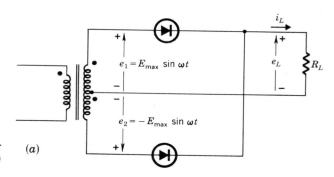

Fig. 14-3 (a) A full-wave-rectifier circuit; (b) its load current.

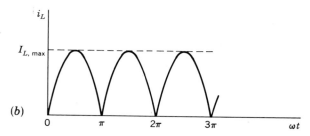

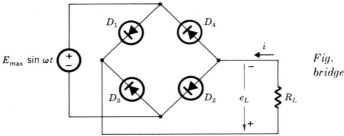

Fig. 14-4 A full-wave bridge rectifier.

required. In many applications, the transformer is required to vary the value of the input voltage so that the required value of $E_{L,dc}$ can be obtained. The transformer also provides isolation between the power line and the circuit. A transformer can be used with a half-wave rectifier, but the direct current through it would tend to saturate the core. Thus, a large, expensive transformer would be required (see Sec. 6-19). In the full-wave rectifier, the net direct flux through the core is zero, and the direct current does not saturate it. This is an important advantage of the full-wave rectifier.

In some applications, a transformer is not required to vary the power-line voltages. In such circumstances, it would be desirable to construct a transformerless full-wave rectifier. Such a circuit is shown in Fig. 14-4. When the voltage $E_{max} \sin \omega t$ is positive, diodes D_1 and D_2 will conduct. When this voltage is negative, diodes D_3 and D_4 will conduct. Thus, the current i_L will have the form shown in Fig. 14-3b, and we shall have achieved full-wave rectification. Because of the circuit configuration, this is called a *bridge rectifier*. It uses four diodes instead of the two used in Fig. 14-3a. However, especially when semiconductor diodes are used, their cost, size, and weight are much less than those of a transformer.

When vacuum-tube diodes are used, some means of heating the filaments must be provided. Often, a separate winding is placed on the power transformer, and this supplies the filament voltage. Such a circuit is shown in Fig. 14-5. The negative lead of the power supply and the transformer case

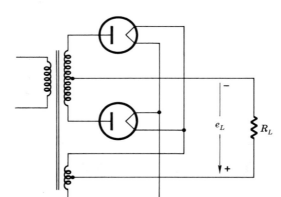

Fig. 14-5 A full-wave rectifier using vacuum tubes.

and core are often connected to the metallic chassis. Thus, the full output voltage appears between the filament winding of the transformer and the core of the transformer. High-voltage insulation must be provided for this winding, even though the voltage drop across it may only be several volts. Although it might appear as though this problem could be eliminated by using separately heated cathodes in the vacuum-tube diodes, this is usually not done. The electric insulation between the cathode and the heater always has a relatively low breakdown voltage (200 volts or less), since there must be good thermal conductivity between the heater and the cathode. Higher voltage tubes also use directly heated cathodes, since the low-work-function oxide-coated cathodes will not withstand positive-ion bombardment.

In vacuum-tube devices, a third winding is often placed on the transformer to supply heater power to the vacuum tubes. In vacuum-tube circuits that do not use transformers, the filaments of the vacuum tubes and a current-limiting resistance are usually connected in series with the supply lines.

The cathodes of the bridge rectifier of Fig. 14-4 are at three different potentials. If vacuum tubes were used in this circuit, three separate filament transformers would be required. For this reason, semiconductor rectifiers are almost always used in bridge rectifiers.

14-4 General discussion of power-supply filters

The ripple factor of a rectifier circuit is quite high. A power-supply filter reduces these alternating components. A typical power-supply filter circuit is shown in Fig. 14-6. e_i is the output voltage of the rectifier, and e_o is the output voltage of the filter. Note that the direct component of e_i is unaffected by the filter, while the alternating components of e_i are attenuated by it. The series elements of the filter should present a high impedance to the alternating components, while the shunt elements should present a low impedance to these components. The converse should be true for the direct components. If e_i is known, then it can be expanded in a Fourier series. Ordinary network analysis can then be used to obtain e_o. If e_i has a waveform such as that of the output of the half-wave rectifier of Fig. 14-2a, then its Fourier series is

$$e_i = E_{max}\left[\frac{1}{\pi} + \frac{1}{2}\sin \omega t - \frac{2}{\pi}\sum_{k=1}^{\infty}\frac{\cos 2k\omega t}{(2k+1)(2k-1)}\right] \tag{14-25}$$

Fig. 14-6 A typical power-supply filter.

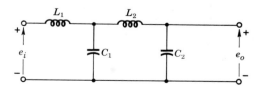

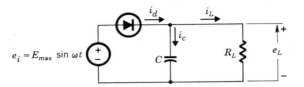

Fig. 14-7   A half-wave rec-tifier with a capacitor filter.

Similarly, the output of the full-wave rectifier of Fig. 14-3a is given by

$$e_i = E_{\max}\left[\frac{2}{\pi} - \frac{4}{\pi}\sum_{k=1}^{\infty}\frac{\cos 2k\omega t}{(2k+1)(2k-1)}\right] \tag{14-26}$$

The lowest frequency of Eq. (14-26) is twice the power-line frequency. It is important to realize that the output voltage of a half-wave or full-wave rectifier will depend upon the type of filter that is used and will *not* always be of the form of Figs. 14-2b or 14-3b, respectively. Thus, Eqs. (14-25) and (14-26) cannot always be used in the analysis of power-supply filters.

14-5   The capacitor filter

A simple power-supply filter consists of a capacitor placed in parallel with the load resistance. Such a circuit is shown in Fig. 14-7. We shall assume in our discussion that the forward resistance of the diode is zero. The load voltage e_L, after the first cycle, will have the form shown in Fig. 14-8a. Because of the diode, the capacitor C can only discharge through R_L. When $\omega t = \pi/2$, the voltage $e_L = E_{\max}$. As e_i decreases, e_L falls off with e_i for a time. However, the rate of falloff of $e^{-t/R_L C}$ will become less than that of $\sin \omega t$. Thus, e_L will tend to be higher than e_i. At this time, the diode will cut off (i.e., become an open circuit). This occurs at $\omega t = \theta_2$ in Fig. 14-8a. The voltage e_L then has the form

$$e_L = E_{\max}\sin\theta_2 e^{-t/R_L C} \qquad \theta_2 \leqslant \omega t \leqslant \theta_1 + 2\pi \tag{14-27}$$

During the next cycle, e_i will eventually become equal to e_L and the diode will conduct. Thus, the output voltage will have the form

$$e_L = E_{\max}\sin\omega t \qquad \theta_1 \leqslant \omega t \leqslant \theta_2 \tag{14-28}$$

This waveform is repeated periodically. Let us consider the currents in the circuit. The load current i_L will have the same waveform as the load voltage. During the time that the diode is not conducting

$$i_c = -i_L = -e_L/R_L \qquad \theta_2 \leqslant \omega t \leqslant \theta_1 + 2\pi \tag{14-29}$$

When the diode does conduct, the current through C is just what it would be if the capacitor were connected directly across e_i. (There are no transients, since the diode starts to conduct at the instant $e_i = e_L$.) Thus

$$i_c = E_{\max}\omega C \cos\omega t \qquad \theta_1 \leqslant \omega t \leqslant \theta_2 \tag{14-30}$$

The diode current is

$$i_d = i_c + i_L \tag{14-31}$$

These waveforms are shown in Fig. 14-8b. The peak current through the diode occurs at $\omega t = \theta_1$ (this assumes that $R_L \gg 1/\omega C$) and is

$$I_{d,\max} = E_{\max}\left(\omega C \cos \theta_1 + \frac{\sin \theta_1}{R_L}\right) \tag{14-32}$$

The diode must be capable of passing this peak current. If the value of C is increased, the decay of e_L in the period $\theta_2 \leqslant \omega t \leqslant \theta_1 + 2\pi$ will decrease. In the limit, as C approaches infinity, e_L will approach a pure direct voltage. Increases in C are accompanied by increases in $I_{d,\max}$.

In order to obtain the direct load voltage and the ripple factor, the value of θ_1 and of θ_2 must be known. A transcendental equation must be solved to obtain them. This is quite tedious. We shall now make some approximations that simplify the calculations. [Note that the Fourier series of Eq. (14-25) cannot be used here, since the output of the rectifier is *not* of the form of Fig. 14-2b.] We shall assume that the load voltage varies linearly[1]

Fig. 14-8   (a) *The load voltage of the circuit of Fig. 14-7; (b) the currents in this circuit.*

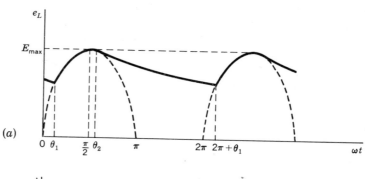

(a)

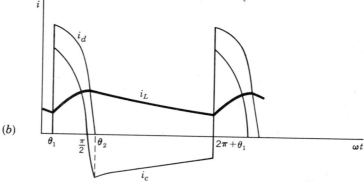

(b)

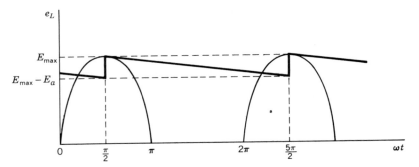

Fig. 14-9   The approximate load voltage that is to be used in the analysis of the capacitor filter.

with time as shown in Fig. 14-9.   This waveform appears to be quite different from that of Fig. 14-8a.   However, the results obtained using it are quite satisfactory.   The average value of Fig. 14-9 is

$$E_{L,dc} = E_{\max} - \frac{E_a}{2} \tag{14-33}$$

If ΔQ represents the change in charge stored in C between $\pi/2$ and $5\pi/2$, then

$$E_a = \frac{\Delta Q}{C} \tag{14-34}$$

Since the voltage is assumed to vary linearly with time, the charge stored in C must decrease at a constant rate.   Thus, current i_C is constant over this period.   (Note that this leads to a paradox since $i_L = i_C$ during the discharge period of the capacitor.   If i_L is constant, then e_L must be constant and not vary as shown.   This paradox results because we have not assumed that the capacitor voltage varies exponentially with time.   However, the results obtained with this analysis are quite satisfactory.)   The constant value of i_C is $I_{L,dc}$, the direct load current.   Since the time of one period is the reciprocal of the frequency, we have

$$E_a = \frac{I_{L,dc}}{fC} \tag{14-35}$$

Thus

$$E_{L,dc} = E_{\max} - \frac{I_{L,dc}}{2fC} \tag{14-36}$$

Even though we have assumed that all the components of this circuit are ideal, its voltage regulation is not.   That is, the output voltage will fall off as the output current increases.   The direct load current and voltage are related by

$$I_{L,dc} = \frac{E_{L,dc}}{R_L} \tag{14-37}$$

Substituting in Eq. (14-36), we obtain

$$E_{L,dc} = \frac{E_{max}}{1 + 1/(2fR_LC)} \tag{14-38}$$

To calculate the ripple factor, we must determine $E_{L,ac}$, the rms value of the alternating component of e_L. This is a triangular waveform that varies from $-E_a/2$ to $E_a/2$. Thus

$$E_{L,ac} = \frac{E_a}{2\sqrt{3}} \tag{14-39}$$

Substituting Eqs. (14-37), (14-39), and (14-35) into Eq. (14-4), we have

$$\gamma = \frac{1}{2\sqrt{3}\,fR_LC} \tag{14-40}$$

To calculate the peak diode current, we must determine the value of θ_1 [see Eq. (14-32)]. The angle θ_1 can be approximately obtained[1] by assuming that the diode starts to conduct when $e_i = E_{max} - E_a$. Thus,

$$E_{max} \sin\theta_1 = E_{max} - E_a \tag{14-41}$$

Substituting for E_a using Eqs. (14-35), (14-37), and (14-38) and solving, we obtain

$$\theta_1 = \sin^{-1}\frac{2fR_LC - 1}{2fR_LC + 1} \tag{14-42}$$

The peak diode current is found from Eq. (14-32). If the value of fR_LC is increased, the value of $E_{L,dc}$ will more closely approach E_{max} for all values of time, the ripple factor will be reduced, and the peak diode current will be increased.

The ripple factor is usually quite small, so that $e_L \approx E_{max}$. Thus, the peak inverse voltage for this circuit is $2E_{max}$.

When a single capacitor filter is used with a full-wave rectifier, the results are quite similar to those of the half-wave rectifier. The approximate output voltage for the full-wave rectifier is shown in Fig. 14-10. The approxi-

Fig. 14-10   The approximate load voltage that is to be used in the analysis of a full-wave rectifier with a capacitor filter.

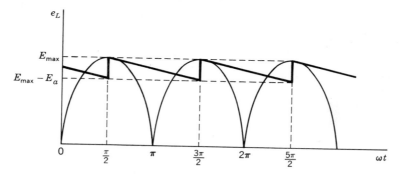

mate waveform is the same as that of Fig. 14-9, but its period is halved. Thus, the half-wave rectifier relations can be applied to the full-wave rectifier if we replace f by $2f$.   Then

$$E_{L,dc} = E_{max} - \frac{I_{L,dc}}{4fC} \tag{14-43}$$

$$E_{L,dc} = \frac{E_{max}}{1 + 1/4fR_LC} \tag{14-44}$$

$$\gamma = \frac{1}{4\sqrt{3}\,fR_LC} \tag{14-45}$$

and

$$\theta_1 = \sin^{-1}\frac{4fR_LC - 1}{4fR_LC + 1} \tag{14-46}$$

The peak diode current is again found by substituting in Eq. (14-32).

When a power supply is designed, the values of $E_{L,dc}$, $I_{L,dc}$, and γ are specified and the values of E_{max} and C are to be found.   This can be done for the half-wave rectifier by simultaneously solving Eqs. (14-38) and (14-40). This calculation yields

$$C \geqslant \frac{1}{2\sqrt{3}\,fR_L\gamma} \tag{14-47}$$

and

$$E_{max} = E_{L,dc}(1 + \sqrt{3}\,\gamma) \tag{14-48}$$

If the greater-than sign is used in Eq. (14-47), the actual value of γ should be used in Eq. (14-48).   If the amount that $E_{L,dc}$ is allowed to vary as $I_{L,dc}$ varies between given limits is specified, then Eq. (14-36) may actually specify the minimum value of C.

For the full-wave rectifier, these design relations become

$$C \geqslant \frac{1}{4\sqrt{3}\,fR_L\gamma} \tag{14-49}$$

$$E_{max} = E_{L,dc}(1 + \sqrt{3}\,\gamma) \tag{14-50}$$

and Eq. (14-43) is used to determine the minimum value of C if voltage regulation is specified.   Note that the value of C that is required when the full-wave rectifier is used is one-half of the value required when the half-wave rectifier is used.   Typical values of C range from 10 μf to several hundred μf. Electrolytic capacitors are usually used.

This analysis has neglected the voltage drop in the forward resistance of the diode.   The primary effect of this voltage drop is to reduce the value of $E_{L,dc}$.   Experimentally determined plots of $E_{L,dc}$ versus $I_{L,dc}$ for various values of C are often supplied by diode manufacturers.   Thus, the effect of the forward resistance as well as that of the circuit can be accounted for.

14-6   The inductor-input filter

In theory, the simple capacitor filter can be used to obtain as small a ripple factor and as good a voltage regulation as desired.   However, the size of the capacitor can become extremely large.   This may result in a filter that is too large, too heavy, and too expensive.   In addition, the peak diode currents can be quite high, and, thus, a high-current-capacity diode will be required.   In such cases, it is often desirable to use more-complex filter circuits.   A typical one is shown in Fig. 14-11.   This is called an *inductor-input filter*, since the input element is an inductance.   This is also called an *L-section filter*, since its shape resembles that of an inverted *L*.   If the design requirements are stringent enough to require an inductance, then it usually is desirable to obtain the advantages of a full-wave rectifier.   [There is less alternating voltage in the output of a full-wave rectifier, and this voltage is of higher frequency than it is in the half-wave rectifier—see Eqs. (14-25) and (14-26).]

The output current of a full-wave rectifier, with a resistance load, equals zero only twice during any one cycle (see Fig. 14-3*b*).   The presence of the inductance tends to maintain the current at all times.   For the time being, let us assume that i_i is never zero.   Thus, one of the diodes must be conducting at all times.   If we neglect the voltage drop in the diode, then e_i will have the form of Fig. 14-3*b*, and it can be expanded in the Fourier series of Eq. (14-26).   That is,

$$e_i = E_{\max}\left(\frac{2}{\pi} - \frac{4}{3\pi}\cos 2\omega t - \frac{4}{15\pi}\cos 4\omega t - \cdots\right) \tag{14-51}$$

To determine the output voltage e_L, we can use the circuit of Fig. 14-12 and consider that e represents each of the components of Eq. (14-51) in turn. Thus, the direct load voltage is given by

$$E_{L,dc} = \frac{2E_{\max}}{\pi} \tag{14-52}$$

Fig. 14-11   A full-wave rectifier with an inductor-input filter.

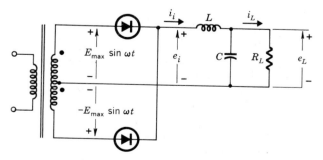

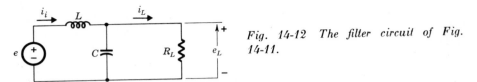

Fig. 14-12   The filter circuit of Fig. 14-11.

The load voltage is not a function of the load current if the components are ideal.   Hence, the voltage regulation will be ideal.   If the inductance has a series resistance R, then the direct load voltage is given by

$$E_{L,dc} = \frac{2E_{max}}{\pi} - I_{L,dc}R \tag{14-53}$$

The effective series resistance of the diodes can also be included in R.

Now let us determine the alternating components of output voltage.   In general

$$\frac{1}{\omega C} \ll R_L \tag{14-54}$$

so that we can ignore R_L in these calculations.   Thus, the component of the load voltage at frequency 2ω is

$$e_{L2} = \frac{-4E_{max}}{3\pi(1 - 4\omega^2 LC)} \cos 2\omega t \tag{14-55}$$

In general, the element values are such that

$$\omega L \gg \frac{1}{\omega C} \tag{14-56}$$

so that $4\omega^2 LC \gg 1$.   Thus, the rms value of the second-harmonic voltage is

$$E_{L2} = \frac{E_{max}}{3\pi \sqrt{2}\, \omega^2 LC}$$

Similarly, the rms value of the fourth harmonic is

$$E_{L4} = \frac{E_{max}}{60\pi \sqrt{2}\, \omega^2 LC}$$

Thus, E_{L4} is $\frac{1}{20}$ of E_{L2}.   The higher harmonics are even smaller fractions of E_{L2}.   Hence, very little error is introduced by assuming that the rms alternating voltage is given by E_{L2}.   Therefore, the ripple factor is

$$\gamma = \frac{1}{6 \sqrt{2}\, \omega^2 LC} \tag{14-57}$$

where it is assumed that the direct voltage drop in the resistance R is negligible.

In this analysis, we assumed that the current i_i was never zero. It cannot be negative, because of the diodes. However, if the load current becomes sufficiently small, then i_i will become zero for finite periods of time. The previously developed relations for $E_{L,dc}$ and γ will no longer be valid, since e_i can no longer be expressed by Eq. (14-51). A typical curve of $E_{L,dc}$ versus $I_{L,dc}$ for an inductor input filter is given in Fig. 14-13. If the load current drops below a critical value, the load voltage rises and the regulation is no longer ideal. If R_L becomes an open circuit, the voltage across the capacitor becomes E_{max}, as it does in the capacitor filter. The capacitor cannot discharge and, thus, neither diode in the rectifier circuit will conduct. Let us determine the constraints that must be impressed on the circuit elements if the previous analysis is to be correct. We shall again assume that relations (14-54) and (14-56) are valid. Then, harmonics above the second can be neglected. Therefore,

$$i_i = \frac{2E_{max}}{\pi R_L} + \frac{2E_{max}}{3\pi \omega L} \cos \left(2\omega t - \frac{\pi}{2} \right) \tag{14-58}$$

Since i_i cannot become negative, this expression is only true for positive values. If it is negative, then $i_i = 0$. If $i_i > 0$ for all times (except possibly for intervals of zero length), then

$$\frac{2E_{max}}{\pi R_L} \geqslant \frac{2E_{max}}{3\pi \omega L}$$

or

$$L \geqslant \frac{R_L}{3\omega} \tag{14-59}$$

The value of $L = R_L/3\omega$ is called the critical inductance L_c. Thus, the value of the inductance should always be greater than the critical value. At times, R_L is a variable. (This can occur instantaneously when an ordinary amplifier circuit is the load, and the signal level varies with time.) The maximum value of R_L should be used in Eq. (14-59). If the maximum

Fig. 14-13   A curve of direct output voltage versus direct output current for an inductor-input filter.

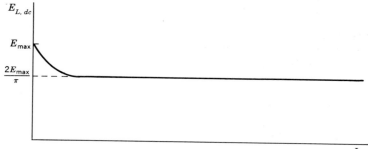

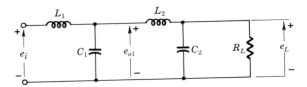

Fig. 14-14 A two-section inductor-input filter.

value of R_L is very large, then the value of the critical inductance will be excessive.   In these cases, a resistance can be placed in parallel with the load resistance.   This effectively limits the maximum value of the load resistance and thus the value of L_c.   This resistance is called a *bleeder resistance*.   It serves another function.   If high-quality capacitors are used in a power supply, the capacitors can hold their stored charge for a long time if the load resistance becomes disconnected.   Thus, the power supply can present a serious shock hazard even if it is turned off.   The bleeder resistance provides a discharge path for the capacitors, and should be connected directly across them.

The design of the filter consists of the choice of $E_{\max}$, L, and C when $E_{L,dc}$, $I_{L,dc}$, and γ are specified.   The value of $E_{L,dc}$ determines $E_{\max}$ and, hence, the turns ratio of the transformer. $R_L = E_{L,dc}/I_{L,dc}$.   This can then be substituted into Eq. (14-59) to determine the minimum value of L.   If this is excessive (or for safety reasons), a bleeder resistance should be included. The value of the product LC can then be determined from Eq. (14-57). L and C are then chosen so that size, and/or weight, and/or cost will be minimized.

If the value of γ is very small, then the sizes of L and/or C can become unreasonably large.   A smaller, cheaper, and lighter filter may then be constructed if more filter elements are used.   Such a filter structure is shown in Fig. 14-14.   In general, the element values are chosen so that

$$\omega L \gg \frac{1}{\omega C} \tag{14-60}$$

and

$$\frac{1}{\omega C} \ll R_L \tag{14-61}$$

where L and C refer to either inductor and either capacitor, respectively. As a consequence of these assumptions, e_{o1} will have the same form as e_L of Fig. 14-11.   The filter section consisting of L_2 and C_2 acts in essentially the same way as the one consisting of L_1 and C_1.   Thus, the rms value of the alternating component of e_L can be obtained by multiplying the rms value of the alternating component of e_{o1} by $1/4\omega^2 L_2 C_2$.   Hence, the ripple factor is

$$\gamma = \frac{1}{24\sqrt{2}\,\omega^4 L_1 L_2 C_1 C_2} \tag{14-62}$$

If this analysis is to be valid, the current i_i must never be zero.   Then L_1

should be greater than the critical value given by Eq. (14-59). Even though this two-section filter has more elements than the one-section filter, the over-all filter can have less volume. Note that Eq. (14-62) is smaller than Eq. (14-57) by a factor of $4\omega^2 L_2 C_2$.

14-7 The capacitor-input filter

If an additional capacitor is added to the inductor input filter as shown in Fig. 14-15, the ripple factor will be reduced. However, the direct voltage across the capacitor will be essentially the same as that given by Eq. (14-43). Hence, we have reduced γ at the expense of voltage regulation. The direct load voltage is equal to the direct voltage across C_1 minus the drop in R, the series resistance of the inductor. Thus, using Eq. (14-43), we have

$$E_{L,dc} = E_{\max} - \frac{I_{L,dc}}{4fC} - I_{L,dc}R \tag{14-63}$$

Substituting the relation $I_{L,dc} = E_{L,dc}/R_L$, we obtain

$$E_{L,dc} = \frac{E_{\max}}{1 + 1/4fR_L C + R/R_L} \tag{14-64}$$

In order to analyze the effect of the filter section consisting of L and C_2, we shall determine the Fourier series of the current i_i. This is

$$i_i = I_{L,dc} + I_{2,\max} \cos 2\omega t + I_{4,\max} \cos 4\omega t + \cdots \tag{14-65}$$

Note that the full-wave rectifier produces only even harmonic components and that i_i will be an even function of time. Using the usual Fourier-series relationships, we obtain

$$I_{dc} = \frac{1}{2\pi} \int_0^{2\pi} i_i \, d\omega t \tag{14-66}$$

$$I_{2,\max} = \frac{1}{\pi} \int_0^{2\pi} i_i \cos 2\omega t \, d\omega t \tag{14-67}$$

Fig. 14-15   A full-wave rectifier with a capacitor-input filter.

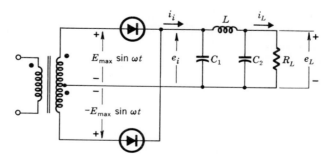

The current i_i in a capacitor filter is nonzero only for short periods of time near $\omega t = \pi/2$ and $\omega t = 3\pi/2$. The value of $\cos 2\omega t$ is approximately -1 during these intervals. Thus,

$$|I_{2,\max}| \approx \frac{1}{\pi} \int_0^{2\pi} i_i \, d\omega t = 2I_{dc} \tag{14-68}$$

We shall assume that the filter components are such that

$$\omega L \gg \frac{1}{\omega C_1} \tag{14-69}$$

$$\omega L \gg \frac{1}{\omega C_2} \tag{14-70}$$

and

$$\frac{1}{\omega C_2} \ll R \tag{14-71}$$

Thus, the magnitude of the second-harmonic component of e_i can be obtained by multiplying Eq. (14-68) by $1/2\omega C_1$. Then the rms value of the second harmonic of E_i is

$$E_{i2} = \frac{I_{dc}}{\sqrt{2}\,\omega C_1} = \frac{E_{dc}}{\sqrt{2}\,R_L \omega C_1} \tag{14-72}$$

The attenuation of the filter section consisting of L and C_2 can be obtained using the procedures of Eqs. (14-54) to (14-57). Thus,

$$E_{L2} = \frac{E_{dc}}{4\sqrt{2}\,R_L\omega^3 C_1 C_2 L} \tag{14-73}$$

As in the case of the inductor input filter, the higher harmonics can usually be neglected. Then, the ripple factor is given by

$$\gamma = \frac{1}{4\sqrt{2}\,R_L\omega^3 C_1 C_2 L} \tag{14-74}$$

The design of this filter proceeds in a manner similar to that of the inductor input filter. The value of $E_{\max}$ and the minimum value of C_1 for the required voltage regulation are obtained from Eqs. (14-63) and (14-64). Then, Eq. (14-74) is used to determine the product $C_1 C_2 L$. The capacitor input filter is sometimes called a *pi-section filter* because it resembles the Greek letter π.

The ripple factor of this filter can be further reduced if a multiple-section filter is used. Each additional LC section will reduce the ripple factor by $1/4\omega^2 LC$.

14-8   Resistance-capacitance filters

An inductance is a relatively expensive, large, and heavy component. At times, it can be replaced by a resistance in a filter section. This tends to

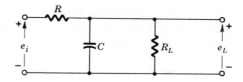

Fig. 14-16   An RC filter section.

increase the ripple factor and worsen the voltage regulation. However, sometimes it may be feasible to use several sections of filtering instead of one when a resistance replaces the inductance. A typical *RC* filter section is shown in Fig. 14-16. We shall assume that

$$R \gg \frac{1}{\omega C} \tag{14-75}$$

$$R_L \gg \frac{1}{\omega C} \tag{14-76}$$

Then, if we are dealing with a full-wave rectifier and assume that all the harmonics above the second can be neglected, the alternating component of the voltage will be reduced by a factor of approximately $1/2\omega RC$.

Resistance-capacitance filter sections are usually not used by themselves but are cascaded with other filter sections. Such a filter is shown in Fig. 14-17. The ripple factor can be obtained by multiplying Eq. (14-57) by $1/2\omega RC$ and accounting for the direct voltage drop in *R*. Thus,

$$\gamma = \frac{1 + R/R_L}{12\sqrt{2}\,\omega^3 R L C_1 C_2} \tag{14-77}$$

This is not as small as the ripple factor of the two-section inductor-capacitor filter given by Eq. (14-62), but it is considerably smaller than the ripple factor of Eq. (14-57). Note that Eq. (14-77) takes the direct voltage drop in *R* into account.

There will be a voltage drop $I_{L,dc}R$ in the filter resistance. This worsens the voltage regulation of the power supply. However, sometimes it is an advantage. Many times a power supply is required to produce several different output voltages. For instance, in an amplifier, the output stages usually require larger direct voltages than the input stages. The ripple voltage must be much lower at the input stages, since the signal levels are lower here. The filter of Fig. 14-17 could be used in this case. The power supply is designed to produce the required value of $E_{1,dc}$. The value *R* is then chosen so that $E_{L,dc}$ is reduced to the required amount. The direct-voltage drop

Fig. 14-17   A cascade of an inductor-input filter and an RC filter section.

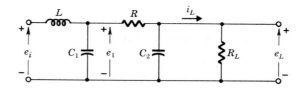

across R is $I_{L,dc}R$. The ripple factor of e_L will be less than that of e_1. If it is desired to reduce the ripple factor at e_L still further, the value of C_2 can be increased, or additional RC sections can be used. The total series resistance should be kept constant so that the correct output voltage will be obtained.

14-9 Output impedance of filters

A power supply for an electronic device should ideally present a zero impedance to all signal components. For instance, in the analysis of amplifier circuits, we replaced the power supply by a short circuit in the linear equivalent circuits. When several cascaded amplifier stages use the same power supply, it is especially important that the power-supply impedance be low, since if it is not, signal voltages may appear across it. Thus, feedback can be introduced between the various stages and the amplifier may oscillate. The output element of a power supply filter is a shunt capacitance. Hence, the impedance down to fairly low frequencies can be kept small. The zero (or very low) frequency impedance of the filter is determined by the voltage-regulation equation. For instance, for an inductance-input filter, Eq. (14-53) gives the low-frequency resistance as

$$R_{dc} = R \tag{14-78}$$

while for the capacitor-input filter we can use Eq. (14-63) to obtain

$$R_{dc} = \frac{1}{4fC} + R \tag{14-79}$$

Note that f is the power-line frequency and not the signal frequency. If this low-frequency impedance is too high, the voltage regulation will be poor, and an amplifier which uses this power supply may oscillate. If the voltage regulation is ideal, then the low-frequency resistance will be zero. Voltage-regulator circuits are used to reduce this low-frequency power-supply impedance. These will be discussed in the next section.

14-10 Voltage-regulated power supplies

In many applications, it is necessary to construct a power supply whose output voltage remains quite constant even if the load resistance changes or if the supply-line voltage varies. For instance, oscillators and direct-coupled amplifiers often require such power supplies. A well-regulated power supply will have a low output resistance (see Sec. 14-9). We shall consider several circuits that can be used to regulate the voltage of a power supply.

Voltage-regulator diodes

When the reverse bias voltage of a semiconductor diode is increased sufficiently, it breaks down. Its breakdown voltage-current characteristic is such that the voltage across the diode is almost independent of the current through it, so the diode can be used as a voltage regulator. The symbol for such a diode is given in Fig. 14-18a. It is sometimes called a *Zener diode* and its voltage-current characteristic is given in Fig. 14-18c. In a similar way, the voltage drop across a "vacuum-tube" diode which has a small amount of gas introduced into it is almost independent of the current through it. The symbol for such a regulator tube is given in Fig. 14-18b. The small open circle is the cathode, which is usually not heated. The voltage-current characteristic of this tube is also given in Fig. 14-18c. A typical circuit that uses these devices is given in Fig. 14-19. Its operation is as follows. If E or R_L should increase, then i_d would increase greatly (see Fig. 14-18c) and the voltage drop across R would rise. This would tend to maintain e_L constant. Similarly, if E or R_L decreases, then i_d would decrease.

Fig. 14-18 (a) The symbol for a voltage-regulator semiconductor diode; (b) the symbol for a voltage-regulator gas diode; (c) their voltage-current characteristics.

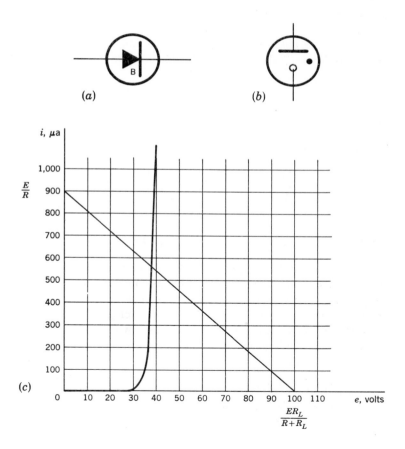

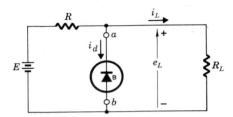

Fig. 14-19   A simple voltage-regulator circuit.

To analyze this circuit, replace the circuit consisting of E, R and R_L as viewed looking into terminals ab by its Thévenin's equivalent circuit. A load line can then be drawn on the characteristics as shown. The voltage across the diode and, hence, the load voltage, is given by the intersection of the load line and the characteristic. Thus, e_L will remain essentially constant for large variations in E or R_L.

This circuit has two disadvantages. First, it is very inefficient. Power is dissipated in both the resistor R and in the diode. If the regulation is to be good, $i_d > i_L$, so that the current through R depends on i_d to a great degree. Thus, the efficiency will be quite small. Secondly, the output voltage cannot be chosen at will, but is a function of the available diode breakdown voltages. We shall next consider some more-complex circuits that eliminate these difficulties and, in addition, provide better voltage regulation.

Series voltage-regulator circuits

Consider the two circuits shown in Fig. 14-20a and b. Their operation is similar, and we shall describe them simultaneously. We have used n-p-n transistors so that most of the polarities of the voltages of both circuits would be the same. The battery E represents the output of a filtered, but unregulated, power supply. The resistance of T_3 is in series with the power supply and the load. The variation of this resistance produces the voltage regulation. This resistance is a function of the grid-to-cathode or base-to-emitter voltage of T_3. This, in turn, depends upon the current through T_2. The grid or base voltage of T_2 depends upon the difference between e_a and the reference voltage e_r. Device T_1 is included to establish a fixed reference voltage with which the output voltage is compared. (R_4 and T_1 form a simple voltage-regulator circuit of the type of Fig. 14-19.) The voltage e_a is a fraction of the output voltage e_L. If e_L increases, then the bias of T_2 will shift so that T_2 draws more current. This will increase the current through R_3 and cause e_b to decrease. Thus, the grid-to-cathode or base-to-emitter voltage of T_3 will change in such a way as to increase the resistance of T_3 and, thus, to reduce e_L. Thus, the variation in e_L will be reduced. In a similar way, a reduction in e_L will be accompanied by a decrease in the resistance of T_3. Increases in the gain of T_2 or of T_3 tend to reduce the variations in

e_L, since they make the change of the resistance of T_3 more sensitive to these variations. The function of the capacitor C is to provide a low output impedance at high frequencies. If the relative sizes of R_1 and R_2 are changed, the effective input bias of T_2 will be varied. This will result in a change in e_L. Thus, the voltage of this power supply can be varied. An alternative way of considering this circuit is to redraw it as in Fig. 14-21. The generator e_r symbolically replaces the voltage-reference tube. Thus, this is a two-stage direct-coupled amplifier whose input is e_r and whose output is e_L. Negative voltage feedback is incorporated, so the output voltage tends to remain independent of the fluctuations in the load resistance and the power supply voltages (see Secs. 10-3, 10-4, and 10-6). If the open-loop gain is increased, the fluctuations in e_L and the output impedance will be reduced. For this reason, T_2 is often a pentode in vacuum-tube circuits. The voltage-regulator circuit is a feedback amplifier; hence, it is subject to oscillation. The procedures of Secs. 10-8 to 10-13 should be used to ensure that the circuit is stable.

Fig. 14-20   Voltage-regulated power supplies using a series device.   (a) Vacuum-tube circuit; (b) semiconductor circuit.

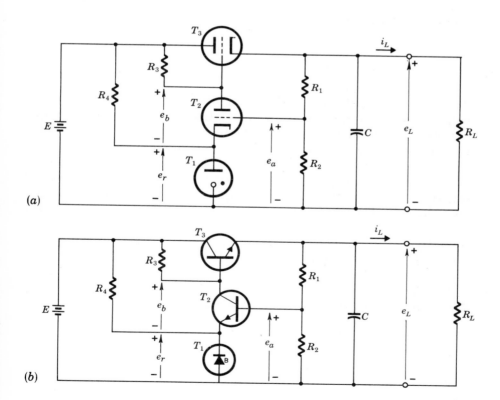

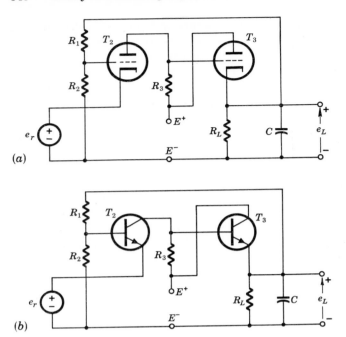

(a)

(b)

Fig. 14-21   (a) The circuit of Fig. 14-20a redrawn; (b) the circuit of Fig. 14-20b redrawn.

14-11   Controlled rectifiers

There are many high-power applications where it is desirable to vary the output voltage of a power supply without introducing a series resistance that dissipates power.   One means of doing this is to control the rectifier so that it conducts for only a fraction of the cycle.   For instance, consider Fig. 14-2. If the diode conducted for only a portion of the half-cycle, the average value of i would be reduced and control would have been achieved.   Consider that the diode circuit of Fig. 14-2 can be controlled so that the current i has the form shown in Fig. 14-22.   We shall assume that the time of the diode's

Fig. 14-22   Current in a controlled rectifier.

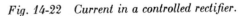

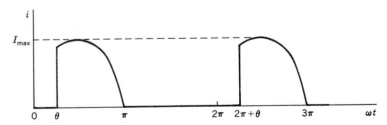

initial conduction occurs θ radians after the start of each cycle. The current i_L is then

$$i_L = \frac{E_{\max}}{r_f + R_L} \sin \omega t \qquad \theta \leqslant \omega t \leqslant \pi$$

The direct load current is given by the average value of i_L. Thus

$$I_{dc} = \frac{E_{\max}(1 + \cos \theta)}{2\pi(r_f + R_L)} \tag{14-80}$$

If θ can be varied from π to 0, the direct load current will vary from zero to a maximum value of $E_{\max}/\pi(r_f + R_L)$. If the diode were ideal ($r_f = 0$), then no power would be dissipated in it even though control had been achieved. The output waveform of this circuit is very rich in harmonics if θ is close to π; consequently, it is difficult to filter. In addition, the ripple factor will change as θ is varied. Hence, these circuits are usually used in applications where low ripple factors are not required (unless substantial filters are used). Let us now briefly consider two devices that can be used as controlled rectifiers.

The *p-n-p-n* controlled rectifier

Consider the *p-n-p-n* structure shown in Fig. 14-23a. It has three leads labeled *anode, cathode*, and *gate*, and its symbol is shown in Fig. 14-23b. This device can be considered to be the interconnection of a *p-n-p* and an *n-p-n* transistor as shown in Fig. 14-23c. To explain the operation, consider the simple circuit of Fig. 14-23d. Assume that i_g is zero or negative, so that T_1 is almost cut off. Then i_1 will be almost zero and T_2 will also be essentially cut off. If i_g is made positive, so that T_1 conducts, i_1 will be nonzero and T_2 will start to conduct. The current i_2 will divide into i_2' and i_2''. If R is much larger than the base-emitter impedance of T_1 when it is conducting, most of this current will pass through T_1. This will increase i_1, which will increase i_2. Thus, this process will repeat itself until both T_1 and T_2 are saturated. Hence, the gate current can switch the connection between the anode and cathode from a very high to a very low impedance. Once conduction has started, the gate loses control. Consider that i_g is reduced to zero. The base current of T_2 will still be maintained by i_2 and the device will not switch off. Thus, the gate can be used to initiate conduction but not to terminate it. However, if E_1 is reduced to zero or made negative, i_L will become zero and the gate will regain control. (The anode current cannot be in the reverse direction because of the *p-n* junctions.) Thus, if this device is used in a half-wave rectifier circuit (with the anode and cathode connected as though they were the anode and the cathode, respectively, of an ordinary diode) and the gate voltage was turned on at the same angle θ of each cycle, the output current would have the form shown in Fig. 14-22. Thus, the desired controlled-rectifier action would be achieved.

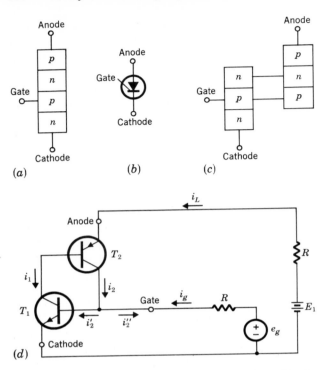

Fig. 14-23   (a) *A p-n-p-n controlled rectifier;* (b) *its symbol;* (c) *a "two-transistor" representation of this device;* (d) *the schematic representation of part c connected into a simple circuit.*

There are several ratings that must be considered. If the anode-to-cathode voltage is made too large, conduction will be initiated by breakdown phenomena even though gate current has not been applied. Breakdown can result from the application of too large an inverse voltage also. Power dissipation is quite important, since the current in a *p-n* junction varies markedly with temperature. Thus, the turn-on characteristic will vary greatly with junction temperature.

The thyratron

Another type of controlled rectifier is the thyratron, which is shown in Fig. 14-24a. Its symbol is shown in Fig. 14-24b. It basically consists of a triode-type structure, into which a small amount of gas has been introduced. The grid is a large solid structure which tends to shield the cathode from the plate. If the gas within the tube is not ionized, then plate current is essentially zero. However, once the gas is ionized, many electrons are available for conduction and the positive ions drift into the space charge cloud

and neutralize it.   Then, the potential drop across the tube is quite low
even if the plate current is large.   The ionization of the gas occurs because
of collisions with emitted electrons and, hence, depends upon the electric
field at the cathode.   This depends more on the grid voltage than on the
plate voltage.   Consider the circuit of Fig. 14-24c.   Assume that $i_b = 0$,
that E_1 is relatively large, and that e_g is quite negative.   Now reduce the
magnitude of e_g.   Eventually, the field at the cathode will be such that the
electrons are accelerated toward the plate.   When this field becomes strong
enough, the gas will *ionize* (or break down).   For the usual thyratron, if
E_1 is sufficiently large, breakdown occurs at negative grid voltages.   If the
magnitude of the negative grid voltage is increased, the thyratron will not
stop conducting, because the positive ions will be attracted to the grid and,
thus, its negative potential will be neutralized.   If the thyratron is to be
switched off, its plate voltage must be made zero or negative, and then the
grid regains control.   Thus, operation of the thyratron is quite similar to
that of the *p-n-p-n* controlled rectifier.   The ratings of the thyratron are
similar to those of the controlled rectifier.

Since the *p-n-p-n* controlled rectifier and the thyratron are quite similar,
we shall only use one in actually describing a controlled-rectifier circuit.
Such a circuit is shown in Fig. 14-25.   Assume that two sinusoidal voltages
are available and that the phase angle between them can be varied.   When
e_g just becomes positive, the rectifier will switch on provided that e_a is
positive.   Actually, e_g may have to be slightly positive, but if E_{max} is very
much greater than this voltage, very little error is introduced by assuming
that the controlled rectifier conducts when e_g just becomes positive.   Thus,
the current i will have the waveform shown in Fig. 14-22.   Now consider
Fig. 14-26, which can be used to produce a varying phase angle θ.   The two
transformers are used for isolation purposes.   Assume that the resistance

Fig. 14-24   (a) A thyratron; (b) its symbol; (c) a simple thyratron circuit.

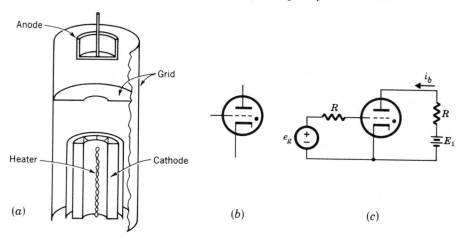

(a)　　　　　　　　　　　　　　　　(b)　　　　　　　　　　　　(c)

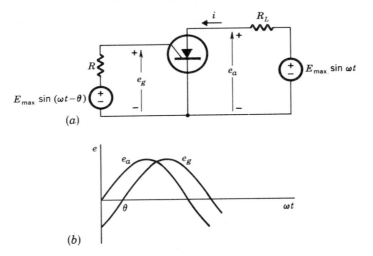

(a)

(b)

Fig. 14-25 (a) A simple controlled-rectifier circuit; (b) waveforms in this circuit (assuming that the controlled rectifier is not conducting).

R_i is infinite. If $R_2 = R_3$, then in complex form, we have

$$\mathbf{E}_1 = \frac{\mathbf{E}_i}{2} \cdot \frac{1 - j\omega R_1 C}{1 + j\omega R_1 C} = \frac{\mathbf{E}_i}{2} \underline{/-2 \tan^{-1}\omega R_1 C} \tag{14-81}$$

Thus, as R_1 is varied from a short circuit to an open circuit, the phase angle θ between e_i and e_1 will vary from 0 to 180° and the current can be varied continually from a maximum value to zero. We have, thus, achieved the desired control.

Fig. 14-26 A controlled rectifier which uses a phase-shifting circuit.

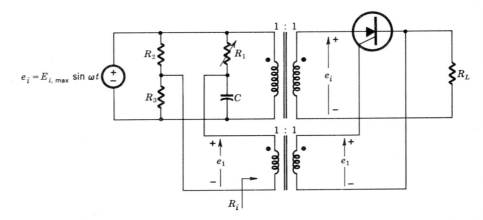

REFERENCES

[1] G. E. Happell and W. M. Hesselberth, "Engineering Electronics," pp. 417–423, McGraw-Hill Book Company, New York, 1953.

BIBLIOGRAPHY

Greiner, R. A.: "Semiconductor Devices and Applications," chap. 16, McGraw-Hill Book Company, New York, 1961.
Happell, G. E., and W. M. Hesselberth: "Engineering Electronics," chap. 14, McGraw-Hill Book Company, New York, 1953.

PROBLEMS

In all the following problems that call for numerical answers, assume that the power-line frequency is 60 cps. If it is not specified otherwise, the diodes can be assumed to be ideal in these problems.

14-1. Compute expressions for $I_{L,dc}$, $E_{L,dc}$, γ, and η_r for the half-wave rectifier of Fig. 14-2a. Do not assume that the back resistance of the diode is infinite or that the forward resistance is zero.

14-2. Repeat Prob. 14-1 for the full-wave rectifier of Fig. 14-3a.

14-3. Repeat Prob. 14-1 for the full-wave bridge rectifier of Fig. 14-4, but now assume that the back resistance of the diodes is infinite. Do not assume that the forward resistance of the diodes is zero.

14-4. Find an expression for the load current in the full wave bridge rectifier of Fig. 14-4. Do not assume that the back resistance of the diodes is infinite or that the forward resistance is zero.

14-5. Determine the output voltage e_o for the circuit shown in Fig. 14-27. How will the output voltage vary if a load resistance is placed across terminals ab?

14-6. Repeat Prob. 14-5 for the circuit of Fig. 14-28.

14-7. The half-wave rectifier with a capacitor filter shown in Fig. 14-7 has the following circuit values: $E_{max} = 150$ volts, $C = 20$ μf and $R_L = 10,000$ ohms. Compute the values of $E_{L,dc}$, $I_{L,dc}$, γ, the peak diode current and the peak inverse voltage.

14-8. Repeat Prob. 14-7, but now consider that a full-wave rectifier is used and that $150 \sin \omega t$ is the voltage across one-half of the transformer secondary.

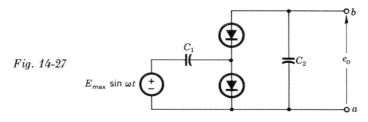

Fig. 14-27

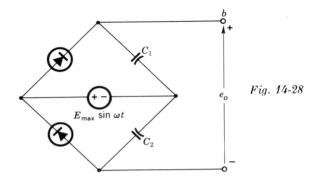

Fig. 14-28

14-9. Design a power supply using a half-wave rectifier with a capacitor filter as shown in Fig. 14-7. The specifications of the filter are: $E_{L,dc} = 150$ volts, $I_{L,dc} = 20$ ma, and $\gamma = 0.01$. Determine the values of C and E_{max}. What is the peak diode current? Assume that the diode is ideal.

14-10. Repeat Prob. 14-9, but now use a full-wave rectifier.

14-11. Repeat Prob. 14-10, but now assume that the design specifications are: $E_{L,dc} = 350$ volts, $I_{L,dc} = 100$ ma, and $\gamma = 0.001$.

14-12. The full-wave rectifier with an inductor-input filter shown in Fig. 14-11 has the following circuit values: $R_L = 1,000$ ohms, $C = 20$ μf, and $E_{max} = 300$ volts. The inductance is the minimum value that satisfies relation (14-59). Compute the values of $E_{L,dc}$, $I_{L,dc}$, and γ. Assume that the resistance of the inductance is 20 ohms.

14-13. For the circuit of Fig. 14-11, the circuit values are: $E_{max} = 300$ volts, $L = 2$ henrys, $C = 20$ μf, and $R_L = 10,000$ ohms. What is the minimum value of bleeder resistance that can be used if the inductance is not to be less than the critical value?

14-14. Assume that there is no bleeder resistance, that the load resistance is removed from the power supply of Prob. 14-13, and that the power supply is turned off at some later time. The leakage resistance of the capacitor is 10^9 ohms. At the instant that the power supply is turned off, what will the output voltage be? How long will it take for the output voltage to drop to 10 volts? Repeat the calculations if a 10^5-ohm bleeder resistance is connected across the capacitor.

14-15. Design a power supply using a full-wave rectifier and an inductor-input filter that meets the following specifications: $E_{L,dc} = 350$ volts, $I_{L,dc} = 100$ ma, and $\gamma = 0.001$. Use a value of inductance that satisfies relation (14-59) but is less than 20 henrys. The values of E_{max}, L, and C should be specified. Compare these results with those of Prob. 14-11. Assume that the inductance has no resistance associated with it.

14-16. Repeat Prob. 14-15, but now use a two-section inductance-input filter. Assume that the values of both inductances and of both capacitances are equal.

14-17. Repeat Probs. 14-15 and 14-16, but now assume that $\gamma = 0.00001$.

14-18. Repeat Prob. 14-15, but now assume that the inductance has a series resistance of 500 ohms.

14-19. Repeat Prob. 14-16, but now assume that each inductance has a series resistance of 500 ohms.

14-20. The capacitor-input filter of Fig. 14-15 has the following element values: $C_1 = 20\ \mu f$, $C_2 = 30\ \mu f$, $L = 10$ henrys, $R_L = 1,000$ ohms, and the series resistance of the inductance is 100 ohms. If $E_{max} = 350$ volts, what are the values of $E_{L.dc}$, $I_{L.dc}$, γ, and the peak diode currents?

14-21. Repeat the design of Prob. 14-15, but now use the capacitor-input filter of Fig. 14-15. Assume that $C_2 = 2C_1$ and that the resistance of the inductance is zero. What is the peak diode current? Does the critical inductance have any significance here?

14-22. Repeat Prob. 14-21, but now assume that the resistance of the inductance is 500 ohms.

14-23. Repeat Prob. 14-21, but now assume that an additional LC section is added to the filter. Assume that the values of both inductances are equal and that the three capacitors have equal values. The maximum allowed value for the inductances is 20 henrys.

14-24. A filter of the type shown in Fig. 14-17 is to be used in a power supply with two different outputs. The first output is to be such that $E_{L1.dc} = 350$ volts, $I_{L1.dc} = 100$ ma, and $\gamma_1 = 0.001$. The second output is to be such that $E_{L2,dc} = 250$ volts, $I_{L2,dc} = 10$ ma, and $\gamma_2 = 0.00001$. Design the power supply using a full-wave rectifier. Note that the power supply must supply a total current of 110 ma.

14-25. The output resistance of the capacitor input filter of Fig. 14-15 is to be equal to or less than 10 ohms. What is the minimum value that C_1 can have? Assume that the inductance has zero resistance.

14-26. Assume that the characteristics of the voltage-regulator diode of Fig. 14-19 are given in Fig. 14-18c. Plot a curve of e_L versus E as E varies from 0 to 220 volts. The values of the circuit elements are: $R = 200,000$ ohms and $R_L = 200,000$ ohms.

14-27. Obtain an expression for the voltage gain of the circuit of Fig. 14-21a. The answer should be in terms of the parameters of the vacuum tubes and the circuit elements. Discuss the voltage regulation of this circuit using these results.

14-28. Repeat Prob. 14-27 for the circuit of Fig. 14-21b. The answer should be in terms of the h parameters of the transistors and the circuit elements.

14-29. Assume that the controlled rectifier of Fig. 14-26 conducts when the gate voltage exceeds $bE_{i,max}$, where b is a constant that is less than $\frac{1}{2}$. Derive an expression for the angle θ of Fig. 14-22. Assume that all components are ideal and that R_i is infinite.

14-30. Consider Fig. 14-26. Derive an expression for e_1. Do not assume that R_i is infinite. What relation must there be among R_i and the circuit elements if Eq. (14-81) is to be valid?

Index